Artificial Intelligence

EARL B. HUNT

Department of Psychology
University of Washington
Seattle, Washington

ACADEMIC PRESS   New York   San Francisco   London   1975
A Subsidiary of Harcourt Brace Jovanovich, Publishers

ACADEMIC PRESS, INC.
111 Fifth Avenue, New York, New York 10003

United Kingdom Edition published by
ACADEMIC PRESS, INC. (LONDON) LTD.
24/28 Oval Road, London NW1

Library of Congress Cataloging in Publication Data

Hunt, Earl B
    Artificial intelligence.

    (Academic Press series in cognition and perception)
    Bibliography: p.
    1.   Artificial intelligence.   [DNLM: 1.   Computers.
2.   Cybernetics.   Q335 H939a]
Q335.H79 1974   001.53'5   74-1626
ISBN 0−12−362340−5

PRINTED IN THE UNITED STATES OF AMERICA

ERRATA

Artificial Intelligence
By Earl B. Hunt

Page	Correction

Page   *Correction*

9   Middle term of Equation (2) should read: $7(7\mathbf{A} \cup \mathbf{B})$

28   s in line above Equation (8) should be **s**

39   Figure 2-8. First row of the left-hand column should read:

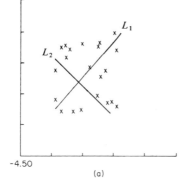

Delete the asterisk in the second line of the legend.

62   Equation (8) should read:

$$\Pr(E_j) = \sum_{i=1}^{k} \Pr(E_j : H_i) \cdot \Pr(H_i)$$

69   Equation (33) should read:

$$\text{EL}(\mathbf{x} \in R_j) = \sum_{i \neq j}^{k} q_i \cdot f(\mathbf{x}; \mathbf{\Sigma}, \mathbf{\mu}^i) \cdot c(i).$$

77   Part (a) of Figure 4-7 should appear as follows:

-4.50

(a)

Page	Correction

94 The left-hand term of Equation (95) should read:

$$\mathbf{w}_i^{(t+1)}$$

95 Line 3 should begin $k - 1$.

Line 19 should read, "Equation (97)"

104 Equation (3) should read:

$\psi(X) = (X)$ contains only l's in the diagonals

105 Remove the number (3) beside the equation in the center of the page

106 Line 39: Insert Φ to read, "Define Φ to be. . . ."

118 Line 24: The expression in parentheses should read, "(mask of under 2)"

127 Line 2: Final expression should read $\mathbf{x} \in D$.

Line 17 should begin, "*length of v, v* $\leq$ *m.*"

129 Equation (5): Numerator should read:

$$\Pr(S_v(y) \cdot C_j)$$

Equation (8): First letter on the right-hand side should read w_{ji}

152 Substitute f for g in Equations (13) and (14)

159 Equation (31) should read:

$$\mathbf{A}_j \rightarrow v\mathbf{A}_j\mathbf{x}; \qquad \mathbf{A}_j \rightarrow \mathbf{w}.$$

181 Line 6: Change "noise" to "noisy."

Line 11: Change $\square$ to $\boxed{}$.

189 Line 8 should read, "Assume that $P(i)$ and. . . ."

Line 28: Second equation should read:

$\sigma(1) = \{1, 5, 7, 9, 13, 17, 19, 21, 25\}$

190 Figure 8-3: Type under left-hand part should read:

$P(1) = \{1, 5, 7, 9, 13, 17, 19, 21, 25\}$

193 Lines 31 and 32: Number sequence should read:

$(4 \subseteq 5, 4 \subseteq 6, 6 \subseteq 4, 2 \subseteq 5, 2 \subseteq 7)$

213 Line 1: Should read $s \in S$

Line 34: Should read $o \in O$

214 Line 13: Change "left-hand peg" to "right-hand peg"

Line 14: Change "peg" to "disk" in both places

217 Equation (10), line 3 should read: $\rightarrow B + (X+C)$ associativity of $+$

220 Line 14 should end $\text{BE} = \text{ED}$

224 Figure 10-1: Delete the line from San Francisco to Las Vegas; add a line from San Francisco to San Bernadino, with the label "300"

228 Line 17 should read:

$\hat{g}_i(n_j) < \hat{g}(n_j)$, *for any* n_j *closed prior to* n_i, *then*

233   Equation (24): Left-most term should read $\hat{g}_k(n_k)$

234   Line 15: Change $(n_g \quad S_g)$ to $(n_g \in S_g)$
          Equation (25): Add carets over both h's
          Line 27: Substitute "of" for "or"

242   Figure 10-5: In the left-hand part, delete the arc adjoining the right-hand B and C endpoints. In the right-hand part, the second endpoint from the right should be labeled B.

259   Figure 11-1: The two right-most endpoints should read C and D

262   Equation (4d) should read:
          $u = v$ implies $w \cdot u = w \cdot v$, where u, v, w are well-formed expressions

267   Line 4 should begin: "may be applied to $(A+B) + C. \ldots$"
          Figure 11-7 should appear as follows:

          Line 17: Replace "left" by "right" in Condition (2)

268   Table 11-4, line R3: Left-hand side should read $-Y+XY \rightarrow X$

307   Line 17 should read: "$\ldots$ the set $S^* \cup \{C\pi\}$ is similarly"

315   Fifth line from bottom: Change (75) to (74)
          Fourth line from bottom: $B^1 = C^2$ to $B^1 = C2$
          Second line from bottom: Change (75) to (74)

316   Line 2 should begin "may be resolved with $C1. \ldots$"
          Figure 12-9: Top line should read $B^0 = C3$
          Equation (77): Replace x_3 by x_1
          Equation (78): Right-hand side should read:

$$\left(7P(x_1, h(x_1, x_3), x_1)\right) \cdot \left(P(x_1, h(x_1, x_3), x_3)\right) = (\quad),$$

322   Figure 12-11: Delete the last sentence of the figure legend.

328   Line 16: Change $j = 1$ to $j = i$

352   Figure 13-6: The numeral "1" should appear in the upper left-hand corner of the rectangle in part (b)

381   Figure 14-4: Add the word *Plays* between *Tennis* and *John*

422   Line 11: Change NP(B) to NP(C)

424   Figure 15-6: Change C to B in part (b)

Stephen Pittick

Ann Arbor, 1975

Artificial Intelligence

ACADEMIC PRESS
SERIES IN COGNITION AND PERCEPTION

SERIES EDITORS:
Edward C. Carterette
Morton P. Friedman
Department of Psychology
University of California, Los Angeles
Los Angeles, California

Stephen K. Reed: *Psychological Processes in Pattern Recognition*

Earl B. Hunt: *Artificial Intelligence*

IN PREPARATION
James P. Egan: *Signal Detection Theory and ROC-Analysis*

CONTENTS

PREFACE

For the artificial intelligence field, this is a very conservative book. My motivation for writing it developed after a number of observations of how people with one background zestfully approach another area with very little awareness of what has been done before. I also believe that training in the artificial intelligence field, and to a lesser extent, in computer science in general, is too bound to fads. Too much effort is placed on putting the student at the *forefront of the field* and too little in defining and presenting basic information. In my university, for instance, the first course in artificial intelligence (obviously not taught by me) deals with the interesting but tangentially relevant theories of Piaget on human cognitive development, and then plunges the first-year graduate students into detailed studies of the latest (often good) doctoral theses from Massachusetts Institute of Technology. The trouble with this approach, as I see it, is that the student is offered a good view of a few trees (chosen by the professor), and no idea either of the forest or of botany. In other words, I think that the professors and the texts should assume more responsibility for analyzing the basic principles and problems. After this is done, it is appropriate to have seminars dealing with the latest, hot-off-the-press research.

So what is to be done? I have tried to gather together, in one place, a reasonably detailed discussion of the basic mathematical and computational approaches to problems in the artificial intelligence field. Emphasis has been on principles, not details. Also, I have tried to focus on the major unsolved *conceptual* problems, especially in the fields of machine comprehension and perception. You will find no descriptions of robots in this book. Neither will you find a machine playing chess. You will find discussions which, if you will wade through them, will help you understand the basic approaches of machine pattern recognition, robot perception, deductive question answering, and computer game playing.

The level of discussion is appropriate for seniors and graduate students in any of the computer related sciences, or in experimental psychology. You must be easily familiar with algebra, and should be passingly familiar with the concepts of probability theory, calculus, and symbolic logic. Persons who do not have some mathematical background, however, probably will not find this text very illuminating.

ACKNOWLEDGMENTS

Dr. J. Ross Quinlan, of the University of Sydney and I had intended to write this book together, and did work on one or two chapters. Alas, we were defeated by the Pacific Ocean. It simply proved impossible to communicate frequently enough, especially in the light of the rapidly expanding literature. Nevertheless, Ross is responsible for a high proportion of those good ideas I have proposed and probably should be blamed for very few of the bad ones . . . and I certainly don't know which. Thanks, Ross.

My second thanks for scientific collaboration goes to Dr. Sharon Sickel, who forced me to keep my nose to the grindstone of mathematical theorem proving, just to be sure I knew what she was talking about. My discussion of theorem proving owes a great deal to her clear and precise reasoning.

A number of other associates have helped in various ways, either by their assistance in some of the specific research problems described here, or by their comments on various proposals and on earlier drafts of the text. I would like to mention particularly, Mark Stickel, David Garnatz, Patrick Russell, Edward Strasbourger, and Michael Delay, all of the University of Washington. Very helpful comments on the text have been received from Edward Carterette of U.C.L.A., Cordell Green of Stanford University, and A. A. Marley, of McGill.

Most of the original research reported here was sponsored by the U.S. Air Force, Office of Scientific Research (Air Systems Command). Indeed, the general plan of the book arose from discussions I had with those charged with various Air Force computer applications, when I asked what sort of consulting guidance they could use. It was there that a need for a book of basic techniques was most apparent, and most clearly stated. Dr. Glenn Finch, now retired, but then with the Office of Scientific Research, was a staunch source of encouragement and support for several years.

Many secretaries worked on this manuscript at various stages. I won't try to name them. They all did a good job. Without the courtesy of the various scientists who responded to preprint requests and put me on their mailing lists, I could not have written a book of this nature, nor could anyone else.

During the period in which I wrote this book I held the post of Chairman of the Psychology Department at the University of Washington. My colleagues in that department respected the idea that their administrator should have a scholarly life as well, and regulated their requests for services so that it was possible for me to maintain a scientific career. I appreciate this.

Neither Academic Press nor my family left me during long periods when I failed to communicate and did not seem to have produced any tangible results. Completing this book provides Academic Press with a manuscript and my family with more of my time. I hope both press and people will be pleased.

Part I
Introduction

Teil

Chapter I

THE SCOPE OF ARTIFICIAL INTELLIGENCE

1.0   IS THERE SUCH A THING?

There are over 100 computer science curricula in universities in the United States. Practically every one of them includes a course entitled *artificial intelligence*. In fact, it appears that more people study programming techniques developed for artificial intelligence research than study techniques for business-data processing (Elliot, 1968). The educational programs are matched by comparable research activity. There is a journal called *Artificial Intelligence* and a series of scientific conference reports on *machine intelligence*. What gives rise to this activity?

If you asked physicists or chemists to offer an abstract definition of their field, you would expect to find them in substantial agreement. It is doubtful whether you would find such agreement if you were to gather together the various scientists studying artificial intelligence. Interestingly, however, you probably would find agreement if you examined the details of the courses they teach and the research they do. The Association for Computing Machinery's recommended computer science curriculum contains an outline for course *A9, Artificial Intelligence*, which lists theorem proving, game playing, pattern recognition, problem solving, adaptive programming, decision making, music composition by computer, learning networks, natural-language data processing, and verbal and concept learning as suitable topics (ACM Curriculum Committee, 1968). Similar veins run through the research literature. No one can question the existence of a scientific field of activity. But what is its significance?

One of the tests that has been proposed to determine the viability of a scientific field asks the question, "Is it having an effect on fields closely related to it?" By this criterion, artificial intelligence rates rather well. Programming techniques originally developed for artificial intelligence research have become widespread in computer programming. Psychology has undeniably been influenced by the concepts of artificial intelligence in a number of fields (Hunt, 1968; Frijida, 1972;

Loehlin, 1968; Miller, Galanter, & Pribram, 1960; Weisstein, 1969). In chemistry, artificial intelligence techniques have been applied to the analysis of data from mass spectroscopes (Lederberg & Feigenbaum, 1968) and in planning the synthesis of organic molecules (Corey & Wipke, 1969).

There appears to be a meaningful body of knowledge whose unifying principles are difficult to identify. The problem seems to lie in the definition of *intelligence*. Psychologists, who have faced the problem of defining intelligence for some time, have adopted the pragmatic approach that intelligence is what the intelligence test measures. I shall do the same. For the first 90% of this book, "artificial intelligence" will simply be the collection of things taught in artificial intelligence courses. I shall select a subset of these topics which appear to me to be most interesting or important, and discuss them in some detail. By taking this approach, I postpone such broad philosophical issues as, "Can a machine think?" and "Is it possible to speak of machine understanding?" until a common background of factual knowledge has been established. To do this, the book has been divided into four sections. The first section contains, in this chapter, an overview of the various fields of artificial intelligence and, in the next chapter, an attempt to connect artificial intelligence problems to some of our notions of computability and abstract computing devices. No attempt will be made to give a comprehensive history, but a book of this nature should contain some overview and at least a few, possibly idiosyncratic, notions of how the field developed historically. Similarly, the chapter on abstract computing is not intended to be a rigorous introduction to the field, but rather an overview of the general notion of computability, with emphasis on the interaction between computability theory and artificial intelligence.

The remaining chapters are divided into sections dealing with substantive knowledge in three areas that are basic to all artificial intelligence: pattern recognition, problem solving, and machine comprehension. No attempt has been made to provide a comprehensive literature review. (There are well over 1500 relevant articles.) The goal has been to explain in detail those approaches and principles which appear to have the greatest promise in each of the fields under discussion. Completeness of coverage has thus been sacrificed; many artificial intelligence projects are simply not mentioned.

When I began work on this book, it soon became apparent that an analysis of previously published reports simply would not provide answers to several important questions which could be raised. Therefore, in conjunction with the discussion, previously unpublished research will be presented. For the most part, this work is concentrated in the fields of theorem proving and pattern recognition, which are the fields most crucial to other artificial intelligence endeavors. Most of the studies can be characterized as attempts to fill gaps, rather than to extend our knowledge of given approaches to a problem.

In the final chapter, I have confronted the philosophical questions which I had been avoiding. My answer to the "Can a machine think?" will probably be an unsatisfactory one to enthusiasts on both sides.

1.1   Problem Solving

"Problem solving" has a rather restricted meaning in the artificial intelligence lexicon. A problem is said to exist when one is given a *present state*, a description of the characteristics of a *desired state*, and the *operations* that can be used to go from one state to another. There may be constraints specifying that certain states are not to be visited at any point. This formulation is known as the *state–space* approach. A few examples will show how generally applicable it is.

In the "missionaries and cannibals" problem, three missionaries and three cannibals wish to cross a river from the left bank to the right. They have available a boat which can take two people on a trip. All can row. The problem is to get all six to the right bank, subject to the culinary constraint that at no time may the number of missionaries on either side of the river be exceeded by the number of cannibals on that side. To translate the puzzle into a formal problem, let a state be defined by the number of missionaries and cannibals on the left bank and the position of the boat. The starting position is (3, 3, L) and the goal state (0, 0, R). The permissible moves of the boat define the operators.

In theorem proving, one is given a set of true statements (premises) and a statement whose truth is not known (the theorem to be proved). By applying a sequence of allowable operations, such as the inference rules of algebra or trigonometry, expand the set of true statements to include the theorem. The states are defined by the statements proven thus far; the inference rules define the operators.

Given a chess position, change it into a position in which the opponent's king is checkmated. En route to this position, avoid any position in which your own king is checkmated or in which a stalemate occurs. The board positions define the states, and the piece moves the operator.

It has been said that modern artificial intelligence research began with the efforts of Allen Newell, Herbert Simon, and J. C. Shaw to write problem-solving programs (Fiegenbaum, 1968). Their studies were conducted jointly at the RAND Corporation and the Carnegie Institute of Technology (now Carnegie-Mellon University). Intellectually, the RAND–Carnegie work was important both in its own right and because it set the tone for many other efforts. Technologically, the programming methods developed in the course of the research have become widely used throughout computer science.

Newell *et al.* (1957) first produced the *Logic Theorist* (LT), a program designed to prove theorems in the sentential calculus. The LT successfully proved 38 of the 52 theorems of Chapter 2 of Whitehead and Russell's *Principia Mathematica*.[1] As the *Principia* is regarded as one of the basic works establishing the logical foundations of mathematics, LT's feats were bound to attract interest. It is easy

---

[1] Twelve of the 14 unsolved problems were not completed because of the physical limitations of the computer then available. The others were beyond the capacity of the algorithm for logical reasons. A modified LT operating on a larger computer later solved all 52 theorems (Stefferud, 1963).

either to overstate or unduly minimize the significance of LT's success in reproducing the *Principia*'s results (references are purposely omitted here), so one wants to be aware of precisely what was done.

The proofs of the theorems in Chapter 2 of Whitehead and Russell would not be considered deep by a mathematician. Bright university students can generally produce most of them. The brilliance of Whitehead and Russell's accomplishment was not in proving the theorems, but in realizing that their proof could be used as the basis for a development which leads from logic to mathematics. This realization was an act of creative insight which Newell, Shaw, and Simon made no attempt to mimic on a machine. On the other hand, the problems of Chapter 2 are not exactly trivial. These proofs probably are beyond the grasp of 60% of humanity, a fact one is likely to overlook if his circle of acquaintances is restricted to present and future Ph.D.'s. Newell *et al.* have repeatedly stated that the real significance of LT lies in how it produced proofs, not in the proofs it produced. Theorem proving is an example of a large class of problems for which there are solution techniques which are known to work, but which are not practical to execute. For example, the following exhaustive technique is guaranteed to produce a proof for any provable theorem—but it may take a while. . . .

> Beginning with the premises, write down all inferences that can be made by combining two or more known true statements in various ways. Examine the set of statements so produced, to see if it contains either the theorem or its negation. In the former case, the theorem is proven; in the latter, it is disproven. If neither case occurs, add the new set of statements to the premises and repeat the procedure. There will be some number, n, such that a proof (or disproof) will be produced on the nth step, but there is no guarantee what n will be.[2]

Newell, Shaw, and Simon called this procedure the "British Museum algorithm," since it seemed to them as sensible as placing monkeys in front of typewriters in order to reproduce all the books in the British Museum. They suggested instead following a *heuristic* approach, a term they took from Polya (1954, 1957), who believed that most mathematical proofs are achieved by guessing the nature of a solution, then proving that the guess is correct. Polya contrasted this with the *algorithmic* technique of mechanically going through steps which are bound, eventually, to result in the correct answer.[3] The British Museum algorithm is clearly algorithmic. What Newell and his colleagues set out to do was to write a set of rules (i.e., a program) for generating guesses, then proving that they were correct. The idea caught on quickly, and today "heuristic programming" is spoken of

---

[2] The procedure may not terminate if the "theorem" to be proven is not derivable from the axioms. This point is discussed in more detail in Part III.

[3] Polya did not give a formal definition of either algorithm or heuristic, nor did Newell *et al.* Currently within computer science the term *algorithm* is used to mean a procedure for operating on strings of input sentences from a specified set of legal strings (Glushkov, 1967). By this definition, any program is an algorithm, and the Newell *et al.* program should be thought of as algorithms for generating guesses.

respectfully, and somewhat mysteriously, as an advanced programming technique, even though it is not a programming technique at all, but rather a way of thinking about what a program is supposed to do when it is used to attack a certain problem.

In writing the Logic Theorist, Newell, Shaw, and Simon encountered problems that forced them to develop an important new programming tool, *list processing*. This is a method of organizing a computer's memory so that ordered sets (lists), instead of variables, are the basic operands. List-processing techniques have found wide application throughout computer science (Knuth, 1969). It can also be argued that in thinking about complex information processing the appropriate language to use is a language for the manipulation of lists, since list processing has proven to be a very important tool in many applications involving symbolic rather than numeric processing.

The RAND–Carnegie approach to problem solving was characterized by a strong interest in how humans solve problems. A program is a precisely defined set of rules for attacking a given class of problems. Suppose a reasonable correspondence were to be established between the input and output of a program and the stimuli and responses observed in the psychological laboratory. Then one could say that, at the level of information processing, the program was a model of the man (Newell, Shaw & Simon, 1958; Newell & Simon, 1961, 1972). Simulating human thought, however, is a different goal from creating a good problem solver, since in one case, the criterion of success is that good problem solving be produced. Newell and Simon (1961) saw no incompatibility in the joint pursuit of these goals, and appear to have used knowledge of human problem-solving to suggest the structure of heuristic programs, and vice versa. Intuitively, this can be justified on the grounds that people are the most flexible problem solvers of which we have knowledge; so if we want to construct artificial intelligences, we should first study how the natural ones work.

The argument that programming should mimic human intelligence is weak if you are interested in solving problems within a specialized area in which "inhuman" methods may work well. The Newell *et al.* work on mathematical theorem proving was criticized on the grounds that more efficient exhaustive search methods than the British Museum algorithm existed, and that by using better exhaustive methods, better results could have been obtained (Wang, 1960). This criticism somewhat misses the point, since Newell and his co-workers were more interested in the generality of their methods than in substantive results in theorem proving. By the same reasoning, it was appropriate for Newell *et al.* to investigate the theorems of the *Principia* as an example of a general class of problems, even though group theory might have provided problems that would be more interesting to a mathematician.

The skeptics' retort is that general problem solving skills, divorced from content areas, may not exist. Newell and his associates' next project, the General Problem Solver (GPS) program, attempted to show (*a*) that such skills do exist and (*b*) that they can be discussed at the very concrete level of computer programming. Whereas the LT had had built into it the operations used in Whitehead and Russell's formalization of the propositional calculus, the GPS was a program for manipulating states and operators in the abstract. To use the GPS on a specific problem, one first had to define the structure of specific states and operators (e.g., the locations of missionaries and cannibals and the moves of the boat) to the program. The act of specification was called describing the *task environment*. The GPS program was capable of attacking any problem that could be translated into a suitable task environment. The goal of GPS research has been to show that well specified generally applicable procedures (i.e., programs) lead to the sort of solutions which, when they are produced by humans, are applauded as clever. The list of problems attacked by the GPS and similar programs includes elementary logic, chess, high school algebra word problems, and the answering of questions phrased in somewhat ambiguous English, but confined to a very small data base. In one of the most extensive investigations the GPS was used to attack ten different small problems in fields ranging from symbolic integration to solution of the missionaries and cannibals puzzle (Ernst & Newell, 1969).

On several occasions Newell and Simon have offered comparisons of traces of a theorem proving program's progress toward solution with comments recorded as a person "thinks out loud" as evidence in support of their contention that their program modeled human thought. In 1972, they published a large body of such data and proposed a general technique for designing programs intended as general simulations (Newell & Simon, 1972).

About the same time that the RAND–Carnegie group began to attract attention, a closely related and similarly active group formed at the Massachusetts Institute of Technology, under the leadership of Marvin Minsky and John McCarthy. Subsequently McCarthy and Feigenbaum, a member of the Carnegie group, both moved to Stanford University, which, together with the Stanford Research Institute, has also become a major center of the artificial intelligence studies. Both directly through the research of members of the groups, and indirectly because of the prestige of the institutions involved, the M.I.T. and Stanford groups have heavily influenced the American study of computer problem solving.[4]

In contrast to the early Carnegie–RAND studies, the M.I.T. research was more concerned with formal mathematical representations. Typical problems studied included symbolic integration (Slagle, 1963), question answering using trivial data bases (Raphael, 1964), the combining of deductive arguments and information retrieval (McCarthy, 1959; Slagle, 1965; Green, 1969), and that hardy perennial, chess playing by machine (Greenblatt *et al.*, 1967). McCarthy, Minsky, and their co-workers seem to see artificial intelligence as an extension of mathematics and symbolic logic, rather than as a parallel discipline to psychology. They have been extremely careful to formalize their computing procedures and to relate them to

---

[4] Since 1965, the M.I.T. and Stanford groups have devoted a good deal of effort to the design and construction of robots, a problem which does not appear to have involved Newell, Simon, and their colleagues. Similarly, since 1965, the Newell–Simon group seems to have moved more toward the study of psychological problems. Naturally, any statement cannot cover all the members of a group.

more conventional mathematics, in particular to recursive function theory (McCarthy, 1961; Berkeley & Bobrow, 1964). Attempts by Amarel (1968) and Banerji (1969) to formalize problem solving processes are also worth examination, as they represent independent efforts directed to the same goal. An emphasis on formalization is of great potential value, since an adequate formalization will be necessary if we are to have a precise, viable theory of the problem solving process. On the other hand, such a theory does not now exist, and it is our feeling that in many specific artificial intelligence projects the informal approach of the Newell–Simon variety would have been just as satisfactory as the often forbidding formalisms that have been presented.

A complementary approach to problem solving, based on the ideas of the mathematician J. A. Robinson (1965), has also greatly influenced the study of mechanical thought. Narrowly conceived, Robinson dealt only with a new approach to theorem proving in formal logic; but his methods can be applied to virtually any situation we normally call problem solving. As we shall see, the technical details of the method can be formidable. The basic logic is quite simple. Any statement can be proven true by showing that its negation is false. In theorem proving one must show that the statement

$$\mathbf{A} \supset \mathbf{B} \tag{1}$$

is true, where $\mathbf{A}$ is the hypothesis of the problem and $\mathbf{B}$ the desired conclusion. Now suppose that $\mathbf{A}$ and $\mathbf{B}$ are sets of statements. If we were to use the Newell and Simon approach to proving that (1) is true, we would begin with the set $\mathbf{A}_0$ of axioms, and then apply some selected rules of inference to produce a new set, $\mathbf{A}_1$ of axioms and inferred statements. Rules of inference would be applied to $\mathbf{A}_1$ to produce a second set, $\mathbf{A}_2$, and then a third, and fourth, until some $\mathbf{A}_1$ was found that contained $\mathbf{B}$, the set $\mathbf{B}$ of statements to be proven, as a subset.

An alternative way to prove (1) would be to show that its negation

$$7(\mathbf{A} \supset \mathbf{B}) = 7(7\mathbf{A} \cup 7\mathbf{B}) = (\mathbf{A} \cdot 7\mathbf{B}) \tag{2}$$

was false.[5] This can be done by showing that the simultaneous assertion of A and $7B$, leads to a contradiction. Robinson proposed that this be done by the use of a single rule of inference, called *resolution*. We introduce the idea with a trivial example. Consider the musical comedy problem:

> *If the lady is Charley's aunt, then she will visit with Charley. But the lady is never seen with Charley.*

Using a rather obvious translation to the formalisms of logic we have the clauses

$$\text{C1} \quad (\text{Aunt(lady, Charley)} \supset \text{Present(lady, Charley)}) \tag{3}$$
$$\text{C2} \quad (7\text{Present(lady, Charley)})$$

---

[5] Throughout the text "7" will indicate negation, "∪," disjunction, and "·," conjunction. Note that if $\mathbf{B}$ is a set of statements which, taken together are, to be interpreted as a single statement, then $7\mathbf{B}$ is the disjunction of the negation of each statement in $\mathbf{B}$.

Let A stand for "Aunt(lady, Charley)" and P for "Present(lady, Charley)." The clauses of (3) are the axioms of the problem. The hypothesis is that the lady is not Charley's aunt.[6] This would be written (7A). To prove this conclusion by the resolution method we want to negate it [producing (A)], and add the resulting clauses to the axioms. Doing this, and rewriting clause C1 in disjunctive form, the set of clauses

$$\text{C1} \quad (7A \cup P), \qquad \text{C2} \quad (7P), \qquad \text{C3} \quad (A). \tag{4}$$

is produced.

We now introduce the second inference step in Robinson's method. Suppose two clauses are of the form $(A \cup B)$ and $(7A \cup C)$. It follows that

$$(A \cup B) \cdot (7A \cup C) \supset (B \cup C) \tag{5}$$

An inference of this sort is called a *resolution* of the clauses on the left of the $\supset$ to produce the *resolvent* clause on the right. A contradiction exists if two clauses of the form (A) and $(7A)$ are simultaneously asserted. Formally, two such clauses can be resolved to produce the empty clause, (   ). Inference of the empty clause is an indication that the original set of clauses contained a (perhaps implied) contradiction.

In view of this background, we now have two ways of proving by resolution that the lady is not Charley's aunt. In one line of proof clauses C1 and C2 are resolved to produce the clause $(7A)$. This resolves with clause C3 to produce the contradiction. Discovery of the other proof is left to the curious.

In practice there are many complications which have not been illustrated. Nevertheless, it can be shown that resolution is a complete proof method. This means that if a contradiction can be obtained from a set of clauses by any valid proof method, then it can be obtained by resolution. In Polya's terminology, therefore, resolution is an algorithm rather than a heuristic. We shall see that heuristic techniques do play a prominent part in practical applications of the resolution method.

There have been very many amplifications of the basic resolution method. The major results are discussed in Part III. Quite apart from the specific results, one of the effects Robinson's work had was to shift the emphasis in artificial intelligence from attempts to mimic human solutions on machines to concern for machine-oriented problem solving methods. A second effect of Robinson's work has been a renewal of interest in practical applications of theorem proving techniques, especially to mechanized information retrieval.

1.2   Pattern Recognition

It may be true that every object is unique, but life would be impossible if we treated this idea too seriously. For many purposes we find it convenient to treat

---

[6] "She" was Charley in disguise.

unique beings as typical—typical service station attendants, elevator operators, or collectors of internal revenue. We let our knowledge of the characteristics of the general class determine our reaction to the specific example. To avoid disaster we must learn to make appropriate classifications. It has been suggested that the ability to do this is basic to intelligent behavior (Bourne, 1965; Bruner, Goodnow, & Austin, 1956; Guilford, 1967; Hunt, 1962). People make subtle classifications so routinely that we do not realize how impressive their performance is. A man returning home will instantly recognize his wife, children, and the family dog. Obviously, the differences between the way the wife, and certainly the dog, looked in the morning and evening are trivial, but this is precisely the point. How do we specify to a computer what is a trivial change in a pattern and what is a change sufficient to require a new classification?

In an influential early paper, Selfridge (1958) proposed that pattern recognition be achieved by computing the weighted sum of a number of "recommended" classifications, each based on different features of the object to be recognized (descriptors). The individual recommendations would need be only slightly more accurate than chance, but the system might be quite accurate. This idea has been developed into what will be called the *parallel* method of pattern recognition. Every object can be considered to have a most primitive description, representable as a vector, whose elements serve as the arguments for a number of functions, whose values are always computed. These, in turn, serve as the arguments for a decision function which determines the eventual classification.

The preceding description, which does not do full justice to Selfridge's ideas, presents pattern recognition as a problem in classifying vectors, or points in n-dimensional space. This view has been made more explicit by Sebesteyen (1962) in a monograph relating pattern recognition problems to mathematical decision theory, and by Miesel (1972) in an excellent discussion of pattern recognition techniques. These aspects of pattern recognition are closely related to classical statistical techniques in multivariate analysis (Anderson, 1952; Tatsuoka, 1971).

Pattern recognition may also be approached by analogy to biological processes. In some circumstances animals' capacity for pattern recognition exceed those of any buildable machine. For simplicity, consider only human capabilities. When we are dealing with classification based on immediate sensory experience, e.g., recognizing faces or spoken words, humans can easily outperform machines. In nonsensory situations human performance is less impressive. For example, people cannot compete with pattern classification programs if the correct classification rule involves logical combinations of abstract properties, such as color, size, and form (Hunt, Marin, & Stone, 1966). To make the problem more complex, these are situations in which it is not clear on what basis people perform erratically, either very well or very poorly. What pattern recognition is involved in reasoning by analogy? The topic is worth study.

Since pattern recognition must be a neural function in animals, one might look for the key to biological pattern recognition in the properties of the neuron itself. For many purposes it may be assumed a neuron is a threshold detection element.

That is, it either produces a constant output when the sum of its inputs reaches a certain point, or it is quiescent. McCulloch and Pitts (1943) have proven that any computable function can be realized by a suitably organized network of *idealized neurons*, threshold detection elements whose logical properties can reasonably be attributed to an actual neuron. The question, then, is whether any reasonable network reorganization principle can be found which would make it possible for an initially randomly connected group of idealized neurons to organize themselves into a "computing device" capable of solving an arbitrarily selected pattern recognition problem.[7] Such a reorganization principle would be a theory of learning applicable at the level of the individual neuron. It is intuitively obvious that such a principle must exist, since animals demonstrably do learn new classification rules, and it is ridiculous to believe that they are born "prewired" for all the classifications which they might learn.[8]

A neurological learning theory put forward by the Canadian psychologist, D. O. Hebb (1948), although originally intended strictly as a model for psychology, has proven quite influential in artificial intelligence. A modification of it was used to define the *Perceptron* pattern recognizer (Rosenblatt, 1958, 1962). The Perceptron, or rather, perceptrons, since what Rosenblatt described was a principle for building programs rather than a single program, exist both as programs and as specially designed analog computers. Substantial effort has been devoted to an analysis of the general class of pattern recognition systems which perceptrons represent. The concepts of *linear pattern recognition* systems and of *threshold logic* systems have been developed. The first term refers to the method used for combining the individual judgments of different feature-recognition elements, and the second to the use of devices which give a constant signal once the level of their input signals exceeds a fixed value. A substantial mathematical theory describing such devices has been developed (Nilsson, 1965a), culminating in an analysis of the type of problems which can be solved by linear, threshold logic systems (Minsky & Papert, 1969).

In research on perceptrons the emphasis has been on adjusting the weights assigned to a fixed set of feature detectors. This is consistent with Selfridge's formulation of the problem. An alternative pattern-recognition technique is to search for "good" features, which discriminate among classes so clearly that an appropriate feature weighting rule will be easy to detect. This approach has been

---

[7] Suppose that every object to be classified is completely described by a vector of not more than k binary digits. Therefore, there will be at most 2^k possible distinguisable objects. We desire a function which, upon receiving one of the 2^k possible descriptions, will produce a 1 if and only if the described object is in class "A," and a 0 otherwise. One of the implications of McCulloch and Pitts's work is that such a function can be constructed from a network of idealized neurons.

[8] It is not so ridiculous to believe that animals are predisposed toward learning certain types of functions. The nervous system as a whole certainly is not random. On the other hand, the genetic message does not contain enough information to specify all the details of the adult nervous system.

stressed in a number of research projects, notably those of Uhr and his associates (Uhr, 1965; Uhr & Vossler, 1963) and in the Soviet literature (Bongard, 1970). An examination of recent articles in the journal *Pattern Recognition* indicates that increasingly greater concern is being paid to feature detection than to feature weighting.

The pattern recognizers mentioned so far are at least analogs to biological pattern recognition. In biology the term "pattern recognition" is implicitly assumed to refer to classification at the sensory level. This orientation is shown by frequent reference to visual pattern-recognition examples. Psychologists have used the term "concept learning" to refer to a task that is mathematically identical to pattern recognition but different at a psychological level. The contrast is easy to illustrate. Imagine that a program has been written to distinguish between pictures of men and women. Now what does "showing a picture to a computer" mean? It means that shades of gray in small areas of a picture are by some method coded into numbers, and the resulting vector used as input to a pattern recognition program. A very simple example is shown in Figure 1-1.

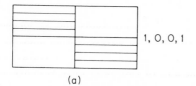

(a)

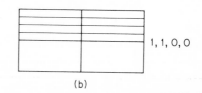

(b)

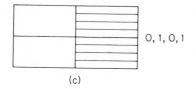

(c)

Fig. 1-1.   Simple example of how a picture is mapped into a vector for pattern recognition. The large square is divided into four quadrants. If the upper left quadrant is shaded, the first component of the vector is 1; otherwise it is zero. Similar rules apply to other quadrants and vector components.

The program, then, is required to classify vectors, not pictures per se. We can contrast this to a program which is to be used to classify animals into their appropriate species and genus. Training would proceed by showing the program descriptions of the animals and indicating the correct species and genus. At the atomic level, the program would be reading sets of characters describing an animal, and converging the descriptions into ordered sets of codes. The pattern recognition program would again be classifying vectors. Since the problems are identical at the machine level, it seems reasonable that the same program would be used to derive a pattern classification rule in each case. Yet if we think of how a person might go about learning these tasks, we suspect that there could be a difference between perception and cognition.

Those scientists interested in the more cognitive pattern recognition tasks have, in fact, developed rather different algorithms than those developed by workers who began with a sensory orientation toward pattern recognition. Instead of making a number of tests in parallel, and then evaluating the joint results, logical classification algorithms tend to proceed by first making a few tests, and then, depending upon the outcome of these, either making a second test or classifying the object. The nature of the second test made will depend upon the outcome of the first. The process can obviously be extended to any number of tests. Classification rules of this nature are called *sequential decision* procedures. Until recently, there was little development of sequential decision procedures in the artificial intelligence literature, although such procedures were studied in detail in statistics and operations research. It is interesting to note that in at least one case in which logical pattern recognition was approached from a strictly statistical viewpoint (Morgan & Sonquist, 1963) the resulting computing algorithms were very similar to those developed from independent work in artificial intelligence (Hunt, Marin, & Stone, 1966). In the last few years greater appreciation of the importance of sequential procedures has been evidenced in the pattern recognition literature (Fu, 1969).

Human vision may well be the finest pattern recognition system in existence. It is obvious that computers ought to be able to look at a scene and analyze it in the way that a human does. In fact, most science fiction scenarios on television assume that the computer of the future will do this routinely. The truth is that computer vision presents a number of very difficult problems. Analysis of a visual scene appears to be all but impossible unless the analyzing device contains a logical model of the scene being viewed, in order to determine how to resolve ambiguities in the visual input. This conclusion is hardly surprising to those psychologists who have studied the perceptual illusions and constancies, and a number of suggestions about how computers ought to process visual data have been adopted from contemporary research on human vision. Similarly, the efforts to give a computer eyes have produced ideas which may be of use in the construction of theories of human vision, although the nature of the contribution is not clear (Weisstein, 1969). At present we can only present a glimpse of this fast moving field, which may not yet have found its basic techniques.

1.3   Game Playing and Decision Making

Attempts to program computers to play games have been a feature of modern artificial intelligence from its beginning. Undeniably, one of the reasons for this is the sheer challenge of the problem. People play complex games. It is quite easy to show that *in principle* a computer program can be written to play a perfect board game.[9] Somehow, no one seems to be quite able to produce a program which matches the best human play.

A second, more general reason for studying game-playing programs is that they may represent a general class of problems which, at present, computers attack rather poorly. In an excellent article on early attempts at chess playing, Newell, Shaw, and

---

[9] More precisely, an algorithm exists for determining the optimal move at any stage of an *n*-person game in which each person has perfect information and there are a finite number of moves on each play (Luce & Raiffa, 1956).

Simon (1963) point out that there are too many alternatives for a computer to examine each move, so an adequate chess playing program must contain heuristics which restrict it to an examination of reasonable moves. Also, to win a game you need not select the best moves, just the satisfactory ones. Hopefully the study of games will teach us how to use computers to search for satisfactory, though sometimes suboptimal, solutions to very complex problems. More pessimistically, it may be that all the efforts in game playing will lead only to a formalization of strategies for the particular games which are studied.

A third reason for studying game playing is that it represents an area in which learning plays an important but not well understood role. Telling a bright person the rules of chess does not make him an expert player. One must have experience, although it is not clear what experience does. If we could define effective game playing programs which profited from their experience then we might have some idea of just what it is to be learned by practicing intellectual tasks. Samuel (1961, 1963, 1965), whose work on checkers is perhaps the most sophisticated work on self-modifying programs for game playing, has stressed that his research is an exploration of machine learning using checkers as a vehicle, and not a study of checkers for its own sake.

Studies of game playing programs have developed almost independently of the mathematical study of "game theory." In part, this may be because the two efforts are really directed at different goals. The mathematical analysis of games concentrates on the strategy to be followed by an idealized perfect player. In programming a game player one tries to produce acceptable play within certain limits on the use of resources. Simon (1956) has summed up the problem neatly by distinguishing between strategies that optimize and those that satisfy. There may be a wide gulf between the description of a perfect player and the construction of an adequate one. Nevertheless, one can reasonably ask why there has not been more coordination between the two fields of study.

We shall treat game playing as part of problem solving and, in fact, shall deal with it only briefly. This approach has been taken for two reasons. In order to write a game playing program one must solve the problem of representing the structure of the game at hand. It is not clear that the solution to a particular game problem tells us anything general about either games or programming. Game playing becomes of interest when aspects of individual games can be shown to be specializations of a definable general class of problems. Our discussion will stress the class of problems and not the details of any one game. We do point out, though, that our approach leads us away from an interesting and developed field. There are regularly scheduled computer chess matches. A number of other games have been studied less intensively. The publication of a volume summarizing this work and the ideas behind it would be of considerable value.

1.4   Natural Language and Machine Comprehension

There have been many attempts to process natural language by computer. These studies are motivated by intensely practical considerations. The biggest bottleneck in the use of computers is the time it takes to write programs. Think how much easier it would be to use computers if the machines could understand simple statements in a natural language. It has been suggested that the ideal computing system would be an "advice taker" which would receive its input in natural language, then respond to queries by deducing implications from the facts it already knew (McCarthy, 1958). Such a program would be extremely important from a theoretical viewpoint, since intelligent answers to complex queries would imply "understanding," something which machines are not supposed to be able to do. There are obvious practical applications.

A quite different application requiring analysis of linguistic data is the recurring effort to produce an automatic language translator. In the early 1950s there were many optimists who believed that mechanical translation was largely a matter of creating hardware large enough to hold a dictionary, since the translation process itself would be straightforward. Today the optimists are few and far between, since virtually the only contribution to technology of the various early mechanical translation projects was to show how little we know about linguistics. A case study suggests that the quality of mechanical translation may not have advanced from 1964 to 1971. (Sinaiko, 1971). In fact, if one's goal is to create a common language for scholars and diplomats, it might be easier to go back to teaching classic Latin on a world-wide basis than to build a perfect machine translator! Fortunately, more modest goals are both attainable and useful.

A third motivation for computer processing of written data is provided by the sheer volume of words in our society. Although more and more of our records are being placed in machine readable form, most of our transactions are still conducted in a natural language. Through these records society produces a vast traffic of information about itself. In order to control organizations of hundreds of millions of people, there must be a rapid way to record, abstract, and analyze the traffic. In some cases, such as the recording of bank checks, we now use computers to manage the information flow. At the other extreme, we rely on human journalists to abstract and comment upon the week's political news. There is an intermediate area in which we still need humans, but where much of the burden of the task could be assigned to the computer. Automatic abstracting and indexing of technical documents is a case in point. The power of computers to do this and similar tasks will depend greatly upon our ability to write programs that can master the intricacies of natural human languages.

Efforts to develop natural language processors fall between artificial intelligence and information retrieval. There is no hard and fast rule to distinguish when a particular application is in one field or the other. We can distinguish some end points. Programs that search for a particular sequence of letters in a text, but do nothing more than record the occurrence or nonoccurrence of the sequence, although very useful in indexing and abstracting, are seldom considered artificial intelligence examples. Programs that compose complex and varied replies to a user, even though those replies are keyed by single words in the input stream, are in the artificial intelligence field. Perhaps deciding how to make the distinction will have to await the creation of a good pattern recognizer!

1.5   Self-Organizing Systems

Much of our intellect, and certainly most of our research capital, is spent in the design and production of machines. Could this task itself be relegated to an automaton? If you accept the view that animals are subject to the same laws as machines, the answer to the question must be "yes," since the evolutionary sequence can be considered an example of the action of physically understandable laws.[10] In principle, it should be possible to mimic evolution in machine design. There might be other ways of building automata.

Von Neumann (1956) sketched a proof showing that it was logically possible to build a device which could either (a) reproduce itself or (b) reproduce variations of itself. His reasoning was based upon McCulloch and Pitt's previously cited proof that any computable function can be realized by a network of idealized neurons. From the beginning, then, the mathematical argument had a strong biological flavor. Von Neumann's proof showed only that the self-reproducing machine was possible. He did not discuss its structure, nor did he discuss the relative efficiency of different schemes for "evolution." These questions have been explored subsequently, without conclusive results.

A slightly different question has also been raised about self-organizing systems. Consider a device that has the capability to make changes in its internal state, and hence the ability to alter its reaction to specific stimuli. Here the analogy is to learning, rather than to evolution. There is also a question of control involved. The total system must contain a mechanism for keeping itself in a "viable" region of its space, by adjusting its reactions as a function of both environmental and internal conditions. How should this system be organized?

Weiner (1948, 1952) stressed that the key to building a system capable of adjusting to a changing environment was the proper use of the *cybernetic* principle. Roughly, a cybernetic device is one which receives as one of its inputs some function of its previous output. More colloquially, if a marksman wants to keep making good shots, he has to know where the bad shots are going; and half the advice to the lovelorn seems to be "watch the reaction you get." We have purposely chosen wide-ranging examples. The concepts of systems which reorganize themselves under feedback control can be applied to any organization whose state can be described by specifying mutually dependent variables, from the neurological examples that interested Weiner to international power politics. At such a level of generality, "cybernetics" refers more to a view of the world than to a precisely defined mathematical technique.

Abstract theories of evolution and learning are as broad topics as one could imagine. Many devices embody the ideas introduced by Von Neumann and Weiner, yet we would hesitate to call them intelligent. An automatic thermostat is a good example. Can anything of content be said about self-organization itself? A number

---

[10] The converse is not true. You could maintain that the evolutionary sequence, or the creation of man, was an event outside natural laws and still agree that principles of self-organization did exist.

of people think so, but I am not among them. I believe that much of the work done is so general as to border on the vacuous. Because of this prejudice, self-organizing systems will not be discussed.

1.6   Robotology

From the Golem to astounding science fiction, robots have fascinated humanity. You could look on all the programs we have mentioned as part of the brain of a robot. To complete the design we need "only" to put them together and to attach the resulting program to some effectors and sensors. The "only" is justified because, once we had the program running, adding the necessary hardware would present technological, but not scientific problems. The quotes are justified because there is no assurance that the technological problems could be solved.

Modern robot studies follow along two general lines, which for lack of better names, we shall call "scientific" and "commercial." At times the scientific goal has seemed to be quite literally to shoot at the sky. At the 1965 Fall Joint Computer Conference, McCulloch stated that he was trying to design an object, weighing not more than 5 pounds, which could survive a landing on Mars and would have the perceptual capacities of a frog. Since then "Shakey," a robot (of sorts) designed at Stanford Research Institute, has been featured in the now-defunct *Life* magazine. Several scientists have implied that, given the necessary support, it would be possible to place some sort of complex automated explorer on the moon or a planet in the near future and, indeed, quite complex devices have already been placed there. Whether these are robots or not depends on your definition of the term. The commercial robot builders have been content to design simpler devices to function closer to home.

Let us arbitrarily define the study of robots as the actual building of realistic devices, ruling out studies in which one builds toys to illustrate a certain principle that would be useful in an unspecified robot. We are aware of substantial robot design projects at three institutions—M.I.T., Stanford University, and Stanford Research Institute. Some work has also been done at the University of Edinburgh. While many people have been involved, to an outsider the work clearly bears the stamp of McCarthy, Minsky, and their colleagues, in that it follows their engineering and mathematically oriented approach to artificial intelligence rather than the more psychological approach of Newell and Simon. The only exception to this approach has been in the design of the robot's visual system. Here psychological and physiological models have made a marked impact on robot design. Particularly noticeable aspects of the robot work are the reliance on list-processing techniques in computer programming and a tendency to view robot perception problems as problems in engineering rather than as simulations of biological perception.

Another characteristic of the scientific approach to robots has been the concern for general solutions to classes of problems, sometimes at the expense of clumsy

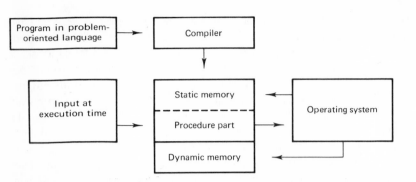

Fig. 2-1.   Steps in generating the special-purpose machine defined by a program.

finite size, and hence can take only a finite number of states. (Suppose that finite memory contained k bits of information. Then it could take on only 2^k different states.) The procedure part can be thought of as a set of rules for changing static memory from one state to another as a function of (*a*) the current state of static memory, (*b*) the information received from the input stream, and (*c*) information that can be retrieved from dynamic memory. The procedure part also specifies rules for writing data into the output stream and into dynamic memory, which plays the role of a storage system for intermediate results.

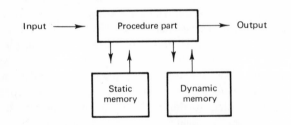

Fig. 2-2.   Control of operations during program execution.

The operations on input, output, and changing the state of static memory are conceptually trivial. Operations that manipulate dynamic memory are more interesting. The procedure part of a program is itself finite, as it can contain only a finite set of rules. Therefore the program cannot contain rules for responding directly to any state of dynamic memory, as there are an infinite number of such states. The program must contain a retrieval scheme for obtaining data from dynamic memory in such a way that only one of a finite set of possible retrievals actually occurs. In the following sections of this chapter we shall be concerned with four retrieval schemes. In one of them it will be assumed that any piece of information in dynamic memory can be obtained (by sufficiently complex programming) without altering the other information in dynamic memory at the time. We will then progressively restrict the permissible operations until we reach

solutions to specific problems. For example, in designing a robot to pick up blocks, McCarthy and his group have concentrated on schemes for visual scene analysis and hand-eye coordination, where a commercial robot might have moved light beams of known intensity over a surface of known reflectance, assuming that the scene before it would always obey rigid restrictions. Despite the remarks about the utility of robots in exploring hostile environments, scientific robot projects have displayed only secondary concern for topics such as miniturization, protective packaging, and economy. In a panel session at the fall 1968 Joint Computer Conference, it was noted that the Standord University robot had its brains in a PDP-10 computer, its ears in a conventional microphone, its single hand mounted on a fixed shaft, and its cyclops eye in a television camera. One word for such a system was "robot"; the speaker also suggested "kludge."[11] This is not a damning criticism since the first goal is to find general solutions. Practical techniques will come later . . . hopefully.

Commercial robot projects have taken exactly the opposite route. Obviously, it would be nice to have an economic machine that is as general-purpose an object manipulator as man is. This would be particularly true if the machine were less subject to heat, radiation, and overtime pay than is man. Such a device is not extant, nor will it be very soon. On the other hand, there are hundreds of thousands of jobs, now done by man, that can be automated by specifically engineered devices. One could consider these to be "special purpose manipulators," just as an analog computer is a special-purpose information processor. What commercial robot designers are attempting to do is to produce easily programmable general-purpose object manipulators. In doing so, the commercial designer must strike a trade-off between generality efficiency at specific tasks, and cost. The location of this optimum point will depend on the technology and the application, and will vary from time to time. Presentations at computer conferences in the late 1960s suggested to us that current commercially made robots are fairly general devices which cleverly and properly avoid difficult issues such as the processing of visual input by making it easy for a man to program new decisions into them as he "instructs" his robots to do a new task.

For these reasons, little will be said about either commercial robots or about the technology needed to build the small computers, flexible mechanical arms, and T.V. cameras capable of surviving the bump of an extraterrestrial landing. When this restriction is placed, the robot problem becomes a specialization of problem solving, pattern recognition, and vision. It will be treated as such.

---

[11]"A more or less functioning system created by mating components whose original designers had never intended to have used together."

Chapter II

PROGRAMMING, PROGRAM STRUCTURE, AND COMPUTABILITY

2.0   The Relevance of Computability

"Creating an artificial intelligence system" usually means "writing a computer program." Every programmer knows that a running program is a compromise between conceptualization and practicality. Such a concern applies in artificial intelligence research as much as in another field. What is not so widely realized is that there are theoretical restrictions on what can be computed, with which there can be no compromise. Of even more importance is the fact that certain classes of functions can be computed only by machines that have certain definable capabilities. In this chapter, an attempt will be made to present some of the basic results relating to computation in the abstract and to relate them to the programming problems which appear in artificial intelligence research. The chapter stands somewhat apart from the rest of the text. The reader not interested in (or already familiar with) the theory of computation may prefer to skip to Chapter III.

The crux of the matter is the relation between the computability of a function on an abstract machine and the structure of the program that realizes the function on an actual machine. It is important to maintain a distinction between real and abstract machines and the programs for them. The theory of computability deals with how conceptual machines compute classes of functions. Programmers try to realize specific functions on the computer with which they have to deal. Since the programmer's choice is of a program and not of a machine, why should he be concerned with computability at all? The answer is that a program in operation can be thought of as a simulation of a special purpose machine on a general purpose machine. The combination of program and actual machine, then, defines a special purpose computer.

When we ask, "What classes of functions require automata with property x to compute them?" we could equivalently ask, "What classes of function require a program that has property x in its structure?"

To pursue this topic, consider how a program defines the separate parts machine.[1] Physically, a program is simply the contents of an ordered se locations in the primary memory of a computer. Since the locations associated a running program may contain either code or data, it is convenient to div program into three separate parts. The *procedure part* consists of all program that cannot be modified by the program during its execution. For those who li think in terms of hardware, the procedure part consists of those loc associated with a program which could be placed into a "read only" memor before run time, without affecting the execution of the program. A progra has two distinct *memory* areas, called the *static* and *dynamic* areas. These hold all data used by the program during a given run, including any code whic be modified and any intermediate results. The static area contains a structures and modifiable program code areas whose size can be predi advance of the program's execution. The dynamic area contains any variab memory structures. To illustrate, in the simple ALGOL program,

> Begin array A [1 : 20] ; integer k, j;
>   read k, j:
>   begin array B [1 : k; 1 : j] end
> end,

array A is part of the static memory, since its size is constant throug execution of the program, while array B is part of dynamic memory, as determined by the values of k and j, which are known only at run time.

As a practical matter, it is customary to specify the program part and memory areas when a program is first constructed. For example, in F compilations a reservation is made in an actual machine for the space the procedure part and fixed memory of a program at compilation time required for dynamic memory must be requested from a supervisor during execution. It is easiest to think of the program as being a user pr the supervisory program as being an operating system, but the distinction would be the same if two user programs were running subordinate to the other. The situation is summarized in Figure 2-1, w the steps involved as a program is constructed in a higher-order langu FORTRAN, or, better, ALGOL or PL-1.

Next, consider the relationship between a program, its memory a input and output during execution. Figure 2-2 is a graphic represent interdependencies. The procedure part of the program determines the which data will be read in from the input stream, stored in either mem finally, the order in which information will be transferred from the me the output stream. Writing data into a memory area is equivalent to memory area's state. This leads to a most important point. Static

[1] See Wegner (1968) for a more detailed discussion of the concepts which here.

the most restricted case, in which there is no dynamic memory section at all. Most FORTRAN programs fall into this latter category. We shall show that the computing power of the programs having different degrees of control over dynamic memory varies considerably and in ways relevant to artificial intelligence.

2.1   Computations on Strings

We cannot study all possible programs, so we must proceed indirectly. The preceding section presented an argument for classifying programs by the nature of the abstract machine that they define. Any limits on the computational capacity of an abstract machine therefore apply to programs that are specific cases of the machine. Conversely, it may be possible to find those properties of an abstract machine which are required to compute defined functions. Any program which is to compute one of these functions must simulate the appropriate machine.

The problem, then, is to find out how the characteristics of a function affect the structure of an abstract machine on which the function can be computed. To do this we shall introduce a second level of indirectness. Instead of discussing the computation of mathematical functions in a conventional sense, we will ask questions about the machine capabilities needed to recognize "sentences" in formal language. It will be shown that this can be done, and that by establishing limits on language recognition we also establish limits on function computability. The approach to be used follows closely that of Hopcroft and Ullman (1969) except that their formal proofs will usually be replaced by illustration and heuristic argument.

Computers are normally thought of as number manipulators, but they could equally well be thought of as devices for writing strings of symbols from one language into another. A computing machine can read and print only finite sets of characters. Call these the *input alphabet I* and the *output alphabet O*, and let I^* and O^* be the sets of strings of finite length composed from the members of I and O.[2] Any program's set of permissible inputs, L and possible outputs, L^o, will be subsets of I^* and O^* respectively. A program computes the function f if it maps every string $s \in L$ into a string $f(s) \in L^o$.

This terminology can be applied to the most prosaic computations. Consider a machine capable of reading and/or printing any decimal digit, the alphabetic characters, and the symbols +, −, ., ,, *, and /.

$$I = O = 1, 2, 3, 4, 5, 6, 7, 8, 9, 0 \tag{1}$$

A, B, C, D, E, F, G, H, I, J, K, L, M, N, O, P, Q, R, S, T, U, V, W, X, Y, Z

+, −, ., ,, *, /.

Clearly $I^*=O^*$. Suppose the computer is programmed to calculate the greatest

---

[2] In general if S is a finite set S^* will be the set of strings composed of members of S. Note that S^* is infinite and that it includes the null string (   ).

integer contained in the square of a real number. The input language is the character representation of the real numbers, and the output language is the character representation of the positive integers. In more conventional terms we would say that the program realizes a function whose domain is the real numbers and whose range is the positive integers. The two descriptions are equivalent.

The logical steps involved in computing a function of a string of symbols will now be considered in detail. The discussion will be based on the action of a program's procedure part and its static and dynamic memories. It has already been shown that finite memory has only a finite set S of states. Let S^t be the state which the machine (program) is in at time t. The notation S_i will be used to indicate a particular one of the states in S, without regard to time. Similarly, we will use M^t and M_j to refer to the state of dynamic memory. Recall that M, the set of possible states of dynamic memory, is infinite but countable, since at any one time M^t will consist of a finite number of filled locations, each of which contains k bits of information, and an infinite set of unused locations. Each of these locations is addressable, in the sense that it is physically possible for the general-purpose computer to access any location. A particular program, however, may be restricted in its access to dynamic memory. To give this discussion some concreteness, it helps to think of static memory as the information in a fixed section of a computer's primary memory, and dynamic memory as a conceptually infinite scratch tape. Finally, the procedure part of a program must consist of a finite set of rules specifying changes in either static or dynamic memory, or both, as a function of the current state of each memory and of the information input at each step in the computing process.

The operations of printing (i.e., output) and halting have not yet been considered. These can be associated directly with the state of static memory. Two not necessarily disjoint subsets of S, P and F, are distinguished as printing and halting states. Whenever the machine reaches any $S_p \in P$, an associated message is to be printed. As soon as the machine reaches any state $S_f \in F$, it halts.

Figure 2-3 is a "generic flow chart" for the action of any conceivable program. The program begins at $t = 0$ in state $S^t = S_0$, i.e. in its normal starting state. At Step (1) any print message associated with S^t is output. At Step (2) the computer is stopped if a halt state has been reached. Assuming that this has not happened, the next symbol x is read from the input stream, at Step (3). Steps (4a) and (4b) reflect the use of dynamic memory. The figure shows first the retrieval of a string $\mathbf{y}$ of symbols from locations R^t in dynamic memory. This is more complex. The set R^t of locations to be read at time t is determined as a joint function of S^t and x, the symbol just read. Let $\mathbf{y}$ be the information so retrieved. At Step (4b) information $\mathbf{y}'$ is written into locations W^t of dynamic memory. Both $\mathbf{y}'$ and W^t are functions of S^t, x, and $\mathbf{y}$. Although Steps (4a) and (4b) are shown as happening in series, in practice the reading and writing operations are normally intermingled. Note, however, that they can be separated logically without loss of generality. Also, we allow the situation in which either R^t or W^t is the empty set, in which case there is no reading or writing. Finally, in Step (5), the state of finite memory is changed

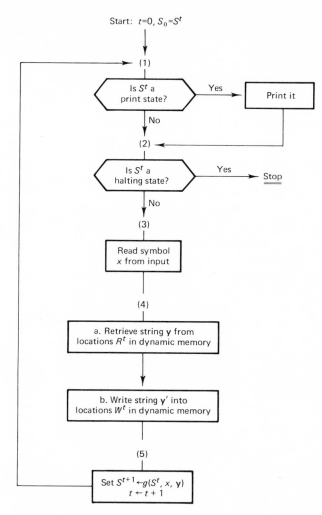

Fig. 2-3.   Steps in computing a function of a string of symbols.

from S^t to S^{t+1}, as a function of S^t, x, and $\mathbf{y}$, and t is incremented by 1. The cycle then begins again at Step (1).

This picture corresponds closely to a programmer's idea of what a program does. A trivial simplification assigns the printing function to a separate machine. The resulting configuration is shown in Figure 2-4. Instead of printing during program execution, the computer sends a record of the states of finite memory through which it passes to the printing machine. Let this record be the string

$$\mathbf{S} = S^0, S^1, \ldots, S^t, \ldots, S^x \tag{2}$$

$\mathbf{S}$ is a string in S^*. The printing machine is capable of recognizing when a state S^t is

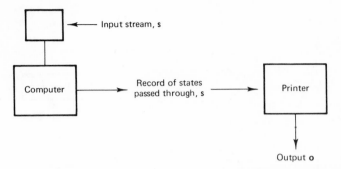

Fig. 2-4. Simplification of program action to do printing after computation.

a print state, at which time it prints the associated output symbols. The printing machine, then, is a simple device for mapping from strings in S^* to strings in O^*. Clearly if the computer maps from the input string s to $\mathbf{S}$, the computer plus printer maps from s to $\mathbf{o} \in O^*$.

A nontrivial simplification collapses Steps (4) and (5), in which dynamic memory is changed from state M^t to state M^{t+1} by manipulation of the contents of locations R^t and W^t, then static memory is changed from state S^t to state S^{t+1}. Changing from the temporal notation to the notation indicating specific states of memory, the transition that takes place at any one step can be written

$$(S_i, M_j, x) \to (S_{i'}, M_{j'}). \tag{3}$$

This has the intuitive interpretation:

> *Having been in static memory state S_i and dynamic memory state M_j, the program read input symbol x and moved to static state $S_{i'}$ and dynamic memory to state $M_{j'}$.*

We can think of the input string s as driving the program through a sequence of such transitions and, as a by-product, producing the string $\mathbf{S}$ which is the input to the printing machine. Each symbol of s forces the transition by activating orders within the procedure part of the program, causing the desired action to take place.

What can be said about the orders contained in the procedure part? First, there must be a finite number of them, since the procedure part itself occupies a finite region of a digital machine. Second, the orders are orders to take specific action upon occurrence of a condition which can be recognized by a digital device *in a single step*. Such a condition must be one of a finite set of possible conditions.[3] Program steps, then, can be written in the form

$$\text{Given condition } A \to \text{Produce condition } B \tag{4}$$

---

[3] To see this, consider a program which reads Hollerith coded cards and prints the contents of a card if it contains the letter Q. Obviously such a program can read any of an infinite set of finite sequences of cards. At any one step of its operation, however, the computer must have a rule to tell it what to do with one of the 2^{960} possible configurations of a single card.

but a form such as the left side of (3) is not suitable as a description of condition A in (4), since (S_i, M_j, x) makes reference to the state of M_j, which is one of the infinitely many states of dynamic memory. To avoid this problem, we associate with each state of static memory a *dynamic memory reading function* h_i and a *dynamic memory writing function* g_i. The reading function maps from the infinite set of combinations of dynamic memory state and input symbol (i.e., the set $M \times I$) into a finite set of possible retrievals of information from dynamic memory. In the terms used in describing Figure 2-3, the reading function determines the locations R to be read from dynamic memory, and then produces one of a finite set $\{y\}$ of possible strings y of symbols by reading these locations. The writing function takes as its arguments the input symbol, the retrieved information y, and the current state of dynamic memory, and produces a new state of dynamic memory by determining locations W and writing some function of x and y into them. Thus each program step can be written in the form

$$(S_i, x, y) \rightarrow (S_i{}', g_i(M^t, x, y)), \tag{5}$$

where y is a string in the (finite) range of h_i and M^t is whatever state dynamic memory happens to be in when g_i is activated. A program is equivalent to a finite set of rules of the form of (5). The program is executed in the following steps.

1. Determine that $S^t = S_i$. If $S_i \in F$, halt. Otherwise go to 2.
2. Read x and execute $h_i(M^t, x)$, thus determining y.
3. Scan the production part for a rule whose left part is (S_i, x, y). If no such rule is found, an error has occurred and the machine halts with s unread. If two such rules exist only the first one found by the scan of the program part will be used. Assume an appropriate rule is found:
4. Change static memory to state $S_{i'}$. Execute $g_i(M^t, x, y)$. Set t to $t + 1$ and return to Step 1.

It may seem by this point that the description is fairly well removed from a programmer's view of a program. In fact, the reading and writing functions may not be at all exotic. A typical example of h_i, one which in fact does map from the infinite set $\{M_j\}$ to the finite set $\{y\}$, is simply

$h_i(M^t, x)$ = Contents of the first location in dynamic memory following (6)
the first location from the start of memory which contains
the symbol x.

Similarly, a possible writing function is

$g_i(M^t, x, y)$ = Concatenate x to y and place the resulting string in (7)
consecutive locations beginning at the first location in
dynamic memory which the program has not yet used.

Transition rules such as (5) are not normally written down explicitly by a programmer.[4] Rather, they are defined by inference. Consider a FORTRAN

---

[4] A glaring exception to this statement is the use of decision tables in computer programming.

program being executed on a machine with a 32-bit word, which uses logical tape 5 for input and logical tape 10 as a dynamic memory area. The program fragment

READ(5) I

READ(10) J

J=I+J

WRITE(10) J

together with its associated program counter (which is part of static memory), specifies 2^{64} possible transition rules. Many of these rules will produce the same result at the end of the program fragment.[5]

To sum up, what can be done with this somewhat unusual view of computation? It has been shown that if a string $s \in I^*$ is an acceptable input to a program (i.e., if $s \in L$, where L is the input language of the program), then the symbols of s drive the machine simulated by the program through a sequence of states **S**. A trivially simple machine can receive **S** as input and produce the required output. The role of dynamic memory is to enable the simulated machine to keep a record of its past actions, so that its response to symbol s_t (the tth symbol of s) can be a function of the sequence $s_0 \ldots \ldots s_{t-1}$. The types of records that can be kept will be determined by the reading and writing functions which the machine can use to manipulate dynamic memory, so we again suspect that describing these functions will turn out to be a useful way to distinguish classes of machines which programs can simulate.

In the next section we shift our attention from a concern with a generic flow chart for all programs to a generic description for sets of strings. More particularly, we consider ways in which a language L can be characterized. Why do we do this? We have shown here that if s can be accepted by a machine, then we can compute

$$S = f(s) \tag{8}$$

and from this, trivially, produce the value of $f(s)$ in a desired output language. Typically in computing we are given a function f, of known domain L, and asked to produce a program that will construct $f(s)$ for all s in L. If we can find a way to describe L that dictates the construction of machines which can accept the strings in L, then we will know a good deal about the required program.

2.2   Formal Grammars

If the computing power of a machine is to be characterized by the complexity of the languages which it can recognize, some way of ordering the complexity of languages is needed. The one which is used is due to the mathematical linguist Naom Chomsky (1963). To understand Chomsky's concept of a language is it first

---

[5] The possibility of halting on overflow has been ignored in this example.

necessary to grasp his idea of a *grammar*. A grammar, G, is a quadruple $\langle N, T, S, P \rangle$ where N is a set of *nonterminal symbols*, or *variables*, T is a set of *terminal symbols* disjoint from N (in terms of the previous discussion, $T = I$, the set of input symbols), $V = N \cup T$ is called the *vocabulary* of G. S is a *distinguished symbol* in the set of nonterminals. It is sometimes called the *head* or *sentence* symbol. P is a finite set of *production rules* or *rewriting rules*. Each rule of P has the form

$$\mathbf{x} \rightarrow \mathbf{y} \qquad (9)$$

where $\mathbf{x}$ and $\mathbf{y}$ are strings in V^*. If the rule $\mathbf{x} \rightarrow \mathbf{y}$ is in P, then $\mathbf{y}$ is *directly derivable* from $\mathbf{x}$. If the rules

$$\mathbf{x_0} \rightarrow \mathbf{x_1}; \quad \mathbf{x_1} \rightarrow \mathbf{x_2}; \dots; \mathbf{x_i} \rightarrow \mathbf{x_{i+1}}; \dots; \mathbf{x_{n-1}} \rightarrow \mathbf{y} \qquad (10)$$

are in P, then $\mathbf{y}$ is *derivable* from $\mathbf{x_0}$, which is written $\mathbf{x} \overset{*}{+} \mathbf{y}$. There must be at least one rule of the form $S \rightarrow \mathbf{x}$, and for every variable symbol $A \in N$ there must be a rule of the form

$$\mathbf{x} A \mathbf{y} \rightarrow \mathbf{w} \qquad (11)$$

where $\mathbf{w}$, $\mathbf{x}$, and $\mathbf{y}$ are (possibly empty) strings in V^*. The language generated by G, $L(G)$, is the set of strings of terminal symbols that can be derived from S. Thus $L(G) \subseteq T^*$ and is equivalent to L in the previous notation. The symbol L will be used for $L(G)$ in places where, hopefully, no confusion can arise.

As an illustration of the idea of a rewriting system consider the language defined by the vocabulary

$$N = \{S, A, B\}, \qquad T = \{\mathbf{x}, \mathbf{y}\} \qquad (12)$$

and the grammar

$$
\begin{array}{lll}
S \rightarrow AB & \text{(R1)} & \qquad (13) \\
A \rightarrow \mathbf{x} & \text{(R2)} & \\
A \rightarrow A\mathbf{x} & \text{(R3)} & \\
B \rightarrow \mathbf{y} & \text{(R4)} & \\
B \rightarrow B\mathbf{y} & \text{(R5)} &
\end{array}
$$

This language contains all strings consisting of $n > 0$ x's followed by $k > 0$ y's. The string **xxxyy** could be generated in the following steps:

String	Rule applied	
S	Starting state	(14)
AB	R1	
ABy	R5	
Ayy	R4	
$Axyy$	R3	
$Axxyy$	R3	
$xxxyy$	R2	

Rules such as those in (13) are called *phrase structure* rules. They always involve expansion of a variable symbol into a string. The successive application of phrase structure rules to produce a string of terminal symbols can be illustrated by a *phrase marker*, which is a tree diagram showing the derivation of each terminal symbol from S. As an illustration, the phrase marker for example (14) is shown in Figure 2-5.

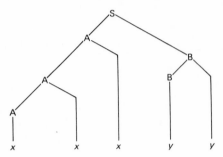

Fig. 2-5.   Phrase marker for *xxxyy* generation by grammar (6).

If the rewriting rule

$$AB \to BA \qquad (15)$$

is added to G to form the grammar G', we have a qualitatively different language, since this rule changes the order of the symbols in a string without expanding a nonterminal symbol. This is called a *transformational rule*, and grammars which contain such rules are called *transformational* grammars. In dealing with transformational rewritings it is often necessary to distinguish between distinct occurrences of the same nonterminal symbol. To illustrate, let T_i stand for a term in a simple arithmetic expression. The commutativity of + can be expressed by the transformation

$$T_1 + T_2 \to T_2 + T_1, \qquad (16)$$

but it is necessary to indicate which term is moved to which location.

Transformational grammars are more powerful and much more complex than phrase structure grammars. The fact that a transformational grammar does not always associate a phrase marker directly with a string of terminal symbols is particularly important.

There is one additional and important rewriting rule which does not fit well with the formalisms introduced. This is the familiar substitution rule, which states that a variable symbol may be replaced by a structure derivable from it, provided that the replacement is made consistently in all situations in which the replaced variable occurs. For example, in school algebra the substitution rule permits the transformation

$$(A + V) - V \to [A + (3B - 4)] - (3B - 4). \qquad (17)$$

It is possible to define the substitution rule as a phrase structure rewriting rule, but to do so would involve a number of circumlocutions. Hopefully the example has made the idea clear.

TABLE 2-1

A Language Abstracted from the ALGOL 60 Definition of Simple Arithmetic Expressions

Vocabulary	$V = N \cup T$
	$N = S$, *term, adop, multop, factor, variable, constant*
	$T = +, 1, *, /, (,)$, "any letter," "any integer"

Grammar G

P1. $S \rightarrow term$	P7. $factor \rightarrow variable$
P2. $S \rightarrow S\ adop\ term$	P8. $factor \rightarrow constant$
P3. $adop \rightarrow +$	P9. $factor \rightarrow (S)$
P4. $adop \rightarrow -$	P10. $variable \rightarrow$ "any letter"
P5. $term \rightarrow factor$	P11. $constant \rightarrow$ "any integer"
P6. $term \rightarrow term\ multop\ factor$	P12. $multop \rightarrow *$
	P13. $multop \rightarrow /$

Typical expressions

$$a, \quad a + (b * 2), \quad b - 3 * (c + 4)$$

Strings in T* but not in L

$$a -, \quad b(x + a), \quad + b -)a + 2 \ (\ , 2(\ ) + 3 - c/$$

The usual convention is to illustrate grammars of different classes by simple example, so that linguistic principles are clear. To motivate future discussion two more interesting but more complex examples will be given here. Table 2-1 describes a grammar consisting of phrase structure rules only. It is a simplification of the grammar used in ALGOL 60 to define simple arithmetic expressions. The language generated by this grammar consists of expressions such as

$$a; \quad a + b; \quad a + b*c; \quad a - b*(c + d).$$

Obviously recognizing that a string is a well-formed simple arithmetic expression is an important part of practical computing.

Table 2-2 presents a set of transformation rules. If these rules and the algebraic rule of substitution (that any simple arithmetic expression can replace a free variable) are added to the rules of Table 2-1, we obtain a language for rewriting arithmetic expressions into equivalent ones. Suppose the language also has added to it a new head symbol, S', and the rule

$$S' \rightarrow s, \tag{18}$$

where s is some arithmetic expression. The language generated will be the set of

TABLE 2-2

Rewriting Rules for Algebraic Manipulation

Vocabulary $V' = N' \cup T'$
$N' = N$ *free variable, bound variable*
$T' = T$ $w_i,$ $i = 1, \ldots, n$

Grammar G   *Phrase structure rules* P1–P13 of Table 2-1, with the following changes:
   bound variable replaces *variable* in P10.
   Add the following rules:
   P14 *variable* → *bound variable*
   P15 *variable* → *free variable*
   P16 *free variable* → w_i $i = 1, \ldots, n.$

Substitution rule
   SO $w_i → S$ provided the replacement is made at all points at which w_i
      appears in a string.

Transformation rules
   T1 $S_1 + S_2 → S_2 + S_1$
   T2 $S_1 + (S_2 + S_3) → (S_1 + S_2) + S_3$
   T3 $(S_1 + S_2) + S_3 → [S_1 + (S_2 + S_3)]$
   T4 $S_1 → (S_1 + S_2) - S_2$
   T5 $(S_1 - S_2) + S_3 → (S_1 + S_3) - S_2$
   T6 $(S_1 + S_2) - S_3 → (S_1 - S_3) + S_2$
   T7 $S_1 * S_2 → S_2 * S_1$
   T8 $S_1 * (S_2 \, adop \, S_3) → S_1 * S_2 \, adop \, S_1 * S_3$
   T9 $S_1 * S_2 \, adop \, S_1 * S_3 → S_1 * (S_2 \, adop \, S_3)$
   T10 $(S_1 + S_2) - S_2 → S_1$

---

strings which are algebraic equivalents of the string s. For example, if s is replaced
by $x + 2 * (a - 3)$ in (11) the resulting language includes the strings

$$x + (a - 3) * 2 \qquad \text{and} \qquad x + 2 * a - 2 * 3.$$

Given this background, consider the "state space" problem

> *Using the rules of algebra given in Table 2-2, prove that B + (A − C) is
> equivalent to A + (B − C).*

This may be recast as a linguistic recognition problem by letting $A + (B − C)$
replace s in (18).

Consider the capabilities of the machines that accept the strings generated by
these grammars. A machine which could accept the simple arithmetic expressions
could also output a string of machine order codes which would compute the
arithmetic value of an expression. A machine which could recognize a string of
symbols as derivable from another string could check algebraic derivations,
although, as we shall see, its assertion that a derivation was incorrect should be
treated with caution. Both these applications present nontrivial computing problems.

Formal grammars present a natural way to order languages, by the restrictions which can be placed on the rewriting rules. Ordering from most powerful to least, we have:

A *type 0 language* or *unrestricted rewriting* system is generated by a grammar in which all rules are of the form

$$x \rightarrow y \tag{19}$$

where x and y are strings in V^*.

A *type 1* language, or *context sensitive* language is generated by a grammar in which all rules are of this form and, in addition, the number of symbols in y (written |y|) is not less than the number of symbols in x. The force of this restriction is best appreciated by examining a rewriting rule which violates it. Rule T10 of Table 2-2 is an example. It can be shown (although we shall not do so) that a language generated by a context sensitive grammar can also be generated by a grammar in which all rules are of the form

$$xAy \rightarrow xwy \tag{20}$$

where w, x, and y are strings in V^* and A is a variable symbol. Since (20) can be interpreted as

String w *may be derived from A if A appears in the context of* x *and* y,

(20) provides a more intuitive definition of a context sensitive grammar.

Context free or *type 2 languages* are generated by grammars in which all the rules are of the form

$$A \rightarrow x \tag{21}$$

where, as before, A is a variable symbol and x is a string in V^*.

Finally, *regular* or *type 3* languages are generated by grammars whose rules are written either

$$A \rightarrow aB \tag{22a}$$

or

$$A \rightarrow a \tag{22b}$$

where a is a terminal symbol and B is a variable symbol.

It is straightforward to see that all type 3 languages are type 2 languages, all type 2 languages are type 1 languages, and type 1 are type 0 languages. Therefore it is not surprising to find that very powerful automata are required to accept type 0 languages, somewhat less powerful to accept type 1 languages, and so forth.

2.3   Turing Machines

2.3.0   TURING MACHINES DEFINED

A *Turing machine*[6] (TM) is an automaton that has all the logical capabilities an actual computing machine could possibly have. For this reason the accepted

---

[6] Named after the English mathematician A.M. Turing, who used these automata to establish a number of basic results concerning computability.

definition of a computable function is one that can be computed by a Turing machine. A TM consists of an infinitely long tape, a read head, positioned at some point along the tape, and a computer which must be in one of a finite set S of internal states. A program for the machine is a finite set of transition rules of the form

If the computer is in state S_i and symbol a_j is read on the tape, move the read head k steps to the right (left if k is negative) and write symbol B_r on the tape. Then switch the machine to state S_m.

A rule for a TM can be written

$$(a_j, S_i) \rightarrow (k, B_r, S_m) \tag{23}$$

in which the symbols are defined as in the verbal description. In the subsequent discussion it will be assumed that no two transition rules have the same left-hand side, i.e., that we are dealing with a *deterministic* machine.

A TM can be described in the terms of a program with a procedure part and static and dynamic memories. The finite set of transition rules is equivalent to the procedure part. The internal states of the machine are equivalent to the possible states of static memory. The TM's tape serves a tripartite function, as the input and the output streams and as dynamic memory. Since the TM can write on the tape and can move it in either direction, it can use the tape to store any arbitrary number of intermediate results. As there is no limit on the size or direction of the moves of the tape, before a symbol is written, any symbol on the tape is accessible to a TM without altering the tape's contents. The reading and writing functions of a Turing machine, then, may specify retrieval of information from or insertion of information into any location in dynamic memory.

The idea of accepting and rejecting a string can also be stated in terms of the actions of a TM. Initially the machine is started in state S_0 with its tape blank, except for the string s whose first symbol is immediately under the read head. The appropriate transition rules are applied until the machine reaches some state $S_f \in F$, where F is the set of halting states, as before. The machine accepts s as a member of its input language L if, after reading the last symbol of s, the machine reaches a state in F for the first time. There is no restriction on the amount of tape manipulation that may occur before S_f is reached.

A language $L \subseteq I^*$ is said to be *recursively enumerable* if a TM that will accept all strings in L and no other strings can be constructed. A language is *recursive* if both L and its complement, the set $I^* - L$, are recursively enumerable. It is worth pondering for a moment what these properties imply. If L is recursive, then a TM, or, equivalently, a program, can be written to recognize whether a given string is or is not a member of the set L. The program may require very powerful dynamic memory manipulation functions. The TM in question actually consists of two submachines, one of which recognizes strings in L and one which recognizes strings in $I^* - L$. The main machine simply notes which of the two submachines accepts the input string. On the other hand, suppose that L is recursively enumerable but not recursive. Then the main machine cannot be constructed, for the sub-component for recognizing strings in $I^* - L$ cannot be constructed. The sub-component for recognizing strings in L would not be sufficient, for if it did not stop, we would not know whether it was caught in a loop in manipulating dynamic memory or whether it simply needed more time to accept the string.

These concepts are illustrated in an important artificial intelligence application. Let L be the set of well-formed expressions (wfe's) which can be derived from a set S of axiomatic statements by applying the rules of inference associated with the logical connectives *and*, *or*, and *not* and the quantifiers *some* and *all*. This set is recursively enumerable, but not recursive. Answering the question, "Do facts S imply conclusion s?" is equivalent to asking "Is s a member of L?" Suppose the true answer is "no." Then s is a string in $I^* - L$, and it *may* not be possible to recognize this fact in finite time. A study by Biss, Chien, and Stahl (1971) offers an interesting concrete example. Biss *et al.* wrote a theorem proving program intended to recognize examples of illegal behavior in automobile driving. The axiomatic statements were the rules of the road, as defined by the *Illinois Driver's Manual*. The program's task was to determine whether these rules proscribed certain definable behaviors. Abstractly, this is a problem in determining whether behavior s is included in the language L which can be generated by applying rules of logical inference to the basic description of illegal behavior. By reference to the fact that L is recursively enumerable, we know that the program cannot work in all cases, although any positive identifications which it produced would by valid.[7]

2.3.1 TURING MACHINES AND TYPE 0 LANGUAGES

Since a Turing machine is the most powerful automaton we shall define, it is not surprising to find that a Turing machine has a powerful linguistic capacity. The following statement is the basic finding concerning turing machines:

> *A turing machine can be constructed to accept any language which has been generated by an unrestricted rewriting system.*

To illustrate the importance of this conclusion, examine the grammar G' defined by Tables 2-1 and 2-2. The transformation rules of G' which are found in Table 2-2 could equally well be called rules of inference for algebraic derivations, or operators in a state–space problem. More generally, given any state–space problem as outlined in Chapter 1 (and dealt with in more detail in Part III), it is possible to construct rewriting rules that define states and operations on states. In general it will be

---

[7] Biss *et al.* made an interesting use of the fact that positive identifications are valid. If after an arbitrary time an input statement had not been identified as forbidden behavior, processing was ceased and a statement describing a counterexample of the behavior in question was input to the program. If this statement could be identified as an illegal act, then the original behavior could be assumed not to be illegal. While such a strategy may be useful in particular cases, it does not represent an escape to the limits imposed by TM capabilities. There is no certainty that the original statement might not be accepted in a finite time, but a time greater than that which Biss *et al.* were willing to wait.

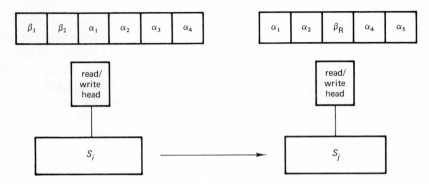

Fig. 2-6.   Transition from one state to another in a Turing machine. In this example, the machine read α_1, then moved the read head two spaces to the right and wrote β_R on the tape.

necessary to use transformational rules, as in the example of Table 2-2. From this we conclude that any problem which has a state–space representation can be thought of as a type 0 language, and hence can be solved by a program which, like a Turing machine, has unrestricted access to a conceptually infinite dynamic memory area.

A second major conclusion of formal linguistics is

Any language generated by a type 0 grammar is recursively enumerable.

It is now generally accepted that the natural languages cannot be generated by any grammar less powerful than a type 0 grammar (Chomsky, 1965: For a less technical argument, see Thomas, 1965). The need for a type 0 grammar is easily demonstrated. Thomas (1965, p. 100) points out that English requires the rule.

$$\text{(Noun Phrase Singular) be (Past)} \rightarrow \text{(Noun Phrase Singular) was} \qquad (24)$$

In order to derive sentences like *John was* from *John be* (Past). Rule (24) violates the type 1 restriction that derivations be of nondecreasing length. English also requires a number of rules for rearrangement of a sentence. Passive statements provide an example. The sentences

$$\textit{John threw the ball to Mary} \qquad (24a)$$

and

$$\textit{The ball was thrown to Mary by John} \qquad (24b)$$

have the same meaning, and intuitively, should have the same underlying structure. Figure 2-7 shows a reasonable parsing diagram, using a simple grammar. The actively voiced sentence can be generated by a parsing tree directly. The passively voiced sentence requires a rewriting rule such as

$$\langle\text{noun phrase}_1\rangle \langle\text{verb}\rangle \langle\text{noun phrase}_2\rangle \rightarrow \langle\text{noun phrase}_2\rangle \qquad (25)$$
$$\langle\text{passive (verb)}\rangle \langle\text{preposition}\rangle \langle\text{noun phrase}_1\rangle$$

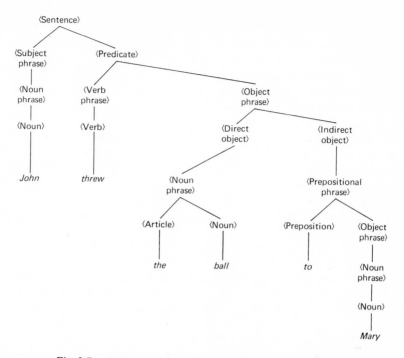

Fig. 2-7. Phrase structure of a natural language sentence.

in order to replace the active form by the passive form. Rule (25) is a transformational rule, similar to the $AB \rightarrow BA$ example of Section 2.2.

The relevant point for artificial intelligence research is that any program which is to compute a function whose domain is the set of sentences in some natural language must be a program modeled by no less an automaton than a Turing machine. Therefore the program will require unrestricted access to its dynamic memory system.

2.4   Linear Bounded Automata and Type 1 Languages

A *linear bounded automaton* is a Turing machine that is not permitted to move the read head beyond the area of the input tape occupied by the input string. This can be achieved by adding to the input language two special symbols (conventionally ¢ and $). These are placed at the front and end of the input string, which then becomes ¢s$. The transition rules of the linear bounded automaton are similar to those of a TM except that whenever the symbols ¢ or $ are read the read head moves one space right or left.

A linear bounded automaton is a model of a program that has unrestricted access to a finite region of the "dynamic" memory area, where the appropriate size of this region can be determined by examining the input string at run time, before conducting an analysis of the input for acceptance purposes. In fact, we can simply regard that portion of the tape required by the input as a scratch area.

The linear bounded automaton model has a nonobvious implication for programming. Recall that an automaton is said to be deterministic if, for each of its combinations of input and internal state, there exists at most one transition rule specifying the next action to be taken. An automaton is nondeterministic if a given input–internal state configuration is the left hand side of more than one transition rule. In dealing with Turing machines the distinction between deterministic and nondeterministic automata was ignored, since it can be shown that for every nondeterministic Turing machine there exists an equivalent deterministic one. It is not known whether or not this is true for linear bounded automata, so until the question is answered, the prudent programmer must assume that if he has to write a program which has a linear bounded automaton as a model, then he ought to assume that the automaton is nondeterministic. A nondeterministic automaton may be faced with choices as to the transition rule to use when a particular memory configuration presents itself. If the wrong choice is made, the automaton will subsequently reach a stopping state without accepting the string. It will then be necessary to back up to the choice point and try to accept the string by taking the alternative computing path. This cannot be done unless fairly elaborate records of previous actions taken are kept.

A theoretical finding concerning linear bounded automata is

A language L is accepted by a linear bounded automaton if and only if it is a type 1 language.

This result in itself is not of a great deal of use since, as we have just argued, the linear bounded automata are models of complex programs. On the other hand, proving that a function f has a domain which is a context-sensitive language can be of some help, since it establishes the memory manipulating and record-keeping capabilities which the program must have to compute f.

The observation

All context-sensitive languages are recursive

is of more use. This states that if a function f has a domain L which can be generated by a type 1 language, then we know we can write a (perhaps complicated) program that is guaranteed to accept all strings $s \in I^*$ and either produce the value of $f(s)$ or produce a reliable signal that f is not defined for s. On the other hand, failure to prove that L is a type 1 language, or even proof that it is a type 0 language, does not guarantee that L is not recursive. There are recursive languages that cannot be generated by a type 1 grammar.

2.5   Pushdown Automata and Type 2 Languages

A pushdown automaton (PDA) is an automaton with limited access to a conceptually infinite storage tape. The structure of a PDA and the form of its transitions are shown in Figure 2-8. The PDA is only allowed to move its read head to the right; i.e., it must accept each input symbol in order. The PDA also has a storage tape which it may move "up" or "down." If the motion of the tape places a symbol "above" the storage tape read head that symbol is lost. By analogy to the movement of plates in a stack of dishes in a cafeteria, the operations of moving the symbols up and down are sometimes called "popping" and "pushing." In the terminology of operations research, the storage tape acts as a last in–first out (LIFO) queue. The storage tape represents limited access to infinite memory, since if the jth from the last symbol to be written on the tape is to be read, then the $j - 1$ intervening symbols must first be erased.

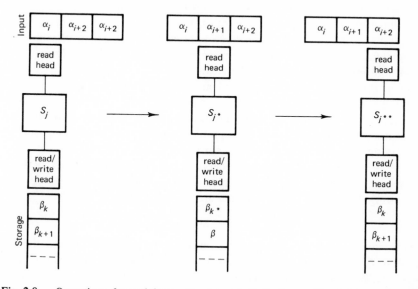

Fig. 2-8.   Operation of a pushdown automaton. Initially the machine is in state S_j, reading symbol α_i on the input and symbol β_{k*} on the storage tape. At the first transition, the input tape is moved forward and β_{k*} pushed onto the storage tape. The machine goes to state S_{j*}. At the second step, the input tape is moved (α_{i+1}) read, β_{k*} is read and popped from the storage tape, and the machine moves to S_{j**}.

In operation a PDA begins in state S_0 with the input string s on the input tape and with blanks on the storage tape. Subsequent configurations are defined by the name of the symbol read, the internal state of the PDA, and the name of the symbol under the storage tape read head. The machine's transition rules can be stated in the form

$$(\alpha, S_i, b_r) \rightarrow (S_j, b_q) \tag{26}$$

which has the intuitive interpretation

If in state S_i with b_r on top of the storage tape, then if input symbol α is read, push the storage tape and write b_q on it.

A special "pop symbol," b°, is required in the alphabet of the storage tape. The command "write b°" is interpreted as "pop the storage tape."

> *A language can be accepted by a pushdown automaton if and only if it is a type 2 language.*

This is an extremely important result for computer science, since most conventional programming languages are (with minor exceptions) type 2 languages. In fact, the majority of compilers are consciously designed as specific examples of pushdown automata. The programming techniques for dealing with dynamic memory management in pushdown automata have been highly developed. The interested reader is referred to Gries (1971) for a discussion.

Within artificial intelligence there are a number of problems which, although superficially quite nonlinguistic, can be phrased as the problem of computing a function whose domain is a type 2 language. Surprisingly, many problems in picture recognition and manipulation can be treated this way. (Examples will be given in Part II of this book.) As soon as a problem can be formulated as one of recognizing a type 2 language we have at our call the impressive amount of knowledge computer science has built up to handle such languages. Therefore it is often worth investigating the relation between the problem at hand and type 2 languages when one is trying to decide upon a structure for the required program.

There is an interesting relationship between type 2 and the more restrictive type 3 grammars. The rewriting rules of a type 2 grammar each expand a single variable into a string. If the rules of a grammar G are such that the relation

$$A \overset{*}{\to} xAy \tag{27}$$

holds for some variable symbol A (i.e., if a string containing A can be derived from A), then G is said to be *self-embedding*. If a type 2 grammar G is *non self-embedding* there exists a type 3 grammar, G', which generates the same language. In the next section it will be shown that there is a very simple model of an automaton which accepts type 3 languages, and that this model dictates program structure directly. Sometimes one may encounter cases in which the most obvious grammar for some language is a type 2 grammar that, upon inspection, turns out to be non self-embedding. In this case it is usually worthwhile to construct the (perhaps less intuitive) type 3 grammar which generates the same language and use it to guide programming.

2.6   Finite Automata and Regular (Type 3) Languages

A *finite automaton* is a machine without any dynamic memory. In familiar programming terms, a FORTRAN program without scratch tapes defines a finite automaton, since this program has no dynamic storage. Similarly, PL-1 and ALGOL programs that do not define dynamic data structures can be represented as finite automata, so the class of programs is of no little practical importance.

Formally, a finite automaton M is defined by the quintuple

$$M = (S, I, P, S_0, F) \tag{28}$$

where S is a finite set of internal states of memory, including a unique starting state S_0, $I = \{\alpha_k\}$ is the finite input alphabet, and $F \subseteq S$ is the set of finish states; P is a mapping from the set $S \times I$ into S, defining the rules of transition from one state to another as a function of the current state and the input symbol. The intuitive organization of a finite automaton is shown in Figure 2-9. The machine begins in S_0. At each step it reads one symbol from the tape, advances the read head one space to the right and changes static memory to a state whose identity is determined by the present state and the input symbol. The cycle is then repeated, until some state $S_f \in F$ is reached. The machine accepts an input string $s \in I^*$ if it reaches S_f for the first time immediately after reading the last symbol of s.

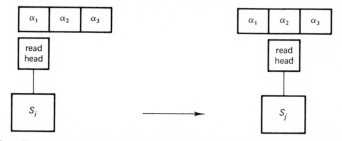

Fig. 2-9.   Finite automaton moving from state S_i to state S_j after reading symbol α_k.

A useful way to represent a finite automaton is by a graph in which the nodes represent states of the machine and the labeled arcs indicate the symbols to be read at each transition. An example is shown in Figure 2-10. Thinking of a finite automaton as a graph leads directly to a method for writing the corresponding program, since there is a simple transformation of graph theoretic operations into operations on arrays. If M is a graph, then it can be represented by the connection matrix C, where

$$C_{ij} = k \qquad \text{if the rule } (S_i, \alpha_k) \rightarrow (S_j) \text{ exists in the automaton;} \tag{29}$$
$$C_{ij} = 0 \qquad \text{if no rule of the form } (S_i, \alpha_k) \rightarrow (S_j) \text{ exists;}$$
$$C_{ii} = -1 \qquad \text{if } S_i \in F. \text{ In this case } C_{ij} = 0 \text{ for } j \neq i.$$

A very simple control program is all that is needed to read matrix C and simulate the actions of the finite automaton which it defines.

> *A language L is accepted by a finite automaton if and only if L is a regular (type 3) language.*

Recall that the rules of a regular language are of the form

$$A \rightarrow x \tag{30a}$$

or

$$A \rightarrow xB, \tag{30b}$$

where x is a terminal symbol and A and B are variable symbols. Rule (30a) can be interpreted as

When in state S_A if x is read move to state S_f in F.

While rule (30b) is interpreted as

When in state S_A if x is read move to S_B.

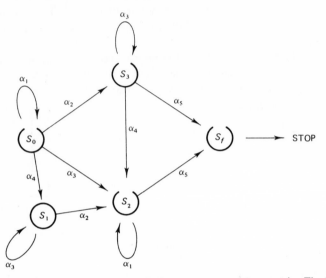

Fig. 2-10.   A finite automaton represented as a state transition matrix. The labels on the arcs name the symbol to be read at each transition.

These interpretations provide the basic building blocks for a graphic representation of a finite automaton. The graph is composed of arcs entering and leaving the same node and arcs connecting distinct nodes. Figure 2-11 illustrates the three types of node–arc combinations possible, the terminating arc corresponding to (30a) and the two possible arcs for (30b), one for the case in which A and B are distinct symbols and one for the case in which A and B are identical. This illustrates a simple way to move from the definition of a regular language to a graph defining an automaton which accepts the language, and from there to a representation of the graph as an array. A program to automate the process is not hard to write. Such a program would receive as input the definition of a type 3 language and produce as output a program which accepted the language.

The following fact is often of practical importance:

If L is a finite set of strings in I^*, L can be generated by a regular grammar.

In practice this means that any function whose domain is a finite set of strings can be computed by a (sufficiently large) program without access to a dynamic memory area.

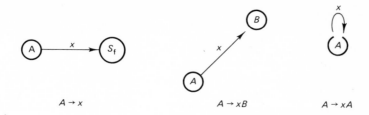

Fig. 2-11.   Graph components corresponding to rule types in finite automata.

2.7   Summary and Comments on Practicality

Four types of languages have been defined, from the relatively unstructured type 0 languages to the highly structured type 3 languages. Each of the higher-order languages is a proper subset of all lower-ordered languages. Corresponding to the sequence of languages there is a sequence of progressively more restricted automata, from Turing machines through linear bounded and pushdown automata to finite automata. The four classes of automata differ in the access they have to a conceptually infinite storage tape. Each machine can be throught of as a master plan for a class of programs with similarly restricted access to a conceptually infinite dynamic storage area.

Actual computing practice may hide the relationship between programs and automata. In programming either TMs or PDAs, one often simulates the "first part" of the conceptually infinite storage tape within the finite memory of an actual computer. The language actually accepted is the language which does not require more tape than this. To appreciate this, observe that in the "pure" definition of FORTRAN as a phrase structure language one should be able to nest parentheses to any level. This would permit arithmetic expressions such as

$$(B + (C + D1 * (D2 / (. . . . .). .). .) + Z \qquad (31)$$

which might contain, say, 974 nested parentheses. In practice, the length of storage tape required by the PDA being simulated by the compiler would exceed the amount of core storage reserved by the program in the actual computer, and the statement would be rejected. This is the "theoretical" reason behind the restriction written into most programming manuals which cautions the programmer not to write statements with more than about 12 levels of nested parentheses.

If a program simulates the top of a storage tape in a finite memory area then, no matter how that area is treated, the program itself defines a finite automaton rather than a PDA. How can we be sure that this limited device will accept a subset of a language which, like pure FORTRAN or ALGOL, has been generated by a constituent structure grammar? The answer is that the subset of the language acceptable to the program will be finite, and it can be shown that any language which contains a finite set of strings can be generated by a regular grammar and, hence, is acceptable by a finite automaton. In practice it is far simpler to think of a translator program as a PDA and remember the side conditions which restrict its operation. The same thing holds for a number of other "pseudo-PDA" programming applications.

A language that can be accepted by a Turing machine is said to be recursively enumerable. If the complement of the language is also recursively enumerable, then the language is recursive. The set of well formed expressions derivable from a set of axiomatic statements in the first-order predicate calculus is recursively enumerable, but not recursive. Therefore there is no way of ensuring that a program designed to recognize such statements will terminate in finite time for any arbitrary well formed expression. This is an important theoretical limitation on Artificial Intelligence. Consider an "ultimate" information retrieval system which is first given a very large data bank, and then asked, "Does statement x follow from this data and the rules of logical inference?" If statement x is not, in fact, derivable, the program may loop.

Other interesting situations have even more formidable restrictions. There are problems in which the desired input language is not recursively enumerable. The set of all true statements in number theory is an example. In practice, however, restrictions due to nonrecursiveness are more important than restrictions due to lack of recursive enumerability.

Virtually all interesting languages for well-formed expressions in mathematics and logic have context-free grammars. Therefore any program which is to process such statements must be at least a PDA. Natural languages, however, require transformational grammars and hence can only be processed by programs defining Turing machines. This implies that natural language analysis programs will have to have complicated mechanisms for addressing a conceptually infinite storage area. A similar conclusion holds for programs designed to perform algebraic manipulations or to prove theorems.

These results may seem discouraging, since they tell us that there are a number of interesting problems that cannot be solved by an algorithm, and many more that cannot be solved by a simple one. We conclude with the more optimistic reminder that in practice one can almost always restrict one's attention to a finite subset of the conceivable sentences in the input language and, pragmatically, solve the problem by writing a program which, although it may be large, does not access a conceptually infinite external storage device. By far the majority of computer applications are of this nature.

Part II
Pattern Recognition

Chapter III

GENERAL CONSIDERATIONS IN PATTERN RECOGNITION

3.0   Classification

Classification is basic to intelligence. We classify so easily that we seldom pause to think of how important it is, or how fine are the classifications we make. You can recognize your own name, spoken by a man or a woman, with or without a cold, against a background of airplane engines or a Beethoven sonata. If you were to analyze the physical stimuli which impinged on your ear in each case, you would find almost no obvious similarities. Now turn to a quite different case. When a physician makes a diagnosis he is not just choosing a name for a man's complaint. He must decide whether or not this particular patient is one of the class of patients for whom treatment X is indicated. Finally, consider a third classification problem. Radar and sonar observers must decide whether or not the particular configurations shown on their displays have been produced by a target, background noise, or a nonrandom target other than the one they are looking for. In general, there will be no perfect rule by which they can do this, since both "target" and noise conditions are capable of producing almost any display configuration. The difference is in the probability with which target or background conditions will give rise to certain displays.

From a psychological point of view, these examples are quite different. The first would normally be treated as a topic in perception, the second as a problem in logical reasoning, and the third as a problem in signal detection. Here is a point at which the man and the computer may differ. It may well be that different psychological processes are involved in each case. On the other hand, the tasks can all be described by the same mathematical formalisms, and, perhaps, should be analyzed by the same algorithms. In each case the observer is given a set of *objects* which can be described by stating the values on each of a known set of *attributes*. Each object is a member of one or more of a fixed set of classes. In the *pattern classification* problem the observer must apply a previously established rule in order to decide to which class an object belongs. In the *pattern recognition* problem the classifying rule must be developed from examination of a set of objects of known class membership. These objects are called, collectively, the *organizing set* or *sample*. In the *pattern formation* problem the objects are presented to the observer without identification of class names. The observer must decide upon an appropriate definition of classes.

For the most part we shall be concerned with the recognition problem. (The discerning reader may have noticed that the classification problem is identical to the problem of recognizing whether a string is a sentence in a formal language.) In this chapter a classification of pattern recognition problems will be presented. The classification scheme generates a number of distinct subclasses of recognition problems. An overview of these types of problems will be given. Subsequent chapters treat the same topics in greater detail.

3.1   Categorizing Pattern-Recognition Problems

3.1.0   GENERAL

Pattern-recognition problems vary along three dimensions: the manner in which the organizing set is presented to the observer, the type of pattern classification rule which the recognizer is to produce, and the way in which the objects to be classified can be described. Figure 3-1 shows these three variations combined into a cubelike schema. Each edge of the cube represents one of the dimensions of problem variation. Each cell within the cube represents a certain class of problems. For example, the cell labeled A in the figure includes those problems in which a pattern classification procedure is to be developed from the information in a single

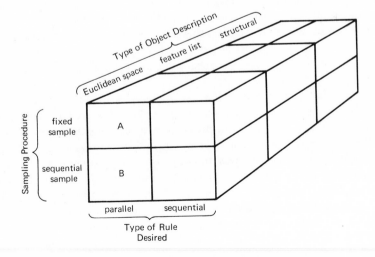

Fig. 3-1.   Variations in pattern recognition problems.

sample, providing that each of the objects can be described as a point in a multidimensional Euclidean *description space,* and assuming that the classification rule to be produced may require full knowledge of an object's description. We can contrast such problems with the problems in cell B of Figure 3-1, where the Euclidean description space and type of classification rule are retained, but there is a shift from classifying on the basis of a single sample to classifying on the basis of a sequence of samples, with the classifying rule being updated after each sample.

The three dimensions of Figure 3-1 will now be described in more detail, as they will be referred to continually when we develop the techniques for solving specific classes of problems.

3.1.1 PRESENTATION OF THE ORGANIZING SET

Two cases will be considered: pattern recognition based upon a single sample and pattern recognition situations in which a sequence of samples is used. In the case of a single sample a number of objects of known class membership are made available to the pattern-recognition system at the start of the problem. Based upon the observations in this sample, a classification rule is formed by the pattern recognizer, and is then applied to objects that are defined but not included in the sample. The classifying rule itself is not changed, even though errors in classification may be observed. In pattern recognition based on sequential sampling the information in the first sample drawn is only a beginning, used to extract the first classification rule. After a rule is developed, a new sample is drawn and the current classification rule is applied to it. (Often the new sample consists of only one object.) The performance of the classifying rule is observed and, if appropriate, a new rule is found. The procedure may be repeated indefinitely, or until some criterion of performance is reached.

Developing a classification procedure on the basis of a fixed sample is generally considered a problem in statistics rather than in artificial intelligence. There are many texts which describe appropriate techniques (e.g., Anderson, 1958; Tatsuoka, 1970), especially if Euclidean description spaces can be used. Statisticians have also been interested in a closely related question: Do the members of different groups exhibit systematic differences when measured on a single dependent variable? This question is very important in the experimental sciences, where the "classification" is of observations gathered under varying experimental conditions.

The sequential sampling case is one of the most intensively studied artificial intelligence problems. It is often labeled *machine learning.* This is probably because of the strong analogy between continuous changing of a classification rule and the ability of most animals to learn by experience. Since, almost by definition, what an animal does is intelligent, an artificial intelligence system should have a similar learning capability. Indeed, a number of philosophical papers have placed great stress on learning by example as the definition of cognition (Uhr, 1965, presents a collection of the most important references).

When a pattern recognizer can learn by adjusting its classification rules over successive samples the problem of estimating the benefit and cost of each change arises. Typically changing a classification rule involves more computation than the act of classification using a given rule. Physicians cannot change their diagnostic procedures after each patient, nor can universities change their admission policies each time they learn whether a given student graduated or not. On the other hand, failure to change any erroneous rule may increase the frequency of classification errors beyond tolerable limits. Probably the most commonly used rule in experimental studies or pattern recognition has been to change the classification rule whenever an error occurs. An obvious alternative is to change the classification rule only when the frequency of errors exceeds some a priori tolerable level. This may be closer approximation to pattern recognition in a practical situation.

It is possible to design a pattern recognizer that does not depend upon errors at all. For example, one could keep a running average of the values of members of a class on each dimension of variation, and classify all new objects by observing how close they were to the current average point of each class. An interesting use of this technique is "unsupervised learning," in which the averages are adjusted by the pattern recognizer on the assumption that classifications are correct, without any reliance on feedback.

The way a pattern recognizer changes a tentative classification rule is determined largely by the records that the recognizer can keep. Every time a new object is presented for classification, the recognizer learns something about its environment—if only an improvement in its estimate of the frequency of occurrence of certain types of objects. How should this information be recorded? In general, there are two techniques. One is the *specific memory* method, in which information about each object is recorded at the time the object is presented. In medical situations, for instance, physicians usually record every examination result and diagnosis. A second technique is the *statistical recording* method. Associated with each class one keeps summary statistics, representing some sort of averaging of the data for all previously observed cases in this class. This case is exemplified by the weather bureau basing its forecasts upon typical readings. Instead of keeping detailed information about one day, they use each day to update their idea of a "typical" rainy or clear day.

By stating the information stored and the type of rule to be developed one specifies a computing problem: Define an algorithm which effectively maps from the set of possible configurations of "memory"—i.e., the set of records about the environment that might have been stored—into the set of possible classification rules. In most cases there will be a number of algorithms which might be defined. They will differ in ways which can be quite important in application. The program properties of most interest to us here are *convergence, optimality*, and *computational complexity*.

Consider a pattern-recognition device that behaves in the following way. The device is initially set to use an arbitrarily chosen classification rule. As it obtains more information, by being shown objects and told their true classification, the device produces a sequence of new classification rules. If, at some point, the device stops producing a new rule no matter how much more information is presented, the device is said to have *converged* to a final rule. In describing an algorithm the conditions required to guarantee convergence are important. We may also ask whether the successive rules produced en route to the final solution will, in the same sense, be "more like" the final solution than previous rules in the sequence. A pattern recognizer is *optimal* if the rule to which it converges is guaranteed to be the rule which minimizes some function defining cost of misclassification. Often this function is simply a count of the number of errors in classification, but it could be more sophisticated. We shall sometimes refer to a pattern recognizer as being *optimal within a class of pattern recognizers* if it produces a final rule which has a value for the misclassification function which is not higher than the value of the misclassification function associated with the final rule produced by any of a stated set of pattern recognition devices.

Computational complexity is a more ill defined, and hence less studied, notion. Intuitively, it refers to the difficulty of using a particular algorithm. This could be defined in terms of the amount of computer memory required to execute the algorithm, the number of computing steps needed, the nature of those steps, or the time required to execute them. There are two important types of computational complexity: complexity of the pattern recognition algorithm itself and complexity of the classification rule it produces. The complexity of the pattern recognition rule is closely related to the convergence question; in both cases we are asking how difficult it is to obtain an answer using a certain method. The question of complexity of the classification rule is directed more at the practicality of the results, for we are essentially asking how good a rule is once it is obtained.

3.1.2 THE TYPE OF RULE REQUIRED

A pattern-recognition procedure is an algorithm that abstracts a pattern classification rule from the organizing set. Obviously the type of classification rule desired will determine the structure of the recognition procedure. There are two general types of classification techniques, *parallel* and *sequential* classification. Assume for simplicity that we may write an object's description as a vector of characters. (This is true for most cases, although we shall introduce exceptions in the following section.) A parallel procedure applies a number of tests to all elements in the vector, and then makes predictions of an object's class membership on the basis of the joint outcome of these tests. A sequential classification procedure first tests some subset of the elements of the description vector, and then, depending upon the outcome of the tests, either makes a classification or selects a new set of tests and a new subset of description elements, in order to repeat the process.

The formal expression of parallel and sequential procedures is revealing. Let $\mathbf{x} = \{x_i\}$ $i = 1, \ldots, n$ be the description vector of an object, and assume there are c

classes into which the object can be classified. In parallel classification there exists a set $F = \{f_j\}$ $j = 1, \ldots, c$ of functions of at most n arguments. The classification algorithm requires that

$$w_j = f_j(x_1, \ldots, x_n) \tag{1}$$

for $j = 1, \ldots, c$, and then that an object be classified as a member of class j if and only if

$$w_j = \max_k \{w_k\}, \qquad k = 1, \ldots, c. \tag{2}$$

The term "parallel" is justified because there is no inherent order in which the f_j need to be computed and hence, if possible, they could be computed simultaneously. The time required to make the classification will be determined by the longest time required to compute any of the f_j, while the total amount of computing resources required to compute a classification is equal to the sum of the resources required to compute each f_j.

Selfridge (1959), in a widely quoted paper, has given an illustrative example of a parallel procedure. Suppose each f_j were replaced by a small demon whose task it was to examine the description and shout the name of his class if he thought that the object fell into it. The demon is instructed to shout loudly if he is certain, softly if he is relatively uncertain. The total noise the demon makes, however, will be determined both by his effort and his capacity for shouting. The latter quality is determined by an omnipotent decision demon, who endows each first-order demon with a large or small voice. Upon presentation of an object to be classified, each demon shouts his class name, with an intensity dependent upon his own computations and the strength of the voice he has been given. The decision demon, acting rather like a chairman at a meeting where a voice vote is taken, decides which class name has been howled the loudest.

Sequential decision procedures are a bit more cumbersome to treat formally, although this can be done. It is more convenient to represent them by a *tree graph*[1] showing the order in which tests are to be applied. A fragment of a tree depicting a sequential decision procedure in medical diagnosis is shown in Figure 3-2. The first test to be made is assigned to the topmost node of the tree; depending upon the outcome of the test, the next test is chosen from either the right- or left-hand node below the node corresponding to the test just made. A class name is associated with the end of each branch, e.g., node A in Figure 3-2.

---

[1] A tree graph is a graph in which

    (a) there is a single node, called the *root*, which has no nodes above it (no predecessors of the root).

    (b) every other node has exactly one node about it (one predecessor).

    (c) no node is included in its own set of successors (no loops).

A node with no successors is called a *leaf* or *endpoint*. Nodes with successors are *interior nodes* of the tree.

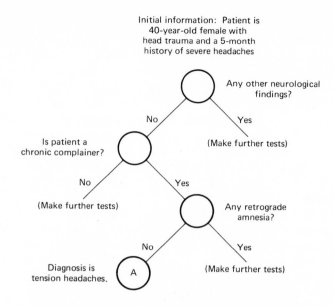

Fig. 3-2. Example of sequential decision process in medical diagnosis. Circles represent path traced in classification of a case. (From Kleinmuntz, 1968.)

Given the same set of tests, sequential decision procedures will generally require the computation of fewer tests than an equivalent parallel computation, hence they will utilize fewer resources. On the other hand, if the potential for true parallel processing exists, the sequential procedure may take considerably longer. Obviously, if we are forced to simulate a parallel procedure on a sequential machine (as is normally the case in using a digital computer) the sequential procedure will, at worst, take as long as the parallel procedure.

A marked disadvantage of the sequential decision procedure is that it is prone to errors if the individual tests are themselves unreliable, either in the sense that they are computed by an unreliable device or in the sense that each element x_i of the description vector is probabilistically determined by the identity of the object. (Note that the same formal mathematics apply in either case.) When this happens the sequential procedure may activate the wrong path through the tree without having any way to recover from the measurement error. A parallel procedure can recover from measurement error, since the extent to which a particular classification is recommended will depend upon all available measures.

3.1.3 VARIATION IN OBJECT DESCRIPTIONS

The third dimension of variation in pattern-recognition problems is in the ways in which the objects themselves can be described. In most classification problems an object can be regarded as a *set of measurements*. We ask, "What is the nature of these measurements, and what does their nature imply for classification and recognition procedures?" The question is decidedly nontrivial. For example, in the most studied cases (especially in statistics) measurements are thought of as defining a *Euclidean description space*, and each object is treated as a point in that space. This permits us to combine measurements to locate a "typical" point in the description space for each class. This procedure works well in measuring and grouping physical objects. For instance, it seems reasonable to develop a concept of "healthy largeness," based on height and weight, and use it to group students into potential athletes and nonathletes. The sensibleness of such a classifying concept, however, depends entirely on the properties we impute to the dimensions of the description space. In the case just given the idea of "closeness by a Euclidean distance measure" is interpretable as "similarity in height and weight," which is reasonable. There are other cases in which there is no reasonable interpretation of a distance measure. This would certainly be the case, for instance, if the basic measurements were attributes with nominal values, such as sex, place of birth, and race.[2] That is, the description of an object is a *list of features* rather than a set of measurements. In either case an object can be represented by a vector of descriptive statements, but the sensible mathematical operations on these vectors will be quite different.

Structural descriptions provide an interesting alternative way of describing objects. Roughly, a structural description stresses the relationship among the components of an object rather than the object's value on a series of measurements. Linguistic objects provide the clearest example of structural descriptions. In the discussion of formal languages (Chapter 2) it was shown that a sentence can be usefully described by its phrase-structure diagram, which summarizes relations between sentence components. One could certainly not develop a very useful measure on sentences by counting the number of times different elements appeared in them. Of what use would it be to say that an English sentence contained three nouns and two verbs? It has been found that the same sort of reasoning can be applied in a number of areas quite removed from conventional linguistics. One of the most interesting applications of structural description has been in the analysis of pictures (Miller & Shaw, 1968). For example, we see no way of describing the defining characteristic of the set of symmetric two-dimensional drawings without using a structural description. Unfortunately, relatively little is known about the appropriate pattern-recognition techniques.

The process of description is itself important. There must be a "most primitive" sensory system for converting the physical stimuli incident upon the classifying device into an internal code. Conventionally, this is called the *transduction* process.

---

[2] In point of fact, there are a number of scales intermediate between scales defining a Euclidean distance and purely nominal scales. Most psychological scales, such as intelligence or masculinity–femininity, are ordinal scales. In these scales objects are ranked relative to each other, but the difference between two adjacent ranks is undefined. For a discussion of the issues involved in scaling, see Krantz *et al.* (1971).

Eyes, ears, and other sense organs serve as transducers for animals, computers rely on devices to sense holes in cards or respond to electrical voltage changes. Let us call the internal code produced by transduction a *level 0* code. Any two physically distinct objects which give rise to the same level 0 coding will be indistinguishable to a pattern recognizer. In computing, level 0 distinctions are apt to sound trivial. "Obviously" it is true that a computer program cannot be written to distinguish between red and blue cards. Still, information is lost.

Level 0 conversion produces a string of binary digits, where each digit represents a most primitive distinction of the computing system. These strings are clumsy to handle directly, so they are normally recoded into units which, hopefully, will make the pattern-recognition process easier. This will be called *level 1* coding. It involves partitioning the input stream into subunits. A familiar computing example is alphanumeric input, in which the 960 bits on a computer card are grouped into 80 alphanumeric symbols. This forces a further information loss, since not all bit configurations will have an interpretation in the alphanumeric code. Similar, and much larger, losses of information occur in biological systems. For example, Hunt and Makous (1969) have estimated the information reduction in silent reading to be from an input rate of 10^9 bits per second to an output rate of 35 bits per second.

The effect of level 1 coding is to produce manageable data for a pattern-recognition algorithm. In biological systems this is achieved largely by throwing away unnecessary data, but simple recoding of data can be almost equally effective. This is illustrated by the example shown in Figure 3-3, in which the "correct" coding changes a very hard pattern-recognition problem into a very easy one. The upper table in the figure shows two classes of binary vectors, arbitrarily labeled X and O. The rule for classifying vectors into each class can be found, but it is not immediately obvious to most people. In the middle table the octal equivalents of the binary vectors are shown. If anything, the classification rule is harder to find. In the lowest table the binary vectors are again rewritten, this time into hexadecimal vectors, and the answer is obvious.

There is nothing magic about a level 0 to level 1 transition; we could easily have level 1 to level 2 transitions, or 2 to 3, and so forth. The number of transitions would make no difference to a pattern recognizer which did not control them. Thus if a computer program is written to classify words, and a bit to character conversion is always applied before the data is presented to the program, it makes no difference whether we regard the program as operating on bits or characters. There is a much more important distinction between feature extraction programs which can and cannot be changed by the pattern recognition program itself during the search for a solution. For instance, the problem of Figure 3-3 could be solved by a complicated algorithm which accepted bit or octal patterns, or by a simple algorithm which tried out different codings until it found that hexadecimal coding produced an easy problem. More generally, we must distinguish between pattern recognition programs which accept a fixed coding of the data and programs which have the capability of changing the coding.

Class X vectors	Class O vectors

Binary coding

Class X vectors	Class O vectors
0 0 0 1 1 0 0 1 0 1 1 0	0 0 0 1 1 1 1 1 0 1 1 0
1 0 1 0 1 0 0 1 0 1 0 0	1 0 1 0 0 1 1 0 0 1 0 0
1 0 0 0 1 0 0 1 1 1 0 0	1 0 0 0 0 1 0 1 0 0 1 1
0 0 0 0 1 0 0 1 1 1 0 0	0 0 0 0 0 1 0 0 1 1 0 0
0 1 0 0 1 0 0 1 0 0 0 0	0 1 0 1 0 0 1 1 0 0 0 0
0 0 1 1 1 0 0 1 0 0 0 1	0 0 1 1 0 0 1 0 0 0 0 1
1 1 1 1 1 0 0 1 0 0 1 0	1 1 1 1 0 0 0 1 0 0 1 0
1 1 0 0 1 0 0 1 1 0 1 1	1 1 0 0 1 0 1 0 1 0 1 1
0 0 1 0 1 0 0 1 0 1 1 1	0 0 1 0 1 0 1 1 0 1 1 1
1 0 1 1 1 0 0 1 1 1 1 1	1 0 1 1 1 1 0 0 1 1 1 1
0 1 0 1 1 0 0 1 1 0 1 0	0 1 0 1 1 1 0 1 0 1 0 1
1 1 1 0 1 0 0 1 0 0 0 1	1 1 0 1 1 1 1 1 1 0 1 0

Octal coding

Class X vectors	Class O vectors
0 6 2 6	0 7 6 6
5 2 2 4	5 1 4 4
4 2 3 4	4 1 2 3
0 2 3 4	0 1 1 4
2 2 2 0	2 4 6 0
1 6 2 1	1 4 4 1
7 6 2 2	7 4 2 2
6 2 3 3	6 2 5 3
1 2 2 7	1 2 6 7
5 6 3 7	5 7 1 7
2 6 3 2	2 7 2 5
3 2 2 1	6 7 7 2

Hexadecimal coding

Class X vectors	Class O vectors
1 9 6	1 F 6
A 9 4	A 6 4
8 9 D	8 5 3
0 9 D	0 4 C
4 9 0	5 3 0
3 9 1	3 2 1
F 9 2	F 1 2
C 9 B	C A B
2 9 7	2 B 7
B 9 F	B C F
5 9 A	5 D 5
E 9 1	D F A

Fig. 3-3.   Example of effect of coding on pattern recognition.

3.2 Historical Perspective and Current Issues

If you were to peruse those journals in which original research on pattern recognition appears, you would find that only a few of the possible types of pattern-recognition problems generate a great deal of interest today. The number of articles on structural descriptions is rapidly increasing, especially with respect to applications in computer recognition of visual data. Clearly this is a field where "the action is." Now if you were to browse through the journals of a few years before, you would find a different emphasis. In the early and middle 1960s there was much interest in the general topic of machine learning and, in our terms, parallel pattern recognition using sequential sampling. Usually these studies assumed a Boolean or Euclidean description space. Prior to that time there was interest in pattern recognition techniques based upon a single sample, so that many of the research reports could be treated equally well as reports in statistical analysis and as reports in artificial intelligence. Finally, throughout the last 10 years there has been a steady, low-key interest in sequential classification and recognition techniques. Interestingly, this work has been paralleled by increased interest in sequential classification procedures on the part of statisticians.

Chapter IV

PATTERN CLASSIFICATION AND RECOGNITION METHODS BASED ON EUCLIDEAN DESCRIPTION SPACES

4.0 General

4.0.0 INTRODUCTION

This chapter describes some parallel pattern-recognition techniques that can be applied to objects represented as points in a Euclidean description space. The basic assumptions are that each object to be classified can be described by a set of measurements defining the axes of a Euclidean space, and that all measurements on an object will be known to the pattern classifier at the time that the categorization is to be made. The restricted problem is often considered to be part of statistics or measurement theory, rather than artificial intelligence. Nevertheless, anyone interested in pattern recognition should have an understanding of the statistical approach. The statistical methods are powerful ones which depend on strong assumptions. When these assumptions can be made, they should be. On the other hand, it is important that the nature of the assumptions be understood, for when they are unwarranted their use may lead to very misleading results.

Since statisticians have devoted much time to the topics of this chapter, it is not surprising that there exists a large literature. We make no attempt to cover it in detail. Tatsuoka (1972) has offered a good basic text. Duda and Hart (1973) and Meisel (1972) have covered the literature with particular reference to applications in computer science.

4.0.1 FORMALISMS

We assume that there exists a known set $C = \{C_i\}$ of k mutually exclusive classes of objects. Each object is represented by a set of measurements, called its *description*. A measurement is a point on a scale, and the scales in turn define a *description space*, D. The description of an object, then, is a point x in the space D.

Note that two objects might have the same description but be in different classes. A *pattern-classification procedure* is a procedure that assigns an object to membership in class C_i if and only if the description of the object falls into that region R_i of D which is associated with class C_i. The pattern classification procedure is correct if the object is, indeed, a member of class i. A *pattern-recognition procedure* is a procedure that defines the regions $\{R_i\}$ by examining the descriptions of a set S of objects whose true class membership is known. Here, S will be called the *sample* on which the pattern recognition procedure operates.

4.0.2   THE EUCLIDEAN ASSUMPTION

The procedures discussed in this chapter all depend upon the notion of the distance between two points in the description space. Roughly, the argument is that if two objects have descriptions which lie close to each other in *D*, then they are likely to belong to the same class. It was pointed out in Chapter 3 that this reasoning is intuitively correct for most physical scales, such as height and weight, but makes less sense if a description is based on the presence or absence of features. That theme can be developed further, to indicate just what the distance assumption does imply about the descriptive measurements themselves.

Let D be an *m*-dimensional description space. A point $\mathbf{x} \in D$ is defined by a vector of m components, $(x_1, x_2, \ldots, x_m)$. The distance between two points, $\mathbf{x}$ and $\mathbf{y}$, in D, is

$$d(\mathbf{x}, \mathbf{y}) = \left(\sum_{i=1}^{m} (x_i - y_1)^2 \right)^{\frac{1}{2}} \qquad (1)$$

This equation implies that the distance between two points depends upon their relative positions in D and not upon their absolute positions. More precisely, two points $\mathbf{x}, \mathbf{y}$ and $\mathbf{x}', \mathbf{y}'$ are the same distance apart if

$$x_i - y_i = x_i' - y_i' \qquad \text{for all } i \qquad (2)$$

Equation (2) assumes that it is meaningful to compare differences between measurements on each scale. A scale on which this can be done is called an *interval scale*. Time is an example of an interval scale, since it is meaningful to say that the difference between z and $z + 2$ minutes is the same regardless of the value of z. Weight and height are also clearly interval scales, and, in fact, they can satisfy more rigorous assumptions. On the other hand, many interesting scales do not satisfy the requirements of an interval scale. For example, *hardness* is defined by the relationship "x is harder than y if x scratches y." On this scale diamonds are harder than glass, and glass harder than butter. Hardness is an example of an *ordinal scale*, since hardness can be used to assign numbers to objects, but these numbers reflect a rank ordering and not necessarily the equal interval property. Clearly Eq. (2) would not be appropriate for hardness.

Interval scales are invariant over linear transformations. This means that it is possible to replace the description space D with a new space D' where the mapping of points from $\mathbf{x} \in D$ to $\mathbf{x}' \in D$ is achieved by

$$x_i' = a_i x_i + b_i, \qquad a_i \neq 0 \tag{3}$$

without affecting the conclusions one draws from analysis of the sample.

There are scales which are both stronger and weaker than interval scales. We have already mentioned ordinal scales. Absolute scales have a unique unit and zero point, as well as the interval property. The Shannon measure of information (Shannon & Weaver, 1948) is an example. At the other end of a scale of scales, the assignment of numbers to telephones is a nominal, or arbitrary scale, since the numbers identify the instruments but do not reflect any physical property of them. The interested reader is referred to Coombs, Dawes, and Tversky (1970) for further brief treatment, and to Suppes and Zinnes (1963) or Krantz *et al.* (1971) for progressively deeper discussions. The purpose in discussing scaling here was twofold: (1) to justify the transformations of the description space that will be used in subsequent sections of the chapter, and (2) to make the reader aware of the basic assumption that lies behind any pattern-classification argument based on the concept of distance.

4.1 . Bayesian Procedures in Pattern Recognition

4.1.0   BAYES'S RULE

Pattern classification is an example of a more general problem: choosing from alternate explanations on the basis of available evidence. Bayesian inference is a procedure for making such decisions. The Bayesian method has been proposed both as a normative model of how one ought to behave and as a descriptive model of how people do behave (Lee, 1970). We shall encounter applications of Bayesian decision making at several points in this book. In this section we introduce the basic procedure, and then apply it to the parallel and Euclidean classification problem.

Let $A, B, C, \ldots$ denote discrete events. The following notation will be used for the probability of occurrence of various combinations of events:

$\Pr(A)$ = probability of event A occuring. $\tag{4}$
$\Pr(A, B)$ = probability of joint occurrence of A and B.
$\Pr(B : A)$ = probability of occurrence of B given that A has occurred.

The joint probability of two independent events is

$$\Pr(A, B) = \Pr(A) \cdot \Pr(B : A). \tag{5}$$

In a Bayesian problem, one begins with a fixed set $H = \{H_i\}$ of *hypotheses*, which define all possible "states of the world." The H_i are mutually exclusive since the world must be in just one state. Associated with each H_i is a (subjective) probability $\Pr(H_i)$ that H_i has, in fact, occurred. It follows that

$$\Pr(H_i, H_j) = 0 \qquad \text{(mutual exclusiveness)} \tag{6}$$

$$\sum_{i=1}^{k} \Pr(H_i) = 1 \qquad \text{(exhaustiveness)}.$$

The fact of H_i's being true or not cannot be verified by direct observation. Instead it is assumed that one can conduct an experiment which has a set $E = \{E_j\}$, $j = 1, \ldots, n$ of observable outcomes. Associated with each H_i there is a known probability of observing each of the possible outcomes of the experiment, i.e., a known $\Pr(E_j : H_i)$. Since the experiment can have only one outcome, the E_j's are mutually exclusive. Again in summary:

$$\Pr(E_j : H_i) \geqslant 0, \qquad \Pr(E_j, E_{j'} : H_i) = 0, \qquad \sum_{j=1}^{m} \Pr(E_j : H_i) = 1. \qquad (7)$$

Note also that since the world must be in exactly one state, then

$$\Pr(E_j) = \sum_{i=1}^{k} \Pr(E_j : H_i). \qquad (8)$$

Let us give a concrete illustration. Suppose that the hypotheses are that it is, or is not, raining and that the experiment consists of looking out the window and observing whether (a) there are no people on the street or (b) that at least one person on the street has an umbrella, or (c) there are people on the street, but none with umbrellas. Given a somewhat wet winter climate, the a priori probabilities of rain or no rain might be

Symbol	Explanation	Value	(9)
$\Pr(H_r)$	Probability of rain	.3	
$\Pr(H_{-r})$	Probability of no rain	.7	

If it is raining the street is more likely to be empty, and if one must go into the street, then one is more likely to carry an umbrella. Thus,

Symbol	Explanation	Value	(10)
$\Pr(E_1 : H_r)$	Rain, people on street with at least one umbrella	.4	
$\Pr(E_2 : H_r)$	Rain, all people on street without umbrellas	.2	
$\Pr(E_3 : H_r)$	Rain, street empty	.4	
$\Pr(E_1 : H_{-r})$	No rain, people on street with at least one umbrella	.05	
$\Pr(E_2 : H_{-r})$	No rain, no one on street has umbrella	.75	
$\Pr(E_3 : H_{-r})$	No rain, street empty	.2	

A man with an umbrella is observed. What is the probability that it is raining? The problem is to calculate $\Pr(H_r : E_1)$, the probability of rain given that a man with an umbrella has been observed. From the definition of compound probability,

$$\Pr(E_1, H_r) = \Pr(H_r : E_1)\Pr(E_1) = \Pr(E_1 : H_r)\Pr(H_r). \tag{11}$$

By rearrangement,

$$\Pr(H_r : E_1) = \frac{\Pr(E_1 : H_r)\Pr(H_r)}{\Pr(E_1)} \tag{12}$$

Since

$$\Pr(E_1) = \Pr(E_1 : H_r) + \Pr(E_1 : H_{-r}), \tag{13}$$

then

$$\Pr(H_r : E_1) = \frac{\Pr(E_1 : H_r)\Pr(H_r)}{\Pr(E_1 : H_r)\Pr(H_r) + \mathrm{Pe}(E_1 : H_{-r})\Pr(H_{-r})}. \tag{14}$$

In the example

$$\Pr(\text{Rain : Umbrella observed}) = \frac{(.4)(.3)}{(.4)(.3) + (.05)(.7)} \approx .78. \tag{15}$$

Equation (14) is readily generalized, by substitution of $\Pr(E_j)$ as written in (8).

$$\Pr(H_i : E_j) = \frac{\Pr(E_j : H_i)\Pr(H_i)}{\sum_{a=1}^{k} \Pr(E_j : H_a)} \tag{16}$$

Equation (16) is *Bayes's rule* for adjustment of the probability of an hypothesis on the basis of observed evidence. It is applicable provided that there exists a fixed set of hypotheses which exhaust the space of possible hypotheses, and that the probabilities of various observations are known under each of the possible hypotheses. The rule can be applied either to parallel pattern recognition procedures, as will be done in the immediately following sections, or to sequential pattern recognition. The second application will be treated in a subsequent chapter.

4.1.1   APPLICATION OF BAYES'S RULE TO PARALLEL PATTERN CLASSIFICATION

In applying Bayes's rule to parallel classification the class names play the role of hypotheses, and the description of the object to be classified plays the role of the experimental observation. Recall that every object to be classified belongs to exactly one class, and that what is observed is a set x of measurements on an object. It is possible that two distinct objects, from two different classes, will give rise to identical description vectors. To take a concrete example, suppose we were asked to classify athletes into the categories "basketball player" and "football player" on the basis of their height and weight. It would generally be true that short, heavy individuals would be football players, and tall, lean individuals basketball players, but this is not an infallible rule. Given only a man's height and weight, an observer could at best state what sport the athlete was most likely to play.

Let x be the event "an object with description x is observed" and let j be the event "the object to be classified is a member of class j." A pattern classifier should predict that an object of description x is a member of class j if and only if

$$\Pr(j : \mathrm{x}) \geqslant \Pr(j' : \mathrm{x}) \qquad \text{for all} \quad j' \neq j. \tag{17}$$

A pattern-recognition procedure partitions the description space D into regions, $\{R_j\}$, such that (17) is satisfied for all points in region R_j and only those points. Objects are then classified by noting the region into which x falls.

This simple principle hides some counterintuitive notions. It is not necessarily true that objects which are "typical" of class j will be categorized as members of that class. Both the probability that the class might give rise to the observation and the probability that the class was sampled at all must be considered. To illustrate by example, imagine that a personnel consultant has been given the job of interviewing all those employees of a company whom he considers to have serious psychiatric problems. If the company is at all large, an extensive interview with every individual will be out of the question. A reasonable alternative might be to give each employee an inexpensive paper and pencil personality test, then interview those who have suspicious test results. In pattern-recognition terminology, the employees are the objects to be classified, and the test score provides a one-dimensional description space. Now suppose that previous research has shown that in the population of actual psychiatric problems test scores follow a normal distribution with a mean of 130 and a standard deviation of 10, whereas the distribution of test scores for psychologically healthy individuals is normal with a mean of 110 and a standard deviation of 20. A rough graph of the distributions for each population is shown in Figure 4-1. The test clearly appears to differentiate the two populations. To use the test in classification, however, one must allow for the fact that healthy individuals are, say, ten times more numerous in the population than psychiatric patients. What

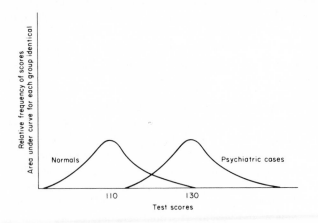

Fig. 4-1.   Hypothetical test score distributions.

this means graphically is that we should shrink the distribution shown for psychiatric cases to one tenth the area of the distribution representing normals, while retaining its shape. This has been done in Figure 4-2. We then ask, "For what range of test scores does the absolute number of psychiatric cases exceed the absolute number of normals?" The answer to this question is also shown in Figure 4-2. Individual employees should be classified as "psychiatric risks" (and hence given an interview) only if their scores exceed the critical value C, marked on the figure. This is true even though $C > 130$, the "most typical score" of a psychiatric patient. One of the results of minimizing the total number of incorrect classifications has been to classify more than half of the psychiatric patients as normal!

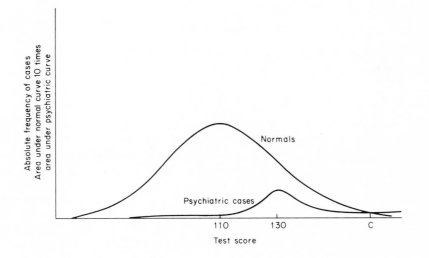

Fig. 4-2. Hypothetical distributions corrected for relative population size.

Is the preceding result an unusual case? Not at all! It is a direct consequence of Bayes's rule, for when we write (16) in the pattern-recognition notation, we have

$$\Pr(j : \mathbf{x}) = \frac{\Pr(\mathbf{x} : j)\Pr(j)}{\sum_{i=1}^{k} \Pr(\mathbf{x} : i)\Pr(i)} \qquad (18)$$

and this expression clearly depends upon the values of the class a priori probabilities, $\{\Pr(i)\}$, as well as the $\Pr(\mathbf{x} : i)$ values.

One may be unhappy with the result. It seems that we are missing a point. As presented, Bayes's formula concentrates on minimizing the number of misclassifications without considering the relative cost of particular misclassifications. In the illustrative example, it might be more serious to fail to interview a true psychiatric risk than to waste time by interviewing people without psychiatric problems. Fortunately there is a simple way to introduce this consideration into Bayesian classification. Let $c(i : j)$ be the cost of classifying a member of class j as a member of class i. If the recognition procedure assigns point x to region i, then the expected loss due to misclassification at point x is

$$EL(x \in R_i) = \sum_{\substack{j=1 \\ j \neq i}}^{k} [Pr(x : j)Pr(j)c(i : j)] \qquad (19)$$

To minimize the expected loss due to misclassification, the regions R_i are defined so that (19) is minimized for all points in D. Equation (19) can also be used to define the boundary between two adjacent regions, R_i and R_j. The boundary equation is

$$EL(x \in R_i) = EL(x \in R_j). \qquad (20)$$

It is often of interest to consider the shape of this boundary, for it can give us an intuitive feeling for the nature of the categorization procedure.

4.1.2   SPECIALIZATION TO A EUCLIDEAN DESCRIPTION SPACE

The preceding discussion is equally valid if we regard D as a Euclidean description space or as an abstract set of possible descriptions with the R_i as subsets. In the case in which D is in fact a Euclidean description space a somewhat different notation is useful to indicate the continuity of the space. Let

$$p_j(x) = \text{probability density function over } D \text{ for members of class } j \qquad (21)$$

and

$$q_j = \text{the probability that a randomly chosen object will be a member} \qquad (22)$$
$$\text{of class } j$$

To determine the proportion of cases of a particular class whose description falls into a given region, R of D, the probability density function is integrated over that region.

$$Pr(\text{object in class } j \text{ will have a description } x \in R) = \int_R p_j(x) \, dx. \qquad (23)$$

Now let region R_j be the region of D which some pattern classification procedure associates with class j. The expected relative frequency of misclassifications due to the definition of this region is given by

$$q_j \int_{D-R_j} p_j(x) \, dx + \sum_{\substack{i=1 \\ i \neq j}}^{k} q_i \int_{R_j} p_i(x) \, dx \qquad (24)$$

The first term of (24) is the expected relative frequency of misclassifications due to failure to classify correctly those members of class j whose descriptions lie outside region R_j. The second term is the relative frequency of misclassification of objects which are not members of class j, but whose descriptions fall within R_j. Point x should be assigned to R_j if

$$q_j p_j(\mathbf{x}) \geqslant \max_{\substack{i=1 \\ i \neq j}} \{q_i p_i(\mathbf{x})\} \tag{25}$$

If it is advisable to consider the cost as well as the frequency of misclassification, the expected loss at point x is given by

$$\mathrm{EL}(\mathbf{x} \in R_j) = \sum_{\substack{i=1 \\ i \neq j}}^{k} q_i p_i(\mathbf{x}) c(j : i), \tag{26}$$

which provides an alternate definition of the classification criterion.

4.2   Classic Statistical Approach to Pattern Recognition and Classification

4.2.0   GENERAL

Bayesian pattern classification assumes knowledge of the probability of encountering an example of a particular class and of the probability that objects within a class will have certain descriptions. In many interesting pattern-classification situations this information is not available. In statistical pattern classification the problem is often resolved by assuming that the probabilities of class membership may be estimated from the proportions of the sample which fall into various classes, and by assuming that the distribution of descriptions over the description space follows some reasonable, known function for each class. That is, it is assumed that for each $p_i(\mathbf{x})$

$$p_i(\mathbf{x}) = f(\mathbf{x}, \boldsymbol{\theta}) \tag{27}$$

where f is a known function dependent upon a vector $\boldsymbol{\theta}$ of parameters. The value of the components of $\boldsymbol{\theta}$ are estimated from the sample, and the Bayesian classification procedures then applied. The details of this procedure vary depending upon the assumption made about f. In the following section the statistical pattern recognition method is illustrated for the commonest assumption, that f is a multivariate normal distribution.

4.2.1   THE MULTIVARIATE NORMAL DISTRIBUTION PROBLEM

This case will be developed as an example of the statistical classification method. The general line of treatment follows that of Tatsuoka (1970). Although the primary reason for presenting this example is to illustrate statistical classification, the example itself is of interest since the assumption of a multivariate normal distribution can often be justified on the following logical grounds. Suppose that for each class there exists an ideal or typical object. Let $\boldsymbol{\mu}$ be the vector of (interval scaled) measurements obtained from this object. The point $\boldsymbol{\mu}$, then, represents the point in the description space which describes the ideal member of a class. Any actual object chosen from the class will have a description x which is not necessarily identical to $\boldsymbol{\mu}$. It may be reasonable to assume that any deviation of x from $\boldsymbol{\mu}$ is due to an accumulation of small, independent variations in each of the measurements. In the basketball–football player example, for instance, one might assume that there is an ideal "basketball type," but that any particular player randomly differs in height and weight from this type. Note that the variations along each dimension might be correlated across players—e.g., if a person is taller than usual, he is likely to be heavier than usual. Such correlations in variation from the ideal are allowed for in the classification method to be presented.

In any case, if the data is generated by this process, then the observations within each class will follow the multivariate normal distribution over the description space D, centered at point $\boldsymbol{\mu}$.

As usual, some special definitions are needed. For each class i the following statistics are defined:

$\mu_j{}^i$ = mean value of the objects in class i on measure j. $\qquad$ (28)

$\sigma_j{}^i$ = standard deviation on measure j of items in class i.

r_{jk}^i = product moment correlation between measurements on class j.
$\qquad$ and k, computed over objects in class i.

In place of the general vector $\boldsymbol{u}$ representing an "ideal" description, the vector of mean measurements of objects in the sample from the class i is

$$\boldsymbol{\mu}^i = (u_1{}^i, u_2{}^i, \ldots, u_m{}^i). \qquad (29)$$

The *dispersion matrix* for class i is the $m \times m$ matrix

$$\boldsymbol{\Sigma}_i = [r_{jk}^i \, \sigma_j^i \, \sigma_k^i], \qquad j, k = 1, \ldots, m. \qquad (30)$$

Since each measure is assumed to correlate perfectly with itself, the diagonal entries of $\boldsymbol{\Sigma}_i$ are simply the elements $(\sigma_j^i)^2$, i.e., the variances of the measures when computed over class i.

In order to simplify the notation, we shall consider in detail only the case in which the dispersion matrices are identical for all classes. This permits us to consider a single dispersion matrix $\boldsymbol{\Sigma}$ with appropriate entries. For each class, and each point $X \in D$, define the quantity

$$X_i^2 = (\mathbf{x} - \boldsymbol{\mu}^i)' \, \boldsymbol{\Sigma} \, (\mathbf{x} - \boldsymbol{\mu}^i), \qquad (31)$$

where $(\mathbf{x} - \boldsymbol{\mu}^i)$ is an appropriately computed column vector, and $(\mathbf{x} - \boldsymbol{\mu}^i)'$ is its transpose. The multivariate normal density function defined over D for class i is

$$f(\mathbf{x}; \boldsymbol{\Sigma} \ \boldsymbol{\mu}^i) = 2\pi^{-1}/\Sigma/e^{-\frac{1}{2}X_i^2} \qquad (32)$$

where $/\Sigma/$ is the determinant of $\boldsymbol{\Sigma}$. Let $c(i)$ be the cost of failing to classify correctly a member of class i. The cost of misclassification due to assigning $\mathbf{x}$ to some region R_j is

$$EL(\mathbf{x} \Sigma R_j) = \sum_{i \neq j}^{k} q_i \cdot f(\mathbf{x}; \Sigma, \mu_i) \cdot c(i). \tag{33}$$

Equation (33) will be minimized if R_j is chosen so that

$$q_j \cdot f(\mathbf{x}; \Sigma, \mu^j) \cdot c(j) \geqslant q_i \cdot f(\mathbf{x}; \Sigma, \mu^i) \cdot c(i) \tag{34}$$

is true for all $x \in R_j$ and all i, j. This is equivalent to

$$\frac{f(\mathbf{x}; \Sigma, \mu^j)}{f(\mathbf{x}; \Sigma, \mu^i)} \geqslant \frac{q_i c(i)}{q_j c(j)} \tag{35}$$

By substituting the definition of the multivariate normal distribution,

$$\frac{e^{-\frac{1}{2} X_j{}^2}}{e^{-\frac{1}{2} X_i{}^2}} \geqslant \frac{q_i \cdot c(i)}{q_j \cdot c(j)} \tag{36}$$

Converting to logarithms and making simple rearrangements

$$X_i{}^2 - X_j{}^2 \geqslant 2 \cdot \{\ln[q_i c(i)] - \ln[q_j c(j)]\}. \tag{37}$$

The element on the right-hand side of (37) will be a constant K_{ji}, which does not depend on $\mathbf{X}$. On the other hand, $X_i{}^2$ and $X_j{}^2$ do depend on $\mathbf{X}$. The pattern-classification rule is

Assign a point $\mathbf{x}$ *to region* R_j *if the set of values* $\{X_i{}^2\}$ *associated with* $\mathbf{x}$ *satisfy*

$$X_j{}^2 \leqslant X_i{}^2 - K_{ji}, \qquad \text{for all } i \neq j. \tag{38}$$

A graphic summary of the multivariate case is instructive. For simplicity, consider the case of two measurements, so that the description space is a plane. This will not restrict the generality of the argument. The density of a class at any point on the plane can be represented by an "altitude marker" orthogonal to the plane. Each class defines a "density hill" whose base lays on the plane. Unlike real hills, however, the density hills from different classes can overlap. We can picture each hill by drawing *isodensity functions*, similar to the contour lines on a topographic map. The points on each of the isodensity functions represent points for which the probability of encountering an object in the appropriate class is a constant. This value depends both upon the absolute frequency of the class and the relative frequency of examples of the class at the point. In fact, it is

$$g_i(\mathbf{x}) = \text{density of class } i \text{ at point } \mathbf{x} \tag{39}$$

$$= q_i \cdot f(\mathbf{x}, \Sigma, \mu^i).$$

The multivariate normal distribution assumption ensures us that the isodensity functions will be ellipses, and that the centroid of the ellipses will be the point μ^i. Parenthetically, μ^i will also be the point of maximum density, which is the degenerate case of an ellipse, and the value of the density for a particular isodensity line will be a direct function of the closest approach of that line to μ^i. Thus each isodensity line will contain all isodensity lines with a higher density value, and will be contained in all functions with a lower value. By tracing out the ellipses for several isodensity values we can obtain a picture of how different distributions for different classes abut on each other. This is done for two classes in Figure 4-3. Note

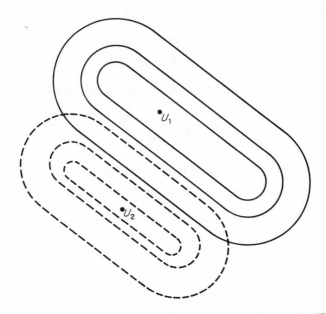

Fig. 4-3.   Density contours about two points in multivariate normal classification.

that the density hills for the two classes in this figure are of identical orientation, although of different size. This is because the dispersion matrices were assumed to be identical for each class, and it is the dispersion matrix which determines the orientation of the ellipses. If the dispersion matrices were not identical, the different density hills might lie at any orientation to each other. An example of this situation is shown in Figure 4-4, which shows three density hills, corresponding to classes which are distributed according to the multivariate normal function, but with unique dispersion matrices.

The boundary between regions R_i and R_j is defined by the set of points which could be assigned either to class i or class j without affecting the cost of misclassification, i.e., the points for which (38) is an equality. It can be proven that the boundary will always be a hyperplane of dimensionality one less than the number of measurements, so, in the two measurement case, the regions are bounded by straight lines. It can further be proven that the boundary hyperplane will always be perpendicular to the line between the centroids of the distributions; i.e., between points μ^i and μ^j in the description space. The point at which the hyperplane crosses this line will depend upon the relative frequency of each class and the cost of misclassification. This is what the value of K_{ji} reflects. An example for more than one region is shown in Figure 4-4. Since K_{ji} can be manipulated by altering either the costs of misclassification or the frequency of the class, without altering the probability density functions for descriptions within a class, it is

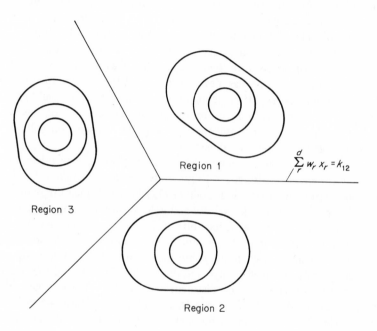

Region 1

$$\sum_{r}^{d} w_r x_r = k_{12}$$

Region 3

Region 2

Fig. 4-4. Boundary between regions.

possible to arrange the boundary hyperplanes so that the "typical" member of class i (point μ^i) actually falls into the region R_j. This is the mathematical explanation for the intuitive conclusion given in discussing the psychiatric screening example.

Two more characteristics of the classification regions are worth commenting upon. Clearly if there are k classes, then a region can be bounded by at most k-1 hyperplanes. It may be bounded by fewer. In fact, a region need not be closed, as is shown in the example of Figure 4-4. Finally, it is possible that there will exist a class for which there is no associated region. In such a case, of course, the class is one to which no observation is ever assigned.

4.3   Classification Based on Proximity of Descriptions

4.3.0   General Discussion and Illustration

What happens when the assumptions of the classical approach cannot be made? Quite similar classification techniques can be applied based upon the weaker assumption that objects whose descriptions are close to each other in the description space are likely to belong to the same class. This will be called the *proximity assumption*. To take a simple illustration, a person's sex can usually be determined by asking if the person looks more like a randomly chosen man or randomly chosen woman. More precisely, a classification measure can be based on the average distance between the descriptions of an unknown object and each of a set of known objects. The procedure retains the assumption that it makes sense to average over measures taken on objects within a set. In addition, the properties of a Euclidean description space, with the corresponding measurement assumptions, will be used. Sebesteyen (1962) has developed a complete discussion of the use of description proximities in pattern recognition. His monograph should be consulted for algebraic development and for proofs of the correctness of the computing techniques which will be presented here. The present discussion will be intuitive and will rely largely on geometric illustration.

To set the stage for the discussion, an actual classification problem will first be presented, and then used throughout to illustrate a variety of points. The problem is based upon a study by Craig and Craig (1972) in which measurements originally designed for physics were applied to archeology and history. Determining the source of material for a particular bit of masonry or statuary is called the determination of provenance. Craig and Craig attempted to determine the provenance of classical Greek statuary by measuring the relative proportions of different isotopes of chemical elements in the marble. They found that marble from different ancient quarries can be distinguished by the relative concentrations of carbon-13 to carbon-12 and of oxygen-18 to oxygen-16. Figure 4-5 plots measures taken by Craig and Craig using a number of fragments from different quarries.[1] Table 4-1 shows the values of the same measurements for chips from masonry and statuary at various sites. Craig and Craig did in fact assign chips to quarries based on this data but did not state their basis for making the assignment. In the following sections the Craig and Craig data will be used as a running illustration to demonstrate how rules can be developed to assign each of the chips to a quarry, with varying indicators of the reliability of this assignment. No appeal will be made to a probabilistic model, nor will particular probability density functions be assumed.

[1] The measurements defining the axes of Figure 4-5 are derived from the $^{13}C/^{12}C$ and $^{18}O/^{16}O$ ratios by a rather complicated formula which compares the measurements in a fragment to the same measurements made on a standard item. Craig and Craig (1972, footnote 14) gives the details. The ratios for isotopes of other elements than carbon and oxygen ratios could be used. Obviously it is easier for us to deal with a two dimensional description space, for clarity of presentation. The methods readily apply to an m dimensional space.

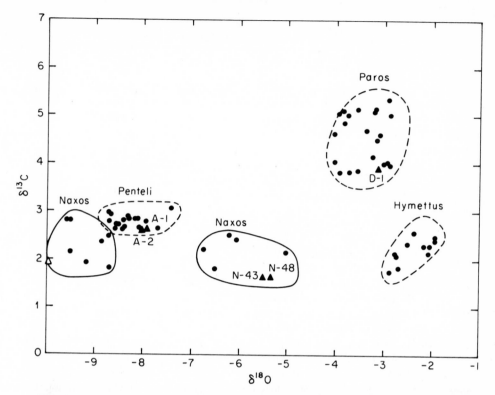

Fig. 4-5. Carbon-13 and oxygen-18 variations in marble samples from ancient Greek quarries relative to the PDB isotopic standard. Triangles denote some of the archeological samples listed in Table 4-1. (From Craig, H. and Craig, V. Greek marbles: Determination of provenance by isotopic analysis. *Science*, 28 April, 1972, pp. 401-402, Table 1. Copyright © 1972 by the American Association for the Advancement of Science. Reproduced by permission.)

4.3.1 DEFINITIONS

From the definition of Euclidean distance [see (1)] it follows trivially that the squared distance between two points **x, y** in D is

$$d^2(\mathbf{x}, \mathbf{y}) = \sum_{i=1}^{m} (x_i - y_i)^2.$$ (40)

Intuitively, a point **x** is similar to a set of points, $Y = \{\mathbf{y}_i\}$ if the mean squared distance between point **x** and the members of Y is small. Thus **x** is close to the set Y if

$$d_1^2(\mathbf{x}, \mathbf{y}) = \frac{1}{n_y} \sum_{i=1}^{n_y} d^2(\mathbf{x}, \mathbf{y})$$ (41)

TABLE 4-1
Isotopic Analyses of Archeological Marble Samples[a]

Sample no.	Description	$\partial^{13}C$ (per mil)	$\partial^{18}O$ (per mil)	Probable prove- nance
A-1	Athens: "Thescion" (Hephaesteion) in the Agora, column on north side	2.63	−7.90	Pentelic
A-2	Athens: basal slab on south side of "Theseion"	2.63	−8.03	Pentelic
D-1	Delphi: carved block lying inside Treasury of Siphnos	3.89	−3.10	Parian
D-2	Delphi: drum of column of the Naxian Sphinx	1.96	−4.15	?
E-1	Epidaurus: carved block (lintel?), 10 m from Tholos	2.01	−1.12	?
E-2	Epidaurus: Corinthian capital next to the "triple circle" of Tholos	2.16	−0.78	?
E-3	Epidaurus: cut slab of white marble, 13 m from Tholos	2.58	−3.96	?
N-43	Naxos: Apollon Gate, Palatia, Naxos Harbour; flake from inside of gate	1.67	−5.51	Naxian
N-46	Naxos: Apollon Gate, large block at foot of hill toward Naxos	1.64	−5.35	Naxian
C-1	Caesarea, Israel: Corinthian capital of grey marble	3.51	−2.64	?

[a]From Craig, H., and Craig, V. Greek marbles: Determination of provenance by isotopic analysis. *Science*, 28 April 1972, pp. 401-402, Table 1. Copyright © 1972 by the American Association for the Advancement of Science. Reproduced by permission.

is small. Figure 4-5 provides examples. *A*-1 and *A*-2 are closer to points in the Penteli set of points than they are to the members of the Naxos set.

To compare two sets, we ask if the average distance between pairs of points, one drawn from each set, is small or large. Suppose X and Y are sets containing n_x and n_y points, respectively. The mean squared distance between points in X and Y is

$$d_2^{\,2}(X,\ Y) = \left(\frac{1}{n_x \cdot n_y}\right) \sum_{i=1}^{n_x} \sum_{j=1}^{n_y} d^2(x_i, y_j) \qquad (42)$$

The further apart the members of X and Y are, on the average, the larger value (42) will have. By this criterion, for instance, the Penteli points in Figure 4-5 lie closer to the Naxos points than they do to the Paros or Hymettus points.

Within a set a measure is needed to determine how closely the points are packed together. The measure is the mean squared distance between the points in the same set, i.e.

$$d_3(X) = \left[\frac{1}{n_x(n_x-1)}\right] \sum_{i=1}^{n_x-1} \sum_{j=i+1}^{n_x} d^2(\mathbf{x}_i, \mathbf{x}_j). \tag{43}$$

The measure is smaller if the points within a set lie close to each other. By this criterion the Penteli cluster is more closely packed than the Naxos cluster.

The general idea behind proximity analysis is to transform the description space D into a space D^* in which all points within a set lie close to each other and in which all points in different sets lie at some distance from each other. For the most part we will be concerned only with linear transformations. Here D^* is a linear transformation of the m-dimensional space D if every point $\mathbf{x} \in D$ is mapped into an $\mathbf{x}^* \in D^*$ by the relation

$$\mathbf{x}^* = \mathbf{x}W \tag{44}$$

where W is an $m \times m$ symmetric matrix. This means that the elements of $\mathbf{x}^*$ are given by

$$x_j^* = \sum_{i=1}^{m} x_i w_{ji}. \tag{45}$$

4.3.2 CLASSIFICATION BY MAXIMIZING INTRASET SIMILARITY

The first proximity based method distorts D in such a way that the mean squared distance between points within a set $[d_3(X)]$ is minimized. It will be illustrated by the Craig and Craig data from the Paros quarry. The original measures are shown in Figure 4-6a.

A trivial solution to the minimization problem would be to map all points in the cluster to the same point. This could be done by the linear transformation in which W is a matrix of zeros. The problem is that this would map all points in D, whether in the cluster or not, to the origin in D^*, and thus would hardly be useful for classification purposes. It clearly does not help to shrink the volume of D uniformly in order to bring the points closer to each other, rather we must rearrange the points themselves. Therefore, let us impose the constraint that the transformation minimize $d_3(X)$ for some X (Paros, in this case), subject to the constraint that the volume of D be maintained. Mathematically we require that

$$\prod_{i=1}^{m} w_{ii} = 1. \tag{46}$$

Equation (46) ensures that the unit hypercube will have the same volume in D and D^*. For D^* both to satisfy (46) and to minimize $d_3(X)$, the points in X must be

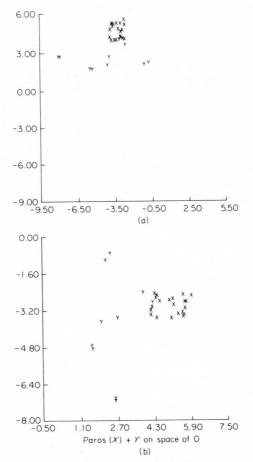

Fig. 4-6. Transformation of Paros data from original to best clustering space. X: Known data. Y: Unknown points. Note that scales have been changed.

packed together into a spheroid, rather than ellipsoid, cluster. The resulting transformation is shown in Figure 4-6b. The question is, "What transformation matrix W achieves this distortion of D into D^*?"

Both graphically and algebraically, the transformation can be pictured as a two-step operation. The graphic sequence is shown in Figures 4-7a–c, again using the Paros data as an illustration. The points are assumed to be clustered in an ellipsoid in D. The first step is to determine the axes of the ellipsoid (lines L_1 and L_2 in Figure 4-7a) and rotate the axes of D to the axes of the ellipsoid. This step is shown in Figure 4-7b. Call the resulting space D^z, and let its axes be $z_1, z_2, \ldots, z_m$. The set X of points in D will map into a set of points X^z in D^z, as shown in Figure 4-7b. Obviously volume has not been changed by rotation. By changing the scale units for each of the dimensions of D^z, we can produce a new

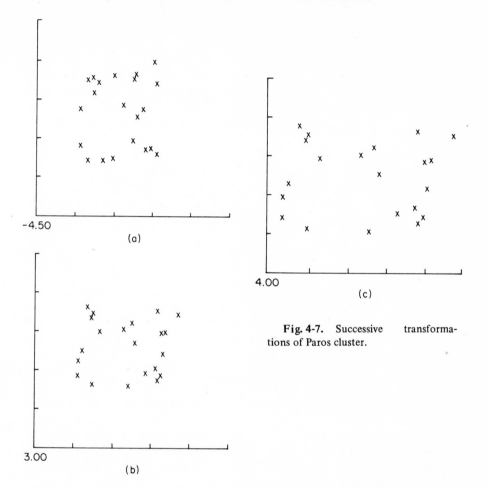

Fig. 4-7. Successive transformations of Paros cluster.

space D^* which is simply D^z shrunken along some axes and expanded along others so that the ellipsoid traced out by X^z becomes a spheroid traced out by X^* in D^*. At this point, however, we must worry about balancing expansion in one dimension against shrinkage in another, so that volume is maintained.

We now state the algebraic operations required to achieve the transformation from D to D^*. Let X be the set of m points for which $d_3(X)$ is to be minimized. The $m \times m$ matrix U is defined with respect to X, as having elements

$$\mu_{ij} = n^{-1} \sum_{q=1}^{n} (x_{qi} - \bar{x}_i)(x_{qj} - \bar{x}_j) \tag{47}$$

where $\bar{x}_i$ and $\bar{x}_j$ are the mean values of components i and j, respectively, of the points $x_i \in X$. [2] Note that the variance of the value of measure i, in set X, is

$$\sigma_i^2 = \mu_{ii}. \tag{48}$$

Let C be the matrix whose rows are the eigenvectors of U, ordered in accordance with the value of the associated eigenvalue, from greatest to least. Each eigenvector defines the direction of one of the axes of the ellipse traced by X in D, hence C is the transformation matrix required to define D^z. Thus we have, for all $x \in D$, $x^z \in D^z$,

$$x^z = xC'. \tag{49}$$

We now need to change scales to move from D^z to D^*, while maintaining the constant volume constraint. In a scale change the transformation matrix A will be a diagonal matrix A whose nonzero elements are

$$a_{ii} = \left(\prod_{i=1}^{m} \sigma_{z_i} \right) m^{-1} (\sigma_{z_i})^{-1}. \tag{50}$$

The effect of the scale change is to introduce a fine scale along those (derived) dimensions which show little variation from point to point within a given class, and to introduce a gross scale along any measurement axis where the known points show a good deal of variation. The rotation followed by the scale change defines the transformation matrix

$$W = (C'A). \tag{51}$$

In the recognition phase a separate space is determined for each class of objects represented in the sample. Let D^{*i} be the space associated with class i. In the classification phase a new object y is presented, and mapped into each of the k spaces D^{*i}. The distance from y^{*i} to the defining set is determined in the same space. That is, if set X^i was used to define D^{*i}, the distance measure $d_1(y^{*i}, X^{*i})$ is determined. Point y is assigned to class j if and only if

$$d_1(y^{*j}, X^{*j}) = \min_{i=1,k} [d_1(y^{*i}, X^{*i})]. \tag{52}$$

To complete our illustration of the method, we have computed the appropriate similarity measurements for all the statuary fragments and all the quarry observations reported by Craig and Craig. The resulting data are shown in Table 4-2. It is interesting to compare these classifications with the classifications made by Craig and Craig, apparently on the basis of visual inspection of Figure 4-6.

---

[2] The reader may have noted that U is the matrix used to estimate Σ in maximum likelihood classification. The reason for differentiating between them is that Σ is an approximation to a presumed population matrix, whereas here U is presented without justification except in terms of the observed points.

TABLE 4-2
Similarity Measurements for Statuary Fragments and Quarry Observations

Sample no.	Description	Naxos I	Penteli	Paros	Hymettus	Naxos II
A-1	Athens: "Theseion" (Hephaesteion) in the Agora, column on the north side.	2.20	.31	26.04	30.44	3.74
A-2	Athens: basal slab on south side of "Theseion"	1.87	.23	27.27	31.89	4.22
D-1	Delphi: carved block lying inside Treasury of Siphnos	40.40	28.25	.92	3.47	12.36
D-2	Delphi: drum of column of the Naxian Sphinx	26.19	17.91	8.11	3.25	4.37
E-1	Epidaurus: carved block (lintel?), 10 m from Tholos	66.10	52.07	11.45	1.89	25.49
E-2	Epidaurus: Corinthian capital next to the "triple circle" of Tholos	71.66	56.85	12.26	2.85	28.97
E-3	Epidaurus: cut slab of white marble, 13 m from Tholos	28.13	18.88	4.95	2.70	5.23
N-43	Naxos: Apollon Gate, Palatia, Naxos Harbour; flake from inside of gate	14.52	9.07	14.07	10.05	1.09
N-46	Naxos: Apollon Gate, large block at foot of hill toward Naxos	15.77	10.05	13.54	9.12	1.34
C-1	Caesarea, Israel: Corinthian capital of gray marble	45.18	32.53	1.91	1.92	14.22

4.3.3 DISCRIMINATION FUNCTIONS BASED ON INTERPOINT DISTANCES

There are two major objections to classification based on intraset similarity. One is that a separate transformation is required for each class, thus complicating the pattern classification process. The other is that considering each class separately may not provide any indication of contrasts between classes in the basic measurement space. An alternative criterion does meet these objections. The criterion is maximization of the difference between points in different sets, while holding the sum of the distances between points within and between sets constant. Such a criterion is called a *discriminant* criterion. Intuitively, it should result in a single (composite) measurement, on which points within a set have similar values and points in different sets have dissimilar values.

This criterion has an interesting geometric interpretation. We can think of a composite (linear) measurement as a line in m space, extending from the origin of the description space D. Any point will have a projection on that line. We seek the line for which points within a set project to the same region, and points in different sets project to different regions. An illustration is shown in Figure 4-8, which is a plot of Craig and Craig's data for the Paros, Hymettus, and Penteli quarries and shows their projection on a line L defined by a weighted sum of the oxygen and carbon ratios.

In order to define the appropriate computing procedures, three auxiliary matrices, G, V, and T are required. For any pair of points $\mathbf{x}, \mathbf{y} \in D$, define the $m \times m$ matrix $G(\mathbf{x}, \mathbf{y})$ with elements

$$g_{rs}(\mathbf{x}, \mathbf{y}) = (x_r - y_r)(x_s - y_s) = g_{sr}(\mathbf{x}, \mathbf{y}), \tag{53}$$

i.e. the product of the difference between $\mathbf{x}$ and $\mathbf{y}$ on measures s and r. Suppose that the original data consist of k sets, $X^1, X^2, \ldots, X^k$ of observations from each of k classes. The matrix V is obtained by averaging the matrices $G(\mathbf{x}, \mathbf{y})$ computed over all pairs of points such that $\mathbf{x}$ and $\mathbf{y}$ are members of distinct sets X^i and X^j. The matrix T is obtained by averaging the matrices $G(\mathbf{x}, \mathbf{y})$ for all pairs of points regardless of their set membership. Algebraically

$$V = \left[\frac{2}{k(k-1)} \right] \sum_{i=1}^{k-1} \left(\frac{1}{n_i} \right) \sum_{j=i+1}^{k} \left(\frac{1}{n_j} \right) \sum_{q=1}^{n_i} \sum_{p=1}^{n_j} G(\mathbf{x}_q^{\,i}, \mathbf{x}_p^{\,j}) \tag{54}$$

and if

$$X = \bigcup_{i=1}^{k} X^i; \qquad n = \sum_{i=1}^{k} n_i, \tag{55}$$

then

$$T = \left(\frac{n}{2} \right) \sum_{i=1}^{n-1} \sum_{j=i+1}^{n} G(\mathbf{x}_i, \mathbf{x}_j). \tag{56}$$

If W is a matrix whose rows are the eigenvectors of the matrix (VT^{-1}), then $\mathbf{w}_1$ is the eigenvector associated with the largest eigenvalue. Eigenvector $\mathbf{w}_1$ defines the direction of the maximum discriminant line extending from the origin in D. More precisely, the line L that we seek will be the line extending from the origin at such an angle from the jth axis of D (d_j) so that

$$\cos(L, d_j) = w_{1,j} \tag{57}$$

Fig. 4-8.   (a) Projections of points from five plots on best discriminating eigenvector. (b) Projections of points from six plots on best discriminating eigenvector.

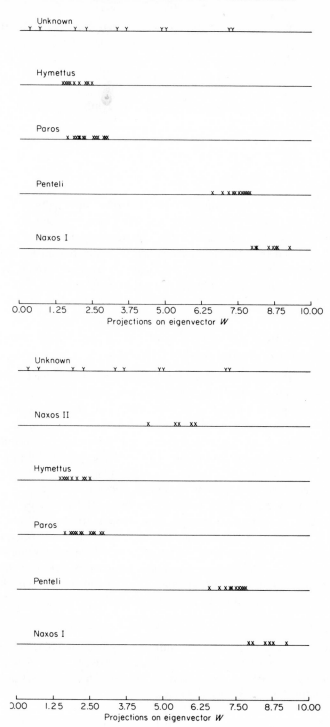

Determination of L completes the pattern-recognition phase. In the pattern classification phase an object is assigned to class i by observing the projection of its description $\mathbf{y}$ on L. For any point $\mathbf{x} \in D$, let

$$x^* = \mathbf{x}\mathbf{w}_1'. \tag{58}$$

Classify $\mathbf{y}$ as a description of an object in class i if and only if

$$r_i(\mathbf{y}) = n_i^{-1} \sum_{j=1}^{n_i} [y^* - (x_j^i)^*] \tag{59}$$

is a minimum for $i = 1, \ldots, k$.

The weak point of the discriminant criterion is that although it provides a good measure for classification over all classes, it will not necessarily provide a good measure for each class. The problem is easily illustrated by inspection of Figure 4-6. No line can be passed through this space which separates out all the classes, since the best line for a Penteli–Naxos discrimination is oriented differently than the optimum line for discriminations not involving the Naxos data.

4.3.4   RELATIONSHIP BETWEEN STATISTICAL ANALYSIS AND PATTERN RECOGNITION BASED ON PROXIMITIES

The Bayesian statistical classification method presented in Section 4.2 is quite similar to pattern recognition based upon minimization of intraclass distance. In both cases one seeks a transformation for each class which clusters the objects within a class close to each other. The Bayesian approach using the multivarite normal assumption can be looked upon as a transformation which minimizes the distance from each point within a cluster to the cluster centroid. In the proximity technique the mean squared interpoint distance between pairs of points within the class is minimized. The two solutions are almost identical.

There is a similar relationship between discriminant techniques and statistical discriminant analysis. Imagine that a linear combination y of the descriptive measures $\{x_i\}$ has been found. Define SS_b to be the sum of the squared distances from the mean y value of each point within a class to the mean y value of the entire sample. Define SS_w as the sum of the squared distances from the value of each individual point to the mean value for the class containing that point. In statistical discriminant analysis y is chosen to maximize the ratio

$$K = SS_b/SS_w. \tag{60}$$

This is similar to the maximization criterion used in Section 4.3.3. The difference is that proximity analysis concentrates on distances between pairs of points whereas statistical analysis concentrates on distances between the individual points and the mean values defined across appropriate classes.

4.3.5 NONLINEAR CLASSIFICATION

A pattern-classification rule based on a sample should, ideally, correctly classify the sample points themselves. This is not always possible if the form of the classification rule is restricted. In particular, if the classification rule is based on a linear transformation of the description space, perfect classification will be possible only if one can draw hyperplanes between each pair of classes such that all members of one class lie on one side of the hyperplane and all members of the other class lie on the other side. Referring back to the Craig and Craig data in Figure 4-5, it is at once obvious that such hyperplanes can be drawn between data points from any pair of quarries except Naxos and Penteli. When the necessary hyperplane exists the classes it separates are said to be *linearly separable* in the description space D, and the pattern-recognition problem is reduced to one of locating the necessary hyperplanes. If there are pairs of classes that are not linearly separable, any of the methods described thus far will make errors in classifying some of the objects of the original sample.

There is a straightforward way to transform a problem containing classes which are not linearly separable into a problem containing only linearly separable classes. What is required is a new description space $D\#$ which is a nonlinear distortion of D such that all classes are linearly separable in $D\#$. The definition of $D\#$ is based on the fact that any function of m variables can be approximated by a function of the form

$$g(x_1, x_2, \ldots, x_m) = \sum_{i=0}^{K} \sum_{j=0}^{K} \cdots \sum_{n=0}^{K} a_{ij\cdots n} x_1{}^{i} x_2{}^{j} \cdots x_m{}^{n} \qquad (61)$$

provided that K is chosen to be sufficiently large. Given a pair of classes that are not linearly separable in D, we can expand D to a new space D^K whose dimensions are defined by all possible expressions of the form

$$f(\mathbf{x}) = x_1{}^{i} x_2{}^{j} \cdots x_m{}^{n} \qquad (62)$$

If the boundary between two classes in D can be expressed by a function of the form of (61), then two classes will be linearly separable in D^K. The pattern-recognition techniques already given can then be applied to the problem in D^K to find W and, by implication, $D\#$, which will be a linear transformation of D^K. (Sebesteyen, 1962, Chap. 3)

The problem with this approach is that it may require a great deal of computing. The dimensionality of D^K grows exponentially with K, and as the matrix operations require computing effort which grows exponentially with the dimensionality, the problem is serious indeed. Empirically, of course, there are situations in which markedly nonlinear problems in space D can be solved with fairly low K. Figure 4-9 is an example, for which Sebesteyen obtained a solution with $K = 6$. Of course, one could also find pathological examples for which impossibly high values of K were required.

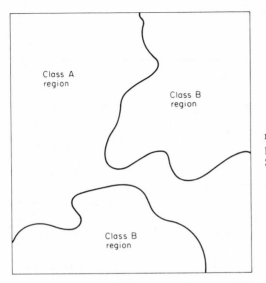

Fig. 4-9. Space partitioned into regions defined by terms indicating cross products of sixth degree. (After Sebesteyen, 1962, Fig. 3-8.)

We have three suggestions for dealing with nonlinear problems by methods other than the brute force technique just described. One is based on interactive computing. The impracticality of successive tests of D^K is due to the time needed to solve the eigenvector problem (i.e., the solution for W) when K is large. Prior to solving for W, however, one might be able to recognize whether a solution was, or was not, possible by visual examination of the distribution of data points in the description space D^K to determine whether the different classes were linearly separable. If one could find out, quickly, that they were or were not, one could decide whether the particular space should be further investigated. One way of deciding would be to display suitable projections of the sample points on a graphic display, and let a man guide the subsequent computations. Although there has been some discussion of interactive techniques in pattern recognition (Brick, 1969, Garnatz & Hunt, 1973), it is not known whether this particular technique has been used, or how successful it would be. At least one of the requirements for its execution would be the development of clever techniques for displaying multidimensional distributions so that a human could understand them.

A second intuitive procedure is to consider classes of transformations of D which are less broad than the set of linear polynomials. This is typically what is done in statistical classification. Given that the initial distributions of points are nonellipsoid, one seeks some transformation that will produce ellipsoids, then proceeds with the linear solution method. If one has an idea of how the data were generated, or if one recognizes a common nonellipsoid form in the data, this is often quite useful. An example is shown in Figure 4-10. The distribution shown in Figure 4-10a was generated by assuming uniform probability of placing a point at any position on the ordinate, and an exponential probability of placing a point at an arbitrary nonzero point on the abcissa. By making a transformation to standard normal deviation units (Hoel, 1971) on the ordinate and a logarithmic transformation on the abcissa Figure 4-10b was obtained, approximating the desired ellipsoid form. The approach of choosing transformations cleverly is a common one in pattern recognition and in statistics generally. While less general than the method of generating D^K sequentially, it may lead to the desired results with much less computation. A caution to be observed is that the transformation to be applied should make sense, given the nature of the data. This question is closely related to the earlier measurement question, given the nature of the basic data, what transformations are allowable?

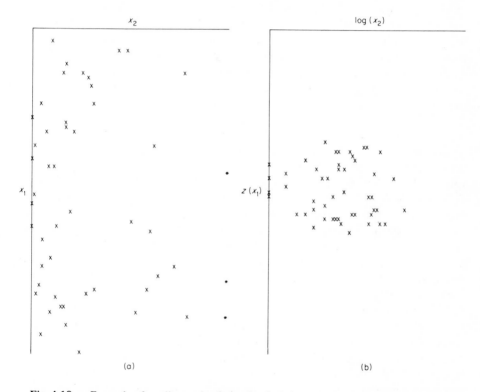

Fig. 4-10. Example of nonlinear transformation based on selected distorting functions. (a) Original distribution. (b) Transformed distribution.

4.3.6 NEAREST NEIGHBOR CLASSIFICATION

The proximity analyses presented thus far allow us to drop the assumption that probability density functions are known for each class, while retaining the concepts of Euclidean distance and of averaging measures over a set of points. In this section a very simple classification technique is presented which drops the averaging concept and is impervious to violations of linear separability. The technique is called *nearest neighbor classification*. In addition to its lack of assumptions, it requires very little computing during the pattern-recognition phase. Its drawbacks are that it may require substantial amounts of computing resources during the pattern-classification stage and that it does not satisfy any reasonable criterion for optimal pattern classification. We shall, however, illustrate the sense in which it may be considered a satisfactory but nonoptimal method.

Before describing the method itself a word of explanation about the averaging concept may be in order. Why would one object to the assumption that it makes sense to average over measures? The answer to this question is that averaging makes sense only when it can be assumed that a measure of central tendency is representative of measures on individual cases. To see when this is, or is not, an appropriate assumption turn again to the Craig and Craig data shown in Figure 4-5. The data points for four of the quarry fragments are clearly packed around a central point, so that it makes sense to average over samples from each of these quarries in order to define a typical data point. The data from the Naxos quarry, however, appear to fall into two distinct clusters (Craig and Craig so regarded these data, although they did not present their reasons for the assumption). Averaging over all points in both Naxos clusters produces a central tendency data point which, in fact, is not representative of any individual data point. Similar examples can, of course, be constructed for even more obvious cases. For instance, the "human of average height" ought to be computed over both men and women, which is not reasonable. In general, problems where averaging is not appropriate are obvious to a person, but how do we define to a machine what is obvious to a man?

The nearest neighbor classification algorithm is extremely simple. Imagine the sample S to be a sequence of data points of known classification, $x^{(1)}, x^{(2)}, \ldots, x^{(n)}$. At each step a data point is observed, its classification is guessed, and the classifier informed of the correct answer. The guess for datum $x^{(j)}$ is made by examining the $j - 1$ preceding data points and finding the k closest points to point $x^{(j)}$. If $k = 1$, the point found is the nearest neighbor to $x^{(j)}$, and $x^{(j)}$ is assigned to the same class as the nearest neighbor. If k is greater than 1 the classification rule could be more complex, but simple rules (e.g., majority vote) generally are used.

The nearest neighbor method was introduced in a technical report by Fix and Hodges (1951). Since then it has not received nearly the attention that other pattern recognition procedures have, perhaps because it appears too simple to be interesting! Surprisingly, however, those studies which have used nearest neighbor classification generally report good results. Cover and Hart (1965; see also Cover, 1969) proved a theorem for the case $k = 1$ which explains why.

Let R_n be the probability of making an error using the nearest neighbor technique based on a sample of size n. We cannot know R_n exactly without knowing the probability distributions (including the parameters) which generate S, but we may estimate R_n by the statistic

$$C_{n-1} = \text{(number of observations } \{x_i\} \text{ in the sequence } x^{(1)} \cdots x^{(n)} \quad (63)$$
which would be misclassified by using a nearest neighbor technique based on the sample $S - x^{(i)}$)

Note that this is a valid estimate only on the assumption that the $x^{(i)}$ are each independent random samples with replacement from U. C_n is a random variable with expectation

$$E(C_n) = R_n. \tag{64}$$

It is intuitively clear that R_n approaches R_∞ as n increases. (For a formal proof, see Cover and Hart, 1965.) Now, let R^* be the risk of misclassification of any randomly chosen observation using the unknown Bayesian optimal classification method. Cover and Hart proved that for the case of two classes

$$R^* \leqslant R_\infty \leqslant 2R^*(1 - R^*). \tag{65}$$

Table 4-3 shows the upper bound on R_∞ associated with some typical levels of Bayesian risk (lower bounds). To decide whether these bounds are acceptable, consider the following "thought experiment." Imagine that we are given two black boxes containing classifiers. They are either both Bayesian classifiers, both nearest neighbor classifiers, or one of each. Our job is to determine which of these possibilities is the case. To do this, we require that each classifier categorize *different* samples of N objects. Since the samples are different, we would expect a nearest neighbor classifier to make more errors. We decide, therefore, to identify one categorizer as nearest neighbor and one as Bayesian if there is less than 1 chance in 100 that the error rates observed would have been observed if the classifiers were the same. If the discrepancy is not large enough, we will assume the classifiers to be identical. How large should N be so that we either (*a*) have an even chance of correctly identifying classifiers as different every time the experiment is conducted with different classifiers or (*b*) make the correct identification three times out of every four in the same situation? The answer to this question can be obtained by using (65) to estimate the limits on performance of the classifiers, then

TABLE 4-3

Upper and Lower Bounds on Asymptotic Risk Using Nearest Neighbor Rule,
and Size of Sample Required to Discriminate between
Worst Nearest Neighbor and a Bayesian Optimal Classifier[a]

1. Bayesian risk (lower bound)	2. Upper bound	3. Size of sample required to discriminate	
		a. Power = .5	b. Power = .75
.050	.095	470	930
.100	.180	220	430
.150	.225	170	340
.200	.320	160	310
.250	.375	160	320

[a] The values in columns 3a and 3b were obtained by the power analysis method described by Cohen (1969), using linear interpolation into his Table 6.41

applying the statistical technique of power analysis (Cohen, 1969). Rather than explain the statistics, we simply assert the results. Columns 3a and 3b of Table 4-3 indicate the required sample size for each experiment for varying levels of Bayesian risk. If anything, these are underestimates, since in preparing the table it has been assumed that the nearest neighbor classifier operates at the highest possible risk.

The problem in nearest neighbor pattern recognition is that finding the nearest neighbor at classification time is not trivial. Sufficient memory must be available to store the entire sample and there must be an information retrieval scheme which enables one to locate the nearest neighbor to a new observation quickly. Imagine, for example, the problem imposed by using the United States Census Data, where the number of *cases* is in the millions, although the number of variables is on the order of 100. In general, the nearest neighbor method is sensitive to the number of cases in the sample, while the other methods are sensitive to the number of variables. This should be remembered when choosing a technique for an actual problem.

In conclusion, the nearest neighbor method gives surprisingly good results considering its simplicity. It is particularly useful in situations in which the assumption of linear separability is badly violated. The major drawbacks to the nearest neighbor method are not lack of accuracy, but rather its large memory requirements and the fact that it, like all proximity techniques, depends very much upon Euclidean distance assumptions.[3]

4.4   Learning Algorithms

4.4.0   INTRODUCTION

An important modification of the pattern recognition problem has been called, by analogy, "machine learning." The less exciting term "adaptive pattern recognition" is also used. Suppose that instead of being given a fixed sample X be analyzed, the pattern recognizer observes the sequence

$$S_x = \mathbf{x}^{(1)}, \mathbf{x}^{(2)}, \ldots, \mathbf{x}^{(i)}, \ldots, \mathbf{x}^{(t)} \tag{66}$$

in which every possible observation appears infinitely many times. We can think of S_x as a sequence obtained by choosing $\mathbf{x}^{(i)}$ repetitively, with replacement, from the set of possible descriptions of objects. The pattern recognition and classification stages are combined. Assume that a current classifying rule exists. As each $\mathbf{x}^{(i)}$ appears it is classified using this rule, and the pattern recognizer is informed of the correct classification. The rule is then corrected. Instead of asking "What decision rule should be inferred from a finite sample?" as has been the case in the previous discussion, we ask "What algorithm will develop an appropriate decision rule by

---

[3] Minsky and Papert (1969, Section 12.3) give an example where the nearest neighbor method actually does worse than chance, but the example is unfair because the Euclidean assumptions are violated.

successive approximation?" Such an algorithm will be called a *learning rule*. The output of a learning rule is a sequence of decision rules

$$S_w = W^{(1)}, W^{(2)}, \ldots, W^{(t)} \tag{67}$$

where the ith rule is used to classify the ith observation. A learning rule is said to converge if there is a positive integer t^* such that

$$W^{(t^*)} = W^{(t^*+j)}, \qquad j \geqslant 0. \tag{68}$$

More simply, (68) states that the learning rule will eventually stabilize on a single, unchanging categorization procedure. The learning rule is a good one if the procedure on which it stabilizes maximizes some criterion for good classification.

The analogy to learning is clear-cut, an algorithm which satisfies these definitions will have learned from experience. It is interesting to note that some of the learning algorithms which have been proposed could be implemented by a network of elements similar in some ways to a nerve cell. In fact, much of the early work on machine learning was at least partly motivated by a desire to model learning in biological systems. The *perceptron*, a well publicized type of learning machine, was first described by Rosenblatt (1958) in an article in the *Psychological Review*, and Rosenblatt's 1965 book *Principles of Neurodynamics* includes an extensive discussion of the relation of perceptron algorithms to neurophysiology. Beyond noting this bit of history, we shall not discuss the plausibility of various learning schemes as biological models. (In general they are naive.) Instead we shall present a discussion (modeled after Nilsson, 1965a) of the mathematics of the learning problem.

4.4.1 DEFINITIONS AND NOTATION

The notion of a sequence of observations has already been presented. Each member of the sequence is assumed to belong to exactly one of $k \geqslant 2$ classes. An important difference from some of our previous treatments is that we assume that no two classes ever give rise to an identical observation. Previously we had only assumed that each class had a probability associated with each point in the description space, we now require that each point $x \in D$ be assigned to a unique class. Instead of developing a learning rule for the sequence S_x a rule will be developed for

$$S_y = y^{(1)} \cdots y^{(t)} \tag{69}$$

where $y^{(i)}$ is an $m + 1$-element vector derived from $x^{(i)}$ by appending a 1 as the $m + 1$st element. We will say that $y^{(i)}$ is a member of class j if $x^{(i)}$ is the description of an object in class j. Obviously a rule for classifying S_y will also classify S_x.

The k classes are said to be separable if there exists a set of functions $\{g_j\}$ such that

$$g_{j^*}(y^{(i)}) = \max\{g_j(y^{(i)})\} \tag{70}$$

if and only if $\mathbf{y}^{(i)}$ is a member of class j^*. The classes are said to be linearly separable if the functions are linear,

$$g_j(\mathbf{y}^{(i)}) = \sum_{s=1}^{m+1} w_{js} y_s^{(i)} \tag{71}$$

$$= \sum_{s=1}^{m} w_{js} x_s^{(i)} + w_{j,m+1}.$$

Note that these definitions are essentially the same as the previous definitions of separability and linear separability, with appropriate changes in notation. If (71) holds a classification rule $W^{(i)}$ can be defined as a $k \times m + 1$ matrix, each of whose rows is the vector $\mathbf{w}_j$. In this case it is convenient to write (71) in dot product notation, as

$$g_j(\mathbf{y}^{(i)}) = \mathbf{y}^{(i)} \cdot \mathbf{w}_j. \tag{72}$$

In general there will be infinitely many matrices W satisfying (70) and (71). Unless it is explicitly stated to the contrary, it will be assumed throughout this section that some W exists. The task is to show that certain learning rules derive a satisfactory $W^{(t)}$.

The case $k = 2$ is of particular interest for three reasons; (1) because it has an elegant treatment, (2) because it is common in practice, and (3) because it is a special case to which the general case $k > 2$ can be reduced. Suppose there exists at least one set of linear functions, $G = \{g_1, g_2\}$, satisfying (70) and (71). The *discriminant function*

$$g^* = g_1 - g_2 \tag{73}$$

exists and, by substitution, is equal to

$$g^*(\mathbf{y}^{(i)}) = \sum_{s=1}^{m+1} w_s{}^* y_s^{(i)} \tag{74}$$

$$= \sum_{s=1}^{m+1} (w_{1s} - w_{2s}) y_s^{(i)}.$$

Therefore the relation

$$g^*(\mathbf{y}^{(i)}) > 0 \tag{75}$$

is satisfied if and only if $\mathbf{y}^{(i)}$ is a member of class 1. Now let Y_1 and Y_2 be the vectors in classes 1 and 2, respectively, and define

$$Z = Y_1 U - Y_2. \tag{76}$$

The relation

$$g^*(\mathbf{z}) > 0 \tag{77}$$

holds for all $z \in Z$. A function g^* is said to *linearly contain* a set Z if (77) is true. From the method of construction of Z it follows that if we can find a function that linearly contains Z, this is equivalent to finding a function that satisfies (75) and thus linearly separates Y_1 and Y_2.

4.4.2 A TWO-CATEGORY TRAINING PROCEDURE

A learning rule for the two-category problem will now be developed. By hypothesis there exists a set of vectors $\{w^*\}$ which will linearly separate Y_1 and Y_2. The task is to find one such vector. This will be done by the following algorithm, which is known as an *error correction procedure* since the classification rule is adjusted only following errors.

Two-class error correction algorithm:

(1) *Let* $w^{(i)}$ *be the approximation used to classify* $y^{(i)}$.

(2) $w^{(1)} = (0, 0, \ldots, 0)$.

(3) *Given* $w^{(i)}$, *the following case rules are to be followed.*

case 1 $y^{(i)} \in Y_1$

     a. *If* $y^{(i)} \cdot w^{(i)} > 0$, $w^{(i+1)} = w^{(i)}$.

     b. *If* $y^{(i)} \cdot w^{(i)} \leq 0$ *an error has occurred.*

        The adjustment is $w^{(i+1)} = w^{(i)} + y^{(i)}$.

case 2 $y^{(i)} \in Y_2$

     a. *If* $y^{(i)} \cdot w^{(i)} < 0$, $w^{(i+1)} = w^{(i)}$.

     b. *If* $y^{(i)} \cdot w^{(i)} \geq 0$, $w^{(i+1)} = w^{(i)} - y^{(i)}$.

It would be possible to propose and prove the necessary theorems about a slightly more general algorithm in which $w^{(1)}$ is an arbitrary vector and the adjustment after errors is $\pm c y^{(i)}$, with c an arbitrary positive constant, but this complicates the algebra unduly.

The two-category learning theorem is

> *If* Y_1 *and* Y_2 *are linearly separable and the two-class error correction algorithm is used to define* $w^{(i)}$, *then there exists an integer* $t > 0$ *such that* $w^{(t)}$ *linearly separates* Y_1 *and* Y_2, *and hence* $w^{(t+j)} = w^{(t)}$ *for all positive j.*

The theorem states that the algorithm works.

There are several proofs. The following one shows that $w^{(t)}$ can be found which linearly contains Z, as defined in Eq. (76). Let S_z be the sequence of z's corresponding to the elements of S_y. The algorithm is first translated into a procedure operating on S_z.

The translated two-class algorithm:

(1) $w^{(1)} = 0$, *as before.*

(2) $\mathbf{w}^{(i+1)} = \mathbf{w}^{(i)}$ if $\mathbf{z}^{(i)} \cdot \mathbf{w}^{(i)} > 0$. *This corresponds to the correct classification cases in the original algorithm.*

(3) $\mathbf{w}^{(i+1)} = \mathbf{w}^{(i)} + \mathbf{z}^{(i)}$ if $\mathbf{z}^{(i)} \cdot \mathbf{w}^{(i)} \leqslant 0$. *This corresponds to the incorrect classification cases in the original algorithm.*

Let S_e be the sequence $\mathbf{e}_1, \mathbf{e}_2 \ldots , \mathbf{e}_j$, where $\mathbf{e}_j$ is the jth error in classification. Thus S_e is a subset of S_z, and $\mathbf{e}_j$ is the vector which causes the jth turn to Step 3 of the modified algorithm. If S_e is finite, there must be a last visit to Step 3, producing a rule $\mathbf{w}^{(t)}$, which is never changed. By assumption, however, S_z is an infinitely long sequence containing every possible data point an infinite number of times, hence $\mathbf{w}^{(t)}$ must be capable of classifying all points and, thus, linearly separating Y_1 and Y_2. The next step, then, is to show that S_e is finite.

By hypothesis there exists a weight vector $\mathbf{w}^*$ which linearly contains Z. Therefore there is a positive number such that

$$\min_{\mathbf{z} \in Z} \{(\mathbf{z} \cdot \mathbf{w}^*)\} = a > 0. \tag{78}$$

Define $\mathbf{w}(t)$ to be the weight vector developed after the tth error. From the algorithm we know that

$$\mathbf{w}(t) = \sum_{j=1}^{t} \mathbf{e}_j \tag{79}$$

and, therefore

$$\mathbf{w}(t) \cdot \mathbf{w}^* = \sum_{j=1}^{t} \mathbf{e}_j \cdot \mathbf{w}^* \geqslant t \cdot a \tag{80}$$

Equation (80) can be used to establish a lower bound on the quantity $[\mathbf{w}(t)]^2$. The *Cauchy–Schwarz theorem* of the calculus of inequalities states that the product of the squares of two vectors is equal to or greater than the square of the product of the two vectors. Applied to the case at hand,

$$[\mathbf{w}(t)^2 \cdot (\mathbf{w}^*)^2] \geqslant [\mathbf{w}(t) \cdot \mathbf{w}^*]^2. \tag{81}$$

By rearrangement

$$[\mathbf{w}(t)]^2 \geqslant \frac{[\mathbf{w}(t) \cdot \mathbf{w}^*]^2}{(\mathbf{w}^*)^2}. \tag{82}$$

Combining (80) and (82)

$$[\mathbf{w}(t)]^2 \geqslant \frac{a^2 \cdot t^2}{(\mathbf{w}^*)^2} \tag{83}$$

$$\geqslant t^2 \cdot M_1$$

where M_1 is an unknown constant whose value depends on $\mathbf{w}^*$. The point is not to specify a value for M_1 but to show that the lower bound of $[\mathbf{w}(t)]^2$ is proportional to t^2.

A different line of reasoning shows that the upper bound is proportional to t. The algorithm ensures that

$$\mathbf{w}(t+1) = \mathbf{w}(t) + \mathbf{e}_{t+1}. \tag{84}$$

Squaring (84)

$$[\mathbf{w}(t+1)]^2 = (\mathbf{w}(t))^2 + 2\mathbf{w}(t) \cdot \mathbf{e}_{t+1} + (\mathbf{e}_{t+1})^2 \tag{85}$$

Since using $\mathbf{w}(t)$ produced error $\mathbf{e}_{t+1}$, $\mathbf{w}(t) \cdot \mathbf{e}_{t+1} \leqslant 0$, so

$$[\mathbf{w}(t+1)]^2 - [\mathbf{w}(t)]^2 \leqslant (\mathbf{e}_{t+1})^2. \tag{86}$$

By summing (86) for $j = 1, \ldots, t$, we have

$$\{[\mathbf{w}(t+1)]^2 - [\mathbf{w}(t)]^2\} + \{[\mathbf{w}(t)]^2 - [\mathbf{w}(t-1)]^2\} + \{[\mathbf{w}(t-1)]^2 - [\mathbf{w}(t-2)]^2\}$$

$$+ \cdots + \{[\mathbf{w}(2)]^2 - [\mathbf{w}(1)]^2\} + \{[\mathbf{w}(1)]^2 - [\mathbf{w}(0)]^2\} \leqslant \sum_{j=1}^{t+1} (\mathbf{e}_j)^2 \tag{87}$$

Since $\mathbf{w}(0) = \mathbf{w}^{(1)} = 0$, $[\mathbf{w}(0)]^2$ may be disregarded. All other terms cancel, leaving

$$[\mathbf{w}(t+1)]^2 \leqslant \sum_{j=1}^{t+1} (\mathbf{e}_j)^2 \tag{88}$$

By reindexing

$$[\mathbf{w}(t)]^2 \leqslant \sum_{j=1}^{t} (\mathbf{e}_j)^2. \tag{89}$$

As Z is finite, it must contain a longest vector. Since $S_e \subset S_z$, this vector is at least as long as the longest vector in S_e.

$$M_2 = \max_{z \in Z} \{(\mathbf{z}^2)\} \geqslant \max_{e_i \in S_e} \{(\mathbf{e}_i^2)\} \tag{90}$$

Combining (89) and (90)

$$[\mathbf{w}(t)]^2 \leqslant \sum_{j=1}^{t} (\mathbf{e}_j)^2 \leqslant t \cdot M_2 \tag{91}$$

Combining (91) with (83)

$$M_1 t^2 \leqslant [\mathbf{w}(t)]^2 \leqslant M_2 \cdot t \tag{92}$$

This relationship is possible only if

$$t \leqslant M_2 / M_1 \tag{93}$$

which places an upper bound on t. Therefore, S_e is finite, and there is a last error. The algorithm must converge to produce some $\mathbf{w}(t)$ linearly containing Z. The theorem is proven.

Two words of caution are needed. Although a limit on t must exist, it cannot be calculated without knowledge of $\mathbf{w}^*$. Since the whole point of the algorithm is to find some $\mathbf{w}^*$, then, no a priori limit on the computation can be established. Second, the assumption that S_y contains every member of Y infinitely many times is central. If the training sequence consists of a specified but repeated subsample, $Y^* \subset Y$, the algorithm would produce a vector $\mathbf{w}^*$ sufficient to classify Y^* but its classification of items outside the sample (i.e., in $Y - Y^*$) might be erroneous.

4.4.3   GENERALIZATION TO THE CASE OF K CLASSES

In the multiple-category problem Y (and X) is partitioned into k cells, $Y_1, Y_2, \ldots, Y_k$. Here Y is linearly separable by the matrix $W^* = \{W_i^*\}$ of weight vectors if and only if

$$\mathbf{y} \cdot \mathbf{w}_i^* > \mathbf{y} \cdot \mathbf{w}_j^* \qquad \text{for all} \quad y \in Y_i, \quad j = 1, \ldots, k, \quad j \neq i. \qquad (94)$$

We regard W^* as a matrix whose rows are the vectors $\mathbf{w}_i^*$. Assume that W^* exists. The training algorithm takes a sequence S_y of observations and develops from it a finite sequence S_w of matrices such that the last member of S_w linearly separates Y. The following algorithm is used.

Multiple-category error correction algorithm:

(1) *Let $W^{(1)}$ be the initial matrix. As before, $W^{(1)}$ will be arbitrarily set to a matrix of zeros, although this is not a necessary restriction.*

(2) *Establish the sequence S_y as before. Consider any $\mathbf{y}^{(t)}$ in S_y, and let Y_i be the class to which it belongs. The observation $\mathbf{y}^{(t)}$ will be classified by $W^{(t)}$. $W^{(t+1)}$ is calculated by the following rules.*

2a. *If the classification is correct, $W^{(t+1)} = W^{(t)}$.*

2b. *If the classification is erroneous there is at least one j such that $\mathbf{y}^{(t)} \cdot \mathbf{w}_j^{(t)} \geqslant \mathbf{y}^{(t)} \cdot \mathbf{w}_i^{(t)}$.*

For each i and each such j

$$\mathbf{w}^{(t+1)} = \mathbf{w}_i^{(t)} + \mathbf{y}^{(t)} \qquad (95)$$

$$\mathbf{w}_j^{(t+1)} = \mathbf{w}_j^{(t)} - \mathbf{y}^{(t)} \qquad (96)$$

As before, we could replace $\mathbf{y}^{(t)}$ by $c \cdot \mathbf{y}^{(t)}$, $c > 0$, in (95) and (96), but do not do so for simplicity.

To prove that the algorithm works, the sequence of errors S_e will again be shown to be finite. By the same reasoning as before, if S_e is finite the algorithm must solve the classification problem.

Let Z be a set of vectors of $k \cdot (m + 1)$ elements derived from Y in such a way that if Z is linearly contained by a vector $\mathbf{v}$, then $\mathbf{v}$ contains the components of the matrix W^* in defined order. To derive such a set, each $\mathbf{y} \in Y$ is used to establish $K - 1$ vectors in Z. Suppose $\mathbf{y} \in Y_i$. The $k - 1$ z's derived from $\mathbf{y}$ are the vectors $\{Z_{i:j}(\mathbf{y})\}$ for $j - 1 : \cdots k, j \neq i$. Each $Z_{i:j}(\mathbf{y})$ is a single vector of k blocks of $m + 1$ elements, where

a. The ith block of $Z_{i:j}(\mathbf{y})$ is identical to the $m + 1$ elements of $\mathbf{y}$.

b. The jth block of $Z_{i:j}(\mathbf{y})$ is identical to the $m + 1$ elements of $-\mathbf{y}$.

c. All other elements of $Z_{i:j}(\mathbf{y})$ are zero.

Thus for any $\mathbf{y}$ in class i there are $k - 1$ vectors in Z, corresponding to the contrasts between $\mathbf{y}$ and the classes to which it does *not* belong. These vectors contain an ith block associated with the correct class.

By hypothesis, W^* exists. We will search for a vector $\mathbf{v}^*$ consisting of the concatenation of the k vectors $\mathbf{w}_i^*$ which are the rows of W^*. Algebraically

$$\mathbf{v}^*_{((i-1)\cdot(m+1)+j)} = w^*_{ij} \tag{97}$$

for $i = 1, 2, \ldots, k$ and $j - 1, \ldots, m + 1$. Then for every $Z_{i:j}$ if $\mathbf{y} \in Y_i$

$$(Z_{i:j}(\mathbf{y})) \cdot \mathbf{v}^* = \mathbf{y} \cdot \mathbf{w}_i^* > 0 \tag{98}$$

because, as Y is linearly separated by W^*, $\mathbf{y} \cdot \mathbf{w}_i^* > \mathbf{y} \cdot \mathbf{w}_j^*$.

Now suppose we reversed the process and assumed that Z was known to be linearly contained by $\mathbf{v}^*$. Equation (86) could then be used to define the vectors of W^*, which would linearly separate Y. An appropriate $\mathbf{v}^*$ can be found by using the two-class algorithm. Thus the multiple-category problem is solved, since once $\mathbf{v}^*$ is found the definition of W^* is trivial.[4] In fact, a moment's consideration will show that the algorithm for finding $\mathbf{v}^*$ is identical to the algorithm proposed for generating S_w directly.

4.4.4 EXTENSION TO NONLINEAR AND NON-EUCLIDEAN PROBLEMS

The reader may have noted that nowhere in the algorithm has any use been made of the Euclidean distance measure. The algorithm has been justified in terms of limits on the numerical values of the sum of squares of vector components, without any necessary interpretation of what this operation corresponds to in a measurement sense. Thus we could equally well apply the rule to objects described in terms of the integers, or in terms of binary vectors. The latter case is of particular interest because of its many interpretations. Suppose a pattern-recognition device receives input from "feature detection" devices, each of which has the result 0 or 1 depending on whether or not the object to be classified has a certain property.

---

[4] Strictly speaking, the problem has been solved for the case $W^{(1)} = 0$ and $c = 1$. The generalized case is again easy to prove, by reference to the generalized case of the two category problem.

"Property" in this context could refer to any quality of the object. The pattern-recognition device will deal with vectors of binary elements. If these elements are linearly separable, in the algebraic sense, regardless of whether the geometric interpretation of linear separability is sensible, then the error correction algorithms can be applied. In doing so, we only have to be concerned with the restrictions imposed by linear separability itself. We shall have more to say about this in the next chapter.

4.4.5 CONVERGENCE

A practical pattern-recognition procedure ought both to get the correct answer and get it fast enough. The convergence methods that have been described are called *fixed-interval* methods. When a vector $y^{(i)}$ is misclassified, each element in $w^{(i)}$ is changed by a fixed amount which depends on the type of error made, but not how badly it was classified, where this is interpreted as the extent to which the necessary inequality was violated. Intuitively, one might want to make a large change in $w^{(i)}$ if $y^{(i)}$ was badly misclassified, and a smaller change otherwise. Nilsson (1965a) has shown that more rapid convergence can be obtained in the two category problem by replacing the fixed constant c of the algorithm by the variable

$$c_i = \lambda \frac{w^{(i)} y^{(i)}}{(y^{(i)})^2} \qquad (99)$$

The resulting algorithm converges provided that λ is in the interval 0–2. C. Chang (1971) has developed a similar algorithm which handles the case $k \geqslant 2$, and has shown that it converges reasonably rapidly on a number of problems.

Throughout we have assumed that the classes are linearly separable. Suppose that they are not, but the learning algorithm is used anyway. What will happen to the weight vectors? Weight vectors can be thought of as points in a $m + 1$-dimensional *weight space*. Minsky and Papert (1969) have proven that the length of $w^{(i)}$ (the weight vector at the ith step) will not grow beyond a fixed bound. Hence although the sequence of errors is infinite, the weight vectors that are generated will remain within some region of the weight space. Minsky and Papert also observed that if the basic observation vectors (the x's) are vectors of integers, including binary digits, then the weight vectors are restricted to a finite number of possible values. In other words, as the sequence S_y is continued in a nonlinear problem the pattern recognizer will cycle its current answer through a finite set of states. Unfortunately, there is no guarantee that the pattern recognizer will spend most of its time in a state in which the rule satisfies some criterion for probabilistic classification.

4.5   Clustering

4.5.0   THE CLUSTERING PROBLEM

In pattern recognition, the assignment of at least some objects to classes must be known. The task is to find the rule that gave rise to this assignment. In the closely related *clustering problem* it is up to the classifier to decide which objects are to be grouped together. Clustering problems arise in many disciplines. In medicine a variety of illnesses caused by distinct organisms are grouped under the omnibus headings "cold" and "intestinal disorder." In psychiatry the classification of disorders of personality into "schizophrenia," "manic-depressive psychosis," and "psychopathology" are not at all as distinct as one might like. In biology the clustering problem has an interesting variation. It is usually assumed that the groupings of species into families and genera reflects a common evolution. Traditionally the evolutionary line has been traced by the appearance of a few arbitrarily selected common traits, but more recently numerical techniques similar to some we shall discuss have been proposed as more appropriate ways of defining a taxonomy (Sokol & Sneath, 1963). In artificial intelligence the clustering problem has been studied under the title "unsupervised learning." The *code breaking* problem is illustrative. Suppose that one receives a coded message in which each letter of the alphabet may have several alternate codes; for example, "a" might be written "b," "c," or "+." The problem is to assign the received code symbols to the letters they represent. Intuitively, this is more like the sort of task one might assign to a computer than the disease classification or taxonomic problems mentioned, yet from a formal standpoint they are all the same.

Meisel (1972) has suggested three characteristics by which clustering algorithms can be described.

(1) Is there a criterion function by which the result of a clustering procedure can be evaluated, or is the clustering to be justified by the reasonableness of the procedure used to define it? In the former case the clustering technique is said to be *indirect*, since it is the by-product of an attempt to minimize or maximize some criterion function, in the latter case the clustering technique is said to be a *direct* one.

(2) Are the clusters to be defined unrelated or are they assumed to be related in some hierarchial fashion, as in a taxonomy?

(3) Is the primary interest in assignment of data points to clusters or in determination of the parameters of a function which is presumed to be generating the data?

There are many algorithms which can be described as clustering procedures. We could not possibly cover them all. Instead we shall present three illustrative methods; one involving estimation of data generating functions by use of an indirect clustering method, one a nonhierarchical and one a hierarchial direct clustering technique. Additional algorithims are given by Duda and Hart (1973).

4.5.1 STATISTICAL CLUSTERING

This particular formulation of the clustering problem is very close to the statistical formulation of the pattern-recognition problem. The observations comprise a set X of n data points of unknown class membership. The process by which the observations were created is assumed to be a two step one. In the first step one of k classes was chosen, with the ith class being chosen with probability p_i. Associated with class i was a *known* probability density function f_i with an unknown set of parameters θ_i. (For example, if f_i were the normal distribution, θ would be the mean and variance of class i.) The point x in the description space is then chosen with probability $f_i(\mathbf{x} : \theta_i)$. The clustering task is to choose values for the sets $P = \{p(i)\}$ and $\theta = \{\theta_i\}$ of parameters which best account for the observed data X.   This is a straightforward although computationally difficult problem in statistical estimation. Hoel (1971) has discussed the mathematical problems involved, and Cooper (1969) has considered them from a more computer oriented viewpoint. Rather than deal with this highly technical literature, we shall present a widely used example computation, *chi square minimization*.

Let the description space D be partitioned into r mutually exclusive, exhaustive regions $D_1, D_2, \ldots, D_r$, and let o_j be the number of points in X falling into region D_j. For any fixed values of P and θ the expected number of observations in a region is

$$E_j(P, \theta) = n \cdot \sum_{i=1}^{k} p_i \int f_i(\mathbf{x} : \theta_i)\, dx, \qquad \mathbf{x} \in D_j \tag{100}$$

The *chi-square statistic* to be minimized is

$$\chi^2 = \sum_{j=1}^{r} [(o_j - E_j(P, \theta))^2 / E_j(P, \theta)] \tag{101}$$

The problem is solved when values are found for P and θ which minimize (101). In some problems the value of k is also to be found. The exact way in which we would proceed depends on the identity of the probability density functions $\{f_i\}$. If we are fortunate there will be a closed form best estimate. In other cases it may be necessary to explore different numerical values of the parameters in some systematic way. On occasion problems are found for which an exhaustive parameter enumeration is unfeasible, even on a very large computer. Garnatz and Hunt (1973) have shown that in such cases a computer-aided graphic estimation procedure may be a sufficiently accurate practical alternative.

4.5.2 k MEANS

MacQueen (1967) has developed a very simple direct clustering technique which he calls *k means*. In addition to representing a direct clustering method for unrelated classes, it also illustrates *adaptive clustering* since, as in the adaptive pattern-recognition problem, the current answer is adjusted as new data is observed. As in the pattern recognition case, the data points are ordered into the sequence S_x consisting of observations $\mathbf{x}^{(1)}, \mathbf{x}^{(2)}, \ldots, \mathbf{x}^{(n)}$ in an m dimensional description space. In the simplest case it is assumed that exactly k classes exist and that each class has a mean point $\mathbf{m}_i{}^*$. We require an algorithm which estimates $\{\mathbf{m}_i{}^*\}$ based on S_x. MacQueen's algorithm is

1. Compute a set of initial estimates, $M^0 = \{m_i^{(0)}\}$ by assigning each of the first k points in S_x to a distinct class. At this point

$$m_i^{(0)} = x^{(i)}, \qquad i = 1, 2, \ldots, k \qquad (102)$$

2. When point $x^{(i)}$ is presented $(k < i \leqslant n)$ assign it to the cluster j for which $d(m_j^{(i)}, x^{(i)})$ is minimized. Ties are resolved in favor of the lowest indexed cluster.

3. Calculate new mean estimates, $\{m_j^{(i+1)}\}$ by computing the new means of the points in each cluster.

    3a. If $x^{(i)}$ was not assigned to class j, $m_j^{(i)}$ is unchanged.

    3b. If $x^{(i)}$ was assigned to cluster j the new mean estimate is made based on the current items in the class. Let $w_j^{(i)}$ be the number of data points in a cluster at the time the ith data point is presented. Then

$$m_j^{(i+1)} = \left[\frac{1}{w_j^{(i)} + 1}\right](w_j^{(i)} \cdot m_j^{(i)} + x^{(i)}). \qquad (103)$$

MacQueen has proven that if S_x is actually generated by samples from k different probability distributions, then the k estimates $m_j^{(i)}$ will asymptotically converge to the means of the distributions.

A constructive algorithm such as the k means procedure can only be justified by its results, since it is not based on a criterion function. Some of MacQueen's original examples are particularly illustrative. In one study words were rated along a variety of scales indicating emotional connotation (e.g., "good, bad," "passive, active"). The ratings defined X. The clusters found included {calm, dusky, lake, peace, sleep, white}, {beggar, deformed, frigid, lagging, low}, and {statue, sunlight, time, trees, wise}. The technique was also applied to multidimensional ratings of student life at various universities. Two contrasting clusters were {Reed, Swarthmore, Antioch, Oberlin, Bryn Mawr} and {Cornell, Michigan, Minnesota, Illinois, Arkansas, Georgia Tech, Purdue}. In both applications the results seem reasonable.

The algorithm as stated suffers from sensitivity to the order of presentation of data points and to the correct choice of k. MacQueen reports that empirically variation in the order does not make a great deal of difference, although it would be possible to construct pathological examples. To avoid complete dependence on an initial estimate, the value of k may be adjusted by the use of a coarsening parameter c and a refinement parameter, r. The modified algorithm calls for reexamination of all assignments of points to clusters after each step. Two means, $m_j^{(i)}$ and $m_{j*}^{(i)}$, are defined as being too close to each other if their Euclidean distance is less than c units. If this happens the j and $j*$th clusters are coalesced into one and k decreased by one. On the other hand, if any point $x^{(q)}$ is ever found to be greater than r units from the nearest cluster mean, then that point is made the initial mean vector of a new cluster and k is increased by one. Note that this could happen if the mean vector was moved away from a point originally close to the center of the cluster as a result of cluster assignments after the point was presented.

Sebesteyen and Edie (1966) independently proposed a variation of the k means algorithm in which the Euclidean distance measure was weighted to correct for intracluster variation along each dimension of the description space. The rationale for doing this is very similar to the rationale for a similar weighting in pattern recognition, it introduces a scale change which moves the cluster into a spheroid pattern. They also suggest that points not be unassigned to clusters if, when they are presented, they are not within a certain distance of any current cluster. Such points can be held in abeyance until a cluster mean moves toward them.

Meisel (1972) has described a class of center adjustment algorithms very similar to the k means procedure except that they are applied to the data without regard to the order of observation. Instead of dealing with a sequence S_x of data points one deals with a set X of points which is to be divided into subsets. The algorithm is

Center Adjustment Algorithm
1. *Select an arbitrary set $\{m_j^{(0)}\}$ of initial means.*
2. *Assign each point in X to the cluster to whose mean it is closest.*
3. *Calculate $m_j^{(i+1)}$ by determining the mean vector within each cluster.*
4. *Repeat steps 2 and 3 until no points change their cluster.*

Like the k means algorithm, the center adjustment algorithm is sensitive to the initial choice of mean points and to the proper choice of k. Despite these defects it is often very useful. Diehr (1968) has pointed out that it can be generalized to the case in which only certain prototypical points are permissible as mean points. In this case we consider the loss associated with the treatment of each data point as if it were actually one of the prototypical points. This is rather like the elevator maker's assumption that all humanity can be treated as if everyone weighs 150 pounds. Diehr's formulation can be used to attack a number of problems in operations research, such as the location of warehouses or the assignment of customers to service centers.

4.5.3 Hierarchical Clustering

Hierarchical clustering algorithms assume that the data to be clustered are drawn from a single class that can be split into subclasses and sub-subclasses. One of the most widely used methods of hierarchical clustering is due to Johnson (1967). The technique can be applied to both Euclidean and non-Euclidean spaces, provided only that the distance measure between two points, $h(\mathbf{x}, \mathbf{y})$ can be treated as an ordinal measure defined for any two points in X.

Johnson's Hierarchical Clustering Method

1. Define the matrix H whose elements are the distances between pairs of data points,

$$h_{ij} = h(\mathbf{x}_i, \mathbf{x}_j) \tag{104}$$

2. Develop a clustering $C^{(0)} = \{c_s^{(0)}\}$ in which each data point is assigned to a

clustering containing only itself. Clearly the distance between any two clusters, $c_i^{(0)}$ and $c_j^{(0)}$ in this clustering is

$$h(c_i^{(0)}, c_j^{(0)}) = h_{ij} \qquad (105)$$

3. Assume the clustering $C^{(t-1)}$ has been defined, with clusters $c_a^{(t-1)}$, $c_b^{(t-1)}$, etc. Further assume that a distance matrix H is defined for these elements, with entries h_{ij} as in (105). Let a and b be the indices of the two closest clusters, i.e., h_{ab} is the minimum entry in H. Clustering $C^{(t)}$ is formed from $C^{(t-1)}$ by coalescing the a and b elements into a single cluster $[a, b]$.

4. The distance matrix H is redefined by dropping all elements referring to a and b, and adding the distances from the new cluster $[a, b]$. These are defined for the cluster and a third element c by either the *maximum rule*

$$h[(a, b), c] = \max[h(a, c), h(b, c)] \qquad (106)$$

or the *minimum rule*

$$h[(a, b), c] = \min[h(a, c), h(b, c)]. \qquad (107)$$

5. Steps 3 and 4 are repeated until all the original data points are coalesced into a single cluster.

The clusters formed by the algorithm have interesting intuitive interpretations. For a given cluster the *diameter of the cluster* is defined to be the maximum distance between any two points in the cluster. If the maximum rule (106) is used clusters of minimum diameter will be formed at each stage. To understand the effect of using the minimum rule (107), consider a *chain* from point x to point y to be a sequence of data points $z_0, z_1, \ldots, z_k$ such that $x = z_0$ and $y = z_k$. The size of the chain is defined as the maximum distance between any two points on the chain. The use of (107) minimizes the size of the smallest chain between any two data points in a cluster at a given stage. Thus in both cases the clustering process is reasonable. The maximum rule produces a hierarchy of clusters such that within each cluster the distance between any two points is minimized, while the minimum rule produces clusters in which the distance of steps between adjacent points in chains within a cluster is minimized.

As was the case for k means, Johnson's hierarchical procedure is normally justified by examples. One application considered acoustic confusability. People were asked to identify phonemes heard in bad listening conditions. The resulting data could be ordered in a "confusion matrix" whose entries were the probability that phoneme i would be recognized given that phoneme j was spoken. The confusion matrix was treated as the H matrix in the analysis. The resulting clusters were, at one level, the unvoiced stops (j, t, k), the voiced stops (b, d, g), the unvoiced fricatives $(f, \theta, s, \int)$, the voiced fricatives (v, γ, z, ξ), and the nasals (m, n). Thus the algorithm recovered groupings which make sense acoustically. Similarly sensible results have been obtained by others in a number of behavioral science applications.

Chapter V

NON-EUCLIDEAN PARALLEL PROCEDURES: THE PERCEPTRON

5.0   Introduction and Historical Comment

We shall now consider some parallel pattern recognition and classification procedures analogous to those described in Chapter IV, but without the restriction that objects must be describable as points in a Euclidean space. Instead we shall assume only that objects can be described by an ordered list of features which they do or do not have. Mathematically, we shall discuss classification procedures for binary vectors. The interpretation of a binary vector is that the information "the jth bit is one (zero)" is equivalent to "the jth feature is present (absent)."

This problem has an interesting history. It first became a prominent part of computer science when Frank Rosenblatt, a psychologist then at Cornell Aeronautical Laboratory, described a machine-oriented pattern recognition and classification system he called a *perceptron* (Rosenblatt, 1958, 1962).[1] The perceptron was presented partly as a model of biological pattern-recognition and partly as a proposal for the construction of a special-purpose computer. Scientists in a number of fields found perceptrons interesting for rather different reasons. It was once hoped that the analysis of perceptrons might lead to the development of visual input systems for computers, a hope that was certainly encouraged by Rosenblatt's use of terms such as "retina" and "perceptron." The way this was to work is shown in Figure 5-1. Visual scenes were to be presented to a feature analyzer, which would record the presence or absence of components of the scene. The scenes themselves were to be from interesting classes, e.g., pictures of men versus pictures of women. A pattern-recognition system would then develop ways to classify the binary records as coming from a visual scene of a specific class.

Perceptrons were limited to the production of certain types of classifications

---

[1] Rosenblatt's 1965 book, *Principles of Neurodynamics*, was originally published and widely circulated as a technical report in 1961.

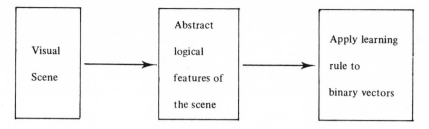

Fig. 5-1. Steps in visual pattern recognition by a perceptron.

rules. Rosenblatt proposed a specific example of Selfridge's (1959) "Pandemonium" model of parallel pattern recognition, described briefly in Chapter III. Pandemonia devices compute a fixed set of functions of the object to be classified, and then compute a function which has as its arguments the results of the previous computations. The output of the last function is the classification decision. If the final function is a test to see if a weighted sum of the values of the first stage functions exceeds a set threshold, then one has a perceptron. As we shall see, this leads to a precise mathematical description.

In the early stages of perceptron research it was found that the application of learning algorithms within perceptrons produced surprisingly powerful classification rules. For this reason a great deal of attention was focused on "machine learning" as described at the end of Chapter IV. A major step in a new direction was taken when Minsky and Papert (1969) asked what sort of classification rules could be produced, assuming that a perceptron could eventually learn any classification rule expressible as a weighted sum of primitive features. In effect, Minsky and Papert changed the question from "How fast can a perceptron learn to do something?" to "What things can a perceptron learn to do?" Newell, in reviewing Minsky and Papert's book, remarked that this is analogous to the distinction psychologists make between learning and performance. No action can be learned unless it can be performed. Thus an understanding of Minsky and Papert's work is essential for anyone who plans extensive work in the pattern-recognition field. In the following sections of this chapter Minsky and Papert's basic results will be presented and an attempt will be made to illustrate their method of analysis.

5.1 Terminology

5.1.0 PERCEPTRON PROBLEMS AND COMPONENTS

By analogy to vision, the input to a perceptron is defined as an ordered set of binary elements, collectively called the retina R. Then, R is a collection of variables,

$$R = (x_1 \cdots x_r). \tag{1}$$

At times it is convenient to think of the elements of R as being arranged in rows and columns on a plane. In this case the notation x_{ij} will refer to the variable in the *i*th row and *j*th column. The reader must be careful to distinguish between arguments that depend upon the two-dimensional representation for their validity and arguments that are convenient to illustrate by this interpretation.

A *picture X* is an assignment of values to the elements of R. To specify X we shall write x_i to indicate that the *i*th variable is to take the value 1 and $\bar{x}_i$ to indicate that it is to take the value zero. Thus any X can be written

$$X = (x_1, x_2, \bar{x}_3, \ldots, x_i, \ldots, x_j, \ldots, x_r). \tag{2}$$

If there are r variables in the retina, then there exists a set of 2^r possible pictures. A *pattern-recognition problem* assigns each of these pictures to exactly one of c classes. The number of possible problems mounts rapidly, as there are c^{2^r} ways to assign pictures to classes. The purpose of the following analysis is to determine which of the many possible problems could ever be solved by different types of perceptrons.

5.1.1 PREDICATES

A predicate ψ is a logical function which maps from the set of pictures into the set {*true, false*}. We can think of a predicate as a logical function of r binary variables. In many interesting cases, however, the value of ψ may be determined by examining fewer than all of the points (variables) of R. If this is true ψ is said to be a *partial predicate*, and the set of variables in R that must be examined to determine the value of $\psi(X)$ is called the *set of support* $S(\psi)$ of the predicate.

To illustrate these concepts, consider the retina defined by an arrangement of elements into a 5 x 5 square, as shown in Figure 5-2. Let the predicate of interest be

$$\psi(X) = X \text{ contains only 1's on the right to left diagonal.} \tag{3}$$

The elements of the set of support for predicate (3) are circled in Figure 5-2. Obviously $\psi(X)$ is true if and only if all the circled elements are ones.

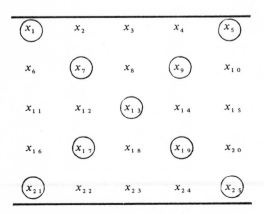

Fig. 5-2. Twenty-five element retina arranged as a 5 x 5 field.

5.1.2   CLASSIFICATION OF PREDICATES

It is often useful to classify predicates by the characteristics of their sets of support.

Local Predicates: R is interpreted as a set of points on a plane. A predicate ψ is local if $S(\psi)$ is a convex set of points in R.[2]

Conjunctively Local Predicates: A predicate ψ is conjunctively local if there exists a set $\Phi = \{\sigma_i\}$ $i = 1, \ldots, p$ of local predicates and if $\psi(X)$ is the conjunction of the values of the $\sigma_i(X)$ in Φ.

Predicate Order: A predicate ψ is of order n if $S(\psi)$ contains n variables.

5.1.3   TRANSLATION BETWEEN LOGICAL AND ARITHMETIC EXPRESSIONS

It will be necessary to map from logical to arithmetic expressions and vice versa. If a logical expression appears within an arithmetic expression it will be treated as having value 1 if its logical value is *true*, 0 otherwise. For example, if $\{\sigma_i\}$ $i = 1, \ldots, p$ is a set of predicates and $\{a_i\}$ a set of real numbers, the expression $\sum_{i=1}^{p} a_i \sigma_i(X)$ is the sum of the a_i for which the corresponding predicate is *true* for the picture X.

Similarly, we must map from logical and relational expressions into arithmetic expressions. Let $[Q]$ indicate that Q is to be assigned the appropriate arithmetic values. A predicate can then be interpreted as an arithmetic expression which takes the value 0 or 1 using this convention. If $f(X)$ is an arithmetic expression, θ a constant, and $\mathbf{R}$ an arithmetical relation, a predicate can be written

$$\psi(X) = [f(X)\mathbf{R}\theta].\tag{3}$$

The *Linear predicates* have the form

$$\psi(X) = \left[\sum_{i=1}^{p} a_i \sigma_i(X) > \theta\right].\tag{4}$$

An expression such as (4) defines a predicate ψ that is linear with respect to the set Φ of partial predicates. The set $L(\Phi)$ is the set of all such predicates.

5.1.4   DEFINITION OF PERCEPTRONS

A perceptron is a hypothetical device that can compute all predicates which are linear with respect to a fixed set of partial predicates. A linear predicate is a

---

[2] A set X of points on a plane (or higher-order Euclidean space) is convex if, for all points p and q in X, the points on the line segment from p to q are also in X. For example, a circle and a square are convex figures, whereas a crescent moon figure is not. The definition generalizes readily to higher-order spaces. Thus a sphere is a convex set of points in three-dimensional space, while a torus is not.

classification rule, since it assigns all pictures X to either the class 0 or 1. A perceptron, then, is an "ultimately powerful" pattern-recognition device for producing linear classification rules. By application of the convergence theorem proven in Chapter IV we know that such a pattern–recognition device exists. To make this connection more obvious, think of the predicates of Φ as the dimensions of a Euclidean *feature space*. If the points represented by the 2^k possible vectors are grouped into linearly separable classes, then there exists a function ψ which satisfies (4). It can be found by searching for an appropriate weight vector $\{a_i\}$ using the algorithms presented in Chapter IV.

Minsky and Papert established classes of primitive predicates by placing constraints upon their sets of support, i.e., upon the sets of points in R that each primitive predicate "looked at" in classifying a picture. They then asked what a constraint implied in terms of the sorts of classifications which could be made by the resulting perceptron. This leads us to the next set of definitions:

k-order limited perceptrons are perceptrons for which no $\sigma_i \in \Phi$ has a set of support of more than k points. Intuitively, the order of a device indicates the extent of complexity of its primitive operations.

The idea of a *perceptron of finite order* is closely related to that of a k-ordered perceptron. If a perceptron is of finite order then there is some k for which it is a k-order limited perceptron. At first thought, it might seem that asserting that a perceptron is of finite but unstated order is a very weak statement, but this is not true. Suppose the order of the perceptron is as great as the number of points in R. This means that the perceptron contains some σ_i which "looks at" the entire retina. Since there are no limits to the complexity of the σ_i except their order, then such a σ_i could simply be a map indicating for each of the 2^r possible X's whether the appropriate classification was 0 or 1. If the order of the perceptron is limited to less than the size of the retina, this powerful partial predicate is no longer available, and the existence of a linear predicate for every one of the 2^{2^r} possible classifications is not assured. This will normally be the case. We want the perceptron to develop linear combinations of logical functions of local properties of X in order to make a classification based upon a global property of X. For what problems is this possible?

Diameter Limited Predicates: A diameter limited predicate is a predicate whose set of support must consist of points within a fixed distance of each other when R is interpreted as a set of points on a Euclidean plane.

Masks: A predicate e_A is a *mask* if it is true if and only if all the points in a finite set $A \subseteq R$ are ones, i.e., if all points in subset A of R are in the "on" condition. A mask is itself a linear predicate of order 1. Let $N(S)$ be the number of elements in the set S. Define to be the set of predicates $\{``x_i = 1"\}$ for all $x_i \in A$. The mask e_A can be defined by

$$e_A(X) = \left[\sum_{\sigma_i \in \Phi} \sigma_i(X) > N(A) - 1 \right] \qquad (5)$$

The *size* of a mask is defined as the number of elements in its set of support.

5.2 Basic Theorems for Order-Limited Perceptrons

5.2.0. COMMENT

Since pattern recognition is a compound of feature detection and feature weighting, it is of interest to know what sort of recognition can possibly occur with fixed limits on the complexity of the detection and weighting stages. The restriction to linear weighting in the perceptron establishes the weighting system. Order limits determine the complexity of the feature detection. We have previously noted that finite order is essential to ensure that the classification procedure is not hidden within an overly complicated feature detector. In any analysis of a physical classifier (e.g., the visual system) one would have to face the fact that each feature detector must be connected to a limited number of sensory elements, and thus, if the classifier is a perceptron, then it must be a k-order perceptron. There are two reasons, then, for studying perceptrons of finite order. The theorems are of interest because they show limitations on the capabilities of buildable linear machines. The proofs are of interest because they illustrate the use of formal techniques in analyzing the capabilities of an artificial-intelligence system.

The first two theorems are presented in detail both to illustrate the proof techniques and because they are building blocks for the other theorems. Substantive theorems are then sketched.

5.2.1 MASKING THEOREM (POSITIVE NORMAL FORM THEOREM)

Every predicate ψ is linear with respect to the set of all masks.

Comment: This is a very strong statement. If $\psi \in L(\Phi)$, where Φ is a set of masks, then the order of ψ can be determined by finding the size of the largest mask in Φ. The theorem also states that any classification can be realized by a linear predicate if all masks, but no other predicates, are included in Φ.

Proof: We know that ψ is a Boolean function of the logical variables $x_1 \cdots x_r$ in R. We can write any Boolean function of a set $\{x_i\}$ of logical variables in its disjunctive normal form.

$$\psi(X) = C_1(X) \cup C_2(X) \cup \cdots \cup C_k(X) \tag{6}$$

where each $C_j(X)$ is a logical product of the r terms. Since each of these products is distinct, it follows that

$$[C_j(X) = 1] \supseteq [C_{j*}(X) = 0], \qquad j \neq j^*; j, \quad j^* = 1 \cdots k \tag{7}$$

This means that at most one of the logical products will be *true*. Therefore ψ can be written in linear form

$$\psi(X) = \left[\sum_{i=1}^{k} C_j(X) > 0 \right] \tag{8}$$

If each of the C_j's can be written as linear combination of masks, then $\psi(X)$ will be a linear combination of linear combinations, and hence linear in the set of masks. The next step is to show that the C_j's can be so written.

Any logical product C_j can be written as a product of variables and their negations,

$$C_j(X) = x_1 \bar{x}_2 x_3 \cdots x_i \bar{x}_{i+1} \cdots x_r. \tag{9}$$

Let $\bar{x}_s$ be the first negation, and write (9) as

$$C_j(X) = \$_j \bar{x}_s \phi_j, \tag{10}$$

where

$$\$_j = x_1 x_2 \cdots x_{s-1}, \tag{11}$$

and

$$\phi_j = x_{s+1} \bar{x}_{s+2} \cdots x_r. \tag{12}$$

Note that $\$_j$ contains only unbarred terms, while ϕ_j may contain both barred and unbarred terms. By algebraic manipulation

$$C_j(X) = \$_j \bar{x}_s \phi_j, \tag{13}$$
$$= \$_j (1 - x_s) \phi_j$$
$$= \$_j \phi_j - \$_j x_s \phi_j.$$

Here $C_j(X)$ has been written as a linear combination of two logical products, one of which contains x_s as an unbarred term, and one of which does not contain x_s at all. Each application of (13) removes one barred term. If we repeat this for all C_j, and for all logical products derived from them, and for all products derived from the first application, etc., we will eventually arrive at an expression in which $\psi(X)$ is stated in terms of a linear combination of logical products containing only unbarred terms. A logical product without unbarred terms is a mask. The theorem is proven.

Illustration: Let R consist of three points, x_1, x_2, x_3, and let $\psi(X)$ be the predicate "There are an odd number of points in X". The predicate is true if all the points of R are in X or if only one of the points of R is in X. Therefore $\psi(X)$ can be written as

$$\psi(X) = [(x_1 \bar{x}_2 \bar{x}_3 + \bar{x}_1 x_2 \bar{x}_3 + \bar{x}_1 \bar{x}_2 x_3 + x_1 x_2 x_3) > 0] \tag{14}$$

If we apply (13) successively to (14) we obtain

$$\psi(X) = [((x_1 \bar{x}_3 - x_1 x_2 \bar{x}_3) + (x_2 \bar{x}_3 - x_1 x_2 \bar{x}_3) \tag{15}$$
$$+ (\bar{x}_2 x_3 - x_1 \bar{x}_2 x_3) + x_1 x_2 x_3) > 0]$$
$$= [(x_1 - x_1 x_3) - (x_1 x_2 - x_1 x_2 x_3)$$
$$+ ((x_2 - x_2 x_3) - (x_1 x_2 - x_1 x_2 x_3)$$
$$+ (x_3 - x_2 x_3) - (x_1 x_3 - x_1 x_2 x_3) + x_1 x_2 x_3) > 0]$$

$$= [((x_1 - x_1 x_2 - x_1 x_3 + x_1 x_2 x_3)$$
$$+ (x_2 - x_1 x_2 - x_2 x_3 + x_1 x_2 x_3)$$
$$+ (x_3 - x_1 x_3 - x_2 x_3 + x_1 x_2 x_3) + x_1 x_2 x_3) > 0]$$
$$= [(x_1 + x_2 + x_3 - 2x_1 x_2 - 2x_1 x_3 - 2x_2 x_3 + 4x_1 x_2 x_3) > 0],$$

which is a linear predicate in the set of masks.

The expression of $\psi(X)$ as a linear combination of masks is called the *positive normal form* of $\psi(X)$. It can be shown that the positive normal form ψ is unique and that ψ is of order k if and only if the largest mask with nonzero coefficient in the positive normal form is of order k (Minsky & Papert, 1969, Theorems 1.5.2 and 1.5.3). If this mask does not depend upon the size of R it follows that ψ is of finite order.

5.2.2 THE GROUP INVARIANCE THEOREM

At the most abstract level, a perceptron is a device for classifying ordered sets of variables. If the particular ordering used to define R is arbitrary, then classifications should remain invariant over permutation of the elements of R. Consider a set of patterns **X** and a set of transformations $G = \{g\}$ of R. Each transformation maps the set of elements of R into itself. We will first ask what sets of patterns can be recognized by a perceptron if R may be rearranged by any arbitrary member of G, so that X and $g(X)$ are in the same class for all $X \in \mathbf{X}$. That is, we wish to know if a perceptron can recognize a class of patterns whose distinguishing features are invariant over G. Philosophically, this is of interest because it has been argued that the mathematically crucial properties of a class are those which are invariant over some important set of transformations. Practically, many pattern-recognition tasks require the ability to recognize invariance over certain transformations, such as the geometrical transformations of translation and rotation. Finally, if we think of the perceptron as a model of a visual system, as the terminology encourages us to do, we know from psychology that certain types of transformations should not pose a problem. For example, people rather quickly learn to adjust to a visual world which is inverted by special eyeglasses, indicating that visual classifications are invariant over reflection of the visual world about its horizontal axis.

Definitions

1. Let G be a finite set of transformations of R. Each $g \in G$ maps each of the x_i of R into some x_j of $g(R)$. For example, if g is an inversion of the order of elements of R then if R is (x_1, x_2, x_3), $g(R)$ is (x_3, x_2, x_1).

2. Φ is a set of predicates on R which is closed over G. This means that for every $\sigma \in \Phi$ and $g \in G$ there exists $\sigma' \in \Phi$ such that

$$\sigma(X) = \sigma'(g(X)). \tag{16}$$

A useful way to interpret (16) is to note that if $\sigma(X)$ has a given value (*true* or *false*) then there is some σ' such that if the transformation g is used to rearrange the retina, then $\sigma'(g(X))$ will have the same value as σ did with the original ordering.

3. The *equivalence class over G* of a predicate $\sigma \in \Phi$ is the set $\{\sigma_{g_i}\}$, $g_i \in G$, such that (16) is satisfied if g is chosen to be g_i. Formally, the predicate σ' is in the equivalence class of σ if and only if

$$(\exists g \in G)(\forall X \in X)(\sigma(g(X)) = \sigma'(X)) \qquad (17)$$

By the definition of a group, if $g \in G$, then its inverse g^{-1} is also in G. Therefore, the relation "σ' is in the equivalence class of σ" is reflexive. Since if g_1 and g_2 are in G, then $g_1 g_2$ is in G, the equivalence relation is also transitive.

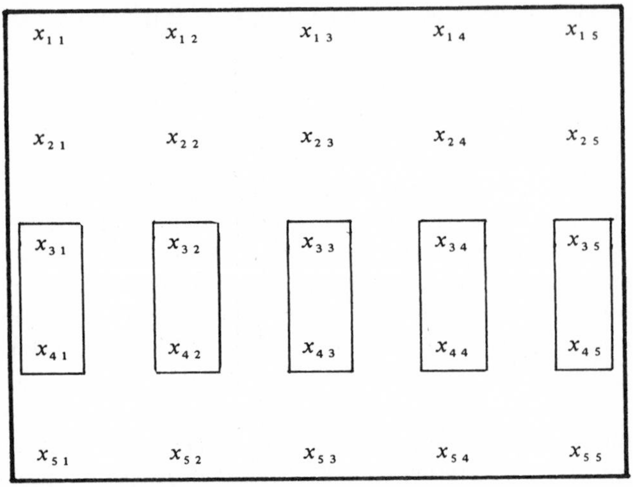

Fig. 5-3.   Example of equivalence class. The predicate "There is a vertical bar of length 2 in column 1, rows 3 and 4" has the equivalence class indicated by rectangles over the set of transformations that interchange the columns.

Example of the Definitions: Figure 5-3 shows a retina arranged as a 5 x 5 matrix. Suppose Φ is the set of detectors of vertical bars of length two. Using the two-dimensional matrix notation referred to earlier, $R = \{x_{ij}\}$, $i, j = 1, \ldots, 5$. Any predicate σ_k in Φ can be written as the logical product

$$\sigma_k = x_{ij} x_{i+1, j}, \qquad i = 1, \ldots, 4, \quad j = 1, \ldots, 5 \qquad (18)$$

Let G be the set of transformations which maps columns into columns. Any $g \in G$ will shift the field of σ_k to the right or left, as shown in Figure 5-3 for vertical bar detectors in rows three and four. The equivalence class of a given σ_k is the set (σ_k') of predicates which have the same row indicator (i) since each allowable transformation shifts the set of support of the detector right or left, but not up or down.

The Group Invariance Theorem

If $\psi \in L(\Phi)$ and if ψ is invariant over G [i.e., $\psi(X) = \psi(g(X))$ for all $g \in G$], then there is a representation of ψ such that

$$\psi(X) = \left[\sum_{\sigma_i \in \Phi} \beta_i \sigma_i(X) > 0 \right] \tag{19}$$

and if σ_i is in the equivalence class of σ_j (written $\sigma_i \underset{G}{\equiv} \sigma_j$) then $\beta_i = \beta_j$.

Proof: Since ψ is a linear predicate it has a representation

$$\psi(X) = \left[\sum_{i=1}^{k} a_i \sigma_i(X) > 0 \right] \tag{20}$$

for some set $\{a_i\}$ of real numbers.

As Φ is closed under G, any element $g \in G$ defines a correspondence $\sigma_i \longleftrightarrow \sigma_{g(i)}$.[3] For all X and any g

$$\sigma_i(g(X)) = \sigma_{g(i)}(X) \tag{21}$$

The assignment of indices in Φ is arbitrary; $\Phi = \sigma_1, \sigma_2, \ldots, \sigma_k$ and $\Phi_g = \{\sigma_{g(1)}, \sigma_{g(2)}, \ldots, \sigma_{g(k)}\}$ are identical sets. Thus, any g can be thought of as assigning an ordering to Φ. As the value of an addition is not determined by order, it is clear that

$$\sum_{i=1}^{k} a_i \sigma_i(X) = \sum_{i=1}^{k} a_{g(i)} \sigma_{g(i)}(X). \tag{22}$$

Now suppose $\psi(X) = 1$ for some X. As ψ is invariant over G, and since if $g \in G$, its inverse, g^{-1}, is also in g, it must be true that

$$\sum_{i=1}^{k} a_{g(i)} \sigma_{g(i)}(g^{-1}(X)) > 0 \tag{23}$$

If we apply (21) to $\sigma_{g(i)}(g^{-1}(X))$

$$\sigma_{g(i)}(g^{-1}(X)) = \sigma_{g^{-1}(g(i))}(X) = \sigma_i(X) \tag{24}$$

By substituting (24) into (23)

$$\sum_{i=1}^{k} a_{g(i)} \sigma_i(X) > 0. \tag{25}$$

---

[3] In this expression $g(i)$ should be interpreted as "that j for which $\sigma_i = \sigma$ and $\sigma_j = \sigma'$" in Eq. (17).

This is true for all $g \in G$. Summing (25) over the g's then must produce a positive quantity.

$$\sum_{g \in G} \sum_{i=1}^{k} a_{g(i)} \sigma_i(X) > 0. \tag{26}$$

By interchanging the order of summation

$$\sum_{i=1}^{k} \left(\sum_{g \in G} a_{g(i)} \right) \sigma_i(X) > 0. \tag{27}$$

Now define

$$\beta_i = \sum_{g \in G} a_{g(i)}. \tag{28}$$

If i and j are in the same equivalence class, then $i = g(j)$ and $j = g'(i)$ for some g and g'. More generally,

$$\sum_{g \in G} a_{g(i)} = \sum_{g \in G} a_{g(j)} \tag{29}$$

if i and j are in the same equivalence class. Thus we have shown that $\beta_i = \beta_j$.

The argument assumes that $\psi(X) = 1$. Exactly the same argument can be applied, with $\leq$ replacing $>$, for the case $\psi(X) = 0$, completing the proof. Starting from the assumption that there is some linear representation of ψ it has been shown that there is a representation in which members of an equivalence class have identical coefficients.

Corollary 1 to the Group Invariance Theorem

A group invariant predicate of order k can be represented by a linear predicate in the set Φ^* of masks of order $\leq k$, in which masks (of the same size) which can be mapped into each other by some $g \in G$ have identical coefficients.

The corollary follows from the masking theorem, which establishes that there is a representation of ψ in $L(\Phi^*)$ and the group invariance theorem applied to that representation.

Corollary 2 to the Group Invariance Theorem

Let Φ be partitioned into $\Phi_1, \Phi_2, \ldots, \Phi_m$, where Φ_t is the tth equivalence class established by G. A linear group-invariant predicate ψ can be represented as

$$\psi(X) = \left[\sum_{i}^{k} a_i N_i(X) > 0 \right] \tag{30}$$

where $N_i(X)$ is the number of predicates σ_j in Φ_i for which $\sigma_j(X) = 1$.

Reasoning: Consider the constructive technique for defining the β_i. For any X, exactly $\mathbf{N}_i$ of the $\sigma_j \in \Phi_i$ will be "on" if $\Phi(X) = 1$.

This corollary may seem obscure at first, but it turns out to be quite useful, for it states a precise requirement on each equivalence class. If we can show that some predicate establishes equivalence classes which do not possess this property, then the predicate cannot be linear in Φ.

5.3   Substantive Theorems for Order-Limited Perceptrons

5.3.0   COUNTING PREDICATES

Let G be the group of all permutations of R, so that G contains all mapping of points into R into other points in R. Let $/X/$ be the number of points of R which are "on" (i.e., the number of unbarred terms in X) for the figure X. The only first-order predicates which are invariant over G are the *counting* predicates

$$\psi(X) = [/X/ > m] \qquad (31)$$

and

$$\psi(X) = [/X/ \geqslant m] \qquad (32)$$

and their negations.

Intuitive Argument for the Counting Predicate Theorem: A first-order predicate is simply a test of a weighted sum of the points on the retina, i.e.,

$$\psi(X) = [\textstyle\sum a_i x_i > \theta] \qquad (33)$$

Since any x_i can be mapped into any x_j by some member g of the very broadly defined group of transformations G, all points are in the same equivalence class, of size N_1, and must have the same weight. Therefore, any predicate which is invariant over G has the representation

$$\psi(X) = [a/X/ > \theta]. \qquad (34)$$

This is equivalent to

$$\psi(X) = [/X/ > \theta/a] = [/X/ > m] \qquad (35)$$

where $m = \theta/a$. Note that in this argument θ can be regarded as the coefficient of the zero-order mask, or constant term, of the linear predicate. Since $/X/$ must be an integer, θ can be chosen to determine the precise inequality desired.

Comment: In a sense, a perceptron of order 1 is a "most general" learning machine. Its designer has not built in any biases by specifying $\emptyset$, since he simply presents to the perceptron the pictures placed on R, together with their correct classification, and lets the convergence procedure find what is important. The theorem states that when this is done and the classification must be invariant over any transformation, then the perceptron can only develop a classification rule which separates figures X_1 and X_2 on the basis of their areas. Whether this result is encouraging or discouraging and surprising or unsurprising, depends on your point of view. In some of the early perceptron research order-1 perceptrons were found to be capable of learning reasonably accurate and interesting discriminations. Handwritten letters or numerals were frequently used to indicate the perceptron's capability. In fact, the perceptron was classifying a digitalized version of the picture. Subtle differences in the area of the various letters and numerals would be translated into a difference in the number of ones on the retina, and hence a counting predicate could be applied. The convergence theorem of Chapter IV guarantees that such a predicate could be found.

It should be pointed out that the counting limitation on first-order perceptrons applies only if invariance is required over all possible transformations of the retina. This is an unusually strong constraint. When it is relaxed some less trivial problems can be solved.

5.3.1   PARITY

We state the theorem without proof. The predicate

$$\psi(X) = \text{The number of points in } X \text{ is odd.} \tag{36}$$

cannot be found by a perceptron of order less than the size of the retina—i.e., if the retina can be increased without limit the necessary perceptron is not of finite order. (Recall that when the parity predicate was used as an example of the positive normal form theorem one of the masks used was of order 3, equal to the size of the retina.)

Parity is an interesting mathematical concept, so, somehow, the fact that a perceptron cannot classify on the basis of parity suggests that perceptrons do not have some aspect of what an intelligent machine should have. A very simple *sequential* pattern recognizer can be constructed which will classify figures on the basis of parity. This machine needs two components, a point scanner and a one-bit memory. The machine begins with its memory bit set to 0 (even). It then scans R, one point at a time, and changes the state of its memory bit whenever it encounters an element of R in the "on" state. At the end of the scan the state of memory is the classification of the figure.

5.3.2   BOOLEAN COMBINATIONS

If we think of a predicate as an elementary property of objects, we may want to construct some other predicate which can classify objects based upon a Boolean combination of presence or absence of primitive properties of objects. One can think of a number of practical classifications that are made in our everyday life, especially in the fields of law and medicine. For example, a voter in a town is a (United States citizen) *and* (legal resident) *and* [*not* (convicted of certain felonies entailing loss of voting privileges)]. A good deal of psychological study has been devoted to the question of how people learn and make such classifications. It turns out to be surprisingly hard for people to learn fairly simple combinatorial rules by example. (Bourne, 1965.) To what extent can a perceptron learn Boolean classifications?

Boolean functions of two variables can be defined by perceptrons of small order. For example, the logical product of two variables $(x_1 \cdot x_2)$ is represented by the linear predicate

$$\psi(X) = [(x_1 + x_2) \geqslant 2] \tag{37}$$

which is of order one. In fact, of the 16 possible Boolean functions of two variables, all can be represented by a linear predicate of order 1 except the predicates "exclusive or" (x_1 or x_2 but not both) and its complement, "equivalence" (x_1 if and only if x_2). Interestingly, these are the hardest Boolean predicates for a human to recognize (Hunt, Marin, & Stone, 1966; Neisser & Weene, 1962).

The next step is obviously to ask about Boolean functions with more complicated primitive predicates. There are two results, one encouraging and one discouraging.

Boolean Combinations Based on Exclusive or and Biconditional

If ψ_1 and ψ_2 are predicates of order k_1 and k_2, respectively, then the predicates $\psi_a = \psi_1$ exclusive or ψ_2 and $\psi_b = \psi_1$ if and only if ψ_2 are both of order $k^* \leqslant (k_1 + k_2)$.

Boolean and/or Theorem

There exist predicates ψ_1 and ψ_2 of order one such that $\psi_a = \psi_1$ and ψ_2 and $\psi_b = \psi_1$ or ψ_2 are not of finite order.

These theorems establish that a finite order perceptron can solve a classification problem based upon the exclusive disjunction or biconditional combination of two perceptron-solvable classifications, but it may not be true that a finite-order perceptron can solve a problem based on the conjunction or disjunction of two solvable problems.

5.3.3 GEOMETRIC CLASSES

Many projects in machine pattern-recognition are motivated by a desire to classify two-dimensional figures of one sort or another. To make such a classification the perceptron must be able to pick out definable geometric properties of the pictures it is to classify. We saw that under the very general requirement that the properties be invariant over any group of all permutations of R, then the only geometric property to which a perceptron can respond is area, which is equivalent to the number of "on" points on the retina. A more realistic requirement is that the perceptron be able to classify pictures on the basis of topologically invariant predicates. Consider any line drawing on a plane. It will consist of one or more components, each of which may contain a hole. As an

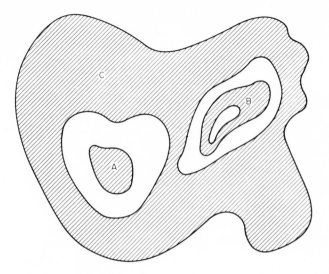

Fig. 5-4.   A geometric figure containing three subfigures. A contains no holes; B contains one hole; and C contains two holes.

example, Figure 5-4 shows a figure containing three components, one with no hole, one with one hole, and one with two holes. A *topological transformation* is any transformation of the plane that does not change the number of components or the "inside-out" relations of the picture. Figure 5-5a is a possible topological transformation of Figure 5-4, while Figure 5-5b is not. The *Euler number* of a figure X is defined as

$$E(X) = \text{Number of components in } X - \text{number of holes in } X. \qquad (38)$$

Minsky and Papert developed a technique for converting an arbitrary figure into a canonical figure whose identity depends only upon the Euler number of the original figure. The method uses only topological transformations. If topologically invariant, a perceptron that is able to distinguish between two figures, X_1 and X_2, must also be able to distinguish between their topologically equivalent canonical forms. Thus any property upon which the classification is to be made must be a function of the Euler number.

This proves to be a surprisingly strong condition. The predicate

$$\psi(X) = X \text{ is a connected figure} \qquad (39)$$

cannot be found by a perceptron of finite order. This follows from the Euler number theorem, since we can construct both unconnected and connected figures with the same Euler number, as illustrated in Figure 5-6.

5.3.4   PREDICATES OF SMALL ORDER

We can extend our analysis from finite order to "reasonably sized" perceptrons and from all transformations to "reasonable" transformations. The geometric

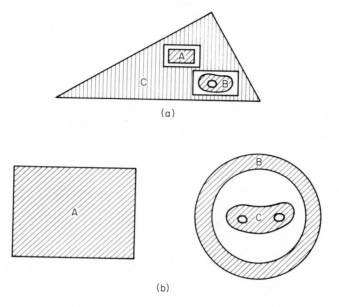

(a)

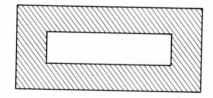

(b)

Fig. 5-5. Transformations of Figure 5-4. (a) Topological transformation. (b) Non-topological transformation.

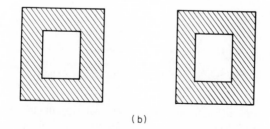

(a)

(b)

Fig. 5-6. Connected and disconnected figure with the same Euler number. "Number of components minus number of holes equals zero."

transformations of retention and translation are especially interesting. If we think of the retina as a two-dimensional plane, we would want to be able to recognize common geometric shapes (e.g., triangles, rectangles, circles) as such regardless of their position and orientation. We might also want to be able to recognize them regardless of size, so in some cases dilation or expansion must also be allowed.

Only limited translation invariant predicates can be achieved by perceptrons of order 1. The reason is that translation places all points of the retina in the same equivalence class, so that an argument similar to the argument used to prove size invariance (see the discussion of the counting predicates) applies.

Given any two figures, it is possible to determine whether or not an order 2 perceptron can be designed to distinguish between them without actually constructing the perceptron. This is done by calculating a property called the *spectrum* of a figure. Think of any $x \in R$ as being a point on a two-dimensional plane and, hence, distinguishable by its two coordinate values. For any two points, x_1, x_2, in R the *difference vector* of $\mathbf{x}_1$ and $\mathbf{x}_2$, written $\overrightarrow{x_1 - x_2}$, is defined as the vector $[(x$ coordinates of $x_1)-(x$ coordinates of $x_2)]$, $[(y$ coordinates of $x_1)-(y$ coordinates of $x_2)]$. Two masks of order two, $x_1 x_2$ and $x_1{}^*, x_2{}^*$, are equivalent over translation if and only if

$$\overrightarrow{(x_1 - x_2)} = \pm \overrightarrow{(x_1{}^* - x_2{}^*)}. \tag{40}$$

The reason for this is straightforward. The difference vector expresses the position of point x_2 relative to point x_1, while translation permits positioning of x_1 anywhere on the plane of the retina. It is necessary to allow for reversed signs of the difference vector to indicate that $x_1 x_2$ and $x_2 x_1$ are the same mask. Finally, for consistency we can treat a single point (mask of under 1) as a "two point" mask $(x_1 x_1)$ with the difference vector $(0, 0)$.

Let $n_\mathbf{v}(x)$ be the number of single points or pairs of points in x which have difference vector $\mathbf{v}$. The *difference spectrum* of a picture x is a list $\{n_\mathbf{v}(x)\}$ of the number of pairs of points having a given difference spectrum $\mathbf{v}$, for all $\mathbf{v}$ appearing in x. These concepts are illustrated by Fig. 5.7, which presents two pictures with identical spectra. The spectrum is listed in Table 5-1.

X	X
X X	X X
X	X

Fig. 5-7.   Two pictures with identical spectra.

A perceptron of order 2 can only develop translation invariant predicates which place all pictures with the same spectrum in the same class. The proof of this statement is a straightforward application of the basic theorems. By the masking theorem the predicate to be developed is expressible as a linear predicate in the set

TABLE 5.1.
Difference Spectrum of Pictures in Figure 5-7

Component	Description	Difference vector	Number of vectors
X	Point	(0, 0)	4
XX	Horizontal Line	(1, 0)	1
X	Vertical Line	(0, 1)	2
X X	Right−left diagonal	(−1, −1)	1
X X	Left−right diagonal	(1, −1)	1

of masks. By the group invariance theorem, all masks with difference vector **v** must be assigned the same coefficients. Therefore, linear discrimination between pictures x_1 and x_2 is possible only if $n_{\mathbf{v}}(x_1) \neq n_{\mathbf{v}}(x_2)$ for at least one difference vector **v**.

If order-2 perceptrons are so limited, what about slightly higher order perceptrons? Order 3 and order 4 perceptrons can solve a number of interesting pattern classification problems, such as the distinction between convex and nonconvex figures. A major problem, however, is that perceptrons of limited order cannot always be constructed to recognize a component of a picture in the context of other components. As an example, the predicate "X is a square" is of order 2, but the predicate "X contains a square as one of its components" is not of finite order. This is a serious limitation on perceptrons, since there are important pattern-recognition problems, such as the recognition of items in aerial photographs, which require in-context recognition.

5.4 Capabilities of Diameter-Limited Perceptrons

Diameter-limited perceptrons are, in general, much less powerful than perceptrons of finite order. This is hardly surprising, since the restriction is more severe. A diameter-limited perceptron may be constructed to recognize any shape, provided that the shape always appears in a fixed position and size on the retina. This implies that practical pattern-recognition by a diameter-limited perceptron requires that the image first be preprocessed to center it on the retina at a standard magnification. The combined preprocessor and classifier could not be considered a perceptron, although it might be a fairly simple device to build. Diameter-limited perceptrons also cannot recognize topological invariances other than the predicate that the Euler number exceeds (or does not exceed) a fixed integer. This is, of course, a stronger restriction than the corresponding limit on the finite-order perceptron.

5.5 The Importance of Perceptron Analysis

The mathematical structure that Minsky and Papert defined to be a perceptron is more restricted than the range of devices described by Rosenblatt (1958, 1965) when he introduced the term. In Figure 5-8 we show the block diagram of a machine that fits the Minsky–Papert definition. In Rosenblatt's original terminology, this diagram shows a single layer, series-coupled perceptron. More complicated perceptrons (in Rosenblatt's sense) can also be defined. Two interesting configurations are shown in Figure 5-9. One of these is a multilayer device in which the first level predicates are themselves perceptrons of order one. The other device is a perceptron with loops, or, a "back-coupled perceptron." In it the classification of a figure input at time **t** is fed back onto the retina, so that it is a part of the figure presented at time **t** + 1. The Minsky-Papert analysis applies only to devices that fit their definition of perceptron, schematized in Figure 5-8. There is no reason why a similar analysis of the more exotic perceptrons such as those of Figure 5-9 should not be attempted. This will probably be a difficult task, and in some cases an impossible one, but there is a potential for useful results. Considering how the tremendous enthusiasm generated by early perceptron studies was dampened, to say the least, by Minsky and Papert's formal analysis, it seems advisable that analysis precede the construction of multilayered, cross-back-coupled perceptrons for use in applied pattern recognition. Of course, advocating further theoretical development before commitment to an application is not the same as advocating stopping research in the field!

If Minsky and Papert's results are, in one way, narrower than the field of perceptrons, in another way they are wider. Most of their theorems are about the existence or nonexistence of linear discriminant solutions to specific classification

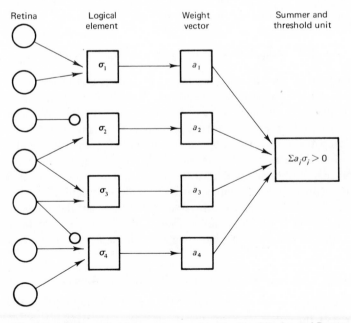

Fig. 5-8.   Schematic of perceptron as described by Minsky and Papert.

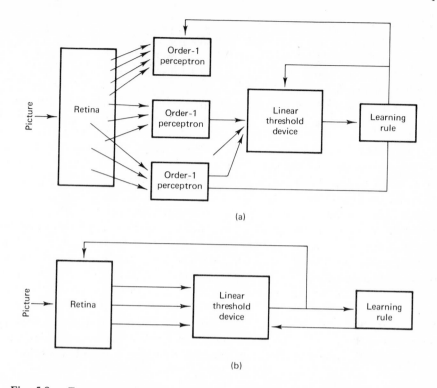

Fig. 5-9. Two more complex perceptrons. (a) Multilayer ("Gamba") perceptron. (b) Back-coupled perceptron.

problems, without concern for how such solutions were to be developed. Thus, the conclusions apply equally well to statistical procedures as to learning machines. The relation of linear classification procedures to the classification of two-dimensional plane figures is of special importance. There are many classification problems in which the data are, inherently, presented as two-dimensional plane figures. Any application involving the sorting of photographs serves as an example. Geometric properties such as connectedness or the presence of one type of picture component in the context of other components are likely to be an inevitable part of the problem solution. Anyone faced with a problem involving plane figure classification would do well to consider which of Minsky and Papert's results are relevant.

A third general point about the analysis of perceptrons is that this work may herald a new approach to pattern recognition research. From 1950 until the mid 1960s most research on pattern-recognition devices had a strong experimental bias. If a person thought of an interesting pattern-recognition technique he constructed the appropriate machine (usually by computer programming) and illustrated its powers by example. One of Minsky and Papert's major theses is that logical analysis is essential if we are going to assert that we "know" a certain method will or will not solve a specified class of problems.

Some of the Minsky–Papert results apply to parallel processors in general. If a perceptron limitation occurs because the presence or absence of feature A may mean different things depending on whether feature B is or is not present, then the problem is probably better solved by a sequential than a parallel machine. Problems like this appear to be particularly common in the analysis of complex visual scenes, where fairly straightforward sequential algorithms can solve problems that can only be handled by very large parallel systems (see Guzman, 1968 and the discussion of related work in Part III of this book).

Chapter VI

SEQUENTIAL PATTERN RECOGNITION

6.0 Sequential Classification

Parallel pattern-classification algorithms can be thought of as designs for machines of the sort shown in Figure 6-1. The object to be classified is presented to a set of n feature detectors which, independently and in parallel, compute n measurements to form a *description vector* $\mathbf{x} = (x_1 \cdots x_n)$. Weights $\{a_i\}$ are assigned to these measurements and the weighted sum is determined. If the sum exceeds a threshold θ the object is treated as a member of class 1; otherwise it is treated as a member of class 0. By contrast, consider the *sequential pattern classification* machine shown in Figure 6-2. This is a device which also contains n feature detectors, but connects them together in a more complex way. First, feature detector 1 is applied to all objects, determining the measurement x_1. This measurement is then input to a switching rule, which determines which of several possible intervals the value of x_1 falls into. (Alternatively, we could think of the

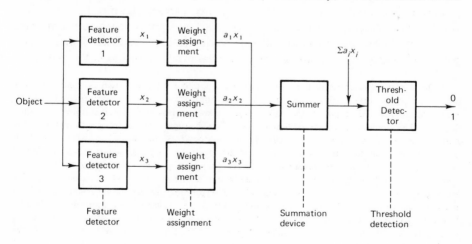

Fig. 6-1.   A parallel pattern classification machine.

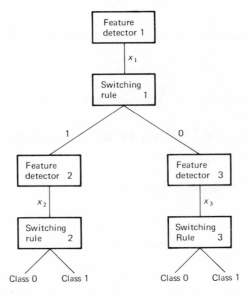

Fig. 6-2.   A sequential pattern classification machine.

range of x_1 as being confined to a narrow set of integers, so that the switching rule simply notes the value of the measurement.) Depending upon the outcome of the switching decision, any one of several feature detectors will be chosen to make the next measurement. A switching rule will be applied to the second measurement to choose the third measurement, etc., until enough information is obtained to make a classification. The sequential machine can be described by stating the switching rules and the location of each feature detector in the tree of tests. Clearly the sequential machine is more complex than the parallel machine, which can be described simply by stating the weight vector $\mathbf{a} = (a_1 \cdots a_n)$. It is also more powerful than parallel machines, since for any parallel classification procedure which can be described in this way, there exists an equivalent sequential machine using the same features, although there are sequential procedures which do not have parallel equivalents.[1] In addition, the sequential machine minimizes the number of

[1] The statement is precisely true for linear discriminant procedures such as those of Figure 6-1, in which the final classification is based on the summation. An "absolute" parallel machine might be constructed in which the weight vectors were replaced by interval detectors which digitized the elements of the description vector. It could assign a unique integer to each possible description vector, and treat this integer as the "address" of the object the vector described. The addressing mechanism could then be attached to an "information-retrieval machine," consisting of a store containing one address for each possible description vector. The appropriate class would be stored at the address. Classification would be made by a table look-up to find a class name given an address. The problem is that the information retrieval machine would have to be very big. We might be able to achieve some economy by finding blocks of addresses, corresponding to objects in the same class, and associating all description vectors in the block with a single address. The function for mapping addresses into blocks would, itself, be a pattern classifier.

features measured before a classification is made. The disadvantages of a sequential machine are its greater complexity, the correspondingly greater complexity of the algorithms required to discover it in the pattern recognition phase, and the longer time required to make a sequential classification, since the features are evaluated in series rather than in parallel.[2]

In this chapter we will deal with sequential pattern classification and recognition procedures. Unless stated otherwise, we will assume that each measurement x_i in the feature vector ranges over the integers $1 \cdots v_i$, where v_i is typically fairly small. Values of the features will be regarded as arbitrary characters rather than as numbers. In general we shall assume that there exists some correct rule $\mathbf{R^*}$ that has been used to assign all members of the universe of possible object descriptions to classes. (We will allow the possibility that the assignment is probabilistic.) We are going to consider algorithms which accept as input a set S of descriptions and class names of objects, and from this set infer a rule $\mathbf{R}$ that approximates $\mathbf{R^*}$. The degree to which $\mathbf{R}$ approximates $\mathbf{R^*}$ will be determined by comparing the classifications made by $\mathbf{R}$ and $\mathbf{R^*}$ over the space of all possible descriptions of objects.

Although sequential pattern recognition is basically a simple process, it requires a formidable notation to describe it. To avoid losing sight of the forest for the trees, we will first provide an illustrative example. Let the objects to be classified be the set of tetrads of four letters generated by the rules:

The first letter must be H, G, E, or W.
The second letter must be X, K, L, or S.
The third letter must be Q, B, F, or T.
The fourth letter must be A, R, M, or Z.

We have chosen a rule that assigns each of the 256 (4^4) possible four-letter sequences to class 1 or class 0. Some of the classifications this rule produces are:

Class 0 objects

GKFA   GLFR   HSTA   GLFM   WLBR   GSFZ

Class 1 objects

GKQA   GSQZ   HKFM   EXQM   HSTM   GLTM   GXBR   WLBM

What is $\mathbf{R^*}$? The reader is urged to try to guess for himself, before glancing at Figure 6-3, which diagrams the rule actually used. While solving the problem, try to note the processes which you use to arrive at an answer.

In fact there are several other rules which are consistent with the classifications given. This is generally the case. If S is a proper subset of the set of all descriptions U, there will be several rules which agree in their classification of objects in S but

---

[2] This contrast, of course, assumes that the parallel procedure is truly parallel. If a sequential device is used to simulate a parallel procedure, as, for example, is done when a standard, single processor digital computer is programmed to execute a digital procedure, then a parallel pattern classification algorithm will require at least as much time for feature evaluation as an equivalent sequential processor.

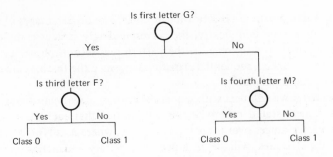

Fig. 6-3.   Example of sequential classification of tetrads of letters.

disagree in their classification of objects in $U - S$.[3] There is no reason for preferring one rule to another unless we are given additional further criteria for a good rule beyond the requirement that it should classify known examples correctly. It is easy to construct reasonable criteria, such as minimization of the number of features used or minimization of the length of the longest path through the graph.

6.1   Definitions and Notation

We first review our notational conventions and introduce some specializations for this problem.

Objects and Descriptions

An object is an abstract entity that has a description associated with it. The description is a vector $\mathbf{x} = (x_1 \cdots x_m)$ of m integers. The ith component of this vector is the value of measurement i. The possible values of measurement i range over the integers from 1 to v_i.

Description Space

D is the set of all possible descriptions. N is the number of elements in D, and

$$N = \prod_{i=1}^{m} v_i \tag{1}$$

Classes

There is a finite set $\{C_j\}$, $j = 1 \cdots c$ of c classes, such that each object belongs to exactly one class. A class defines a probability distribution, $\Pr(\mathbf{x} \mid C_j)$ over the set of

---

[3] Let N be the number of objects in U and n the number of objects in S. Since S is a proper subset of U, $n < N$. Suppose that there are k possible class names for objects. This means that there are k^n possible ways in which class names can be assigned to objects in U. By definition, each of these is a classifying rule. As there are k^n ways of assigning class names to objects in U, there must be k^{N-n} rules which are identical in their assignment of class names to objects in S but not identical in their assignment of names in $U - S$.

possible descriptions. It is assumed that two classes are always distinct, i.e., that for any two classes C_i and C_j there exists at least one description vector $\mathbf{x} \in C$ such that

$$\Pr(\mathbf{x} \mid C_j) \neq \Pr(\mathbf{x} \mid C_i). \tag{2}$$

Sequences of Observations

Some motivation is necessary to explain the definition. Suppose that we pass an object through a sequential classification procedure, or *decision tree* such as the one shown in Figure 6-3. As we pass the object from one node to another we shall progressively build up our knowledge of the object's description vector. At any one point in the classification we can summarize this knowledge by an ordered set of pairs of integers, where the components of the *j*th pair define the *j*th measurement applied and its outcome. Each node in the tree will have a unique ordered set of pairs associated with it. For example, the lower right-hand node of Figure 6-3 has associated with it the set $\{(1, -G), (4, -M)\}$, which states that if an object is passed to this node, then we know that the first letter is not G and the fourth letter is not *M*.

These notions are stated symbolically by defining a *description sequence of length v*, $v, < m$. A description sequence is an ordered set $S_v(y)$ of pairs of integers (a, b), fulfilling the following restrictions.

1. $1 \leqslant a \leqslant m$, since a indicates a possible measurement.
2. $1 \leqslant b \leqslant v_a$, as b is a possible value of measurement a.
3. The set $S_v(y)$ contains no two members whose a components are identical, i.e., each measurement appears not more than once in the sequence.

A sequence $S_v(y)$ contains a sequence $S_w(y)$ if $w < v$ and if the first w components of $S_v(y)$ are identical to the components of $S_w(y)$.

Classification Rules

A classification rule $\mathbf{R}$ is a set of pairs, in which each pair consists of a sequence and a class name and in which the sequences can be diagrammed by a tree graph, as in the example of Figure 6-3. Each sequence corresponds to the path from the root node to one of the endpoints of the tree. Note that this has two interesting implications for the set $\mathbf{R}$. All elements of $\mathbf{R}$ must have an identical first element in their sequences, and $\mathbf{R}$ itself must consist of either (*a*) a single element or (*b*) it must be possible to partition $\mathbf{R}$ into k subsets, $\mathbf{R}^{(1)} \cdots \mathbf{R}^{(k)}$ such that if the (common) first element is disregarded in the sequences, each of the $\mathbf{R}^{(i)}$ are themselves classification rules describing the subtrees immediately below the root.

An object *fits a sequence* if the values of the measurements specified in the sequence are identical to the object's values for those measurements. When $\mathbf{R}$ is used to classify an object, the object is fit to one of the sequences of $\mathbf{R}$ (exactly one of these will fit) and the object is then assigned the class name associated with the sequence. Graphically, this is equivalent to "passing the object through the tree" to an endpoint.

Sample

A sample S is a set of vectors determined by choosing randomly from objects in U and assigning their description vectors to S.

Augmentation of a Sequence

The *augmentation* of a sequence, $S_v(y) \# x_r$, is the set of sequences of length $v + 1$, each of which contains $S_v(y)$ and which each have as their $v + 1$st element one of the v_r possible pairs (r, b). In graphic terms, the augmentation of $S_v(y)$ consists of those paths that branch one node beyond the node $S_v(y)$ by making a test of the rth measurement at this node.

Sequential Pattern Recognition Algorithm

A sequential pattern recognition algorithm is a procedure for producing a rule **R** from examination of a sample. If the algorithm first takes a sample S_1 and produces rule $\mathbf{R}_1$, and next expands to a new sample S_2 (which may or may not have S_1 as a subset), to produce a second rule $\mathbf{R}_2$ from S_2, etc., then the rules will be numbered in the order that they are produced.

Costs

The *misclassification cost* w_{ij} is defined as a real number representing the cost of classifying an object as a member of class C_i when, in fact, it is a member of C_j. The *measurement cost* f_i is a real number representing the cost of making the ith measurement on an object.

Probability of Classification or of Observation

We review briefly the notation used for the unconditional, conditional, and marginal probabilities of an object's being in a particular class or having a particular description.

$\Pr(C_j)$ = probability that a randomly chosen object is a member of class C_j, $j = 1 \cdots k$.

$\Pr(S_v(y))$ = probability that a particular sequence of length v will be satisfied by a randomly chosen object's description vector.

$\Pr(S_v(y) \mid C_j)$ = probability that an object randomly chosen from class C_j will satisfy the sequence $S_v(y)$.

$\Pr(C_j \mid S_v(y))$ = probability that an object randomly chosen from the set of objects satisfying $S_v(y)$ will be a member of class C_j.

6.2   Bayesian Decision Procedures

In Chapter IV the idea of a Bayesian decision procedure was introduced.

Bayesian analyses prove particularly useful in studying sequential pattern classification and recognition.[4]

Suppose that we have discovered that the partial description of a randomly chosen object is $S_v(y)$. We need a rule for deciding the class to which the object should be assigned. The joint probability that the partial description will be satisfied *and* that the class is C_j is

$$\Pr(S_v(y) \cdot C_j) = \Pr(C_j) \cdot \Pr(S_v(y) \mid C_j). \tag{3}$$

This, however, turns the problem around. What we want to know is the probability of C_j given the sequence of observations. An alternative to (3) is

$$\Pr(S_v(y) \cdot C_j) = \Pr(S_v(y)) \cdot \Pr(C_j \mid S_v(y)) \tag{4}$$

from which a specialized version of Bayes's rule follows.

$$\Pr(C_j \mid S_v(y)) = \frac{\Pr(S_v(y) \mid C_j)}{\Pr(S_v(y))} \tag{5}$$

The denominator on the right of (5) is the sum of all the ways that the sequence could have arisen; i.e., the sum of the probabilities that the sequence would be observed over all classes, weighted by the probability of each class. Therefore

$$\Pr(S_v(y)) = \sum_{i=1}^{k} \Pr(S_v(y) \mid C_i) \cdot \Pr(C_i). \tag{6}$$

By substitution of (6) into (5) we have a sequential pattern classification version of Bayes's theorem,

$$\Pr(C_j \mid S_v(y)) = \frac{\Pr(S_v(y) \mid C_j) \cdot \Pr(C_j)}{\sum_{i=1}^{k} \Pr(S_v(y) \mid C_i) \cdot \Pr(C_i)} \tag{7}$$

The expected loss associated with the decision to assign an object satisfying $S_v(y)$ to class C_j is

$$EL(j \mid S_v(y)) = \sum_{i=1}^{k} w_{ij} \cdot \Pr(C_i \mid S_v(y)) \tag{8}$$

A *Bayesian optimal* classification rule is a rule that chooses j to minimize (8).

---

[4] Bayesian decision rules are based on a philosophical understanding of statements about probability which may not always be appropriate. Kanal and Chandresakaran (1969) point out that although the philosophies behind Bayesian and non-Bayesian approaches to pattern recognition are different, in practice they lead one to the same computing procedures. Accordingly, we shall not discuss the controversy. It is *not* always the case that Bayesian and non-Bayesian philosophies lead to the same computations, especially in statistical hypothesis testing (Edwards, Lindeman, & Savage, 1963).

This reasoning applies when a decision maker has already established the sequence of observations and the probability estimates he will use, so minimization of (8) is a pattern *classification* rule. Pattern *recognition* procedures are aimed at discovery of the best sequences to observe and their associated classification rules. Suppose that, for some arbitrarily chosen sequence of observations, the expected loss is somewhat too high to be acceptable. An alternative course of action is to choose some measurement x_r not in $S_v(y)$, and determine which sequence of observations the object to be classified satisfies in the augmented set of sequences, $S_v(y) \# x_r$. It may be possible to find an acceptable classification loss for sequences within this set. The alternative, however, has associated with it the fixed cost of making the rth measurement. When should we take this alternative and how should x_r be chosen? These are the topics of the next two sections.

6.3   Bayesian Optimal Classification Procedures Based on Dynamic Programming

We will first search for a way of defining the best possible sequential classification procedure when marginal and conditional probabilities are known. The analysis will follow Fu's (1969a) treatment of the problem, in terms of dynamic programming, or optimization of a recursively defined function.

A classification procedure must tell us what to do after observing any sequence $S_v(y)$ of observations, including the null sequence $S_0(y)$. Given a particular sequence, the classification procedure may either specify the classification decision or the way in which the sequence of observations is to be expanded before a decision is to be made. How do we decide which of these alternatives to follow? Let $g(S_v(y))$ be the expected loss due to following the optimal classification procedure given $S_v(y)$.

$$g(S_v(y)) = \min \begin{cases} \min_j \{EL(j \mid S_v(y)) \\[2ex] \min_r \{f_r + \sum_{i=1}^{v_r} \Pr(x_r = i \mid S_v(y)) \cdot g(S_{v+1}(y + (r, i)))\} \end{cases} \quad (9)$$

where $S_{v+1}(y + (r, i))$ is the $v + 1$ element sequence which contains $S_v(y)$ and has the pair (r, i) as its $v + 1$st element. Note that the range of i is $1 \cdots v_i$. If the value of (9) is established by the upper right-hand term, the decision is to assign an object to class j, otherwise measurements are continued. Unfortunately, in order to find the optimal treatment for any v length sequence of measurements, it is necessary to find the optimal treatment for all $v + 1$-length sequences which can be created from the original sequence. This is shown by the lower right-hand expression of (9). In the worst possible case, determining the optimal procedure can require that we consider the optimal procedure for all possible sequences of observations of length m or less. This can easily create a problem. Suppose, for simplicity, that all measures had the same number of values, b. The number of possible sequences for m such measures is $\sum_{i=1}^{m} b^i$, which rapidly mounts to an astronomical number. To give some idea of how quickly the increase is, Table 6-1 shows the number of

TABLE 6-1
Number of Possible Description Sequences as a Function of
Number of Measurements and Value per Measure

Values per measure	Number of measures					
	1	2	3	4	5	6
2	2	6	14	30	62	126
3	3	12	39	120	367	1096

sequences to be considered for the various combinations of $m \leqslant 6$ and $b \leqslant 3$, which covers only very small classification problems.

6.4 Approximations Based on Limited Look Ahead Algorithms

6.4.0 ALGEBRAIC TREATMENT

In many cases a straightforward procedure of "looking ahead" to consider the possibility of *at most k* further measurements before classification provides an adequate and computationally much smaller pattern recognition algorithm. The argument for this approximation is that nature is unlikely to be infinitely complex, so one should only consider the lower order interactions between predictor variables in attempting to predict class membership. We will first demonstrate the procedure for a one-step look ahead algorithm.[5]

As before, given $S_v(y)$ we will consider two possible alternatives. The first is that we make the best possible classification given the available observations. The cost of this alternative is defined by (9). Call this alternative A_1, and let it have cost $C(A_1)$. Alternative A_2 considered in the one-step look ahead procedure is that we make exactly one further measurement (choosing the best possible measure, of course), and then classify the object. The cost of A_2 is

$$C(A_2) = \min_r \{ f_r + \sum_{i=1}^{v_r} \left(\Pr(x_r = i \mid S_v(y))\right) \cdot \min_j(EL(j \cdot S_v(y + (r, i)))\} \quad (10)$$

The estimated cost of classification at this node using the procedure produced by the one-step algorithm is

$$h_1(S_v(y)) = \min\{(C(A_1), C(A_2)\} \quad (11)$$

If $C(A_1) \leqslant C(A_2)$ the look ahead algorithm designates node $S_v(y)$ as an endpoint

---

[5] Our treatment follows that of Hunt, Marin, and Stone's (1966) CLS-9 algorithm. Fu (1969) also considers the look ahead procedure as an alternative to his dynamic programming formulation.

associated with the best possible classifying decision. Otherwise the node is made an interior node whose test is the measurement r that minimizes $C(A_2)$. It is important to realize that this does *not* mean that the v_r nodes immediately beyond the current node will necessarily be endpoints. To make that decision the algorithm will be applied to each of them in turn. This is one of the senses in which we can call this an "approximate" procedure; it bases its estimates for the cost of each action on assumptions which, in general, will not be true.

6.4.1 SAMPLE PROBLEM

In presenting both the optimal and the approximate procedures, we have spoken as if the various conditional and marginal probabilities were known. In practice, we would estimate them from observed frequencies in the sample S. To illustrate this and several other points about the look ahead procedure, which is really much simpler than the rather forbidding notation required to describe it makes it appear, we will follow the procedure using as set S a set of four tetrads shown in Table 6-2. For simplicity costs of misclassification are assumed to be 0 for a correct classification and 1 for an error. We also assume that any measurement has a cost of .10. Therefore

$$w_{ii} = 0; \qquad w_{ij} = 1 \qquad \text{for all } i, j \text{ with } i \neq j \qquad (12)$$

and

$$f_r = .1 \qquad \text{for all } r. \qquad (13)$$

TABLE 6-2
Example Problem for One-Step Look Ahead Algorithm

Class 1 objects				Class 2 objects			
GSQA	GLBR	GKFM	GXBZ	GXFZ	WXTA	GKFR	EKFR
HSQM	ELBM	WKFM	HXTM	WLQZ	GSFA	HSBA	GLFM

At the start classification must be based on the null sequence $S_0(y)$, and the probability of obtaining particular values or classes is estimated by their relative frequency in the sample. In this case initially $\Pr(C_1) = \Pr(C_2) = .5$ and the expected loss due to classification based on the null sequence is .5, regardless of which classification is made. To determine the expected loss due to testing just one measure and then classifying, we must estimate, for each measure, the expected loss if the best possible classifications are made after that measure is taken. This can be done by making a cross classification of classes against measurement values, with a separate classification for each measure. In the example, then, we begin with the classification tables and associated tests shown in Table 6-3. Since using the fourth position as a measurement minimizes A_2 and brings its estimated cost below A_1, the first node is made a test of feature 4. Splitting the sample on measure 4 produces the four subsamples shown in Table 6-4. Each of these subsamples is associated with one of the nodes immediately below the first node.

When we carry out the same computations on each of these subsets, we find that in subsample 1 measure 1 can be used to discriminate between classes, that in subsample 2 measure 2 can be used, that in subsample 3 the best thing to do is to cease measurement, and that in subsample 4 measure 3 can be used. The resulting decision tree is shown in Figure 6-4. In some cases the decision tree ends in a "?." This indicates that the particular sequence of values of measures associated with that node did not appear in the sample, and hence no classification rule can be

TABLE 6-3
Cross Classification Tables of Classes Against Measurement Values[a]

First measurement: Expected loss using measure 1 = .4375 + .1 = .5375 > .5

Letter	Class 1	Class 2
H	(2)	1
G	(4)	4
E	(1)	1
W	1	(2)
	8	8

Second measurement: Expected loss for using measure 2 = .50 + .10 = .60 > .50

Letter	Class 1	Class 2
X	(2)	2
K	(2)	2
L	(2)	2
S	(2)	2
	8	8

TABLE 6-3–*cont.*

Third measurement: Expected loss using measure 3 = .3125 + .1 = .4125 < .50

Letter	Class 1	Class 2
Q	(2)	1
B	(3)	1
F	2	(5)
T	(1)	1
	8	8

Fourth measurement: Expected loss using measure 4 = .25 + .10 = .35 < .50

Letter	Class 1	Class 2
A	1	(3)
R	1	(2)
M	(5)	1
Z	1	(2)
	8	8

[a]Best classification for each case is circled. Class 1 chosen in case of ties. Cross-classification tables for first step of algorithm.

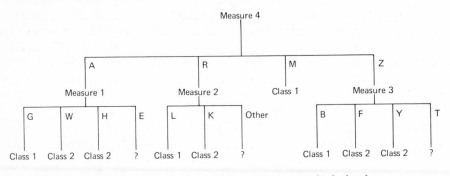

Fig. 6-4.   Decision tree developed by one step look ahead.

TABLE 6-4
Subsamples After Division on Measure 4

Subsample 1, x_4 = A		
	Class 1 objects	Class 2 objects
	GSQA	WXTA, HSBA
Subsample 2, x_4 = R		
	Class 1 objects	Class 2 objects
	GLBR	GKFR, EKFR
Subsample 3, x_4 = M		
	Class 1 objects	Class 2 objects
	GKTM, HSQM,	GLFM
	ELBM, WKFM, HXTM	
Subsample 4, x_4 = Z		
	Class 1 objects	Class 2 objects
	GXBZ	GXFZ, WLQZ

proposed. Various strategies can be offered for such situations. A common one is to choose as the appropriate decision the class that would have been optimal had measurement ceased at the node immediately above the endpoint in question.

6.4.2 GENERALIZATION TO k STEPS

There is no reason to restrict look ahead to only one step. More complex problems can be solved by looking ahead k measures at a time. The algorithm to do so is a straightforward extension of the one step look ahead. The major problem with a k-step look ahead procedure is that the number of cross-classification tables needed increases very rapidly. Even when k is large, however, there may be considerable reduction over the amount of classification required by the dynamic programming method, although this savings is of little help if the approximation method is itself too large a computing problem to be practical.

6.4.3 A COMMENT ON RELIABILITY

Sequential pattern classification procedures are sometimes criticized because of their vulnerability to sampling error. Since **R** is produced by analysis of a randomly chosen sample S it is possible that at some stage of pattern recognition the "wrong" measurement, i.e., a measurement which is appropriate for predicting class names within the sample but not within the universe of objects, will be inserted in the classification procedure being developed. At the classification stage, there is no way to recover from this error. Graphically, once an object is passed down the wrong branch of a tree there is no way to move it back to a correct branch.[6]

---

[6] An analogous argument cannot be made against parallel pattern classification procedures, since the effects of one irrelevant test can be swamped by the results of numerous relevant ones.

It has been suggested (Hunt, 1967) that the appropriate way to avoid this problem is to compute statistical measures during pattern recognition which indicate the confidence with which we may extrapolate a measurement classification relation observed in the sample of the population. The particular statistic suggested for use is the χ^2 contingency measure.

To specialize this measure to pattern recognition, the following definitions will be used:

$$n = \text{number of objects in } S$$

$$n_j = \text{number of objects in } S \text{ and members of class } C_j$$

$$n_j(a, b) = \text{number of objects in } S \text{ and } C_j \text{ for which } x_a = b.$$

We wish to measure the extent to which the association between class name and measure value indicated by tables such as those of the preceding section might have arisen by chance, on the assumption that in the population the measurement values and class names are independent. Suppose that this is the case. The number of times we would expect to find objects satisfying the conditions (class name $= j$) and $(x_a = b)$ in a sample of size n is

$$e_j(a, b) = (n_j/n) \sum_{i=1}^{k} n_i(a, b) \tag{14}$$

The chi square statistic on d degrees of freedom is

$$\chi_d^2 = \sum_{i=1}^{k} \sum_{b=1}^{v_a} [n_i(a, b) - e_i(a, b)]^2 / e_i(a, b) \tag{15}$$

where

$$d = (k - 1)(v_a - 1) \tag{16}$$

A high value of χ_d^2 indicates that the relation observed in the sample would be unlikely to occur unless there was also an association between measure a and class membership in the universe. More complete justifications are given in introductory statistics texts, which also provide tables giving the probability of obtaining different values of χ_d^2 under the null hypothesis. In cases in which it is felt that reliability is a problem it is advisable to set a maximum probability level (equivalently a minimum χ_d^2 value) and insist that during the pattern recognition stage test nodes only be added when this value is exceeded.

6.5   Convergence in Sequential Pattern Recognition

6.5.0   INTRODUCTION

There is a widespread common belief that pattern recognition and "machine learning" are intimately connected. We have seen that this belief motivated much of the work on perceptron convergence theorems. Unfortunately, we know of no analogous theorems for the case in which the correct classification procedure is *not* a linear discriminant procedure. In fact, if there are no restrictions on the form of the correct classification procedure, then there is no way of being certain that an appropriate procedure has been deduced, short of keeping a record of what to do for each distinguishable case.

6.5.1   SIMULATION OF SEQUENTIAL BY PARALLEL PROCEDURES

On the other hand, there are some situations for which convergence theorems can be found, and others in which convergence usually occurs, although it cannot be guaranteed. It may be possible to convert what is intuitively a sequential classification procedure into a parallel linear procedure. Consider the case in which the measurements, $\{x_i\}$ are all binary variables as in the perceptron. Suppose further than the correct classification rule $\mathbf{R}^*$ is "An object is a member of class C_j if and only if j is the largest index such that $x_j = 1$, i.e., the jth feature is the highest indexed feature found in the object's description." This rule can be depicted by the sequential classification tree shown in Figure 6-5, which classifies a vector by first

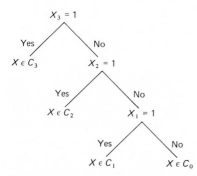

Fig. 6-5.   Sequential rule that can be simulated by parallel pattern recognition. Case $m = 3$ is shown.

determining whether x_m is one, then x_{m-1}, etc., until one of the features is found to be present. Algebraically, the conditions of the classification rule state that

$$(x \in C_j) \supset (x_j = 1), \tag{17}$$

$$(x \in C_j) \supset (x_i = 0), \qquad i > j.$$

Let us consider the single linear discriminant procedure ψ_j which, if it exists, has weights $\{a_i\}$ such that $\sum_{i=1}^{m} a_i x_i > 0$ if and only if (17) is satisfied. It is easy to show that ψ_j does exist. For example, if we take any real number $b > j$, and let

$$a_i = ib^i \qquad i \leqslant j \tag{18}$$

$$a_i = -ib^i \qquad i > j$$

then

$$\sum_{i=1}^{m} a_i x_i > 0 \tag{19}$$

if and only if $\mathbf{x} \in C_j$. Unfortunately, the size of the coefficients rapidly becomes so great that a practical "machine" would have trouble storing them! Thus even in this restricted case simulation of a sequential by a parallel machine is not practical.

6.5.2   SEQUENTIAL   DECISION   RULES   DEVELOPED   FROM   FINITE   SAMPLES

The algorithms given in Section 6.3 will always produce some rule $\mathbf{R}$ adequate to classify S. With what confidence can we say that $\mathbf{R}$ applies to all members of U? Another way of putting the question is to ask how large S must be before we can assert something about the relation of $\mathbf{R}$ to $\mathbf{R}^*$ with a fixed level of confidence.

One way of approaching this question is by statistical analysis. The literature is quite helpful if we are willing to assume that $\mathbf{R}^*$ is, in fact, a linear discriminant procedure. In this case we can establish "confidence limits" for the $\{a_i\}$ of $\mathbf{R}$. Beginning with S, assumed to be randomly drawn from U, we compute the best estimates for $\{a_i\}$, and establish an interval about each of them. We can then calculate the probability that a_i would have been observed given that the true values, a_i^* lies outside the appropriate interval.

Unfortunately we know little about analogous procedures for establishing confidence limits for nonlinear rules. In the preceding section we advised testing to make sure that the classification procedure produced from $\mathbf{R}$ was not likely to be a random one. Unfortunately, there are so many ways that nonrandomness could be produced that it is almost impossible to say anything general. For instance, the χ^2 test proposed in Section 6.4 is an appropriate test of the hypothesis that the association between measurement and class membership is not random, but it is not an appropriate test of the hypothesis that the measurement being tested is the best possible measurement. Such a test can be constructed, but implementing it involves substantial computation.

Hunt and his associates (Hunt, Marin, & Stone, 1966; Hunt, 1967) conducted empirical studies of how quickly one-step look ahead procedures converge to $\mathbf{R}^*$. In these experiments a known classification rule was chosen and used to classify a universe of objects. A sample was then chosen and presented to a pattern-recognition algorithm. In one version of the experiment the sample was increased, one object at a time, until the correct pattern classification rule was found. Alternatively a sample of fixed size was presented and the rule developed by the algorithm compared to the correct classification rule. The general conclusion drawn from these studies was that reasonable approximations to nonlinear classification rules can be produced, providing that the correct rule is not "terribly complex." Of necessity, this statement is imprecise. To give it some content we shall describe one of the experiments reported by Hunt et al. (1966).[7]

In this experiment, U was defined to be the set of vectors $\{\mathbf{x}\}$ of length 4, in which each component took on an integer value from 1 to 4. There are 256 (4^4)

[7] The description is of their Experiment IX, extended to complete the presentation here. Hunt et al. used a slightly different terminology.

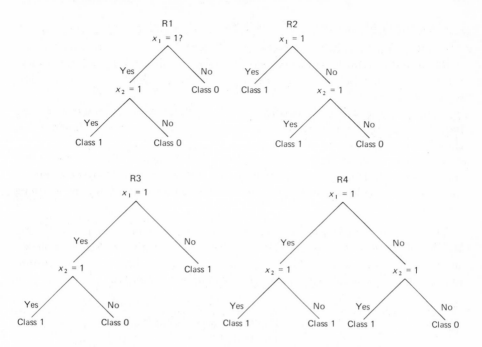

Fig. 6-6. Rules used by Hunt, Marin, and Stone in convergence study.

such vectors. Each vector was assigned to Class 1 or 0, using an arbitrarily chosen classification procedure **R***. Four different versions of **R*** were used, corresponding to the definition of the commonly used logical connectives, AND, INCLUSIVE OR, EXCLUSIVE OR, and IMPLICATION. (In other experiments the connective BICONDITIONAL, which is the negation of EXCLUSIVE OR, was also considered, but in this particular experiment the two problems were equivalent to the pattern recognition algorithm being used.) These rules are diagrammed as sequential classification trees in Figure 6-6. In words they can be stated as follows:

R1. A vector is in class 1 if the statement ($x_1 = 1$ AND $x_2 = 1$) is true, otherwise it is in class 0.

R2. A vector is in class 1 if the statement ($x_1 = 1$ OR $x_2 = 1$) is true, otherwise it is in class 0.

R3. A vector is in class 1 if the statement ($x_1 = 1$ IMPLIES $x_2 = 1$) is true. Alternately, this can be stated ($x_1 \neq 1$) OR ($x_2 = 1$). Otherwise, the vector is in class 0.

R4. A vector is in class 1 if ($x_1 = 1$ AND $x_2 \neq 1$) OR ($x_1 \neq 1$ AND $x_2 = 1$) is true, otherwise it is in class 0.

Rule R1 defines necessary conditions for class membership, while rule R2 defines sufficient conditions. Rule R3 contains a negation. Rule R4 is a two-step process, and requires a more complex tree to diagram it.

The experiment was conducted as follows.

1.   A rule was chosen from R1–R4. Call this **R***.

2.   An object was chosen at random, with replacement, from U, and its class was determined by **R***. Let $\mathbf{x}(t)$ be the descriptive vector of the tth object chosen. The vector was added to S.

3.   Let $\mathbf{R}(t)$ be the trial classification rule in effect at the time $\mathbf{x}(t)$ is chosen. Initially $X(R(1)) =$ "All objects belong to class 1." When $\mathbf{x}(t)$ was chosen it was classified by both $\mathbf{R}(t)$ and **R***.

4.   If the classifications produced by $\mathbf{R}(t)$ and **R*** agreed, $\mathbf{R}(t + 1) = \mathbf{R}(t)$ and control was returned to Step 2. Otherwise $\mathbf{R}(t + 1)$ was generated by examining S using the one step look ahead algorithm described in Section 3.4 before returning control to step 2.

The cycle through Steps 2–4 was continued until the sample contained 10, 20, 30, or 100 objects. The experiment was replicated 10 times for each possible **R*** and number of objects in S. At the completion of each replication a "computation gain" score (CG) was calculated. Let R be the final rule produced.

$$CG = 1 - \cfrac{\text{Number of items in } U \text{ incorrectly classified by } R}{\text{Min}\begin{bmatrix}\text{Number of items of class 0 in } U, \\ \text{Number of items of class 1 in } U \end{bmatrix}} \qquad (20)$$

The CG measure can be thought of as the efficiency of the final classification rule relative to the simple classification rule "Call all objects in U members of the largest subclass of U." A score of 1 indicates that R is a perfect classifier. A score of 0 indicates that the rule developed by the algorithm is no better than the simple "most likely alternative" rule and a negative score indicates that the algorithm has actually produced a worse classification procedure than the most likely alternative rule. Figure 6-7 shows the CG score as a function of the form of **R*** and the size of the sample. There is a tendency to converge toward the correct rule, but the strength of this tendency depends upon the complexity of the (unknown) correct rule.

The question of how big a sample is needed to achieve a given level of accuracy is also of interest, since it addresses the problem of extracting a rule when memory is finite. Diehr and Hunt (1968) noted that in machine pattern recognition the limiting factor is often not the number of data points that can be investigated but instead the amount of computer storage needed to execute the pattern-recognition algorithm. Since sequential pattern recognition programs require specific records of objects which have been previously added to the sample, they may produce a substantial storage problem. The algorithm designer, then, should be concerned with economy of use of the computer storage space.

Diehr and Hunt referred to the computer storage area in which sample records were kept as the "memory bank." There are basically two ways in which a memory bank can be organized. We can look on it as a *fixed record length* file, in which case each record contains enough storage for the n components of a vector, plus an

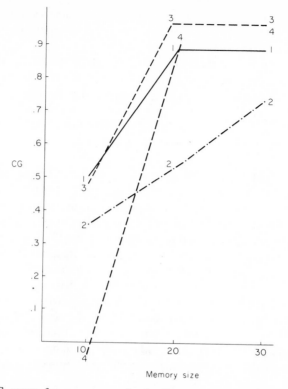

Fig. 6-7.   CG scores for convergence in the Hunt, Marin, and Stone studies. Numbers indicate data for R1–R4.

additional character storage space for the class name. Alternatively, we can treat the memory bank as a collection of *variable length records*, where each record requires space for the class name of an object and some selected data from the vector describing the object. (Some additional space is also needed for information concerning the layout of the variable length records. See Lefkovitz, 1968, for details.) Diehr and Hunt found that in pattern-recognition studies such as those of Hunt *et al.* the trial hypotheses [the $R(t)$] are progressively closer to being correct as the sample size increases. In particular, the relevant components of the vector typically appear in the trees of the $R(t)$ before they are correctly placed.[8] To make use of this fact Diehr and Hunt modified the Hunt *et al.* experiments as follows:

1.   Instead of presenting a fixed number of objects, they cycled through the set of 256 objects several times. However, they restricted the number of objects which

---

[8] Bourne (1965) cites evidence that this is true for human logical pattern recognition. People evidently solve classification problems ("concept learning problems" in the psychological literature) in two stages; first they note what is relevant to solution and then they note how it is relevant. Williams (1971) has simulated human concept learning by incorporating the Diehr and Hunt memory management scheme within the framework of a model of human memory.

could be in memory at any one time. They treated memory as consisting of a fixed set of locations, each capable of storing precisely one component of a vector, and modified data storage in the following way;

2. When an object was presented and correctly classified [so that $R(t + 1) = R(t)$], they stored only those components of the object description which were used to classify the object. For example, suppose that $R^* = R1$ and $R(t)$ was "If $x_1 = 2$ or $x_2 = 1$ then the object is in class 0," and let $x(t) = (3, 1, 2, 4)$. By the definition of R1, $x(t)$ is in class 0. $R(t)$ also makes this classification (though not for the right reason), so the information stored in the memory bank is ($x_1 = 3$, $x_2 = 1$, class = 0).

3. When an object was presented and incorrectly classified the entire description vector was stored. Following incorrect classifications a new trial hypothesis [$R(t + 1)$] was developed, using the same pattern-recognition algorithm except that it was modified to allow for the possibility that the value of some components of some objects would be unknown.

Diehr and Hunt conducted a number of experiments similar to those of Hunt *et al.*, except that in addition to using the Hunt *et al.* rules, they used some more complicated ones. Their results for problem R4 are diagrammed in Figure 6-8. It can be seen that the modified memory utilization procedure produces efficient pattern recognition at a fixed memory size.

Strictly speaking, these results show that in a certain artificial environment it is possible to demonstrate convergence. Somehow one should be able to say more than this. Since both the environment and the pattern-recognition algorithm are

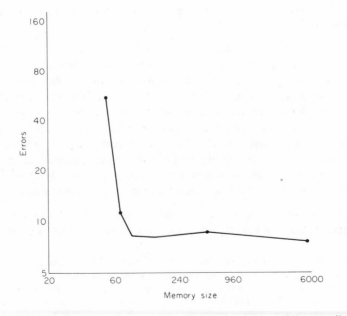

Fig. 6-8.   Mean errors on problem D-4. Obtained in Diehr and Hunt studies.

well defined, we ought to be proving theorems instead of proceeding inductively from experimental observations. Much of the experimental work on nonlinear pattern recognition has the same flavor as the earlier work on perceptrons; work which lead to conjectures that were later shown to be false or misleading. On the other hand, today we do not have theorems about sequential pattern recognition.

A second objection to artificial experiments is that they are too artificial. Suppose that all the conjectures are correct. Suppose even, that the experimental results are replaced by deductions about pattern recognition algorithms operating in the artificial environments. Does this tell us anything about more complex "real" pattern recognition situations? There is no clear answer to such an objection. Whether experiments in an artificial, tightly controlled situation will lead or mislead us in practical application is a question to be answered on a case by case basis.[9]

[9] Simon (1969) presents an excellent discussion of this issue in much more detail.

Chapter VII

GRAMMATICAL PATTERN CLASSIFICATION

7.0   The Linguistic Approach to Pattern Analysis

In this chapter we shall approach pattern recognition from quite a different direction. The concepts of mathematical linguistics which were presented in Chapter II will be reintroduced and related to pattern recognition. The reader who is not familiar with the basics of formal linguistics may wish to review Chapter II before proceeding.

The reason for studying formal linguistics in computer science is that there is a correspondence between a program and the design of a machine that can recognize the strings of symbols which are well formed expressions (sentences) in a language defined by a generative grammar. As in Chapter II, let G be the grammar, $L(G)$ the language it generates, T the set of terminal symbols used in G, x a string of terminal symbols, and T^* the set of all strings of symbols which can be constructed from T. The language recognition problem (or, equivalently, the linguistic pattern classification problem) is to sort any string $x \in T^*$ into the sets $L(G)$ or $7L(G)$ [$=T^* - L(G)$] in a finite number of steps. If it is possible to construct an algorithm for doing this, $L(G)$ is said to be a *recursive* language, and G a *decidable* grammar. There are some languages generated by rewriting systems which are not recursive. For these languages an algorithm can be constructed which will recognize any $x \in L(G)$ but it is impossible to guarantee that the algorithm will halt for all strings $x \in 7L(G)$. Such languages are said to be recursively enumerable, but not recursive. Any language generated by a generative grammar is recursively enumerable. If the generative grammar is a type 1 grammar (context sensitive, constituent structure grammar), or some subset of such grammars, then $L(G)$ is recursive. Obviously the string classification problem is solvable only if G is at least a type 1 grammar.

String classification provides a more general approach to pattern recognition than the vector classification approach taken up to this point. Vectors are strings of finite length,[1] and can be described using a generative grammar. Since there are only a finite number of vectors in any class, the "language" corresponding to the vectors in some (not necessarily continuous) subspace of the Euclidean description space can be thought of as a finite language.[2] Finite languages can be generated by a regular (type 3) grammar. But we have already argued that the linguistic pattern classification problem is solvable for the less restrictive type 1 (context free) grammars. Thus the linguistic pattern-classification approach must be more general. Furthermore, it was pointed out in Chapter II that the recognition algorithm for a type 3 language could be achieved by a program that did not utilize dynamic storage. This leads us to believe that vector-classification programs tend to be computationally simple. This is indeed the case, although they may also be quite large. All the algorithms given for pattern classification in Chapters III through VI can be written in FORTRAN, provided that enough fixed storage is available. Although it may not be obvious, this is as true for the sequential as for the parallel algorithms (Hunt, 1967).

Granted that the vector classification problem could be handled as a string classification problem, doing so is often neither intuitive nor particularly useful. But what about the string classification problems that have no vector classification formulation? In a very general sense, these are the problems in which membership of an object in a class does not depend on any Boolean combination of presence or absence of features, but rather upon the (possibly complex) relationship between the component parts of the object. Intuitively linguistic problems certainly have this feature. Miller and Shaw (1968) point out that there is no other way the translation algorithm of a compiler can operate. There is, for instance, no set of features which distinguishes a FORTRAN program from a meaningless string of keypunch characters.

In the process of linguistic classification a great deal of information about the structure of the string is uncovered. This can be useful—as is certainly the case of analyzing programming languages. The importance of structure can also be shown by a natural-language example. Which of the following strings are equivalent?

> *Loves Mary John*
> *John loves Mary*
> *Mary loves John*
> *John is loved by Mary*

Any English speaking person knows that only the last two strings have the same meaning. The first string is not an English sentence. The second, third, and fourth

---

[1] The statement assumes that each element of the vector can take on only a finite set of values. In theory, this is not the case for vectors defining points in a Euclidean space. In practice, however, there will be a limit to resolution in the space, so for any computing application the assertion is correct.

[2] A language which contains only a finite number of strings.

are all English sentences, but the second has a different deep structure than the third and fourth. In order to do anything sensible with these sentences one must both classify them and uncover the relationships among components.

Structural classification is not restricted to sets which are language by our intuitive notion. There is a great deal of interest in the design of a computing system which could recognize spoken words. Such a machine has proven very hard to build for a number of reasons. One is that in the acoustic phase of speech recognition the structure of the physical signal is more important than the presence of any absolute physical property. For instance, words must be recognized as being the same regardless of the sex of the speaker, although the speaker's sex obviously is a major determinant of the physical signal received at the machine's microphone. In another nonintuitive application, linguistic classification techniques have been applied to the recognition of classes of two-dimensional diagrams (Miller & Shaw, 1968). We shall deal with this topic in more detail later.

Given that linguistic methods can be applied in pattern classification, what about the corresponding pattern recognition task? This is called *grammatical inference*, and is the major focus of the chapter. Some formal definitions are given in the next section. Here we present a few generalities. In the inference problem the input data is a set of strings, each of which is identified as having been generated or rejected by an unknown grammar. We can think of the strings as the descriptions of certain objects in the environment which have been grouped together by an unknown law of nature. For example, the set of acceptable strings might be the descriptions of records obtained from a bubble chamber during a nuclear physics experiment. (Such an application has actually been studied by Narashiman, 1965). If we can uncover a grammar generating the strings, perhaps that grammar's rules can be related to our ideas of the physical processes operating in the experiment. Now let us turn to quite a different example. Suppose that we write down a set of assertions about political issues, such as

> *Appeasing Communists leads to further attacks on capitalism.*
> *Poor people ought to be supported by the government.*
> *No one who refuses an opportunity to work should be given government support.*

We then ask an informant to sort these strings into statements with which he agrees and statements with which he disagrees. The sorting establishes the sets of strings accepted or rejected by the (assumed) grammar our informant uses to generate political beliefs. If we could uncover the grammar, then would we not learn something about the informant's way of thinking about politics?

This, very briefly, is the rationale for studying grammatical inference. It has been claimed that the uncovering of grammars is, in a nontrivial sense, analogous to the construction of a theory in science. After all, a theory is nothing more than a set of rules for generating all possible observations. Is this not what a grammar is? A compelling argument can be made for the analogy. To date, however, no particularly useful results have been obtained by grammatical inference. At least to our knowledge, no one has yet written a program which has output an interesting theory in the form of a grammar. This may be too stringent a criterion. Work on grammatical inference is very new. In the following two sections we outline what little is known and how it might be applied.

7.1   The Grammatical Inference Problem[3]

7.1.0   NOTATION AND BASIC IDEAS

The first step is to develop a formal definition of both the grammatical inference problem and its solution. Most of the ideas to be introduced are based upon work by Feldman (Feldman, 1972; Biermann & Feldman, 1972), who in turn drew upon previous work by himself and his collaborators (Feldman, Gips, Horning, & Reder, 1969) and by Gold (1967). For formal proofs, the interested reader may wish to examine Feldman's (1972) presentation, which is particularly clear. For the most part we shall rely on intuitive illustration rather than formal proof.

A *sample* S_t is defined to be a sequence $x_1 \cdots x_t$ of t strings of symbols chosen from T^*. We assume that some of these strings have been generated by the unknown grammar G^*. We will denote by S_t^+ those strings in the sample which are acceptable to G^*, and by S_t^- those strings which are rejected by G^*.

$$S_t^+ = S_t \cap L(G^*), \qquad S_t^- = S_t \cap \daleth L(G^*). \tag{1}$$

The sentences in S_t^+ will be called *positive sentences* and the sentences in S_t^- *negative sentences*. A grammatical inference algorithm is a procedure for examining S_t and producing some grammar G_t. In most cases, we shall be interested in situations in which S_{t+1} is derived from S_t by adding exactly one more string,

$$S_{t+1} = S_t \cup \{x_{t+1}\}. \tag{2}$$

Equivalently, we can speak of the machine M which examines the successive sets $S_1, S_2, \ldots, S_t$, and produces a grammar G_i after each examination. The grammatical inference problem is solvable if a machine can be constructed which will eventually stabilize on the production of a grammar G which generates the same language as G^*,

$$L(G) = L(G^*). \tag{3}$$

In this case, G is said to *match* G^*. This is the strongest reasonable definition of a solution. We cannot require that a machine be built which will eventually reproduce G^*, since there may be infinitely many grammars which match G^*. The information in a sample does not discriminate between any pair of these grammars.

The trial grammars $\{G_t\}$ must be chosen from the *hypothesis space* **G** of

---

[3] In preparing this section I have benefited greatly by discussion of a review prepared by Binod B. Nayak as part of his Master of Science studies in computer science at the University of Washington.

grammars which M can produce. If the machine produces the members of **G** in some fixed order then it is said to *enumerate* **G**. At each stage t a good grammatical inference machine ought to choose from **G** the grammar that "most adequately accounts" for the finite sample S_t. There are three conditions that a grammar ought to meet to give an account for a sample. At the least, G_t must correctly classify all strings in S_t. In addition, it should give a "natural" account for S_t. This is closely linked to the statistical idea of likelihood—do the positive sentences of S_t follow naturally from the grammar G? For example, is G the grammar which derives the sentences of S_t^+ by shorter derivations than any other grammar $G'' \in$ **G**? A third consideration is that a trial grammar G ought to meet some criterion for simplicity of explanation. This notion is analogous to the statistical idea of "degrees of freedom." Grammar G should be preferred to grammar G'' if it contains fewer rules which are simply restatements of a specific situation which occurs in the sample. To be concrete, suppose that sample S_3 consists of the positive sentences

$$S_3 = \{a, ab, aba\}.$$

The grammar G_a

$$H \to a, \qquad H \to ab, \qquad H \to aba. \tag{4}$$

obviously is consistent with S_3. However, it is an ad hoc explanation good only for this sample. On the other hand all the derivations are short! We can compare G_a to grammar G_b

$$H \to a, \qquad H \to aA, \qquad A \to b, \qquad A \to bH. \tag{5}$$

This grammar contains more rules than G_a and requires more complex derivations to account for S_3, but it is preferable in that it is not a specialized explanation. Instead it treats S_3 as only one of many samples that might have been generated. Finally, we consider the grammar G_c

$$H \to a, \qquad H \to b, \qquad H \to HH, \tag{6}$$

which generates the set of all strings of a's and b's. Our intuition is that G_b is the preferred explanation for S_3, since G_a is too specialized and G_c too general. The problem is to utilize these intuitive notions in computation.

Gold (1967) has shown that the way in which the sample is constructed may limit the inferences that can be drawn and the efficiency of the inference process. The most important distinction is between samples which contain positive sentences only and samples which contain both positive and negative sentences. The former case is called *text presentation*, since it is analogous to the task of a person trying to decipher a language by examination of texts which contain only proper usage. The latter case is called *informant presentation*, since it is analogous to the case of a person trying to understand a language by questioning a native speaker. The advantage to informant presentation is that the learner can determine what is *not* allowed by the correct grammar G^*. This information can be very important.

Unfortunately, many applied problems in grammatical inference are inherently text presentation problems. A good example is the problem faced by an archeologist who is trying to understand a "dead" language by examining recovered manuscripts. He has no way of determining what string of symbols would be improper Sumerian or Phrygian.

A reasonable inference machine ought to make better inferences if it has more information. *Limit questions* study the assertions that can be made about the properties of the successive grammars $\{G_t\}$ that are derived from samples S_t as t is increased, and finally as t approaches infinity. Under what conditions are we assured that G_t will match G^* for sufficiently large t? This will be called the *matching question*. The *approach question* is closely related. In an inference process we begin with the set **G** of grammars which the inference machine could conceivably propose. We assume that G^* can be matched by some member of this set. At each step we find that certain grammars can be rejected; either they fail to generate some positive sentence in S_t or they accept a negative sentence in the sample. Let **G**(t) be the set of grammars that are still available for consideration at step t. If the inference machine is making progress **G**(t) should grow progressively smaller. We require that

$$\mathbf{G}(t + 1) \subset \mathbf{G}(t) \tag{7}$$

If the inference process can match G^*, then at some point **G**(t) will be restricted to grammars G' for which $L(G') = L(G^*)$. In other cases, however, **G**(t) may be an infinite set containing some grammars which do not match **G**(*). In this case the inference process does not match G^*. It may also be the case that **G**(t) does *not* include any grammar which matches G^*.

Finally, we will need to use the idea of adequacy functions. For the moment, we define an adequacy function $g(S_t, G)$ to be a measure of the extent to which grammar G is a good account for sample S_t. The range of g is from 0 to $+\infty$, with 0 being interpreted as a "perfect account" of S_t, and $+\infty$ as an indication that G is not compatible with S_t, either because $L(G)$ does not include all the positive sentences of the sample or because it does include one of the negative sentences. We will be interested in knowing something about the behavior of g as t increases without limit.

7.1.1 DECIDABILITY RESULTS

Imagine a hypothetical machine M, which infers grammars in the following manner. The machine is capable of enumerating the grammars in a possibly infinite set **G** of candidate grammars. An omniscient experimenter selects a grammar $G^* \in \mathbf{G}$ as the correct grammar. The experimenter then generates progressively increasing samples, $S_1, S_2, \ldots, S_t$ using either informant or text presentation. For each S_t the machine generates a corresponding G_t, by finding the first grammar in its enumerating sequence which satisfactorily explains S_t. We shall consider specific definitions of "satisfactory explanation" later, for the moment let us assume that this term implies that the conditions

$$S_t^+ \subseteq L(G_t); \qquad S_t^- \cap L(G_t) = \emptyset \tag{8}$$

must be met, and that G_t meets some criteria for adequate explanation of S_t and simplicity of its own internal structure. The machine M is said to solve the grammatical inference problem if, for any choice of G^*, there is some t^* such that $t > t^*$ implies that G_t matches G^*. Note that if M cannot match G by this criterion, then there is no machine that can, for M is simply a very general automaton capable of (a) recognizing one member of $\mathbf{G}$ from another and (b) determining whether or not a given string x is accepted by any $G \in \mathbf{G}$.

Gold (1967) has proven two important results concerning the inference problem. The first will be called the *general solvability theorem for informant presentation.*

> Let $\mathbf{G}$ be any set of decidable (i.e. recursive) grammars. If informant presentation is used the grammatical inference problem can be solved for any $G^* \in G$.

The proof is direct. Let M enumerate $\mathbf{G}$ in the order $G^1, G^2, \ldots, G^k$. Suppose that G^k does, in fact, match G^*. At any stage t in the inference process M takes as its trial hypothesis grammar the first grammar in the enumeration $G^1 G^2, \ldots, G^i$ which satisfies (8) by correctly classifying all sentences in S_t. Suppose grammar G^i is the first such grammar, so $G^i = G_t$. For $i < k, G^i$ does not match G^*, so as t is increased eventually a sentence will be found which is erroneously accepted or rejected by G^i. Grammar G^i is then dropped from consideration and the next acceptable grammar, $G^j, j > i$, is selected. Eventually G^k will be chosen. Let t^* be the stage at which this happens. Grammar G^k will never be subsequently rejected. Hence the inference problem has been solved.

The proof relies upon the fact that for any $G^i, i < k$, either a string in $L(G^*)$ will be rejected *or* a string in $7L(G^*)$ will be accepted. Under text presentation $(S_t = S_t^+)$ only the first type of error can be made. This is sufficient to destroy the solvability condition. Theorems by Gold, and Feldman (Feldman, 1972; Feldman *et al.*, 1969) support the following *unsolvability result for text presentation.*

> Suppose $\mathbf{G}$ contains grammars for all finite languages and any one infinite language. If text presentation is used, there is no machine which can solve the inference problem for arbitrary $G^* \in \mathbf{G}$.

The basis of the proof is that for any grammar $G \in \mathbf{G}$ which generates a finite language, there will always be another grammar $G' \in \mathbf{G}$ which includes that language. Thus for any finite t we have

$$S_t \subseteq L(G) \subset L(G'). \tag{9}$$

If $\mathbf{G}$ contained only finite languages we might avoid the problem, by noting that for any $G^* \in \mathbf{G}$ there would be a point at which no new sentences could be generated for S_{t+1}. Since there is at least one grammar, $G'' \in \mathbf{G}$ that generates an infinite language, however, the sample S_t might not terminate. So long as (9) holds, the machine cannot distinguish between G and G' (and, indeed, G' is one of an infinite set of such grammars). The possibility that (9) holds is always present if $G'' = G*$, since in this case a new sample can always be generated.

The inadequacy of text presentation is a serious problem, since, as was illustrated in the introduction, in many actual problem solving situations text presentation will be the only way in which the sample can be generated. Fortunately it is possible to use text presentation to define grammars which are progressively closer to the correct grammar in a precisely defined way. Feldman (1972) defines two interpretations of "closer," one of which includes the other.

Approach Condition

An enumerating machine M is said to approach $G* \in \mathbf{G}$ if

A1. After some $t*$, the grammars G_t $(t > t*)$ selected as a trial hypotheses by M accept any string acceptable to $G*$.

$$(\forall x \in L(G*))((t > t*) \supset (x \in L(G_t))) \tag{10}$$

A2. Any grammar G whose language properly includes $K(G*)$ will eventually be rejected.

$$(\forall G \in \mathbf{G})((L(G*) \subset L(G)) \supset ((\exists t')(t > t') \supset (G_t \neq G))) \tag{11}$$

An interesting implication of the two approach conditions is that if a machine approaches $G*$, then any incorrect grammar G will be the trial grammar G_t only for finitely many t, i.e., any particular wrong guess will be made only for a finite number of trials. We can think of $\mathbf{G}$ as being divided into progressively smaller subsets, each representing the set of answers that have not yet been ruled out. Even so, $G*$ will not necessarily be chosen, because the "progressively smaller" sets of still viable hypotheses could be infinite.

The machine M *strongly approaches* $G*$ if in addition to A1 and A2, the next condition is fulfilled.

Strong Approach Condition

A3. If there is a $G \in \mathbf{G}$ such that matches $G*$ $[L(G) = L(G*)]$, then $G_t = G$ for infinitely many t.

The strong approach condition states that any grammar which matches $G*$ will be chosen infinitely many times. The difference between this condition and the matching condition is that if matching occurs M eventually restricts its guesses to a set $G*$ of hypotheses which contain only matching grammars, while if M strongly approaches $G*$, the machine keeps rechoosing any $G \in \mathbf{G}$ which is a matching grammar, although in between these choices other choices of nonmatching grammars are permitted. Feldman has shown that a machine can be constructed which can strongly approach $G*$ using text presentation for any class of recursive grammars $\mathbf{G}$. This is interesting in one sense, since it shows that a machine can be constructed which will cycle about a correct grammar. On the other hand, the machine may never stabilize in its guesses. This is true even for a very restricted class of grammars, such as the finite state grammars.

Suppose we shift attention from matching to choosing the best explanation to account for the sample. This, of course, is what we would be doing in most practical applications. The first step is to define a best explanation. Let $g(S_t, G)$ be the *incompatibility function* for sample S_t and grammar G. The function g should be a computable function of the complexity of G and of the extent to which S_t fits naturally with G. Let $c(G, \mathbf{G})$ be the *intrinsic complexity* function relating G to a class of grammars $\mathbf{G}$, and let $d(S_t, G)$ be the *derivational complexity* function, measuring the extent to which S_t follows naturally from $L(G)$. For example, $c(G, \mathbf{G})$ might be an ordering of $\mathbf{G}$ by the number of nonterminal symbols in each grammar, whereas $d(S_t, G)$ could be the length of the longest derivation required to generate S_t from G. In general, c and d cannot be minimized simultaneously.

We assume that G is an acceptable explanation of S_t. That is, the conditions of (8) must hold. To choose between acceptable explanations we seek to minimize g subject to the following conditions.

C1. The incompatibility function must be a computable function of intrinsic complexity of the grammar and the derivational complexity of the sample given the grammar

$$g(S_t, G) = f(c(G, \mathbf{G}), d(S_t, G)).   \qquad (12)$$

C2. Given two equally complex grammars, the incompatibility function must be less for the grammar which provides the least complex derivation.

C3. Given two grammars with equal derivational complexity, the simpler of the two grammars is the least incompatible.

Conditions C2 and C3 may be summarized algebraically by noting that for any constant k, and any two real numbers a, b such that $a > b$, we require

$$g(k, a) > g(k, b)   \qquad (13)$$

and

$$g(a, k) > g(b, k).   \qquad (14)$$

Since $c(G, \mathbf{G})$ is a computable function of G with respect to $\mathbf{G}$, an enumerating machine could be designed which generated the elements of $\mathbf{G}$ in order of intrinsic complexity. Such an enumeration is called an *occam's enumeration*.[4] If $G^1, G^2, \ldots, G^i, \ldots, G^j$ is an occam's enumeration then $c(G^i, \mathbf{G}) < c(G^j, \mathbf{G})$ for $i < j$. What can a machine capable of an occam's enumeration do?

Clearly the machine could find the best explanation for any finite sample S_t. To do this the machine considers the grammars G^i in order of enumeration. Suppose

---

[4] After the English philosopher William of Occam, who stated the principle that simple explanations were to be preferred to complex ones.

that G^i is the first grammar that is acceptable by (8) given S_t. The machine computes $d(S_t, G^i)$, and since it already "knows" $c(G^i, \mathbf{G})$, it can establish

$$g(S_t, G^i) = m \tag{15}$$

as an upper bound on the incompatibility of the grammars to be considered. The best possible explanation of the sample would be a grammar for which $d(S_t, G)$ was equal to zero. By the definition of an occam's enumeration, either $\mathbf{G}$ is finite, in which case there is no problem, or there is some $k > i$ such that

$$f\big(c(G^k, \mathbf{G}), 0\big) > m. \tag{16}$$

Suppose G^k is the first grammar in the occam's enumeration which is so complex that it cannot be considered, even if $d(S_t, G^k) = 0$. Clearly the incompatibility function for any $G^s, s > k$, will be greater than m. Therefore M can restrict its choices of grammars to the finite set $\{G^i, G^{i+1}, \ldots, G^{k-1}\}$. It is worth noting that this proof applies to any set $\mathbf{G}$ of grammars for which the appropriate functions can be defined. In particular, the theorem is not restricted to decidable grammars.

Stronger results can be obtained if the sample is generated by informant presentation. Feldman (1972) has proven that as t approaches infinity the sequence of best guesses will approach G^* for any set $\mathbf{G}$. In fact, if the derivational complexity function has an upper bound as t is increased without limit, then an incompatibility minimizing machine using an occam's enumeration can match G^* in the limit. This is important, since the assumption of an upper limit to derivational complexity is quite a reasonable restriction. For example, suppose that there is some defined probability $p(\mathbf{x} \mid G)$ that a sentence would appear in a sample assuming that G is the correct grammar. We define $d(S_t, G)$ to be the probability that G would generate some sample of size t other than S_t. This is

$$d(S_t, G) = 1 - \prod_{i=1}^{t} p(\mathbf{x}_i \mid G) \tag{17}$$

which has an upper bound of 1. It can also be shown that the expected value of $d(S_t, G)$ is, in the limit, lower for those grammars for which $p(\mathbf{x}_i, \mathbf{G}) = p(\mathbf{x}_i, G^*)$ for all $\mathbf{x}_i \in T^*$. Thus the machine using an occam's enumeration will eventually choose the least complex grammar which both matches G^* and agrees with G^* in respect to the probability with which a sentence is to be generated.

We close with a caution and a speculative analogy. The caution is that these results are proofs about what grammatical inference algorithms can do. They are not necessarily practical instructions for writing the algorithms. A machine that must generate and evaluate each grammar in a sequence could spend an excessively long time examining incorrect grammars. Intuitively an incompatibility minimizing machine should be better, but would it be good enough? Also, it is often difficult to determine appropriate complexity measures. The problem is not that there is none available, but that a number of different ones can be proposed, and there seem to be no compelling arguments for using one or the other.

The speculation is addressed to psychologists. How can a child learn a language? It was once assumed that language learning was a process of "verbal conditioning" similar to the learning of mechanical skills. This proposition is not supported by the facts. Throughout the world children begin by speaking simple grammars, then progress to more complex ones. Furthermore, the order in which types of grammars are "considered" by the child appears to be relatively independent of the language which is being learned (Dale, 1972). To what extent can the idea of a natural enumeration of grammars be applied in constructing a model of first language learning? The idea may at first seem far fetched, but an examination of the proposals of some of the modern structural linguists (Lenneberg, 1967, 1969; Kelly, 1967) indicates at least a superficial resemblance between the ideas of an ontogenetic sequence of trial grammars and an occam's enumeration.

7.1.2 COMBINING BAYESIAN PROCEDURES WITH ENUMERATION

Linguistic enumeration results in selection of the best trial grammar, for a given sample. A statistical approach to grammatical inference would assign probabilities of being the "correct" grammar to each of a set of candidate grammars. The two approaches have been combined by Horning (1969) and in tangentially related papers by Hunt (1965) and Watanabe (1960).

The concept of a grammar must be modified to include the idea of "probability of occurrence of a sentence." Let G be a generative grammar. Each production of G will be of the form $\mathbf{r} \to \mathbf{s}$, where $\mathbf{r}$ and $\mathbf{s}$ are strings in the vocabulary of G. The k productions which have $\mathbf{r}$ as their left-hand element can be identified by $\mathbf{r}1$, $\mathbf{r}2, \ldots, \mathbf{r}k$. A *stochastic grammar* $S(G)$ is derived from G by assigning a probability measure[5] $p(\mathbf{r}i)$ to each production. This measure defines the probability that rule $\mathbf{r}i$ will be used to rewrite string $\mathbf{r}$, given that $\mathbf{r}$ is produced. Nyak (1972) offers the following example.

	Rule	Probability of use	(18)
$S1$	$S \to aA$	2/3
$S2$	$S \to aSB$	1/3
$A1$	$A \to bA$	1/4
$A2$	$A \to b$	3/4
$B1$	$B \to cB$	1/4
$B2$	$B \to c$	3/4

---

[5] If $\{p(\mathbf{r}i)\}$ is a set of probability measures, then $0 > p(\mathbf{r}i) \geqslant 1$, $\sum_{i=1}^{k} p(\mathbf{r}i) = 1$.

The string aabbcc is derived by the following steps.

String	Rule applied	Probability	(19)
S	S2	1/3	
aSB	B1	1/4	
aScB	B2	3/4	
aScc	S1	2/3	
aaAcc	A1	1/4	
aabAcc	A2	3/4	
aabbcc			

By multiplying the probabilities in the right-hand column of (19) the probability of generation of $x = aabbcc$ $[p(x \mid G)]$ is found to be 18/2304. This may seem small, but this is to be expected. Given our intuitive ideas of a language, any specific sentence in a language ought to have small probability of occurrence.

The previously used definition of matching is inadequate for stochastic grammars, since two stochastic grammars could generate the same language but differ in their assignment of probabilities of occurrences to specific sentences. *Stochastic matching* is defined as

> Two grammars G_a and G_b stochastically match if $p(x \mid G_a) = p(x \mid G_b)$ for all $x \in T^*$.

Recall the fiction of an experimenter who selects a grammar $G^* \in \mathbf{G}$ and uses it to generate sentences for a sample from which the identity of G^* is to be inferred. We shall assume that there exists a probability $p(G)$ that any particular $G \in \mathbf{G}$ will be selected for use as G^*. Furthermore, we assume that the learner (or inference machine) is capable of computing $p(G)$. The measure $p(G)$ will be called the a priori probability of selection of G. If the learner follows a Bayesian inference procedure to infer G from S_t he will assign a posteriori probabilities in accordance with the algorithm

$$p(G \mid S_0) = p(G) \tag{20}$$

$$p(G \mid S_t) = \frac{p(x_t \mid G) \cdot p(G \mid S_{t-1})}{\sum_{G' \in \mathbf{G}} p(x_t \mid G') \cdot p(G' \mid S_{t-1})} \tag{21}$$

Equation (21) presents a problem, for its computation requires summation over the elements of an infinite but not differentiable set $\mathbf{G}$. The "most obvious" way to avoid this problem is to restrict the computations to the set $\mathbf{G+}$ of grammars with a priori probabilities $p(G)$ greater than some arbitrary small value e.[6] Unfortunately

[6] Another alternative, which suffers from the same defects, is to consider only $\mathbf{G+} = G^1 \cdots G^k$, where $\sum_{i=1}^{k} p(G^i) = 1 - e$.

there is a defect in this solution. Whenever attention is restricted to any subset $\mathbf{G}+$ of the possible grammars $\mathbf{G}$, there is some arbitrarily small probability that G^* will be outside the set under consideration, i.e., it will lie in the set $\mathbf{G} - \mathbf{G}+$. Fortunately, there is a way the problem can be solved using the idea of minimization of the incompatibility function. Assume that the grammars of $\mathbf{G}$ can be enumerated in order of their a priori probabilities. Let the ordering be G^1, $G^2, \ldots, G^i, G^{i+1}, \ldots, G^j$, where $i > j - i$; $i < j$ implies that $p(G^i) \geqslant p(G^j)$. The same ordering will be produced by an occam's enumeration which uses the intrinsic complexity function

$$c(G, \mathbf{G}) = -\log_2\big(p(G)\big). \tag{22}$$

The derivational complexity measure may be made to reflect the probability of the sample,

$$d(S_t, G) = -\log_2\big(p(S_t \mid G)\big)$$

$$= -\sum_{i=1}^{t} \log_2\big(p(\mathbf{x}_i \mid G)\big). \tag{23}$$

A Bayesian decision maker forced to select a single grammar at each stage in the inference process should select that grammar which maximizes the quantity

$$q = p(S_t \mid G) \cdot p(G). \tag{24}$$

This is equivalent to minimizing the incompatibility function

$$g(S_t, G) = d(S_t, G) + c(G, \mathbf{G}),$$

where d and c are defined by (22) and (23). This shows that there is an enumeration procedure which minimizes an incompatibility function at each step of the sampling process and which selects the same grammar as would a Bayesian procedure. We have already observed that an enumeration procedure can select that grammar which minimizes the incompatibility function over an infinite set of grammars. Logically, this settles (affirmatively) the question of whether a Bayesian inference algorithm can be constructed which will select the Bayesian optimal grammar for every sample, even if the set of possible grammars is infinite. An appropriate algorithm is

Bayesian Enumeration Algorithm for Stochastic Text Presentation

1. *Let* $G^1, G^2, \ldots, G^i, G^{i+1}$ *be an occam's enumeration of an infinite set* $\mathbf{G}$ *using the intrinsic complexity function of (22).*
2. *Given* S_t, *find the lowest integer i such that* $S_t \subseteq L(G^i)$. *Calculate*

$$q = p(S_t \mid G^i) \cdot p(G^i). \tag{25}$$

3. *Find the lowest integer k such that* $p(G^k) < q$.

Comment: Clearly

$$p(S_t \mid G^k) \cdot p(G^k) \leqslant p(G^k) < q. \tag{26}$$

Furthermore, (26) is true for any $m > k$. Therefore, the integer j that maximizes $p(S_t \mid G^j) \cdot p(G^j)$ over **G** must lie in the interval from i to $k - 1$ inclusive.

4. *Select G^j from the set* $\mathbf{G+} = G^i, \ldots, G^{k-1}$ *using the normal Bayesian inference procedure. This will identify the Bayesian optimal selection of a grammar from* **G** *to account for S_t. Add x_{t+1} to S_t, forming S_{t+1}, and repeat the process from step 2.*

This reasoning establishes that Bayesian induction can be applied to choose the best grammar to explain a fixed sample. Naturally, we are also interested in the limiting behavior of the selection process. Are we assured that the correct grammar G^* will always be considered (i.e., will eventually become a member of **G+**) and what are the chances that it will be selected as the optimal grammar, once in **G+**?

Regardless of the location of G^* in the enumeration, there is some stage at which G^* must become a member of **G+** if it has not already been included. Let $G\#$ be the first grammar in the enumeration such that $L(G^*) \subset L(G\#)$. Under stochastic text presentation there will be some stage $t\#$ at which all earlier grammars in the enumeration will have been eliminated from consideration, due to their inability to accept some sentence in $S_{t\#}$. At this point $G\#$ will become the first grammar in **G+**. If $G\# = G^*$, then, of course, G^* will be in **G+**. The grammar G^* could also be inserted into **G+** at stage $t\#$ if the relationship

$$p(S_{t\#} \mid G\#) \cdot p(G\#) \leqslant p(S_{t\#} \mid G^*) \cdot p(G^*) \tag{27}$$

holds. In either case $t\# = t^*$. If (27) does not hold at stage $t\#$, it will at some subsequent stage $(t\# + k)$, since if $G\#$ does not stochastically match G^*,

$$\lim_{k \to \infty} \frac{p(S_k \mid G\#)}{p(S_k \mid G^*)} = 0. \tag{28}$$

Once G^* is included in **G+**, Bayesian induction will converge toward selecting it as the most likely grammar to explain S_t, as t increases without limit. To show that this is so, let X be the set of distinct sentences in S_t, regardless of the number of appearances of each. Let $f(\mathbf{x})$ be the frequency with which sentence $\mathbf{x}$ appears, and let $e_G(\mathbf{x})$ be the expected number of occurrences of $\mathbf{x}$ on the assumption that grammar G is being used to generate the sample. It can be shown (Hunt, 1965) that if Bayesian inference is used to select an hypothetical "best" grammar from a fixed set of grammars,[7] then the grammar selected will minimize the quantity

$$C = \sum_{\mathbf{x} \in X} \frac{[e_G(\mathbf{x}) - f(\mathbf{x})]^2}{f(\mathbf{x})} . \tag{29}$$

As t increases without limit, this function approaches its absolute minimum, zero, only for a grammar for which

$$e_G(\mathbf{x}) = e_{G^*}(\mathbf{x}) \tag{30}$$

---

[7] Strictly speaking, Hunt's result was proven for any finite set of hypotheses. Grammatical inference is a special case.

for all $x \in T^*$. This is a restatement of the stochastic matching condition. In the limit, then, the Bayesian enumeration algorithm will select the first grammar in the enumeration which stochastically matches G^*. This is a different result than the corresponding result for formal linguistic inference. By using information about frequencies, the Bayesian procedure can achieve stochastic matching from text presentation alone, whereas the formal linguistic enumeration procedures based on incompatibility minimization cannot even approach G^* using text presentation.

The fact that Bayesian inference uses, and in fact requires, text presentation, whereas linguistic inference is more efficient with informant presentation raises an interesting point. Would it be possible to combine stochastic text presentation with an efficient manner of informant presentation, using the fact that Bayesian induction indicates both which grammar is the best explanation for S_t and which other grammars are reasonable alternative explanations? For example, suppose that the Bayesian enumeration procedure indicates that G_a maximizes the a posteriori probability of selection, but that G_b's a posteriori probability measure is nearly as high. Would it not be reasonable to select x_{t+1} under informant presentation to be that string which was acceptable to only one of the two grammars? What would this do to the inference and enumeration algorithms? There has been no direct study of this issue. The interested reader is referred to tangentially relevant discussions by Hunt (1965) and Watanabe (1960, 1969).

The argument for creating Bayesian inference by enumeration methods depends upon our ability to produce the necessary occam's enumeration of **G**. It is intuitively reasonable to suppose that a machine could be designed to generate progressively more complex examples of some class of grammars. But could a machine be designed to produce progressively *less likely* grammars? The answer to this question probably belongs in the realm of philosophy, since it depends on what one's definition of "less likely" is. Some may feel that the intuitive argument for an enumeration based on probability is weaker than the argument for an enumeration based on complexity.

There is some question as to how widely the concept of a stochastic grammar can be applied. In some cases it seems useful. Swain and Fu (1972) have applied a very similar concept, stochastic programmed grammars, to the analysis of simple line drawings. The utility of their proposal is as yet unevaluated. Serious objections have been raised as to the appropriateness of a stochastic description of a natural language. There are two distinct objections. One is that the concept of symbols probabilistically following symbols in a natural language is fundamentally false, since this analysis takes no account of the meaning of what is being said. This is essentially a philosophical argument. The other attack is more pragmatic. Suppose that we grant that a statistical description of language generation via a stochastic grammar is possible in principle. In practice, natural languages appear to be so complex that the parameter estimation task in unmanageable, hence some other mode of linguistic descriptions must be found (Miller & Chomsky, 1963). This argument is by no means answered by showing that enumeration is valid, for Miller and Chomsky's point is that the enumeration procedure itself is unmanageable.

7.1.3 CONSTRUCTIVE PROCEDURES FOR GRAMMATICAL INFERENCE

In enumeration a sequence of grammars is generated independently of the sample, and each grammar evaluated against the sample. This is a helpful conceptualization of inference but is not likely to be a practical procedure. A great deal of time may be spent rejecting grammars that "obviously" ought not to be considered given the particular sample obtained. An alternative inference technique is to examine the sample, and, from it, construct a grammar which is (a) simple and (b) generates a language which includes all positive sentences in the sample. The construction procedure should restrict attention to "reasonable" grammars, i.e., grammars which at some stage t of the inference process are capable of generating S_t. Unfortunately fully satisfactory methods for doing this have not been found. The techniques proposed to date are restricted in the classes of grammars which they can produce and have a tendency to produce inelegant grammars from fairly small samples. It is likely that a number of new and better methods will appear in the next few years. Three somewhat different procedures will be used as illustrations. A fourth constructive technique specialized for two dimensional drawings will be presented in the section on picture grammars.

Solomonoff's Method

In an early discussion of the problem, Solomonoff (1964a,b) proposed a technique for inferring context free grammars from a finite sample. His method is based on the "uvwxy theorem" for context free languages (Hopcroft & Ullman, 1969), which is:

uvwxy Theorem

If L is a context-free language, then there are constants p and q > 0, dependent upon L, such that if there is a string z of length greater than p in L, then z may be written as a concatenation of the strings uvwxy, *where* vwx *has length less than q and* v *and* x *are not both the empty string,* λ. *We write* s^i *to symbolize the concatenation of string s with itself i times. If z, as described above, is in L, then for any integer i > 0 the string* uv^iwx^iy *is in L.*

Let us consider what this means. It states that if S_t is a sample from language L, and if L is generated by a context-free language, then if we can find a sufficiently long string $z \in S_t$, this string will consist of a *core* w, flanked by two repeating strings, v and w, only one of which may be null, and a *front* string u and *tail* string y, both of which may be null. The grammar of L must contain productions capable of generating such sentences. In particular, it must contain productions which can derive the infinite set of substrings of the form v^iwx^i from some nonterminal symbol $A_j (j = 0 \ldots n)$. One way this could happen would be for the grammar to contain the productions

$$A_j \rightarrow vA_ix; \qquad A_i \rightarrow w. \tag{31}$$

The problem becomes one of identifying the appropriate strings v, w, and x.

In a *simplified* version of Solomonoff's procedure the sample is searched for strings of the form $v^i wx^i$, making appropriate allowance for positions in which strings of null symbols can be found. Suppose that a set of strings is found which contains the same v and x strings, with possibly different w's. A nonterminal symbol Aj is chosen and the necessary productions are added to the grammar. This will, in general, leave us with a set W_j of core strings associated with the nonterminal A_j. The procedure may be applied recursively to W_j, to generate new nonterminal symbols and productions, until no more nonterminals can be added. The resulting grammar will generate a language which includes the sample.

To illustrate the method, a grammar will be inferred from

$$S_t = \{abccdef, abbbcdeeef, abcccdef, abbbccccdeeeef\}. \tag{32}$$

The grammar is inferred in the following steps.

(1)   All strings in S_t are of the form $a^1 wf^1$. Add to G the productions

$$
\begin{aligned}
A0 &\to aA0f, &\tag{33}\\
A0 &\to bcccde,\\
A0 &\to bbbcdeee,\\
A0 &\to bcccde,\\
A0 &\to bbbbccccdeeee.
\end{aligned}
$$

At this point the grammar is already an overgeneralization, since it permits strings of the form $a^k wf^k$, which may not be in the language. This is a specific illustration of the point already made concerning the theoretical limitations of text presentation.

The algorithm is next applied recursively to the set of strings $W_0 = \{bcccde, bbbcdeee, \cdots\}$. All these strings are of the form $b^k we^k$. Replace the last four productions of (33) by $A0 \to A1$ and add the productions

$$
\begin{aligned}
A1 &\to bA1e, &\tag{34}\\
A1 &\to cccd,\\
A1 &\to cccd,\\
A1 &\to ccccd.
\end{aligned}
$$

to the grammar. Now examine the core set W_1. The strings are of the form $c^k w\lambda^k$. Replace the last three productions of (34) with $A1 \to A2$ and add

$$A2 \to cA2\lambda, \qquad A2 \to d \tag{35}$$

to the grammar. Of course, λ may be dropped wherever it occurs. The set $\{d\}$ cannot be further reduced. The final grammar is

$$
\begin{aligned}
A0 &\to aA0f, &\tag{36}\\
A0 &\to A1,\\
A1 &\to bA1e,\\
A1 &\to A2,\\
A2 &\to cA2,\\
A2 &\to d.
\end{aligned}
$$

This grammar generates a language which includes but is not limited to S_t.

In applying the *uvwxy* algorithm one can choose several ways of defining the **v**, **w**, and **x** strings. The grammar inferred depends heavily upon the choice made. This point is illustrated by an example which, instead of being made up to demonstrate the algorithm, was constructed from the definition of an arithmetic expression.[8] For convenience the strings within S_t will be numbered;

$$S_4 = 1. \quad v; \tag{37}$$
$$2. \quad v + v;$$
$$3. \quad v + v + v;$$
$$4. \quad v + v + v + v.$$

If we define strings to be of length one, as was implied in the previous example, then all strings except 1. are the form $v^1 \mathbf{w} v^1$, and the initial set of productions is

$$A0 \rightarrow vA0v \tag{38}$$
$$A0 \rightarrow v \qquad \text{(to handle 1)}$$
$$A0 \rightarrow + \qquad \text{(to handle 2)}$$
$$A0 \rightarrow + v +$$
$$A0 \rightarrow + v + v +$$

This set of productions will lead to trouble. Subsequent steps in the analysis will produce a complex set of productions to handle a simple case. In addition, the production of (38) will permit strings such as $vvv + vvv$, which are not desired in the language. An alternative approach is to note that $A0 \rightarrow v$ clearly must be in the language, to handle string 1, and that string 3 has the form $(v+)^1 v(+v)^1$. Following this line of reasoning, the initial set of productions is

$$A0 \rightarrow v, \tag{39}$$
$$A0 \rightarrow v + v,$$
$$A0 \rightarrow v + A0 + v.$$

These productions alone will generate the required language, but they have an esthetic disadvantage, as first two productions define two different types of basic arithmetic expression. This difficulty can be avoided if the scanning algorithm takes yet another view of the sentences of (37). Recall that the *uvwxy* theorem allows either **v** or **x**, but not both, to be null. Suppose (37) is viewed as being a set of sentences in which **v** is the null string, λ. Then the final three sentences in the sample take the form $\lambda^k \mathbf{w}(+v)^k$. Suppressing λ^k, the resulting grammar is

$$A0 \rightarrow A0 + v, \tag{40}$$

$$A0 \rightarrow v.$$

These two productions will generate the required arithmetic expressions in such a way that the nesting in the grammar corresponds to a reasonable sequence of computations.

---

[8] My thanks to Mr. Patrick Russell for calling this example to my attention.

In summary, the *uvwxy* algorithm establishes a basis for the design of several grammatical inference algorithms. As the second example shows, the utility of the method in a particular case will depend heavily upon the precise choice of a scanning method to detect **v**, **w**, and **x** strings. Thus, the simplified Solomonoff method does not, in itself, dictate the design of a set of equivalent grammatical inference algorithms. The complete procedure used by Solomonoff is somewhat more elegant and restrictive in the grammars it generates, but many of the problems raised in the illustration remain. The interested reader should examine Solomonoff's (1964a,b) original papers and Biermann's (1971) discussion of Solomonoff's work.

GRIN1

Feldman (1967; Feldman *et al.*, 1969) has developed a grammatical inference program GRIN1, which infers finite state (regular) grammars, i.e., grammars whose productions are of the form $Aj \rightarrow aAk$ or $Aj \rightarrow a$. A regular grammar can always be found that will generate every sentence in a fixed sample, since the finite languages can be generated by regular grammars.

The program operates in three stages. In stage 1 a set of rules sufficient to generate the sample is produced. This set includes certain rules, called *residual rules*, which are of the form $Ai \rightarrow ab$. In the second inference stage the residual rules are dropped, leaving a regular grammar which generates the same language as that generated by the grammar found in stage 1. In the third state redundant productions are merged without affecting the language generated.

To illustrate the method a grammar will be inferred from the set

$$S_7 = \{caaab, bbaab, caab, bbab, cab, bbb, cb\}. \qquad (42)$$

In its initial stage GRIN1 searches for productions sufficient to account for the longest strings, then the next longest, then the next next longest, etc., adding as few productions as possible at each step. The last production used to account for a string of maximum length must contain a right hand side with exactly two terminal symbols. Such productions are *residuals productions* which will be removed in the next stage.

Let us go through the first stage. The first string to be analyzed is *caaab*. GRIN1 produces the production rules

$$
\begin{aligned}
A0 &\rightarrow cA1 \\
A1 &\rightarrow aA2 \\
A2 &\rightarrow aA3 \\
A3 &\rightarrow a\,b \text{ (residual rule).}
\end{aligned}
\qquad (43)
$$

A0 will be the "head symbol" of the grammar, and thus is to be used as the first symbol in each derivation. The next string to be analyzed is *bbaab* which is also a "longest string". The new production rules required are

$$
\begin{aligned}
A0 &\rightarrow bA4 \\
A4 &\rightarrow bA5 \\
A5 &\rightarrow aA6 \\
A6 &\rightarrow a\,b \text{ (residual rule).}
\end{aligned}
\qquad (44)
$$

The next string is *caab*. This can be partly derived from previously developed productions. By applying A0 → *c*A1, A1 → *a*A2, A2 → *a*A3, in order, the string *caa*A3 is produced. Adding the production

$$A3 \rightarrow b \tag{45}$$

completes the derivation. To account for *bbab* we begin with A0 → *b*A4, A4 → *b*A5, A5 → *a*A6 to produce *bba*A6, and then add

$$A6 \rightarrow b. \tag{46}$$

By similar treatments of the remaining strings, the rules

$$A1 \rightarrow b, \qquad A2 \rightarrow b, \qquad A5 \rightarrow b \tag{47}$$

are added. The complete grammar is

$$
\begin{array}{ll}
A0 \rightarrow c A1 & A0 \rightarrow b A4 \\
A1 \rightarrow b & A1 \rightarrow a A2 \\
A2 \rightarrow b & A2 \rightarrow a A3 \\
A3 \rightarrow b & A3 \rightarrow ab \text{ (residual rule)} \\
A4 \rightarrow b A5 & \\
A5 \rightarrow b & A5 \rightarrow a A6 \\
A6 \rightarrow b & A6 \rightarrow ab \text{ (residual rule).}
\end{array}
\tag{48}
$$

The first stage is ended.

In the second stage residual rules are merged into the rules that use them. For example, A5 → *b* is a rule which is redundant to A6 → *b*. To produce the *ab* sequence, we write A5 → *a*A5 instead of A5 → *a*A6. This permits us to drop the A6 residual rule. In a similar fashion A3 may be merged into A2. The resulting grammar is

$$
\begin{array}{ll}
A0 \rightarrow c A1 & A0 \rightarrow b A4 \\
A1 \rightarrow b & A1 \rightarrow a A2 \\
A2 \rightarrow b & A2 \rightarrow a A2 \\
A4 \rightarrow b A5 & \\
A5 \rightarrow b & A5 \rightarrow a A5
\end{array}
\tag{49}
$$

Note that the new grammar contains recursive constructions, and thus is capable of producing an infinite language.

In stage 3 additional simplification is achieved, without changing the language generated, by merging any two rules which are identical except for the naming of a variable symbol. In (49) A1 may be substituted for A2 in the second and third lines to produce two identical lines. A1 and A5 may be merged similarly. Note that to merge an expression the replacement must be made throughout the set of productions. The result of merging is the final, simplified grammar

$$
\begin{array}{ll}
A0 \rightarrow c A1 & A0 \rightarrow b A4 \\
A1 \rightarrow a A2 & A1 \rightarrow b \\
A4 \rightarrow b A1 &
\end{array}
\tag{50}
$$

A similar, but more complex program, GRIN2, has been written to infer *pivot grammars* from strings. This class of grammars can generate most of the features of simple programming languages.

Inference Using Semantics

Practical grammars are not abstract rules for generating strings, they are instructions for generating sentences which have meaning. In particular, consider the programming languages. The FORTRAN statement

$$A = B + C \tag{51}$$

is a command to a compiler to generate machine instructions for fetching the value of C, placing it in a temporary register, fetching the value of B, adding this value to the temporary register, and then placing the contents of the temporary register in A. Using nested brackets to indicate the order of operations, the semantic structure of (51) is

$$[[A] = [[B] + [C]]] \tag{52}$$

where each level of nesting corresponds to an elementary operation in the FORTRAN language. Crespi-Reghizzi (Crespi-Reghizzi, 1971; Crespi-Reghizzi, Melkanoff, & Lichter, 1973) has developed a grammatical inference procedure which makes use of knowledge of the semantics of sentences in a sample to infer the underlying grammar of the language. Crespi-Reghizzi *et al.* have suggested that the procedure could be used to aid designers of programming languages, by permitting them to illustrate the language they wish to use rather than requiring that they define it formally. An appropriate grammar would then be generated from the examples by inference.

The inference algorithm proceeds in three steps; (1) a *trial* grammar is first generated for each string in $S+$. (No consideration is given to "nonsentences.") The resulting grammar for a string is sufficient to generate precisely that string. (2) Each trial grammar is then generalized in a manner to be described. (3) Finally, the various trial grammars are merged, so that the final grammar is the union of the generalized trial grammars. The details of the method can be illustrated by considering the derivation and generalization steps for a single sentence.

$$s = [[a] + [[a] + [a]]] \tag{53}$$

in which a has the intuitive definition "variable name." (53), then, is an example of a string of summations. The semantic structure dictates right to left order of evaluation.

In order to derive the trial grammar, let z be a string in s which exists at the deepest level of brackets. The string z will consist entirely of terminal symbols. The rule $Ni \rightarrow z$ obviously must be in the language. Substituting Ni for z removes one level of bracketing. Now let y be a string at the (new) deepest level of bracketing. Note that y may contain nonterminal symbols. Add $Nj \rightarrow y$ to the grammar, and proceed as before. Continue the addition of rules until the outermost string of brackets is removed. In the case of example (53) the results are, in sequence

Step	String	Rule	(54)
0	$[[a] + [[a] + [a]]]$	$N1 \to a$	
1	$[N1 + [N1 + N1]]$	$N2 \to N1 + N1$	
2	$[N1 + N2]$	$N3 \to N1 + N2$	
3	$N3$	$S \to N3.$	

Grammar (54) generates exactly string (53). To generalize the grammar nonterminal symbols are merged into classes which are defined by the similarity of the terminal strings derivable from the nonterminals within a class. The simpler of two algorithms developed by Crespi-Reghizzi *et al.* will be described. In it two nonterminal symbols are merged into one if the sets of terminal symbols which may appear as the first and last terminal elements of the strings derivable from each nonterminal symbol are identical. More precisely, let $Ni \to z$ be a rule in the trial grammar. The left terminal set, $Lt(z)$, of the string z is defined to be the set of terminal symbols which can appear as the leftmost *terminal* symbol (not necessarily the leftmost symbol) in a string derivable from z. We define $Rt(z)$ similarly for rightmost terminal symbols. The *terminal* profile of Ni, $Tp(Ni)$, is the ordered pair $\langle Lt(z); \quad Rt(z) \rangle$. Two nonterminal symbols, Ni, Nj, are merged if their terminal profiles are identical.

The application of the generalization method to grammar (54) is a convincing exercise. First, however, a rule is needed for calculating the terminal profile of a nonterminal symbol.

Let z be a string and z_j the first terminal symbol in z. The leftmost terminal set $Lt(z)$ consists of the union of z_j and the union of the left terminal sets of all nonterminal symbols which precede z_j in z. An analogous definition holds for $Rt(z)$, excepting that z_j is interpreted as the rightmost terminal symbol in z, and the union is over the right terminal sets of all nonterminals following z_j in z.

Now to generalize grammar (54). The first step is to find $Tp(N1)$. This is done by

$$N1 \to a; \qquad Lt(a) = Rt(a) = \{a\} \tag{55}$$

$$Tp(N1) = \langle a; \quad a \rangle.$$

Substituting the terminal profile of $N1$ for $N1$ makes it possible to calculate $Tp(N2)$.

$$N2 \to N1 + N1 \to \langle a, a \rangle + \langle a; a \rangle, \tag{56}$$

$$Lt(\langle a; a \rangle + \langle a; a \rangle) = \{a+\}, \qquad Rt(\langle a; a \rangle + \langle a; a \rangle) = \{a+\},$$

$$Tp(N2) = \langle a+; a+ \rangle.$$

Substituting again, this time to calculate $Tp(N3)$,

$$N3 \to N1 + N2 \to \langle a; a \rangle + \langle a+; a+ \rangle, \tag{57}$$

$$Lt(\langle a; a \rangle + \langle a+; a+ \rangle) = Rt(\langle a; a \rangle + \langle a+; a+ \rangle) = \{a+\},$$

$$Tp(N3) = \langle a+; a+ \rangle.$$

Since $N2$ and $N3$ have identical terminal profiles, $N2$ replaces $N3$ wherever the latter occurs. The resulting grammar is[a]

$$N1 \to a, \tag{58}$$
$$N2 \to N1 + N1,$$
$$N2 \to N1 + N2,$$
$$S \to N2.$$

Grammar (58) produces strings such as

$$[[a] + [a]], \qquad [[a] + [[a] + [a]]], \tag{59}$$
$$[[a] + [[a] + [a[a] + [a]]]],$$

which is a reasonable generalization of string (53). In fact only 10 judiciously chosen sentences are required to produce a grammar for all arithmetic expressions involving addition operators except the single term $[a]$. Clearly the algorithm has some interesting properties. Nevertheless, it also has its drawbacks. Crespi-Reghizzi *et al.* note that it is limited to the generation of a restricted set of operator-precedence grammars (Irons, 1961). To remedy this, they propose an amplication of the generalization technique in which nonterminals are merged only if their terminal profiles are identical when restricted to at most k derivations. The resulting inference procedure generates a more powerful class of grammars. Another important characteristic of their method, which is not clearly an advantage or disadvantage, is that it is very dependent on the provision of a good set of sample sentences. This forces the human language designer to be on his toes, which is perhaps a good thing.

7.1.4 CONCLUSIONS CONCERNING FORMAL GRAMMATICAL INFERENCE

This is a new and challenging field. The mathematical problems posed are well defined and interesting, and very little is known. We have presented here only a few of the approaches that might be taken. The interested reader should consult the review by Biermann and Feldman (1972) for details. None of the methods of inference proposed to date appear to be remotely practical devices for inferring the grammar of an artificial language as complex as, say, A L G O L, although it is possible to infer grammars for fragments of such a language. Certainly we are in no position to begin to attack the natural languages! In the next section we shall explore the

---

[9] In this example it is always the case that $Lt(y) = Rt(y)$. This need not be true. The string

$$s_2 = [[([[a] + [a]])] + [a]]$$

produces the trial grammar:

$$A1 \to a, \qquad\qquad Tp(A1) = \langle a;a \rangle,$$
$$A2 \to A_1 + A1, \qquad Tp(A2) = \langle a+;a+ \rangle,$$
$$A3 \to (A2), \qquad\qquad Tp(A3) = \langle (;) \rangle,$$
$$A4 \to A3 + A1, \qquad Tp(A4) = \langle +(;a+ \rangle.$$
$$S \to A4,$$

question of whether or not it is possible to apply gramatical techniques in describing classes of two-dimensional figures. This application is interesting, but raises some specialized questions. Setting aside such practical applications, Feldman (1972) points out that there remain a host of interesting theoretical questions. For instance, what is the effect of noisy data, i.e., erroneous identification of some sentences as positive or negative? What rules should a grammatical inference machine follow in interacting with an informant? Finally, as Crespi-Reghizzi's work suggests, some consideration of the semantics of the sentences in the sample may be of great help.

7.2 Grammatical Analysis Applied to Two-Dimensional Images

7.2.0 PICTURES AS LINGUISTIC ENTITIES

It would be nice if computers could accept two-dimensional pictures as input. For one thing, they could give the correct change for various currencies. Similar devices could analyze photographs from weather satellites, conduct information retrievals based on fingerprint photographs, and sort medical specimen slides. The reader does not need to be very imaginative to think of many more applications. Science fiction writers have assumed that the picture reading machine is a routine bit of technology that we have not quite yet developed, but certainly will have well in hand by A.D.2001, which is just over 25 years away. George Orwell assumed that face recognition would be possible in 1984. The truth may be a bit more sobering. Computer vision at a level of proficiency approaching human vision is certainly several years away. The capability of analyzing line drawings may be closer, but even that is surprisingly elusive. This section discusses a method for the analysis and classification of very simple line drawings, based on grammatical classification and inference. The reader will probably be willing to agree that in principle, the analysis could be extended to quite detailed pictures. He should also note that the extension would rapidly become very, very complicated. The analysis of pictures which seem simple to a person can involve considerable computing effort.

We have already seen that the concept of an acceptable input to a computing process is intimately tied to the concept of a well-formed expression in a formal language. On the other hand, although grammatical analysis can always be applied to define inputs to a computer program, it is not always the most natural way to characterize a program and its action. Early attempts at picture classification involved a preprocessing step in which the picture to be analyzed was mapped into a fixed-length vector. Each element of the vector was a variable indicating the value of a grayness function at a specified point on the picture plane. Vector classification methods were then applied to manipulate the "pictures" internally. This approach was not notably successful. This may have been because some interesting classes of pictures are defined by relationships between their components, rather than by the possession of any absolute characteristic. An excellent example is the distinction between the classes of picture "circle inside square" and "square inside circle." We have already noted that concepts such as this are quite hard to handle using normal vector classification techniques (Minsky & Papert, 1969).

In discussions of the "state of the art" in artificial intelligence (Minsky, 1959, 1963) and computer science generally (Ledley, 1962) it was noted that formal grammars provide concepts that are at once familiar to computer science and appropriate for describing classes defined by relations between components. These suggestions have lead to the development of a number of "grammars" for the analysis and classification of line drawings. This work has been well reviewed (Fu & Swain, 1971; Miller & Shaw, 1968) and we shall not attempt to do more than present the basics of the approach. Having done this, we shall examine the grammatical inference problem for picture grammars. We conclude with a few critical comments on the linguistic approach to picture classification.

7.2.1   ILLUSTRATION OF BASIC CONCEPTS

In order for grammatical analysis to work, the class of pictures of interest must be specified in terms of component relationships, which can be mapped into strings of symbols. These well-formed expressions correspond to "well-drawn pictures," and can be regarded as a language with an associated grammar. In most cases we need only consider the languages generated by phrase structure grammars.

Consider the figure ⌂

TABLE 7-1

Binary Operations for Pictorial Expressions[a]

Symbol	Meaning	String example	Picture described by string
↑	is above	○ ↑ ▢	
→	is next to	○ → ▢	
⊙	in inside of	○ ⊙ ▢	
◐	is inside on bottom of	○ ◐ ▢	
↨	rests on top of	△ ↨ ▢	
↦	rests next to	▢ ↦ ▢	

[a] After Ledly (1962).

This can be described by the string □ ↑ △ where ↑ is interpreted as "is on top of." Ledley (1962) used this and similar operations (listed in Table 7-1) to define a language for describing cartoon drawings of houses. The context-free grammar generating the language is presented in Table 7-2. It generates for the pictures in Figure 7-1a but not those in Figure 7-1b.

To use a picture grammar three steps must be executed. First the grammar capable of generating descriptions for the class of pictures of interest must be defined. This often requires ingenuity. Next a way of parsing suitable for the grammar must be found. This is usually a straightforward problem. Finally, we must find a way of mapping from a picture into its associated string. This can be quite difficult. It is often not at all trivial to go from a visual image to a string of computer-readable symbols. Continuing with the cartoon house example, we shall use a picture-to-string mapping method that works with simple grammars and sharply defined line drawings.[10] To illustrate the technique we shall develop a linguistic string for the cartoon house shown in Figure 7-2.

TABLE 7-2
Language for Describing Line Patterns of Houses

Vocabulary

N = ⟨door⟩, ⟨window⟩, ⟨chimney⟩, ⟨wall⟩,
    ⟨gable⟩, ⟨roof⟩, ⟨front view⟩, ⟨side view⟩, S

$T = \left\{ \quad \right\}$

Grammar

⟨door⟩	:: =					
⟨window⟩	:: =					
⟨window⟩	:: =					
⟨chimney⟩	:: =					
⟨wall⟩	:: =					
⟨gable⟩	:: =					
⟨roof⟩	:: =	⟨window⟩ →	⟨door⟩	⟨wall⟩	⟨window⟩	
⟨front view⟩	:: =	⟨wall⟩	⟨chimney⟩	⟩gable⟩	⟨chimney⟩	⟨roof⟩
⟨side view⟩	:: =	⟨gable⟩	⟨wall⟩	⟨roof⟩	⟨wall⟩	
S	:: =	⟨front view⟩ | ⟨side view⟩				

[10] The method is not solely a pedagogical device. Ledley (1964) has applied it successfully in the analysis of chromosome slides.

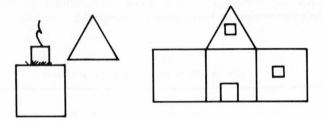

Fig. 7-1. Pictures corresponding to strings in a picture grammar. (a) Two well-formed "houses." (b) Two ill-formed "houses."

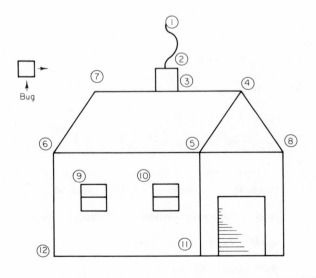

Fig. 7-2. Cartoon house to be analyzed.

Assume that the picture has been digitalized, so that a program can "follow lines" by following continuous 1's in the matrix representation of the picture. *Conceptually* line reading is done by moving a "bug" (shown in the upper left of Figure 7-2), from left to right and top to bottom until a line is encountered. The bug then follows the line until it returns to a point it has previously visited. When faced with a choice between untraversed paths the bug turns clockwise. The movements of the bug will successively trace out the different components of the picture. In Figure 7-2, the bug will encounter its first line at location 1, and will then trace the element ⌷ , a chimney. In order to produce what is, linguistically, a string of terminal symbols there must be a grammar defining each element in terms of basic moves of the bug—e.g., horizontal line followed by vertical line at its right end, connecting to a horizontal line at lower end of the vertical line, etc. Such grammars are rather tricky to write, since the lines must terminate at the appropriate vertices. See Clowes (1969) or Rosenfeld (1969a,b) for details and Shaw (1969) or Narashiman (1965) for examples. In any event, assume that when point 2 is reached the bug can recognize that it has traced out a basic element. It will also have detected, at 3, a line that it did *not* traverse. The scan, therefore, is resumed at 3, tracing the figure defined by 3-4-5-6-7-4, a roof.[11] Since the co-ordinates of both roof and chimney are known, the string $\square^5$ ↑ $\square$ can be inferred. The scan then returns to 4, which is a point at which the line 4-8 was detected but not followed. The element 4-8-5 will be traced next. Eventually the entire house will be traced, excepting the windows. To detect these the bug must resume its interrupted left–right scan at 1, and continue, ignoring lines already traced, until it contacts the windows at points 9 and 10. When the windows are traced their coordinates may be used to locate them inside the wall defined by 6-5-11-12. At this point a string of terminal symbols will exist. This can be examined by conventional parsing techniques to make sure that the picture is, indeed a "well-formed house."

This description is very brief, and may have made things seem simpler than they are. It is worth repeating that the methods work well for simple line drawings, but rapidly become complicated as the pictures become complex or when the "straight" lines become just a little wavy. Unfortunately the really interesting pictures are precisely of this sort. As this is a specialized topic, it will not be dealt with. (The presentation by Rosenfeld, 1969b, provides a good introduction.) The inference problem posed by picture analysis is more directly relevant.

7.2.2 INFERRING PICTURE GRAMMARS

Despite the frequent admonition to use visual aids in teaching, very little is known about the logical process of inferring relationships from pictures. The most

---

[11] There are other scanning strategies that could be followed. The reader is invited to try some of them. Note that in this example, as in other element tracings, the bug must somehow recognize that single lines can be parts of two elements—as is the case for the line segment shared by the top of the roof and the bottom of the chimney.

advanced study in this field is by Evans (1971). Evans pointed out his research is only a beginning and has yet to achieve any notable results. Nevertheless, the problems encountered by Evans's method seem typical of the problems that will have to be solved by future picture-grammar inference programs, and so the work is worth discussing for this reason alone. In addition, Evans's approach embodies a number of ideas that may well be retained in future approaches.

Evans uses a somewhat different linguistic notation than the generative grammar notation we have been using. His formalisms are more tied to those of the LISP programming language than to Comsky's development of rewriting systems. It will become clear as we proceed, however, that Evans's notation is equivalent to the more conventional notation for a phrase-structure grammar. The "terminal elements" in Evans's system are *primitive object types* and *predicates*. The object types are the building blocks of the pictures to be recognized. Examples of primitive object types are line segments, arcs, circles, and squares. The initial representation of a picture (i.e., the data from which the inference is begun) is simply a list of the primitive object types in the picture, together with some information about their size and location on the picture plane. The second type of terminal elements, the predicates, are relationships that may hold between any two picture components, regardless of whether the components are primitive object types or compound objects. The latter correspond to nonterminal symbols in a conventional grammar. For example, *inside* (x, y) ("x is inside of y") is a predicate which has the value *true* if and only if all components of the (possibly compound) object x are located within the perimeter of object y. Note that the definition of *inside* implies that there is a program that can examine the digitalized picture to locate y, determine whether it has a perimeter, and then determine whether the locations of the elements of x are inside the perimeter. In general it is true that a predicate names a subroutine which examines a digitalized picture to determine whether a particular spatial relationship holds between its arguments.

A *grammar*, in Evans's terms, is a set of productions, each of which defines a (compound) object in the picture language under discussion. A production consists of three parts, a production name, a list of production arguments, and a list of statements that must be true of the arguments. The latter list is broken into two components: a list of object types, with one entry for each of the arguments, and a predicate which must have value *true* when applied to the arguments. If the left-hand part of the production is the head symbol, H, of the grammar, then the production defines a *scene*, or picture which can stand alone. This corresponds to a well formed expression. Otherwise a production defines various types of sub-expressions.

We can illustrate these concepts with the "face" of Figure 7-3a. Suppose that the terminal vocabulary is

> *Object types:*   dot, square, line segment, circle
> *Predicates:*   inside, above, left, horizontal, and

A possible grammatical description of 7-3a is the production

      face → (x, y):   features (x), head (y); *inside (x, y)*   (60)
         A face is features inside a head.

    head → (x):   *circle (x)*
      A head is a circle.

    features → (x, y, z) eyes (x), nose (y), mouth (z); *and (and (above (x, y),*
      above (x, z)), above (y, z))
      A features is eyes above a nose and a mouth, and a nose above a mouth.

    eyes → (x, z):   *dot (x), dot (y); left (x, y)*
      Eyes are a pair of dots, one to the left of the other.

    nose → (x):   *square (x)*
      A nose is a square.

    mouth → (x):   *line segment (x); horizontal (x)*
      A mouth is a horizontal line.

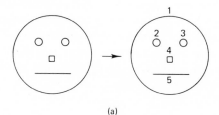

(a)

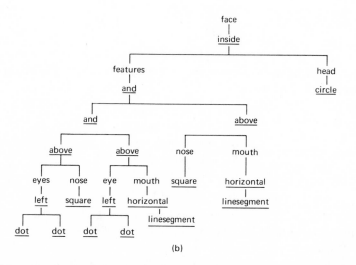

(b)

Fig. 7-3.   Grammatical analysis of a cartoon face. (a) Face → face with labeled components. (b) Parsing of face by arbitrary grammar.

The productions of (60) can be represented as a parsing tree, in typical phrase structure manner. This is shown in Figure 7-3b.

The inference problem is to develop grammars similar to (60) by analyzing sets of scenes, $S_1 \cdots S_n$, where each scene is a complete picture. The resulting grammar should contain productions sufficient to account for each scene, and in addition meet other (rather ill defined) criteria for power and complexity. There are three stages in the inference process.

Object Construction Stage

Each scene is initially represented by a list of the primitive objects in it. New objects are created and added to each scene's list by finding all predicates which are true for any subset of objects already on the list. This requires that we evaluate each *n*-ary predicate against every ordered subset of size *n* in the list. The resulting computing problem is of little concern so long as we are studying simple pictures such as we have illustrated, but could rapidly pose problems if we were to study scenes approaching the complexity of, say, an aerial photograph, simply because of the number of subsets. In any case, the process of applying predicates and creating new objects is continued until no new objects can be produced. The list is then examined for objects which contain every primitive component of a scene as subcomponents. Such objects are possible grammatical descriptions of the scene.

To obtain an intuitive feeling for first stage actions, consider the following example. We label the primitive components of Figure 7-3a as shown, producing (61) as a "first pass" list of objects in a face.

$$
\begin{array}{ll}
1: & (1)\ circle\ (1) \hfill (61)\\
2: & (2)\ dot\ (2)\\
3: & (3)\ dot\ (3)\\
4: & (4)\ square\ (4)\\
5: & (5)\ line\ segment\ (5)
\end{array}
$$

Application of the predicates *inside*, *above*, and *left*[1,2] to all pairs of objects in (61) produces a second pass list,

$$
\begin{array}{ll}
6: & (4, 5)\ above\ (4, 5) \hfill (62)\\
7: & (1, 2)\ inside\ (2, 1)\\
8: & (1, 3)\ inside\ (3, 1)\\
8: & (1, 4)\ inside\ (4, 1)\\
10: & (1, 5)\ inside\ (5, 1)\\
11: & (2, 3)\ left\ (2, 3)
\end{array}
$$

The process is repeated using the expanded list. Note that during the expansion the location information must be created for new objects. For instance, it is reasonable to say that object 11, the eyes, is above the nose, 4, since the center of gravity of the dots is directly above the nose. Individually, the dots are not above the nose.

[1,2] The predicates *horizontal* and *and* have been dropped for simplicity of illustration.

The third pass list is

$$
\begin{array}{rl}
12: & (1, 6) \ inside \ (6, 1) \\
13: & (1, 11) \ inside \ (11, 1) \\
14: & (4, 11) \ above \ (11, 4) \\
15: & (5, 11) \ above \ (11, 5) \\
16: & (6, 11) \ above \ (11, 6)
\end{array}
\tag{63}
$$

The final pass produces

$$
\begin{array}{rl}
17: & (1, 14) \ inside \ (14, 1) \\
18: & (1, 15) \ inside \ (15, 1) \\
*19: & (1, 16) \ inside \ (16, 1) \\
20: & (5, 16) \ above \ (16, 5) \\
*21: & (1, 20) \ inside \ (20, 1)
\end{array}
\tag{64}
$$

Objects 19 and 21 have been marked in (64) because they contain all primitive objects as components. The appropriate parsing trees for these objects are shown in Figure 7-4. Note that constant names replace the variables of a grammar. To

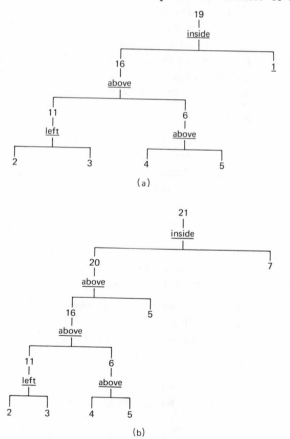

Fig. 7-4.   Two object structures for a face.

produce a grammar from an object description the constant names (1, 2, 3, etc.) are replaced by object type indicators with variables as arguments. Since there are two structural descriptions we produce two grammars,

$$H \rightarrow (x, y): circle\ (x),\ A16\ (y);\ inside\ (y, x); \qquad\qquad (65)$$
$$A16 \rightarrow (x, y):\ A6\ (x),\ A11\ (y);\ above\ (x, y);$$
$$A6 \rightarrow (x, y):\ dot\ (x),\ dot\ (y);\ left\ (x, y);$$
$$A11 \rightarrow (x, y):\ square\ (x);\ line\ segment\ (y);\ above\ (x, y),$$

which has been derived from 19, and

$$H \rightarrow (x, y):\ circle\ (x),\ A20\ (y);\ inside\ (y, x); \qquad\qquad (66)$$
$$A20 \rightarrow (x, y):\ line\ segment\ (x),\ A16\ (y);\ above\ (y, x);$$
$$A16 \rightarrow (x, y):\ A6\ (x),\ A11\ (y);\ above\ (x, y);$$
$$A6 \rightarrow (x, y):\ dot\ (x),\ dot\ (y);\ left\ (x, y);$$
$$A11 \rightarrow (x, y):\ square\ (x),\ line\ segment\ (y);\ above\ (x,, y).$$

Note that two grammars have been derived from one scene. In the more general case, we would have n scenes, and want to derive a single grammar which generated them all. To do this we take all possible unions of grammars, one from each scene. Thus if we had three scenes, with three grammars derived from the first scene, two from the second, and three from the third, we could produce $3 \times 2 \times 3 = 18$ distinct grammars, any of them capable of generating all scenes in the original sample. Each of these grammars is then subjected to simplification, in the next stage.

Grammatical Simplification Stage

The goal of this stage is to reduce an unwieldy grammar by three operations: removal of redundant rules, insertion of new nonterminal symbols to define classes of terminal symbols, and identification of two nonterminals with each other in order to unify two or more productions into a single production. The operations used are best shown by an illustration involving the scenes "triangle" and "square." The only primitive object permitted is the line segment (*seg*). The two predicates are *join* (x, y), which is interpreted as "the head of x attaches to the tail of y" and *close* (x, y), which is interpreted as "the ends of x and y are joined." The initial scenes and operations are shown in Figure 7-5. Suppose that an inference process has generated the following grammar for a square:

$$H \rightarrow (x, y):\ seg\ (x),\ A1\ (y);\ close\ (x, y); \qquad\qquad (67)$$
$$A1 \rightarrow (x, y):\ seg\ (x),\ A2\ (y);\ join\ (x, y);$$
$$A2 \rightarrow (x, y):\ seg\ (x),\ seg\ (y);\ join\ (x, y),$$

and the grammar for a triangle

$$H \rightarrow (x, y):\ seg\ (x),\ A3\ (y);\ close\ (x, y); \qquad\qquad (68)$$
$$A3 \rightarrow (x, y):\ seg\ (x),\ seg\ (y);\ join\ (x, y).$$

The goal is to simplify and perhaps generalize these grammars. The first rules of both (67) and (68) would be identical if A3 and A1 were the same symbol. This can be achieved by using the second line of (68) as an alternative production for A1,

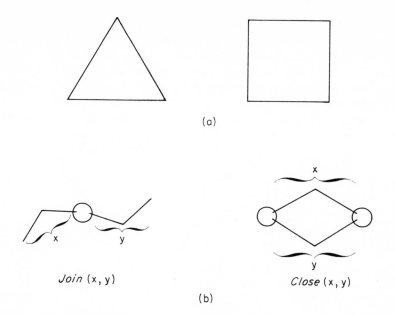

Fig. 7-5. Data for derivation of grammars (67) and (68). (a) Scenes used. (b) Operations of *join* and *close*.

which does no violence to the idea of a grammar, for a single nonterminal may serve as the left side for any number of rewriting rules. Making the identification and merging, the grammar becomes

$$H \rightarrow (x, y):\ seg\ (x),\ A1\ (y);\ close\ (x, y) \qquad (69)$$
$$A1 \rightarrow (x, y):\ seg\ (x),\ A2\ (y);\ join\ (x, y)$$
$$A2 \rightarrow (x, y):\ seg\ (x),\ seg\ (y);\ join\ (x, y)$$
$$A1 \rightarrow (x, y):\ seg\ (x),\ seg\ (y);\ join\ (x, y)$$

The right hand sides of the last two productions are identical. Therefore we can eliminate the higher-numbered nonterminal, making appropriate replacements of A2 by A1 whenever A2 appears. We now have the final grammar,

$$H \rightarrow (x, y):\ seg\ (x),\ A1\ (y);\ close\ (x, y); \qquad (70)$$
$$A1 \rightarrow (x, y):\ seg\ (x),\ A1\ (y);\ join\ (x, y);$$
$$A1 \rightarrow (x, y):\ seg\ (x),\ seg\ (y);\ join\ (x, y),$$

which is a recursive grammar defining the class of closed polygons. Note how the grammar has been simplified while the language which it generates has been expanded. The method of expansion, however, insures that the grammar will always be able to generate the original sample.

Weakening of Type Restrictions

The operations applied in the first and second stages are syntactically justified, in the sense that one can prove what their results will be in terms of expansion of the grammar. In the final stage a heuristic technique for grammar expansion is introduced. The argument is simply that it seems to be useful. The device is to weaken the requirement that the productions in the grammar carry with them all the object type and relation information present in the sample from which the grammar was derived. Suppose that a grammar contains n rules (usually $n = 3$) which are identical except that at one position the object type or predicate names vary. By replacing the varying names by the permissive "any" (i.e., a predicate which has value *true* for all arguments) the n rules may be collapsed into a single one. This procedure, of course, has no linguistic justification whatsoever.

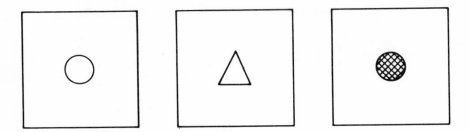

Fig. 7-6.   Scenes for inferring the grammar of (71) and (72).

Nevertheless, it is intuitively appealing because it frees us (sometimes) from depending on the vagaries of the sample. For example, suppose that the scenes from which the grammar is to be inferred are the figures shown in Figure 7-6, and that the primitives are the object types *square, triangle, circle,* and *dot* and the predicate *inside*. At the end of the second-stage analysis the grammar is

$$H \rightarrow (x, y): triangle\ (x), square\ (y); inside\ (x, y) \tag{71}$$
$$H \rightarrow (x, y): circle\ (x), square\ (y); inside\ (x, y)$$
$$H \rightarrow (x, y): dot\ (x), square\ (y); inside\ (x, y)$$

The rules differ only in the type of the first argument. Disregarding this produces

$$H \rightarrow (x, y): any\ (x), square\ (y); inside\ (x, y) \tag{72}$$

defining the class of all figures with square borders. Intuitively this seems a good solution to the problem.

Grammatical inference itself is in its infancy, so picture grammatical inference must be a neonate. As Evans's work shows, pattern-grammar inference leads to more reliance on ad hoc rules, such as the type weakening rule, than do purely formal approaches to the inference problem. Applying inference to pictures also forces us to consider some real practical problems, such as the combinatorial explosion which occurs when we attempt to apply all possible predicates in all possible ways. Despite these drawbacks, grammatical inference in picture recognition offers a new and challenging approach to an old problem, drawing inferences from visual patterns. Its success will depend upon the success of the linguistic approach to pattern classification. We have already offered the argument for this approach. In the next section we make a few cautionary observations.

7.2.3 CRITIQUE OF PICTURE GRAMMARS

Picture grammars are appealing to the computer scientist because they provide a way in which complex entities can be reduced to familiar formalisms. Such situations can be a seductive trap for any discipline. The question is not whether formal linguistic methods can be applied to picture processing; we know that they can by appeal to the theory of computability. The question is "When is it useful to apply the concepts of linguistics?" Clearly there are some cases in which picture grammars do illuminate our understanding of a distinction between classes of pictures. Our examples have stressed such situations. But what are the characteristics of situations in which we would recommend against using a linguistic analysis?

A fundamental assumption of linguistics is that our understanding and ability to deal with pictures will be enhanced if we know the process by which the pictures were generated. Watanabe (1971) has provided some examples of picture classes for which this is not true. Consider the classes of pictures shown in Figure 7-7.

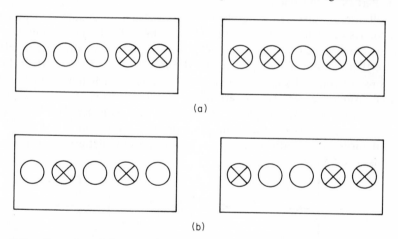

(a)

(b)

Fig. 7-7.   Examples of classes with useless generating rules. (a) Pictures generated from π. (b) pictures generated from a random number table.

Class (a) is the set of pictures generated from five circles, by picking an arbitrary digit as a starting point in the string $\pi = 3.14159\ldots$ and for the starting and subsequent circles placing an X in the circle if and only if the corresponding digit is five or more. Class B pictures were produced by using a table of random numbers to make the same assignment of X's to circles. Knowing the generating rule helps us little in our understanding of the structure of the pictures. One may object that this is a forced example. It is not, it is a sharpening of a general point. In many interesting cases pictures are defined by complex statistical dependencies between components, and not by relationships in the sense that the term is used in grammatical analysis. Pictures whose classification depends upon the perception of depth provide an excellent case in point. One of the major cues to depth perception is the change in gradient of the background texture in a picture (Gibson, 1950). In the case of stereoscopic pictures the crucial statistical dependencies between points on the picture plane are considerably more complex (Julesz, 1970) although the same principle holds. It is hard to see what sort of grammar could summarize this information.

A second point that will be familiar to psychologists is that many pictures are grouped together by semantic rather than syntactical rules. Perhaps the most striking examples are the various perceptual illusions. We can classify very different retinal images as "pictures of a box about six feet long" by using our knowledge about the real-world characteristics (size, shape, etc.) of various other objects depicted with the box. For instance, we can recognize projections of a square box viewed from different angles. No purely syntactical approach can achieve this sort of classification, since the classification is based on our knowledge of shapes and optics, rather than an analysis of the information present in the picture itself. This point is particularly important in scene analysis, which will be discussed in more detail in Part IV of this book.

Not all useful rules can be stated as phrase-structure grammars. One of the characteristics of such a grammar is that substitutions of equivalent components do not alter the character of a string. This permits a syntax driven compiler to recognize that $A + A + A + A + A$ and $A + A + B + B + (D - E)$ are both arithmetic expressions. In some classes of two-dimensional images such substitutions are not permitted. Watanabe uses Islamic art forms to illustrate this. Some examples are shown in Figure 7-8. Any sequence of repeating figures is permissible (providing some other restrictions are met), but component substitution is *not* allowed. A somewhat more mathematical example is based upon the definition of a group of operations. The figures

are members of the class of figures which are mapped into themselves by a 90° rotation. How is this to be expressed grammatically?

These objections can be considered theoretical ones. There are a number of practical issues which also must be resolved in any specific application. The problem of unmanageable complexity has already been mentioned. An even more critical problem concerns the definition of the terminal elements. Strictly speaking, this is not a linguistic problem since formal linguistics assumes the existence of a known terminal alphabet. In practice, this may be the hardest step in the analysis process. About 300 of the 400 papers cited in a review by Rosenfeld (1969a) were concerned with some phase of the feature definition problem! Another practical problem is the criterion for determining that a component or relation exists in a

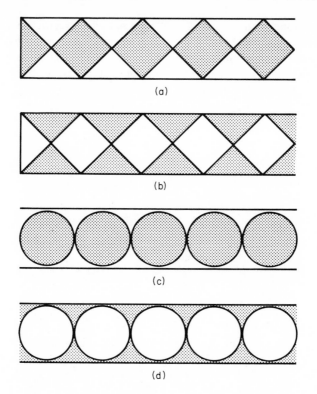

Fig. 7-8.   Islamic art patterns. Color and phase may be shifted, but the components of (a) or (b) and (c) or (d) are not interchangeable on an element-by-element basis.

picture. In our cartoonlike examples this problem has been ignored; it is clear in our context that either the roof is on the wall ⌂ or it is not □△!

Parents and teachers (usually) recognize houses drawn by first graders, although the location of roof relative to wall may be somewhat variable. Similar indeterminacies arise if we have to deal with noise aerial photographs, or if a primitive relationship may be expressed between objects which are not contiguous in a picture.

The existence of noise in the data does not, in itself, pose any unsolvable conceptual problem. One can simply use some variant of a stochastic grammar (e.g., Swain & Fu, 1972) to recognize that squares are usually drawn as □ but may be □ . The practical problem remains, since stochastic grammars require much more complicated parsing algorithms. Also, a single picture may map into several well formed expressions, with varying probability. We do not have a good grasp of the resulting difficulties for pattern classification, let alone an understanding of the implications of this for grammatical inference.

In conclusion, there is no question that the grammatical viewpoint in picture classification is an important one. It is an excellent way of approaching some problems, including many which are ill represented in vector classification. The converse statement is true. Statistical distinctions, especially, are often well handled by vector classification methods. Finally, there are a number of picture processing applications for which neither grammatical nor vector classification procedures are suitable. The field awaits new ideas.

Chapter VIII

FEATURE EXTRACTION

8.0 General

Vector and grammatical classification methods presuppose the existence of features that can be measured. Finding the features is often itself a considerable step toward solving the problem. We can think of any machine as having a set of "most primitive" measurements to which it can respond. These measurements may not correspond to the true properties of the objects being classified. The object itself may be composed of a (possibly small) number of features, all of which are reflected in different ways in the basic measurements. For example, suppose we were trying to classify the state of water pollution in a river on different days. A natural way to do this would be to measure the amount of sulphur, arsenic, and other chemical compounds in the water. Now, in fact, oxygen, sulphur, arsenic, mercury and other compounds would not be placed in the river as such. What would be happening is that upstream from the measuring instrument there might be a sawmill, factory, and any number of other waste-producing sources, with each source providing a particular type of waste, which would be a compound of the basic chemicals being measured. In order to describe the pollution state of the river accurately, however, one might want measures of the amount of (compound) waste from each source on a given day, rather than a record of the downstream chemical measures.[1] But suppose we did not know of the existence of the upstream sources. Would it be possible to infer their existence from an analysis of the downstream measures? This is an example of the feature-detector problem.

There are two general ways to approach feature analysis, depending upon the assumptions one wants to make about the most primitive measures. In the *multivariate analysis* approach, each primitive measure is treated as a continuously measurable combination of the underlying features. The problem is seen as one of reducing the description space from the m-dimensional space defined by the

---

[1] Of course, for other purposes, just the opposite might be true.

original measures to a smaller k-dimensional space defined by the features. The classification problem is then studied in the reduced space. The problem of defining the k-dimensional space has been studied intensely under the rubric "factor analysis." The basic mathematics involved are described by Tatsuoka (1971). Harman (1967) has produced a definitive work describing techniques currently in use. Meisel (1971) and Fukunaga (1972) discuss pattern recognition as a branch of applied mathematics. Because of the existence of this literature, and because we are not sure that this is what most scientists mean when they speak of "feature detection," we shall describe the method only briefly.

The second approach to feature detection regards the basic measurements on an object as a sequence of binary vectors. The features are assumed to be subsets of the basic measurements. The problem is to define a useful set of such subsets. An illustrative and important practical example arises in machine detection of handwritten characters. Imagine that the alphanumeric characters to be classified are projected on a 10 x 10 grid. The squares of the grid are numbered in normal left–right, top-to-bottom reading order, so that each point of the grid can be thought of as a binary variable that is on if and only if a line crosses it. A simple optical system can then be used to transform the character into a vector of 100 primary measures, $x_1 \cdots x_{100}$. A typical input is shown in Figure 8-1. It is

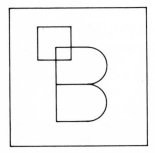

```
0 0 0 0 0 0 0 0 0 0
0 0 0 0 0 0 0 0 0 0
0 0 0 1 1 1 1 0 0 0
0 0 0 1 0 0 1 0 0 0
0 0 0 1 1 1 0 0 0 0
0 0 0 1 0 0 1 0 0 0
0 0 0 1 0 0 1 0 0 0
0 0 0 1 0 1 1 0 0 0
0 0 0 1 1 1 0 0 0 0
0 0 0 0 0 0 0 0 0 0
```

Projection on grid   Digital representation

Fig. 8-1.   Representation of hand-printed character. 2 x 2 local figures shown in interior square.

reasonable to assume that any actual character will be formed from the union of a number of features, such as a diagonal left to right line, a horizontal line, and right to left diagonals. For example, from the set of components $\{-, |, /, \backslash, ^D, D, (\}$ we can construct the letters **A**, **B**, **C**, **P**. If we did not know what these components were, we ought to be able to determine them by noting local regularities in the various letters. Mathematically, this means that we should develop an algorithm that detects regularly recurring clusters of values of the binary variables $\{x_i\}$.

8.1   Formalization of the Factor-Analytic Approach

Let X be an $n \times m$ matrix, each of whose rows describes an object in terms of the m basic measurements. Thus the row vector describing the ith object is

$$x_i = x_{i1}, x_{i2}, x_{i3}, \ldots, x_{ij}, \ldots, x_{im}. \tag{1}$$

If each basic measurement reflects a weighted sum of the values of the object on a number of primitive object features, $f = 1 \cdots k, k < m$, then

$$x_{ij} = a_{1j}f_{i1} + a_{2j}f_{i2} + \cdots + a_{kj}f_{ik}, \tag{2}$$

where the coefficient a_{pj} reflects the contribution of the pth feature to the jth measure and the value f_{ip} is a measure of the extent to which object i possesses feature p. Given these definitions we can define X in terms of the $n \times k$ matrix of individual feature values and the $k \times m$ matrix of contributions (called *loadings*) of the pth feature (or factor, to be consistent with the factor analytic literature) to the jth measure. The matrix equation is

$$X = F \cdot A \tag{3}$$

The problem is to determine F and A given the observations of X. Clearly there will be infinitely many matrices for which (3) will hold, so some additional restriction is needed. A number of different criteria have been considered; the interested reader is referred to Harman's (1967) discussion of the question. The commonest technique, called *principle components analysis*, will be described.

Let R be the matrix of correlations[2] between the basic measures. The diagonal elements r_{ii} are determined by the multiple correlation of r_i with the remaining $m - 1$ measures.[3] Let Q be a matrix whose rows are the eigenvectors associated

---

[2] If x and y are two measures, on a collection of n objects with mean $\bar{x}, \bar{y}$ and standard deviations σ_x, σ_y, the correlation between them is

$$r = \frac{\sum_{i=1}^n (x_i - \bar{x}) (y_i - \bar{y})}{n \sigma_x \sigma_y}.$$

[3] The multiple correlation between a measure x and a set of measures $Y = \{y_j\}$ is the correlation between $\{x_i\}$ and a linear combination $z_i = \Sigma a_j y_{ji}$ of the y_j's, where the coefficients a_j are chosen to maximize the correlation between x and z.

with the k largest eigenvalues of R, in order from largest to smallest. Finally, let λ_p be the pth eigenvalue. The matrix A is obtained by the normalization

$$a_{ij} = q_{ij}(\lambda_j)^{1/2} \left(\sum_{s=1}^{m} q_{sj}^2 \right)^{-1/2}. \tag{4}$$

The factor matrix can then be obtained by rearrangement of (3).

$$F = X \cdot A^{-1}. \tag{5}$$

The only problem that remains is to establish the value of k. This is normally done by a statistical criterion. Let V^2 be the sum of the squared distances of each point x_i from the centroid of the n points in the original, m-dimensional measurement space, and let W_k^2 be the same measure for the points $\{f_i\}$ in the k-dimensional factor space. Beginning with $k = 1$, the size of the feature space is steadily increased until either $V^2 - W_k^2$ or $1 - (W_k^2/V^2)$ becomes sufficiently small.

The principle components technique has a clear-cut visualization. The method finds the best fitting ellipsoid in m space for the points x_i defining the objects at hand. Each factor corresponds to one of the axes of this ellipsoid, with the largest axis being found first, then the next largest, continuing until the stopping criterion is met.

8.2   Formalization of the Binary Measurement Case

Suppose that the matrix X is a binary matrix, in which a 1 in position x_{ij} indicates that on measuring object i the jth "on–off" measure was set to "on." We will say measure j is in the on state in this case. The feature model assumes that in the presence of certain object properties certain measuring devices will be set on, and that several features may combine to set the same measure. A feature, then, can be thought of as a binary vector f_j, of length m, for which $f_{js} = 1$ if and only if feature j sets measure s on. Let $\oplus$ be the operation of Boolean addition, i.e.,

$$1 \oplus 1 = 1; \qquad 1 \oplus 0 = 1; \qquad 0 \oplus 0 = 0. \tag{6}$$

We write $\sum_{i=1}^{n \oplus} x_i$ for the Boolean summation of several binary variables. Let S_i be the unknown set of features present in object i. Then, to obtain the description vector,

$$x_i = \sum_{f_j \in S_i}^{\oplus} f_i \tag{7}$$

Equation (7) can be written in a neater form. Let $*$ be the multiplication operation on Boolean matrices, i.e., an operation in which $\sum^{\oplus}$ replaces $\sum$, but otherwise matrix multiplication is as normally defined. Finally, let B be the $n \times k$ matrix with entry b_{ij} if and only if object i possesses feature j.

$$X = B * F. \tag{8}$$

Equation (8) establishes a set of Boolean equations. Unfortunately, finding their solution may not be practical, so a number of heuristic constructive methods for feature detection have been developed. These are described in the next section.

8.3   Constructive Heuristics for Feature Detection

8.3.0   UHR AND VOSSLER'S IMITATION METHOD

A series of experiments by Uhr and Vossler (1963) have shown that a simple procedure of imitating parts of the input patterns can produce quite good feature detection. They were concerned with classification of two-dimensional images, such as cartoon faces, hand-printed letters, and speech spectrograms, rather than abstract vectors, and therefore the concept of distance between variables is sensible. Their program relies heavily upon this fact. The input to the program was a series of 25×25 binary patterns, similar to the one shown in Figure 8-1. From these large patterns they constructed sets of 5×5 "local operators" by comparing the 5×5 pattern at a given location across several 25×25 pictures. If a number of the original pictures had a nearly identical 5×5 configuration of bits at *any* coordinate location, then the subpicture was accepted as a feature. The 25×25 pictures were then described by the identity and location of the features in them. This permitted the program to distinguish between, say, "horizontal line at the top" and "horizontal line at the bottom." For example, **A** would be described by the location of Λ, -, /, \. This information was summarized in a vector **z** describing the object in terms of its features. A simple clustering algorithm was then used to classify the **z** vectors.

Uhr and Vossler also used the clustering process to indicate when new features were needed. At any one time, the program used only a fixed number of features. The clustering algorithm would weight each component of the **z** vector in terms of its usefulness in distinguishing among different classes. If a component had near zero weight the associated feature would be dropped, and the 25×25 input picture reexamined to define a new feature. The process of feature generation, clustering, and new feature generation produced a very powerful pattern-recognition system. In fact, their program could actually learn visual discrimination tasks more rapidly than people, provided that the objects to be classified were *not* familiar to humans (Uhr, Vossler, & Uleman, 1962). The flavor of this conclusion is illustrated by knowing that the program outperformed people in recognizing classes of abstractly defined mathematical forms, but was outperformed by people in recognizing cartoon faces.

8.3.1   BLOCK, NILSSON, AND DUDA'S FORMALIZED IMITATION METHOD

A more formal approach to the same problem has been taken by Block, Nilsson, and Duda (1964). To explain their method, a slight extension of the notation is needed. Instead of representing a primitive description as a binary vector we will represent the description of the *j*th object by a set of integers,

$$P(i) = \{j\} \tag{9}$$

where $1 \leqslant j \leqslant m$, and $j \in P(i)$ if and only if in the description vector of the *i*th object $x_{ij} = 1$. Figure 8-2 shows a cross projected on a 5×5 grid, the grid represented as a set of variables, and the vector and set representations of the cross on the grid. Define a *mask* σ to be a subset of the integers from 1 to *m*. If a mask is present in object *i*, then $\sigma \subseteq P(i)$.[4]

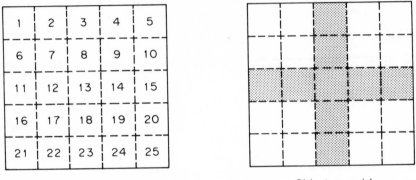

Basic grid   Object on grid

Fig. 8-2.   Different representations of the description of a picture on a grid. Vector representation of object:

$$x = (0,0,1,0,0,0,0,1,0,0,1,1,1,1,1,0,0,1,0,0,0,0,1,0,0)$$

Set representation of object:

$$P(j) = 3,8,11,12,13,14,15,18,23.$$

Given a set of descriptions, $S = \{P(i)\}$, $i = 1, \ldots, n$, the problem is to find a minimum set $\Phi = \{\sigma\}$ of masks such that for every description, $P(i)$, there exists a set of masks $M(i)$ with the properties

$$M(i) \subseteq \Phi; \tag{10}$$

$$P(i) = \cup \sigma, \qquad \sigma \in M(i). \tag{11}$$

Note that for a given set of masks, Φ and $P(i)$, $M(i)$ may not be unique.

To find a minimal set Φ of masks we want to find those masks which are included in many descriptions. Block *et al.* define a procedure for doing this even though the individual masks are not known initially. Let $\mathbf{F}(\sigma)$ be the set of object

---

[4] Block *et al.* use the term "feature." We distinguish between masks and features because the Block *et al.* definition is identical to the definition of mask used in the analysis of perceptrons.

descriptions containing mask σ. Block *et al.* propose that σ be defined as the intersection of these descriptions, i.e.,

$$\sigma = \overset{i}{\underset{P(i)\in F(\sigma)}{\cap}} P(i) \tag{12}$$

Thus if $F(\sigma)$ is known, we can define σ. In most cases, however, $F(\sigma)$ will not be known. It is necessary to decide when two patterns, $P(i)$ and $P(i*)$ do contain a common mask, since if they do, then the intersection of the two descriptions will also include the mask. This is done by setting a threshold θ for common nonzero elements in two patterns. Assume that $p(i)$ and $P(i*)$ and contain a common mask if and only if

$$\eta(P(i) \cap P(i*)) > \theta \tag{13}$$

Consider first the problem of defining exactly one mask. Let the sample S be ordered in some arbitrary fashion, so that $S = P(1), P(2), \ldots, P(n)$. The mask σ will be defined by successive examination of each of the descriptions in S. Let $\sigma(i)$ be the tentative definition of σ after the ith description in S has been examined, so that $\sigma = \sigma(n)$. The algorithm is

$$\sigma(0) = \{j\}, \qquad j = 1 \ldots m \tag{14}$$

$$\sigma(i + 1) = \begin{cases} \sigma(i) \cap P(i + 1) & \text{if and only if} \quad \eta(\sigma(i) \cap P(i+1)) > \theta \\ \sigma(i) & \text{otherwise} \end{cases}$$

We use Figure 8-3 to illustrate the procedure by example. Examination of these figures immediately suggests several possible masks: diagonals, horizontals, and vertical lines in particular locations. (This is a major difference between the Uhr–Vossler and Block *et al.* techniques; the masks are tied to specific locations on the grid. This is also true of the perceptron definition of a mask.) The illustration extracts a left-to-right diagonal.

To restrict consideration to masks of size 3, set $\theta = 2$. The successive steps in definition of the first mask are

$$\sigma(0) = \{1, 2, 3, \ldots, 25\}; \tag{15}$$

$$\eta(\sigma(0) \cap P(1)) = 8 > 2; \qquad \sigma(1) = \{1, 5, 7, 13, 17, 19, 21, 25\};$$

$$\eta(\sigma(1) \cap P(2)) = 5 > 2; \qquad \sigma(2) = \{1, 7, 13, 19, 25\};$$

$$\eta(\sigma(2) \cap P(3)) = 1 \leqslant 2; \qquad \sigma(3) = \sigma(2);$$

$$\eta(\sigma(3) \cap P(4)) = 5 > 2; \qquad \sigma(4) = \{1, 7, 13, 19, 25\};$$

$$\eta(\sigma(4) \cap P(5)) = 5 \leqslant 2; \qquad \sigma(5) = \sigma(4);$$

$$\sigma = \sigma(5).$$

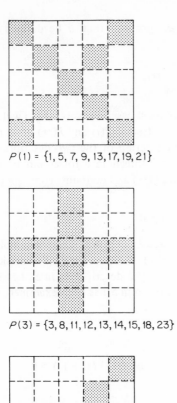

$P(1) = \{1, 5, 7, 9, 13, 17, 19, 21\}$

$P(2) = \{1, 7, 11, 12, 13, 14, 15, 19, 25\}$

$P(3) = \{3, 8, 11, 12, 13, 14, 15, 18, 23\}$

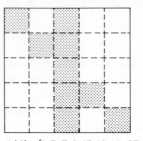

$P(4) = \{1, 3, 7, 8, 13, 18, 19, 23, 25\}$

$P(5) = \{5, 9, 11, 12, 13, 14, 15, 17, 21\}$

Fig. 8-3.   Figures to be used in mask development example.

The final mask is the left to right diagonal,

```
X _ _ _ _
_ X _ _ _
_ _ X _ _
_ _ _ X _
_ _ _ _ X
```

which, in fact, was one of the features used to construct the objects shown in Figure 8-3.

This algorithm will, in general, produce a different σ for each of the $n!$ possible orderings of S. Also, the set of masks produced is not minimal. A more efficient algorithm passes through the set of descriptions k times, to produce k masks, one on each iteration. To describe the algorithm, let σ_j be the mask produced after the jth iteration, and let $\sigma_j(i)$ be the tentative definition of mask σ_j after the ith description has been examined on the jth iteration.

We define K_{ij} to be the set of integers $\{k\}$ such that

$$k < j; \qquad \eta(P(i) \cap \sigma_k) > \theta; \qquad \sigma_k \subseteq \sigma_j(i). \tag{16}$$

Thus K_{ij} lists those previously developed masks which are subsets of the mask currently being developed and which are contained in the description currently being examined.

The algorithm is

$$\sigma_j(0) = 1, 2, \ldots, m \tag{17}$$

$$\sigma_j(i + 1) = \begin{cases} \sigma_j(i) \cap P(i + 1) & \text{if and only if} \\ \qquad \eta(\sigma_j(i) \cap P(i + 1)) > \theta + \eta\left(\bigcup_{k \in K_{i+1,j}} \sigma_k\right), \\ \sigma_j(i) & \text{otherwise.} \end{cases}$$

$$\sigma_j = \sigma_j(n)$$

By definition of $\sigma_j(i + 1)$ it can be seen that the decision as to whether σ_j should be modified or not is made by comparison to a variable threshold which is modified to take into account the extent to which the description $P(i + 1)$ has already been accounted for by other features. Any two features σ_j and σ_{j*} must differ in at least θ components.

Block et al. show that if, in fact, there are k features which are sufficient to reconstruct all descriptions in S, with $N_{\min}$ components in the smallest mask, and at most $N_{\max}$ components share by any two masks, then if θ lies in the range

$$\left(\tfrac{1}{2}k(k - 1)\right) \cdot N_{\max} \leqslant \theta \leqslant N_{\min} - (k - 1)N_{\max} \tag{18}$$

the algorithm will generate the appropriate masks.

8.3.2 COMPARISON OF UHR-VOSSLER AND BLOCK ET AL. TECHNIQUES

Block et al. also assert that even when condition (18) is not met the algorithm will generate useful features. Their article gives several examples. We have also conducted a few informal tests and note that this, indeed, is true. Empirically, however, the Uhr-Vossler procedure has been observed to give even better results. One reason has already been noted, Uhr and Vossler look for the same local operator at a number of positions on the grid, while the Block et al. procedure is tied to specific points.

It is interesting to examine the relationship of these ideas to Minsky and Papert's definition of perceptron predicates. Block et al. give a procedure for defining masks.

Uhr and Vossler have provided a method for defining sets of diameter limited predicates that are equivalent over translation. Which procedure is most desirable in a given case depends upon whether the concept of "diameter limited predicate" makes sense. In the geometric examples given here it does. Block *et al.* point out (in different terminology) that the problem of finding components of line figures is trivial for people largely because the idea of a diameter limited predicate is sensible in the visual world, and we have evolved to be visual animals. Suppose, however, that the grid patterns were distorted by a random permutation of grid elements. For example, one permutation of variables changes the left-to-right diagonal into

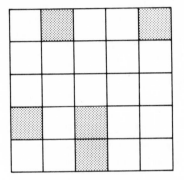

The mathematical problem of identifying features or masks would be identical, insofar as the Block *et al.* algorithm was concerned, but a procedure which assumed that the concept of a "local region of the grid" made sense could not do so. Thus the Block *et al.* algorithm is more powerful, but the Uhr and Vossler procedure is quite probably more efficient for the limited (but very important) set of situations in which its implicit assumption of spatial continuity is valid.

There is another feature of the Uhr and Vossler method which we have not yet mentioned, but which is very important. This is the concept of "don't care" variables. Given a particular 5 x 5 subpattern, the Uhr and Vossler program categorizes its elements as a vector of *ternary* components, with values 1, 0, and X. When searching for this subpattern in a larger grid pattern, the program looks for a 5 x 5 area of the larger pattern in which all the zeros and ones of the feature can be matched, but disregards the values of any of the X-valued components of the subpattern. Roughly, the decision to mark a component with an X is made on the basis of borders. Recall that the original feature is defined by copying a 5 x 5 area of a description. An exact match (0 or 1) is insisted upon at "borders," i.e., at locations where one of the neighbors of a 1 is a zero or vice versa. The result is that a feature defines a border region of a larger figure. For example, the left to right diagonal would be defined by

1	0	0	X	X
0	1	0	0	X
0	0	1	0	0
X	0	0	1	0
X	X	0	0	1

and could fit either of the two figures

1	0	0	0	0
0	1	0	0	0
0	0	1	0	0
0	0	0	1	0
0	0	0	0	1

which contains exactly a left-to-right diagonal, or

1	0	0	0	1
0	1	0	0	0
0	0	1	0	0
1	0	0	1	0
1	0	0	0	1

which contains an embedded left-to-right diagonal. The effect of this addition is to insist on an exact match at the borders between "white" and "black" regions of a picture, but to permit stray spots of light on dark areas and vice versa. In dealing with two-dimensional figures this is often a sensible strategy.

8.3.3 THE ATTRIBUTE INCLUSION METHOD

The two algorithms just described develop features by comparing object descriptions. Abdali (1971) has proposed an alternative approach, in which features are developed by noting those measures whose on state co-occurs. The basis for Abdali's idea is that if a feature of the object turns on instruments 4, 5, and 6, say, in the set of measuring instruments, then the fact that 4 is on will imply that 5 and 6 are also on. Now suppose that a second feature turns on measures 2, 5 and 7. The two features set up the inclusion relationships $(4 \subseteq 5, \quad 4 \subseteq 6), (2 \subseteq 5, \quad 2 \subseteq 6, 2 \subset 7)$. Each such set of inclusion relationships can be used to define a feature.

Let us consider the algebraic relationships involved in the preceding statements. If X is the $n \times m$ matrix whose rows are object descriptions in terms of m measurements, then the columns of X can be considered vectors x_j' whose elements indicate that measure j is on or off, depending on whether x_{ji}' is 1 or 0, for object i. A measure x_j' implies a second measure x_{j*}' if the nonzero elements of x_j' are included in x_{j*}'. By examining X, then, we can find the necessary inclusion relationships, and thus define features. These ideas are summarized in the illustration of Figure 8-4. This figure shows a set of patterns on a 3 x 3 grid and the

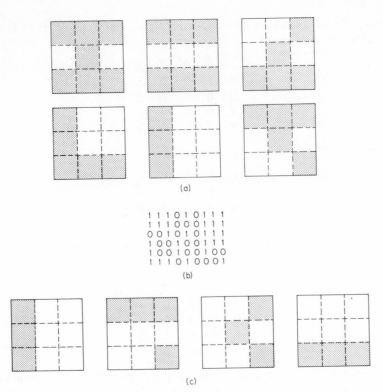

(a)

```
1 1 1 0 1 0 1 1 1
1 1 1 0 0 0 1 1 1
0 0 1 0 1 0 1 1 1
1 0 0 1 0 0 1 1 1
1 0 0 1 0 0 1 0 0
1 1 1 0 1 0 0 0 1
```

(b)

(c)

Fig. 8-4.   Illustration of attribute inclusion technique. (a) Grid patterns to be described. (b) Matrix description of patterns. (c) Masks generated. (After Abdali, 1971.)

associated matrix X. Examination of X detects that the sets of inclusion relationships are $(4, 1, 7)$, $(2, 1, 3, 9)$, $(5, 3, 9)$, and $(8, 7, 9)$. The features thus generated are illustrated graphically, and are sufficient to generate the set of patterns.

Abdali's technique, like that of Block *et al*, finds masks. There is one case in which it will not work. Suppose that within a mask, there exists a submask which can occur independently. For example, suppose that we added to Figure 8-4 a pattern in which the mask $(4, 7)$, a subset of $(1, 4, 7)$, appeared alone. This situation is easy to detect. The steps are as follows:

(1) Count the number of occurrences of on states for each measure. Consider the measures in order from the one with the fewest nonzero occurrences of the on state to the one with the most nonzero occurrences of the on state.

(2) For each measure, x_j' in the indicated order, determine the measures implied by that measure. This set defines as mask.

(3) For all measures x_{j*}' not yet considered, check to see if all occurrences of on states have been accounted for by the masks found to this point. If this is so, drop

the measure from further consideration. Otherwise return to step (2), until all measures have been considered.

In practice, some consideration should be given to the bookkeeping required to execute the procedure. Details are given by Abdali (1971). He has shown that this method is a rapid way of detecting masks. It has the advantage of not depending upon proper choice of a threshold, as the Block *et al.* algorithm does. Like any mask-finding procedure, it can be applied to abstract binary vectors, since it is not justified by an interpretation of the input as pictures on a plane. The main disadvantage of the method is that it insists on an exact implication relationship. It is possible that this could be weakened to accept "implication" by some statistical criterion for co-occurrence if it were reasonable to assume that the basic measurements were subject to error.

8.4   An Experimental Study of Feature Generation in Pattern Recognition

The various combinations of feature detection and pattern recognition present a bewildering number of possibilities. Do the feature-detection and pattern-recognition phases interact and, if so, how? To shed some light on this question an experiment was conducted by Mark Stickel and myself. The results provide an interesting example of how feature detection can alter the logical characteristics of a pattern-recognition problem.

The basic logic of the experiment is outlined in Figure 8-5. The objects

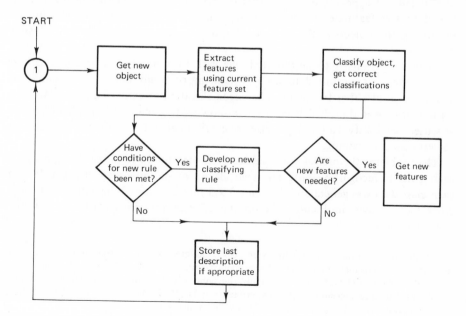

Fig. 8-5.   Procedure in pattern recognition studies.

presented to the program were digitalized two-dimensional plane figures projected on a 25 x 25 grid. The program described these patterns to itself in terms of the location of two 5 x 5 features subpatterns, similar to those used by Uhr and Vossler. Initially the program chose its two features randomly, subsequently they were chosen by imitation of features in the data being classified. The vector y of detected features defined the input to the pattern recognizing part of the program. It specified how many times each feature appeared and the feature's average horizóntal and vertical position. The pattern recognizer then applied its current "best guess" (i.e., its best guess as to the correct classification procedure) to classify the object. This answer was compared to the correct answer and the z vector describing the object in terms of features was stored in the program's memory.

Whenever the program incorrectly classified an object a new classification rule was developed, using one of three procedures. The *linear classification program* simply cycled through all objects currently in the program's memory, using the perceptron training algorithm, until a linear discriminant function was developed which could correctly classify all objects. The *cluster program* applied to the objects in memory Sebesteyen's (1962) technique for deriving clusters based on the average distance between a point and other points in a given class. The *CLS program* applied the "one step look ahead" procedure for constructing decision trees. All these algorithms have been described in previous chapters. Once the classification rule was developed, but before new data were accepted, the program examined the classification rule it had developed to see if both of the currently active features were used. If one of the features had low weights associated with it, or if it did not appear in the decision tree, then that feature was dropped and a call issued to the feature-extraction subprogram, which produced a new feature by examining the objects in the program memory using a variant of the Uhr–Vossler procedure.

In the experiments to be reported[5] we varied the number of descriptions that the program was permitted to store in its memory at any one time. Training was continued until either 100 pictures had been classified or until 15 min of IBM 7094 central processor time had been used. Following training, the last rule developed was used to classify 100 new patterns, selected independently for the selection of patterns used in training.

The problems themselves were purposely chosen to illustrate the strong point of each pattern recognition program. Two classes of patterns were defined. Within each class data was generated by placing 5 x 5 subfields containing either a "+" or a cross "x" (shown in Figure 8-6) on the 25 x 25 grid in accordance with the following rules.

---

[5] A number of other experiments were also conducted which we shall not report. They support the conclusions drawn here. Experiments similar in logic to parts of our study were reported by Nilsson (1965b) with essentially the same results. After we completed our studies we obtained data from a similar set of experiments by Dr. Paula Diehr of the UCLA Biomedical Data Processing Center. She obtained essentially the same results.

(1) In the *linear* problem in Class I the probability of placing a "+" in a subfield was greater than .5 for the two top rows of 5 x 5 subfields, while the probability of placing an x in a subfield was greater than .5 in the two bottom rows. In Class II the probabilities were reversed.

(2) In the *cluster* problem the probability of placing a "+" or an "x" on a 5 x 5 subfield varied depending upon the distance of the subfield from the center 5 x 5 grid. Both classes were "clustered" about the center point, at which the probability of placing either figure on a subfield was highest for the subfield. In one class the probability of placing a + on a peripheral subfield decreased more rapidly than the probability of placing an x as one moved outward from the center point; in the other class the probability of placing an x decreased more rapidly than that of placing a +.

(3) In the *sequential* problem classes were defined by the relation between the locations of +'s and x's. In Class I, +'s were placed in the *upper left* corner with high probability *and* x's in the *lower right* with high probability, or the +'s were placed in the upper right with the x's in the lower left. In the Class II examples, +'s were most likely to be found above the x's, in either the right or left portion of the grid. Thus this problem presented a classification based on two "model" patterns per class.

For Class I these were

```
+-----------------+        +-----------------+
| +  +  +         |        |         +  +  + |
|                 |        |                 |
| +  +            |   or   | +  +  +          |
|                 |        |                 |
|       +   x  x  |        | x          +    |
|                 |        |                 |
|       x  x  x   |        | x  x  x          |
|                 |        |                 |
|       x  x  x   |        | x  x  x          |
+-----------------+        +-----------------+
```

as opposed to

```
+-----------------+        +-----------------+
| +   +   +       |        |    +   +   +    |
|                 |        |                 |
| +   +           |   or   |    +   +   +    |
|                 |        |                 |
| +   +   x       |        | x   +   +       |
|                 |        |                 |
| x   x   x       |        |    x   x        |
|                 |        |                 |
| x   x   x       |        |    x   x        |
+-----------------+        +-----------------+
```

in Class II.

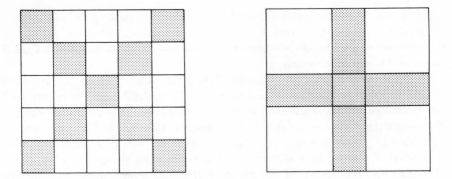

Fig. 8-6.   Components used to generate patterns in experimental study.

By varying the parameters of this basic situation (such as memory size and introduction of random blanks, +'s, and x's) we could create many experiments. Fortunately, we soon found that our basic conclusions were almost impervious to parameter variation, and thus can be summarized in the single drawing of Figure 8-7. This shows the number of correct classifications of the second sample of 100 drawings, following training on the first sample. The figure shows clearly that although problem types vary in difficulty, the different pattern-recognition programs do not vary markedly on their performance on a given problem. The only thing that the figure does not show is the variability in obtaining solutions. This was quite low, except for the sequential problem which is sometimes not solved by the linear pattern recognizer. Otherwise the mean is a reasonable summary of the data.

These results surprised us, since we had thought that the different pattern recognizers would do differentially well on the problems designed for them. In particular, we did not at first see how the linear program could ever solve the sequential problem since we thought we had ensured that the feature extraction method would destroy the information needed to reach a solution. On the contrary! What happened was that the feedback from the pattern recognizers forced the feature extraction part of the program to define features which converted the classification problem to one suitable for the particular pattern recognizer being used. The neatest illustration of this is how the linear pattern recognizer forced a solution of the sequential problem. Recall that to solve the sequential problem one must notice whether the +'s tend to appear above the x's or not, anywhere on the 25 x 25 large grid. The linear pattern recognizer kept calling for new features until the feature extractor developed features shown in Figure 8-8. These are features that are useful in detecting "the bottom half of a + over a blank field," or "a blank field over a x: or "a + over a x." In other words, the program found features characteristic of the border between areas with high or low densities of +'s and x's. Perhaps we should have known before-hand that the program would do this. People to whom we recite this example tell us this—after we have told them how the program solved the problem.

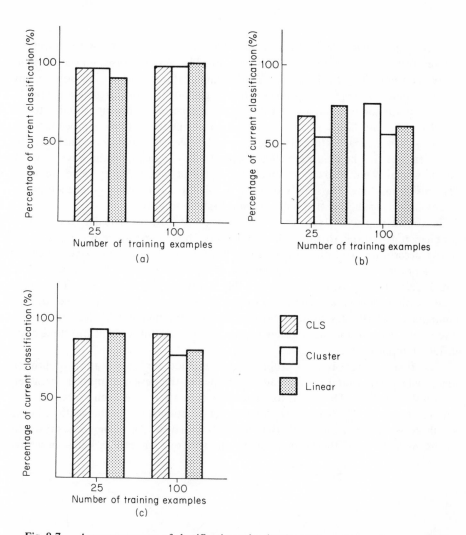

Fig. 8-7. Average accuracy of classification rules developed for various pattern recognition programs on different problems. (a) Linear problems. (b) Cluster problems. (c) Sequential problems.

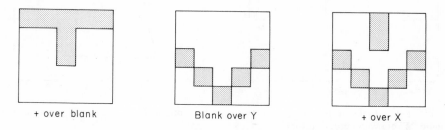

+ over blank   Blank over Y   + over X

Fig. 8-8. Features generated by a linear pattern recognizer solving a sequential problem.

8.5   On Being Clever

Advocating cleverness is always reasonable, even if such advice is frustrating to the receiver. In our experiments we were fooled because our program was, in some sense, cleverer than we had been in defining features. In fact, to solve many practical pattern-recognition problems one ought not to look for general methods, but rather for some locally powerful but very specialized techniques suitable to the problem at hand. This is nicely illustrated in Ledley's (1964) procedure for applying grammatical pattern-classification techniques to chromosome analysis. The basic features that he used were chosen because they represented the ways in which chromosomes were known to break. No attempt was made to generate these features by machine. The man with a real problem is quite willing to take advantage of any knowledge he has that will help him find the solution.

In considering what features should be used to solve a particular classification problem it is natural to think first of features that represent components of the object description; e.g., thinking of a person as a collection of hands, feet, and legs, or of a printed letter as a collection of arcs and lines. There are a number of cases in which careful analysis has shown that this is *not* the way to proceed. There may exist features which are quite useful in classification but cannot be tied to components of the description. No general rules for finding such features can be given, but, because the method has proven quite powerful, we will cite three quite different applications.

The first of these is the "probe vector" method for classification of printed digits, which has found widespread acceptance in the design of optical character-recognition systems. The task is to recognize a digit after it has been precentered on a field. The way this is done is to construct a network of "probe vectors," lines which cross the field on which the figure is displayed. An example is shown in Figure 8-9a. Each of the vectors can be thought of as a feature. When an actual

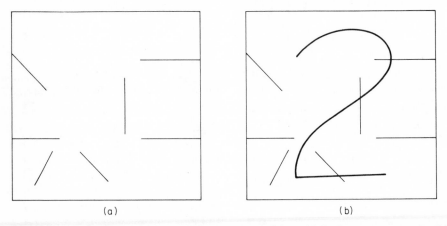

Fig. 8-9.   Probe vector method of character recognition. (a) Probe vector network. (b) Figure "2" drawn on probe vectors.

character is projected onto the network, as is done with the figure "2" in Figure 8-9b, different probe vectors will be crossed. The crossing of probe vectors corresponds to a feature being present in our previous terminology. The different digits produce different patterns of crossing of the probes, and thus form the basis for character recognition.

Bongard (1970) reports an even more imaginative method of applying feature extraction techniques to an unusual pattern recognition task. Consider the two tables shown in Figure 8-10. Each of them consists of lines from two mathematical functions, Table I of Figure 8-10 shows entries for a table of $g(A,B) = A + B = C$, while Table II of Figure 8-10 shows entries for $g(A,B) = A - B = C$.

A	B	C
3	5	8
7	6	13
6	2	8
4	9	13

I

A	B	C
4	5	-1
7	9	-2
10	3	7
5	5	0

II

Fig. 8-10.   Function tables to be recognized. (I) $g(A, B) = (A + B = C)$. (II) $g(A, B) = (A - B = C)$.

Given a number of tables such as these could a program be written which would examine all the tables belonging to a given function and then extract descriptors which could be used to assign new tables to their appropriate function? Nowhere in this process would the function be defined explicitly to the program. Bongard reports a program, called ARITHMETIC, which apparently does this. We are particularly impressed by its feature-extraction procedure, and discuss it for that reason.

In ARITHMETIC feature extraction is done in three stages. In the first stage a particular number of arithmetic features are generated. Each arithmetic feature combines two of the three table entries (A, B, C) with an elementary arithmetic operation. Thus at this stage we could develop real-valued features such as $A + B$, $A + C$, A/C, $B \times C$. Given that there are only three possible operands and a limited number of operators, there is only a small set of possible arithmetic features. Each of these can be evaluated for each row of the table. The arithmetic operations are then converted to logical variables using one of six possible conversion rules. All the rules are based upon the value of the arithmetic operation. For example, the rule $L_1(f(x, y)) = T$ if and only if f is greater than 0, is a possible logical conversion rule. This can be applied to functions such as $A + B$, or A/C, and when the arguments of

f are specified, a logical value of $L_1 f$ is implied. Following our example, we could define $L_1(A + B)$ of the first row of Table I as "True." We have now produced features which can map from the row of a table to a vector of logical variables.

In the next stage pairs of logical variables are combined. The combination rule is chosen from one of the ten possible logical operations which apply to two variables. That is, the combination rule might be $F(a, b) = a$ OR b, a AND b, etc., where a and b are logical variables. Here a typical feature might be

$$F(a, b) = L_1(A + B) \quad \text{OR} \quad L_1(A/B) \tag{19}$$

Again, the feature F has its value defined for a particular row of a table. To define F for the table as a whole its logical product is determined over all rows of the table. In summary, this procedure allows us to define a number of features which apply to partial tables of arithmetic, functions, rather than rows.

ARITHMETIC is given a number of tables, each associated with a different (but unknown) function. Table features (F's) are generated until the program has obtained 33 functions, each of which is True for approximately half of the tables. (The number of functions to be chosen was determined by characteristics of the machine on which the program was run, and has no particular significance.) The program then examines a new set of tables generated from the same functions, and attempts to identify which of the new tables is to be paired with which of the training tables. The decision is made by a simple clustering algorithm based on the similarity of the pattern of F's on each pair of tables. Bongard reports that for simple arithmetic functions his program correctly classified all but about 3% of the test cases. This is somehow an impressive figure, although one is not quite clear how to proceed next. On the one hand, there is a sense in which the program has "inductively defined a function," since it can recognize new examples of the function. On the other hand, the function itself has not been defined. The program could not be trained to give the value of C for a particular pair of arguments A, B, although it could be modified to make an educated guess as to which of two possible values of C was most likely to be correct.

If nothing else, Bongard's results suggest that multiple choice tests are not good devices for measuring the intelligence of a machine. They certainly represent an application of pattern recognition to an unusual situation.

As a final illustration of useful, nonobvious feature analysis, we consider a method for processing two-dimensional pictures by dealing with them as mathematical abstractions. A black and white picture can be defined by a "grayness function," $g(x, y)$ whose value is the intensity of grayness at point (x, y) on the picture plane. The grayness function may be broken down into independent components using an analytic technique called *two-dimensional Fourier analysis*. No attempt will be made to explain the mathematical details. (The interested reader is referred to a brief discussion by Duda and Hart, 1973, who give further references.) An intuitive presentation of the idea follows.

To set the stage, consider a function of one argument $f(x)$ and assume that this function can be regarded as periodic in the range $-\pi \leqslant x \leqslant \pi$, when x is measured in radians. Fourier's theorem states that $f(x)$ can be represented by the converging, infinite summation

$$f(x) = \tfrac{1}{2}a_0 + \sum_{n=1}^{\infty} (a_n \cos nx + b_n \sin nx). \tag{20}$$

Clearly the infinite sum may be approximated by a summation over a finite number of terms. An example is shown graphically in Figure 8-11, in which a complex function is shown to be the sum of suitably weighted harmonic components.

How might a pattern-recognition problem involving classification of complex waveforms, such as 8-11A, be solved? One way to proceed would be to describe each waveform by a vector **z** consisting of the coefficients of its first k harmonic components, and then apply a pattern-recognition algorithm for vector classification to the set $\{z\}$ of coefficient vectors. *Fourier analysis* is a well-known

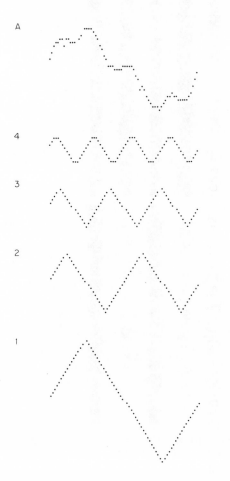

Fig. 8-11.   Example of decomposition of A function. Curve A was produced by a weighted summation of the harmonic curves 1-4.

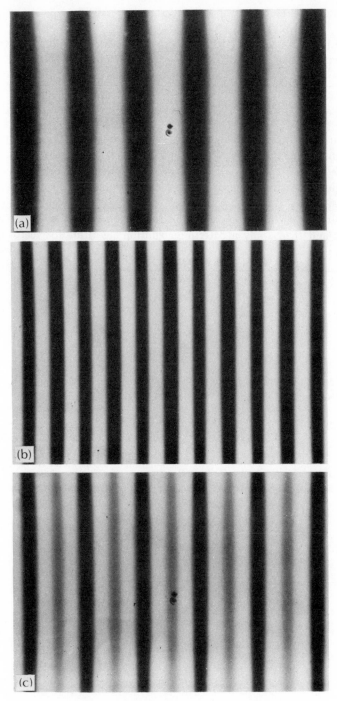

Fig. 8-12. Logic of spatial Fourier analysis. The bottom picture was reproduced by summing the two upper pictures.

204

mathematical procedure for discovering the coefficients, given the waveform, so this step would pose no problem.

To apply this method to picture recognition, consider first a simple picture consisting of a sequence of identically shaded vertical lines. Such a picture could be regarded as a weighted sum of a set of "gratings" of varying frequency of alternation of white and black vertical lines. An example is shown in Figure 8-12. Similarly, a picture consisting of uniform horizontal shadings could be produced by summing horizontal gratings. In such a picture the grayness value would only be a function of the horizontal or vertical dimension $[g(x)$ or $g(y)]$, and the coefficients of the harmonic grayness functions used to produce the picture could be recovered by Fourier analysis. Now, suppose that a picture produced by summing horizontal gratings were superimposed on a picture produced by summing vertical gratings. The result would be a picture composed of blocks of varying grayness levels. The only limit on the resolution would be the limit on the frequencies used to construct the gratings; the use of high frequencies, and thus frequent, thin lines, would produce a fine mosaic of very small blocks. Blocks alone, however, are not sufficient to define most pictures, since an edge may, in general, be on a diagonal. Very roughly, diagonal lines correspond to ratios between frequencies f_x, fy in the x and y dimensions. That is, if f_x and f_y are frequencies represented by vertical and horizontal gratings, then the pair (f_x, f_y) is represented by a set of lines with slope $-(f_x/f_y)$. (Note that f_x, f_y may be negative, corresponding to sine and cosine terms.) The spacing between lines is determined by the values of f_x and f_y; the higher these values, the closer the lines are spaced together. An example of a grating is shown in Figure 8-13. The fundamental result of spatial Fourier analysis is that any picture [i.e., grayness function $g(x, y)$] can be approximated by a finite weighted summation of gratings corresponding to the f_x, f_y pairs. Intuitively, then, we can think of a picture as being a weighted sum of gratings of varying orientation, spacing, and intensity. In terms of pattern recognition by a digital computer, any picture can be represented (to an arbitrary degree of accuracy) by a vector whose elements are the coefficients representing the weight assigned to a grating of a

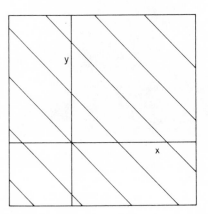

Fig. 8-13.   Grating correspondence to nonzero contribution of (f_x, f_y) pair to a grayness function $g(x, y)$.

particular orientation and spacing. Sharp edges correspond to high intensity, tightly spaced gratings at the appropriate orientation.

At first glance, breaking a picture into its Fourier components may seem an operation which, whatever its mathematical justification, is not likely to package the information in the picture into a convenient form. Some surprising research into sensory functioning suggests that this is not the case. It appears that the mammalian visual system performs an approximate Fourier analysis of the retinal image, and uses this analysis to order the visual world. Evidence for this proposition comes from several sources. An unusually interesting experiment arguing for it was performed by Harmon and Julesz (1973). They first quantized a high-resolution photograph of a portrait of Abraham Lincoln into blocks, and assigned all points within blocks the average grayness value for the block. The resulting picture is shown in Figure 8-14a. The effect of such quantizing is to introduce high-frequency "noise" components associated with the borders between blocks. Harmon and Julesz then produced a second picture by filtering *from the blocked picture* almost all frequencies which were higher than the components which could have been transmitted from the original photograph to the blocked picture. (The size of the blocks establishes an upper limit to the frequency information which can be transmitted from the original to the blocked picture.) The reconstruction is shown in Figure 8-14b, it is a clearly recognizable portrait of Abraham Lincoln.

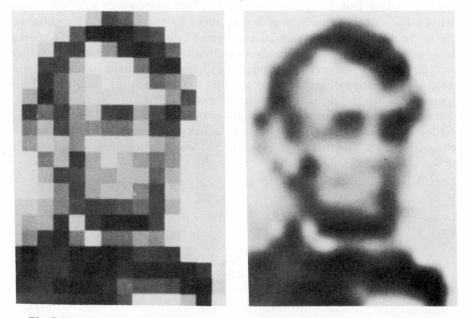

Fig. 8-14. Pictures obtained by (a) quantizing a high-resolution picture and then (b) filtering high frequencies from (a), thus blurring the edges. [From L. D. Harmon and B. Julez. Masking in Visual Recognition: Effects of two-dimensional filtered noise. *Science*, 1973, **180**, 1194. Copyright© 1973 by the American Association for the Advancement of Science and reproduced by permission.]

This excursion into sensory psychology illustrates an important point for pattern recognition by computer. The feature-detection system used in a pattern recognizer need not retain picture information packaged into the same units that are *perceived* by a human observer. Indeed, the human visual system itself evidently does not do this. A good feature-detection system retains information sufficient to recreate the objects to be classified at the level of detail needed for classification. Furthermore, it presents this information to the pattern-recognition algorithm in a manner that is convenient for the latter to handle.

Part III
Theorem Proving and Problem Solving

Chapter IX

Chapter IX

COMPUTER MANIPULABLE REPRESENTATIONS IN PROBLEM SOLVING

9.0   The Use of Representations

In artificial intelligence the term "problem solving" is used in a rather restricted way. We say that a problem exists if there is a discrepancy between the perceived and the desired state of the world. The problem is solved by altering the world so that this discrepancy disappears. This implies that the problem solver has the capability of taking actions which can effect the needed changes. Making these actions blindly does not qualify as problem solving, as there should be some sort of selection process by which appropriate actions are chosen. Our concern is with computer programs which make this selection.

Thinkers do not deal with problems directly; they deal with representations of problems. This fact is so commonplace that we do not realize its importance until we attempt to construct a problem-solving program. The program, of course, does not deal with the physical world. It deals with a symbolic representation of the world, on the assumption that there is a translation between symbols and operations on symbols in the computer and states and actions in the external world. The whole of applied mathematics can be looked upon in the same way. Numbers and operations on numbers are used to represent the physical world and actions in it. We first solve the numerical problem and then translate the solution into physical terms. Sometimes the translation is an obvious one. This would be the case, for instance, if we were asked to find the average weight of a football team. We would assign a number to each individual player, corresponding to his weight, do the appropriate arithmetic, and produce an answer. Sometimes the translation is more subtle. Consider the problem of finding an optimal route for a school bus. Given any particular route we can calculate the mileage traveled and the time each child spends on the bus. We become uneasy when we attempt to define "best route" by combining these variables. Should an additional bus be purchased if the average transit time is greater than 15 min with only one bus, or should we wait until the transit time is greater than half an hour? How does the price of the bus affect this decision? How do we balance the average transit time for all students against maximum transit time for an individual student? In this example we can measure the individual variables, but are uncertain about the meaningfulness of combining operations. In many "real life" situations the crucial variables themselves may elude measurement. It has been claimed by a number of observers that the failure of United States military policy in Vietnam was because of this. Policy decisions in this conflict seem to have been based upon mathematical models of the "cost-effectiveness" of the use of different tactics and weapons systems. Effectiveness was measured in terms of the number of target personnel killed, equipment destroyed, and similar quantifiable variables. No satisfactory way was found to measure the social and psychological reactions of either the hostile North Vietnamese or the allied South Vietnamese to the different military measures. The result was a stunning setback for United States foreign policy despite many victories in local actions.

The first question we want to ask about a representation, then, is whether it is a sufficiently accurate model of reality. A second criterion of the utility of a representation is that it should be one that the problem solver finds easy to use. "Easy to use" is a concept which implies something about the problem solver as well as the problem. For example, an arithmetician equipped with a slide rule will find an analog representation of numbers useful for multiplication, while one equipped with an abacus will use a digital representation. In artificial intelligence we are often concerned with differences between those representations which are natural for a human problem-solver and those suitable for machine problem solving.

To illustrate the interaction between representations and processes, let us examine a problem in social communication. It is well known that scientists rely a great deal upon personal contacts for information about recent developments. Also, not all scientists exchange information with all other scientists. Suppose that a particular scientist who is a member of some, but not all, "invisible colleges" of colleagues, makes a discovery, and announces it through his entries into the informal network. How long will it take for news of the discovery to spread as far as it is going to spread?

As a first approximation, we assume that all communication between scientists takes place at scientific meetings, and that at each meeting each scientist exchanges information with all his friends concerning all discoveries of which he has knowledge. This is certainly an oversimplification of the actual communication process, since we have constructed an artificial clocking mechanism for the exchange of information and since we have not allowed for the possibility that a man's acquaintances will change. Nevertheless, the model is perhaps not too inaccurate.

In a *list representation* we can write down the names of the scientists and the people to whom they talk. The list might read

1. Jones		Smith, Thomas
2. Smith		Jones, Brown, Green
3. Thomas		Jones, Baker, Brown

4. Green	Smith, Brown
5. Brown	Smith, Green, Thomas
6. Baker	Thomas, White
7. White	Baker
8. Bennett	Mason, James
9. Mason	Bennett
10. James	Bennett

Arbitrarily, let Jones be the discoverer. To solve the problem, list the people Jones talks to: Smith and Thomas. These are the people who will hear of the discovery at the first meeting. Next add to the list the people whom Smith and Thomas will tell at the next meeting, so that the list now reads Jones, Smith, Thomas, Brown, Green, Baker. At each succeeding stage add the names of people who are reached for the first time. Eventually (in this case after three meetings) no new names will be added. This tells us how long it will take for the news to spread, and to whom it will spread.

A *graphic representation* has exactly the same correspondence to reality as the list model, but has some advantages in revealing the answer visually. The communication network is depicted by a graph (shown in Figure 9-1) in which the nodes are individuals and the arcs connect individuals who speak to each other. By glancing at the figure we see that there are two clusters, so that there is no way to pass a message from Jones to the Bennett-Mason-James group. A slightly more detailed examination shows that the furthest reachable point from Jones is White, three arcs away. The graphic representation is an improvement over the list representation when people are solving the problem. Why? Probably because people are outstanding processors of visually presented information. Of course, we could overwhelm the graphic representation by increasing the number of names, thus making the graph complex beyond reason. Then we would have to fall back on the list expansion approach. People could do this, for arbitrarily complicated problems, but they would have a great deal of trouble because of the human proneness toward clerical errors.

The final representation to be considered, the *matrix representation* (suggested by Harary, Norman, and Cartwright, 1965), is suitable for problem solving by

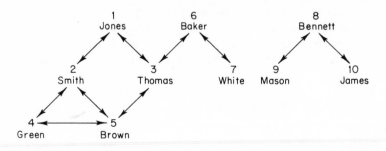

Fig. 9-1.   Graphic portrayal of a communication net.

	1	2	3	4	5	6	7	8	9	10
1	0	1	1	0	0	0	0	0	0	0
2	1	0	0	1	1	0	0	0	0	0
3	1	0	0	0	1	1	0	0	0	0
4	0	1	0	0	1	0	0	0	0	0
5	0	0	1	1	0	0	0	0	0	0
6	0	0	1	0	0	0	1	0	0	0
7	0	0	0	0	0	1	0	0	0	0
8	0	0	0	0	0	0	0	0	1	1
9	0	0	0	0	0	0	0	1	0	1
10	0	0	0	0	0	0	0	1	1	0

Fig. 9-2.   Connection matrix for Figure 9-1.

machine, but is not a technique that a man could use easily by himself. Let a *path* be a route by which information can be transmitted from one person to another, and the *length* of the path be the number of steps in it. Thus the sequences Jones–Thomas–Brown and Jones–Smith–Green–Brown in Figure 9-1 are paths from Jones to Brown, and are of length two and three, respectively. Let C be a binary matrix whose elements c_{ij} are one if and only if person i communicates with person j, and zero otherwise. By convention, c_{ii} is always zero. Figure 9-2 presents the matrix corresponding to Figure 9-1. Note that one way of interpreting C is to say that c_{ij} states the number of paths (at most one) of length one from person i to j. This seems a clumsy way of describing the meaning of the matrix until we consider a more general form of the question. How many paths of length two are there from i to j? To answer this question we must consider the number of paths of length one from i to k, and then of length one from k to j, for all possible k. This is

$$\text{Number of paths of length two from } i \text{ to } j = \sum_k c_{ik}c_{kj} \tag{1}$$

$$= c_{ij}^{(2)}.$$

Expressing (1) as a matrix equation, (2)

$$C^{(2)} = [c_{ij}^{(2)}] = C \cdot C.$$

To find the number length three from i to j determine for all k, the number of paths of length 2 from i to k and of length 1 from k to j. This is

$$\text{Number of paths of length 3 from } i \text{ to } j = c_{ij}^{(3)} \tag{3}$$

$$= \sum_k c_{ik}^{(2)} c_{kj}$$

and, in matrix form

$$C^{(3)} = C^{(2)} \cdot C. \tag{4}$$

Equation (4) generalizes to the case of paths of length n,

$$C^{(n)} = C^{(n-1)} \cdot C \tag{5}$$

$$= C^n.$$

The communication process terminates at the point at which increasing the length of a path does not increase the number of paths. Mathematically this is reflected by the condition

$$C^{n+1} = C^n. \tag{6}$$

Let n^* be the lowest integer for which (6) holds. A nonzero value of $c_{ij}^{(n^*)}$ indicates that there is at least one path of length n^* or less leading from person i to person j. If $c_{ij}^{(n^*)}$ is zero there is no path from i to j.

The contrast between the matrix and the graphic representation is obviously not in the translation from the real to the symbolic world, since there is a one to one correspondence between the representations. The choice between these two systems depends upon the problem solver's predilection for numerical or visual operations.

The next section presents a typology of problem solving representations, modeled after those developed by Newell and Simon (1972) and Nilsson (1971). It is not a rigorous typology. It is likely that formal equivalence can be established between at least some of the different types of representations presented, a point which Banerji (1969) develops in some detail. Despite this conjecture it seems doubtful that all representations are pragmatically as equivalent. Representations are heuristic devices for looking at problems. A good representation suggests a good problem-solving method. That a good representation is formally equivalent to a bad one is an interesting mathematical fact, but is of less moment for problem solving.

9.1   A Typology of Representations

9.1.0   ENUMERATION

An *enumerative representation* begins with a set $\mathbf{U}$ of potential solutions and a rule for evaluating them. If $\mathbf{U}$ is finite, solutions may be examined in some order, and a correct answer selected. If $\mathbf{U}$ is infinite but denumerable the members of $\mathbf{U}$ can be generated in order and tested for correctness of solution. Enumeration methods are sometimes scored in artificial intelligence research, in part because early writings in the field[1] implied that they relied on "brute force and ignorance" to keep generating trial solutions blindly until a correct one was formed. In practice, however, some quite elegant enumerative techniques have been developed. An abstract representation of the method itself suggests when enumeration is likely

[1] See, in particular, Newell, Shaw and Simon's *Remarks on the British Museum Algorithm*, 1956.

to be useful. Let f be a function which selects at least one solution $s \notin S$ for any $S \subseteq U$. An enumerative technique is executed in the following steps

(*i*) Begin with a set $S_0 \subseteq U$ of trial answers. Set i to 0.
(*ii*) If S_i contains an answer, end. Otherwise go to (*iii*).
(*iii*) Construct $S_{i+1} = f(S_i)$, increase i by one, and go to (*ii*).

The feature of an enumerative method that separates it from other methods is that at each step S_{i+1} is produced solely from consideration of S_i. The next step is, then, a function of the value of the current step and does not depend upon a comparison between the current step and the answer. Intuitively, this seems like blind problem solving, and indeed it is *unless the characteristics of an answer are always the same.* If this is true, then an implied comparison between the answer state and the members of S_i can be built into the definition of the enumerating function f. An important example of such a problem was given in Chapter I, where we noted that many problem situations can be described by a conjunction of statements of the form "*A* or *B* or *C*." If the goal of problem solving is to show that the conjunction of such statements is *false* (i.e., that the statements are incompatible), this can be done by deriving the null statement *false* from the original statements. Thus *false* becomes a constant goal state for a number of different problems, and an enumeration approach to problem solving becomes feasible. This method has proven to be useful in computer implementations of theorem proving.

9.1.1   STATE-SPACE PROBLEM SOLVING

The *state-space* approach is a very popular problem-solving representation. It assumes the existence of a countable set S of *states* and a set O of *operators* which map the states of S into themselves. The problem solver is seen as moving through space defined by the states, in an attempt to reach one of a designated set of goal states. A problem is solved when a sequence of operators

$$\mathbf{o} = o^{(1)}, o^{(2)}, \ldots o^{(k)} \tag{7}$$

is found such that the following relationship holds for some state s_0 in the set of possible starting states and s_g in the set of goal states

$$s_g = o^{(k)}(o^{(k-1)}(\ldots\ldots o^{(2)}(o^{(1)}(s_0))\ldots\ldots)) \tag{8}$$

There is a useful isomorphism between the problem of finding the sequence $\mathbf{o}$ and the problem of finding a path through a graph. Think of S as defining the nodes of a graph, with arcs between nodes i and j if and only if there is an operator $\mathbf{o} \in O$ which maps s_i into s_j. A path from one state to another, then, is equivalent to a sequence of operators mapping from the first state to the second. The graphic representation of state-space problem solving has three advantages. It is intuitively easy to grasp, a point that is far from trivial. It leads to a natural extension in which we associate a cost, c_k with the application of each operator o_k. Graphically this can be represented by labeling each arc in the graph by its cost. Finally, in many cases the next step to be explored can be made a function of a comparison between a goal state and a final state. The details are discussed further in Chapter X.

9.1.2. PROBLEM REDUCTION

In the *problem reduction* method one identifies subproblems which, if solved separately, will constitute a solution of the original problem. Each subproblem is then attacked, and the results combined to create a solution to the total problem. The process can be applied recursively, to generate subproblems, subsubproblems, etc. until finally a trivial set of "problems" whose solutions are known is identified. The solution of these problems thus can be combined into the solution of a larger problem. Nilsson (1971) offers an interesting illustration, a "Three Peg Tower of Hanoi" problem. The problem begins with three pegs with disks placed on them as shown in Figure 9-3a. The goal is to move the disks to the left hand peg, within the constraints that (*a*) only one peg may be moved at a time and (*b*) a larger peg may never be placed on top of a smaller one. To solve the problem, the large disk must be placed on peg 3. This, of course, implies that disk C is exposed on peg 1 and that peg 3 is empty, a situation which could only occur if peg 2 contained disks A and B in the proper order. The problem, then involves two subproblems, to be solved in order. These are shown in Figures 9-4 and 9-5. Note that the problem of Figure 9-5 is trivial, we can assert solution in a single move. After these problems have been solved, however, there remains an additional problem, moving disks A and B into place. This problem is shown in Figure 9-6. The reader can easily apply the preceding reasoning to generate further subproblems, thus arriving at solutions for all the unsolved subproblems.

The subproblems discussed so far are collectively called *and* subproblems, as they all must be solved in order to solve the main problem. It is often the case that several *or* subproblems can be located, subproblems such that if any one of them is solved, the main problem is solved. This occurs in the Tower of Hanoi problem. Figure 9-7 shows two configurations of disks such that if either of them is reached, the main problem is trivial to solve.

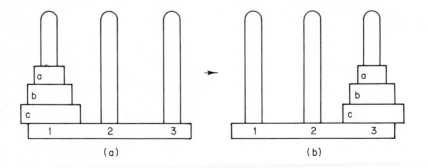

Fig. 9-3.   Three disk Tower of Hanoi problem, original statement.

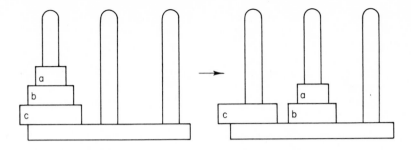

Fig. 9-4. A nontrivial Tower of Hanoi subproblem.

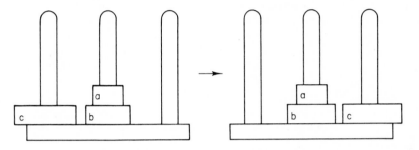

Fig. 9-5. A trivial Tower of Hanoi problem, which can be solved in one move.

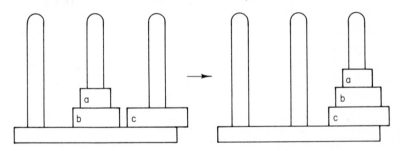

Fig. 9-6. Remaining Tower of Hanoi problem after solving Figures 9.4 and 9.5.

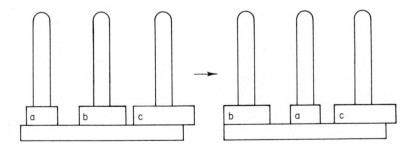

Fig. 9-7. OR subproblems of the Tower of Hanoi problem.

The problem reduction representation can be depicted by a special sort of graph, called a *tree graph*. In graph theory a *tree* is a directed graph with the following properties.

(*i*) There is a distinguished node called the *root*, which is not the successor of any other node.

(*ii*) There are no loops or slings—i.e., there are no paths from a node back to itself, and there is no arc from a node to itself. Such a graph can be arranged in the form of a family tree, hence the name. An abstract example is shown in Figure 9-8. Note the arc connecting subproblems 1 and 2 to each other. This indicates that both subproblems must be solved before the main problem is solved. Subproblems 1 and 2, then are *and* subproblems. The arc would be removed if the subproblems were *or* subproblems, as is done below subproblems 1 and 2.

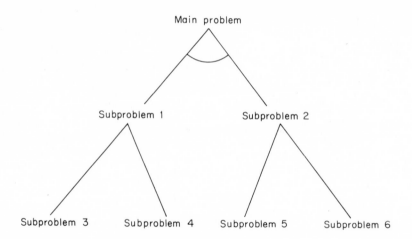

Fig. 9-8.   A tree representation of the problem reduction method. To solve the main problem, subproblems 1 and 2 both must be solved. To solve subproblem 1, either subproblem 3 or 4 may be solved; to solve subproblem 2, either subproblem 5 or 6 must be solved.

The process of problem solving is seen as a process in which each node is marked as solved until the root is reached. We begin with the root node, which represents the original problem. Subproblems of the original problem are generated and attached to the root node, as either *and* or *or* successors. Subproblems of subproblems are generated, until a subproblem that can be solved directly is found (i.e., the problem solving program "knows the answer" to the subproblem). The appropriate node is marked *solved*, and the tree reexamined. All nodes for which any *or* subproblem has been solved are marked *solved*, as are all nodes for which all *and* subproblems have been solved. The process terminates when the root node can be marked *solved*, indicating solution of the original problem.

9.1.3   STRING REWRITING

In the *string rewriting* representation, possible "states of the world," including starting and goal states, are treated as well formed expressions in some language. Operators mapping from one state of the world to another are treated as rewriting rules which map one well-formed expression into another. High school algebra provides an excellent example of the string rewriting approach. Suppose we wish to prove that

$$X + (B + C) = B + (X + C) \tag{9}$$

using the rules of commutivity and associativity. The proof is

$$X + (B + C) \rightarrow (X + B) + C \qquad \text{associativity of } + \tag{10}$$
$$\rightarrow (B + X) + C \qquad \text{commutivity of } +$$
$$\rightarrow B + (X + C) \qquad \text{associativity of } X +$$

The selection of the operation (rewriting rule) to use at each step is based upon a comparison of the structures of the current and desired well formed expression. There is clearly an identity between the state–space representation and the string rewriting procedure. In addition, one can argue that all programmable problem solvers must be string rewriting systems, since the content of a computer's memory can be expressed as a string, and any change of the memory contents is then a rewriting of the string. As a matter of heuristics, however, only some problems are easily conceptualized as string rewriting problems, and some are not.

9.2   Combining Representations

The problem reduction representation works because problem solving is often a hierarchical affair. Problem reduction alone, however, hides an important point. It is not necessary that the main problem and all the subproblems be attacked using the same representation. If any generalities are permissible, we might say that the problem-reduction method is a useful device for representing very global aspects of a problem, while state–space, rewriting and enumeration methods are of more use when more specific problems are to be attacked. We can see this best if we consider very broad problems of a scope not yet attacked by computer. Think of the "problem" alluded to by President Kennedy in his inaugural address—how to restore American prestige on a worldwide basis? He saw this in terms of a number of subproblems, which included a more active civil liberties program, increased effectiveness of military forces, and an expanded space exploration program. The last program contained as a subproblem the task of putting a man on the moon. So far we are speaking in problem reduction terms. Lunar exploration required the construction of certain space vehicles. This task is best represented by a critical path analysis graph. Construction of the vehicle, in turn, required the solution of a number of engineering mathematical problems, tasks which required either an enumerative or rewriting approach.

The use of mixed representations does not just occur in the problems facing national and international leaders. One of the most publicized projects in modern artificial intelligence is "Shakey the robot," a computer controlled vehicle constructed at Stanford Research Institute. Shakey has the capacity to determine what route it[2] will follow to reach a goal and what actions are necessary for the robot to change the environment in a certain way. The system architecture of Shakey's programming system makes use of a mixture of representations (Munson, 1971). When Shakey is ordered to change the environment, the main problem faced by the robot is broken down into subproblems, and a graphic (state–space) representation is used to determine the sequence in which subproblems should be attempted. Theorem proving techniques are applied to specific steps of the sequence to demonstrate that applying a certain operation will have the desired effect. The methods used are enumeration methods similar to those to be described in Chapter XII. Within the enumeration methods, however, it is necessary to find which algebraic expressions are equivalent. Serious consideration has been given to representing this problem as a string rewriting problem. The robot project thus provides a good example of how we are forced to mix representations when we attack a problem that is at all complex—it also illustrates the point that what is complex, by computer standards, may be terribly simple for a human. Despite rather lurid reports in the public press, Shakey's most ardent admirers freely admit that the robot's actions are not impressive in themselves. In a number of public presentations (e.g., those by Nilsson and Feldman at the 1972 ACM western regional meetings) it has been pointed out that the chief reason for working on robots in the 1970s is to learn how to construct complex problem-solving systems that require multiple representations, rather than to construct a device which will be useful in itself.

When computing techniques are used to solve very complex problems the "typical" mistake the program makes is to generate so many trial solutions that, even at computer speeds, there is not time to examine each one. Hence a correct solution may not be found, simply because the data processing problem is impossible. Humans, on the other hand, appear to have as their typical mistake a failure to generate a correct solution. This suggests that people have some way of (perhaps overly) restricting their search space to a space of feasible solutions. The mathematician Polya (1954, 1957) among others, has suggested that the way this is done is by the use of *plans* and *analogies*. To remove the discussion from psychology to computer science, we can define a plan as a solution to a reduced problem which contains only some of the original problem's key features. Solving a problem in a planning representation will establish a series of subproblems which, hopefully, will be easy to solve in sequence when the original problem is attacked. While we could demonstrate this idea with an example from computing, the

---

[2] Following a debate between EH and Dr. Naomi Weisstein, Shakey's sex will be indeterminate.

principle is just as well, and more simply, illustrated by the "traveling professor" problem. Suppose a professor in Seattle, Washingron wishes to visit a colleague at the University of California's Santa Barbara campus, in southern California. Eventually this problem can only be solved by a series of actions that involve taxi, limousine, airplane trips, and even a bit of walking. Initially the trip will be planned from airport to airport, on the assumption that the local transportation problems will somehow be solved when they arise.

While planning fits naturally into a computer-oriented notion of hierarchical relations between problems and subproblems, analogies seem to be more difficult to deal with in a formal way. They are best understood by reference to the problem reduction representation. Suppose that at some stage an *or* set of subproblems has been identified. The problem solver should, ideally, choose the easiest of these to solve and attack it. If any member of the set is unsolvable, it is clearly a waste of time to attack it. The problem is, "How does the problem solver know a problem is easy or difficult or impossible to solve until the problem is attacked?" To break out of this logical circle, suppose that the problem solver had available a (perhaps not completely accurate) way of representing subproblems that was very easy to manipulate. We shall say that this representation is an analogy to the representation in which the problem is to be solved. The problem solver could solve all the subproblems in the analogy, or at least identify those which could be solved, and use this information to attack the subproblems in the original representation. Note the difference between the analogical and the hierarchical mixture of representations. In the hierarchical mixture different subproblems have their own representation. In the analogy mixture a given subproblem has two representations.

Perhaps one of the clearest and most sophisticated uses of analogical representations appeared quite early in modern artificial intelligence research, in Gelernter's (1963) Artificial Geometer, a program which solved problems in plane geometry. Formally, plane geometry is an axiomatic system in which one defines well-formed expressions from premises, following precisely stated rules of inference based largely on the properties of congruent triangles. To prove something in plane geometry it is necessary to show that the rules of inference can be applied to the premises to derive the desired conclusion. This implies that a mechanical proof technique should rely on a rewriting approach. The problem is that geometry contains so many rules of inference that the number of permissible rewritings from a set of premises is very large, so that it is time consuming to discover the path from the premises to the conclusion. The saving grace is that plane geometry can be interpreted as a set of statements about the relations between lines in a diagram drawn on a flat surface.[3]

---

[3] To solve a geometry problem you "look at the diagram and see how the thing has to work." The relationship between the statements of the geometry problem and the physical arrangement of the diagram are not exact, because the diagram is not perfect, but this can generally be ignored. The same statements could be made about the relationship between a symbolic plane geometry statement and numerical representation of a diagram which could be read by a computer. Any statement in the symbolic representation should be "approximately true" in the diagram.

The Artificial Geometer made use of diagrams as analogical representations of geometry problems. The program was given both a symbolic statement of a problem and a description of an appropriate diagram. (Generating the diagram from the statement would be fairly easy to do, but in fact was not done.) The symbolic premises and conclusions were examined to generate subproblems—which were also expressed as statements to be inferred. The diagram was then examined to determine which of the subproblems were statements which were true in the diagram. Only subproblems that passed this filter were considered further.

The method is illustrated by the problem

Prove that the diagonals of a parallelogram bisect each other.

Formally this problem is stated as

Premise: Figure ABCD;   AB//DC,   AD//BC;   (11)

AB = DC;   AD = BC;   Line AEC;   Line DEB.

Conclusion: AE = EC *and* BE = EB.

An appropriate diagram is shown in Figure 9-9. For simplicity we will deal only

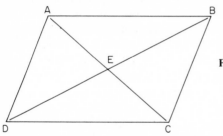

Fig. 9-9.   Parallelogram problem diagram.

with the first problem, AE = EC.[4] Since rules of inference in geometry depend on congruences between triangles, AE and EC can be shown to be equal if they are corresponding parts of congruent triangles. AE appears in the triangles AEB and AEC, EC in the triangles ECB and ECD. Possible congruencies are, from purely symbolic considerations,

---

[4] The reader will no doubt have recognized that the solution of AE = EC is identical to the solution of BE = EB, except that the names of points and lines must be interchanged. The Artificial Geometer, which was a very sophisticated program for its time, was also capable of recognizing this. More formally, if the Geometer solved a problem, and then discovered that it had another problem which could be stated in the same form, excepting only a change in names, it asserted proof of the second problem by syntactic symmetry between the first and second problems. The program could also "draw a line" in the diagram and add to the premises statements about that line.

$$AEB \cong ECB, \tag{12a}$$

$$AEB \cong ECD, \tag{12b}$$

$$AED \cong ECB, \tag{12c}$$

$$AED \cong ECD. \tag{12d}$$

Examination of the diagram, however, shows that only (12b) and (12c) are "graphically congruent." Thus only these subproblems are placed on the list of subproblems to be attacked.

Analogical reasoning is potentially a very powerful heuristic device. In fact, Polya (1954) devoted one entire volume of his two volume work to the discussion of the use of analogy and induction in mathematics. Unfortunately, he presents ad hoc examples but no general rules. Gelernter's work is an example of the application of analogical reasoning to a very specific calculus. Becker (1969) has attempted to develop some general principles about the use of analogies in problem-solving programs, but the results thus far have not been spectacular. One of the problems appears to be that analogies are very specific to the content field in which they are used. Recent artificial intelligence studies have concentrated on the

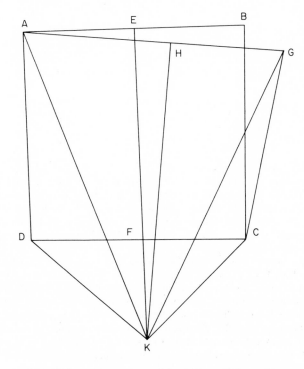

Fig. 9-10.   Inaccurate model of obtuse angle problem.

study of problem solving in the abstract. A second caution we would add is that any inaccuracy in the analogy may lead to an invalid inference. Therefore it is important to maintain a separation between heuristic reasoning using the analogy and formal proof in the original representation.[5]

[5] Many of the most puzzling mathematical puzzles are challenging simply because their wording leads the user either to use an inaccurate analogy or to mix reasoning in the two representations. The nineteenth century English logician, H. L. Dodgson (better known as "Lewis Carroll," the author of *Alice in Wonderland*) was famous for his ability to construct such puzzles. Figure 9–10 is Dodgson's "proof" that obtuse angles are sometimes right angles (Gardner, 1971).

Let ABCD be a square. Bisect AB at E, and through E draw EF at right angles to AB, and cutting DC at F. Then DF = FC. From C draw CG = CB. Join AG, and bisect it at H, and from H draw HK at right angles to AG. Since AB, AG are not parallel, EF, HK are not parallel. Therefore they will meet, if produced. Produce EF, and let them meet at K. Join KD, KA, KG, and KC. The triangles KAH, KGH are equal, because AH = HG, HK is common, and the angles at H are right. Therefore KA = KG. The triangles KDF, KCF are equal, because DF = FC, FK is common, and the angles at F are right. Therefore KD = KC, and angle KDC = angle KCD. Also DA = CB = CG. Hence the triangles KDA, KCG have all their sides equal. Therefore the angles KDA, KCG are equal. From these equals take the equal angles KDC, KCD. Therefore the remainders are equal: i.e., the angle GCD = the angle ADC. But GCD is an obtuse angle, and ADC is a right angle. An obtuse angle is sometimes a right angle.

Chapter X

GRAPHIC REPRESENTATIONS IN PROBLEM SOLVING

10.0   Basic Concepts and Definitions

In a state-space formulation a problem can be represented as a directed graph and a problem solution as a path between selected nodes in the graph; a natural question is "How does one find a path through a graph?" This chapter is devoted to a presentation of some appropriate algorithms. In the main, these algorithms have been taken from or are modifications of algorithms presented by Nilsson (1971), who has presented a very thorough discussion of graphic methods in problem solving. There are a number of "puzzles" that do not fit the restricted definition of problem solving considered here, but can still be handled by graphic methods. The interested reader is referred to Harary, Norman, and Cartwright's (1965) textbook on the topic.

Let $N = \{n_i\}$ be a denumerable set of *nodes*, and $E = \{e(n_i, n_j)\}$ be a set of labeled arcs between nodes. (In the cases of most interest e will be a real-valued function interpreted as the cost of traversing the arc.) Together E and N define a *graph*, G. Let S_0 and S_g be subsets of N called the *starting* and *goal* sets. A *solution* is a sequence of nodes $n_0, n_1, n_2, \ldots, n_k$ such that $n_0 \in S_0$ and $n_k \in S_g$. Two nodes, n_j, n_{i+1} may be in the sequence only if $e(n_i, n_{i+1})$ is defined. The cost of the solution is simply the sum of the labels of the arcs, i.e.,

$$\text{Cost of solution} = \sum_{i=0}^{k-1} e(n_i, n_{i+1}). \tag{1}$$

A solution is minimal if there is no other solution with lower cost. The length of a solution is the number of nodes in it.

These ideas may be illustrated graphically. Figure 10-1 shows a hypothetical route map for the West Coast of the United States. Clearly there are several routes from Seattle to San Diego, each with an associated cost in terms of miles. This is a

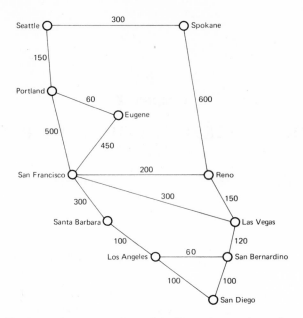

Fig. 10-1.   Transportation map to be used in illustrating graph searches. (Distances have been chosen for illustration and are not geographically correct.)

finite problem. Figure 10-2 shows part of an infinite, denumerable graph indicating the well-formed expressions of simple algebra that can be derived from x using the equivalence relations

$$x + y = y + x,$$

$$x = (x + y) - y,$$

$$x + (y + z) = (x + y) + z, \qquad (2)$$

$$(x + y) - z = (x - z) + y.$$

The derivation of $(y - y) + x$ from x can be made in three or five steps.

Although these problems are trivial, they can illustrate a number of points about graph searching. First, why are they trivial? Probably because a person can take a

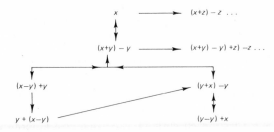

Fig. 10-2.   Example of graph representation in algebraic problem solving.

global view of a graph. Consider how the graph would appear to a computer or, equivalently, to a bug with total recall. All such a device would know about the graph would be information about the arcs actually visited. This is the viewpoint from which a computational algorithm must work. The following definitions will be used.

$$g(n) = \text{Cost of minimal path from any node in } S_0 \text{ to node } n, \qquad (3)$$

$$h(n) = \text{Cost of a minimal path from } n \text{ to the closest member of } S_g.$$

Note that n is not required to be in S_0.

$$f(n) = \text{cost of a minimal path from } S_0 \text{ to } S_g \text{ constrained to include } n.$$

From these definitions it is trivially true that

$$f(n) = g(n) + h(n) \qquad (4)$$

The information needed to compute f, g, and h may not be available if the entire graph is not known. In this case estimates $\hat{f}$, $\hat{g}$, and $\hat{h}$ may provide the basis for a decision. The caret indicates that the function is being estimated and may be reevaluated with more information.

The set of nodes that can be reached directly from node n [i.e., the set of nodes $\{m\}$ for which $e(n, m)$ is defined] will be referred to as the *successor* nodes of n, and written $\mathbf{S(n)}$.

To complete the preliminaries, note that if n_i and n_j are nodes on a minimal path, then

$$f(n_i) = f(n_j). \qquad (5)$$

10.1   Algorithms for Finding a Minimal Path to a Single Goal Node

10.1.0   GENERAL

Four basic algorithms for graph searching will be discussed. Each starts by designating some node $n_0 \in S_0$ as the initial node, finding its successors, $\mathbf{S}(n_0)$, and then ordering the set $V = \mathbf{S}(n_0) \cup \{S_0 - n_0\}$ in accordance with an estimate $\hat{f}(n)$ of the cost of the solution path for each $n \in V$. Nilsson uses the following general way to describe how the algorithms work. When a node is assigned an $\hat{f}(n)$ value for the first time, it is placed in an ordered set called OPEN. Nodes are removed from OPEN in ascending order of $\hat{f}(n)$. When a node is removed from OPEN, it is placed in a set called CLOSE (This will be called "*closing* node n"). When a node is closed the $\hat{f}$ values associated with each node in OPEN may be recomputed. Therefore, we must complicate our notation slightly, by letting $\hat{f}_i(n_j)$ stand for "The value of $\hat{f}(n_j)$ computed as node n_i is closed." A similar definition will hold for $\hat{g}_i(n_j)$. Every node in either OPEN or CLOSE is assumed to have recorded with it the node that was closed at the time that its *current* $\hat{f}$ value was established.

10.1.1   BREADTH FIRST ALGORITHM

The Algorithm

1. Place all nodes of S_0 into OPEN in arbitrary order.
2. If OPEN is empty, exit with a failure. There is no solution.
3. Close the first node in OPEN. Let this be node n. If $n \in S_g$ quit with a success. The solution is given, in inverse order, by node n, the node that was closed at the time node n was placed in OPEN, the node that was closed at the time that node was placed in OPEN, etc., until some node $n \in S_0$ is reached. If $n \in S_g$ go to 4.
4. Find $\mathbf{S}(n)$. Place all nodes in the set $\mathbf{S}(n) - (\text{OPEN} \cup \text{CLOSED})$ in OPEN, in arbitrary order excepting that they follow any node already in OPEN. Record the fact that n was used to place each of the new nodes in OPEN.

Example

Consider the problem of finding a route from Seattle to Reno in Figure 10-1. The successive entries on OPEN and CLOSED are:

OPEN	CLOSED
1. Seattle (Start)	
2. Portland (Seattle)	Seattle (Start)
Spokane (Seattle)	
3. Spokane (Seattle)	Portland (Seattle)
Eugene (Portland)	Seattle (Start)
San Francisco (Portland)	
4. Eugene (Portland)	Spokane (Seattle)
San Francisco (Portland)	Portland (Seattle)
Reno (Spokane)	Spokane (Seattle)
	Portland (Seattle)
	Seattle (Start)
5. Reno (Spokane)	San Francisco (Portland)
Santa Barbara (San Francisco)	Eugene (Portland)
San Bernardino (San Francisco)	Spokane (Seattle)
	Portland (Seattle)
	Seattle (Start)

At the next step the solution is detected. The route is, in *inverse* order, Reno–Spokane–Seattle.

The breadth first method will always find the solution path with the fewest links, as all nodes not more than $k - 1$ steps from some node in S_0 are examined before any nodes k steps from S_0. By definition, a node in S_0, being zero steps away from itself, is zero steps away from the starting set.

10.1.2   UNIFORM COST SEARCH

This is a modification of breadth first to minimize the cost of the final solution.

The Algorithm

1. Place all nodes $n \in S_0$ on OPEN in arbitrary order.
   Let $\hat{g}(n) = 0$.

2. If OPEN is empty, exit without a solution.

3. Let n_i be the node in OPEN for which $\hat{g}(n_i)$ is a minimum. If $n_i \in S_g$ quit with a solution, tracing a path back to some node $n_0 \in S_0$ as before. Otherwise close n_i and go to 4.

4. For all $n^* \in S(n_j)$, compute $\hat{g}_i(n_i) + e(n_i, n^*)$. This is the estimated minimum path from some node in S_0 to n^*, constrained to go through n_i, as calculated when n_i is closed. If n^* is not in OPEN, place it there with $\hat{g}(n^*) = \hat{g}_i(n^*)$. If n^* is in OPEN, and $\hat{g}_i(n^*) < \hat{g}(n^*)$, then replace the current value of $\hat{g}(n^*) = \hat{g}_i(n^*)$, and record that n^* was placed on OPEN via n_i. Otherwise, leave $\hat{g}(n^*)$ and OPEN as they were. Note that this procedure may vary the estimate $g(n^*)$ as new nodes are closed.

5. Go to step 2.

Example.

The algorithm can be illustrated by solving the problem of going from San Francisco to Los Angeles, again using the map of Figure 10-1. (Again, recall that the distances are chosen for illustration only.) The successive contents of OPEN and CLOSE, this time shown with their distance estimators and the link to other nodes, are

OPEN	CLOSE
1. San Francisco (0, Start)	
2. Reno (200, San Francisco) Santa Barbara (300, San Francisco) San Bernardino (300, San Francisco) Eugene (450, San Francisco) Portland (500, San Francisco)	San Francisco (0, Start)
3. Santa Barbara (300, San Francisco) San Bernardino (300, San Francisco) Las Vegas (350, Reno) Eugene (450, San Francisco) Portland (500, San Francisco) Spokane (800, Reno)	Reno (200, San Francisco) San Francisco (0, Start)
4. San Bernardino (300, San Francisco) Las Vegas (350, Reno) Los Angeles (400, Santa Barbara) Eugene (450, San Francisco) Portland (500, San Francisco) Spokane (800, Reno)	Santa Barbara (300, San Francisco) Reno (200, San Francisco) San Francisco (0, Start)
5. Las Vegas (350, Reno) Los Angeles (360, San Bernardino) Eugene (400, San Francisco) Portland (500, San Francisco) Spokane (800, Reno)	San Bernardino (300, San Francisco) Santa Barbara (300, San Francisco) Reno (300, San Francisco) San Francisco (0, Start)
6. Los Angeles (360, San Bernardino) Eugene (400, San Francisco) Portland (500, San Francisco) Spokane (800, Reno)	Las Vegas (350, Reno) San Bernardino (300, San Francisco) Santa Barbara (300, San Francisco) Reno (200, San Francisco) San Francisco, 0, Start)

Solution is achieved at the next step, with the route San Francisco–San Bernardino–Los Angeles.

This algorithm is an improvement over the previous one because nodes are placed in CLOSE in the order of their distance from the START. Thus, any node in OPEN will be further from START than any node on CLOSE. If we can assume that when n is closed its true distance from the closest node of S_0 has been established, then the uniform cost method will always produce the shortest solution path. This assumption is established by the following theorem:

Uniform Cost Theorem.

Using the uniform cost method, when n is closed, the minimum path from S_0 to n will have been established and hence, $\hat{g}_i(n_i) = g(n_i)$ for all i.

Proof of Theorem:

Two lemmas are required

Lemma 1.

If any $n_j \in S(n_i)$ is placed on OPEN when n_i is closed, or if already in OPEN, if $\hat{g}_i(n_j) < \hat{g}(n_j)$, for any n closed pair PRIOR to n_i, then

$$\hat{g}_i(n_j) = \hat{g}_i(n_i) + e(n_i, n_j) \geq \hat{g}_i(n_i). \tag{6}$$

Proof of lemma:

The right-hand side of the equality is the definition of an adjustment of $\hat{g}_i$. The weak ordering follows since $e(n_i, n_j) \geq 0$.

Corollary:

Suppose n_k is a successor to some node n_j, and when n_k is closed, that $\hat{g}_k(n_k) = \hat{g}_j(n_k)$. Furthermore, suppose that $\hat{g}_j(n_j) = \hat{g}_i(n_j)$. Then

$$\hat{g}_k(n_k) \geq \hat{g}_i(n_i). \tag{7}$$

Any node n_k which, when it is closed, can have its current estimate of distance from S_0 traced back to an estimate based upon the distance of n_i from S_0 when n_i was closed will be called a *descendant* of n_i. Conversely, n_i will be called an *ancestor* of n_k. The weak ordering of (7) holds for all n_k descended from n_i.

Lemma 2.

If node n_j is closed after node n_i, then $\hat{g}_j(n_j) \geq \hat{g}_i(n_i)$, i.e., the order in which nodes are closed is in ascending order of their $\hat{g}$ estimates at time of closing.

Proof of lemma:

Let N^* be the set of nodes in OPEN at the time n_i is closed, and let n_k be any node in N^*. The relation

$$\hat{g}_i(n_k) \geq \hat{g}_i(n_i) \tag{8}$$

must be true, otherwise n_k would have been closed instead of n_i. Now consider any node n_j which is closed after n_i is closed. If n_j is a descendent of n_i, then by the Corollary to Lemma 1, $\hat{g}_j(n_j) \geqslant \hat{g}_i(n_i)$. If n_j is not a descendent of n_i, then it must be a descendent of some node $n_k \in N^*$ that was closed after n_i was closed, but was not itself a descendent of n_i and was closed with $\hat{g}_k(n_k) = \hat{g}_i(n_k)$. In this case we have

$$\hat{g}_j(n_j) \geqslant \hat{g}_k(n_k) = \hat{g}_i(n_k) \geqslant \hat{g}_i(n_i) \tag{9}$$

and the lemma is proved.

After n_i has been closed, we might subsequently close some node n_j such that $n_i \in S(n_j)$. In doing so, we could obtain a new estimate of $\hat{g}(n_i)$, as $\hat{g}_j(n_j) + e(n_j, n_i)$. By application of the two lemmas, this new estimate would have to obey the relation

$$\hat{g}_j(n_j) + e(n_j, n_i) \geqslant \hat{g}_j(n_j) \geqslant \hat{g}_i(n_i), \tag{10}$$

hence, $\hat{g}_i(n_i)$ would not be recomputed. This means that when n_i was closed, its estimated distance from some member of S_0 was at a minimum, so the path traced from n_i back to its ancestor in S_0 was a minimum path, and therefore

$$\hat{g}_i(n_i) = g(n_i) \tag{11}$$

proving the theorem.

10.1.3   ORDERED SEARCH

Although the solution obtained by the uniform cost search is optimal the search for a solution is not. This was illustrated in the example, where at one stage the algorithm considered routes from San Francisco to Los Angeles via Portland. A person would avoid this by making use of concepts like "north," "south," and "in the general direction of." Such criteria for choosing the next step do not always work, but they often help. The next algorithm, the *ordered search* method, uses a similar idea. The node to expand is chosen partly on the basis of the estimated solution path length $(\hat{f})$, rather than its distance from the starting states.

Ordered Search Algorithm

1. Place S_0 in OPEN in increasing order of estimate of $\hat{f}(n)$, $n \in S_0$.
2. If OPEN is empty exit with a failure.
3. CLOSE that node n on OPEN for which $\hat{f}(n)$ is a minimum.
4. Place $S(n)$ on OPEN. If any node $n^* \in S(n)$ is already in OPEN, recompute $\hat{f}(n^*)$ if the new estimate, based on closing n, is less than the previous estimate. If a new $\hat{f}(n^*)$ value is computed, it is necessary to extend this to computations of new $\hat{f}$ values for all descendants of n^* in OPEN.
5. Go to 2.

Clearly the algorithm is vacuous without a definition of $\hat{f}(n)$. A commonly used one is presented below. The other algorithms can all be considered special cases of the ordered search algorithm using a suitable definition of $\hat{f}(n)$. If

$$\hat{f}(n_i) = 0 \quad \text{if} \quad n_i \in S_0 \tag{12}$$

$$\hat{f}_j(n_i) = \hat{f}_j(n_j) + 1 \quad \text{if} \quad n_i \in S(n_j)$$

we obtain the breadth first. The uniform cost method can be obtained by letting $\hat{f}_i(n_k) = \hat{g}_i(n_k) =$ for all i, k.

10.1.4   DEPTH FIRST SEARCHING

For completeness, a fourth graph searching technique, known as *"depth first"* searching, should be mentioned. The name comes from its application in tree graphs. Instead of going down all paths simultaneously, an equal distance on each, the depth first method first follows on path to its end, then the next path, etc. In the transportation example, a depth first search might proceed from San Francisco to Portland, to Seattle, to Spokane, to Reno, and then back to San Francisco. On detecting this loop, the depth first algorithm would back up to Reno and explore alternate routes, if any existed. Following this, alternatives from Spokane would be examined.

Depth First Algorithm

1. Place all nodes in S_0 on OPEN in any arbitrarily chosen order.
2. If OPEN is empty exit with failure.
3. Close the first node on OPEN. If it is a goal node exit with success.
4. Place the successors to the node just closed on OPEN *preceding* any node already on OPEN. If any node in the successor set already occurs on OPEN remove the earlier occurrence. If any node in the successor set is on CLOSE do not place it on OPEN.
5. Go to 2.

A depth first search can be trapped in a nonterminating search if the graph is not finite. For example, consider the graph of Figure 10-1b. Suppose the task is to find a path from X to $Y + (X - Y)$. A possible sequence of states explored by the depth first method is

$$X$$

$$(X + Y) - Y$$

$$(((X + Y) - Y) + Y) - Y$$

$$(((((X + Y) - Y) + Y) - Y) + Y) - Y$$

etc.

This path neither terminates nor includes the goal path. To guard against such situations it is customary to include in implementations of the algorithm an additional step (3a) which states that the successors of a node are not to be placed on OPEN if the node being closed is on a path of length **k** or greater from the starting set. The value of **k** is set specifically for each problem. While this step is clearly needed in any implementation that might deal with an infinite graph, it destroys the possibility of general analysis of the resulting program.

The depth first algorithm will not in general find the shortest or least cost solution. To consider this, reexamine the San Francisco–Los Angeles problem of Figure 10-1 using a depth first algorithm with the rule that the successor set is placed on OPEN with the northernmost branch first, and branches in counterclockwise order thereafter. The route discovered by the algorithm goes from San Francisco to Los Angeles via Portland, Seattle, Spokane, Reno, and Las Vegas! This is hardly optimal.

In view of these deficiencies, one might well ask why this algorithm is discussed at all. In part, the answer is "for historical reasons." Depth first searching is quite easy to program, since OPEN can be ordered appropriately by pushing and pulling a pushdown list, or stack (Knuth, 1969). As a result, depth first searches have been appealing to people who wanted to get something off the ground. At least one author has acknowledged this explicitly (Slagle, 1965b). There may be another, more subtle, reason. Depth first searching is a method that is easy for people to execute. Breadth first searching often places a large number of nodes on OPEN. It always requires a scheme for keeping track of which nodes are tied to which nodes. Depth first searching, on the other hand, generally holds fewer nodes on OPEN and ties them together by the order in which they are on OPEN rather than by the use of explicit pointers. Modern theories of human memory (Norman, 1969, Kintsch, 1970) stress that people have very limited amounts of storage for active information, and thus must adopt problem solving strategies which do not require that they keep track of a great many things at one time. This, of course, would make depth first searching more attractive.

The argument that depth first searching is psychologically more natural is not entirely a theoretical one. Newell and Simon (1965) noted that in chess play, which can be formulated as a graph searching problem, a very good human player used a modified depth first search. We have conducted a number of experiments in which people are given explicit graph searching problems and asked to solve them using either depth first of breadth first searches. Almost invariably people can follow the depth first instructions, but are unable to execute even fairly simple breadth first searches.

10.2 An "Optimal" Ordered Search Algorithm

10.2.0 DEFINITION OF A HEURISTIC FUNCTION

Nilsson suggests that in using an ordered search, $\hat{f}$ be defined by

$$\hat{f}(n) = \hat{g}(n) + \hat{h}(n), \tag{13}$$

where $\hat{h}(n)$ is an estimate of $h(n)$. He refers to $\hat{h}(n)$ as a "heuristic estimate," which represents a best guess of the difficulty of reaching S_g from n, given knowledge of some of the characteristics of n. This definition of $\hat{f}$ is intuitively reasonable, since if all our estimates were perfect, we would have $\hat{g}(n) = g(n)$ and $\hat{h}(n) = h(n)$, and

$$\hat{f}(n) = g(n) + h(n) = f(n) \tag{14}$$

is obviously optimal from the definitions previously given. Note that the definition in (13) assumes that the difficulty of solving a problem given a partial solution (i.e. arrival at node n) is independent of the way in which the partial solution was reached.

Nilsson has also shown that some intuitively reasonable restrictions on $\hat{h}$ lead to interesting results. Let $h(m, n)$ be the cost of the shortest path from m to n, where neither m nor n need be in S_0 or S_g. We require that

$$h(n) \geqslant \hat{h}(n) \geqslant 0 \tag{15}$$

$$\hat{h}(m) - \hat{h}(n) \leqslant h(m, n). \tag{16}$$

Since $h(n)$ is the "true cost" of moving from n to S_g, the first restriction states that the estimated cost of moving from n to S_g be nonnegative but not an overestimate. Inequality (16) requires that a similar restriction against overestimation apply to the cost of any segment of the solution path.

An algorithm is *admissible* if the solution which it finds is a minimum cost solution. Thus, the uniform cost algorithm is admissible. The following theorem proves that the use of (13) in the ordered search procedure produces an admissible algorithm.

Ordered Search Theorem

An ordered search algorithm using $\hat{f}$ as defined in (13), and $\hat{h}$ subject to the restrictions of (15) and (16), is admissible.

Proof. The algorithm cannot terminate until either a goal is found or all descendents of nodes in S_0 are closed. Hence, if a solution exists, it will be found.

By definition, for any node $n_g \in S_g$, $h(n_g) = 0$.
By (14), this requires that $\hat{h}(n_g) = 0$. Suppose n_g is placed on OPEN by closing some node n_i. At this point we will have

$$\hat{f}_i(n_g) = \hat{g}_i(n_g) + 0 = \hat{g}_i(n_g) \tag{17}$$

$$= \hat{g}_i(n_i) + e(n_i, n_g)$$

Subsequently, $\hat{f}(n_g)$ will be changed only if a node n_j is closed such that

$$\hat{f}_i(n_g) > \hat{g}_j(n_j) + e(n_j, n_g). \tag{18}$$

First a lemma is required.

Lemma 1.

Under the conditions of the theorem, $\hat{g}_i(n_i) = g_i(n_i)$.

Lemma 1 states that when a node is closed its minimum cost path from S_0 will have been determined. The lemma already has been shown to be true for the special case $\hat{h}(n) = 0$ for all n, since this is the uniform cost method. It will be proven for the general case.

Proof. Let n_i be the node that is being closed, and let N^* be the set of nodes on OPEN at that time. Subsequent to n_i's being closed, a less costly path to n_i could only be discovered if some node n_k were closed, $n_i \in S(n_k)$, and

$$\hat{g}_i(n_i) > \hat{g}_k(n_k) + e(n_k, n_i). \tag{19}$$

It will now be shown that this is impossible.

A minimal path from S_0 to n_i cannot contain n_i as an intermediate node. Suppose it did. If, at the time n_k is closed, n_k is a descendent of n_i, then

$$\hat{g}_k(n_k) + e(n_k, n_i) = \hat{g}_i(n_i) + h(n_i, n_k) + e(n_k, n_i) \tag{20}$$

$$\geqslant \hat{g}_i(n_i),$$

violating relation (19).

If n_k is not a descendent of n_i when n_k is closed, then it must be a descendent of some node $n_j \in N^*$, where n_j is not a descendent of n_i. Furthermore, n_j must have been closed without adjusting the estimate $\hat{g}$ below the one it held when n_i was closed, i.e., $\hat{g}_j(n_j) = \hat{g}_i(n_j)$, for the contrary would contradict the assumption that n_j, and hence n_k, are not descendants of n_i.

Therefore

$$\hat{g}_k(n_k) + e(n_k, n_i) + \hat{h}(n_i) = \hat{g}_j(n_j) + e(n_j, n_k) + e(n_k, n_i) + \hat{h}(n_i) \tag{21}$$

$$= \hat{g}_i(n_j) + h(n_j, n_i) + \hat{h}(n_i)$$

by restriction (16)

$$\hat{g}_i(n_j) + h(n_j, n_i) + \hat{h}(n_i) \geqslant \hat{g}_i(n_j) + (\hat{h}(n_j) - \hat{h}(n_i)) + \hat{h}(n_i) \tag{22}$$

$$\geqslant \hat{g}_i(n_j) + \hat{h}(n_j)$$

$$\geqslant \hat{f}_i(n_j)$$

Since n_i was closed before n_j, we know that $f_i(n_i) \leqslant f_i(n_j)$. Therefore

$$\hat{g}_i(n_j) + h(n_i, n_j) + \hat{h}(n_i) \geqslant f_i(n_i). \tag{23}$$

By substituting the left side of (21) for the left side of (23) and subtracting $\hat{h}(n_i)$ from both sides, we have

$$g_k(n_k) + e(n_k, n_i) \geqslant \hat{g}_i(n_i). \tag{24}$$

Therefore $\hat{g}_i(n_i)$ must be at its minimum, $g(n_i)$, when n_i is closed, proving the lemma. A direct application of the lemma shows that when some $n_g \in S_g$ is closed, $\hat{f}_g(n_g) = g(n_g)$, i.e., the cost of a shortest path to that goal node has been established.

It remains to be shown that the goal node closest to S_0 will be chosen. By application of Lemma 1, no goal node will be closed until the immediate ancestor on a least cost path has been closed. Furthermore, we know, from restriction (15), that when any ancestor of a goal node is closed, the cost of the path between the ancestor and the nearest goal node is not overestimated. Since all nodes of S_0 are in OPEN at some time, we are assured that either the goal node on the minimal cost path, n_{g*}, is in OPEN with estimate $\hat{f}(n_{g*}) = g(n_{g*})$ or some ancestor of n_{g*} is in OPEN. In the former case n_{g*} will be closed before any other goal node on OPEN. In the latter case the ancestor of n_{g*} will be closed before the other goal node is closed, placing n_{g*} or yet another of its (closer) ancestors on OPEN, and repeating the situation. Therefore no goal node ($n_g\ S_g$) will be closed until n_{g*} is closed, and the algorithm must discover the minimum cost path.

10.2.1   THE OPTIMALITY THEOREM

This theorem establishes a characteristic of algorithms which search efficiently for an optimal path. The idea of an "informed algorithm" is first introduced by saying that if two algorithms, A and A^*, are ordered search algorithms which are identical except for their heuristic functions, h and h^*, respectively, then A is *no more informed* than A^* if, for all nodes,

$$h(n) \geqslant h^*(n) \geqslant 0. \tag{25}$$

i.e. if A^* and A both underestimate $h(n)$, but if A^*'s estimates are more accurate, then A is no more informed than A^*.

The Optimality Theorem.

Let $\mathbf{A}^*$ be the set or ordered search algorithms which use h^*, and differ among themselves only in the way in which they choose which of two nodes, n_j and n_k, to close when both are on OPEN with estimates $\hat{f}_j(n_j) = \hat{f}_j(n_k)$. $\mathbf{A}^*$ contains some algorithm A^* such that for any A not in $\mathbf{A}^*$, a node closed by A^* is also closed by A. In particular, the algorithm A^* that breaks ties in the same manner as does algorithm A will close only nodes also closed by A. $\mathbf{A}^*$ is *optimal* in the sense that it contains at least one algorithm that closes no more nodes than any $A \notin \mathbf{A}^*$.

Although optimality is, by name, an intuitive idea, the theorem is less interesting than it might be. What it says is that if we restrict ourselves to the set of admissible algorithms based on various "non-overestimates" of the true cost of reaching solution from a given point, then the best of these is the one which does the least underestimating.

Loosely, the optimality theorem is true because each algorithm seeks to close the next node on the minimum cost path at each step. Since A makes lower estimates of path costs than A^*, A may investigate a path that A^* rejects, not vice versa. A formal proof of this statement is given in the paragraph immediately following. It is surprisingly tedious. A good intuitive view of the algorithm can be obtained by skipping directly to the example.

Proof. A lemma is required.

Lemma 1.

If an ordered search algorithm closes nodes in the order $n_0, n_1, n_2, \ldots, n_t$, then $i < j$ implies that $\hat{f}_i(n_i) \leqslant \hat{f}_j(n_j)$.

Proof of Lemma. The proof of the lemma is by induction on the nodes in the order they are closed, $n_0, n_1, n_2, \ldots$.

Base. The first node closed, n_0, is in S_0. Consider any other node n_i in S_0. By definition $\hat{g}_0(n_i) = 0$, and since this is a minimum, $\hat{f}_i(n_i) = \hat{h}(n_i)$ for any n_i in S_0. Since n_0 was chosen before n_i, we have

$$\hat{f}_0(n_0) \leqslant \hat{f}_i(n_i), \qquad n_i \in S_0. \tag{26}$$

Consider any node n_j subsequently added to OPEN. When it is closed, by Lemma 1, of the ordered search theorem, we will have

$$\hat{f}_j(n_j) = g_j(n_j) + \hat{h}(n_j). \tag{27}$$

Since n_j was derived from some node in n_i in S_0, then by applying (15) and (16),

$$\hat{f}_j(n_j) = h(n_i, n_j) + \hat{h}(n_j) \geqslant \hat{h}(n_i) - \hat{h}(n_j) + \hat{h}(n_j) \tag{28}$$

$$\geqslant \hat{h}(n_i),$$

By substitution of the definition of $\hat{f}_i(n_i)$ for $n_i \in S_0$, and application of (26).

$$\hat{f}_j(n_j) \geqslant \hat{f}_0(n_0) \tag{29}$$

proving the theorem for n_0.

Progression. Assume that the lemma is true for all nodes through n_{i-1}. Let n_i be the node being closed. Consider the set of nodes that are on OPEN at this time and for which n_i is not on the shortest path from S_0, i.e., the nodes on OPEN which will not be descendents of n_i when they are closed. Either this set is empty or it includes at least one node n_k whose immediate ancestor, n_a, $a < i$, has been closed. Note that any node on OPEN when n_i is closed must either fulfill the conditions for n_k, or have n_i as an immediate ancestor, or have some node in OPEN which is its ancestor and does fulfill the requirements for n_k. For node n_k we have

$$\hat{g}_i(n_k) + \hat{h}(n_k) = g(n_a) + e(n_a, n_k) + \hat{h}(n_k) \tag{30}$$

$$\hat{f}_i(n_k) = \hat{g}_i(n_k) + \hat{h}(n_k)$$

$$= \hat{f}_k(n_k).$$

Since n_i was chosen for closing instead of n_k, it must be that

$$\hat{f}_i(n_i) \leqslant \hat{f}_i(n_k) = \hat{f}_k(n_k). \tag{31}$$

Now consider any node n_j which either was not on OPEN when n_i was closed, or did not fit the definition of n_k. When n_j is closed one of its ancestors will either be n_i itself or some node n_k satisfying (30) and (31).

In the former case

$$\hat{f}_j(n_j) = g_i(n_j) + \hat{h}(n_j) \tag{32}$$

$$= g_i(n_i) + h(n_i n_j) + \hat{h}(n_j)$$

$$\geqslant g_i(n_i) + \hat{h}(n_i) = \hat{f}_i(n_i).$$

In the latter case, we substitute k for i in (27) then apply (31) to produce

$$\hat{f}_j(n_j) \geqslant \hat{f}_k(n_k) \geqslant \hat{f}_i(n_i). \tag{33}$$

This proves the lemma.

Proof of Theorem. Let f^* stand for the estimates generated by A^*, using h^*. Since both A and A^* are ordered search algorithms

$$\hat{f}_g(n_g) = f(n_g) = g(n_g) = \hat{f}_g^*(n_g) \qquad \text{for all} \quad n_g \in S_g, \tag{34}$$

No node n_i will ever be closed by either algorithm if

$$\hat{f}_i(n_i) > f(n_g), \tag{35}$$

where n_g is a goal node on a least cost path from S_0.

We prove the theorem by induction on nodes in the order they are closed by A^*.

Base. Since n_0^* is in S_0, n_0^* is in OPEN for A and A^* by Step 1 of the algorithm. Since

$$\hat{f}_0(n_0^*) \leqslant \hat{f}_0^*(n_0^*) \leqslant f(n_g), \tag{36}$$

and A must close n_g, then A must close n_0^*.

Progression. Assume that all nodes up to n_i^* have been closed by A, and that $f^*(n_i^*) < f(n_g)$, so that n_i^* will be closed by A.

Either n_i^* is a member of S_0 or it is a descendant of a node that has been closed by A and A^*. In the former case it is on open with $f(n_i^*) < f(n_g)$ and must be closed. In the latter case, either n_i^* will have been placed in OPEN by A or A will have been placed in OPEN some ancestor of n_i^*, n_a, such that

$$\hat{f}_a(n_a) \leqslant \hat{f}_i(n_i^*) \leqslant f(n_g) \tag{37}$$

Thus A must either close n_i^* or one of its ancestors before it can close n_g and terminate. A is required to place n_i^* on open, and once there, it must be closed before n_g is closed. The only case that remains is the case of equality,

$$\hat{f}_j(n_j) = \hat{f}_j^*(n_j) = f(n_g).$$

In this case A^* will either choose to close n_g and terminate or will make an erroneous choice. What will happen will depend on the tie breaking rule. If A^* does make the wrong choice, A^* will contain some other algorithm, A^{**}, which is identical to A^* except that it uses the tie breaking rules of A.

Example. The ordered search algorithm may improve the search for a solution even when using a crude heuristic. To see this, look again at the example of finding a route from San Francisco to Los Angeles, using the following guide.

(1) If the route is generally north let $\hat{h}$ be half the distance traveled to the north.
(2) If the route is generally east let $\hat{h}$ be one quarter the distance traveled.
(3) If the route is generally south $\hat{h} = 0$.

The steps taken in solution will now be, with $\hat{f}$ replacing $\hat{g}$.

OPEN	CLOSE
1. San Francisco (0, start)	
2. Reno (250, San Francisco)	San Francisco (0, start)
Santa Barbara (300, San Francisco)	
San Bernardino (300, San Francisco)	
Eugene (675, San Francisco)	
Portland (750, San Francisco)	
3. Santa Barbara (300, San Francisco)	Reno (250, San Francisco)
San Bernardino (300, San Francisco)	San Francisco (0, start)
Las Vegas (400, Reno)	
Eugene (675, San Francisco)	
Portland (750, San Francisco)	
4. San Bernardino (300, San Francisco)	Santa Barbara (300, San Francisco)
Las Vegas (400, Reno)	Reno (250, San Francisco)
Los Angeles (400, Santa Barbara)	San Francisco (0, start)
Eugene (675, San Francisco)	
Portland (750, San Francisco)	
5. Los Angeles (360, San Bernardino)	San Bernardino (300, San Francisco)
Las Vegas (400, Reno)	Santa Barbara (300, San Francisco)
Eugene (675, San Francisco)	Reno (250, San Francisco)
Portland (750, San Francisco)	San Francisco (0, start)

The solution is discovered at the next step. Only five nodes will have been opened, as opposed to six opened by the uniform cost method.

In complicated transportation problems much more dramatic results have been obtained with only slightly more complex heuristic functions. An example is a problem in route finding for a vehicle with a cross-country capability. Suppose a vehicle is at point X and wishes to move to point Y. The vehicle can move at varying speeds along country roads, across fields, or by freeway. The quickest route from X to Y is desired. As a heuristic function, we let $\hat{h}^*(n)$ be the time that it would take to go from any point n along the best possible road to point X *assuming* *that the appropriate super-highway exists.* This heuristic was used in a study[1] of computer aided tactical planning for military unit movements, where it produced savings in computer time by a factor of a hundred or more in some cases.

10.3   Tree Graphs and Their Use

10.3.0   DEFINITIONS

A *tree graph* is a directed graph containing a single distinguished node, called the *root*, for which there is no input arc. Every other node in the graph has exactly one input arc. Loops and slings (arcs from a node to itself) are not permitted. Nodes which have no output arcs are called *leaves*, nodes with both input and output arcs are *interior nodes*. The resulting graph is depicted in Figure 10-3. Despite the arboreal terminology, the graph is a familial rather than an agricultural variety, a fact which is reflected by the usage that nodes below a node are *descendents*, while a node above a node is an *ancestor*. Note that any node within a tree is the root of a subtree consisting of the node and its descendents. Because of this we shall occasionally speak of a subtree rooted at node *n*.

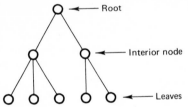

Fig. 10-3.   A tree graph.

Trees are used in two ways in artificial intelligence research, to represent problems solvable by the problem reduction method and to model the play of formal games. In *problem reduction* graphs multiple end points (i.e., a set of leaves) must be reached before a problem is solved . . . or at least before it is solved in the most obvious representation. In *game playing graphs* the tree unfolds bit by bit, and there is no backing up, since making one move may deny a player the option of investigating alternative moves. In both cases it is not possible to apply the state-space search algorithms just presented directly. The usual alternative is to use algorithms specifically designed for a tree searching task. We shall see, however, that this is not always necessary.

10.3.1   PROBLEM REDUCTION TREES

The basic ideas behind the searching of a reduction tree can be illustrated by the problem of finding an expression for the indefinite integral

$$F(x) = \int \frac{x^2 - 2x + 1}{x - 1} \, dx \tag{38}$$

[1] As a master's thesis in computer science by Oren K. Phipps.

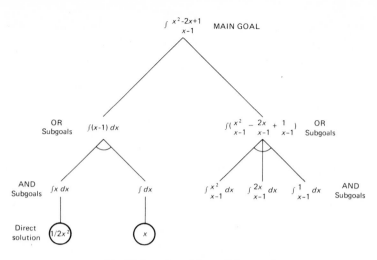

Fig. 10-4.   A problem solving graph.

A problem-solving tree for this problem is shown in Figure 10-4. We could factor the numerator of (38), discovering that it is $(x - 1)^2$, and use this fact to cancel the denominator, giving us a simpler equivalent expression

$$F(x) = \int (x - 1)\, dx. \tag{39}$$

Alternately, we could use the identity $(a + b)/c = a/c + b/c$ to arrange for integration by parts,

$$F(x) = \int [x^2/(x - 1) + 2x/(x - 1) + 1/(x - 1)]\, dx \tag{40}$$

Either (39) or (40) are OR subgoals of the original problem, as is indicated in the figure. Each of the subgoals, in turn, has its own subgoals. Equation (39) can be integrated by parts, provided that the solution to both

$$F_1(x) = \int x\, dx \tag{41}$$

and

$$F_2(x) = \int dx \tag{42}$$

can be found. Integration by parts of (40) produces three somewhat more complicated subgoals. Note that (41), (42) and the tree expressions that compose (40) must all be solved before the problems which generated them are solved. Therefore these subproblems are AND subgoals of the generating goal. This is shown in the figure by an arc across the edges of the graph connecting a goal to its AND subgoals. Finally, let us consider equations such as (41) and (42). These are *directly solvable problems.* That is, they are problems whose answer can be stated without generating any more subgoals. (In this particular case, the solutions can be found in a table of integrals.) The idea behind graph oriented problem solving is to expand the graph until a directly solvable problem is found. This becomes a leaf of the tree and, when it is reached, its solution is recorded. The problem-solving program then enters the solution just found as a component into as many higher order problems as it can, marking each higher order problem solved if that is appropriate. For example, in the illustration we can envisage a program which progressively generated subproblems, noted their relation to the problem generating them, and, as each subproblem was generated, checked it against a table of standard integrals. When the expression $\int x \, dx$ was generated, the program would not its solution and, working backwards, would find that this was one of a set of solutions required to solve the AND subproblems of the problem $\int (x - 1) \, dx$. Next the program would generate $\int dx$, whose answer could also be formed in the integral table. This would complete solution of a set of AND subproblems. Therefore, by appropriate combination, the generating problem would be solved. The program would then note that it had just solved an OR subproblem or the main problem. Therefore the main problem would be marked solved, terminating the program.

What properties would we want to include in a program for searching problem reduction graphs? At every OR branch the program should attack the easiest subproblem. This implies that the program must have some way of evaluating problem difficulty. The heuristic function $\hat{h}$ provided this mechanism in state–space problem solving, in tree searching an analogous function is required. In some situations one subproblem will be a component of several higher order sub-problems. The program should recognize this fact and solve the repeated problem only once. To illustrate, in calculating the double integral

$$F(x, y) = \int_y \int_x (3y + 4)(x - 2) \, dx \, dy \qquad (43)$$

$$= \int_y [\int_x 3y(x - 2) \, dx + 4 \int_x (x - 2) \, dx] \, dy$$

The expression $\int_x (x - 2) \, dx$ appears twice. If the straightforward technique of expanding and solving subproblems that was used in the previous integration example were to be applied here, this expression would be integrated twice, which is obviously unnecessary. On the other hand, a good deal of computing effort would be needed to keep track of solved subproblems and to set up an information retrieval mechanism to determine whether a "new" subproblem was actually an old one. (For a discussion of some of the technical issues involved, see Gelernter and Rochester, 1959.) Another problem which is raised by the multiple occurrence of subproblems is that we must consider both the difficulty and the worth of a subproblem. It may often be rational to attack a hard subproblem which appears as a component of many higher order problems rather than making a piecemeal attack on a number of easy problems. In cases in which a subproblem must be solved in order to solve a main problem this question obviously does not arise.

A number of algorithms have been proposed as guides for efficient searching of problem reduction graphs. We shall present a solution by Chang and Slagle (1971) in which tree searching is treated as a special case of the problem of finding an efficient path from a starting to a goal state in a state–space representation. The algorithm is elegant in that once the transformation from trees to state-space graphs has been accomplished, proof of their algorithm's admissibility and optimality follows directly from the proof of admissibility and optimality of the heuristic search algorithm described in the preceeding section. The basic point behind the algorithm is that if a problem solving tree contained only OR branch points, then a path from the root to *any* leaf node would constitute a solution to the original problem. (The reader might review Figure 10-4 if there are any questions about this point.) A subproblem reduction graph, then, can be viewed as a state–space graph if every branch of the original problem can be rewritten to contain only OR branches. The heuristic search technique already proven to be optimal in state–space problem solving can then be used to find a path from the root to the closest leaf. As before, we must define a heuristic function $\hat{h}(x)$ for all subproblems, x such that $\hat{h}(x) \leqslant h(x)$, where $h(x)$ is the "true" difficulty of solving the subproblem.

A procedure is needed to transform a problem reduction tree graph into a graph in which all nodes except those immediately above leaves are OR branches. The leaf nodes of the graphs will represent conjunctions of "basic" subproblems, such that if all the subproblems attached to a node are solved, then the original problem will be solved. The appropriate functions must be defined for graph traversing. Assuming that the difficulty of solving each of a set Y of distinct problems is independent of the solution of other problems in Y, then the difficulty of solving the set of problems is

$$h(Y) = \sum_{y \in Y} h(y) \tag{44}$$

If $\hat{h}$ satisfies the previous requirements of a heuristic function, then

$$\hat{h}(Y) = \sum_{y \in Y} \hat{h}(y) \leqslant h(Y) \tag{45}$$

Let us interpret the cost $e(x, y)$ associated with an arc from a problem x to any one of its subproblems y as the cost of determining that subproblem y is indeed a component of problem x. Then, if there is a path $x_0, x_1, \ldots, x_n = y$ from the root to subproblem y, the cost of identifying subproblem y is

$$g(y) = \sum_{i=0}^{n-1} e(x_i, x_{i+1}) \tag{46}$$

The necessary conjunctions of subproblems that must be associated with the leaves can be identified algebraically. Suppose that problem A can be solved if *either* subproblem B and C can be solved *or* if D and (C or B) can be solved. We write

$$A = (B \cdot C) \cup (D \cdot (C \cup B)) \tag{47}$$

Equation (47) can be rewritten as a disjunction of conjunctions, i.e.,

$$A = (B \cdot C) \cup (D \cdot C) \cup (B \cdot D). \tag{48}$$

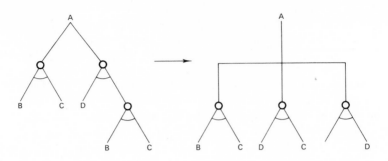

Fig. 10-5.   Transformation of a problem reduction tree graph into a graph in which all interior branches not directly above leaves are OR nodes.

If any one of the conjunctions is solved, then A is solved. The transformation is shown graphically in Figure 10-5.

We next use these notions to rewrite a problem solving tree as just illustrated. Let the initial problem be a root node. Subsequent nodes are identified by writing either the root node or the node being expanded in terms of its subproblems, then rewriting the equation corresponding to the tree in disjunctive normal form, as in (48). At each step the function

$$f = g + \hat{h} \tag{49}$$

with g and $\hat{h}$ as defined above, is used to select the node (subproblem) to be expanded next. As subproblems which can be solved directly are identified they are marked *true*. The problem is solved when one of the terms of the disjunctive normal form statement of the original problem consists only of *true* subproblems.

Figure 10-6 shows an abstract problem solving graph for an arbitrary problem, X, with repeated subproblems. Each subproblem (nonroot node) has been assigned a "heuristic estimate" of its difficulty of solution. We will assume that the cost of identifying a problem as a component subproblem of a higher order problem is always 1. The algorithm is executed on the problem in the following steps.

(i) Write X in terms of its subproblems, i.e.,

$$X = (A \cdot B) \cup C \tag{50}$$

Initially place these components on OPEN, with their estimated solution costs,

$$\text{OPEN} = \{(A \cdot B, 6), (C, 6)\}. \tag{51}$$

Suppose the tie is arbitrarily resolved by attacking the pair $(A \cdot B)$. Since

$$A \cdot B = D \cdot (E \cup F)$$
$$= (D \cdot E) \cup (D \cdot F) \tag{51}$$

we have

$$\text{OPEN} = \{(D \cdot E, 3), (D \cdot F, 4), (C, 6)\}. \tag{53}$$

D is a directly solvable problem, so it is marked TRUE and removed. The result is

$$OPEN = \{(E, 3), (F, 4), (C, 6)\} \tag{54}$$

At the next step D is found to be an equivalent problem to E, i.e., if D is solved, E is solved also. Since D is already solved one of the terms of the disjunctive form of the original problem has been solved, and hence the original problem is solved. This algorithm provides an efficient and effective way of searching through complex problem reduction graphs.

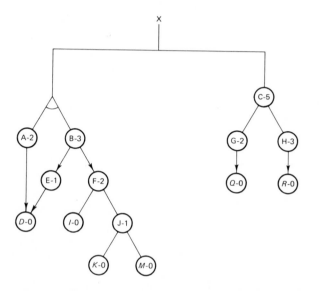

Fig. 10-6.   Abstract problem solving. The numbers beside each letter indicate estimated difficulty ($\hat{h}$) of problem. Arc costs are presumed to be 1 in all cases. (Problem adapted from Chang and Slagle, 1971, page 123.)

10.3.2   GAME TREES

In pure conflict situations two opponents make moves and countermoves in an attempt to reach a terminal situation only one of them desires. When the stakes are low and the rules well defined we call this a game. Business, interpersonal conflict, and war bear a resemblance to games, although the permissible moves, the rules for calculating advantage or disadvantage, and the extent of conflict of interest are usually not clearcut. Even so, there is a temptation to treat real life decision problems involving conflict of interest as if they were games, and hence analyzable by the appropriate mathematics. Since some conflicts of interest may involve rapid decisions requiring analysis of a tremendous volume of data, and since any computerized decision process must have a mathematical basis, the question of how computers should play complex games has a good deal of practical importance.[2] Besides, games and computers both present an intellectual challenge. It is hard to program computers to play interesting games well, and because it is hard, some of us will find that it is fun to try.

Formally, we will be concerned with computable strategies for *two person, zero sum games with perfect information* (cf. Luce & Raiffa, 1956). Less formally, we shall consider the problem of programming a strategy of play for a conventional board game which obeys the following rules: two players move alternately, choosing their moves from a known set of possible moves, any loss of piece, position, or game for one player is unequivocally a gain for the other, all moves are revealed at the time they are made, and the result of each move is deterministic. That is, the position of the players at the end of a proposed move can be predicted perfectly, rather than being predictable up to a chance event. To understand the last constraint consider a change to checkers which would make it *non* deterministic. Suppose that when a piece was jumped the players rolled a die and removed the jumped piece if the result was four or greater. The outcome of a move could only be predicted probabilistically. We could extend the discussion to probabilistic outcomes, but this would lead us into discussion of game theory rather than artificial intelligence.

The play of a two person zero sum game can be represented by a series of moves from one to another until one of a set of terminal configurations is reached. Each terminal configuration has a number assigned to it, which will be called the *outcome* of the game. Player A seeks to maximize the outcome, player B to minimize it. In many situations we can simply assign +1 to all terminal positions representing a win by A, -1 to terminal positions representing wins by B, and 0 to terminal positions representing a tie. The *minimax* strategy is considered rational for virtually all such games. Roughly, this strategy states that one should always play as if the opponent will make his best possible counter to your move. Another way of looking at things is to say that if you make a move then, at your opponent's turn, he will be able to enforce different losses on you, the size of the loss depending upon his cleverness in choosing a move. The safest thing one can do is to assume that your opponent knows what he is doing. In choosing your move, you ought to choose a move which minimizes the maximum loss the opponent can enforce. Hence the name of the strategy, since you play to minimize maximum loss. For example, consider the one move game shown in matrix form in Table 10-1. The game has the following interpretation. Players A and B each choose from one of two moves, $\{A1 \quad A2\}$ and $\{B1, \quad B2\}$, respectively. The value of the game is established by the joint choice. Thus the moves $A1$–$B2$ would produce a game value of 4. Suppose A must move first. What is the minimax move for A? The answer is $A2$, for if $A1$ is chosen then B can choose either a value of 10 or 4, and will surely

---

[2] We will discuss the technical problems associated with the game model, assuming that the model itself is appropriate. Rapoport (1960, 1964) presents a discussion of the moral and philosophical implication of the model itself.

choose 4 ($A1$–$B2$). On the other hand, if $A2$ is chosen, the lowest possible value of
the game is 5.

TABLE 10-1
Simplified Game in Matrix Form

	B's moves	
A's move	$B1$	$B2$
$A1$	10	4
$A2$	5	6

We can represent this game as a tree graph as well as in matrix form. This is done
in Figure 10-7. This figure illustrates some concepts and conventions. Square nodes
are used to represent A's moves, and circular nodes for B. Leaf nodes are
represented either by a number indicating the value of the outcome or by "?" to
indicate that the tree of moves continues beyond this point, but is not shown.

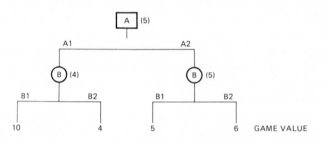

Fig. 10-7.   Tree form of game defined by Table 10-1. The value of outcomes is shown at
the endpoints. Backed up values of positions are shown in parentheses beside each node.

We now ask, *What is the value of this game for A?* Of course, we already know,
since we have shown that A can ensure himself of an outcome of 5. We will
recompute this value from Figure 10-7, illustrating a method that can be extended
to more complex games. The method works backwards from the value of the
outcomes. Immediately above each outcome is a move for B. What is the value of
each of these moves? Since each position represents a choice for B, and since B
wishes to minimize the result of the choice, the value of a position is surely the
minimum of the values of the outcomes that B can enforce from the position.
Therefore, if the outcomes B can enforce are $\{10, 4\}$, then the value of B's choice
of these outcomes is 4. A value determined in this way is called a *backed up value*
of a position. Backed up values for B's positions are shown in parenthesis beside the
nodes in Figure 10-7. To establish the value of A's position, we simply repeat the
operation, but this time backing up from the now known values of B's positions,

and taking maxima instead of minima, since A wishes to maximize outcomes. In the trivial game at hand, A's first (and only) move will offer B positions with value 4 or 5. Since A wants to maximize position value of A's choice (and the game, since this is the first choice) is 5.

Conceptually this method works for all board games. We can imagine considering all possible opening sequences of chess, all possible replies, etc. until we found a guaranteed winning sequence of moves in chess if such exists. If it does not exist we would know this. There would then be no point to playing chess. Fortunately for game players, the method is grossly impractical. To take the most interesting case, in chess there are 40 possible opening moves, with 40 counters. Minsky has estimated that there are 10^{120} nodes in the tree describing a full chess game, far more than could possibly be investigated by man or computer. What has to be done in a practical game playing program is to define a *strategy*, i.e. a highly selective search of interesting sequences of moves, accepting the possibility that the right answer will be overlooked.

The *n step look ahead* is one such simple strategy. Assume that it is A's move at some nonterminal position. A considers all possible situations which could be reached within n steps, where n is chosen to be small enough to lead to a manageable tree. The nonterminal positions in the n step tree are then evaluated using a heuristic function which assigns a "predicted outcome" to each position that can be reached in n steps. If a terminal position can be reached, the computation is straightforward. For nonterminal positions, however, some method must be found to assign worth without actually investigating the further play of the game. This method must, of necessity, be specific to the game being played. For example, in checkers one could use the function

$$\text{Value} = 6 \cdot \text{no. of own kings} - \text{no. of opponent's kings} \atop + 4 \cdot (\text{no. own men} - \text{no. opponent's men}). \tag{55}$$

The power of the n-step look-ahead method will very much depend on how good the value determining function is. We will illustrate the method, and the pitfalls of using a bad function, by showing how one might program a computer to lose at tic-tac-toe while trying to win.

The game will be played using one-step look ahead. To evaluate a position, P_i,[3] use the function

$$f(P) = (\text{number of lines which could be extended to produce a win for X.} \atop - \text{Number of lines which are similarly available for the play of 0}). \tag{56}$$

A will play X and try to maximize $f(P)$. B will play O and try to minimize. The initial position, P, is the empty board. P_1-P_9 defined the set of positions of the board with X in one of the squares and the other squares blank. If we number these by the position of the X in conventional reading order, we have, for P_1, P_5, and P_6

---

[3] The notation P, P_i, P_{ij}, ... will be used to indicate P, the positions below P, the positions below P_i, etc.

$$P_1 \quad \begin{array}{ccc} \mathrm{X} & \_ & \_ \\ \_ & \_ & \_ \\ \_ & \_ & \_ \end{array} \quad f(P_1) = 3$$

(since lines can be extended diagonally, horizontally or vertically from the X),

$$P_5 \quad \begin{array}{ccc} \_ & \_ & \_ \\ \_ & \mathrm{X} & \_ \\ \_ & \_ & \_ \end{array} \quad f(P_5) = 4,$$

and

$$P_6 \quad \begin{array}{ccc} \_ & \_ & \_ \\ \_ & \_ & \mathrm{X} \\ \_ & \_ & \_ \end{array} \quad f(P_6) = 2$$

In fact $f(P_5)$ is the maximum value for the set $P_1 \cdots P_9$, so A chooses it. B can now choose from eight moves, $P_{51}, P_{52}, P_{53}, P_{54}, P_{56}, P_{57}, P_{58}$, and P_{59}. An example is

$$P_{51} \quad \begin{array}{ccc} 0 & \_ & \_ \\ \_ & \mathrm{X} & \_ \\ \_ & \_ & \_ \end{array} \quad f(P_{51}) = 3 - 2 = 1$$

In fact, all these positions have value 1, so we can assume B is indifferent between them. Let B's choice be P_{51}. A now has seven possible moves, several of which have the maximum value 2. Suppose the choice is

$$P_{518} \quad \begin{array}{ccc} 0 & \_ & \_ \\ \_ & \mathrm{X} & \_ \\ \_ & \mathrm{X} & \_ \end{array} \quad f(P_{518}) = 2$$

B now has six responses. "Anyone can see" B ought to make the move

$$P_{5182} \quad \begin{array}{ccc} 0 & 0 & \_ \\ \_ & \mathrm{X} & \_ \\ \_ & \mathrm{X} & \_ \end{array} \quad f(P_{5182}) = 1$$

but the function does not! For consider

$$P_{5183} \quad \begin{array}{ccc} 0 & \_ & 0 \\ \_ & \mathrm{X} & \_ \\ \_ & \mathrm{X} & \_ \end{array} \quad f(P_{5183}) = 0$$

Since B is minimizing $f(P)$ he chooses P_{5183} and A wins on the next move.

Since one ought not to lose at tic-tac-toe (beyond the age of 8) f must be a bad position evaluation function. This bit of reverse cleverness is specific to tic-tac-toe. There is another way that the game has been played, however, that illustrates a sort of poor judgment that could occur in tree searching in general. In making the evaluation A first considered nine positions, then B considered eight, then A seven, for a total of $9 \cdot 8 \cdot 7 \cdot 6 \cdot 5 = 35$ positions. If a two step look-ahead had been considered this number would have increased to $9 \cdot 8 + 7 \cdot 6 + 6 \cdot 5 = 144$.

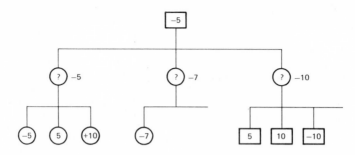

Fig. 10-8.   *A*'s knowledge of the game after his first move.

Remember, this is a very simple game! One of the biggest problems faced by writers of game-playing programs is keeping the machine from spending too much time evaluating fruitless paths. A search method to do this which has been adopted widely is the *alpha–beta* procedure. It is based on the idea that one ought not to explore a set of paths further if they all can be shown to be worse than some other path already explored. The method can be illustrated without going into the details of a specific game, since the alpha–beta procedure is a way of searching any tree graph. Consider the abstract game shown in Figure 10-8. A value of 10 has been assigned to win by *A* and a value of −10 to a win by *B*. To define a general heuristic function let us make the intuitively reasonable assumption that a player can estimate the average worth of the positions P_i which can be reached from position *P*, without examining each of the successor positions. Therefore, the heuristic evaluation of a position *P* with *k* positions below it is

$$f(P) = (1/k) \sum_{i=1}^{k} f(P_i) \qquad (57)$$

if *P* is not an endpoint. If *P* is an endpoint, $f(P)$ is the worth of that outcome. In Figure 10-9 each interior node of the tree has been marked with its *true* $f(P)$ value if one examines the entire tree and applies (57) to all nodes.

We will apply the alpha–beta search procedure to this game tree using a two-step look-ahead. At each step a player will consider available moves, opponent's counters, and the resulting configuration of the game. The player computes $f(P)$ for each of the configurations so discovered, and uses the minimax rule to back up values for each position. A node will not be examined if its $f(P)$ value is known to be irrelevant to the final choice of a move. How this can be predicted will now be shown. Consider first the initial move in the game of 10-9. Player *A* looks ahead always checking from the leftmost to rightmost branch. Call the moves $A1, A2 \ldots$ and $B1, B2 \ldots$ in this order. *A* discovers that if his first move is on the left branch (*A*1), then *B* can choose from the set of position estimates $\{-5, 5, 10\}$. *A* assumes *B* will minimize the value of this set, and so assigns value −5 to move *A*1. Since this is the best move known thus far to *A*, −5 is established as an *alpha cutoff*. *A* then

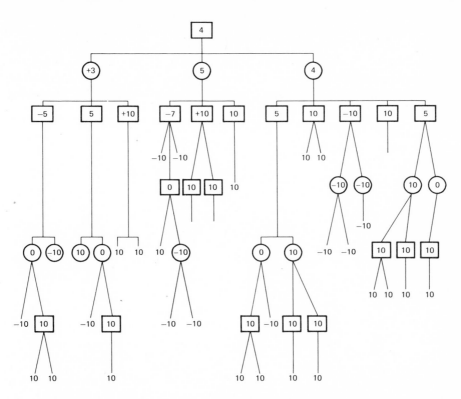

Fig. 10-9.   A full tree showing estimation functions for a hypothetical game.

turns attention to the center move, $A2$. It is discovered that if A makes $A2$, and B counters with $B1$, the estimated worth of the sequence will be -7. This is below the alpha cutoff. In practice, this means that no matter what else B could do, in response to $A2$, he could always do worse (in A's terms) to $A2$ than he could in response to $A1$. Therefore other alternative replies to $A2$ need not be considered, as $A1$ is known to be preferable to $A2$. Attention shifts to $A3$. The counters $B1$ and $B2$ to $A3$ are both above the alpha cutoff. The sequence $A3$–$B3$, however, would leave A in a worse position (-10) than could possibly happen if $A1$ were chosen. Therefore, A chooses move $A1$. A now has incomplete knowledge of the game tree, as depicted in Figure 10-8, which shows the positions actually evaluated by A and their estimated worth to him.

   B now looks two moves ahead from position P_1. Remember that B is trying to minimize the outcome. If $B1$ is played, the game will move to position P_{11}. B examines the positions below P_{11} and finds that their *maximum* estimated value is 0. Surely A will enforce this if he can, therefore the value of P_{11} to B is 0. This is the lowest valued position discovered so far, so it is made the *beta cutoff*. B now considers position P_{12}, resulting from a play of $B2$. If $A1$ is played in counter to $B2$, the game moves to P_{121}, which has a value of 10. This is above the beta cutoff, and is an indication that A has a play against $B2$ which damages B more than A's best play against $B1$. Therefore $B2$ can be dropped from consideration. $B3$ (Position P_{13}) is dropped from consideration for similar reasons. B's current knowledge of the game is summarized in Figure 10-10. $B1$ is chosen and it becomes A's turn to play from position P_{11}. At this time A can look ahead to endpoints, discovering that no matter what he plays, B can force a win. Therefore A resigns.

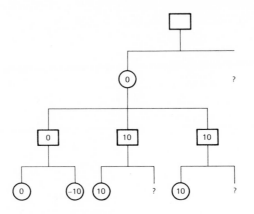

Fig. 10-10. B's knowledge of the game at B's first move.

Several things should be noted about this example. First, and most important, only a few of the possible moves are ever investigated. Second, the picture one has of the game changes as it progresses. If we applied $f(P)$ throughout the tree (as in Figure 10-9) the initial position appears slightly favorable to A. As the game progresses, however, the position appeared to favor B, $(f(P_1) = -4)$, then to be fair $(f(P_{11}) = 0)$, and finally it turned out that B had a win. Third, and most important, the efficiency and justifiability of the alpha–beta procedure, and any game procedure, depends jointly on the heuristic evaluation function, f, that is used and the depth of the look-ahead. If A had looked ahead further than B or, perhaps, used a better heuristic function, the outcome might have been different. If the reader does not see this, we suggest that the game be repeated using different heuristic functions and look ahead parameters.

The example also illustrates a number of basic differences between game tree searching and problem solving graph searching. In game playing there is no going back; making a move rules out returns to other positions that might have been chosen. This means state space search algorithms are not appropriate. As we move through the tree, getting closer to the end point, our heuristic estimates of the worth of a position will probably get better. Even so, at some point we will have to rely on estimates which depend upon averaging over a number of inadequately investigated alternatives. For this reason Slagle and Dixon (1970) have suggested that in addition to the use of the minimax and averaging strategies, one should increase the estimated worth of a position if it opens the way to a number of alternatives. Their argument is that when we reach such a position, and are able to make a better evaluation of the alternatives, we are more likely to find that one of them is good if there are a lot of them. Similar rules have been suggested based upon the variance of the estimates of worth made before backing up values (Slagle, 1971).

In addition to using the alpha-beta cutoff procedure to eliminate exploration of fruitless paths, we can improve efficiency by ordering the search so that the ultimate cutoff is established early in the search process. To see this, the reader can compare the number of nodes explored in the example to the considerably greater number. Therefore some sort of game specific "move proposer" is usually included node, we had explored from right to left. A number of dynamic ordering procedures have been suggested which tend to find the cutoff point early. The problem is discussed in detail by Slagle (1971). He also proposes methods for varying the depth of look-ahead dynamically for promising and unpromising paths.

In closing, some comments on the playing of specific games by computers are in order. In most real games the alpha–beta procedure, even with dynamic ordering, is not sufficient to reduce the number of moves to be investigated to a manageable number. Therefore somesort of game specific "move proposer" is usually included in the program. The move proposer selects moves which accomplish some reasonable purpose in the game. Examples from chess are king safety, center control, or piece advantage. The choice of moves to investigate is made from the set of moves generated by the move proposer, instead of the set of all legal moves. This greatly reduces the number of moves to be considered. The idea of the move proposer also implies that a good game playing program will be specific to that game, since it will have to contain much game specific information. For chess, the most extensively investigated game,[4] this most emphatically is the case. The most frequently cited American chess player, "Mac Hack," of the Massachusetts Institute of Technology, and most modern programs, is good because it contains substantial files of plausible moves to generate in different situations (Greenblatt et al., 1967). In other words, a good chess player knows a lot about chess. How a computer program should acquire chess knowledge is a moot point. One way, of course, is for certain records to be built into the original program. To an extent this is done. Most chess playing programs contain the sequence of moves and counter-moves for standard defenses. The situation at mid game is more complex, since so many positions might arise. One approach that has been taken is to convert the problem

[4] There are now regular man–machine and machine–machine tournaments. Reports of interesting games appear in the newsletter of the special Interest Group on Artificial Intelligence of the Association for Computing Machinery. The growth in chess playing by computer in the late 1960s appears to be due more to the availability of better programming language, more cooperation with chess masters, and faster machinery, than to a breakthrough in understanding how the game should be played. The basic ideas behind the chess playing programs with which we are familiar are contained in an article by Newell, Shaw, and Simon (1963) which also reviewed the work done up to about 1960. Zobrist and Carlson (1973) discuss more recent studies, and include interesting examples and a commentary by a (friendly) chess expert.

to one in pattern recognition. The program is used to play many games, either against itself or a human opponent. The positions encountered are recorded, and an attempt is made to find a classification rule for determining when such a move is appropriate. This has worked well in developing a checkers playing program (Samuel, 1967). Zobrist and Carlson (1973) have suggested that in the more complex game of chess the opponent should be a master player and that the master should have a way of directing the (machine) pupil's attention to key aspects of various board positions as the program accumulates and evaluates experience.

An important concept in actual games is the idea of a static position. Some situations are inherently unstable, and ought not to be evaluated until the instability has been resolved. For example, in chess it would not be sensible to evaluate a position in the middle of a queen exchange, the exchange should be completed first. Game playing programs often look ahead to the next static position, rather than depending on a look ahead of exactly n steps.

Newell and Simon (1965, 1972) and DeGroot (1966) have contrasted human and machine play. DeGroot, in particular, has studied the play of many master chess players. He has noted that master's play is highly stereotyped, suggesting that chess playing, at least, is a very specific skill, which depends as much on knowledge of chess literature as it does on the mastery of general game playing strategies. Newell and Simon, however, feel that the human players they observe show at least the rudiments of the components found in game playing programs; notably minimaxing and the idea of looking ahead to a static position. The chief difference they noticed between human play and the algorithms we have discussed is that humans seem to have a sort of inertia—once they start to develop a line of play they will go a considerable way along a favorable path, and then begin to backtrack to see if they can be thrown off it by the opponent. Thus, it appears that humans are more disposed toward depth first searching than is the properly programmed computer.

Most techniques for programming chess players are based on the assumption that evaluating a chess position requires so much time that a brute force search of possible positions is out of the question. The argument could be obviated by two developments, an advance in computer technology that made very rapid searching possible and/or the development of a very easily computed position evaluation scheme. There is some evidence that both these events may occur. Gillogly (1972) has reported a surprisingly successful "brute force" chess program . . . but, the evaluation algorithm was developed by Hans Berliner, a world correspondence chess champion! A similar approach has been taken by the Soviet grandmaster, M. M. Botvinnik (1970), who is perhaps the finest player to be actively involved in programming chess players. Botvinnik's proposed program relies on sophisticated evaluations rather than on a memory for past positions. The point remains valid, a good computer program for chess must contain a lot of information about chess. It may use that information in a rather different way than a human would.

Chapter XI

HEURISTIC PROBLEM-SOLVING PROGRAMS

11.0 General Comments

The graph-searching techniques presented in Chapter X provide an elegant way to represent a problem, if useful heuristic functions and subproblem definition techniques are available. The formal analysis of graph searching can tell us something about the requirements to place on a "good" $\hat{h}$ function or upon good subproblem definition, but knowing some of the restrictions that must be met is not equivalent to having a program to solve problems.

Ideally we would like to present a universally applicable heuristic function tied directly to $\hat{h}$. In practice this is not possible, nor is it likely to be. Heuristic functions and subproblem definition techniques are almost inevitably problem dependent—a good technique in chess may be quite different from a good technique for algebra. This chapter discusses three problem solving programs with some pretension to generality, the General Problem Solver (GPS) of Newell, Simon, and their co-workers, a program of our own called the Fortran Deductive System (FDS), and a "robot guidance" program called STRIPS which has been developed at Stanford Research Institute. The GPS is a classic artificial intelligence program which introduced many of the basic concepts of heuristic problem solving. The FDS is an extension of certain mechanisms in GPS, while STRIPS attempts to use plans in problem solving. FDS and GPS were both written before the development of the graph-searching methods known today, so it is understandable that these programs cannot be connected directly to graph-searching techniques. The connection to graph searching in STRIPS is much more explicit.

11.1 Terminology

A very general terminology can be used to discuss the programs of interest. Practically anything can be thought of as an object that has values on different attributes. A basketball team can be described by the style of its offense and defense, while a nation can be described by pairs such as economy–industrial, population–200 million, and political organization–democratic republic. The computer format is the same. A problem exists when there is a discrepancy between the description of the present object and a desired object. The discrepancy can be removed by applying *operators* to the present object, and to objects derived from it, until the description of the present object agrees with that of the desired object. Each operator must have an input form and an output form. The input form is a set of constraints on the values of attributes, which must be satisfied before the operator can be applied. The output form is a definition of the values certain attributes (usually not all the attributes) of an object will have after the operator has been applied to the object.

Let us look again at the medical diagnosis and treatment problem, using a problem-solving instead of a pattern-recognition approach. Suppose a physician is faced with a patient who is partially described by

Attribute	Value
temperature	feverish
neurologic symptoms	headache
digestive symptoms	mild stomach upset

The physician identifies the major symptomatic problem to be removal of the fever and headache. The obvious operator is aspirin, an operator whose output form is

Attribute	Value
temperature	reduced
neurologic symptoms	pain reduced
digestive system	aggravated mildly

The input form of aspirin is a definition of people who can take it;

Atrribute	Value
history	no indication of aspirin allergy
condition	no aspirin within four hours
age	six years or more

The patient could take aspirin; however, the output form indicates that aspirin alone will leave him with a rather more upset stomach. Therefore additional medication is indicated before the problem is completely solved. Note that the state-description framework may easily be changed to a graph-searching framework by letting the nodes represent possible states and the arcs the operators applicable to each state. All the arguments for search procedures apply directly. Given a set of possible transformations, we want to apply that transformation which is most likely to move us closer to the goal state. This is what was done implicitly in the medical treatment example. Selecting useful transformations, however, leads us to a subsidiary problem. Suppose a transformation would be useful if it could be applied (i.e., its output form is similar to the goal description) but it cannot be applied because the current state does not satisfy the constraints of the transformation's input form. We must set up the subproblem of changing the present state so that the particular transformation (equivalently, operator) can be applied. The sub-problem may itself generate subproblems. A problem-solving program must solve subproblems and combine their solutions in a way appropriate to the context of the larger problem which generated them.

To summarize, a problem-solving program must be able to describe objects to itself in some general way, select transformations to alter those objects, establish and solve subproblems generated by attempts to apply operators to objects, and finally, the program must be able to arrange the solutions of subproblems and problems in an orderly fashion. We now look at two closely related computer programs that do just this.

11.2   The General Problem Solver (GPS)

11.2.0   HISTORY

The GPS is perhaps the most famous program in the history of artificial intelligence. It was originally reported by Newell, Shaw, and Simon (1959) in a rather obscure conference report, which fortunately has been reprinted in Luce, Bush, and Galanter's (1965) *Readings in Mathematical Psychology*. A cogent, highly readable description can also be found in Newell and Simon (1961). Ernst and Newell (1969) have published a detailed description of the program, its performance, and the programming techniques required to construct it.

The initial motivation for the GPS was an interesting mixture of computer science and psychology. From a computer science point of view, GPS was a logical generalization of the computer programs that had been written to solve problems in specific content areas, such as the propositional calculus (Newell, Shaw, & Simon, 1957), plane geometry (Gelernter, 1963) and integral calculus (Slagle, 1963).[1] From the psychological point of view, GPS was proposed as a model of the information-processing characteristics of the mind. The idea that a computer

---

[1] The dates of these references are apt to be misleading. The research work of Slagle, Gelernter, and several other scientists interested in the construction of problem solving programs was fairly widely known via the medium of technical reports and conference presentation in the period from 1957 to 1960.

program could serve as a model of cognition was broached very early in the history of computer science.[2] Polya (1954) had stressed that the ways in which mathematicians discovered proofs bore little resemblance to the ways in which proofs are presented. To explain how mathematicians operated, Polya coined the word "heuristic" to describe proof discovery methods which were easy to apply and which often but not always discover the desired solution. Polya drew from his own and other mathematicians' experience to give many examples showing that heuristics are used, but he was very inexact about what the heuristics themselves were. One of Newell *et al.*'s major contributions to psychology was the demonstration that heuristic techniques could be made explicit in a computer program. Such a program would, then, be a precisely defined method for "guessing" a solution. If the method was also used by a person to attack the same problem, then the program could be said to be a model of the person. Newell and Simon have been at pains to point out that this model would be fully as precise as any conventional mathematical model, since, after all, any program is ultimately reducible to a sequence of Boolean operations. On the other hand, one can express very complex sequences in a computer program, so a program is potentially capable of describing a far richer repertoire of behavior than could be described by a tractable set of equations. This position has been widely accepted in modern psychology (Miller, Galanter, & Pribaum, 1960; Hunt, 1968; Frijda, 1971; Neisser, 1967; Reitman, 1965), although, naturally, there are conflicting opinions as to whether particular models are good or bad models of the behavior they are supposed to explain.[3]

As we noted in Chapter I, GPS was developed from work on the logic theorist (LT), (Newell, Shaw, & Simon, 1956, 1957), a program for solving problems, the sentential calculus problems in Chapter II of Whitehead and Russell's *Principia Mathematica*.[4] Although the theorems of the *Principia* are basic in establishing the relations between logic and mathematics, their proofs are not terribly difficult. The genius of Whitehead and Russell was not in proving the theorems, but in realizing what they meant. On the other hand, LT's accomplishment was by no means trivial. It discovered proofs that are beyond the ability of most college sophomores to discover on their own, and most human beings (by definition, intelligent) are less intelligent than the college sophomore. Furthermore, the proofs were not discovered by a brute force and ignorance technique. In most cases the program made quite direct progress toward a solution.

[2] It is implied in some of Lady Lovelace's discussions of Babbage's differential analyzer.

[3] In the interests of historical accuracy, it should be noted that proposals for "programs and subroutines" as models of behavior were considered by Hovland (1952) and Bruner, Goodnow, and Austin (1956). Newell et al. however, were clearly the first and prime movers of the current approach to programs as simulation of behavior.

[4] LT solved 38 of the 52 theorems of the *Principia*. Subsequently Stefferud (1963) rewrote the program using a more sophisticated technique for data storage and ran it on a much faster computer. Stefferud's version solved all 52 theorems.

The LT program *conceptually* fell into two sections, a section concerned with problem analysis and subproblem generation and a section concerned with the application of rules specific to the sentential calculus. Programmatically, however, these two sections were intertwined. In the GPS they were separated both conceptually and in the program's code. The idea was that GPS would contain the problem analysis and subproblem generation sections as part of its own code, and that content area specific techniques (e.g., the rules of sentential calculus or the rules of algebra) would be provided as input. We will go into detail in the next section.

The program has generated a great deal of comment. In psychology, the general conclusion seems to be that GPS is not itself a model of human problem-solving, but that it points the way toward what a model of human problem-solving should be. (For a stronger view of the psychological reality of GPS see Newell and Simon, 1972.) In computer science GPS is usually discussed to point up the issues involved in developing programs that handle a very wide range of problems (Newell & Ernst, 1965). As Ernst and Newell's (1969) book provides extensive documentation, the program can serve as an illustration in discussing problem solving by computer. As a practical problem solver it is now superceded by more powerful programs designed to attack the same problems on different principles (J. A. Robinson, 1965) and by programs written "in the spirit" of GPS but using programming techniques not yet developed when the GPS was first constructed (Fikes & Nilsson, 1970; Quinlan & Hunt, 1968, 1969).

11.2.1 BASIC PRINCIPLES OF GPS

The GPS embodies two basic principles: *means–end analysis and recursive problem solving.*

Means–end analysis is a technique for making sure that an attempt is made to apply an operator only if there is some purpose to the application. Suppose the possible attributes for two objects are defined. A difference between objects is, by definition, a discrepancy in their values on some attribute. An operator changes the values of attributes. Define an *operator difference table* by listing the operators and the differences which they effect. The table is then used to guide subproblem selection. The following examples illustrate the method.

The Monkey Problem

A monkey is in a cage. Suspended over the center of his cage, out of reach, is a bunch of bananas. There is a box in the corner. What should the monkey do to get the bananas?

This situation can be described by stating; the altitude of the monkey (high–low), the location of the monkey in the cage, the location of the box, and the location and altitude of the bananas. These are the attributes of the situation. The operators are the things that the monkey can do; walk, climb, reach for bananas, and push the box. The attributes, the implied differences, and the

TABLE 11-1
Operator Difference Table for Monkey Problem

Difference	Climb	Walk	Push	Reach
		Operator		
Monkey location		X	X	
Box location			X	
Banana location				X
Monkey altitude	X			
Banana altitude				X

operators, are shown in the *operator difference* table of Table 11-1. An entry in the body of this table indicates that the operator affects the difference. In fact, Table 11-1 is only one of several different operator difference tables that might have been defined. The definition of the operator difference table is outside the GPS itself, since it is given to the program as part of the definition of the task environment.

Simple Algebra

An "algebra of plus and minus" can be defined by the following rules:

R1 $X + Y = Y + X$,
R2 $X = X + 0$,
R3 $(X + Y) - Y = X$,
R4 $(X + Y) - Z = (X - Z) + Y$,
R5 $(X + Y) + Z = X + (Y + Z)$.

The universal substitution rule that a well-formed expression may be substituted for a free variable is implied for this and all GPS problems. One of the several possible operator-difference matrices is given in Table 11-2. Note that the differences in this table refer to differences between two well-formed expressions in algebra. A

TABLE 11-2

	R1	R2	R3	R4	R5
			Operator		
Type of arithmetic operator		X	X	X	
Number of variables			X		
Location of variables in expression	X	X		X	X
Presence or absence of 0		X			

well-formed expression may contain other well-formed expressions, so one must be able to locate as well as describe the differences. For instance, the expressions

$$(A + B) + (C - D), \tag{1a}$$

$$(A + B) + (C + D) \tag{1b}$$

are similar at their topmost level, in that they are both expressions of the form $X + Y$, but they differ in their right-hand components. In order to detect such similarities GPS represents objects as *tree structures*. As an example, the two expressions of (1) are shown in Figure 11-1. By examining the trees it is immediately apparent that the first difference of Table 11-2, type of arithmetic operator, exists at the right-hand expression in Figure 11-1.

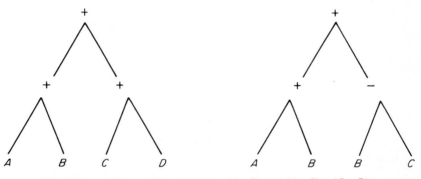

Fig. 11-1.   Tree graphs for $(A + B) + (C + D)$ and $(A + B) + (C - D)$.

It is useful to attach attributes to the nodes of a tree—e.g., the attributes connective type, left-hand operator, and right-hand operator apply to the interior nodes of the trees in the diagram. Note that, as in the example, the value of an attribute may itself be a structure. Thus the value of the left-hand operator of the root node in each tree is the tree structure for the expression $A + B$. The tree representation is useful in a number of situations that are superficially quite unlike algebra. In the degenerate case, a single node is a tree, so problems like the monkey problem can be diagrammed as shown in Figure 11-2.

Means–end analysis uses the difference between objects to guide the problem-solving process. The steps for an analysis of the abstract problem "transfer object A

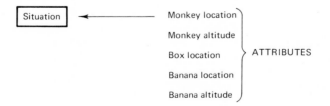

Fig. 11.2.   "Tree structure" for monkey problem.

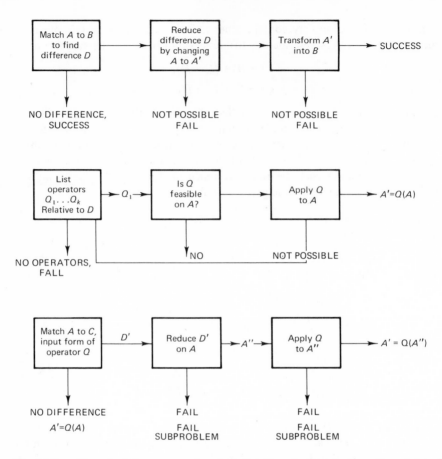

Fig. 11.3.   Flow chart for means-end analysis. (a) Steps in the transformation of A to B. (b) Steps in the difference reduction. (c) Steps in operator application.

into object B" are shown in Figure 11-3. The first step is to find the most important difference D between objects A and B. (If no differences are found, the problem is assumed to be solved.) "Most important" is defined by an a priori ordering of differences which is supplied by the programmer. Once differences have been evaluated, difference reduction is achieved by the use of an *apply operator* sequence. This is shown in Figure 11-3-b. Given D and A, the operator-difference matrix is consulted to determine a list of operators $Q_1 \cdots Q_k$ which, if applicable to A, will alter the characteristic D on A. Let Q_i be the first such operator. A preliminary check is made, in which the form of A is compared to the input form of Q_i. If the two forms are roughly similar the subgoal of applying the operator Q_i to the object A is established. If this succeeds the transformation, $A' = Q_i(A)$, is made, and the result returned to the appropriate point in the controlling program.

One more step must be explained; how do we solve the subproblem of applying Q to A? This is a transformation problem similar to the original one. Recall that a transformation is, by definition, a change of an object from form C to form C', in which C and C' are very general tree structures containing free variables, and hence can be fit by many specific trees. Refer to Figure 11-3c. First A is matched to C to determine if there are any differences in form. If there are not (i.e., if A is a particular example of the general form C) then Q_i is applied directly to form $A' = Q_i(A)$. Suppose, however, that difference D' between C and A is found. The subgoal of transforming A into a special case, A'' of C, is established. The solution to this subproblem may require further difference reduction and operator application. If A'' is finally established, Q_i is applied to construct $A' = Q_i(A'')$. These steps require that GPS be a recursive program, i.e., that it be capable of calling itself as a subroutine. This leads us to a discussion of recursive problem solving and change of context in solving subproblems.

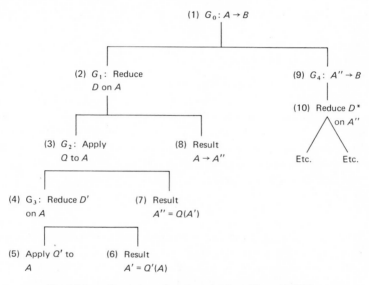

Fig. 11.4.   Operation of goals and subproblems in GPS.

Figure 11-4 is an alternative way of presenting the actions of GPS, with more attention to the context change problem. The required steps are as follows:

(1)   Accept the externally defined goal G_0 of transforming $A \to B$. Generate difference D, by matching the tree structure forms of A and B.

(2)   Goal G_1 is reduction of D in object A. By consulting the operator difference table Q is selected as an appropriate operator.

(3)   Goal G_2 is the application of Q to A. Let Q be an operator with input form C. The difference D' is found between A and C.

(4)   Goal G_3 is reduction of D' on A. The operator Q' is found to be relevant.

(5)   Let the input form of Q' be C'. Suppose that there are no differences between A and C'. Apply Q' to produce $A' = Q'(A)$. We must now climb out of the subproblem generation process, having solved one of the subproblems.

(6)   The difference D' is reduced on A by substituting $Q'(A)$ for A.

(7)   Since D' has been reduced, Q can now be applied to A' to produce $A'' = Q(A')$.

(8)   The difference D is reduced on A by the transformation $A \to A''$.

(9)   The new subproblem of transforming A'' into B is established. The difference between A'' and B will either be nonexistent of will be $D^* \neq D$.

(10) If D^* exists, reduce D^* on A''. The process continues until solution is reached.

In some cases this neat scheme of contexts within contexts is not quite adequate. Problems arise if "loops" occur, in which a problem becomes a subproblem of itself. Appropriate, though rather tedious, programming arrangements can be made. Quinlan and Hunt (1968) and Ernst and Newell (1969) discuss details.

11.2.2   AN EXAMPLE OF GPS PERFORMANCE

It is important to distinguish between the very general ideas of problem solving "in the style of GPS" and the realization of these ideas in the GPS program. In fact, a number of significant variations of GPS have been produced with some interesting differences in performance. We will now go through a detailed example of how the program performed on an example problem discussed by Ernst and Newell (1969). This should give our abstract remarks some content.

The problem is to find the algebraic form of

$$F(x) = \int te^{t^2} \, dt. \tag{2}$$

Figure 11-5 shows the tree form of the expression to be integrated. The goal object is any expression which does *not* contain the symbol $\int$. Two classes of operators are defined, *differentiate* and *integrate*. Within each class a number of possible input–output form changes are specified. For example, the integration rule

$$\int u^n \, du = u^{n+1} \cdot (n+1)^{-1} \tag{3}$$

can be depicted by the change in tree forms shown in Figure 11-6. Further form changes for integration and differentiation are shown in Table 11-3. In addition to these rules, GPS was given implicit definitions of communitivity and associativity of multiplication and addition, a capacity for integer arithmetic, and the following rules of integration

$$\int cf(u) \, du = c \int f(u) \, du, \tag{4a}$$

$$d(cf(u)) = cd(f(u)), \tag{4b}$$

$$d(c + f(u)) = d(f(u)), \tag{4c}$$

u = v implies $wu = w \cdot v$, where u, v, w are any well-formed expressions. $\tag{4d}$

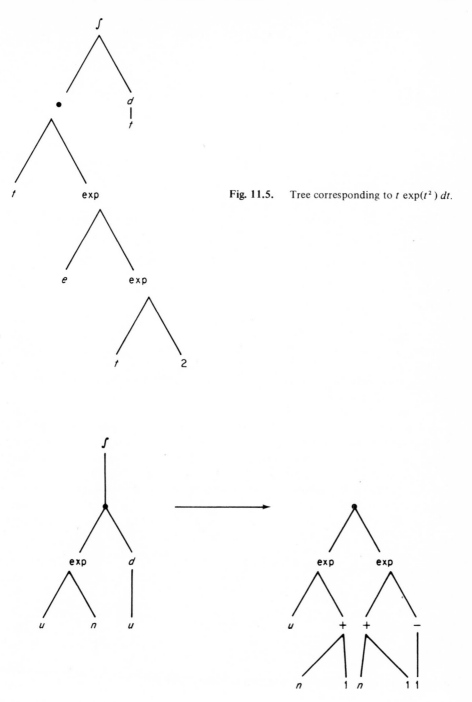

Fig. 11.5. Tree corresponding to $t\,\exp(t^2)\,dt$.

Fig. 11.6. Form change operation in integration.

TABLE 11-3

Integration rules

$$\int u^n \, du = u^{n+1} \cdot (n+1)^{-1}$$

$$\int u^{-1} \, du = \log(u)$$

$$\int \sin(u) \cdot du = -\cos(u)$$

$$\int \cos(u) \, du = \sin(u)$$

$$\int u \, du = u^2 \cdot 2^{-1}$$

$$\int e^u \, du = e^u$$

$$\int (f+g) \, du = \int f \cdot da + g \cdot da$$

Differentiation rules

$$d(\sin(u)) \, du = -d(\cos(u))$$

$$d(\cos(u)) \cdot du = d(\sin u)$$

$$d(u) \cdot du = 2^{-1} \, d(u^2)$$

$$d(u^{-1}) \cdot du = d(\log(u))$$

Rules (4a)-(4d) were applied directly by the program whenever possible without conducting a means–end analysis.

Two classes of differences were defined; *symbol differences* and *set differences*. Symbol differences exist when the symbols in matching positions in the trees of two expressions are not identical. An ordering of importance for the various possible types of symbol differences (e.g., $\int$ versus +, + versus −) was also established externally to the program. A set difference exists whenever the number of factors in two expressions to be integrated differs. In the operator-difference matrix integration was stated to be relevant to reduction of symbol differences and differentiation to be relevant to the reduction of set differences. Clearly, these are not the only nor necessarily the best differences that could be used to contrast algebraic expressions. It turns out, however, that they are sufficient in this case.

The initial goal is

G1   Remove $\int$ from $\int t \cdot e^{t^2} \, dt$.

This generates the goal

G2   Reduce symbol difference $\int$ on $\int t \cdot e^{t^2} \, dt$.

Since the integration operation is relevant to this difference, the new goal is

G3   Integrate $\int t \cdot e^{t^2} \, dt$.

These three steps were needed to establish a workable problem for GPS, even though they appear to have done little. The various input forms of *integrate* were examined, and the form closest to the present expression chosen. This produced

G4   Apply $\int e^u \, du = e^u$ to $\int t \cdot e^{t^2} \, dt$.

A comparison of the input form and the expression generated the set difference produced by comparing $\{e^u, du\}$ and $\{t, e^{t^2}, dt\}$. The second expression had too many factors, so the next goal was

G5   Reduce number of items in $\{t, e^{t^2}, dt\}$

Differentiation was relevant, so

G6   Differentiate $t \cdot e^{t^2} \cdot dt$.

became the goal. The various forms of *differentiate* were examined and the operation

G7   Apply $d(u) \cdot du = 2^{-1} \cdot d(u^2)$ to $d(t) \cdot dt$.

was chosen. This was applicable, producing $2^{-1} \cdot d(t^2)$. By substituting and applying the obligatory transformations we obtain

$$t \cdot e^{t^2} \, dt = e^{t^2} \cdot t \, dt \qquad \text{(commutativity of multiplication)} \qquad (5)$$

$$= e^{t^2} \cdot 2^{-1} \cdot d(t^2) \qquad \text{(successful application of goals G7, G6, G5).}$$

$$= 2^{-1} \int e^{t^2} \cdot d(t^2) \qquad \text{(commutativity of multiplication and application of (4a)).}$$

Since G5 has been achieved, we attempt G4 using the final expression of (5), which contains an expression of the form $\int e^u \, du$. G4 can be achieved, producing

$$\int te^{t^2} \, dt = 2^{-1} \cdot \int \cdot e^{t^2} \cdot d(t^2) \qquad (6)$$

$$= 2^{-1} \cdot e^{t^2}.$$

The achievement of G4 ensures that G3 has been achieved. The symbol difference of G2 has now been achieved, and a comparison of the final form of (6) with G1 shows that the integral sign has been removed, so the problem is solved.

11.3   The Fortran Deductive System—Automatic Generation of Operator-Difference Tables

11.3.0   HISTORY AND GENERAL APPROACH

The power of the GPS program on a specific task depends largely on the definition of differences in the operator difference table. Several investigators have considered the problem of generating this table automatically. In particular,

Quinlan (Quinlan & Hunt, 1968, 1969; Quinlan, 1969) developed the Fortran Deductive System (FDS), a program similar to GPS except that the operator-difference table is derived from the description of the operators.

Although the FDS representation of objects can be shown to correspond to the tree graphs of GPS, it is easier to use linguistic terminology in thinking about this program. States of objects are represented as strings of symbols drawn from an alphabet of *terminal* and *nonterminal* symbols. The nonterminal symbols are *variable* symbols, indicated here by using letters from the end of the alphabet, e.g., X, Y, Z. The terminal symbols consist of a finite set of constants, unary operators, and binary operators, and are redefined for each problem. What in GPS terms would be an object is, in FDS terms, a well-formed expression (w.f.e.). W.f.e.'s are defined by the rules

(1)   A constant or a variable is a w.f.e.
(2)   A binary operator followed by two w.f.e.'s is a w.f.e.
(3)   A unary operator followed by one w.f.e. is a w.f.e.

These rules define the prefix or "Reverse Polish" notation. They also establish a relationship between the trees of the GPS and the strings of FDS. Consider the integration problem presented in the last section. We can define the set T of primitive symbols as follows:

$$T = T_0 \cup T_1 \cup T_2 \qquad\qquad \text{the alphabet;} \qquad\qquad (7a)$$

$$T_0 = \{a, b, c, \ldots ; 1, 2, 3, \ldots , 9, 0\} \qquad \text{the constants;} \qquad\qquad (7b)$$

$$T_1 = \{\text{neg}, d\} \qquad\qquad\qquad \text{unary operators;} \qquad\qquad (7c)$$

$$T_2 = \{\textstyle\int, \cdot, +, -, /, \exp\} \qquad\qquad \text{binary operators.} \qquad\qquad (7d)$$

The expression

$$\int (t \cdot e^{t2}) \, dt$$

thus has the form shown in Eq. (8). Note that we have followed the convention that a binary operator is followed first by its right-hand and then by its left-hand operand.

$$\int (t \cdot e^{t^2}) \, dt \to \int dt \cdot \exp \exp 2tet. \qquad\qquad (8)$$

If the reader will turn back to Figure 11-5 he will find that there is a correspondence between this string and the tree form of expression (8).

The substitution rule is part of FDS, as it is of GPS. This allows treatment of strings such as

$$(A + B) + C \qquad\qquad (9)$$

as special cases of

$$X + Y \qquad\qquad (10)$$

The operators of FDS are called *string rewriting rules*, for they indicate that one string may be substituted for another. For instance

$$X + Y \rightarrow Y + X \tag{11}$$

may be applied to $C + (A + B)$ to produce either $(B + A) + C$ or $C + (A + B)$. As the example of (11) indicates, rewriting rules take the form of $S_1 \rightarrow S_2$, where S_1 and S_2 are w.f.e.'s. The string rule

$$(X + Y) - Z = (Y - Z) + X \tag{12}$$

requires two transformation in the FDS. These are

$$-Z + YX \rightarrow +-ZYX \tag{13a}$$

$$+-ZYX \rightarrow -Z + YX \tag{13b}$$

since the equality relation is not implicitly reflexive.

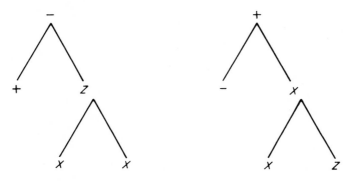

Fig. 11.7.   Tree form for $(X + Y) - Z \rightarrow (X - Z) + Y$.

Rule (13) can also be used to illustrate how differences are defined in creating the operator-difference table. Consider (13a). Both the left- and right-hand sides are w.f.e.'s, and hence, trees, as shown in Figure 11-7. The list of differences between the left- and right-hand side of these trees follows.

(1)   The topmost node is $-$ on the left and $+$ on the right.
(2)   The node to the left immediately below the topmost node is $+$ on the left-hand side and $-$ on the right-hand side.
(3)   The location of the Y and Z terms are interchanged.

Differences (1) and (2) are *absolute* differences, since these changes will be made wherever the rule is applied. The exact nature of the change due to difference (3) however, cannot be specified until we know the structures to which the rewriting rule is to be applied. For example, if the rewriting rule were to be applied to the string

$$(A + B) - C \tag{14}$$

then the constants B and C would be interchanged, while if the same rule is applied to produce

$$(A + B) - (C + B) \rightarrow (A - (C + B)) + B \tag{15}$$

the constant B will be replaced by the binary operator $+$ and its associated operands. These are examples of *context dependent* changes. When operators are defined, the FDS program examines each operator to determine which absolute and context dependent changes the operator is capable of making. The bookkeeping details of how this is done are unimportant. (For a detailed discussion, see Quinlan and Hunt, 1968.) The point is that the definition of the operators implies an operator-difference matrix that the program can derive.

The same scheme is used to detect differences between states and goals during problem solving. Initially the starting state and goal state are expressed as strings. The strings are compared on a component by component basis[5] and the differences between them are noted. The program then consults its operator-difference table and proceeds much as GPS does.

11.3.1   An Example of Problem Solving with Fds

The FDS method will be illustrated by a problem in school algebra. The operators allowed are given in Table 11-4.

TABLE 11-4
Rewriting Rules for Simplified Algebra

R1	$X + Y \rightarrow Y + X$	$+YX \rightarrow + XY$
R2	$X + (Y + Z) \rightarrow (X + Y) + Z$	$+ +ZYX \rightarrow +Z + YX$
R3	$(X + Y) - Y \rightarrow X$	$-Y + XY \rightarrow X$
R4	$X \rightarrow (X + Y) - Y$	$X \rightarrow -Y + YX$
R5	$(X - Y) + Z \rightarrow (X + Z) - Y$	$+Z - YX \rightarrow -Y + ZX$
R6	$(X + Y) - Z \rightarrow (X - Z) + Y$	$-Z + YX \rightarrow +Y - ZX$
R7	$(X - Y) + Z \rightarrow X + (Z - Y)$	$+Z - YX \rightarrow + -YZX$

For readability the rules have been written in both the normal and prefix notation. The program of course deals only with the prefix form.

The problem to be solved is to prove that

$$(A - C) - (B - C) \rightarrow (A - B) \tag{16}$$

---

[5] Recall that "component by component" is determined by the positions of nodes in trees, and not by the ordinal position of an item in a string. Thus in the comparison of $++BA - DC$ to $+XY$ the comparisons are

(1) $+$ to $+$, since first positions are always comparable
(2) $+$ to X and
(3) $-$ to Y

since these symbols occupy the same positions in the tree.

is a valid derivation. In fact this is quite a hard problem, when only the seven rules of Table 11-4 are available. The reader is urged to try to solve (16) before proceeding. The attempt will be an instructive exercise.

To aid in illustrating the algorithm applied, the starting state and its successive derivatives, will be written immediately over the final goal state. Initially

$$- -CB -CA \tag{17}$$

$$-BA.$$

The program detects that the second minus must be replaced by a variable. This can be done by applying Rule 4 to the entire expression.[6]

$$-X + X - -CB - CA \tag{18}$$

$$-BA$$

The X can now be converted to a B by a simple substitution, since X is a free variable.

$$-B + B - -CB - CA \tag{19}$$

$$-BA$$

The + must be converted to the variable A. There is no rule that does this directly. However, A, the desired variable, appears as the last symbol. This is an example of an "in context" difference. Rule 3 transforms a string into its last symbol, so it can affect this difference. The subproblem of converting the string starting at the + in (19) into a string to which Rule 3 can be applied is set up. (Note that a w.f.e. begins at each position in the string.) The subproblem is

$$-B + B - -CB - CA, \tag{20}$$

$$-B - X + XY,$$

with X and Y again free. The + in (20) must be converted into a −. Rule 5 does this, but is Rule 5 applicable? Not until (20) is converted into the proper form. We have a new subproblem.

$$-B + B - -CB - CA, \tag{21}$$

$$-B + X - YZ.$$

Since X, Y, and Z are free variables, substitution can be applied. If we let $X = B$, $Y = -CB$, and $Z = -CA$, the problem now is

$$-B + B - -CB - CA, \tag{22}$$

$$-B + B - -CB - CA.$$

---

[6] This is probably the step that makes the problem hard. Application of rule 4 produces a statement that is more complex than the input statement and that is not immediately obvious as a step toward a solution. Newell and Simon (1972) have compiled an impressive amount of evidence indicating that constructions such as this are difficult ones for people to select.

Rule 5 can be applied to (22) and then substituted into (20). The string now appears as

$$-B - -CB + B - CA, \tag{23}$$

$$-B - X + XY.$$

It is still not in the form desired, but if the substitution $X = -CB$ is made, then

$$-B - -CB + B - CA, \tag{24}$$

$$-B - -CB + -CBY.$$

The third B in the upper string must be converted to $-$. This can be done directly by applying Rule 7 to the substring beginning at $+$. Since

$$-B - -CB + B - CA, \tag{25}$$

$$+Z - XY$$

matches, the substitutions $Z = B$, $Y = C$, and $X = A$ are appropriate. Placing the right-hand side of Rule 7 in (24), and performing the substitutions produces a string of the form

$$-B - -CB + -CBA, \tag{26}$$

$$-B - -CB + -CBY.$$

By making the substitution $Y = A$ the entire string matches. Therefore, the lower string of (26) may be replaced with its right-hand side, which is just Y, and Y replaced with its definition A producing

$$-BA \tag{27}$$

$$-BA$$

and solving the problem.

11.4   Planning

11.4.0   GENERAL

In all the problem-solving methods we have discussed so far, the next step toward solution is chosen from local considerations, without regard to how it might fit into a sequence of steps. We suspect that humans often solve problems by paying more attention to global definitions of progress. To return to a much used example, in planning an itinerary one first decides what cities one wishes to visit. Airline, taxi, and limousine schedules are then fitted into the global plan. Can some provision for global planning be introduced into computer-oriented problem solving? The answer is yes. Two quite different planning techniques have been proposed in the literature. Newell and Simon (1972) have proposed an extension to GPS in which a problem is first solved in a simplified planning space, and then an attempt is made to specialize the planning space solution to the original, more detailed problem space. Fikes, Hart, and Nilsson (1972) have taken a quite different approach, in which they show how generalized plans can be abstracted from solutions to specific problems. The generalized plans are then available for later use.

11.4.1 PLANNING IN GPS

Newell and Simon's proposal[7] for extending GPS to planning will be described first. Their method consists of simplifying a problem by considering only "important" differences between states, solving the problem in the simplified space, and finally using the solution to the simplified problem as a way of setting subgoals, which, if reached in the original problem space, are likely to produce a state from which GPS can easily reach a solution state. This use of planning is consistent with Newell and Simon's general emphasis on recursive problem solving. A difficult GPS problem is (hopefully) made simple by solving a simpler but related GPS problem.

We shall adopt an example given by Newell and Simon to GPS planning. The problem domain of the example is the sentential calculus. Sentential calculus problem solving is equivalent to proving that one w.f.e. can be derived from another. The w.f.e.'s of the sentential calculus are strings of variables, negation symbols (7), and the three binary connectives $\supset$, $\cdot$, and $\cup$. Most of the rewriting rules of the sentential calculus are of the form $x \to y$, where x and y are w.f.e.'s. An example is the rule for commutativity of $\cup$,

$$A \cup B \to D \cup A. \tag{28}$$

A few rules map from pairs of derived expressions into single expressions. One such rule is

$$\left.\begin{array}{c} A \\ \\ B \end{array}\right\} \quad \to \quad A \cdot B, \tag{29}$$

which states that if strings A and B have been derived, then string $A \cdot B$ may be added to the list of derived strings. Table 11-5 lists the GPS operators which were used in Newell and Simon's sentential calculus studies. Each operator has been written as a rewriting rule. In addition to the operators, Newell and Simon defined six classes of differences between expressions. These are shown in Table 11-6. These differences combine with the operators of Table 11-5 to establish the operator difference matrix shown in Table 11-7a. The matrix is used to guide problem solving in the original search space. Suppose GPS were to be given the problem of proving that

$$(R \supset -P) \cdot (7R \supset Q) \to 7(7Q \cdot P). \tag{30}$$

is a permissible rewriting. By applying the methods described in section 11.2 the

---

[7] The planning method was only partially implemented in GPS.

TABLE 11-5
Original and Abstracted Logical Operators for Planning[a]

	Original operator	Abstract operator in planning space
R1	$A \cup B \to B \cup A$ $A \cdot B \to B \cdot A$	Identity
R2	$A \supset B \to 7B \supset 7A$	Identity
R3	$A \cup A \longleftrightarrow A$ $A \cdot A \longleftrightarrow A$	$AA \longleftrightarrow A$
R4	$A \cup (B \cup C) \longleftrightarrow (A \cup B) \cup C$ $A \cdot (B \cdot C) \longleftrightarrow (A \cdot B) \cdot C$	$A(BC) \longleftrightarrow (AB)C$
R5	$A \cup B \longleftrightarrow (7A \cdot 7B)$	Identity
R6	$A \supset B \longleftrightarrow 7A \cup B$	Identity
R7	$A \cup (B \cdot C) \longleftrightarrow (A \cup B) \cdot (A \cup C)$ $A \cdot (B \cup C) \longleftrightarrow (A \cdot B) \cup (A \cdot C)$	$A(BC) \longleftrightarrow (AB)(AC)$
R8	$A \cdot B \to A$ $A \cdot B \to B$	$AB \to A$ $AB \to B$
R9	$A \to A \cup X$	$A \to AX$
R10	$\left.\begin{array}{c} A \\ \\ B \end{array}\right\} \to A \cdot B$	$\left.\begin{array}{c} A \\ \\ B \end{array}\right\} \to AB$
R11	$\left.\begin{array}{c} A \supset B \\ \\ A \end{array}\right\} \to B$	$\left.\begin{array}{c} AB \\ \\ A \end{array}\right\} \to B$
R12	$\left.\begin{array}{c} A \supset B \\ \\ B \supset C \end{array}\right\} \to A \supset C$	$\left.\begin{array}{c} AB \\ \\ BC \end{array}\right\} \to AC$

[a] After Newell and Simon (1972).

GPS would discover that the right and left sides of (30) differ in number of terms $(t-)$, and in sign (s). By referring to Table 11-7a, Rules 2, 5, 6, 8, and 11 are found to be candidates for reducing these differences. Although this defines a starting point, the problem is quite difficult for GPS.

To apply the planning method to problem (30), we first construct the abstracted, simplified search space in which only differences in term, variable appearances, and grouping (t, n, g) are considered when comparing two expressions. Problem (30) becomes the abstract problem

$$(PR)(QR) \to (PQ). \tag{31}$$

TABLE 11-6
Differences Used in Newell and Simon's Studies of GPS Problem Solving in Logic

Difference Name	Explanation
Term difference (t)	There is a term difference between two expressions if terms appear in one expression and not in the other. In the problem $A \rightarrow B$ expression A may have a negative ($t-$) positive ($t+$) or undefined (tX) difference from expression B depending upon whether it is necessary to delete, add, or change the variables in A to eliminate the difference. For example, $P \cup P$ has a $t+$ difference compared to $Q \cup P$.
Variable occurrence difference (n)	Expressions may differ in the number of times a given variable occurs in each expression. As for t, $n+$, $n-$, and nX differences are defined. $P \cdot Q$ has an $n+$ difference when compared to $(P \cdot Q) \supset Q$.
Negation difference (s)	Two expressions may differ in the "sign" of the negation, as in Q versus $7Q$.
Binary connective difference (c)	The main binary connective of two expressions may differ, e.g., $P \supset Q$ versus $P \cup Q$.
Grouping difference (g)	There is a difference in association of variables, as in $P \cup (Q \cup R)$ versus $(P \cup Q) \cup R$.
Position difference in components of an expression (p)	Two expressions have the same components, but in different locations in their tree, as in $P \supset (Q \cup R)$ versus $(Q \cup R) \supset P$.

TABLE 11-7
Operator Difference Matrices for GPS Logic Problems

(a) Original Problem Space

	R1	R2	R3	R4	R5	R6	R7	R8	R9	R10	R11	R12
t								−	+	+	−	X
n			X				X	−	+	+	−	X
s		X			X	X						
c					X	X	X					
g				X			X					
p	X	X										

(b) Planning Space: Operators R1, R2, R5, R5 Never Appear in Plans

	R1	R2	R3	R4	R5	R6	R7	R8	R9	R10	R11	R12
t								−	+	+	−	X
n			X				X	−	+	+	−	X
g				X			X					

The rewriting operators must be similarly reconstructed to ignore differences other than those used in the simplified space. For example, the rule

$$A \cup (B \cdot C) \longleftrightarrow (A \cup B) \cdot (A \cup C) \tag{32}$$

becomes

$$A(BC) \longleftrightarrow (AB)(AC). \tag{33}$$

As a result of the necessary transformations, some of the operators of the original space disappear in the abstract space. The rule

$$(A \cup B) \rightarrow (B \cup A) \tag{34}$$

becomes the identity operator, since it does not affect any difference relevant to the abstract space. The right-hand side of Table 11-5 shows the result of transforming the operators of the original problem into the space of the simplified problem, and Table 11-7b shows the operator-difference matrix that results.

Now consider again problem (30) and its abstract interpretation, (31). By comparing right and left sides of (31) GPS notes that there is a tX difference between them. After trying several solutions, GPS solves the abstracted problem in the following steps, which we shall number $A1, \ldots, Ai$. Notice that each step specifies a valid rewriting of the original string.

A1 $(PR)(QR)$ Original problem
A2 (PR) R8 applied to first component of A1
A3 (QR) R8 applied to produce second component of A1
A4 (PQ) R12 applied to A3, A2

GPS next attempts to apply the plan R8, R8, R12 to the original problem. We number the steps $L1, \ldots, Li$ to distinguish them from the steps of the abstract problem.

L1 $(R \supset 7P) \cdot (7R \supset Q)$ Original problem
L2 $(R \supset 7P)$ R8 applied to L1, left component
L3 $(7R \supset Q)$ R8 applied to L1, second component.

At this point the plan calls for the application of R12 to L3, L2. L3 and L2, however, are not in the appropriate form to be input lines for R12 in the original space. The comparison is to

$(7R \supset Q)$ versus $A \supset B$ and to $(R \supset 7P)$ versus $B \supset C$.

The R term is in the wrong location in L3, so the subgoal of reducing a position (p) difference is established. After consulting the operator difference table the step

L4 $(7Q \supset R)$ R2 applied to L3

is achieved. A new attempt is made to apply R12, this time to L4, L2. It is successful, producing

L5 $(7Q \supset 7P)$ R12 applied to L4, L2.

Although all steps of the plan have been completed, there are still differences between L5 and the goal state. Comparing $(7Q \supset 7P)$ versus $7(7Q \cdot P)$, a sign difference (s) in the main expression is found. Sign differences are reducible by application of R5 (see Table 11-7a), but R5 cannot be applied, since there is a connective difference between $(A \cup B)$, and L5. Rule R6 is appropriate for reducing connective differences, and can be applied, producing

L6 $(Q \cup 7P)$ R6 applied to L5

R5 can be applied to L6, with the result

L7 $-(7Q \cdot P)$ R5 applied to L6,

which is the desired goal state.

In GPS the plan is used to establish subgoals which, if accomplished, may not solve the original problem but "usually" produce a state g reasonably close to the desired goal state. There is no guarantee that planning will always work, but empirically it seems to be a useful technique.

11.4.2 STRIPS

The Stanford Research Institute Problem Solver (STRIPS, Fikes & Nilsson, 1971; Fikes, Hart, & Nilsson, 1972) produces plans by generalizing from solved problems. STRIPS is part of the programming control system for "Shakey the robot," a self-propelled vehicle designed to move about a simplified environment in response to commands in simplified English. To understand STRIPS, some explanation of Shakey is required. Shakey contains four major physical systems; the vehicle and propulsion system, a sensory system consisting of a television camera and a touch bar, a computer (not on the vehicle) which executes programs to analyze the information obtained by the vehicle's sensors, to parse input commands, and to signal the vehicle to activate its propulsion system, and a radio link for data transmission between the computer and the vehicle. STRIPS is the program which determines which commands are to be sent to the robot.

The robot's world consists of rooms, doors between rooms, movable boxes, and, in more complex situations, lights and windows. The particular physical world existing at any time is described to STRIPS by a set of assertions worded as clauses in the predicate calculus. For instance, the appearance of the clause

INROOM (ROBOT, R2)

in the data base is an assertion that the robot is in room R2 at that moment. STRIPS assumes all assertions are true, while another program, PLANEX, tests their truth. The data base must be updated as the physical situation changes. Collectively, the data base describing the world at any one time is called the *model* of the world.

The control programs also contain a number of subroutines which, when executed, will cause the robot to move through a door, push a box through a door, turn off a light, or perform other physical actions. These programs are quite complicated in themselves, but are not of direct concern in problem solving. They bear somewhat the same relation to robot problem-solving that the complex acts of walking or picking up an object bear to human problem solving.

Suppose the model contains the statements

BOX(B1)	B1 is a box	(35)
ROOM(R1)	R1 is a room	
ROOM(R2)	R2 is a room	
DOOR(D1)	D1 is a door	
INROOM(B1, R1)	B1 is in R1	
INROOM(ROBOT, R2)	Robot is in R2	
CONNECTS(D1, R1, R2)	D2 connects R1 to R2	

and the robot is given the problem of placing box B1 in room R2. More generally, let us consider the problem of placing box $b1$ in room $r2$, where $b1$ and $r2$ are variables. (We shall follow the convention of writing variables in lowercase letters and constants in uppercase letters, and of using b, d, and r for box, door, and room where it is appropriate for exposition.) Formally, STRIPS is asked to produce a model containing the clause INROOM(B1, R2). There are three ways the problem could be solved.

(a) The desired clauses might already be in the model. This would be equivalent to giving GPS or FDS the "problem" of deriving a string from itself.

(b) It might be possible to infer the desired clauses from the model without changing the physical world to which the model referred. Suppose that we add to (35) the clauses

BOX(B2)   (36)

ON-TOP-OF(B2, B1)   B2 is on top of B1.

and further suppose STRIPS to be capable of inferring

$$\left. \begin{array}{l} \text{IN}(x, y) \\ \text{ON-TOP-OF}(z, x) \end{array} \right\} \rightarrow \quad \text{IN}(z, y) \qquad (37)$$

INROOM(B2, R1) could be asserted by inference, without the robot's doing anything to the physical world. STRIPS has a powerful inference-making ability, based on the resolution principle, rather than the techniques used for inference in GPS and FDS. Chapter XII describes the resolution principle in detail. For the present, assume STRIPS' capability for logical inference.

(c) Finally, in order to solve some problem it is necessary to change the physical world and, therefore, the model describing it. This is the most interesting situation.

Let us examine a typical operator, PUSHTHRU(w, x, y, z), "Push w through x

from *y* into *z*." This operator can be described by stating ints *preconditions*, its *add list*, and its *delete list*. The preconditions are, as the name implies, the statements which must be in the model before the operator can be applied. PUSHTHRU $(b1, d1, r1, r2)$ can only be accomplished if the model contains the clauses

$$\text{BOX}(b1); \quad \text{DOOR}(d1); \quad \text{ROOM}(r1); \quad \text{ROOM}(r2); \quad (38)$$

$$\text{CONNECTS}(d1, r1, r2); \quad \text{INROOM}(b1, r1); \quad \text{INROOM}(\text{ROBOT}, r1).$$

Note that (38) is stated in terms of requirements on variables. In a specific attempt to activate PUSHTHRU the variables will be replaced by constants. This is called *(ground) instantiation*.

Continuing with the PUSHTHRU example, following the completion of the operation PUSHTHRU$(b1, d1, r1, r2)$ the model must be changed to include

$$\text{INROOM}(\text{ROBOT}, r2); \quad \text{INROOM}(b1, r2) \quad (39)$$

and to drop

$$\text{INROOM}(\text{ROBOT}, r1); \quad \text{INROOM}(b, r1). \quad (40)$$

Note the similarity between the preconditions and add and delete list and the left and right sides of GPS and FDS rewriting rule operators. They are used in very much the same way.

When given a problem STRIPS first tries to retrieve or deduce the solution conditions from the current world model. Assume that this cannot be done. The program next considers what conditions would have to be included in the model so that deduction of the solution conditions would be possible. This is similar to GPS's analysis of the difference between two states. A means–end analysis is then conducted to determine which operators have add lists that include the required clauses. As in GPS, this analysis can lead to a "problem" of changing the model so that an operation can be applied. A problem is said to be solved if a sequence of operations is found such that the first operator can be applied to the current model, the nth operation can be executed on the world model as modified by the $n - 1$st operation, and the solution conditions exist after execution of the last operator in the sequence.[8]

After solving a problem, STRIPS can generalize a solution into a plan. Consider the situation after the robot has solved the problem of moving from R2 to R1, then pushing a box back into R1. The STRIPS solution is

GOTHRU(D1, R2, R1)   "Move from R2 to R1 through door D1"   (41)

PUSHTHRU(B1, D1, R1, R2)   "Push B1 R1 to R2 using door D1."

---

[8] In reality, the problem will be solved only if the sequence can be successfully executed in the physical world. A second module of Shakey's control system (PLANEX) monitors plan execution. PLANEX returns control to STRIPS if the robot's sensors indicate that the world has been changed in some way not anticipated by STRIPS, so that the model which STRIPS used to generate the plan is no longer accurate.

The most obvious way to generalize this solution is to replace each constant with a variable, producing

$$\text{GOTHRU}(d1, r1, r2) \qquad\qquad (42)$$

$$\text{PUSHTHRU}(b1, d1, r2, r1).$$

Plan (42) is overspecialized. It is a prescription for going from one room to another, and then pushing an object in the second room back into the first room. It seems reasonable that the plan STRIPS ought to produce from this problem a plan for going from an arbitrary room into another room, and pushing an object from the second room into a third room. The overspecialization occurs in (42) because each individual constant in the solution was replaced by a single variable throughout the plan. We could use a more general replacement rule, in which a separate variable would be used for each argument of an operator, without regard to the identity of arguments of different operators in the solution. This, unfortunately, is even more unsatisfactory. For suppose we apply such a replacement rule to solution (41). The result will be

$$\text{GOTHRU}(d1, r1, r2) \qquad\qquad (43)$$

$$\text{PUSHTHRU}(b1, d2, r3, r4).$$

Plan (43) implies that the robot can go into room $r2$, and then push an object out of room $r3$, which may be a different room. Obviously this is not correct. The replacement of constants with variables must consider which variables in different steps of the solution necessarily refer to the same object. STRIPS does this by considering which variables in the steps prior to the nth step in the plan are required in the preconditions to the nth step. The technical details of how this is done depend on the mechanics of the resolution principle technique of theorem proving, which we have not yet discussed.[9] For our present purposes, it is sufficient to note that there are valid ways to generalize solutions so that they do not overgeneralize, as in (43), and avoid the excessive specialization illustrated by (42). On the other hand, although Fikes *et al.* (1972) propose a number of useful generalization techniques, they are the first to admit that they are using heuristic procedures that do not always achieve the degree of generalization one would like to have.

The purpose of forming a plan from a solution is to make available a sequence of operators (called a *macrop*) which STRIPS can use as a single operation in solving complex problems. Dealing with macrops is made difficult, however, by the fact that the action of the first n steps in a macrop will, in general, affect the conditions under which the $n + 1$st operation is to be applied. Macrops require a more sophisticated mechanism for determining when they are applicable than the simple precondition list used for single operators. STRIPS makes use of an ingenious

[9] For the cognoscenti, and those who may return to this section after reading Chapter XII, we note that the unifications required to deduce the preconditions of each step provide a vehicle for indicating which variables in a plan must refer to the same object.

device called a *triangle table*. To illustrate the method we shall build a triangle table for the simple GOTHRU–PUSHTHRU plan, correctly generalized[10]

$$\text{GOTHRU}(d1, r1, r2) \tag{44}$$

$$\text{PUSHTHRU}(b1, d2, r2, r3). \tag{45}$$

GOTHRU($d1, r1, r2$) requires as preconditions that the robot be in $r1$ and that $d1$ connect $r1$ to $r2$. The PUSHTHRU operator requires that the robot and the box be in $r2$, and that $d2$ connect $r2$ to $r3$. Finally, observe that the add list of GOTHRU contains INROOM(ROBOT, $r2$), which is one of the preconditions of PUSHTHRU, and that PUSHTHRU deletes this precondition from its model while adding INROOM(ROBOT, $r3$) and INROOM($b1, r3$) to the model. This means that INROOM($b1, r2$) must be in the model prior to execution of GOTHRU, but that INROOM(ROBOT, $r2$) need not be. A plan's preconditions must reflect this.

0	1	2
*INROOM(ROBOT, r1) *CONNECTS (d1,r1,r2)		
	1 GOTHRU(d1,r1,r2)	
*INROOM(b1,r2) CONNECTS (d1,r2,r3)	*INROOM(ROBOT,r2)	
		2 PUSHTHRU(b1,d2,r2,r3)
		INROOM(ROBOT;r3) INROOM(b1,r3)

Fig. 11-8. A triangle table.

A triangle table for plan (44) is shown in Figure 11-8. More generally, if a plan contains k steps, the table will consist of $k + 1$ rows and columns, in triangular form. The rows are ordered from $1 \ldots k + 1$, and columns $0 \ldots k$. The table is constructed in the following steps:

(*i*) In column i, row $i + 1$ place the add list of operator i.

(*ii*) In column i, row $i + j + 1$ [$j = 0 \ldots k - (i + 1)$] place those clauses in column i, row $i + j$ which will remain in the model after operator $i + j$ has been applied—i.e., the clauses that are in column i, row $i + j$ and are not on the instantiated deletion list of operator $i + j$. Referring to Figure 11-8, column 1 lists the result of the operation GOTHRU at various stages. Initially GOTHRU ($d1, r1, r2$) places the robot in room $r2$, so INROOM(ROBOT, $r2$) is added to the

[10] In fact, generalizations and triangle table construction are concurrent processes, as the information obtained from triangle table construction is useful in establishing generalizations.

model, and placed in column 1, row 2. The next operation PUSHTHRU $(b1, d2, r2, r3)$ takes the robot out of $r2$, so column 1, row 3 is empty. Similarly, the statements added to the world model by PUSHTHRU, INROOM(ROBOT, $r3$) and INROOM($b1, r3$), must be added in column 2, row 3. Clearly this procedure can be applied to a plan with an arbitrary number of steps.

(*iii*) Column 0 remains to be constructed. This is done by considering the preconditions of the operator to be applied at step *i*. In column 0, row *i* we place the precondition clauses that must be in the model before operator *i* can be applied, but which do not already appear in row *i* as a result of the previous operations. Thus column 0, row 2 lists the preconditions of PUSHTHRU($b1, d2, r2, r3$) except for INROOM(ROBOT, $r2$) which has been established by the previous action of GOTHRU.

(*iv*) Given these rules for triangle table construction, there will in general be some entries in row *i* which are not preconditions for operator *i*. To distinguish precondition statements in a row from non precondition statements, the former are marked with an asterisk.

An entire plan can be applied if all clauses in column 0 of the plan's triangle table exist in a model or can be inferred from it. In fact, the triangle table can be used to treat parts of plans as a plan. Define the *i*th *kernel of a plan* to be the square within the triangle table containing row *i* and the lower left-hand corner of the table. This square will contain a number of marked statements. A subplan consisting of steps $i, i + 1, i + 2, \ldots, k$ can be applied to any model which contains every marked statement within the kernel. Any other preconditions of the $i + j$th operator will be generated by prior steps in the plan.

Planning using triangle tables has been shown to be a useful feature of STRIPS. Fikes *et al.* cite examples in which the use of plans and triangle tables reduces the time required to solve robot movement problems by a factor of three. On the other hand, as the authors themselves note, the creation of many plans will produce a sizable information retrieval problem, as it becomes nontrivial to decide how many triangle tables can be applied to a given world model.

Although extensive reliance on plans is a fairly new development, we observe that there are at least three earlier programs which generated plans of a sort. Samuel (1967) developed a chess-playing program that kept statistics on situations in which certain sequences of moves had proved useful, and used these statistics to develop a complicated, nonlinear pattern recognizer to indicate how the current game resembled previous games. Quinlan (1969) built a similar extension to FDS and showed that "training" in one field, logic, would generalize to the similar field of simple algebra. Both applications were successful, but seem more an example of pattern recognition in theorem proving than planning, as we have used the word here. Gelernter (1959) used a planning technique called syntactic symmetry, which is similar to the "overspecialized" STRIPS planning illustrated by (42), which he applied within a geometry theorem prover to avoid solving the same subproblem more than once. Kling (1971) has proposed a system somewhat similar to Gelernter's for use in resolution-principle theorem provers. Discussion of Kling's method is not possible without first explaining how a resolution principle theorem prover works, and so will be postponed until the latter stage of the following chapter.

11.4.3 PLANNING LANGUAGES

Throughout the text there has been little discussion of programming details, as languages change rapidly while logical foundations are hopefully more permanent. The need for planning in problem solving systems, however, presents a number of challenges to the programming language designer. Any language sufficient to describe a push down automaton (and thus, any context free language) can be used to express a problem solving plan, but the expression may be clumsy, since a language designed for planning can make good use of linguistic constructs that are unlikely to be found in languages designed to express conventional computation. For this reason a number of attempts have been made to design special programming languages for artificial intelligence. This history has been well reviewed by Sammett (1971), so we shall mention only the highlights. Information Processing Language V (IPL-V), the earliest such language, was essentially a machine order code for a machine designed to perform symbolic rather than numerical calculations (Newell *et al.*, 1964). McCarthy (1961) combined the IPL-V constructs with the formalisms of Church's lambda calculus to produce LISP, a programming language which can be analyzed formally (Wenger, 1969). Many of the ideas of LISP have been incorporated into languages expressly designed for expression of plans for problem solving and theorem proving, notably PLANNER (Hewitt, 1972) and Question Answerer 4 (QA-4, Dirksen *et al.*, 1972). The useful concepts which a language needs will be demonstrated by a discussion of some of the features of PLANNER. No attempt will be made to be faithful to all the formalisms of PLANNER notation, since training PLANNER programmers is not the goal. The discussion is intended only to give the reader some idea of the nature of the language.

A problem solving program must be able to deal with three primitive entities; objects, properties of objects, and relations between objects. Using the prefix notation, (RED, B1) states that object B1 has the property red, while (ON, B1, B2) states that object B2 is on object B1.[11] This presentation agrees with our intuition. Properties, however, can be regarded as functions of one object, and relations as functions of several arguments. Therefore we need not make a distinction between them. Furthermore, whether a symbol refers to a relation or an object of thought depends largely upon context. RED is sometimes a property of colored objects, and sometimes it is an object, the color "red." In order to distinguish the way in which a term is being used, we shall write $\#X$ to refer to the use of term X as a relation, and $:X$ to refer to its use as an object.

Relations may be used to construct complex objects, since the fact of two objects being in a particular relation is itself something that can be an object of thought. This is partially illustrated in the above examples, but is clearer when we consider complex acts. The statement *The robot put block B1 in the box* may refer to a named event, which itself is a datum,

$$:REL1 = (\#PUTIN \quad :B1 \quad :BOX \quad :ROBOT). \qquad (46)$$

A second example is *The robot grasps B2*,

$$:REL2 = (\#GRASP \quad :B2 \quad :ROBOT). \tag{47}$$

A new object can be created to express the event that :REL1 and :REL2 occur in a given sequence, by use of the BEFORE relation,

$$:REL3 = (\#BEFORE \quad :REL2 \quad :REL1). \tag{48}$$

These examples have been taken from the simple world of robots. It is of more than passing interest to apply similar concepts to the description of natural language in natural settings. A sentence such as

$$\text{John saw Mary at Luigi's.} \tag{49}$$

can be described as an event with objects and relations between objects,

$$\text{EVENT I} - (\#LOCATION \; : LUIGI's \; :(\#SAW \quad :JOHN \quad :MARY)) \tag{50}$$

Rumelhart, Lindsay, and Norman (1972; Lindsay & Norman, 1972) have given a number of more elaborate illustrations of how natural language can be converted into structures similar to those found in PLANNER data bases. Their particular notation emphasizes graphs, but, as we have pointed out, graph structures and networks of relations are isomorphic.

In order to reason we must both have knowledge of the objects in the world and the rules of inference which permit us to infer new knowledge from old. That is, we distinguish between explicit events, which have been our concern up to now, and knowledge about relationships which hold in the general case. Again we could appeal to psychology, and in particular to Tulving's (1972) distinction between episodic and semantic memory. Examples such as (50) are part of episodic memory. An example of a semantic statement is

$$E1 = FORALL(X) (\#IMPLIES (\#MORTAL \quad :X) (\#MAN \quad :X)) \tag{51}$$

which says simply that the property of being a man implies the property of being mortal. Such a statement can be interpreted as a plan for proving that something is true. Thus, by (51), to prove X is mortal, prove X is a man. Some plans are much more complex than this and require a more flexible notation. Consider a bit of guidance Winograd (1972) offers to graduate students, *A paper is acceptable as a thesis if it is long or if it contains a persuasive argument*. In PLANNER this becomes

$$E2 = FORALL (X) (\# IMPLIES \tag{52}$$

$$(\# OR (\# LONG \quad :X) \quad (EXISTS (:Y) (\# AND (\# PERSUASIVE \quad :Y)$$

$$(\# ARGUMENT \quad :Y)$$

$$(\# CONTAINS \quad :Y:X)))$$

$$(\# THESIS :X))$$

$$(\# ACCEPTABLE :X))$$

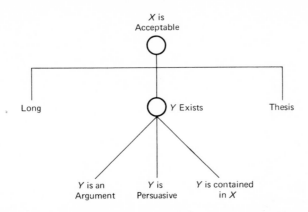

Fig. 11.9. Subproblem reduction graph for proving acceptability of *X*.

It is useful to think of (52) as a definition of acceptability which can be structured as a sequential decision procedure, similar to those discussed in Chapter VI. The appropriate diagram is shown in Figure 11-9. The figure could equally well be thought of as a problem reduction graph. Each node corresponds to a condition which had to be proven true, and the AND and OR nodes indicate how the subproblem solutions are to be tied together to solve the main problem. The use of the problem reduction representation should call to mind the fact that the order in which subproblems are attempted may greatly influence the difficulty of solving a problem. In PLANNER it is possible for the programmer to specify how the search is to take place, both by stating the sequence in which subproblems will be attempted and by providing hints about the solution of each subproblem. This is done by defining *consequence* theorems, which indicate how to prove that a particular fact is a consequence of known facts. An example of such a theorem is

(DEFTHEOREM EVALUATE   (53)
    (THECONSQ(*X, Y*) (# ACCEPTABLE $?*X*)
        (THGOAL (# THESIS $?*X*)),
        (THOR (THGOAL(# LONG $?*X*) (THUSE CONTENTS–CHECK–COUNT))
            (THAND (THGOAL (# CONTAINS $?*Y X*))
                (THGOAL (# ARGUMENT $?*Y*))
                (THGOAL (# PERSUASIVE $?*Y*)))))),

which defines a procedure for determining whether the problem reduction graph of Figure 11-9 can be satisfied. The flow diagram for the data base search is shown in Figure 11-10. The first line is simply an instruction to the PLANNER system to treat the statement as a theorem—i.e., as semantic rather than episodic information. The second line defines the theorem as a "consequent" theorem for proving that something, *X*, has the property of being acceptable. In this line the existence of a

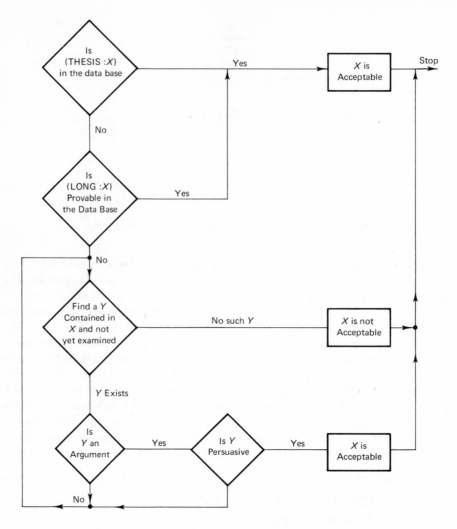

Fig. 11.10.   Flow charge of search procedure defined by statement (53).

second variable, Y, is noted. The notation $\$?X$ and $\$?Y$ states that X and Y are free variables. The following lines state conditions which, if true, are sufficient to assert that X has the property of being acceptable. Each condition is called a *goal*. The first, (THGOAL (#THESIS $\$?X$)), states that if X already has the property of being a thesis, then it has the property of being acceptable by implication. The next goal is actually a set of OR subgoals, as shown by the use of (THOR, which indicates that the goal is established if any of its subgoals are established. The first of the subgoals is (THGOAL(#LONG $\$?X$) (THUSE CONTENTS-CHECK-COUNT)). The subgoal itself is to prove that X has the property long. The second construct directs PLANNER to use a proof method called CONTENTS-CHECK-COUNT (here undefined) to determine the "long" property of X. The second OR subgoal is itself a conjunction of subsubgoals

$$(\text{THAND}$$
$$(\text{THGOAL} (\# \text{CONTAINS} \$?Y \$?X))$$
$$(\text{THGOAL} (\# \text{ARGUMENT} \$?Y))$$
$$(\text{THGOAL} (\# \text{PERSUASIVE} \$?Y)))$$

all of which must be established before the subgoal itself is established. Their interpretation should be clear. What the THECONSQ statement does, in effect, is to establish a particular type of search of a problem reduction graph. Thus the activation of a THECONSQ statement is very similar to the activation of a problem solving program such as GPS or FDS. The difference is that the general programs must use the same graph searching methods for every problem, while PLANNER allows the programmer to give (hopefully) helpful hints about solution methods. In doing so, however, the programmer can concentrate on specifications of useful goals and subgoals, and need not concern himself with how goals are to be achieved unless he wishes to do so.

PLANNER has a number of other features of interest. We have already seen how the programmer may suggest a particular proof method, by the use of the THUSE construct. The same construct would be used to evoke the proof procedure just defined, as in

$$(\text{THGOAL} (\#\text{ACCEPTABLE} \quad :X) (\text{THUSE EVALUATE})) \qquad (54)$$

which directs PLANNER to prove acceptability of a particular document, A, using the THECONSQ procedure named EVALUATE. In some cases more than one plan can be indicated for use in realizing a goal, by concatenating THUSE statements. The appropriate procedures will be tried in order. Finally, there is a "catch all" THUSE statement, (THTBF THTRUE), which instructs PLANNER to attempt to realize a goal using any proof procedure known to the system. This is particularly useful if the system's memory contains a universal proof procedure, which can function as an expensive last resort proof technique.

A very old syllogism illustrates the power of PLANNER. Suppose that

$$(\text{DEFTHEOREM TH1} \qquad \qquad (55)$$
$$(\text{THCONSQ}(X) (\#\text{FALLIBLE} \$?X)$$
$$(\text{THGOAL} (\#\text{HUMAN} \$?X))))$$

has been included in the data base. We also suppose that the data base contains the statements:

$$(\#\text{HUMAN} \quad :\text{TURING}) \qquad \qquad (56)$$
$$(\#\text{HUMAN} \quad :\text{PLATO})$$
$$(\#\text{GREEK} \quad :\text{PLATO})$$
$$(\text{FALLIBLE} \quad :\text{FOOTBALL-COACHES})$$

The question "Is anyone fallible" is evaluated by

$$THPROG(Y) \ (THGOAL(\#FALLIBLE \ \$?Y) \ (THTBF \ THTRUE)), \quad (57)$$

which directs PLANNER first to examine the data base to determine whether there is any constant for which fallibility is listed as a property and then, if the search fails, to use any proof method available to infer fallibility. Since (55) states a theorem whose consequent is fallibility, PLANNER will examine the data base for the appropriate antecedent conditions. If (57) is evaluated on the data base (56) the answer FOOTBALL-COACHES will be returned. If the statement (#FALLIBLE :FOOTBALL-COACHES) is removed from the data base and the question asked again, the answer will be PLATO, on the grounds that (#HUMAN   :PLATO) is in the data base, and, by (55), (#FALLIBLE   :PLATO) is an implied fact. Now suppose we make the question more complex, by asking *Is any Greek fallible*? The program is

$$THPROG(Y) \ (THGOAL \ (\#AND \ (FALLIBLE \ \$?Y) \ (\#GREEK \ \$?Y))) \quad (58)$$

Initially, FOOTBALL-COACHES are found to be fallible, but the program cannot prove that they are GREEK. The "backtrack" feature of PLANNER is then called into play, as the system automatically returns to find a second FALLIBLE object. This time TURING is found to be FALLIBLE, by inference, but TURING is not GREEK. PLANNER backtracks again, proves that PLATO is FALLIBLE by inference, and then finds that PLATO is GREEK. In addition to illustrating backtracking, the example is useful to show how important the sequencing of goals is. Obviously much less data processing would have been done if (58) were rewritten

$$THPROG(Y) \ (THGOAL \ (\#AND \ (\#GREEK \ \$?Y) \ (\#FALLIBLE \ \$?Y))), \quad (59)$$

causing PLANNER to first find Greeks and then prove that they were fallible, rather than the other way around.

Chapter XII

THEOREM PROVING[1]

12.0   Theorem Proving Based on Herbrand Proof Procedures

12.0.1   GENERAL

In mechanical problem solving there must be a formalism by which the elements of the problem are represented in the machine and a set of mechanizable operations for acting on the formal representation. The state–space approach discussed in Chapter XI provides a formalism that is often "natural"; at least, it is easily understood by people. Unfortunately, the mechanical manipulation problem may become formidable, because of the problem of choosing between different possible inference rules. An alternative approach is to use a formalism that is less easily understood by people, but has a more straightforward machine representation and leads to simpler symbol manipulations. A solution that has proven unusually powerful is to represent all "problems," in the loose sense, as theorems to be proven within the first-order predicate calculus. A simple technique for formula manipulation, first proposed by J. A. Robinson (1965, 1967), is then available and easily mechanized. In order to explain the method, it is first necessary to consider the nature of the theorem proving exercise.

In theorem proving one attempts to show that a particular well-formed expression (w.f.e.), B, is a logical consequence of a set $S = \{A1, \ldots, Ak\}$ of w.f.e.'s, collectively called the *axioms* of the problem. A rule of inference is a rule by which new expressions can be derived from previously established ones. For instance, if Ai and Aj are previously established w.f.e.'s,

$$f_q(Ai, Aj) \to Ak \tag{1}$$

indicates that Ak can be derived from Ai and Aj using inference rule f_q. Now

---

[1] In preparing this chapter I have benefited greatly from discussions with my colleague, Dr. Sharon Sickel. Any responsibility for error, is, of course, my own.

consider the sequence of sets of expressions $S0 = S, \ldots, Sj$ obtained from a set of axioms S by the rule

$$S0 = S, \tag{2}$$

$$S(j + 1) = Sj \cup F(Sj)$$

where $F(S)$ is the set of expressions which can be obtained from the set S by making all possible applications of all possible rules of inference f_q in a finite set $F = \{f_q\}$ of rules. Statement B "follows from the axioms of S" if B is a member of S_j, for some j. The rewriting rules of Chapter XI can be thought of as inference rules. The problem there was that F was relatively large, thus leading the sequence of (2) to explode in size. The combinatorial explosion problem might be manageable if F were small. In the extreme, suppose F contained the single rule of inference

$$(A \vee B) \cdot (7A \vee C) \rightarrow (B \vee C) \tag{3}$$

This is sufficient to prove any theorem in the first-order predicate calculus. Rule (3) is the basis for resolution principle theorem proving.

12.0.2   NOTATION

In order to develop the method formally, a notation for the first-order predicate calculus is needed. The initial discussion ignores the problem of quantification; i.e., we will not consider the implication of statements such as "all x are y" or "at least one x is y." The universe of discourse will contain a set of elementary symbols; a, b, $c, \ldots$ which serve as *constants*, a number of *variable* symbols, written from the "end" of the alphabet, x, y, z, and *functions*. Functions are mappings; a function of n arguments maps from the elements of the set D^n (all possible ordered sets of n terms) into the set D. For example, the function $+$ is a binary function, which maps a pair of real numbers into a single real number. The letters f, g, h will be used for functions. Finally, capital letters (usually P, Q) will indicate *relations* or *predicates*. A predicate of n arguments maps from D^n into the set $\{T, F\}$. That is, any n-ary relationship between terms is either true or false.

Now let us consider the structure of a well-formed expression. A *term* is either a variable, a constant, or a function. An n-ary function must have n terms for its arguments. Thus the following are terms:

$$a, b, c, \qquad f(a), \qquad g(f(x), y), \qquad h(g(a, w), f(x)).$$

An *atomic formula*, or *atom* is a predicate and its arguments:

$$R(f(x), a), \qquad P(a, y), \qquad Q(g(a, b), f(x))$$

A *literal* is an atomic formula or its negation. When the structure of an atomic formula is not relevant, we shall write atomic formulas as capital letters, A, B, etc., with negations indicated as 7A, 7B. When the structure of a literal is not important we will write L_i for the ith literal.

TABLE 12-1

Simple Statements about Inequality Expressed in the Predicate Calculus Notation

Expression	Alternate notation	Possible interpretation, comment
Constants and variables		
a, b x, y		a and b are any particular pair of real numbers. x and y are variables whose values range over the real numbers.
Functions, terms		
$f(x, y)$	$x + y$	Functions of the real numbers.
$g(x)$	x^2	
Atoms		
$R_1(x, y)$	$x > y$, A_1	Atom A_1. Either true or false
$R_2(x, y)$	$x < y$, A_2	for any assignment of values to
$R_3(x, y)$	$x = y$, A_3	x and y. Similarly, for atoms A_2, A_3.
Literals		
$7R_1(x, y)$, $R_2(x, y)$	$x \not> y$; $7A_1, A_2$	An atom and its "sign."
Clauses		
$\big(R_1(x, y), R_2(x, y), R_3(x, y)\big)$	$C1$	For all x, either $x > y$, $x < y$, or $x = y$.
$\big((7R_1(x, y), 7R_2(x, y)\big)$	$C2$	Either $x \not< y$ or $x \not> y$.
$\big(R_2(x, a), R_1(g(x), x)\big)$	$C3$	Either $x < a$ or $x^2 > x$. True if $a = 1$ and $x \neq 1$.

A *clause* C is a disjunction of literals, and a set of clauses **S** is interpreted as a single statement that is the conjunction of all of its clauses. Since atomic formulas are predicates that map into the set $\{T, F\}$, the truth values of a set of atoms determines the truth values of the clauses and sets of clauses that can be constructed from them.

These ideas are illustrated in Table 12-1, which shows some simple statements about inequalities written in this notation.[2] The constants of this table $\{a, b\}$ should be interpreted as any two real numbers, whereas the functions should be

---

[2] Most illustrations of theorem proving use mathematically more interesting examples taken from group theory. We have purposely avoided doing so, since we do not want any difficulty in the example to detract from illustration of the principles. For some more complex illustrations of resolution principle applications, see Hayes and Kowalski (1969).

interpreted as single-valued functions on the real numbers. The predicates are the three possible orderings (greater than, less than, equal to) that can hold between any pair of real numbers. Obviously a statement of a particular ordering for a given pair is either true or false, including clauses C1, C2, and C3 in **S** states that they are simultaneously true.

12.0.3   PROOFS BY CONTRADICTION

We noted that a statement **T** follows from a set of clauses **S** if **T** is a logical consequent of the statements (clauses) in **S**. For simplicity, assume that **T** consists of the single clause T. Now consider the set of clauses

$$\mathbf{S} \cup \mathbf{T} = \{C1, \ldots, Cn, T\} \tag{4}$$

The Ci and T must all be true for **S** ∪ **T** to be true. The truth value of the clauses will, in turn, be determined by the truth value of the atomic statements in them—the assignment of truth values to atoms must be such that at least one literal in every clause is true. A particular assignment of truth values to atoms is called a *model*. If **S** implies **T**, then there is no model such that **S** can be true and **T** not be true. However, if **T** is true, then its negation, $7T$, must be false. Therefore, if **S** implies **T**, then the statement

$$\mathbf{S} \cup 7\mathbf{T} = \{C1, \ldots, Cn, 7T\} \tag{5}$$

must be false under every model.

Suppose, for a moment, that there is a finite number of atoms. If so, then there will be a finite number of models, as there are only 2^k distinct assignments of truth values to k atoms. Clearly we could systematically generate these assignments and determine the truth value of the Ci and T under each of them. If (5) proves to be false under all models, then **S** does indeed imply **T**. This argument, called *proof by contradiction*, is basic to the theorem-proving techniques presented in this chapter.

12.0.4   THE RELATION OF MODELS TO CONTRADICTIONS

From the preceding argument, we see that proving the inconsistency of a statement such as (5) is conceptually a trivial problem, providing that the number of atoms is finite. Whether the problem is practically trivial, of course, depends on how many atoms there are and our capacity for generating and examining models. Still, it is interesting to ask what the conditions are which ensure that the number of atoms is finite. **S** is a set of statements which are true of the atoms contained in **S** directly and any atoms which can be derived from **S**. The latter set may be infinite, as is shown by the following trivial example. Let **S** be the single atomic statement

$$\mathbf{S} = \{R_1(a, x)\} \tag{6}$$

and assume that the function $f(x)$ has been defined. From (6) we may produce the infinite sequence

$$R_1(a, x), \quad R_1(a, f(x)), \quad R_1(a, ff(x))), \ldots \tag{7}$$

Although the sequence is infinite it is denumerable; i.e., we can easily produce a numbering scheme which can order any two statements. (In the example, we could simply count the level of nesting in the second argument.) In general, it is always possible to produce a numbering scheme for the infinite set of atoms produced by substitution into a finite set.

Suppose for the moment that **S** contains *no* variables. This is called the *ground case*, and the universe of discourse is the *Herbrand base*. We may enumerate the ground case. To illustrate the procedure we will use a simplified version of the example of Table 12-1, in which we assert that for two particular numbers (a, b) [not for number pairs in general, which we would write (x, y)] the statement

$$a = b \rightarrow a \not> b \tag{8}$$

is true. The atoms to be considered are

$$\begin{array}{lll} \text{A1} & a > b, & \tag{9} \\ \text{A2} & a < b, & \\ \text{A3} & a = b. & \end{array}$$

The clauses of **A** and their interpretations are

$$\begin{array}{lll} \text{C1} & \text{(A1, A2, A3)} & \text{One of the relations holds} \tag{10} \\ \text{C2} & \text{(7A1, 7A2)} & \\ \text{C3} & \text{(7A1, 7A3)} & \text{No two relations hold simultaneously.} \\ \text{C4} & \text{(7A2, 7A3)} & \end{array}$$

In this notation (8) will be A3 ⊃ 7A1, and the negation of (8) is A3 · A1. We will write this as two separate clauses, for purposes of illustration.

$$\begin{array}{ll} \text{7T1} & \text{(A3)} \tag{11} \\ \text{7T2} & \text{(A1)} \end{array}$$

Combining (10) and (11),

$$\mathbf{S} = \mathbf{A} \cup \mathbf{T} \tag{12}$$

$$= \{(\text{A1, A2, A3}), \quad (\text{7A1, 7A2}), \quad (\text{7A}_1, \text{7A}_3), \quad (\text{7A}_2, \text{7A}_3), \quad (\text{A1}), \\ (\text{A3})\}$$

Since there are $2^3 = 8$ possible values of the atomic statements in **S** we can generate all possible models. If each of these models falsifies at least one of the clauses of **S**, then a statement of the form of (5) will have been falsified, and hence (8) will be proven. This is done in a very mechanical (and not very clever) way in Figure 12-1.

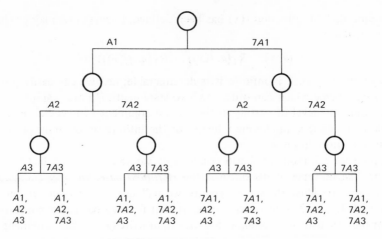

Fig. 12-1.   Tree models for a simple problem with no variables.

This figure shows a tree graph for generating models. At each interior node of the tree an atom is chosen, and the two branches leading out of the node designated as branches for the "true" and "false" values of that atom. Thus since $A1$ is chosen for the first node, all branches to the left of the root node point to models in which $A1$ is true, and all branches to the right point to models in which $A1$ is false. If statement (8) is indeed implied by (10), then each of the models represented by endpoints of the tree will falsify at least one of the clauses of $\mathbf{S} \cup \mathbf{T}$. We can enumerate the models to see that this is true.

Model	Clause falsified
$A1, A2, A3$	$C2, C3, C4$
$A1, A2, 7A3$	$C2, 7T1$
$A1, 7A2, A3$	$C3$
$A1, 7A2, 7A3$	$7T1$
$7A1, A2, A3$	$C4, 7T2$
$7A1, A2, 7A3$	$7T1, 7T2$
$7A1, 7A2, A3$	$7T2$
$7A1, 7A2, 7A3$	$C1, 7T1, 7T2$

Since there is no possible truth table combination of atoms which will make statement (12) true, it follows that (8), the hypothesis, is implied by the axioms.

Unfortunately, the method may not work in more complex cases. Trivially, we could create a statement with so many atoms that the method of enumeration would not be practical. Even more to the point, what about the case in which the Herbrand universe contains an infinite number of atoms? Finally, although the enumeration method is valid, it leads to redundant steps. We could have shown that

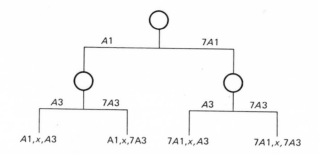

Fig. 12-2.   Tree of general models.

(12) is contradictory by examining fewer models. Consider the "partial tree" shown in Figure 12-2. This tree was derived from Figure 12-1 by considering only the branches involving atoms A1 and A3. The endpoints on the tree of Figure 12-2 correspond to sets of models in which only the truth values of atoms $A1$ and $A3$ are defined. If a clause is falsified by all combinations of $A1$ and $A3$ truth values, however, it is clearly unsatisfiable. In the case at hand we can show this by simply listing the *partial assignments* of truth values to $A1$ and $A3$.

Partial assignment	Clause falsified
$A1, A3$	$C3$
$A1, 7A3$	$7T1$
$7A1, A3$	$7T2$
$7A1, 7A3$	$7T1, 7T2$

12.0.5   THE SKOLEM–HERBRAND–GÖDEL THEOREM

Refutation by examination of partial assignments suggests a way to avoid the impossibility of enumerating all models. We have shown by example that a partial assignment can demonstrate unsatisfiability. The Skolem–Herbrand–Gödel theorem, which provides the logical justification for the techniques discussed in this chapter, states that a partial assignment can be found which will falsify any set of clauses which are mutually contradictory (Robinson, 1967). We now show how this fact can be used in theorem proving.

Let $S(X_1, x_2, \ldots, x_q)$ be a statement (set of clauses) containing q variables. By substitution, each variable may be replaced by a term, which can be either a function term of the form $f(a, b, x_i, x_j)$ or a constant. There are denumerably many such replacements, some of which may contain $q' > q$ variables. A given statement, then, implies its instantiations and denumerably many other statements, and any single statement contains a finite number of atoms. The original statement **S**, then, has associated with it a Herbrand universe containing denumerably many atoms. These atoms can be arranged in an "infinite binary tree" as shown in Figure 12-3.

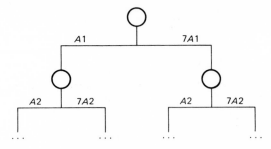

Fig. 12-3. "Infinite binary tree" of atoms. Each node in tree corresponds to a partial assignment of truth values to atoms.

Each node of this tree corresponds to a partial assignment of truth values to atoms in the Herbrand universe. Now, consider the sequence **S**, **S1**, **S2**, . . . , **Si** of statements obtained by substitutions for the variables in **S**. Since each **Si** is a specification of the general statement **S**, **S** ∪ **Si** for all *i*. Suppose that **Si** is falsified by the set of partial assignments in some tree of the form of Figure 12-3. We will say that the tree terminates in this case. This means that **Si** is false (more properly, truth-functionally unsatisfiable). Since **Si** was produced by a substitution into the more general statement **S**, if **Si** is false, then **S** must also be false, for if **S** were to be true, any statement implied by it would also be true.

The Skolem–Herbrand–Gödel theorem states that if **S** is false (truth functionally unsatisfiable), then there will be some **Si** which is truth functionally unsatisfiable. This suggests a mechanical technique for theorem proving. "All" that must be done is to generate from **S** each statement **S1**, **S2**, . . . , **Si** that can be produced by substitutions into **S**, construct the tree of partial assignments containing all atoms of **Si**, the statement just generated, and determine the satisfiability of **Si** by enumeration. If **S** is of the form of (5), containing a set of axioms and the negation of a conclusion, then if **Si** is unsatisfiable, the statement containing the axioms and the desired conclusion [as in (4)] is satisfiable, provided that the axioms themselves may be assumed consistent.

As described, this procedure is not remotely practical. As the inequalities example showed, given a statement and even without considering substitution, simple enumeration of all possible models may produce more models to be examined than are needed to prove that a statement is unsatisfiable. Furthermore, blind generation of substitutions into **S** will produce an impossibly large number of statements **Sj** which are, in fact, satisfiable. It is hard to overestimate this problem. If statements are generated and tested without a plan, then the number of statements needed to solve very simple problems will often exceed the speed and memory capabilities of the largest conceivable computer. What is needed is a method for restricting the number of derived statements to be considered and, given a statement which is, in fact, unsatisfiable, of locating a partial assignment that will demonstrate the fact.

12.1   The Resolution Principle

12.1.0   PLAN

In this section we describe the *resolution principle* and the theorem-proving techniques that are based on it. First we shall show that a method of inference, called resolution, is both valid and complete. This means that the method only produces proofs of true theorems and that, if a theorem is true, the technique will produce a proof after a finite number of steps. As the previous section suggested, we will do this indirectly, since the basic proof strategy involves showing that the converse of a theorem is false, rather than deriving the theorem directly. More precisely, then, resolution is a method for demonstrating that a false statement is false, not that a true statement is true.

Resolution will first be proven valid and complete for *ground resolution*, i.e., for refuting statements **S** that contain no variables. This will be done partly as a demonstration of how proof techniques are proven to have certain properties, and partly to demonstrate resolution itself. Next it will be shown that resolution is appropriate in the general case in which the statement to be refuted does contain variables.

12.1.1   GROUND RESOLUTION

Consider a statement **S** that contains clauses $C1, C2, \ldots, Cn, 7T$, none of which have variable symbols. Suppose **S** contains two clauses such that one contains a literal which is negated in the other. The clauses will have the form

$$C1 = (L_1, L_2, L_4); \tag{13}$$

$$C2 = (L_3, 7L_4).$$

The conjunction of these clauses implies the clause $C3 = (L_1, L_2, L_3)$

$$(L_1, L_2, L_4) \cdot (L_3, 7L_4) \rightarrow (L_1, L_2, L_3). \tag{14}$$

since the truth value of the conjunction clearly does not depend upon the value of L_4. We shall say that $C3$ is deduced from $C1$ and $C2$. Clause $C3$ will also be referred to as the *resolvent* of $C1$ and $C2$, and $C1$ and $C2$ as the *parent* clauses of $C3$. If $C3$ were itself to be used in a subsequent resolution of, say, $C4$, $C1$ and $C2$ would be *ancestors* of $C4$, and $C4$ a *descendent* of $C1$, $C2$, and $C3$. To give a more general definition of the resolution operation, define the clauses Ci and Cj to be sets of literals such that Ci contains the literal L and Cj the literal $7L$. Clause Ck, the resolvent of Ci and Cj, is

$$Ck = \{Ci - \{L\}\} \cup \{Cj - \{7L\}\}. \tag{15}$$

A set **S** of clauses is truth functionally satisfiable if there exists a model under which the conjunction of clauses in **S** is true. Furthermore, if **S** is truth functionally satisfiable, then any set **S'** consisting of **S** and the clauses derived from **S** by resolution must also be truth functionally satisfiable. Therefore, if S' is not satisfiable, it follows that S must have been truth functionally unsatisfiable. This, of course, is simply a restatement of what we have said before, specialized to resolution. Resolution, however, provides an easy way to show that certain sets S' are not satisfiable by any model. Since the truth value of a clause is the disjunction of the truth value of its literals, the truth value of a clause cannot be changed by appending the "universally false" statement F to it. Therefore we can take any clause $C = (L_1, L_2, \ldots, L_k)$ and change it to $C^* = (L_1, L_2, \ldots, L_k, F)$. The set S^* formed from S in this manner has the same truth value as the set S under any assignment. Now suppose we are able, after one or more "rounds" of expansion of S by resolution, to produce two clauses which (except for F) are clauses with single literals ("singletons") and whose literals are complements of each other. The resolvent of these two clauses is

$$(L, F) \cdot (7L, F) = (F). \qquad (16)$$

This is a universally false statement, which cannot be satisfied by any model. Therefore any expansion S' of S which contains the clause (F), being a conjunction of its clauses, must be truth functionally unsatisfiable. S itself must then be truth functionally unsatisfiable. In other words, the production of (F) by resolution from S is sufficient to show that S is truth functionally unsatisfiable. In practice, we can drop this device and speak of generating the *empty clause* (   ) by resolution. The preceding reasoning shows that if (   ) can be derived from S by resolution, S must be unsatisfiable.

To complete the proof of validity of the resolution principle, we must show that if S is unsatisfiable, (   ) can always be produced by resolution. This will be done using a syntactic procedure developed by Anderson and Bledsoe (1970). The proof is by induction on $k(S)$, where $k(S)$ is an "excess literal" count,

$$k(S) = (\text{number of appearances of literals in } S) - (\text{number of clauses} \quad (17)$$
$$\text{in } S).$$

For example, if

$$S = \{(L1), (L1, L2), (7L1, L2, L3, L4)\}, \qquad (18)$$

then there are three clauses in S, and

$$K(S) = (1 + 2 + 4) - 3 = 4. \qquad (19)$$

It is of interest to note that $k(S)$ is a feature of the structure of S, and does not depend on an assignment of truth values to S. Thus, the Anderson and Bledsoe proof illustrates a *syntactic proof*, in which we show that an assertion is true for all possible structures of S. This can be contrasted to a *semantic proof*, in which an assertion about S is shown to be true under all possible models of S. Our previous proofs were, of course, semantic proofs.

The theorem to be proven is

If S is an unsatisfiable set of ground clauses, (   ) can be deduced from S by resolution.

First, suppose that $k(S) = 0$. If this is the case, either every clause is a unit clause (so the number of literal appearances equals the number of clauses) or one clause contains two literals, but another clause is (   ), so that the single excess literal is balanced out. If S contains (   ), then the theorem is trivially true, since (   ) has been "deduced" by being one of the axioms. If every clause in S is a unit clause, then S consists of clauses in the form

$$S = \{(A1), (7A2), (A2), (A3), (A4)\},\qquad\qquad (20)$$

etc. That is, each clause contains exactly one atom, and every individual clause is true under any assignment which establishes its single literal as being true. Since, by hypothesis, S is unsatisfiable, every complete assignment must establish the value of S as F. This means that there must be at least one pair of clauses in S whose literals are complements of each other, so that any assignment which sets one of them T sets the other F, thus ensuring that S always has at least one unsatisfied clause under any model. [In (20) the second and third clauses of S play this role.] If we resolve these two clauses of S against each other we produce (   ), e.g.,

$$((A2) \cdot (7A2)) \rightarrow (\quad).\qquad\qquad (21)$$

The theorem is therefore true for $k(S) = 0$, and the base step is proven.

For the induction step, assume that the theorem has been proven true for $k(S) < n$, that S is an unsatisfiable set of clauses, and that $k(S) = n$. If S already contains (   ) the theorem is trivially true. Suppose this is not so. As $k(S) > 0$, there is at least one clause C containing more than one literal. Let $C = (A, L)$ be such a clause, where L is a literal, and $A = C - \{L\}$. Now let the set S' of clauses be defined by

$$S = S' \cup \{(A, L)\}\qquad\qquad (22)$$

or equivalently

$$S' = S - \{C\}.$$

We can derive two sets from S' by splitting C into its components.

$$S_1 = S' \cup \{(A)\},\qquad\qquad (23a)$$

$$S_2 = S' \cup \{(L)\}.\qquad\qquad (23b)$$

Since S_1 and S_2 have the same number of clauses as S, and S_1 has one less literal appearance and S_2 at least one less, then

$$k(S_2) \leqslant k(S_1) < k(S) = n,\qquad\qquad (24)$$

so, by hypothesis if S_1 and S_2 are unsatisfiable, then (   ) can be derived from them. We can show that they must be unsatisfiable. Let M^* be the set of models such that, for any assignment $m^* \in M^*$, the value of C is T. (Such a set always exists.) Since $S = S' \cup \{(A, L)\}$ is unsatisfiable by hypothesis, it must be unsatisfiable for any model in M^*. Therefore any $m^* \in M^*$ must falsify some clause $C^* \in S'$. In particular, all the assignments for which $A = T$ or $L = T$ are in M^*, and they must each falsify some $C^* \in \mathbf{S}'$. On the other hand, any model not in $\mathbf{M}^*$ must falsify both (A) and (L), otherwise C would not be F. This means that any assignment, whether or not in $\mathbf{M}^*$, must falsify $\mathbf{S}_1$ and $\mathbf{S}_2$, since any assignment in $\mathbf{M}^*$ falsifies $\mathbf{S}'$ and any assignment not in $\mathbf{M}^*$ falsifies both (A) and (L). Therefore, (   ) can be deduced by resolution from either $\mathbf{S}_1$ or $\mathbf{S}_2$.

Let us write $R^k(\mathbf{S})$ for the set produced by k steps of resolution beginning with set $\mathbf{S}$. What we have proven to this point is that there exist i nd j such that

$$(\quad) \in R^i(\mathbf{S}_1), \tag{25a}$$

$$(\quad) \in R^j(\mathbf{S}_2). \tag{25b}$$

Now suppose that we apply the i steps used to produce (25a) not to $\mathbf{S}_1$, but to $\mathbf{S} = \mathbf{S}' \cup \{(A, L)\}$. This will produce either (   ) or (L). [To see this, note that the clause (L) would act much like the F in our discussion of attachment of F to clauses.] If (   ) is produced, then (   ) will have been deduced from $\mathbf{S}$ by resolution. If (L) is produced, then since $\mathbf{S}' \subseteq \mathbf{S}$

$$(\{\mathbf{S}' \cup \{(L)\}\} = \mathbf{S}_2) \subseteq R^i(\mathbf{S}) \tag{26}$$

We can next apply the j resolutions of (23b) to $\mathbf{S}_2$ as a subset of $R^i(\mathbf{S})$, to produce (   ). This proves the theorem.

Example. we will illustrate resolution using the simple inequalities example. For clarity, we repeat the axioms. (Their interpretation, which is irrelevant here, was given in the preceding section.)

$$\begin{array}{ll} C1 & (A1, A2, A3) \\[4pt] C2 & (7A1, 7A2) \\[4pt] C3 & (7A1, 7A3) \\[4pt] C4 & (7A2, 7A3) \\[4pt] 7T1 & (A1) \\[4pt] 7T2 & (A3) \end{array}$$

Resolving $C3$ and $7T1$ we produce

$$R1 \quad (7A1, 7A3) \cdot (A1) \rightarrow (7A3), \tag{27}$$

and then resolving $R1$ and 7T2

$$(A3) \cdot (7A3) \rightarrow (\quad) \tag{28}$$

we establish the contradiction.

Although this example is straightforward, we have omitted saying how the choice of resolution (28) was made. Making the correct choice is in fact the most difficult step in resolution-principle theorem proving. Straightforward algorithms will yield many resolutions which are inessential to the derivation of ( ). For example, consider the following iterative algorithm.

(*i*) Order the clauses from 1 to *n*.

(*ii*) Set *i* = 1.

(*iii*) Make all possible resolutions of clause *i* with clause $i + 1, i + 2, \ldots, n$, adding derived clauses as clause $n + 1, n + 2, \ldots, n^*$.

(*iv*) Increase *i* by 1, set $n = n^*$, and go to step (*ii*).

The process is continued until the empty clause is derived. Clearly this algorithm will generate all resolutions which can be produced, including many unnecessary derivations. On the very simple example given above, the first three clauses generated are

$$(A1, A2, A3) \cdot (7A1, 7A2) \rightarrow (A2, A3, 7A2); \qquad (29)$$

$$(A1, A2, A3) \cdot (7A1, 7A2) \rightarrow (A1, A3, 7A1);$$

$$(A1, A2, A3) \cdot (7A1, 7A3) \rightarrow (A2, A3, 7A3).$$

None of these clauses could figure in a proof, since they are *tautologies*, clauses which contain a literal and its complement, and hence cannot be false under any model. In other cases the iterative algorithm will produce clauses which, although not tautologies, also do not advance the proof.

12.1.2 RESOLUTION AT THE GENERAL LEVEL

To form a resolvent one must find two clauses that contain complementary literals. In the ground case this is fairly easy to do, since complements can be recognized readily. In the more general case complementary literals may be implied by substitution. To illustrate the point, we take another example from the calculus of inequalities. Let x, y, be variables ranging over the positive integers, and for clarity, use E for the equality relation and G for "greater than." Finally, let the product of x_i and x_j be $p(x_i, x_j)$. The set containing the clauses

	Clause	Interpretation
C1	$(E(x, x))$	$x = x$
C2	$(E(p(x, 1), x))$	$x \cdot 1 = x$
C3	$(7G(x, y), 7E(x, y))$	$(x \not> y) \lor (x \neq y)$
C4	$(G(p(x, y), x))$	$(x \cdot y) > x$

is unsatisfiable, because C4 is not true for *y* equal to one. The resolution method as presented cannot be used to prove this, since in no cases do two clauses have complementary literals, and therefore there is no basis for resolution. What we can do, however, is to select two clauses as candidates for resolution, even though they cannot be resolved directly, and then search for a sequence of substitutions such that two clauses which can be resolved against each other are produced from the original clauses. Consider the potential resolution of clauses C3 and C4,

$$(7G(x, y), 7E(x, y)) \cdot (G(p(x, y), x)). \qquad (30)$$

These clauses are reasonable candidates for resolution, since the same predicate, G, appears in normal form in one clause and in complemented form in the other. This is clearly a necessary condition for resolution.

The first step is to find the appropriate substitution. In doing so we must be careful not to confuse the names of the variables in each clause, so the variables in the left clause (C3) are renamed $x1, x2, \ldots$, and in the right clause (C4) $y1$, $y2, \ldots$ Using this convention, (30) becomes

$$(7G(x1, x2), 7E(x1, x2)) \cdot (G(p(y1, y2), y1)). \qquad (31)$$

The rule of substitution states that a term may be substituted for a variable not contained in that term, providing that the substitution is made consistently. The resulting statement is a special instance, or *instantiation*, of the original clause. Substituting $p(y1, y2)$ for $x1$ in (31) produces

$$((7G(p(y1, y2), x2), 7E(p(y1, y2), x2)) \cdot (G(p(y1,y2), y1)) \qquad (32)$$

and, by the further substitution of $y1$ for $x2$,

$$(7G(p(y1, y2), y1), 7E(p(y1, y2), y1)) \cdot (G(p(y1, y2), y1)). \qquad (33)$$

Resolution of (33) is possible, with the result

$R1 \quad (7E(p(y1, y2), y1)).$

C2 and R1 can be resolved. Again renaming variables to avoid confusion,

$$(E(p(x1, 1), x1)) \cdot (7E(p(y1, y2), y1)). \qquad (34)$$

Substituting $x1$ for $y1$ and 1 for $y2$, resolve and produce

$$(E(p(x1, 1), x1)) \cdot (7E(p(x1, 1), x1)) \to (\quad), \qquad (35)$$

deriving ( ) and proving the original set of clauses unsatisfiable.

To apply such reasoning mechanically there must be an algorithm for finding the sequence of substitutions to be made in order to reduce to clauses to resolvable form. Furthermore, the algorithm should fail only if no such sequence exists. The *unification algorithm* developed by J. A. Robinson (1965) has both properties. In order to describe it, some subsidiary definitions are needed.

Let **A** be a set of atoms. A substitution, θ is a replacement throughout **A** of the form

$$\theta = (t_1/v_1, t_2/v_2 \cdots t_i/v_i \cdots t_k/v_k) \qquad (36)$$

in which t_i is a term which appears in $\mathbf{A}$ and v_i is a variable in $\mathbf{A}$. When θ is applied each t_i replaces the corresponding v_i throughout $\mathbf{A}$. The resulting set of atoms is written $\mathbf{A}\theta$. We shall also write $C\theta$ and $S\theta$ for the clause or statement, respectively, resulting from the application of the replacement θ to all atoms in a clause, C, or a statement $\mathbf{S}$. The null substitution will be written e.

For any set $\mathbf{A}$ of atoms, the *disagreement set of* $\mathbf{A}$ is the set of terms starting at the first symbol position within an atom at which there is at least one symbol that is found in one, but not all, the atoms of $\mathbf{A}$. For example, if

$$\mathbf{A} = \{P(x, f(y, z)), P(x, a), P(x, g(h(k(x))))\} \tag{37}$$

then the disagreement set of $\mathbf{A}$, $D(\mathbf{A})$, is

$$D(\mathbf{A}) = \{f(y, z), a, g(h(k(x)))\} \tag{38}$$

The disagreement set of $\mathbf{A}$ is empty if and only if $\mathbf{A}$ is a singleton.

A *lexical ordering* is any ordering of terms in a disagreement set such that all variable symbols in the set (if any) appear before any nonvariable symbol in the set. and all nonvariable terms are ordered in some consistent matter.

The *unification algorithm* for a set $\mathbf{A} = \{A1, A2, A3, \ldots, An\}$ of atoms consists of the following steps.

1. Set $k = 0$, and substitution $\pi_k = $ e.
2. Set $\mathbf{A} = \mathbf{A}\pi_k$. If $\mathbf{A}$ is a singleton terminate with a success, in which case $\theta = \pi_0 \pi_1 \pi_2 \cdots \pi_k$. (Note that from the definition of a substitution, the concatenation of a substitution is a substitution.) If $\mathbf{A}$ is not a singleton, continue.
3. Establish the disagreement set of $\mathbf{A}$ and its lexical ordering.
4. Let V_r, U_r be the first and second elements of the lexical ordering of $D(\mathbf{A})$. If V_r is not a variable or if it is a variable contained in U_r terminate with a failure. Otherwise set $k = k + 1$, $\pi_k = \{U_r/V_r\}$ and go to 2.

The product of the unification algorithm will be either a failure message, if no sequence of substitutions exists that can transform all the atoms of $\mathbf{A}$ into a single atom, or the desired substitution θ, if $\mathbf{A}\theta$ is a singleton. In this case we shall say that θ *unifies* A. Furthermore, θ is a *most general unifier* of $\mathbf{A}$ in the following sense. Suppose there is some other substitution, θ^* which also unifies $\mathbf{A}$, but which is not produced by the unification algorithm. The unifier θ^* will always be of the form

$$\theta^* = \theta\pi, \tag{39}$$

where π is some substitution of terms for variables in $\mathbf{A}\theta$. Then, θ is the substitution that unifies $\mathbf{A}$ with the fewest substitutions of constants and function terms for variables. But θ is not necessarily unique.

The algorithm is illustrated by the following example.

$$\mathbf{A} = \{Q(x, y), Q(a, c)\}; \tag{40}$$

$$D(\mathbf{A}) = \{x, a\};$$

$$\pi_1 = \{a/x\};$$

$$\mathbf{A}\pi_1 = \{Q(a, y), Q(a, c)\};$$

$$D(\mathbf{A}\pi_1) = \{y, c\};$$

$$\pi_2 = \{c/y\};$$

$$\mathbf{A}\pi_1\pi_2 = \mathbf{A}\theta = \{Q(a, c)\}; \qquad \text{singleton}$$

$$\theta = \pi_1\pi_2 = \{a/x, c/y\}; \qquad \text{desired unification.}$$

To use unification with resolution, imagine that two clauses, C1 and C2, have been proposed as candidates for resolution because they contain opposite signed literals with the same predicate. The set $\mathbf{A}$ is defined to be the set of atoms contained in these literals. The unification algorithm is then applied and, if it succeeds, the substitution is applied throughout both clauses, producing $C1\theta$ and $C2\theta$. To illustrate, suppose we wish to resolve

$$(P(x1, b), Q(x1, a)) \cdot (P(y1, c), 7Q(b, y2)). \tag{41}$$

The appropriate renamings have already been accomplished. The literals containing Q are the obvious candidates for resolution, so

$$\mathbf{A} = \{Q(x1, a), Q(b, y2)\}. \tag{42}$$

Applying the algorithm produces the substitution

$$\theta = \{b/x1, a/y2\} \tag{43}$$

and the resolvent of (41) is

$$(P(b, b), P(y1, c)). \tag{44}$$

Resolution with unification is a complete method of inference (Robinson, 1965). A precise statement of the completeness property is

> Let $\mathbf{S}$ be a set of general clauses. The null clause ( ) can be derived from $\mathbf{S}$ by resolution and unification if and only if $\mathbf{S}$ is truth functionally unsatisfiable.

This important result guarantees that if $\mathbf{S}$ is not satisfiable, then ( ) can be derived from $\mathbf{S}$ in a finite number of steps. On the other hand, failure to derive ( ) after a finite number of inferences does not prove that $\mathbf{S}$ is satisfiable, since it might be that ( ) could be derived if sufficiently more inferences were made. The only way $\mathbf{S}$ can be proven satisfiable is to reach a point at which there are no more new resolutions to be made, provided that our method of choosing resolutions is such that the completeness property has been maintained. There are cases in which this will never happen.

12.2 Simple Refinement Strategies

12.2.0 REFINEMENT

The unrestricted application of the resolution principle will generate far too many clauses for practical computation. To obtain a graphic picture of the problem which arises, consider a deduction by resolution of (   ), or for that matter, for any other clause, depicted as a tree, such as is shown in Figure 12-4. Unlike the trees we discussed in problem solving, however, this tree grows downward from the leaves, which represent original clauses, to the root. Every nonleaf node (including the root), represents a clause produced by resolution of the two clauses immediately above it.

In Figure 12-4, only one deduction is shown. We could have other deductions spreading out in other directions from the original clauses, as is shown in Figure 12-5. Some of the deductions will terminate with (   ), and hence be valid proofs of unsatisfiability. Others will not lead to a production of (   ), and, in fact, may never terminate. If resolution is to be made practical we need a guide to tell us which resolutions to make and which deductions to pursue.

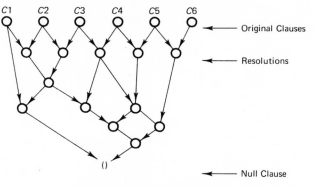

Fig. 12-4. "Tree" of deductions.

An algorithm that selectively chooses resolutions is known as a *refinement strategy*. A rule for changing the order in which resolutions are attempted but not restricting their number will be called an *ordering strategy*. Refinement strategies fall into three general classes: syntactic, semantic, and ancestory strategies. A syntactic strategy selects clauses for resolution by criteria based on structural properties of the clauses themselves, such as the number of literals they contain, without regard to the interpretation of the atoms in the clause as true or false under a particular model. Semantic strategies do the opposite, they select clauses which are known to be true only under certain models. Ancestory strategies select clauses

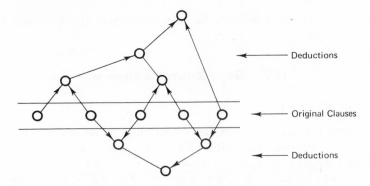

Fig. 12-5.   Examples of spread of deductions from set of original clauses.

for further resolution based upon the history of derivation of the clauses so selected. For example, in the *input strategy* every resolution must involve at least one clause from the original set **S** of clauses.

Refinement strategies are guides for writing theorem-proving programs that compute only a restricted set of the set of all possible resolutions. To show that the resulting program is a valid theorem proving system it is necessary to show that the completeness theorem for resolution holds for the limited set of resolutions permitted by the refinement.[3] The difficulty of proving completeness for different strategies varies greatly. In general we shall not offer proofs, but shall give adequate reference for those interested in proof techniques.

Some refinement strategies are quite sophisticated, and will be treated in separate sections. Others, to be described briefly in the remainder of this section, are simple and easy to implement. Virtually all of the useful ordering strategies are also simple, and will be described here.

12.2.1   UNIT PREFERENCE STRATEGY

If clauses C1 and C2, containing m and n literals, respectively, are resolved against each other, then the resolvent will contain at most $(m - 1) + (n - 1)$ literals. If one of the clauses, say C1, contains only one literal, then that literal must be the literal resolved upon and the resolvent will contain $(n - 1)$ literals. Since the

---

[3] It can be argued that completeness is not really an interesting property of a refinement strategy. Allen Newell (personal communication) has pointed out that, regardless of the strategy used, a logically correct derivation of (   ) is always sufficient to prove that **S** is unsatisfiable. Failure to derive **S**, as we have noted, proves nothing. Of what use, then, is it to know that if a program were run for some unspecified larger amount of time then, if **S** is unsatisfiable (which is unknown), (   ) would be derived? Although this argument has a good deal of pragmatic truth, we would reject it on two grounds. First, as we have also pointed out, if a strategy is complete and, at some point, there are no new resolutions to be made, then **S** must be satisfiable. The more restrictive the strategy, the more likely this is to happen. Second, we feel that completeness is an important property to study if only to shed more light on the logical foundations of mechanical theorem proving.

goal of the program is to resolve a clause with no literals, this is a step in the right direction. The unit preference strategy requires that at each step in an inference all resolutions involving clauses with only one literal (*unit clauses* or *singletons*) be computed prior to computing any other resolutions. More generally, resolutions involving short clauses are generally attempted before resolutions involving long clauses.

Unit preference is an example of a syntactic strategy, since its application depends only upon the structural properties of the clauses involved. Unit preference is an ordering rather than a refinement, since it changes the order in which resolutions will be done, but does not eliminate any possible resolution from consideration.

12.2.2 TAUTOLOGY AND UNIQUE LITERAL ELIMINATION

These are refinement strategies, the goal of which is the removal of irrelevant clauses from **S** before resolution is begun. Let $S^* \subseteq S$ be an unsatisfiable set of clauses such that every proper subset of S^* is satisfiable, i.e., in order to obtain a contradiction from S^*, it is necessary to use every clause of S^* at least once in the proof. In general, it is more efficient to work with S^* instead of **S**. In fact, it can be proven that there exists at least one deduction of (   ) beginning with any clause $C^* \in S^*$ (Anderson & Bledsoe, 1970). Therefore it would be desirable to locate and remove the clauses, if any, in $S - S^*$ before beginning resolution. Tautology and unique literal elimination, when applicable, identify some of these clauses. Both strategies are easy to apply.

A clause C is a *tautology* if it contains two complementary literals, e.g., the literals A and $7A$, where A is any atomic statement. Since the truth value of the clause is determined by the disjunction of the truth values of the literals in it, a tautology obviously cannot be false under any model, for $(A \lor 7A)$ is true regardless of the truth value of A. Therefore the unsatisfiability of a set **S** of clauses containing the tautology C must be determined by the unsatisfiability of the set of clauses $S - \{C\}$.

A clause C can be dropped from **S**, even though it is not a tautology, if it is the only clause containing a *unique literal*, L, whose predicate, P, does not appear negated in any literal of another clause $C^* \in S$. The reason is that no resolution involving C or any clause descended from C can ever result in (   ). To see this, suppose **S** is the set

$$C1: \quad (P(x), 7P(b), Q(y));$$

$$C2: \quad (7P(c), P(y));$$

$$C3: \quad (7P(b), 7P(x)).$$

Any sequence of resolutions containing $C1$ must produce a clause which contains the literal $Q(y)$ or some instantiation of it. As no clause in **S** contains an instance of clause $7Q(x)$, there is no way of removing $Q(y)$ or any of its instantiations.

Therefore, one might as well never begin such a sequence. The general principle is that if C contains a unique literal, then if **S** is unsatisfiable, ( ) can be deduced from **S** − $\{C\}$.

12.2.3 FACTORING

Clauses may be reduced in length by application of an instantiation which reduces several literals within a clause to the same literal. This operation is called *factoring*. To illustrate, the clause

$$C = \big(A(x, f(k)) \quad A(b, y), A(a, f(x)), A(x, z)\big) \tag{45}$$

can be factored by the substitution

$$\theta = \big(b/x, f(k)/y, f(b)/z\,\big) \tag{46}$$

to produce

$$C\theta = \big(A(b, f(k)), A(a, f(b)), A(b, f(b))\big). \tag{47}$$

$C\theta$ is a *factor* of C. Factors of a clause are not necessarily unique. If (46) is replaced by the substitution

$$\pi = (a/x, f(k)/y, f(a)/z) \tag{48}$$

we obtain the factor

$$C\pi = \big(A(a, f(k)), A(b, f(k)), A(a, f(a))\big). \tag{49}$$

Since a clause implies its factors, **S** may be augmented by the factors of C. Although this increases the number of clauses of **S**, the added clauses will be shorter than the clauses that produced them, and may lead to shorter deductions of ( ).

12.2.4 SUBSUMPTION

For any pair of clauses C, $D \in S$, C is said to *subsume* D if there is an instantiation of C, $C\pi$, such that $C\pi \subseteq D$. For instance, if

$$C = \big(A(x)\big), \tag{50}$$

$$D = \big(A(b), P(x)\big),$$

then the substitution

$$\pi = (b/x) \tag{51}$$

produces

$$C\pi = (A(b)).\tag{52}$$

The validity of subsumption may be illustrated by an argument using the propositional calculus, in which the truth value of a set of clauses is defined as the conjunction of the truth value of the clauses it contains. Let $C\pi$ be (L) and D be (L, X), where X is a sequence of zero or more literals, $L_1, L_2, \ldots$. Since the truth value of D is the disjunction of its literals,

$$D = (L \vee X).\tag{53}$$

It is elementary that

$$L \supset (L \vee X)\tag{54}$$

regardless of the truth value of X, so $C\pi \supset D$. Define $\mathbf{S^*} = \mathbf{S} - \{D\}$. Under the propositional calculus interpretation of a set,

$$\mathbf{S^*} \cdot C\pi \supset \mathbf{S}.\tag{55}$$

If $\mathbf{S}$ is false under all assignments, then $\mathbf{S} \supset (\quad)$. This means that $\mathbf{S^*} \cdot C\pi \supset (\quad)$, i.e., if $\mathbf{S}$ is truth functionally unsatisfiable, then the set $S^* \cup \{C\pi\}$ is similarly unsatisfiable. It should be simpler to derive $(\quad)$ from $\mathbf{S^*} \cup \{C\pi\}$ than from $\mathbf{S}$ because both sets contain the same number of clauses, but $C\pi$ contains fewer literals than D.

12.2.5 HYPERRESOLUTION

Resolutions can be made involving several clauses at once. This is called *hyperresolution*. Suppose there exists a finite set of clauses, $\{C1, C2, \ldots, Cn,\}$ and a single clause B which satisfy the following conditions;

(*i*) B contains the n literals $L_1 \cdots L_n$.

(*ii*) For every i, $1 \leqslant i \leqslant n$ clause C_i contains the literal $7L_i$ but does not contain the complement of any other literal which occurs in B, nor the complement of any literal which occurs in any clause Cj, $j \neq i$. The set of clauses $\mathbf{S}_a = \{Ci\} \cup \{B\}$ is called a *clash*. The clause

$$R_a = (C1 - \{7L_1\}, C2 - \{7L_2\}, \ldots Cn - \{7L_n\}, B - \{L_i\})\tag{56}$$

is called the hyperresolvent of $\mathbf{S}_a$, and may be deduced from $\mathbf{S}_a$.

In most cases we will obtain a clash only after appropriate substitutions. That is, we will be given a set $\mathbf{S}_a$ of clauses which do *not* meet the definition of a clash, but there exists a substitution π such that $\mathbf{S}_a\pi$ is a clash. In this case $\mathbf{S}_a$ is called a *latent clash*. Since standard resolution involving only two clauses at a time is a special case of hyperresolution, it follows that if $(\quad)$ can be deduced from S by resolution, it can also be deduced from $\mathbf{S}$, and perhaps more quickly, by hyperresolution.

As an example of hyperresolution, consider the set $\mathbf{S}_a$ defined by

$$\mathbf{S}_a = \begin{cases} C1 = (7A(x), P(a)) & (57) \\ C2 = (P(y)) \\ C3 = (7P(k), Q(a,\ b)) \\ B \ = (A(a), 7P(y), 7Q(x,\ y), A(c)). \end{cases}$$

The substitution $\pi = (a/x,\ b/y)$ produces

$$\mathbf{S}_a \pi = \begin{cases} C1\pi = (7A(a), P(a)) & (57a) \\ C2\pi = (P(b)) \\ C3\pi = (7P(k), Q(a,\ b)) \\ B\pi \ = (A(a), 7P(b), 7Q(a,\ b), A(c)). \end{cases}$$

$\mathbf{S}_a \pi$ is a clash with resolvent

$$R_a = (P(a), 7P(k), A(c)), \qquad (58)$$

and thus $\mathbf{S}_a$ is a latent clash.

Hyperresolution is an example of a semantic strategy. The reason is that the clash at $\mathbf{S}_a$ can only be satisfied by a model that contains some of the literals, and at least one from each clause of the clash, which are contained in the clash resolvent. Thus the clash resolvent points the way toward elimination of all models.

12.3   Ancestory Strategies

12.3.0   Introductory

We now consider some more sophisticated strategies in which the permissible resolutions are determined by requirements placed upon the derivations of the clauses to be resolved. Ancestory strategies are powerful strategies, for they permit savings in both the number of resolutions to be considered and the amount of computer storage required for recording clauses that have been inferred. If a clause is known to have a derivation satisfying none of the requirements for resolution imposed by the strategy, then that clause need not be saved, since it will never be used in subsequent resolutions. In fact, this situation occurs fairly often. The problems that ancestory strategies pose, however, are related to their effect. In order to determine whether a clause can be used in a resolution, it is necessary to keep a record of the clause's derivation and this, of course, requires both computer memory and computer time. Under some strategies a clause that is eligible for resolution at round t of the inference process may not be eligible at round $t + 1$.

(The converse never occurs.) This means that provision must be made for a "garbage collection" routine to erase clauses from storage once they are no longer needed. Whether or not this results in a net savings depends upon the amount of memory saved and the complexity of the computation involved in garbage collection.

12.3.1 SET OF SUPPORT

In most theorem-proving problems S can be divided into two subsets, the *axioms* of the system, $\{Ci\}$, and the *negation* of the hypothesis to be proven, $7T = \{Ti\}$. It is usually reasonable to assume that the axioms are internally consistent, i.e., that the set $\{Ci\}$ is satisfiable. Wos, Robinson, and Carson (1965) have proven that if this is the case, and if S itself is unsatisfiable, then ( ) can be deduced by a sequence of resolutions in which each step involves a resolution in which at least one of the clauses is in the *set of support*, where the set of support is defined as

(*i*) All clauses in $\{Tj\}$ are in the set of support.

(*ii*) A resolvent clause is in the set of support if at least one of its parents is in the set of support.

The practical effect of the set of support strategy is that we need never consider any resolution involving only clauses in $\{Ci\}$. This is useful, since $\{Ci\}$ is often large relative to $\{Tj\}$.

The concept of a minimally unsatisfiable set, is closely related to set of support. Let S be an unsatisfiable set of clauses, and let $S^* \subseteq S$ be a smallest subset of S such that S^* is unsatisfiable, but every proper subset $S^+ \subset S^*$ is satisfiable. S^* is a minimally satisfiable subset of S. In general, S^* will not be unique, as the following example shows. Let E, G, and L be atomic statements with no variables, and define S as

$$S = \{(E, G, L), (7E, 7G), (7E, 7L), (7G, 7L), \tag{59}$$

$$\{(E), (G), (L)\}.$$

Possible minimally unsatisfiable sets are

$$S_1{}^* = \{(7E, 7G), (E), (G)\}; \tag{60}$$

$$S_2{}^* = \{(7E, 7L), (E), (L)\};$$

$$S_3{}^* = \{(7G, 7L), (G), (L)\};$$

Note that ( ) can easily be derived from any of the $S_i{}^*$. Also, given $S_i{}^*$, any clause $C \in S_i{}^*$ can be defined to be the set of support, since all proper subsets of a minimally unsatisfiable set are satisfiable.

12.3.2 LINEAR DEDUCTIONS

The linear deduction strategy is a quite restrictive ancestory method which has the additional advantage of providing proofs that are easy to follow. Let C^0 be any clause in a minimally satisfiable set S^*, and let C^i, $i > 0$, be the ith clause derived in a sequence of resolutions beginning with C^0 and some other clause in S^*. If the ith clause ($i > 0$) of the deduction always has as one of its parents (called the *left parent*) the $i - 1$st clause in the deduction, then the deduction is a linear deduction. In a linear strategy only resolutions permissible in a linear deduction are considered. The technique is illustrated by the deduction of (   ) from the set of ground clauses.

$$S = \{(Q), (P, R), (7P, S), (7R, S), (7P, 7Q, 7S), (7Q, 7R, 7S)\} \qquad (61)$$

One linear deduction of (   ) from S is

$$(7P, 7Q, 7S) \cdot (Q) = (7P, 7S); \qquad (62)$$

$$(7P, 7S) \cdot (P, R) = (R, 7S);$$

$$(R, 7S) \cdot (7P, S) = (7P, R);$$

$$(7P, R) \cdot (P, R) = (R);$$

$$(R) \cdot (7R, S) = (S);$$

$$(S) \cdot (7Q, 7R, 7S) = (7Q, 7R);$$

$$(7Q, 7R) \cdot (Q) = (7R);$$

$$(7R) \cdot (R) = (\quad).$$

The deduction of (62) is shown graphically in Figure 12-6. Each clause C^i has clause C^{i-1} as its left parent and clause B^{i-1} as its right parent. Each B^i is either an input clause or $B^i = C^j$, for some $j < i$.

The linear deduction refinement strategy is complete (Anderson & Bledsoe, 1970),[4] and so can be recommended as a useful guide in writing theorem-proving programs. It is of some interest to consider how a program using this refinement develops a deduction of (   ). Suppose S is a minimally unsatisfiable set. There will be at least one linear deduction of (   ) beginning with each of the clauses in S, but there is no way of knowing a priori, which of these deduce (   ) in the fewest inferences. Also, not all linear deductions from a given clause will terminate with (   ), and those that do not cannot be identified beforehand. As a result the theorem proving program is faced with a tree-searching problem, similar to those discussed in Chapter X. This is shown graphically in Figure 12-7, which depicts the relationship between the various clauses derived by the program. The root of the tree represents the program's start. The nodes immediately below the root represent the different clauses that can act as C^0, i.e., all clauses in the minimally unsatisfiable set. Throughout the rest of the tree the nodes immediately below node n represent the clauses that can be derived from the clause represented by node n

---

[4] The Anderson and Bledsoe article is recommended for those interested in how strategies are proven to be complete, for it introduced a generally accepted and very useful technique for proving completeness.

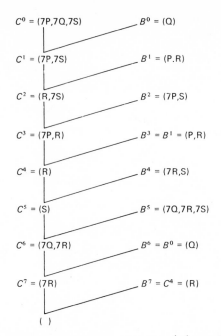

Fig. 12-6. Illustration of a linear deduction of ( ). C^{i-1} and B^{i-1} are, respectively, left and right parents of C^i. Every B^i is either an input clause or a C^j, $j \geqslant i$.

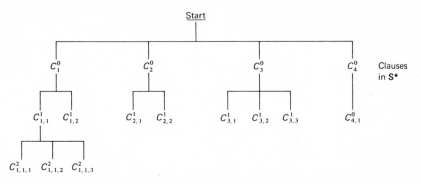

Fig. 12-7. Illustration of branching structure of deduced clauses when linear strategy is used.

by a resolution in which the left parent is the clause represented by node n, and the right parent is either an input clause or some clause whose node lies between node n and the root. At any one time the program need only consider resolutions between clauses associated with the (current) leaf nodes of the tree, the input clauses, and the clauses lying between each leaf and the root. (In fact, as we shall explain below, even more restrictive conditions may be placed on the resolutions to be considered.) On the other hand, the program must do the bookkeeping required to determine which resolutions should be attempted.

12.3.3   LEMMA PROOFS

These are deductions which do not satisfy the conditions of a linear proof. Roughly, a lemma structure proof brings together two or more separate lines of proof. Derivation (63) is a lemma structure derivation of (   ) from (61).

$$(7P, 7Q, 7S) \cdot (P, R) = (7Q, R, 7S); \tag{63}$$

$$(7Q, R, 7S) \cdot (7Q, 7R, 7S) = (7Q, 7S);$$

Lemma 1 $\qquad\qquad (7Q, 7S) \cdot (Q) = (7S);$

$$(7P, S) \cdot (P, R) = (R, S);$$

$$(R, S) \cdot (7R, S) = (S);$$

$$(S) \cdot (7S) = (\quad)$$

A diagram of (63) is shown in Figure 12-8. Note that deductions branch out from several starting points in **S**, and then merge. This is similar to the abstract picture of resolution shown in Figure 12-5. Usually the rules for developing lemma structures are not as clear as the rules for developing linear structures. The notion of a lemma

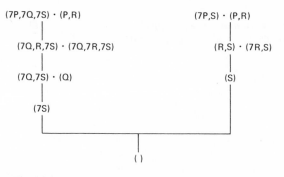

Fig. 12-8.   Structure of lemma deduction [Eq. (63)].

proof has been introduced here primarily as a contrast to the notion of a linear proof. On the other hand, the deduction of (63) is shorter than the linear deduction of (62) and might be considered to be "more elegant" on that ground. While it may often be the case that linear deductions are longer than lemma structure deductions, linear deductions are easier to discover by a mechanical procedure. For example, (63) was developed by a minor amount of ill-defined guesswork, whereas (62) can be developed by an easily explained mechanical procedure.

12.3.4   SUBSUMPTION AND MERGE CONDITIONS

Two further refinements, called the *subsumption* and *merge* conditions, may be applied jointly with linearity to restrict further both the number of resolutions to be considered during the deduction and the number of clauses that must be retained in memory. The combination of all three strategies is called the *merge, subsumption, linear (m.s.l.)* refinement strategy. (Subsumption may also be defined without respect to linearity.)

The subsumption condition restricts the number of resolutions that will be attempted at each round of inference. Let C^i be the clause just deduced, and let $\mathbf{R}$ be the set of previously resolved clauses that have been retained for use as possible right parents in a linear deduction. Thus $\mathbf{R} \subseteq \{C^j\}$ for $j < i$. The left parent of C^{i+1} will, of course, be C^i. The right parent, B^i must be chosen from the set $\mathbf{S} \cup \mathbf{R}$. The subsumption condition states that if $\mathbf{S}$ is unsatisfiable there exists a linear deduction of ( ) in which C^{i+1} subsumes C^i in all cases in which B^i is chosen from $\mathbf{R}$ rather than $\mathbf{S}$. Therefore the search for candidate right parent clauses can be confined to $\mathbf{S}$ and some of the clauses of $\mathbf{R}$. Specifically, if the subsumption condition is to be satisfied, B^i must contain only literals that are unifiable with literals in C^i, with the exception of exactly one literal, which will be the literal resolved upon, and must be unifiable with a complementary literal in C^i. Those clauses in $\mathbf{R}$ which do not fulfill this condition need not be considered as candidates for resolution.

The subsumption condition, then, restricts attention to a subset of $\mathbf{R}$, given C^i. The *merge condition* provides a way of limiting the number of derived clauses to be placed in $\mathbf{R}$ in the first place. A clause C^i is a *merge* of clauses C^{i-1} and B^{i-1} if there is a literal L, other than the literal resolved upon, which occurs in C^i and is an instantiation of two literals, L_1 and L_2, which appear in C^{i-1} and B^{i-1}, respectively. The literal L is called a *merge literal*. A *merge clause* is either the clause C^i or a factor of C^i. An example of a merge resolvent is

$$C^{i-1} = \big(Q(k, b), 7Q(a, c), Q(k, c)\big); \qquad (64)$$

$$B^{i-1} = \big(Q(k, b), Q(a, c), Q(b, c)\big);$$

$$C^i \quad = \big(Q(k, b), Q(k, c), Q(b, c)\big);$$

in which $Q(k, b)$ is a merge literal. Although the notation that has been used to present merging refers to linear deduction, the idea of merging may equally well be applied to lemma structure deductions.

Anderson and Bledsoe (1970) have shown that merging, subsumption, and linearity can be combined, by proving the following theorem.

> Let $\mathbf{S}$ be a minimally unsatisfiable set of clauses. There exists a linear deduction of ( ) from any clause $C = C^0 \in \mathbf{S}$ in which, at every step the right parent, B^i is either an input clause ($B^i \in \mathbf{S}$) or a deduced merge clause. Furthermore, when the right parent is a deduced clause, then the literal of resolution is a merge literal and the resolvent, C^{i+1}, subsumes the left parent, C^i.

This theorem states that a program may choose any clause $C \in \mathbf{S}$ as the first clause in a linear deduction, providing that $\mathbf{S}$ is minimally unsatisfiable. The qualification poses no problem, since if we know the set of support, $\mathbf{T}$, then we can usually be safe in assuming that **T** is included in any minimally unsatisfiable subset. Therefore deduction begins with a clause in **T**. Whenever a clause C^i is deduced, it need be stored only if it is a merge clause. Finally, in seeking previously deduced clauses to resolve with some C^i we can restrict our search to those clauses C^j $(j < i)$ which (a) contain a merge literal unifiable with the atom of a complementary literal in C^i and (b) contain only other literals that are unifiable with literals in C^i, thus ensuring that subsumption will be satisfied.

12.3.5   AN EXAMPLE FROM GROUP THEORY

The m.s.l. refinement strategy is worth illustrating, using the following theorem from group theory:

> *In any associative system which has left and right solutions s and t, for all equations of the form s · x = y and x · t = y there is a right identity element.*[5]

To prove the theorem true m.s.l. and set of support will be used. As an ordering strategy, clauses with few predicates will be given preference. This implies the unit preference strategy. These strategies will dictate choice of the clause C^0 with which the deduction begins, and will subsequently restrict the resolutions to be considered at each stage. Whereas this is clearly desirable, there are other, shorter, proofs of the theorem which may seem more elegant (cf. Slagle, 1972, p. 63).

The first step is to formalize the problem. Let $P(x, y, z)$ be a predicate with the interpretation "$x · y = z$." The set **S** is defined by

$$\mathbf{S} = \begin{cases} C1 = \big(P(g(x, y), x, y)\big) & g(x, y) \text{ is the left solution for} \quad (65) \\ & \text{the pair } (x, y). \text{ If } s · x = y, \text{ then} \\ & s = g(x, y). \\[6pt] C2 = \big(P(x, h(x, y), y)\big) & h(x, y) \text{ is the right solution.} \\[6pt] C3 = \big(7P(x, y, u), 7P(y, z, v), & \text{This is part of the condition of} \\ \quad 7P(x, v, w), P(u, z, w)\big) & \text{associativity. In a more transparent} \\ & \text{notation, } \big((x · y = u) \wedge (y · z = v) \\ & (x · v = w)\big) \supset (u · z = w). \\[6pt] C4 = \big((7P(x, y, x))\big) & \text{There is no } y \in \mathbf{N} \text{ such that} \\ & x · y = x. \text{ Denial of the hypothesis.} \end{cases}$$

[5] Let us provide a brief explanation for those not familiar with group theory. Consider the set **N** of elements and an operation, "·", such that for any $x, y \in \mathbf{N}$, $z = x · y$ is also in **N**. We further require that there exist $s, t \in \mathbf{N}$ such that $s · x = y$ (left solution) and $x · t = y$ (right solution). The association condition states that for all $x, y, z \in \mathbf{N}$ $x · (y · z) = (x · y) · z$. The theorem asserts that there is some element $e \in \mathbf{N}$ such that $x · e = x$ for every $x \in \mathbf{N}$. This element is the right identity element. To take a concrete example, suppose **N** is the set of real numbers and the operation "·" is multiplication. Clearly there exist left and right solutions, since for every pair of real numbers x, y, the numbers (y/x) and (x/y) are real numbers. For multiplication the right (and left) identity element is 1, since $x · 1 = x$. If the operation "·" were interpreted as addition, the identity element would be 0.

In developing this illustration it will be necessary to use x and y instantiations of clauses, to avoid confusing variable names. We shall adopt the convention that the variables x, y, and z in any clause C serving as *left* parent will be renamed x_1, x_2, x_3, etc. Similarly the variables in any *right* parent B will be renamed $y_1, y_2, \ldots$.

Since C4 is the negation of the hypothesis, {C4} is the set of support. Let $C^0 = $ C4, to begin the m.s.l. deduction. Since the deduction will be linear, the set of support strategy is thus assured. After renaming,

$$C^0 = (7P(x_2, x_1, x_2)). \tag{66}$$

Unification is first attempted with unit clauses C1 and C2, failing each time. Clause C3 is then selected as B^0, with the instantiation

$$B^0 = \big(7P(y_4, y_5, y_1), 7P(y_5, y_6, y_2), 7P(y_4, y_2, y_3), P(y_1, y_6, y_3)\big) \tag{67}$$

The only candidate for literal of resolution in B^0 is the rightmost literal. Applying the substitution

$$\pi = (y_1/x_2, y_6/x_1, y_3/y_1) \tag{68}$$

and resolving,

$$C^1 = \big(7P(y_4, y_5, y_3), 7P(y_5, y_6, y_2), 7P(y_4, y_2, y_3)\big). \tag{69}$$

Since C^1 is a resolvent of C^0 and an input clause, it does not have to meet the subsumption or merge conditions. Clause C^1 will be a left parent, so its x instantiation is,

$$C^1 = \big(7P(x_3, x_4, x_2), 7P(x_4, x_5, x_1), 7P(x_3, x_1, x_2)\big). \tag{70}$$

Unit preference is again applied to order the possible resolutions with C^1. The y instantiation of C1 is

$$C1 = \big(P(g(y_1, y_2), y_1, y_2)\big), \tag{71}$$

defining B^1. Unifying C^1 and B^1 by

$$\pi = (x_4/y_1, x_2/y_2, g(x_4, x_2)/x_3) \tag{72}$$

the resolvent

$$C^2 = \big(7P(x_4, x_5, x_1), 7P(g(x_4, x_2), x_1, x_2)\big) \tag{73}$$

is produced. Renumbering its variables, we have

$$C^2 = \big(7P(x_3, x_4, x_1), 7P(g(x_3, x_2), x_1, x_2)\big) \tag{74}$$

At this point (75) is not the only possible definition of C^2, since we could produce a different C^2 by resolving C^1 with $B^1 = C^2$, thus starting a second linear deduction from $C^0 = $ C4. Alternatively, the possibility of a branch to a different deduction at C^1 can be recorded, and the deduction from (75) continued. This alternative has been chosen because of the rule that resolutions involving clauses with fewer literals are to be dealt with before developing a deduction from longer clauses.[6] Clause C^2 may be resolved with C^1, using the second literal of C^2, as the literal of resolution. The result is

$$C_a^3 = \left(7P(x_3, x_4, x_1), 7P(g(x_3, x_2), x_1, x_2)\right) \cdot \left(P(g(y_1, y_2), y_1, y_2)\right) \quad (75)$$

$$= \left(7P(x_3, x_4, x_3)\right)$$

Using the substitution

$$\pi = (x_3/y_1, x_2/y_2, x_3/x_1) \qquad\qquad (76)$$

Note that alternatively the first literal of C^2 could have been resolved upon, using $B^2 = C2$. This will not be pursued here, but is noted as an alternative route in Figure 12-9. Continuing from (78), we find that C_a^3 can be resolved with $B^3 = C2$.

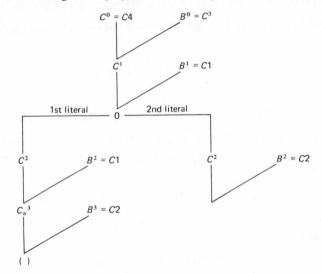

Fig. 12-9.   Tree graph of m.s.l. deduction of (   ) from problem (65).

After renumbering the variables of C_a^3, applying the unifying substitution

$$\pi = (x_1/y_1, h(x_1, y_2)/x_2, x_3/y_2) \qquad\qquad (77)$$

produces the resolvent

$$(C_a^3 \pi) \cdot (B^3 \pi) = \left(7P(x_1, h(x_1, x_3), x_3)\right) \cdot \left(P(x_1, h(x_1, x3), x_3)\right) = (\quad), \quad (78)$$

proving the theorem. The final step in the deduction is shown at the lower left hand branch of Figure 12-9.

---

[6] The rule that deductions are to be continued first from shorter clauses acts as a heuristic search function, in the sense introduced in Chapter X. In fact, an m.s.l. deduction using the "shortest clause available" rule can be viewed as a graph searching problem. What are the circumstances under which resolutions at C1 might be resumed?

12.3.6 INPUT PROOFS

To complete discussion of ancestory strategies, we will examine further the *input proof* strategy mentioned earlier. An input proof is a proof in which at least one of the parent clauses in each resolution is an input clause. The input proof strategy is not complete, but has other interesting theoretical properties. It has been proven that an input proof exists if and only if a unit proof exists (Chang, 1970). This fact permits us to build a bridge between the state-space approach to problem solving developed in Chapter XI and the formal theorem-proving approach. We shall show that an input proof always exists for a problem which can be conceptualized as a state-space problem. A more cogent way of stating this is that any problem which can be solved by a program similar to GPS or FDS can be formulated as a set **S** of clauses from which ( ) can be deduced using either the unit or input strategies.

A GPS or FDS operator can be written as

$$s_i \to s_j, \tag{79}$$

where s_i and s_j are well-formed expressions possibly containing function and variable symbols. Let $S(x)$ be a predicate with the intuitive meaning "x is a state (string) derivable from the statement of the problem." A state-space problem can be interpreted as, "Given the predicate $S(s_0)$ and the rewriting rules (axioms) prove that $S(s_g)$ is derivable." If we are willing to retain the restriction that at every step of a problem's solution, rewriting rules are to be applied only to the string representing an entire state, the rewriting rule $s_i \to s_j$ can be interpreted as "If s_i is a derivable string, then s_j is a derivable string," i.e.,

$$S(s_i) \supset S(s_j). \tag{80}$$

The disjunctive form of (81) is

$$(7S(s_i), S(s_j)). \tag{81}$$

The problem statement, $s_0 \to s_g$, must be treated differently. Following the resolution principle technique, this is to be proven by demonstrating that ( ) can be derived from the set **S** of clauses consisting of the clauses of the form of (80), derived from the rewriting rules, and the negation of the clauses derived from $s_0 \to s_g$. The negation is $(S(s_0) \land 7S(s_g))$, so the set of support is $\{(S(s_0)), (7S(s_g))\}$.

To illustrate, consider the following very simple school algebra problem. Given the rewriting rules

$$\text{R1:} \quad x + y \to y + x \tag{82}$$

$$\text{R2:} \quad x + (y + z) \to (x + y) + z \tag{83}$$

prove that the second rule is symmetric; i.e., that

$$\text{R3:} \quad (x + y) + z \to x + (y + z) \tag{84}$$

is true. If we look at this as a string rewriting problem, a solution is

Step	Justification	
$(x + y) + z$	starting state	(85)
$z + (x + y)$	apply R1	
$(z + x) + y$	apply R2	
$y + (z + x)$	apply R1	
$(y + z) + x$	apply R2	
$x + (y + z)$	apply R1, goal state.	

Rewriting (83) as a set of clauses, and writing $f(x, y)$ for $x + y$,

$$C1 = \big(7S(f(x, y)), S(f(y, x))\big) \tag{86}$$

$$C2 = \big(7S(f(x, f(y, z))), S(f(f(x, y), z))\big).$$

The negation of (84) is

$$C3 = \big(S(f(f(x, y), z))\big) \tag{87}$$

$$C4 = \big(7S(f(x, f(y, z)))\big)$$

and the set of support is $\{C3, C4\}$. Applying the appropriate x and y instantiations, the following proof can be obtained

$$\big(S(f(f(x_1, x_2), x_3))\big) \cdot \big(7S(f(y_1, y_2)), S(f(y_2, y_1))\big) = S(f(x_3, f(x_1, x_2))) \tag{88}$$

$$\big(S(f(x_1, f(x_2, x_3)))\big) \cdot \big(7S(f(f(y_1, y_2), y_3))\big) = (\quad).$$

This refutation is surprisingly short, compared to (85). An alternative proof by resolution could also have been obtained by mimicking the steps of (85) by a simple device. Suppose "$s_i \to s_{i+1}$ by rule k" is the ith step of the rewriting proof. Each such step will translate into the form

$$(L_i\pi) \cdot (7L_i\pi, L_{i+1}\pi) = (L_{i+1}\pi), \tag{89}$$

in which L_i, L_{i+1} are the literals derived from s_i, s_{i+1} without instantiation, so that $L_i\pi = S(s_i)$, and where the second clause on the left is the clause form of rule k. At the first step $L_0\pi$ would be $S(s_0)\pi$, i.e., the precise form of the starting state. The last step will be of the form

$$(L_i\pi) \cdot (7L_i\pi) = (\quad), \tag{90}$$

where

$$(7L_i\pi) = (7S(s_g)), \tag{91}$$

the denial of the goal state. Since resolutions of the form of (89) and (90) are both input and unit resolutions, the existence of an input and a unit proof is assured. Construction of the proof, however, requires prior knowledge of the rewriting proof. Also, as the example of (88) showed, the resolution proof constructed from the rewriting proof may not be the most elegant resolution proof possible.

What happens if we remove the restriction that at each step in the rewriting solution the operator must be applied to an entire string? Clearly we must do this, since in most interesting rewriting problems it is necessary to rewrite string components. We can still produce a conceptual translation from rewriting into the predicate calculus, but the translation becomes much more involved. In fact, it leads us to consideration of an infinite set of axioms! Removing the restriction destroys the correspondence between $s_i \rightarrow s_j$ and $S(s_i) \supset S(s_j)$. To illustrate, consider the problem of using

$$\text{R1} \qquad x + y \rightarrow y + x \qquad\qquad (92)$$

to prove that

$$(a + b) + (c + d) \rightarrow (b + a) + (d + c). \qquad\qquad (93)$$

Obviously this is trivial if R1 can be applied to the substrings $(a + b)$ and $(c + d)$. If we use the predicate calculus translation rules given previously we obtain the theorem proving problem

$$S = \begin{cases} C1 = \big(7S(f(x, y)), S(f(y, x))\big) \\ C2 = \big(S(f(f(a, b), f(c, d)))\big) \\ C3 = \big(7S(f(f(b, a), f(d, c)))\big) \end{cases} \qquad (94)$$

A bit of experimentation should convince the reader that there is no way (94) can be used to deduce (   ), since $C1$ cannot be applied within the term $f(f(a,b), f(c,d))$.

Conceptually, this poses no problem, since if one knows the rewriting proof, one can augment the axiomatization of the problem with a special clause describing each application of a rewriting rule to a substring. Suppose we were to do this for (94), by adding the rule

$$C4 = \big(7S(f(f(x,y),z)), S(f(f(y,x),z))\big) \qquad\qquad (95)$$

This is a statement of

$$R2 \qquad (x + y) + z \rightarrow (y + x) + z \qquad\qquad (96)$$

which is a special case of R1. When (95) is added to (94), we can obtain the solution (with trivial substitutions not spelled out)

$\big(S(f(f(a,b), f(c,d)))\big)$	$C2$	(97)
$\big(S(f(f(b,a), f(c,d)))\big)$	$C5 = $ resolvent $C2, C4$	
$\big(S(f(f(c,d), f(b,a)))\big)$	$C6 = $ resolvent $C5, C1$	
$\big(S(f(f(d,c), f(b,a)))\big)$	$C7 = $ resolvent $C6, C4$	
$\big(S(f(f(b,a), f(d,c)))\big)$	$C8 = $ resolvent $C7, C1$	
( )	. resolvent $C8, C3$	

We would consider the extended predicate calculus formulation as a restatement of an amplified rewriting system, implied by the original one, in which the restriction to rewriting only "whole" states applied. Logically we have retained the correspondence between state–space problems and predicate calculus problems with input and unit proof.[7] However, we paid a heavy price in both practical and theoretical terms. The extended formulation requires either than we know the context in which each rewriting rule is to be applied, so that we can write the appropriate clauses, or we must provide a mechanism within our program for generating context-sensitive clauses of the form of (96) as they are needed. It is hard to see how we can fulfill the first condition without already knowing the rewriting system's answer to the problem. An implementation of a problem-solving program which must have its input based on an already known solution to the problem to be solved strikes us as being of limited interest. If we provide an axiom generating mechanism, the set S will be infinite and countable, rather than finite. Fortunately, resolution is a complete deductive system for countable sets of axioms (Slagle, 1970b), so the basic method is still valid. The generation of large numbers of clauses, however, has serious practical consequences. In general, the whole process of translating from one problem solving formulation into another will have become much more complicated.

12.4   Syntactic Strategies

12.4.0   INTRODUCTORY

Syntactic strategies are procedures for choosing resolutions based solely upon the structural properties of the clauses involved, without regard to the truth or falsity of the clause under a particular model or the derivation of the clause. Unit preference and tautology elimination are examples of simple syntactic strategies. Syntactic strategies are easy to apply because they depend only on examination of the clauses potentially involved in a resolution, and thus eliminate the need for extensive record keeping. In addition, syntactic strategies can often be added to ancestory or semantic strategies, thus further restricting resolution, without sacrificing completeness. We have already seen this done with unit preference and tautology elimination, neither of which are total refinements in themselves.

There are two major syntactic refinement strategies, *A-ordering* and *C-ordering*. (Rieter, 1971). In A-ordering the atoms of a set S are ordered in arbitrary fashion, and the literal of resolution chosen to be the highest ordered atom in the left parent. A-ordering can be combined with merging and linearity to produce the complete *merge, a-ordered, linear* (*m.a.l.*) refinement strategy. This strategy simplifies the choices to be made during development of a linear proof, dictating the choice of a literal of resolution when two such literals are possible. The example

---

[7] This is what Chang (1970, p. 706, ex. 10) did in restating some of Quinlan and Hunt's (1968) problems as first-order predicate calculus problems.

of Figure 12-9 and (65) illustrates such a situation. A-ordering, however, still permits an excessively large number of resolutions. Reiter's second strategy, *C-ordering*, seems to be more restrictive.

12.4.1 C-ORDERING

C-ordering is a complete strategy which can be combined with merging and linearity to form the complete *merge, c-ordered, linear (m.c.l.)* refinement. In fact, C-ordering implies linearity, as a distinction is made between left and right parent in the definition of C-ordering. Let C be a clause of **S**, and $[C]$ be the ordered clause obtained by imposing some arbitrary but fixed ordering on the literals of C. $[S]$ is the set of ordered clauses obtained by ordering the clauses of **S**. If $[C]$ is a derived clause in a linear deduction ($[C] = [C^i]$, $i > 0$), then let $[C^{i-1}]$ and $[B^{i-1}]$ be its ordered left and right parents, with $L_1, \ldots, L_k, L_r$ being, in order, the literals of C^{i-1}, L_r the literal of resolution (and rightmost literal of the left parent), and $M_1, \ldots, M_m$ being the literals of B^{i-1}, in order. Clearly $M_i = 7L_r$ for some i, $1 \geqslant i \geqslant m$. The ordering of C^i is

$$C^i = (L_1, \ldots, L_k, M_1, \ldots, M_{i-1}, M_{i+1}, \ldots, M_m), \tag{98}$$

i.e., the literals of the right parent are appended to the literals of the left parent, with the literals of resolution in each parent omitted and any duplicate literals retained only in their leftmost occurrence. Resolution is permitted only on the rightmost literal of C^i.

To illustrate C-ordering, let X, Y, Z be arbitrary ground atoms, and let

$$[S] = \{(Y), (Z, X), (7X, W), (W, 7Z), (7X, 7W, 7Y), (7Z, 7W, 7Y)\}. \tag{99}$$

Figure 12-10 illustrates a C-ordered refutation. Note that at each step the literal of resolution is predetermined, thus reducing the number of potential right parents. On the other hand, C-ordered derivations are generally longer than derivations which do not satisfy C-ordering, since in the course of a derivation it may be necessary to extend a clause temporarily in order to remove its rightmost literal.

The derivation of Figure 12-10 does not satisfy the merge condition. Figure 12-11 shows a derivation of ( ) from the same set of clauses which satisfies C-ordering, merging, and linearity. As is typical, this is a longer derivation but still fewer alternative right parents were available at each inference step.

Sickel and Hunt (1973) extended C-ordering to combine with merging, linearity, unit preference and subsumption. To do this, they redefined subsumption to require that the subsuming clause contain a subset of the literals of the subsumed clause and in the same order. This was necessary in order to maintain compatibility with C-ordering during a derivation. In addition, they introduced the idea of *overriding unit preference*. By this they meant that a unit resolution could be attempted at any point in the deduction, regardless of the ancestry of the unit clause. In particular, the unit preference strategy was given priority over the linear strategy. The combination of merging, subsumption as defined, overriding unit

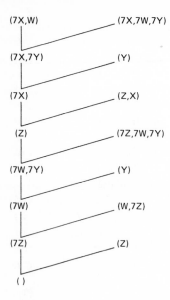

Fig. 12-10.   A *C*-ordered linear refutation of (98).

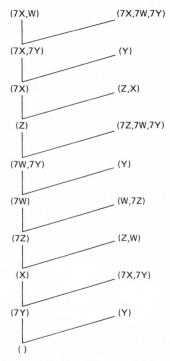

Fig. 12-11.   A merge, *C*-ordered linear refutation of (98). Underlined literals are merges.

preference, and C-ordering is complete. Interestingly, the refinement is not complete if overriding unit preference is removed. Sickel and Hunt's result is most useful in situations in which memory space is a limiting factor, since it allows the removal of a clause from memory after a clause subsuming it is derived.

12.5   Semantic Strategies

12.5.0   GENERAL

If a set of clauses **S** is satisfiable, then there is some assignment of truth values to the atoms of **S** such that all clauses in **S** are satisfied. Any particular assignment of truth values to atoms is called a *model*. Semantic strategies seek to show that **S** is unsatisfiable by showing that there is no model which satisfies **S**. A relationship can be developed between model elimination and linear ancestory strategies (Loveland, 1972), but the explanation is quite technical. The idea of semantic proofs will be illustrated by heuristic presentation of a procedure for theorem proving due first to Hayes and Kowalski (1969). Before doing so, some expansion on the idea of a model is necessary.

Let $\mathbf{A} = \{Ai\}$ be the set of atomic statements in **S** and the clauses derivable from **S**. In general **A** will be an infinite, countable set. Let **L** denote the set of literals derivable from **A**, i.e., the members of **A** and their complements. A *partial model* M_i of S is a subset of **L** that does not contain any literal and its complement. We also require that if L is a member of M_i, then M_i must not contain $7L\pi$, for any substitution π. A partial model, then, is a consistent assignment of truth values to *some* of the literals of **L**. We can think of M_i as representing the set of models $\mathbf{M}_i$ whose members are other models that include, as a subset of their literals, all the literals of M_i or descended by substitution from them. To illustrate, suppose we have

$$S = \{(P(x), Q(a, y), 7R(x)),$$ (100)

$$(7P(x), 7Q(x, f(x)), R(y))\}.$$

A consists of the atoms which are instantiations of $\{P(x), Q(a,y), Q(x,f(x)), R(y)\}$. The set **A** is an infinite countable set, since it contains atoms of the form $Q(x,f(x))$, $Q(f(x), f(f(x))), \ldots$. The set **L** consists of the elements of **A** and their complements, and hence is also infinite and countable. Now consider the two incomplete models

$$M_1 = \{P(a)\}, \qquad M_2 = \{7P(a)\}.$$ (101)

Let $\mathbf{M}_1$ be the set of all complete models including M_1 as a subset, and $\mathbf{M}_2$ be the set of complete models containing M_2 as a subset. Since $P(a)$ is derivable from **A**, every complete model must be in $\mathbf{M}_1$ or $\mathbf{M}_2$ and cannot be in both. Clearly if some clause C_1 in or derivable from S is falsifiable by M_1 it is falsifiable by any member of $\mathbf{M}_1$, and hence no model in $\mathbf{M}_1$ satisfies S. If we can find a similar clause C_2 that is falsified by M_2, we will have proven that S is unsatisfiable.

Doing this is the goal of a semantic refinement strategy. By "judicious" choice of resolutions, we seek models for S which exhaust the universe of models (in the sense $\mathbf{M}_1$ and $\mathbf{M}_2$ did above) and in which at least one clause is falsified. To demonstrate how this can be done, it is necessary to define some special graphs and relate them to theorem proving.

12.5.1   DEFINITIONS

A *tree*, T is a set of nodes $\{n\}$, together with a partial ordering, $>$, of some of the pairs of nodes n_i, n_j, in T. For two nodes, n_i, n_j, if $n_i > n_j$, n_i is said to be *immediately above* n_j. Conversely, n_j is *immediately below* n_i. The ordering is restricted by the following rules:

(*i*) There is a distinguished node, n_r, called the *root* of the tree, such that there is no node immediately above n_r.

(*ii*) Every other node n_i has exactly one node immediately above it.

(*iii*) If a node n_i is not immediately above any other node, then n_i is a *tip node* of T.

Consider any node n_k that is not the root node. The sequence of orderings $n_r > n_1 > n_2 > \cdots > n_i > n_j > \cdots > n_k$ is a *branch* to n_k.

A node n_i is *above* (*below*) a node n_j if it is immediately above (below) it, or if it is immediately above (below) a node n_k that is above (below) n_j. Figure 12-12 illustrates the tree defined by

$$T = \{A, B, C, D, E, F, G\}$$
$$A > B, \quad A > C, \quad B > D, \quad B > E, \quad C > F, \quad C > G. \quad (102)$$

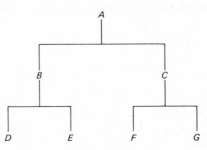

Fig. 12-12.   Tree generated from simple ordering.

A *semantic tree*, T is defined for a set **S** of clauses by attaching literals to the nodes of T according to the following rules:

- (*i*) ( ) is attached to the root of T
- (*ii*) Let n_i, $i = 1 \cdots k$ be nodes of T such that $\mathbf{N} = \{n_1 \cdots n_k\}$ is the set of nodes directly below node n, and let $\mathbf{B}_i$ be the set of literals attached to node n_i. The truth value of $\mathbf{B}_i$ is interpreted as the truth value of the conjunction of the literals it contains. If T is a semantic tree, the disjunction of the set $\{\mathbf{B}_i\}$ must be a tautology.
- (*iii*) The union of the set of literals assigned to nodes in any complete branch, or sequence from the root to a tip node in T must contain every literal in **L** or its complement, and thus is a *complete assignment*, or *complete model* for **S**.

For example, let $\mathbf{S} = \{(A(x)), (7A(x), B(x, y)), (7B(x, y))\}$. Then $\mathbf{A} = \{A(x), B(x, y)\}$. Two semantic trees for **A** are shown in Figure 12-13. Tree (a) was developed by ordering the atoms of **S** and then assigning ( ) to the root, A1 and 7A1 to the two nodes immediately below the root, A2 and 7A2 to the nodes below each of the first level nodes, etc. The definition of a semantic tree is satisfied, since at any level the disjunction of the assignments immediately below a node will have the form $(A \vee 7A)$, which is a tautology. The "bushier" tree of Figure 12-13b is also a semantic tree, since the disjunction of the assignments to nodes below the root (the sole interior node) is a tautology of the form $(A_1 \cdot A_2 \vee A_1 \cdot 7A_2 \vee A_1 \cdot A_2 \vee 7A_1 \cdot 7A_2)$.

A semantic tree, T, is a *finite clash tree* for **S** if, for every node $n \in T$, and set of nodes $\{n_1, \ldots, n_k, n_{k+1}\}$ immediately below n, the following relations hold:

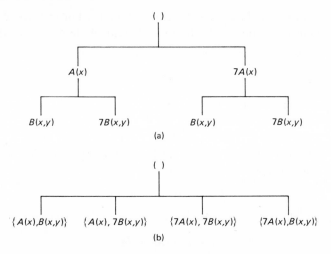

Fig. 12-13. Alternate semantic trees for $\{A(x), 7B(x, y)\}$.

(*i*) Each set $\mathbf{B}_i$ of literals assigned to a node n_i, $1 \leqslant i \leqslant k$, is a singleton $\{L_i\}$

(*ii*) The set $\mathbf{B}_{k+1}$ of literals assigned to n_{k+1} is

$$B_{k+1} = \{7L_i\}, \qquad i = 1, k \tag{103}$$

(*iii*) No literal assigned to a node below n is a member of the set of literals assigned to node n.

A finite clash tree based on the atoms of $\{A(x), B(x,y)\}$ is shown in Figure 12-14. Note that it satisfies the tautology restriction for the nodes immediately under a node.

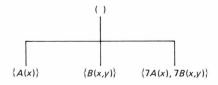

Fig. 12-14. Finite clash tree for $\{A(y), B(x, y)\}$.

12.5.2 MODEL ELIMINATION USING FINITE CLASH TREES

The concept of a finite clash tree can be used to demonstrate that no model exists for a given unsatisfiable set. Any set **S** must be unsatisfiable if it is falsified by every model represented by a sequence of literals from the root to some tip node of a semantic tree. The sequence of literals on the path from the root to each node can be thought of as a partial assignment, or partial model. For instance, consider the leftmost tip node of Figure 12-14. The associated literals define the model

$$M_1 = \{(\ \ ), A(x)\} \tag{104}$$
$$= \{A(x)\}.$$

We can make a similar argument for the model

$$M_2 = \{B(x, y)\} \tag{105}$$

associated with the center tip node of the figure. Finally, at the rightmost node we have the complete assignment

$$M_3 = \{7A(x), 7B(x, y)\}. \tag{106}$$

Taken together, all possible models for $\{A(x), B(x, y)\}$ are included in

$$\mathbf{M} = M_1 \cup M_2 \cup M_3. \tag{107}$$

If **S** is falsified by each of these models, then **S** must be unsatisfiable.

We can generalize the example. Extend the set of atoms to include $C(y)$, i.e., redefine

$$\mathbf{A} = \{A(x), B(x, y), C(y)\}. \tag{108}$$

The tree of Figure 12-14 may be included in the larger finite clash tree shown in Figure 12-15. Note that the assignment $C(y)$ has replaced (   ). Models M_1, M_2, and M_3 are similarly redefined to include the literal $C(y)$, since the node associated with it lies on the path from the appropriate tip node to the root. Failure of **S** under M_1, M_2, and M_3 would demonstrate that **S** could not be satisfied by any model including $C(y)$, but would say nothing about the satisfiability of **S** by models containing $7C(y)$.

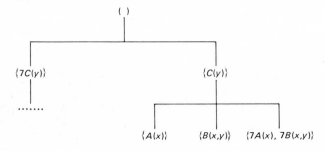

Fig. 12-15.   Inclusion of finite clash tree in a larger tree.

To amplify further on what we mean by "failure of **S** at a node," we shift attention from **S** to the clauses of **S**. The set **S** is unsatisfiable if at least one clause $C \in \mathbf{S}$ is false under every possible model. Let us define Mn to be the model containing the *complement* of every literal associated with a node on the path from the root to node n, and let **Ln** be this set of literals. We say that clause C *fails at* *node n* if **Ln** includes every literal of *C*. Clearly, *C* will have the value false and **S** will then be unsatisfiable under *Mn* if *C* fails at node *n*. This point is illustrated by the rightmost branch of Figure 12-15, where **Ln** is $\{C(y), 7A(x), 7B(x, y)\}$. Clauses such as $(C(y))$ and $(7A(x), 7B(x, y))$ would fail at this node. Note also that **Ln** must include the set of literals **Lm** associated with any node *m* above *n*. Therefore any clause that fails at *m* will also fail at *n*. For example, $(C(y))$ would fail at any right-hand node of Figure 12-15.

We are interested in the highest node in the tree at which **S** can be made to fail. Node *n* is defined to be a *failure point for* **S** if there is a clause $C \in$ **S** which fails at node *n* but does not fail at any node *m* above *n*. Otherwise, node *n* is *free for* **S**. Now suppose **S** fails at the root node. This is an indication that **S** is unsatisfiable under all models, since every model is associated with some node below the root. Therefore, the goal of a semantic procedure is to make **S** fail at the root node. This is done by resolution. Let node **n** be an *inference node* if *n* is free for **S** but all nodes *n'* below are failure points. If *n* is an inference node, then there is a clause *C* which may not be in **S** but can be deduced from **S** by resolution, such that the literals of *C* are contained in the set **Ln**. To see this, consider the set of clauses

$$S = \begin{cases} C1 = (A(x), B(x, y)) & (109) \\ C2 = (C(x), 7B(x, y)) \end{cases}$$

and the finite clash tree of Figure 12-16. The nodes $n1$, $n2$ are associated with the sets of literals

$$L1 = \{A(x) \quad C(x), \quad B(x, y)\} \tag{110}$$
$$L2 = \{A(x) \quad C(x), \quad 7B(x, y)\}$$

and are closed for **S** since **L1** falsifies $C1$ and **L2** falsifies $C2$. The resolvent of $C1$ and $C2$ is

$$C1 \cdot C2 = C = (A(x), C(x)). \tag{111}$$

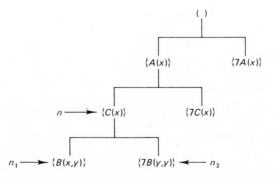

Fig. 12-16.   Fragment of tree showing n_1, n_2 (closed) and *n* (inference node) for $S = \{ (A(x), C(x), B(x, y)), (A(x), C(x), 7BB(x, y)) \}$.

The literals of C are included in, and in this case identical to, the model associated with node n. If by resolution the null clause ( ) is produced, since ( ) is included in all $\mathbf{Ln}$, $\mathbf{S}$ must be unsatisfiable.

The semantic strategy for producing ( ) from $\mathbf{S}$ is simply to construct the appropriate tree. To do this the clauses available are examined to search for a *latent clash resolution*. This is a resolution in which there is a nucleus clause C0 and a set $\mathbf{C} = \{Ci\}$ of *satellites*, where

$$C0 = (\mathbf{A0}, D1 \cdots Dk) \tag{112}$$

and, for each $Ci \in \mathbf{C}$,

$$Ci = (\mathbf{C0}_i, Ei) \tag{113}$$

in (112) and (113) $\mathbf{C0}_i$ and $\mathbf{A0}$ are disjoint sets of literals, and there exists a unification such that

$$Di\pi = 7Ei\pi. \tag{114}$$

From a latent clash we may infer

$$C = (\mathbf{A0}\pi, \mathbf{C0}_1\pi, \ldots, \mathbf{C0}_k\pi). \tag{115}$$

As in hyperresolution, $Ei\pi$ may not occur in any clause $Cj\pi, j \neq 1$, and none of the set of literals $\{Di\pi\}$ may occur in any set $\mathbf{C0}_i\pi$.

An example is in order. Let

$$\mathbf{S} = \begin{cases} C0 = \bigl(P(x1), 7Q(a, x2), 7Q(b, c)\bigr) & (116) \\ C1 = \bigl(R(y1), Q(y2, c)\bigr) \\ C2 = \bigl(R(a), Q(b, z1)\bigr) \end{cases}$$

By applying

$$\pi = (a/x1, a/y2, c/x2, c/z1) \tag{117}$$

the clauses

$$C0\pi = \bigl(P(a), 7Q(a, c), 7Q(b, c)\bigr) \tag{118}$$

$$C1\pi = \bigl(R(y1), Q(a, c)\bigr)$$

$$C2\pi = \bigl(R(a), Q(b, c)\bigr)$$

are obtained. By hyperresolution derive

$$C = \bigl(P(a), R(y1), R(a)\bigr) \tag{119}$$

and factor C by the substitution $\theta = (a/y1)$, producing

$$C\theta = \bigl(P(a), R(a)\bigr). \tag{120}$$

The assembly of this sequence of inferences is shown in the semantic tree diagram of Figure 12-17. Initially each clause $Ci\pi$, $i = 1, \ldots, k$, of (118) is associated with a

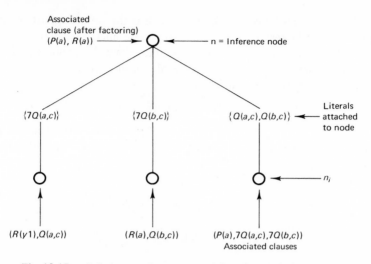

Fig. 12-17.   Inference node constructed from latent clash resolution.

tip node, n_i. The literals $Di\pi$ is also attached to N_i. Finally, clause $C0\pi$ is associated with node n_{k+1} and the literals $\{7Di\pi = Ei\pi\}$ attached. Node n is defined to be the node immediately above nodes $n_1, \ldots, n_{k+1}$. The tree constructed in this manner satisfies the definitions of a finite clash tree. Clauses $C0 \cdots Ck$ fail at their respective tip nodes, providing that the sets of clauses **L**i have the appropriate literals. Assuming this to be true, and if the Ci do not fail at or above n, then n must be the endpoint of a branch whose literals Ln contain the literals of the hyperresolvent clause C. Furthermore, C is either a nucleus or satellite clause in a further latent clash resolution. The chain of such resolutions terminates when ( ) is deduced, equivalently, when the root of the tree is reached.

Despite the complexity of its description, the procedure is simple to execute, as in the following example of a proof of the simple inequalities theorem given in Section 12.0. Unit preference and set of support are also used in this example. We write $L(x, y)$ for $x < y$, with similar interpretations for $G(x, y)$ $(>)$ and $E(x, y)$ $(=)$, to maintain compatibility with our previous notation. The theorem to be proven is that there are no two numbers a and b such that a is both greater than and less than b. The initial set of clauses is

$$S = \begin{cases} C1 = (L(x, y), G(x, y), E(x, y)) & (121) \\ C2 = (7L(x, y), 7G(x, y)) \\ C3 = (7L(x, y), 7E(x, y)) \\ C4 = (7E(x, y), 7G(x, y)) \\ C5 = (G(a, b)) \\ C6 = (L(a, b)). \end{cases}$$

The denial of the hypothesis is $\{C5, C6\}$, which is the set of support and provides the initial nucleus clauses. Satellite clauses for these nucleii must contain negative literals, so $C1$ can be dropped from consideration. Possible satellites for $C5$ are $C2$ and $C4$. Since they are of the same length, arbitrarily choose $C2$. By latent resolution of $C5$ and its single satellite, infer

$$C7 = (7L(a, b)). \tag{122}$$

At this point, we can begin construction of the semantic tree. The two satellite nodes and the inference node are shown in Figure 12-18a. $C7$ is now available for

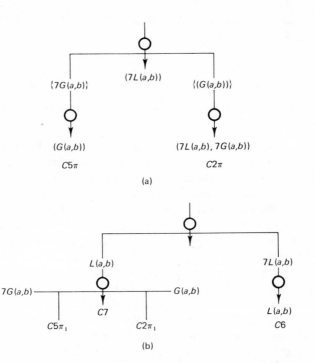

Fig. 12-18.   Construction of a semantic tree by latent clash resolution. (a) First stage. (b) Second stage.

entry into a latent clash resolution. In fact, because of the sign and letter of its predicate, it is eligible to be a satellite clause for the nucleus of $C6$, and because of unit preference, it is the first satellite to be selected. We can then construct the simple ground resolution (a trivial case of latent clash resolution)

$$(7L(a, b)) \cdot (L(a, b)) = (\quad).$$

Thus we have a deduction of ( ), which refutes **S**.

12.6   Heuristics

12.6.0   SIMPLE HEURISTICS

There are a number of pragmatically useful heuristic devices which deliberately sacrifice completeness in the hope of obtaining a rapid solution most of the time. Most of them are simple, and need only be mentioned. One, the use of analogies, requires a detailed discussion.

The *depth limit* heuristic places a temporary limit on the length of the derivations to be considered. Let $k > 0$ be the depth limit. All derivations of length k or less will be developed before extending any derivation to length $k + 1$. The value of k may be adjusted upward during the search for a solution. Depth limit, then, is a slight extension of the notion of breadth first searching, appropriately specialized to theorem proving.

Techniques which try to minimize the complexity of the derived clauses can be considered as heuristic searches, since (   ) can be regarded as the simplest clause possible, and complexity minimizing techniques deal first with clauses which, in some sense, resemble (   ) more closely than do other clauses. Let k, m, and n be positive integers. A *complexity limit* heuristic rejects derivations from any clause which exceeds some combination of nested parentheses to a depth greater than k, more than m symbols, or more than n literals. The value of these parameters may be adjusted during problem solving, as required.

12.6.1   ANALOGIES

In problem solving by analogy a correspondence is noted between problem A and previously solved problem B, and the correspondence used to suggest a way of solving A. As any schoolboy logician knows, the mere existence of the analogy does not prove that B's solution is "like A's," but if the suggested solution can, indeed, be shown to be valid, then the question of how it arose is superfluous. In practice, the utility of analogical reasoning by human mathematicians has been amply documented (Polya, 1954). Is there any way to capture this powerful tool for mechanical problem solving? We have previously seen one approach, in Gelernter's (1963) use of a digitized diagram to suggest symbolic proofs to plane geometry problems. Kling (1971) has proposed a quite different way of introducing analogies in resolution principle theorem proving. His approach has been illustrated by the performance of a program called ZORBA,[8] which successfully proved a number of problems in modern algebra by a combination of analogy and resolution. ZORBA itself must deal with the many special cases that arise when creating an analogy. We shall make no attempt to explain how it handles each problem. Instead we shall demonstrate the broad approach by going through a simple example[9] in which

[8] No explanation has been given for this name.

[9] The example is a modification of an illustrative example developed by Michael Delay for a graduate seminar presentation.

most of the mechanisms of ZORBA are applied, although not in exactly the manner that the program would actually make use of them.

In what sense are analogies applicable to resolution? Imagine a resolution program which is intended to show that certain statements follow from a very large data base, **D**. The straightforward way to proceed is to define **T** as the negation of the statement to be proven, and then show that the set $\mathbf{D} \cup \mathbf{T}$ is unsatisfiable, by deriving the empty clause (   ). In many cases of interest (e.g., deductive question answering) **D** will be quite large, and there will be an unknown subset $\mathbf{S} \subset \mathbf{D}$ such that $\mathbf{S} \cup \mathbf{T}$ is unsatisfiable. It may be that although the problem of refuting $\mathbf{S} \cup \mathbf{T}$ is manageable, attempts to refute $\mathbf{D} \cup \mathbf{T}$ directly will lead to many "nonproductive" derivations which do not terminate in (   ), but do require a great deal of computational time and space. Therefore we would like to have some way of identifying **S** prior to beginning resolution. Now suppose further that there is available a previously solved problem, **T***. That is, the theorem prover "knows" that there is a subset **S*** of **D** such that $\mathbf{S^*} \cup \mathbf{T^*}$ is unsatisfiable and, furthermore, the derivation of (   ) from $\mathbf{S^*} \cup \mathbf{T^*}$ is known. The question is "Can we establish a mapping π from the clauses used to refute **T*** to the clauses of **D** such that $\pi(\mathbf{S^*}) \subseteq \mathbf{D}$ and $\pi(\mathbf{S^*}) \cup \mathbf{T}$ is unsatisfiable?" If the answer to this question is "yes," then we have a way of identifying **S** prior to beginning the resolutions to refute **T**, by analogy to the clauses used to refute problem **T***. This is the sense in which ZORBA is an analogical reasoner. Before sketching the rudiments of the ZORBA method, however, we need to introduce two preliminary notions.

The first of these is the idea of a *semantic template*. Before ZORBA can begin, the user must select the "analogical problem," **T***. In addition, the user specifies a *semantic type*, or class, for each predicate and predicate place in the language of discourse. For example, in the illustration we are about to develop we shall use the predicates $IN(x1, x2)$, $AT(x3, x4)$, $DOING(x5, x6)$, and $SICK(x7)$, and the semantic types

$$Location = \{ IN, AT \} \tag{123}$$

$$Activity = \{ DOING, SICK \}$$

$$Person = \{ x1, x3, x5, x7 \}$$

$$Place = \{ x2, x4, x6 \}.$$

The semantic template of an atomic statement is simply the statement with its predicate name and arguments replaced by their type names. Thus the semantic template of $DOING(x5, x6)$ is *Activity(person, place)* and that of $SICK(x7)$ is *Activity(person)*.

The second preliminary idea is that of a *description* of a clause. This is the set of *features* which the clause contains, where a feature refers to the manner in which a predicate appears in a clause. For an arbitrary clause C and predicate P, C contains the feature $pos(p)$ if P appears in the clause only in positive form, $neg(p)$ if P appears in the clause only in negated form, and $impcond(P)$ if P appears in both positive and negative form. The description of the clause $(\text{AT}(\text{DESK}, X),$ $7\text{IN}(\text{OFFICE}, X))$, then, is pos(AT), neg(IN). A description is said to *satisfy* another if the second description is a subset of the first. Two descriptions *partially satisfy* each other if they have a nonempty intersection.

We are now prepared to deal with the example. Table 12-2 contains a set of clauses, C1–C6, defining a mild version of the Prostestant work ethic. The problem is to prove that "John is not sick" having previously answered the question "Where is Smith?". To answer the question "Where is Smith" the assertion was made that "Smith was nowhere" (T1 in Table 12-2), and this statement was refuted by the derivation,

T1   (7 AT(SMITH, Y))   "There is no Y such that Smith is there." (124)
                           Set of support.

R1   (7 IN(SMITH, OFFICE))   Resolution of T1 and C3

R2   (7 DOING(SMITH, WORK))   Resolution of R1 and C2

R3   (   )   Resolution of R2 and C1,

which will serve as the basis of the analogy. Analogy construction will proceed in three steps. First a mapping will be found between the predicates and terms used in **T** and **T***. Next, this mapping will be used to derive *image clauses*, hypothetical clauses which are similar to the clauses used in derivation (124). Finally, **D** will be searched for clauses whose descriptions are similar to the descriptions of the image clauses. When such a clause is found, it is said to be an *analog* of the clause in the original refutation which gave rise to the image. More than one analog may be

TABLE 12-2
Data and Problem Statements for Analogy Example

	Clauses in Data Base	
C1	(DOING(SMITH, WORK))	"Smith is working."
C2	(7DOING(X WORK), IN(X, OFFICE))	"One works in the office."
C3	(7IN(X, OFFICE), AT(X, DESK))	"When in the office, one is at one's desk."
C4	(IN(JOHN, OFFICE))	"John is in the office."
C5	(7IN(X, OFFICE), DOING(X, WORK))	"When at the office, one works."
C6	(7DOING(X, WORK), 7SICK(X))	"One does not work when one is sick."
	Problem statements	
T1	(7AT(SMITH, Y))	"Smith is nowhere."
T1*	(SICK(JOHN))	"John is sick."

found for a given original clause. The process of mapping and searching for analogs will be continued until at least one analog is found for each clause used in the solution of **T**. An attempt will then be made to derive a refutation from **T*** and the analog clauses.

The first step is to find $\pi 0$, the initial mapping from the language of **T** to that of **T***. Using the semantic templates defined earlier, the atomic statements of **T** and **T*** are grouped separately into sets. In the case at hand, this step is trivial, since there is only one atomic statement in each problem, so the sets must be

$$S1 = \{AT(SMITH, Y)\}; \qquad \text{template } location \text{ (person, place)} \qquad (125)$$

$$S2 = \{SICK(JOHN)\}; \qquad \text{template } activity \text{ (person)}. $$

Certainly there could be more complicated problems. For now, we shall not consider them.[10] Once the sets are established a mapping is established, first from templates to templates, and then from atoms within a given template to atoms within another template. In the general case we would find several mappings and have to explore them all, but in the particular case at hand there is only one mapping. It implies a mapping of predicates and terms, since if AT(SMITH, Y) $\longleftrightarrow$ SICK(JOHN), an obvious component by component mapping is

$$\pi 0 = \{AT \longleftrightarrow SICK; \quad SMITH \longleftrightarrow JOHN\} \qquad (126)$$

Next the image clauses are found. The clauses used in the refutation are

$$\{T1, C1, C2, C3, R1, R2\}. \qquad (127)$$

Mapping $\pi 0$ can be applied to atoms in only one of these clauses, $C3$, producing the image clause

$$A3 \quad \pi 0(C3) = (7IN(X, OFFICE), SICK(X)) \qquad (128)$$

which has the description neg(IN), pos(SICK). Referring to Table 12-2, we find that the "closest" description of A3 is that of clause C5, which also contains the feature neg(IN). Clause C5 is taken as an analog of C3.

We are now in a position to extend the mapping $\pi 0$ to a larger domain. This is done by considering the two mapped clauses, C5 and C3. They have introduced two new atomic statements:

$$IN(X, OFFICE) \qquad \text{and} \qquad DOING(X, WORK).$$

Note that one of these statements was introduced from a clause in the refutation of **T**, the other was introduced through an analog. As before, the new atomic statements are grouped by similarity of template (which is again trivial, since there is only one element in the set being partitioned), and a mapping extended. This produces

$$\pi 1 = \pi 0 \cup \{IN \longleftrightarrow DOING: \quad OFFICE \longleftrightarrow WORK\}. \qquad (129)$$

[10] If there are several different templates represented in **T** and **T***, and several atoms for each template, the process of mapping from atoms to atoms becomes complicated. See Kling (1971) for details of one possible solution.

Mapping 1 can be applied to all the clauses that have not been previously mapped, producing the image clauses

$A1$: $\pi1(C1) = (IN(JOHN, OFFICE))$; $pos(IN)$ (130)

$A2$: $\pi1(C2) = (7\ IN(X,\ OFFICE),\ DOING(X,\ WORK))$; $neg(IN)$,
                                                                          $pos(DOING)$

$AR1$: $\pi1(R1) = (7\ DOING(JOHN;\ WORK))$; $neg(DOING)$

$AR2$: $\pi1(R2) = (7\ IN(JOHN,\ OFFICE))$; $neg(IN)$.

The data base is searched for clauses whose descriptions intersect with the image clauses, and the appropriate analogs selected. At this point we have

Clause	Analog clause(s)	(131)
$C1$	$C4$	
$C2$	$C5$	
$C3$	$C5$	
$R1$	$C2, C6$	
$R2$	$C3, C5$.	

Together, the analog clauses comprise the trial $\mathbf{S}^* = \{C2, C3, C4, C5, C6\}$. Note that $\mathbf{S}^*$ is smaller than $\mathbf{D}$, since $C1$ does not appear in $\mathbf{S}^*$. Furthermore, $\mathbf{S}^* \cup \mathbf{T}^*$ is unsatisfiable, as the following refutation demonstrates.

$T1^*$	$(SICK(JOHN))$	Set of support, $T1^*$	(132)
$R3$	$(7DOING(JOHN, WORK))$	Resolvent of $T1^*$, $C6$	
$R4$	$(7IN(JOHN, OFFICE))$	Resolvent of $R3$, $C5$	
$R5$	$(\ \ )$	Resolvent of $R4$, $C4$.	

Clearly, $\mathbf{S}^* \cup \mathbf{T}^*$ is not a minimally unsatisfiable set, so while the process of analogy has made refutation more efficient, maximally efficient refutation has not been achieved. This will normally be the case.

Kling (1971) used ZORBA to preselect clauses from a large data base designed for proving selected theorems in modern algebra. He reports very efficient data selection, as in most cases $\mathbf{S}^*$ contained only one or two superfluous clauses. There is no way in which we can say how good this particular use of analogy is "in general," since it is not clear how we define the set of problems to which we want to generalize. In fact, we cannot say how useful analogies are in human reasoning, at least in any quantifiable interpretation of "how useful." It is clear that in some cases the method works well, undoubtedly examples of inefficient use of analogies could be constructed. There are two likely weak points. One is that the pair of problems forming the analogy must be presented to the program by a (human) user. To be precise, Kling has offered a method for detailing an analogy once one has been suggested. Genius may lie in being able to think of the analogical problem in the first place. The second weakness is more of a technical one. In the illustration used here only one mapping, and hence one analogy, was possible. In general there may be a very large number of possible mappings and analogies. The technique has not yet been sufficiently studied to enable us to say very much about the rules to be used in restricting our search to useful analogies. It seems unlikely that questions such as these will yield to a logical analysis. As in the case of a comparison of various heuristic and refinement techniques, what may be needed is the data from carefully designed empirical experiments in problem solving.

12.7   Quantification

We have thus far implicitly assumed that every variable is universally quantified, i.e., that it can take on any value in its range. Often one deals with *existentially quantified* statements, assertions that for some value of x, $P(x)$ is true. Existentially quantified statements can be reduced to statements involving only universal quantification by the construction of *Skölem functions* to replace existentially quantified variables. To do this, first write all quantifiers explicitly, using $(\forall x)$ $(P(x))$ for universal quantification and $(\exists x)$ $(P(x))$ for existential quantification. The extension to combinations of quantifiers is straightforward. To assert that for every value of x there is some value of y such that the predicate $Q(x, y)$ is true, write

$$(\forall x) \quad (\exists y) \quad (Q(x, y)), \tag{133}$$

and execute the following algorithm:

    (*i*) Establish a list **L** of universally quantified variables. Initially **L** is empty.

    (*ii*) Let *Ci* be the clause being processed and let j be the index of the Skolem function s_{ij} to be constructed. Initially, set $j = 1$.

    (*iii*) Proceeding from the leftmost quantifier, remove quantifiers in order by applying (*a*) or (*b*) as appropriate.

    (*a*) If the quantifier is $(\forall x)$, remove the quantifier and add x to **L**.

        (*b*) If the quantifier is $(\exists x)$, remove the quantifier and replace x throughout *Ci* with the term $s_{ij}(x_1 \cdots x_k)$, where $x_1 \cdots x_k$ are the variables currently on list **L**, then set j to $j + 1$.

To illustrate, consider

$$C7 = (\forall x) \quad (\forall y) \quad (\exists z) \quad (\forall w) \quad (Q(x, y), 7Q(z, w)) \tag{134}$$

The quantifiers $(\forall x)$, $(\forall y)$ are removed without changing C7. **L** will then be

(x, y). On encountering $(\exists z)$, replace throughout C7 with $s_{71}(x, y)$, producing

$$C7 = (\forall w) \quad (Q(x, y), 7Q(s_{71}(x, y), w)) \tag{135}$$

$(\forall w)$ is then removed, and $C7$ has the final form

$$C7 = (Q(x, y), 7Q(s_{71}(x, y), w)) \tag{136}$$

In words, this can be interpreted as

For all values of x, y either the relation $Q(x, y)$ is true or there is a function of x, y $s_{71}(x, y)$ whose value is such that the relation $Q(s_{71}(x, y), w)$ is false for all values of w.

The negation of a quantified clause requires special treatment. Consider the universally quantified statement

For all x, $Q(x)$ is true.

The negation of this is the existentially quantified statement

There exists some value of x such that $7Q(x)$ is true.

To negate a universally quantified statement, then, we replace universal quantification by existential quantification and negate the statement itself, i.e.,

$$7((\forall x)(Q(x))) \rightarrow ((\exists x)(7Q(x))). \tag{137}$$

The inverse operation is also correct. The statement

There is some x such that $Q(x)$ is true

is negated by

For all x, $Q(x)$ is false.

Symbolically

$$7((\exists x)(Q(x))) \rightarrow ((\forall x)(7Q(x))) \tag{138}$$

The reader may recognize that this arrangement provides the logical basis for the example of Section 12.6.1. There, at one time, we asked the question "Where is Smith?" Another way of stating this question is "Is there some place x, such that $(AT(SMITH, X))$ is a theorem?" Symbolically, we want to derive $((\exists x)(AT(SMITH, X)))$ or equivalently, refute $((\forall x)(7AT(SMITH, X)))$. We can repre-ent parts of this reasoning using an example (due first to Green, 1969), which is very similar to the example of 12.6.1. Let the predicates P and W be interpreted as

$$P(x) = x \text{ is a person} \tag{139}$$

$$W(x, y) = x \text{ works at } y.$$

Variables x and y range over the space of persons and locations. We assert that for every person there is a location at which he works (C1) and that John is a person (C2). We then will prove (T1) that there is a place where John works. The clauses are

$C1 = (\forall x) \quad (\exists y) \quad (7P(x), W(x, y))$ "Being a person implies one works   (140) somewhere."

$C2 = (P(\text{JOHN}))$ "John is a person."

$T1 = 7(\exists z) \quad (W(\text{JOHN}, z))$ "There is no place where John works."

By applying the negation rule this becomes

$$T1 = (\forall z) \quad (7W(\text{John}, z)) \tag{141}$$

By applying the quantification rules to $C1, C2$, and $T1$

$$S = \begin{cases} C1 = (7P(x), W(x, s_{11}(x))), & (142) \\ C2 = (P(\text{John})), \\ T1 = (7W(\text{John}, z)). \end{cases}$$

Applying the substitution $\pi_1 = (\text{John}/x)$ to $C1$ and resolving $C1\pi_1$ and $C2$,

$$C3 = (W(\text{John}, s_{11}(\text{John}))) \tag{143}$$

Let $\pi_2 = (s_{11}(\text{John})/z)$ and resolve $C3$ and $T1\pi_2$ deducing (   ), thus proving the theorem.

12.8   Problems Involving Equality

We have dealt with two ways to derive new clauses: substitution and resolution. Resolution maps pairs of clauses into clauses, whereas substitution replaces a term in a clause by another term of the same syntactic form. In some cases we may want to replace a term by an equivalent term which is not an instantiation of the first term. Consider this simple example from school algebra. Suppose we write $x + y$ as $f_+(x, y)$. If we compare

$$C1 = (Q(f_+(a, b)), \tag{144}$$
$$C2 = (7Q(f_+ (b \ a)).$$

we have no way of detecting the contradiction, since resolution provides no way of substituting for terms of varying syntactic form. In Chapter XI we saw that programs such as GPS and FDS could easily handle such problems by string rewriting, which may be a more natural notation for this problem than is the predicate calculus; for other problems the opposite is true. Ideally we would like to have a theorem-proving method that combines the advantages of both approaches. There are two ways we might do this. The most obvious is to include within the axioms of a problem some axioms defining equality. This is not a practical solution, since it increases the length and number of clauses in a statement, and thus increases very greatly the number of resolutions that can be made but which, in fact, do not lead to a proof. A more generally accepted alternative is to include within the framework of a resolution principle program a special rule of inference to be applied when dealing with equalities. To be compatible with the rest of the theorem prover, the inference rule should meet two criteria. First, it should deal with clauses in which equalities are expressed as atoms. Second, it should be an operation that accepts as input two clauses and produces a third as output. The first condition ensures that special data types are not needed to express equality relations, the second ensures that the mechanics of applying either the new inference rule or resolution can easily be placed within the same program. Such an inference rule, *paramodulation*, has been presented, in slightly modified form, by several authors (Morris, 1969; Robinson & Wos, 1969; Sibert, 1969). For the most part, we follow the Robinson and Wos formulation.

Let A, B, etc. be *sets* of literals, and let α, β, γ, be terms (i.e., variables, constants or function terms). In addition to the usual definition of atoms and literals, (atoms and their complements), we will write *equality atoms* in the form $\alpha = \beta$, indicating that the term α is equal to the term β. Substitution, of course, may be applied to terms.

The *paramodulation rule* is as follows:

> *Given clauses* $C1$ *and* $C2 = (\alpha' = \beta', B)$ *or* $C2' = (\beta' = \alpha', B)$, *with no variables in common, then if the following conditions are fulfilled*
>
> *(i)* $C1$ *contains a term* δ
> *(ii)* δ *and* α' *have a most common general instance* α, *where*
>
> $$\alpha = \delta\pi_1; \qquad \pi_1 = (t_j/w_j), \tag{145}$$
> $$= \alpha'\pi_2; \qquad \pi_2 = (s_i/u_i),$$
>
> *with* u_i *and* w_j *variables in* α' *or* δ, *respectively, then form* $C1^* = C1\pi_1$, *and* $C1\#$ *by replacing* δ *by* $\beta'\pi_2$ *for some one occurrence of* α *descended from* δ *in* $C1^*$. *Finally, infer*
>
> $$C3 = (C1\#, B\pi_2). \tag{146}$$

The idea is actually simpler than its statement, and is easily illustrated. In the simplest case B is null; so that the clauses containing equality statements consist of the single atom expressing an equality. Thus, given

$$C1 = (Q(a)), \tag{147}$$
$$C2 = (a = b)$$

we can infer

$$C3 = (Q(b)). \tag{148}$$

At only a slightly more complex level, if

$$C1 = Q(x), \tag{149}$$

$$C2 = (a = b).$$

The substitution $\pi = (a/x)$ gives us

$$C1^* = (Q(a)), \tag{150}$$

$$C3\ \ = (Q(b)).$$

In a single application of paramodulation the substitution $\alpha = \beta\pi_2$ is applied only once to $C1^*$. Thus if we have

$$C1 = (Q(x), P(x)), \tag{151}$$

$$C2 = (a = b),$$

a single application of the paramodulation rule with $\pi_1 = (a/x)$ can produce first

$$C1^* = (Q(a), P(a)), \tag{152}$$

and then either

$$C3 = (Q(a), P(b)) \tag{153}$$

or

$$C3 = (Q(b), P(a)). \tag{154}$$

A second application of paramodulation is required to produce

$$C4 = (Q(b), P(b)). \tag{155}$$

In more complex cases paramodulation is applied with **B** not null. The next example is taken from the logic of fairy tales. We will prove that the parentage of an alleged royal female child may be ascertained. For a more mathematical example, see Robinson and Wos (1969, p. 140). Our example, although perhaps whimsical, does require the use of equalities to amplify the original clauses of **S**. Table 12-3 states the definitions and initial clauses.

By applying the technique of the previous section, the existential quantifier can be removed from $C1$ and $C2$, thus using f_i for Skolem functions,

$$C1\quad (M(f_1))\qquad \text{``}f_1 \text{ is a man''} \tag{156}$$

$$C2\quad (7M(f_2))\qquad \text{``}f_2 \text{ is a woman''}$$

The universal quantifiers of $C3$ and $C4$ may be dropped. By resolution of $C1$ and $C3$, and then $C2$ and $C4$, we obtain

$$C7\quad (f_1 = k,\ C(f_1))\qquad \text{``}f_1 \text{ is king or commoner''} \tag{157}$$

$$C8\quad (f_2 = q,\ C(f_2))\qquad \text{``}f_2 \text{ is queen or commoner''}$$

TABLE 12-3
Definitions and Clauses for Paramodulation Example

Definitions

x, y, z	variables ranging over the set of persons.
$M(x)$	x is a man
$C(x)$	x is a commoner
$D(x)$	x is capable of detecting a pea placed under twenty featherbeds
$x = k$	person x is the king
$x = q$	person x is the queen
$d(x, y)$	daughter of x and y
$x = p$	x is the princess

Initial clauses and their interpretations

$C1\ (\exists x)\ (M(x))$	"There is a man"
$C2\ (\exists x)\ (7M(x))$	"There is a woman"
$C3\ (\forall x)\ (x = k,\ 7M(x),\ C(x))$	"If x is a man and not a commoner, he is the king."
$C4\ (\forall y)\ (y = q,\ M(y),\ C(y))$	"If y is a woman and not a commoner, she is queen."
$C5\ (d(k, q) = p)$	"The daughter of the king and queen is the princess."
$C6\ (D(p))$	"The princess can detect the pea."

Next we paramodulate $C7$ into $C5$, thus making a substitution into an equality. This produces

$$C9 \quad (d(f_1, q) = p,\ C(f_1))$$

"The daughter of f_1 and the queen (158)
is princess or f_1 is a commoner"

By paramodulation of $C8$ into $C9$

$$C10 = (d(f_1, f_2) = p,\ C(f_1),\ C(f_2))$$

"The daughter of f_1 and f_2 (159)
is a princess or either f_1 or
f_2 are commoners"

Finally, paramodulation of $C10$ into $C6$ produces

$$C11 = (D(d(f_1, f_2)),\ C(f_1),\ C(f_2))$$

"The daughter of f_1 and f_2 can (160)
detect the pea or either f_1 or f_2
are commoners,"

which is the desired test of legitimacy of royal descent.

12.9 Problems and Future Development

A great deal of progress has been made in the automatic theorem proving field. Despite this, resolution-based theorem proving programs tend to generate too many clauses and to try too many fruitless paths. It is easy to find problems that exhaust both computer memory and the time available on present currently conceivable machines. This fact has lead some authors to advocate the use of methods special to a problem area (Hodes, 1970) or the use of more restrictive, although incomplete, inference rules (Bledsoe, Boyer, & Henneman, 1972). The latter approach resembles a return to the earlier incomplete techniques found in FDS, GPS and similar programs. A third alternative has been outlined by Robinson (1969, 1970, 1971), the development of a higher order calculus which can deal with complex relationships more directly than can the often clumsy notation limited to conjunctions of disjunctions. From the programming point of view this changes the problem from one of doing simple operations on many statements to doing complex operations on a few. A closely related approach by Pietrzykowski (1973) has extended a resolution of sorts to the λ calculus, thus allowing variable function and predicate names.

   A drastically different, nonmathematical method has also been suggested. A man could be used to provide "sophisticated" guidance to a theorem-proving machine. The reasoning behind this is that typically automatic theorem provers fail because they expend too much effort pursuing certain approaches long after it would have "become obvious" to a man that a proof is not in sight. It is asserted from time to time that people are good at sensing a fruitful approach, but fall down in the mechanics of applying inference rules at each step. If this is true, the man–machine combination should provide the famous system in which the whole is greater than the sum of its parts. A number of research projects have tried to capitalize on this hope, but without great success. (Allen & Luckham, 1970; Guard, Oglesby, Bennett, & Settle, 1969; Green, 1970; Stickel, 1971). Such projects move us out of the field of artificial intelligence into the even vaguer field of man–machine intelligence. There appear to be three questions that those advocating man–machine systems must answer. It is not at all clear whether, or in what circumstances, man indeed does have the capacity to sense that a certain line of reasoning will be fruitful.[11] Guard *et al.* (1969), who probably have done the most extensive work in the field, remark that observing an automated theorem prover at work is like having a window into the mind of a powerful but very inhuman mathematician. This point can also be illustrated by glancing at the (undeniably correct) proofs produced by a theorem-proving program. To build a man–machine system, then, one must have a language in which the two system components can communicate. We doubt that any common computing language now known is satisfactory, although Planner and QA4 are interesting alternatives. Finally, our own limited personal experience indicates to us that the human engineering aspect of the interaction are going to be quite important. For instance, the sheer amount of noise produced by a teletype is

---

[11] Arguments that man is indeed insightful are generally "proven" by citing anecdotes about mathematical discoveries achieved by very gifted individuals. We acknowledge that Gauss, Liebniz, von Neumann, and Einstein had the ability to get to the heart of a problem, but retain some skepticism as to whether the average mathematician will produce similar insights when he is given access to a powerful enough computer system.

a major distraction when one is working on a difficult theorem-proving problem. Similarly, the psychomotor concentration needed to type a message to a computer disturbs one's thinking about the semantics of the message. There is virtually no research on "human factors" in theorem proving or mathematics in general.

Part IV
Comprehension

Chapter XIII

COMPUTER PERCEPTION

13.0   The Problem of Perception

As servants of man computers have decided limitations. The most annoying is that the masters have to speak the language of the servants. People must translate their understanding of chaotic and ambiguous physical situations into precisely organized sequences of input data. Then, adding insult to injury, machine instructions must be written in stilted, unnatural languages such as FORTRAN and ALGOL instead of the easily spoken, ambiguous phrases of English or Russian. The ancient Romans insisted that their Greek slaves speak Latin. We seem to have slipped backward.

What is needed is a more capable machine, one that can understand the physical world with the same freedom of expression people have. There are two aspects to the problem: machine perception and machine comprehension. The boundary between the two is not at all clear. Very roughly, in perception a sentient being organizes the sensations of the physical world into entities, and establishes an internal representation of the external world which depicts the "important" relationships between the recognized entities. In comprehension the internal representation itself is manipulated in order to derive some output message. The actions required to do this may include a comparison of the internal representation of the current world to any number of real or imagined representations of other worlds.

Man learns about the physical world through his five senses: vision, audition, tactile sensation, olfaction, and taste. Vision and audition are by far the most important channels, and only these have been considered seriously as possible input media for machines. Creating a computer with vision and audition capabilities has proven to be very difficult. In neither case does computer perception remotely approach human perception. Vision computer analysis has been restricted either to the classification of photographs, which is really more of a problem in specialized pattern recognition (Rosenfeld, 1969a,b) and will not be pursued here, or to the analysis of very simple scenes, such as those that can be composed by placing children's blocks on a tabletop. The problems this task poses are formidable. Audition has been restricted almost as severely. The facts of our progress are a far cry from those assumed in science fiction movies, in which computers scan jungles or monitor the replacement of parts in a missile.

The reason why computer perception is so limited is quite simple. The retinal image is an ambiguous representation of the physical world. Imagine an observer looking out a window at a rectangular chimney whose face is at an oblique angle to the line of sight (Figure 13-1a). The retinal image on the back of the observer's eyeball contains a pyramidal form "lying on its side," as in Figure 13-1b. The observer processes and correctly interprets the visual signal as an oblique view of a rectangle because he "knows" that in Western European culture chimneys have a characteristically rectangular face. The point is that the visual input must be interpreted in terms of what we know about the world.

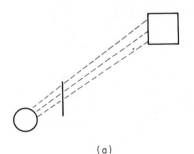

(a)

Fig. 13-1. Ambiguity in viewing a rectangular shape from an angle. The diagram also illustrates how a three-dimensional scene is projected onto a two-dimensional visual plane. (a) Top view, showing visual plane. (b) Visual pattern on plane.

(b)

Similar phenomena can be observed in acoustic signals. Every motor vehicle driver can recognize the sound of an ambulance moving toward (increasing pitch and amplitude) or away (decreasing pitch and amplitude) from him. The acoustic signal is interpreted on the assumption that a constant signal is being generated by a moving vehicle. The identical sound could be produced by a stationary source with a varying signal, but we "know" this is not the case. Again our knowledge of the physical world is used to construct a reasonable interpretation of sensory input. Many psychologists believe that the key feature of all perception is our ability to find some internal world model capable of reconstructing the signal just received. But how are we to program such a process into a computer? Only if we find a way to represent the world in the machine.

13.1   Vision

13.1.0   ON THE IMPOSSIBILITY OF VISION

Imagine a robot whose eye is a cyclopean television camera. The robot gazes at *scenes*, configurations of three-dimensional objects viewed from a particular perspective. The camera, however, transmits to the robot a two-dimensional *pattern* constructed by passing rays from the camera lens to the objects in the scene. Pattern construction, as well as ambiguity, is shown in Figure 13-1. An object in the scene is represented in the pattern by the set of points at which rays from the lens to the object intersect with a plane perpendicular to the line of sight of the camera. The visual perception problem is to reconstruct the scene, given the pattern. In this section we shall present some arguments to the effect that this is an impossible task. Of course, the reader will immediately object that such an argument cannot be correct. After all, the scene analysis problem is faced by humans as well as by robots, and humans solve it. This is true, and it is also true that an implicit goal for every computer vision project is to achieve a perceptual capacity at least close to human perception. No extant robot system comes even close to such performance. Why?

A first approach to scene analysis would be to treat it as a special problem in pattern classification, in which visual patterns are classified as equivalent if they are different views of the same scene. This approach is not fruitful, for reasons that are partly explicable in terms of our earlier discussion of pattern classification problems. The equivalence class defined by a scene viewed from different perspectives is an equivalence class defined over the operation of three-dimensional rotation, and as such is a group theoretic classification of the type Watanabe (1971) has shown to be very difficult to handle by current pattern-classification techniques (see also the discussion in Chapter VII, pages 179–180). More specifically, the analysis of a scene requires that we be able to recognize the objects of which it is composed. Translating to the pattern classification problem, we must be able to recognize the different two-dimensional figures that can be produced by the projection of a three-dimensional object onto the visual plane. In typical scenes, however, there will be more than one object. Therefore the robot must be able to recognize a figure within the context of other figures. Minsky and Papert (1969) have proven that a parallel, linear classifier cannot do this. From these two considerations we must agree that the scene analysis algorithm is going to be a sophisticated one.

The need for a sophisticated algorithm conflicts with another requirement for scene analysis—speed. The sheer amount of data to be handled in computer vision is tremendous. A high quality television camera transmits pictures defined by the grayness value at 1024×1024 different locations. Each point on the picture is typically defined on a three-bit grayness scale. Color vision, of course, would be still more complex. Now suppose the camera transmits 30 pictures per second. (That is just above the rate at which most people would perceive flicker. Fifty frames per second is more typical.) Data input to the computer would be at the rate of $3 \times 30 \times 1024^2$, or about 10^8 bits per second. Detailed real-time processing of data being input at this speed is hard to imagine on any foreseeable computer.

There is still another complication. Despite the amount of data being transmitted, the information in the visual pattern is insufficient to specify the visual scene! This is a point long known, and remarked upon, by psychologists interested in studying visual illusions and perceptual constancies (Day, 1972; Hochberg, 1971). The size constancy phenomenon illustrates the problem. The size of an object's image on the retina varies inversely with the distance of the object from the eye. Still, we have little trouble recognizing that toy cars on a nearby desk are smaller than real cars in a distant parking lot. An even more striking fact is that we can make surprisingly good estimates of an object's size as distance varies. Humans do this by basing their estimate of object size on both retinal image size and perceived distance. When cues for distance are systematically removed the size constancy effect is reduced and may even disappear. It is also possible to reverse the process; the retinal image of an object of known size can serve as a cue to its distance. Such facts are everyday knowledge. Consider, though, what they mean for robot perception. Perception of complex visual scenes is of necessity a process of probabilistic inference based both upon the information present in the visual pattern and the perceiver's knowledge of the likely properties of the visual scene. This means that perception not only poses a sophisticated data processing problem, it also poses an information retrieval problem. How are the necessary computations to take place given the very high rate of data input?

Now obviously vision is possible. One of the reasons that this is so is that the visual pattern is highly redundant in both space and time. Given knowledge of the grayness value of one point on the visual pattern, the adjacent points can be predicted, *unless* the point in question is located on or near the contours of an object. Edges are the points which require intensive processing. Furthermore, when the possible objects to be identified are limited, then only very crude boundary information is needed. To illustrate, is Figure 13-2 a picture of a dog, cat, or horse? Obviously, we see it as a cat. The figure was produced by taking a photograph of a cat and approximating the animal's contours by straight lines (Attneave, 1954). There are two things to note about the example. First, the picture is not "obviously" a cat unless you are first told what the choices are. Second, given these

Fig. 13-2.   Attneave's cat.

choices only the crudest sort of information about figure edges is needed to make the identification.

Figure 13-2 is an illustration of redundancy in space. Redundancy in time is even more marked, for the simple reason that we live in a continuous world. So long as the input rate from the camera to the computer is high with respect to movement of objects in the environment, it will be possible to predict most of the visual pattern at time t from knowledge of the pattern at time $t - 1$. Therefore a second way in which we can achieve economics in information processing is by performing detailed analyses of a visual pattern only when it has changed in some important way from the previously seen pattern.

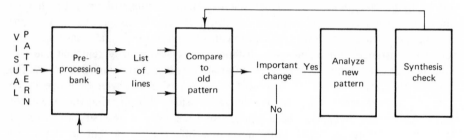

Fig. 13-3.   Schematic of a perceiving machine.

These considerations suggest an outline of a perceiving machine, which is shown schematically in Figure 13-3. The machine consists of four basic mechanisms:

(*i*) An input *preprocessor* receives the visual pattern. The preprocessor consists of a bank of local operators which smooth the input, detect figure edges, and approximate the edges by straight lines. The local operators play the role of feature detectors as defined in our earlier discussion of pattern recognition (see Chapter VIII, page 000). The local operators can perform in parallel without reference to each other, so the total time taken in this step is limited only by the time required of the slowest operator. Since the preprocessor is relatively independent, it can be working on the pattern at time t while the remainder of the mechanism works on previously received patterns.

(*ii*) A *comparator* matches the output of the feature detector against its previous output, to determine if any significant changes have occurred, and, if so, where. The definition of "significant" may be variable, depending upon previous identifications of scenes. If no significant changes have occurred, the comparator merely replaces its record of the last output by the current output of the feature detector.

(*iii*) When a significant change does occur, the comparator interrupts an *analyzer*. The analyzer is a sophisticated, time-consuming device which operates on the output of the feature detectors. The analyzer also has access to a memory containing data specifying the types of figures and objects that are likely to be encountered. It is useful to think of the analyzer as a sort of Bayesian decision maker. Each of the features of the pattern can be regarded as an experiment whose outcome alters the likelihood of a particular scene's being chosen as an explanation for the pattern. The data base provides the necessary probability measures, both for the a priori likelihood of a scene and for the likelihood that a given object will give rise to a particular visual figure. Note this does not mean that the memory need contain explicit data defining the figure obtained by viewing every possible object from every possible direction. All memory need have is an algorithm for computing the figure that would be obtained from a particular object and perspective.

(*iv*) After the analyzer chooses a scene interpretation, a *synthesizer* computes the visual pattern that would result if the analyzer is correct. This pattern is compared to the actual pattern as abstracted from the feature detection process. The analyzer's interpretation is accepted if the match is sufficiently close.

This model is only an outline of a very complex process. To construct a complete model of vision we would have to specify feedback loops between the analyzer and the preprocessor and go into great detail concerning what the comparator should regard as important change in a pattern. We should also have to consider how well the model fits with the known facts about human vision.[1] For our present purposes this is not necessary. The model of Figure 13-3 is sufficient to provide a framework for talking about the specifics of computer vision.

13.1.1   BASIC CONCEPTS IN SCENE ANALYSIS BY COMPUTER

The general principles of scene analysis by computer are readily grasped. These will be presented here. In addition, there are many technical details which are omitted. For further discussion of these, see Duda and Hart (1973).

In its most primitive form, a scene is represented as a matrix, each element of which specifies the gray value of a point in a pattern. Edges in the pattern can be detected by noting sets of connected points (i.e., lines) for which there is a sharp discontinuity in grayness values. Since the data may be noisy, it is often useful to replace "approximately straight" lines derived in this way with straight lines. Such operations can take place on local areas of the pattern. Preprocessing of this sort takes place in virtually every computer vision project of which we are aware. This step will be called *edge processing*.

Following edge processing a pattern is represented in the computer by a list of lines, together with their vertices. Vertices, in turn, are represented both by the lines they connect and by their coordinate locations. For simple line drawings (e.g., particle traces in bubble chambers) no further representation is required. In more

---

[1] Actually, the model is not too bad a description of visual perception (Cornsweet, 1970). This is particularly true if one allows the possibility that the preprocessor is actually a scanning pattern, i.e., only a few features detectors are active at a time but they are moved over the entire visual field. This is consistent with some of the data and speculations concerning the role of eye movements in the recognition and retention of visual patterns (Hochberg, 1971; Loftus, 1972).

TABLE 13-1
List of Lines and Vertices[a]

Line	Vertex, adjoining lines	
Figure (a)		
1	(A)	(B, 2, 3)
2	(B, 1, 3)	(C)
3	(B, 1, 2)	(D)
Figure (b)		
1	(A, 8)	(B, 2)
2	(B, 1)	(C, 3)
3	(C, 2)	(D, 4)
4	(D, 3)	(E, 5)
5	(E, 4)	(F, 6)
6	(F, 5)	(G, 7)
7	(G, 6)	(H, 8)
8	(H, 7)	(A, 1)

[a]Numbers and letters reference Figure
13-3. A separate table of vertex locations
on X and Y coordinates is also required.

complex situations higher-order concepts are needed, since the figures to be
represented may not be easily definable in terms of lines. To demonstrate this,
consider the two "T" figures shown in Figure 13-4. Table 13-1 lists the lines and
vertices for each figure. Although a person will immediately recognize that both the
figures are the same letter, it is clear from the table that a complex algorithm will
be needed to establish a correspondence between the two lists of lines. Intuitively
we suspect that people make the correct recognition by extending lines 7 and 13 of
the "block T" (Figure 13-4b) until they meet and then noting that the relationship
which holds between lines in the "line T" holds between areas I and II in the block T.

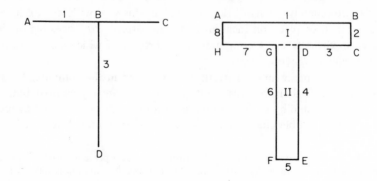

Fig. 13-4. Two block "T" figures. Lines have been assigned numbers and letters,
respectively, for ease of reference to Table 13-1. The dotted line is not represented in Table
13-1. For its use, see text. (Adapted from Clowes, 1971.)

For the moment, we pass by the question of how the decision to extend the lines was made, and note that this example has introduced a new concept, that of *region*. Formally, a region is a closure of a cyclically ordered set of lines having coinciding endpoints. Informally, closures correspond to the visible part of the surfaces of objects in a scene. To see this, imagine an observer facing a table with two children's blocks on it. The situation is shown in cross section in Figures 13-5a and b. Figure 13-5c shows the pattern that the observer sees. To make an inference about the scene, the observer must assign each region to an appropriate object surface and then locate the objects in three-dimensional space.

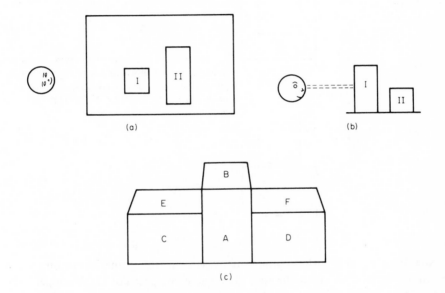

Fig. 13-5. Different views of a simple scene. (a) View from above of observer looking at two blocks on a table. Blocks are labeled for reference. (b) View from side of observer. (c) View as seen by observer. Regions A and B belong to visual surfaces on Block I. Regions C-D and E-F are parts of surfaces on Block II.

Lines, vertices, and regions are properties of two-dimensional visual patterns. They combine to form visual figures. Scenes are composed of objects, whose basic elements are surfaces, edges, and corners. For simplicity, we shall concern ourselves only with objects with plane surfaces unless otherwise noted. In scene analysis the relations between pattern and scene elements are exploited to recover the three-dimensional scene from the two-dimensional pattern. The key to the recovery process is to consider what the shape and orientation with respect to the observer of the objects implies for the observed pattern. Guzman (1968) was the first to use this information in a systematic way. His methods have since been extended by other authors, including Clowes (1971) and Huffman (1971), who prepared catalogues of the types of local patterns that can be produced by different configurations of corners and "in front of–behind" relations.

An edge can be classified as being convex or concave, depending upon whether it joins two surfaces which protrude toward the observer or recede from him. This is illustrated by Figure 13-6, which shows a schematic of two observers looking at a scene in which one block is placed on top of another. The observer at I sees a convex edge at 1 and a concave edge at 2.

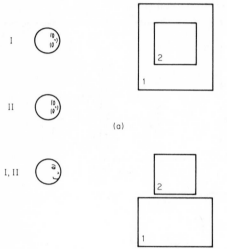

(a)

(b)

Fig. 13-6. Schematic of two observers viewing a scene in which one block rests on top of another. Edge 1 is convex, Edge 2 is concave with respect to Location I. (a) Top view, (b) Side view.

Now consider the pattern produced by viewing this scene from point II, as shown in Figure 13-7. Assuming that the scene is composed of parallelepipeds, the vertex at A can be formed by a corner connecting three surfaces, one of which is hidden. Furthermore, such a vertex implies that the two observable surfaces share a convex edge, with respect to point II, whereas the two edges between the invisible surface and each of the visible ones must be concave (see Figure 13-8a). Still further, if this interpretation of vertex A in Figure 13-7 is correct, then there *must* be a corner which produces a vertex of the form of Figure 13-8b somewhere to the right of and collinear with line 3. (The point need not be on line 3 itself, since line 3 could be broken by the figure produced by an intervening object in the line of sight, as in the example of Figure 13-5.)

Now let us shift our attention to vertex B in Figure 13-7. Such a vertex cannot possibly represent a corner in a scene composed of parallelepipeds. It can be interpreted as evidence for a vertical surface rising in front of the more distant edge of surface A. This interpretation implies a possible vertex, of the type shown in Figure 13-9, at some point along the extension of line 2. The implied vertex may be invisible if there is an intervening vertical surface, as indeed there is in the example.

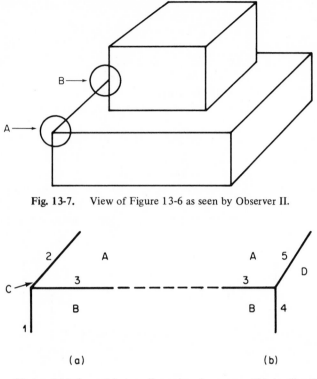

Fig. 13-7.   View of Figure 13-6 as seen by Observer II.

Fig. 13-8.   Vertex (a) is formed in two dimensions by corner. This implies the existence of vertex (b) to the right of (a).

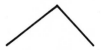

Fig. 13-9.   Vertex formed by the intersection of one visible and two invisible surfaces, with edges concave.

The point to be made is that particular arrangements of the scene dictate the presence of particular vertices in the pattern. Several interpretations may imply the same vertex at a particular point, but unless the visual pattern is truly ambiguous, there will be only one scene interpretation which satisfies all the vertices. A program can identify a few vertices, form a hypothesis about the scene, and check this hypothesis by searching the pattern for the vertices the interpretation implies. This technique is called *analysis by synthesis*. Not only is it a feasible method of computer vision, it is also closely related to principles which have been proposed for human perception (Neisser, 1967). The major weakness of analysis by synthesis is that it presupposes the availability of knowledge about the sort of objects which can occur in a scene. Before discussing just how limiting this is, let us give a detailed example of an analysis-by-synthesis program.

13.1.2   THE INTERPRET SYSTEM

INTERPRET (Falk, 1972) is a computer vision system intended for use in a study of computer-controlled hand–eye coordination. The program is restricted to analysis of visual scenes composed of plane-surfaced blocks of known size and shape. This restriction makes it possible for the program to decompose quite complicated scenes, but limits its generality. The program is also of special interest because it can handle problems that arise when the line representation of a scene has an inaccuracy in it.

In the first stage of INTERPRET the digitized input from the television camera is converted into a line drawing by edge detection. The accuracy of the drawing will depend upon the contrast between light and dark areas of the scene. Poor contrast may cause lines to be erroneously introduced or dropped. An example is shown in Figures 13-10a and b, where the actual scene is one of a block in front of a larger block, but two of the lines in the front block have been lost due to lack of contrast.

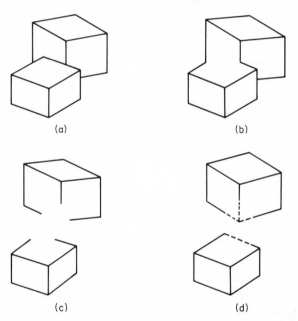

Fig. 13-10.   Successive stages of analysis. (a) Figure with all visible edges shown as lines. (b) Imperfectly drawn figure recovered from input. (c) Different figures obtained by assigning different surfaces (regions) to objects. (d) Completed figures obtained by line proposer.

After the line drawing is produced, INTERPRET examines the vertices, in a manner similar to that described in the last section, to assign edges and surfaces to bodies. This is done by finding all vertices which can be interpreted as the corner of a body, and assigning the corresponding edges and surfaces to that body. At the end of this step INTERPRET will be able to decompose the original visual pattern into figures, each of which arises from a single object in the scene. At this stage, however, the patterns arising from an object will not necessarily be complete, as Figure 13-10c shows. Also, during this stage, INTERPRET will determine the position of some corners in three-dimensional space, and will identify some objects as resting on other objects, by using the simple assumptions that (*a*) no object is suspended in space, and (*b*) if any visual figure has a horizontal boundary which is not above a horizontal boundary, then the associated edge is resting on the table. Identification of the location of corners is particularly useful to INTERPRET, since it "knows" the size of the blocks used in the scene, and thus can compute the expected location of several corners as soon as the block type and location of one corner are identified.

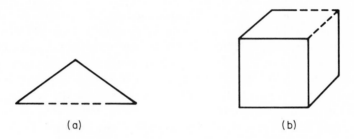

(a)   (b)

Fig. 13-11.   Examples of simple line completion.

The next step is to identify the bodies in the scene. First some fairly obvious methods are attempted to complete lines. These include joining collinear lines and adding corners for intersecting lines, as illustrated in Figure 13-11. Finally, the visual patterns of individual figures located in the picture are compared to stored representations of patterns obtained from known bodies viewed from different perspectives.[2] The best match is accepted. INTERPRET now knows what the bodies in the scene are and where they are located. As a check, the program computes the (line drawing) visual pattern which would be obtained on the assumption that the scene and perspective have been correctly identified. This pattern is compared to the input pattern and the interpretation is accepted if there are no major discrepancies.

INTERPRET and other similar programs are capable of correctly analyzing quite complicated arrays of blocks. INTERPRET itself is also robust, in the sense that it can correct for missing lines and edges in its input data. This is very important in practice, since reduced contrast will markedly diminish the accuracy of a television picture of a scene. So the basic input to the program may be faulty. The defects of the INTERPRET approach are all traceable to the fact that the program can only

---

[2] We stress again that this does not require that INTERPRET prestore all possible representations. All that must be stored is a canonical representation (e.g. a three dimensional description and an algorithm for computing the pattern obtained from any perspective. There is some interesting evidence that this is how humans are able to recognize three dimensional shapes (Shepard & Metzler, 1970).

deal with a specialized world. Falk reports that a large, complex program is needed to deal with scenes of blocks. If this is so, how can we ever expect to deal with worlds which require orders of magnitude more knowledge before they can be predicted? The problem is not simply that more forms are required, but that the shapes of basic forms in the real world are much more complex than those studied to date. For example, inclusion of figures with curved surfaces would greatly complicate the analysis, yet humans live in a world replete with such objects.

INTERPRET and the other computer vision projects reported to date are, in many ways, attempts to replicate human vision on a computer. While this is a laudable goal it may be too ambitious. The problem is not that the visual system of a human is beyond duplication in our technology, but that the memory system of a human may be. It has been suggested that human memory consists of a very large store of elements which become active when they observe their own replication in the current input (Hunt, 1973; John, 1972). In view of this sort of memory, human vision can afford a "passive watching" approach in which preprocessed information coming from the eye to the brain is permitted to arouse memories. Because of current computer memory technology, it might be more appropriate for robot builders to attach a computer to an active scanning device which would emit a physical signal and then analyze the returning echo. Perhaps the analogy in biological systems should be the bat's sonar, instead of the human's eye.[3] This approach seems particularly suited to a situation in which the computer is to scan a "visual world" containing only a limited set of interesting target objects.

13.2   Perception of Speech by Computer

13.2.0   THE SPEECH PROBLEM

In its most general form, auditory perception by computer should refer to a system which translates any acoustic signal into a digital code. Obviously the construction of a device to respond to a specific acoustic signal may be a difficult or an easy task, depending on the nature of the signal and the background noise. In any case, such studies are unlikely to be addressed to any general problem, with one exception. This is speech perception. It is clearly possible to extract information from the acoustic speech signal, encode it as a series of pulses or a continuous electrical signal, and transmit sufficient information so that a human receiver can recognize the semantic content of the original utterance. After all, this is what a telephone does, without making any attempt to automate the recognition process. Computer speech perception goes beyond this. The goal is to develop a machine that can identify the lexical components of a message given the acoustic signal. Lexical identification is intended as a preliminary to semantic analysis, a formidable problem in its own right.

---

[3] Of course, the scanning device need not depend on sound. Reflections from a laser beam might be more useful and more suitable to a memory operating at computer speeds.

Why should we want a speech perceiving machine? One answer is that its construction is an interesting scientific challenge. Another, more immediate one, is that people should not have to communicate with a machine in a machine's language. This is a serious problem. Kemeny (1972), among many others, has noted that the principal stumbling block to widespread utilization of computers is the requirement that the computer user adopt a very restrictive, machine-oriented form of communication. A report prepared for the Defense Research Projects Agency, Department of Defense, identified a number of more specific situations in which a speech perceiving machine would be useful (Newell *et al.*, 1972). Among these projects were the construction of data management systems which could be queried by computer, voice query of the status of a large computer system, data acquisition, and machine controlled instruction in the use of a computer or other complex piece of machinery. If anything, this list is likely to strike one as mundane, for it was intended as a list of reasonable, not ultimate, goals. More glamorous tasks can be imagined for the not too distant future. For example, an earthbound explorer might want to move a remote-controlled vehicle about the lunar surface without going through the annoying intermediary of a teletype. Naturally, modern science fiction assumes that still more striking examples of voice input will soon be an everyday occurrence.[4]

The Department of Defense report distinguished carefully the capabilities required for the different applications. Many interesting applications can be realized on a system capable of recognizing a few key words spoken in restricted contexts. For reporting stock prices a vocabulary of perhaps 500 words (open, close, Standard Oil, volume, etc.) would probably suffice. In other situations limited vocabularies can be combined into simple sentences constructed from the grammar of a formal language. Systems that do this exist, and make possible voice control of a robot hand which moves blocks on a table (Vicens, 1969) and dictation of a simple program directly to a computer (Strasbourger, 1972b). The most interesting class of tasks requires that the user be able to specify commands in some nontrivial approximation of a natural language. Newell *et al.* felt that this task is practical only in a rather limited semantic context, such as vocal specification of moves in a chess game. In such a situation semantics can be used to support other levels of analysis; given a particular board position only a relatively few speakable commands will be sensible.

13.2.1 THE SPEECH SIGNAL

Before we can discuss computer perception of speech in any detail, some consideration of the speech signal itself is in order. Speech sounds are produced by passage of air through the vocal tract, a complex passageway including the throat,

---

[4] The film *Colossus: The Forbin Project*, set in the late twentieth century, assumed speech perception, although one of the characters does caution that the computer's comprehension of a statement is apt to be quite literal. The film *2001, A Space Odyssey* depicted vastly more complicated input devices as being available on business machines as well as sophisticated scientific systems.

mouth, and nasal cavity. We are little concerned with the detailed anatomy[5]; all we need to remember is that the tract is a tube of variable cross section with a number of independently moveable obstructions in it, including the tongue, lips, and vocal cords. Sound is produced when air is forced through the tube. The air pressure itself can be varied precisely, and the different obstructing bits of anatomy can be moved quickly. The result is the awesome collection of grunts, clicks, whistles, oohs, and aaahs of which humans are capable. Any particular language will select roughly 40 or 50 categories of these sounds as speech sounds, or *phonemes*. Meaning bearing units, or *morphemes*, are constructed from the phonemes but, as we shall show, not in a simple manner.

A given speech sound is produced by a specific sequence of muscle movements in the vocal tract. Very generally, two broad classes of speech sounds can be distinguished, the vowels and the consonants. Vowel sounds are produced by relatively long (more than 35 msec) movements of air through the vocal tract, while the tract is in a stable configuration. Vowels are distinguished from each other by the positioning of the tongue and the extent of constriction of the vocal tract while this configuration is maintained. For example, contrast the vowel sounds in *eve* and *at*, reflecting a combination of tongue front with high or low constriction, to the vowel sounds of *boot* and *father*, in which the tongue is held back, with either high or low constriction. The consonants are sharper sounds, produced by sequences of movements in which the configuration of the tract is changed during production of a sound. For each consonant sound there is a precise course of events, such as the release of air in the first letters of *pet* and *top*. Maintenance of this sequence is crucial to the correct production of the consonant. In some cases parts of the tract are completely closed, as in the "z" of *zebra*. Chomsky and Halle (1968) distinguished 12 "present or absent" features that could be used to classify the sounds used to produce general American English dialect. Each of these had implications for the distribution of energy in the acoustic signal. Halle and Stevens (1972) have recently revised this list, but in the main it is a good account of the muscular movements involved in production of the articulatory units of speech.

Obviously the listener analyzes a received acoustic signal, and not the muscle movements that produced it. The acoustic signal is a waveform, varying sound pressure over time. The wave can be analyzed to determine the intensity of the sound at each frequency. Research on speech transmission has shown that there is sufficient information in the ranges from 300 to 4000 Hz to recover the speech signal (Busignies, 1972). There is also considerable energy in the lower frequencies, but this is associated with the permanent characteristics of the vocal cord, and serves to identify the speaker's physical characteristics, such as age and sex. A compilation of the energy level in different frequency bands over some period of time is called the *spectrum* of the waveform over that period. The time over which the spectrum is computed will be called the *window*. In the analysis of speech sounds a "burst" of energy within a particular frequency band over a continuous

---

[5] For detailed discussion at a non-technical level, see Dale (1972).

time interval is called a *formant*. By convention, the formants in an utterance are labeled from the lowest frequency formant (F0) to the highest (Thurlow, 1971). As the vocal cord takes on differing shapes during the production of a phoneme, a characteristic "signature" of formants will be sufficient to identify a phoneme spoken *in isolation*. An example is shown in Figure 13-12, which is an idealized pattern of the energy distribution over time during the production of the syllables *ba* and *ma*.

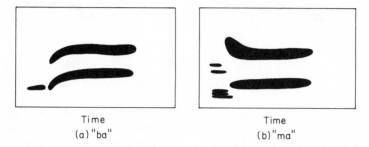

Time
(a) "ba"

Time
(b) "ma"

Fig. 13-12. Idealized sound spectrograms. Dark areas indicate intensity of concentration.

With this information in hand, we are ready to consider a simple (and erroneous) model of speech perception. In this model a machine is built to compute the sound spectrum of a speech signal over some time, identify the formants, and from them the phonemes of a known language. The phonemes are then used to identify the morphemes. We will refer to this as the *cipher model* since all it does is to translate from an acoustic cipher to a phonetic one, on the assumption that there is a one-to-one transformation between the two codes. We admit the possibility of random noise in the speech signal, but this would pose only a minor pattern-recognition problem.

Unfortunately the cipher model must be rejected. Although phonemes obviously are represented acoustically, the coding is more complex than the substitution of specific sound waves for specific muscle movements. This has been shown clearly by Liberman and his associates at the Haskins Laboratories (Liberman, 1970; Liberman, Cooper, Shankweiler, & Studdert-Kennedy, 1967). Consider the acoustic signal of the phoneme /d/, which appears in virtually every language. Figure 13-13 shows two idealized speech spectrograms, one for the syllable *da* and one for *di*, both containing /d/. One can see at a glance that the second formant differs markedly in the two cases. Since the first 50 msec of the speech pattern are responsible for recognizing that the first letter is /d/, and not, say, /b/, this is clearly important. One's interpretation of the second formant depends upon the context in which it appears. This is not an isolated example. It is generally true that the spectrum of a phoneme will be strongly influenced by the context in which the phoneme appears. There are two straightforward reasons why this should be so. Let us assume, as Liberman and his associates do, that there is an invariance between the phoneme the speaker intends to produce and the motor nerve signals that are transmitted

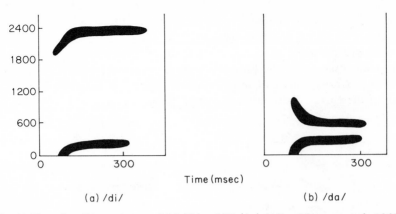

Fig. 13-13.   Sound spectrogram of (a) /di/ and (b) /da/. (After Liberman *et al.*, 1967.)

from the brain to the musculature of the vocal tract. The actual physical movements that take place in the tract, which determine the sound produced, will depend upon the configuration of the vocal tract before the neural signal is received. Equally important, not all muscle groups involved in the production of a particular sound respond with equal rapidity. Therefore the actions of the muscle groups involved in the production of sequentially commanded phonemes may actually take place partly in parallel. Since the sound produced is a product of the entire vocal tract, the acoustic signal associated with a specific phoneme depends on the phonemes produced both before and after the phoneme in question. To use computing terms, we are dealing with a highly asynchronous mechanism without a clearly defined cycle. When this is realized, the apparent anomaly of Figure 13-13 is no longer so puzzling.

What is puzzling is how perception can possibly occur. A number of authors have argued that the analysis-by-synthesis model applies to speech as well as vision (Halle & Stevens, 1972; Liberman, 1970). By this they mean that the acoustic cues are examined and, by a very complex decoding process, the listener discovers a sequence of muscular commands that could have produced the acoustic signal. At first thought this might seem a monumental task, but a closer examination suggests that it is not. Assume a listener who is familiar with the language being spoken. Such a person will know that only those phonetic productions need be considered which are permitted by syntactical, semantic, and phonetic conventions of the language. As in the case of vision, the listener is a receiver who can decode ambiguous messages by knowing that only some messages are likely, rather than having to decode to consider all possible alternatives.

This is not the place to review the evidence for or against the analysis-by-synthesis model as an explanation for human perception. As a proposal for machine perception, however, the model has some major defects. If it were to be adopted literally it would be necessary to include a speech producing machine, or at least a mathematical model of one, as a subcomponent of the speech perceiving machine. This is possible, but not trivial. On the other hand, any scheme for computer perception will have to come to grips with the complex coding considerations which forced psychoacousticians and psycholinguists to the analysis-by-synthesis model in the first place.

13.2.2 RECOGNITION OF ISOLATED WORDS

We do not want to make the problem harder than it need be. The discouraging remarks about the difficulty of recovering phonetic information from acoustic information apply to situations in which many speakers are speaking in many contexts. Suppose that instead the problem is to recognize words chosen from a limited set of words, spoken by a speaker whose vocal characteristics are known to the system. If there are k words permissible, with k reasonably small, it is feasible to store prototypical acoustic patterns for each word and speaker. In fact, several patterns can be stored for a single word, so long as no two words give rise to nearly identical patterns. The recognition problem is then reduced to a conceptually simple pattern classification problem. Both the prototype patterns and the input are described by detecting features in the acoustic waveform which are (usually) sufficient to identify the word being spoken. The speech recognition problem in this limited case reduces to a problem of feature detection. Can we find features which are computationally easy to abstract from the acoustic signal and informationally sufficient to define distinct prototypes for different words? It might be necessary to have several levels of analysis, perhaps using prototype phonemes to identify acoustic signals and then prototype words to identify strings of phonemes. There is no need to match a human-oriented perceptual hierarchy. We shall call this method the *cipher method*, since it is based on a direct mapping of acoustic features into phonemes, and then into words. In theory, the phoneme stage could be by-passed if we could find a way to map from the acoustic signal directly into the words of a dictionary, but in practice this does not seem possible. There are two broad classes of ciphers which have been used, based on *frequency-band filtering* and *Fourier analysis*.

In frequency-band filtering the acoustic signal is broken into bands of varying width and the energy distribution within each band calculated for m time intervals (windows) of t msec each. In most cases the window interval is from 10 to 20 msec, i.e., considerably less than the time required for the production of a phoneme. Thus the parameters describing a given window should be considered subphonemic, rather than phonemic features. Somewhat surprisingly, the method is indifferent to the fineness of the windowing process, and to the choice of parameters to describe the spectrum within a window. Vicens (1969) obtained good recognition by counting zero crossings and peak amplitudes over 10-msec windows in each of six frequency bands. Reddy (1970) notes that very much better recognition is *not* obtained using as many as 40 frequency bands, and suggests that practically any sensible and reliable signal summarization technique will work.

Following the parametrization stage, the speech signal will be represented by an $n \times m \times p$ array, where n is the number of frequency bands, m is the number of windows observed and p the number of parameters extracted from a band. This array is examined for patterns of parameter variations over time which are characteristic of the production of particular phonemes. The prototype phonemic patterns used at this stage typically ought to have been spoken by the person whose speech is to be recognized, for there is a good deal of individual variation in phoneme production.[6] At the least, the person producing the prototypes should be of the same sex and speak the same dialect as the person whose voice is to be recognized. In making the comparison the speech signal must be segmented into "probable phonemes" prior to beginning the match against prototypes. The easiest, and crudest, methods are to use fixed time intervals (Vicens, 1969) or to search for acoustic information indicating pauses, and then divide the data between pauses into equal time intervals (Herscher & Cox, 1972). Again the choice of a specific procedure does not seem to make too much difference. In a few systems this step is by-passed completely. At the final step a match is made between the analyzed and recoded utterances and the prototypic word patterns known to the system. The closest match is chosen as the word spoken.

Despite its limited generality, the cipher method works very well for recognition of isolated words. A number of authors have reported from 80 to 90% correct recognition of isolated words, using vocabularies of about 50 words and, in some cases, multiple speakers. Using more limited vocabularies (10–20 words) accuracies as high as 98% have been reported, even with mixed male and female speakers (Herscher & Cox, 1972). A system constructed by Vicens and Reddy is reported to have obtained 90% correct recognition with a single speaker and a vocabulary of 500 words (Newell *et al.*, 1972).

An alternative to the extraction of simple parameters from a number of frequency bands is to conduct a mathematical analysis of the entire sound signal. There are a number of ways that this can be done, most of which are closely related to the concept of Fourier analysis. The mathematics behind this are involved and only an intuitive presentation will be given. The speech signal is initially represented as a variation in amplitude over time, i.e., as a waveform. The Fourier transformation of a waveform converts this information (the representation in the *time domain*) into an equivalent representation showing amplitude as a function of the frequency and phase angle of the pure sine wave components required to recreate the original waveform (representation in the *frequency domain*). In some studies this representation has been used directly to compare speech to be recognized against prototypic speech. A more useful technique involves a further transformation, called *cepstrum analysis*. (Nakano, Ichikawa, & Nakato, 1972; Strasbourger, 1972a, b). In cepstrum analysis the Fourier transform of the speech signal is separated into high- and low-frequency components. The high-frequency components are generally associated with movements of the vocal tract, while the lower order (less than 400 Hz) components are produced by stable characteristics of the tract. Thus the components below 400 Hz can be regarded as being

---

[6] Individuals differ in their phonetic construct ion of words. Regional dialects offer the clearest examples, e.g., *Car* is pronounced *kar* in the Northwest and *kah* in New England.

characteristic of the speaker's age, sex, and other physical characteristics, while the higher-order components of the speech signal indicate the muscle movements being made as the speaker says something. The product of cepstrum analysis is a time varying signal whose form, then, reflects formant production. This signal can be compared to prototype signals of different phonemes, produced by different speakers if necessary, in order to identify the sounds in the utterance. The question of individual idiosyncrasy is not entirely avoided, since different speakers will use different muscle movements to say the same word.

The fact that the acoustic signature of a phoneme is context specific might lead one to believe that the methods just described have no implication for the recognition of continuous speech. This is not quite true. Although acoustic signals are, *in general*, ambiguous with respect to the phoneme which produced them, there are many situations in which the acoustic signal does uniquely identify a phoneme. The situation is analagous to that in scene analysis, where some vertices have only one three-dimensional interpretation, while other vertices have several possible explanations. Now suppose further that all the utterances to be received by a speech perception system must be spoken in a rigorously defined language with a small lexicon and simple grammar. There will often be sufficient information in the acoustic signal to rule out all but one of the permissible utterances.

The idea of combining acoustic and syntactical knowledge to determine a most probable message has been adopted by a number of investigators, following the lead of Vicens and Reddy (Vicens, 1969; see also the discussion by Newell *et al.*, 1973, Chap. 4), who built an "ear" for the Stanford University hand–eye–ear coordination project (McCarthy, Earnest, Peddy, & Vicens, 1968), in which a computercontrolled hand receives instructions to move blocks on a table. As already noted, the Vicens–Reddy system used a hierarchical cipher scheme. The utterances received by the system, however, had to be legitimate strings in a language for block manipulation, i.e., in a language for programming the robot's hand. The language used can be defined by specifying the substitutions allowed in generating a sentence in a language containing only a finite set of sentences. The substitution rules used are diagrammed in Figure 13-14. By examining the figure one can readily see that by recognizing a few unambiguous acoustic cues at strategic points, it is possible to infer what the utterance must have been. The inference process can be (and was) considerably aided by a judicious choice of lexicon, so that no two words which are syntactically interchangeable are acoustically similar. Although this is cheating, if your goal is to mimic natural language, it is a very practical artifice if your goal is to produce a system capable of accepting a limited set of nontrivial utterances. In justification of the artifice, it can also be argued that natural language selects words using the same principle, and that this selection fails confusions are likely to result.

What sort of performance can be expected from a system using hierarchical decoding ciphers, combined with syntactic analysis? The results depend upon whether or not the person whose speech is being recognized is also the person from whose speech the prototype samples were obtained. Let us call the former person the *tester*, the latter the *trainer*. If the tester and trainer are identical, the

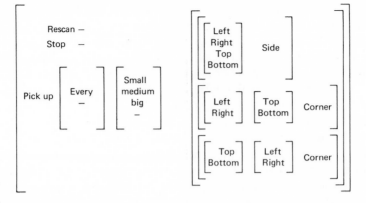

Fig. 13-14. Schematic of language in Vicens-Reddy system. "−" means word or blank is to be ignored. Bracket indicates choice. Seventy-four sentences can be generated. (After Strasbourger, 1972b.)

Vicens–Reddy system will make a semantically correct interpretation of about 85% of the tester's utterances. If the tester and trainer are distinct individuals of the same sex, the recogition rate drops to approximately 60%. An interesting contrast to these figures is provided in a study by Strasbourger (1972b), who combined the cepstrum method of acoustic analysis with a syntax correction method. Strasbourger's language, SPOCOL, however, was considerably richer than the Vicens-Reddy block manipulation language. SPOCOL is a spoken language for computer programming having roughly the same power as the elementary BASIC language. Strasbourger found that 18 of 24 statements could be correctly recognized by the system using the same trainer and tester. If the trainer and tester differed, from 12 to 14 of the 24 statements were recognized. Since the Fourier-transformation technique used by Strasbourger effectively eliminates variations in the acoustic signal due to a speaker's physical characteristics, the drop in accuracy with different speakers is probably due to differences in the motor movements different individuals use to produce phonemes. It is of interest to note that although Strasbourger and Vicens and Reddy used quite different acoustic analytic techniques, and considerably different languages, their two systems were roughly equal in accuracy.

13.2.3 HEARSAY[7]

The limited potential of isolated word recognition systems is widely recognized, and a number of different solutions have been proposed. All of these rely on some sort of interchange between phonetic, syntactical, and semantic analyses of speech utterances. The concepts involved are well illustrated by the HEARSAY system

---

[7] I would like to acknowledge the excellent description of the HEARSAY system provided me by Dr. Raj Reddy.

(Reddy, Erman, & Neely, 1973) now under development at the Carnegie–Mellon University. Unlike the other programs that have been described, HEARSAY is not organized into a hierarchy of ciphers. Not only is there a constant interchange between coding levels, the system can also tolerate errors at one level if they can be compensated for at another.

HEARSAY's organization is best thought of as a set of parallel processors which place information in a central bulletin board. A schematic diagram is shown in Figure 13-15. The first step is a straightforward parametrization of the acoustic signal. The number of zero crossings and the maximum sound pressure observed in five frequency bands, plus an unfiltered band from 200 to 6400 Hz, are recorded every 10 msec. The 10-msec windows are then identified as "subphonemic units," based upon prototype sounds observed from analysis of records produced by a trainer speaking known phonemes. The result of this stage is a conversion of the 10-msec intervals from a sequence of parameter values to a sequence of named acoustic features. The 10-msec intervals are then grouped into larger units, of approximately the length of a phoneme, by lumping together sequences of similarly named subphonemic units, and by breaking strings of named intervals at points at which changes from voiced to nonvoiced or fricated to nonfricated sounds can be distinguished. At this point the acoustic signal will have been translated into an *approximately* correct string of phoneme-like units. Exact correctness cannot be guaranteed because of the inherent unreliability of the speech signal, even when a speaker is trying to mimic himself, and because of the change of the acoustic characteristics of a phoneme due to its context. An important point, though, is that this analysis does break the acoustic signal into word segments with high reliability. To this point, then, HEARSAY is very similar to the earlier work of Vicens and Reddy.

The parallel analyses can now begin. As Figure 13-15 shows, parallel analysis is

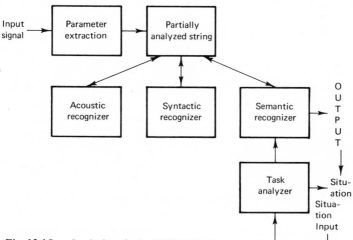

Fig. 13-15.   Logical analysis of HEARSAY.

conducted by three recognizers, each operating in philosophically the same manner. Hypotheses about the utterance being analyzed are generated by combining the partially analyzed signal with special knowledge available to a particular recognizer, resulting in a "suggested interpretation." The suggested interpretation from one recognizer is then forwarded to the other recognizers, where it is evaluated in the light of the special knowledge available to the non-proposing recognizers. Let us consider each of the recognizers in turn:

The *acoustic recognizer* operates on words. It has access to acoustic, phono-logical, and vocabulary information. Acoustic knowledge is contained in a record of the expected subphonemic features of a phoneme spoken in isolation. Phonological knowledge is defined as information about the ways in which certain contexts can modify a phoneme's acoustic signature, e.g., the *di–da* distinction discussed previously. The vocabulary information specifies the sequences of features which represent variants of permissible words.

The *syntactic recognizer* operates at the phrase level. Syntactic knowledge is stored in what Reddy *et al.* refer to as "antiproductions," frames in which particular words or clauses can appear. When one or two words are recognized, the syntactic analyzer is able to propose syntactic hypotheses about the surrounding words. Similarly, the syntactic recognizer can determine whether a proposed word definition would lead to a syntactic error in a partly analyzed phrase. This method of recognition will work well for context-free languages and so, whereas it does not permit us to deal with all natural language, it certainly allows us to deal with an interesting subset of languages.

The *semantic recognizer* is an addition beyond mechanisms studied in previous research. It operates at the level of a complete utterance. The job of the semantic recognizer is (*a*) to propose utterances which would be sensible given the situation, and (*b*) to evaluate the reasonableness of a proposed utterance. To do this the recognizer must control a situation specific (but not speech specific) *task analysis* program that is capable of deciding what is, and what is not, sensible given the external world. The task Reddy *et al.* have considered is chess. For the overall system, the task is to receive spoken instructions in a chess game between a computer and a person. The task analysis program used is a program for chess playing (Gillogly, 1972) which proposes and evaluates moves for any board situation. As recognition of the utterance proceeds, the chess playing program, through the semantic recognizer, indicates which words should be considered likely at certain points in an utterance. In addition, the task analysis program can be used to determine if a certain word or phrase proposed by the acoustic or syntactic analyzers leads to a reasonable move.

Once the parameterization process has been completed, all three recognizers in HEARSAY work in parallel on utterance evaluation, seizing upon special cues to propose or verify an hypothesis, until finally the entire utterance has been proposed and accepted as reasonable. It will take a great deal of research before this model of speech perception can be evaluated in any definitive way. The importance of HEARSAY, however, is not so much as an advance in technology as in its role in advancing our conceptualization of speech processing. HEARSAY is a clear abandonment of the hierarchically oriented acoustic-phonetic-syntactic-semantic model of speech analysis. This is generally recognized as being necessary. In addition, HEARSAY does not rely on analysis by synthesis. Therefore it is an attractive model for mechanical speech perception, even though it may not be an adequate simulation of how humans perceive speech. This is not a damning remark, since simulation is not the goal of artificial intelligence research. Furthermore, the evidence for the analysis by synthesis model is not overwhelmingly strong, and it is by no means universally accepted as the correct model of speech reception.[8] At the least, analysis by hypothesis should be seriously considered by psychologists and linguists.

[8] Lenneberg (1969) has pointed out that children raised in grossly speech defective environments, and thus having little cause to produce speech, readily learn to comprehend it. This is difficult to reconcile with a theory that makes production capacity vital to comprehension.

Chapter XIV

QUESTION ANSWERING

14.0   The Problem

The preceding chapter was concerned with the creation of a communication link to a computer. Suppose that the link had been established, how would it be used? Somewhat naively, computers ought to be of great help in answering questions. Certainly the physical capacity for storing and retrieving data in a computer system is awesome. Nevertheless, interrogating a computer is apt to be a frustrating experience. Why?

Computers and people can store facts. People, however, also store rather subtle implications of facts. If you say that you are going on a trip, but are nearly out of gasoline, then a reasonable person will store in his memory the inferred statement that you will drive by a gasoline station. Only a very few computer programs for simulating thought do this. The question of how general impressions are formed is even subtler. If you are told that a given United States senator has voted against seven foreign aid bills and three civil rights measures, and that he has bitterly opposed the appointment of a former labor lawyer to the Supreme Court, then you are likely to form an impression of the senator in question. This impression can be used to make later inferences about his behavior on new issues. These observations are hardly surprising, "everyone does it." But what computer programmable rules are being activated?

By way of contrast, let us consider a typical computerized information system. These can usually be thought of as large, efficient filing cabinets. They can answer any question if the specific answer is in the data bank *and* marked as an answer to that question. Few systems will retrieve the answer to related questions. Also, in computer systems knowledge is amazingly compartmentalized. If a credit bureau checks to see whether a man is employed or unemployed they will get only that information; they will not get information about the credit rating of, say, his wife. The man's neighbor might volunteer such information if it appears relevant. A still more interesting situation arrives when we consider facts which imply the need for further inquiry. If a lawyer were asked, "How much do you charge to defend a man accused of homicide?" and "Do you know where I can obtain some strychnine?" he might respond with some questions of his own. Computer systems do not do this.

The problem of responding intelligently to facts is closely tied to language comprehension. Computers will execute exactly the orders that are given them, provided that one sticks to a very formal language and providing that there is no ambiguity whatsoever in the order. A machine that truly comprehends what we are trying to say to it should execute the operations that we want it to do, even though we may have failed to follow all the formalisms of the language in which the machine expected to be addressed. Designing such a machine is probably the hardest of all artificial intelligence problems.

In this chapter and the next we shall examine the problem of getting computers to act in a more intelligent manner. Despite the publicity this topic has received, there is less progress in this than in any other field in artificial intelligence. The reader should be warned—some scientists with excellent credentials in artificial intelligence might disagree not only with the answers we give but even with our questions! However, these same scientists would disagree with each other, so the approach here may be as good as any.

Message comprehension is the first problem to be faced by the intelligent machine. In conventional computing, the human speaker learns to write (program) in a precisely defined formal language. This is the problem! Programming is too hard. There are many thoughts in our natural language which we cannot put in computing terms. To quote one of our students, "Try to define freedom in FORTRAN!" Lest the reader feel that this example is too exotic, we point out that there have been periodic attempts to apply computers as an aid in legal and information retrieval. The "obvious" approach is to use computers to look up documents containing key words either in title or in context in the text. Buchanan and Headrick (1970) point out that this is not the way lawyers use the legal literature. The lawyer bases his argument on analogies to cases and upon specific applications of abstract concepts. Buchanan and Headrick argue that the law will not have really adequate computing aid until computers can be made to do the same thing.

We do not have to rely on futuristic examples to illustrate problems in message comprehension. Consider the following straightforward information-retrieval requests

(*i*) What are the populations of New York, Chicago, St. Louis, and Philadelphia?

(*ii*) What are the populations of New York, Illinois, Missouri, and Pennsylvania?

To a human it is clear that "City of New York" is intended in the first question, and "State of New York" is intended in the second. Establishing the correct reference by analogy to other questions being asked at the same time is a subtle bit of reasoning quite within the capability of people and quite outside that of most information-retrieval systems.

Machine comprehension is deeply involved with machine analysis of natural language. Since this is a major topic in its own right, we will postpone detailed discussion of linguistic problems until the following chapter. In many specific cases it is possible to avoid the comprehension problem by providing a formal language which contains a few natural language constructs and at the same time is amenable to machine analysis (Thompson, 1966; Dozstert & Thompson, 1971). We will not deal with this approach at great length, as the solutions are usually problem specific. At least until the next chapter, assume that the message comprehension problem has been solved. Two other problems must also be solved.

Data structures for comprehension have been studied a great deal. How should data be organized so that it can be retrieved when it is needed and not retrieved when it is not? Perhaps the greatest advantage man has over machine is in this area. Somehow we are able to retrieve relevant information from long-term memory very quickly, even with imprecise cues. The difficulty of designing a correct data structure for information retrieval is closely related to the system designer's ability to control the questions asked of the data base. A library restricts its users to asking the sorts of questions that can be answered via the index file, and is seriously handicapped by its filing system if its users suddenly insist on retrieving books by the publisher's name. It would be defeated if users asked for books by the author's place of birth. The problem of indexing for data structures in situations in which the form of question can be anticipated is usually dealt with in discussions of information retrieval, a field of study in its own right (c.f. Lefkovitz, 1969). We shall concentrate on some more "exotic" data structures which have been used within the artificial intelligence field, where every attempt is made to avoid restricting the user's questions.

Inference rules must be included in a comprehending computer system. An inference rule is a method of deducing facts which are implied by but not stated in the data base. We previously discussed inference rules in describing theorem proving and problem solving systems. Many of the inference procedures originally developed for problem solving may be applied directly to comprehension problems. In addition, there are other, more specialized inference procedures that can be applied within data retrieval, although they would not produce valid reasoning in general. Recognizing what inference procedures and data are relevant is a vital first step in question answering. If asked the question

Will DDT affect the population level of Ospreys?

a reasonable biologist will use rules of inference involving set inclusion, and implication applied only to the information he has about DDT distribution, the effects of chlorinated hydrocarbons on egg production, and the eating and nesting habits of fishing birds and hawks. He will not attempt deductions based upon facts about ostriches, because such facts "obviously" are not relevant. The inference problem in comprehension is largely one of deciding which facts are "obviously irrelevant." Once the relevant facts are established the deductions required are generally straightforward.

14.1 Data Structures

14.1.0 GENERAL

There is no agreed upon best way to organize data for a comprehending program, nor is there likely to be one. The reasons are pragmatic. Why does anyone want an "intelligent" computing system in the first place? We can see two reasons: to solve a complex information retrieval problem or to demonstrate some algorithm for inference. If the user has a problem to solve, it undoubtedly will involve a large data base, for otherwise there would hardly be any reason to use the computer. Although the user may want his system to be sufficiently flexible to warrant the label "comprehension" he will usually be able to specify some limits on the sort of questions that are going to be asked.[1] Finally the system that he designs will have to run on the equipment that is available to him. The user will naturally adopt data structures that reflect the logic of his data base and the characteristics of his equipment. It is hardly surprising that the resulting system is likely to have only limited generality. In fact, the extent to which a system is useful for the purpose for which it was designed may be inversely related to the extent to which the system design solution is interesting to other people. This is the danger of an application-oriented approach.

The pure research approach suffers from the opposite problem. Here the emphasis is on generality; upon demonstrating that certain algorithms will correctly answer a wide range of questions. Once this has been illustrated there is little interest in conducting the demonstration again, so a large data base is usually not needed. (Most of our illustrations in this chapter will involve very small bases.) Since the data base is small, and since operating efficiency is not crucial, little attention may be paid to data base structuring. Several experimental systems simply accept whatever in-core data technique is provided in the programming language of choice. The resulting program is often an elegant demonstration of a logical point, but is not a practical data-processing tool, and, worse, is not easily modified to be one.

These problems are relative ones. Obviously data-organization methods for comprehension programs do exist. The remainder of this chapter is a discussion of some techniques which have been used to solve representative programs. These programs have been chosen to illustrate techniques rather than being chosen as being the most modern and up-to-date programs that we can imagine. The

---

[1] For example, most applied systems can ignore the lexical ambiguities of English. *Strike* is an unambiguous term to a system designed to deal with baseball statistics or to one designed to deal with labor law. It is only when the program must be prepared to deal with both fields that resolution of the ambiguity is needed.

professional journals of computing contain periodic discussions of the "state of the art."

14.1.1   BASEBALL–A SIMPLE QUESTION-ANSWERING SYSTEM

Shortly after the introduction of the list-processing technique into computer science, a program called BASEBALL was written to illustrate how the new techniques could be used in question answering (Green, Wolf, Chomsky, & Laughrey, 1961; Green, 1963). The program was designed to answer questions about the 1959 American League baseball scores, hence its name. Although the social utility of this application is questionable, it does provide a good vehicle for testing programming concepts that have since proven to have wide application.[2] Messages to the program were phrased in a simple subset of English, with which we shall be little concerned. What is of more interest is the data structure that was used.

BASEBALL's data was organized into a hierarchical system similar to an outline of a composition. Equivalently, the data structure could be graphed as a tree. The highest level of the outline was YEAR (only 1959 data was used, but provision was made for more years in the program), followed, in order of priority, by MONTH and PLACE. After locating a given combination of YEAR, MONTH, and PLACE, a serial list specified game number, day and score.

In outline format the data structure appeared as

YEAR

  MONTH

    PLACE

      (Game Number, Day, (Team, Score) (Team, Score))

      (Game Number, Day, (Team, Score) (Team, Score))

      . . . .

      (Game Number, Day, (Team, Score) (Team, Score))

This form of data structure is clearly not restricted to baseball, and the data-processing routines of BASEBALL were written to manipulate any hierarchical data structure regardless of the interpretation of the various levels and branches.[3]

The operation of the BASEBALL program can be understood by considering two concepts: *the data path* and the *specification list*. A data path is a sequence of branches required to reach a particular game. Thus YEAR = 1959, MONTH =

---

[2] It was once planned to use BASEBALL to answer questions about voting records, but apparently this application was never programmed.

[3] Search processes for tree structures terminating in serial lists have been studied to determine the optimal sequence of branches and lists (Sussenguth, 1963; Stanfel, 1970).

APRIL, PLACE = BOSTON, GAME = 55, locates GAME 55 and, in the process, specifies some things about this game. A unique data path is associated with each game, with the entries on it establishing the attributes of the game, as the example shows. A simple tree-searching algorithm can be used to generate all possible data paths, since the data tree is guaranteed to be finite.

The specification list is a list of characteristics that the data path must have in order to be an admissible answer to a question. For example, the specification list of the question[4]

$$\textit{In what places did the Rex Sox play in July?} \tag{1}$$

is

PLACE = ?
 TEAM = RED SOX
  MONTH = JULY.

Assume that the English-language processor has generated a specification list for a question. The hierarchical data processor accepts the specification list and systematically generates all data paths that match it. A path matches a specification list if

(*i*) an attribute-value pair (e.g., TEAM = BOSTON) is in both the specification list and path, or

(*ii*) an attribute value pair on the specification list has the value "?" (e.g., PLACE = ?), in which case the corresponding value on the data list is listed as a possible value. Note that in example (1) the list of values will be the answer.

(*iii*) if an attribute value pair on a specification list has the value EACH, it is matched by the value of any attribute on the data path. The type of match is not listed.

As described thus far, the process of generating data paths and matching them to a specification list is independent of any knowledge of the baseball application. *Derived* attribute-value pairs may also match, but in this case they are application specific. For example, consider the question

$$\textit{How many games did the home team win in July?} \tag{2}$$

To answer this question the program must find all data paths that identify games for which the value TEAM is identical to the value of PLACE, and for which the TEAM whose name is identical to the PLACE value has a higher score associated with it for that game than does the team whose name is not the same as the PLACE. The routine that derives the appropriate specification list is clearly based on knowledge of the game of baseball.

---

[4] Throughout this and the next chapter examples in English texts will be numbered, in the manner used in numbering equations in previous chapters.

As data paths satisfying specification lists are located, they are summarized on a *found list*. This is itself a tree. For example, the paths that are answers to question (1) can be summarized by

MONTH = JULY
  TEAM = BOSTON
    PLACE = BOSTON, NEW YORK, CHICAGO, ...

The answer to a question is composed by examining the found list. In the case of (1) the answer would be obtained by simply listing PLACE values on the found list. A slightly more complex question

In how many places did the Red Sox play in July?   (3)

would be obtained by counting the PLACE values of the found list.

The question-answering procedure described so far is summarized in Figure 14-1. The English subset analyzer receives the English question, recognizes the type of question which has been asked, and produces the specification list. This part of BASEBALL is, of necessity, application dependent in two ways. Trivially it must have access to a lexicon about baseball. Nontrivially, it must contain routines which map English phrases such as "how many" and "in which" into appropriate

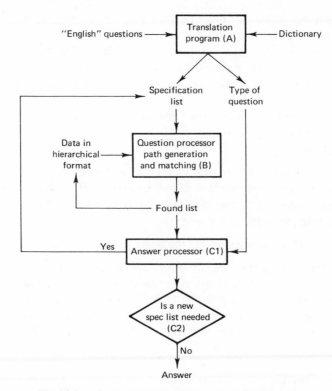

Fig. 14-1.   Steps in question answering in BASEBALL.

specification lists. Thus while Green *et al.* did not limit users to asking index-type questions, as a library does, they did prespecify the sorts of questions that could be asked of the system.

In Step (B), the program generates a found list for the data from the specification list. As has been noted, large parts of Section B are application independent, although specified subroutines may be needed for testing derived attributes. In the final step the answer is generated from the found list (Boxes C1 and C2). Here again the programmer must anticipate the type of questions to be answered and include in the system an appropriate routine for generating found lists for each question type.

As Sections C1 and C2 of Figure 14-1 suggest, BASEBALL is not restricted to questions that can be answered by a single pass through the data. Consider the question[5]

$$\text{How many teams played in 8 places in July?} \tag{4}$$

The initial specification list is

(S1)   TEAM (NUMBER OF) = ?
        PLACE (NUMBER OF) = 8
        MONTH = JULY

The question defined by this specification list cannot be answered directly. Instead, the processor must examine (S1) to generate a new specification list

(S2)   TEAM = ?
        PLACE (NUMBER OF) = 8
        MONTH = JULY

Again (S2) cannot be answered directly, since we need the subsidiary question

(S3)   TEAM = EACH
        PLACE (NUMBER OF) = 8
        MONTH = JULY

(S3) cannot be answered directly either, so it is stored and the question

(S4)   TEAM = EACH
        PLACE = ?
        MONTH = JULY

is generated. (S4) can be answered by the question processor, producing the found list

(S5)   TEAM = BOSTON
        PLACE = NEW YORK, BOSTON, WASHINGTON
        MONTH = JULY
        GAME = GAME NUMBER, etc. etc. etc.

        TEAM = NEW YORK
        PLACE = NEW YORK, BOSTON, etc.

[5] This example is "in the spirit" of BASEBALL, but does not detail the matching process.

Specification (S4) indicates examination of all lists of the form of (S5). By counting place names, the answer to (S3) can then be obtained, which is converted into a list, and is the answer to (S2). The answer to (S1) follows directly.

BASEBALL was apparently not developed beyond the pilot project stage, a common fate for artificial intelligence systems. Indeed, the idea of hierarchical data structure seems to be dropping out of programming for computer comprehension. This is somewhat surprising as hierarchical structures make possible efficient data management, especially if it is necessary to store large amounts of data partially in primary memory and partially on relatively slow, inexpensive storage devices (see Sussenguth, 1963 for details). Hierarchical data structures also lend themselves to implementation by data management techniques compatible with more conventional information management systems (Hunt & Kildall, 1971; Lefkovitz, 1969). Certainly if comprehension programs are going to be used, there will be a time at which practical questions about cost and system compatibility must be asked. Perhaps a wise step in the future would be to go back to the concepts embodied in this relatively old program.

14.1.2   DEACON: Ring Structures and English Approximations

The next example we shall discuss, DEACON (Direct English Access and Control; Craig, Berenzer, Carney, & Loveyear, 1966) is an experimental system for managing a fictitious military data base. Like BASEBALL, DEACON's data structure generalized beyond the particular application. Indeed, DEACON's data base is, strictly speaking, a set of unordered sets, so it is as general a structure as one can hope for. The data structure, however, is not DEACON's most noteworthy feature. In DEACON the structure of the language the user has at his command is more closely linked to the structure of the data base than in most information retrieval programs. At first glance, a meshing of the language analysis and data structure management phases might seem to be a violation of the programmer's commandment to write modular code. In fact, the decision to intertwine the data structure and language analysis was based on Thompson's (1966) model of what a programming language does and of how English might serve as a programming language for information retrieval. Thompson's basic point was that programming languages are vehicles for specifying operations on an environment.[6] For example, FORTRAN programmers manipulate an environment of real and integer variables. Consider the statement

$$A = I + J * I. \tag{5}$$

By applying appropriate syntactical analysis, we know that this is a FORTRAN statement of the form

Real variable = integer variable (1) + integer variable (2) *   (6)

integer variable (1).

[6] All computer programming can be treated in this way. Wegner (1968) presents a detailed discussion.

As soon as we recognize this we can specify the necessary sequence of multiplications, additions, fetches, and stores required to carry out computation. Equivalently, we could say that we have specified the series of changes to be made in the environment. The same approach can be used in designing information management programs. If we have an appropriate data structure for describing the environment and a set of rules that translate from English-like statements into sequences of manipulations of the environment, then there is no need that the translation process be separated from the execution process. Indeed, if an English-like language is used, it may not be desirable to separate the processes because one of the effective ways of distinguishing between the different meanings of ambiguous statements is to determine which of these leads to a reasonable manipulation of the environment.[7]

The basic data structure of DEACON is a *ring*. A ring is an unordered list (set) of elements, physically realized by chaining computer words to each other, and then linking the last word on the list to the first. (See Knuth, 1968, for discussions of linking methods.) Each ring holds a set of names, some of which may name other rings. Figure 14-2 illustrates a set of rings for a hypothetical military application. Each referent term (*artillery, armor, battalion, 638th, 12th*) in the user's language names a ring in the data structure, just as variable names reference computer memory locations in FORTRAN. Linkages between rings correspond to relations between basic terms. Thus in Figure 14-2 we can determine that the "12th" is a *Marine Artillery Regiment* by the simultaneous appearance of "12" in each of the appropriate rings.

DEACON recognizes a command by locating a pattern in the input language which it recognizes as an order to carry out an operation on the data base. Words in the lexicon are divided into two classes: function words and referents. Function words aid in identification of patterns, whereas referent words specify specific ring structures. When an English statement is input it is first scanned for referent and function words, and then the sequence of referent and function words is searched to determine whether it matches one or more of the set of prespecified patterns. If the pattern is found, one of two things may happen: The input string may be further defined or an operation on the data base may be carried out. In the event that two patterns match the same string at any time, the operations specified by each pattern are carried out unless one of the operations is impossible. In this case the corresponding pattern is dropped. As our example will show, DEACON's analysis is very similar to the production system method advocated by Newell and Simon (1972).

We can illustrate the ideas by following an example offered by Craig *et al.* (1966). Consider the data structure shown in Figure 14-3 and suppose that the query is

WHO IS COMMANDER OF THE 638TH BATTALION?   (7a)

---

[7] Interestingly, Thompson seems to have retreated from this position in later work (Dozstert & Thompson, 1971).

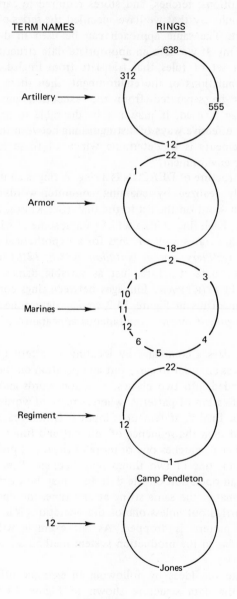

TERM NAMES   RINGS

638
312
Artillery ──────▶
555

12
22
1
Armor ──────▶

18
2
1   3
10
Marines ──────▶   11
12
6   4
5

22

Regiment ──────▶   12

1

Camp Pendleton

12 ──────▶

Jones

Fig. 14-2

This string contains the function words *who, of, the, ?* and the referents *commander, 638*, and *battalion*. Sentence (7a) is first reduced to

WHO COMMANDER (R1) OF THE 638 (R2) BATTALION (R3)?   (7b)

A search for patterns then begins. A DEACON pattern that matches (7b) is described by:

Syntactic rule. If the input string contains the sequence R1 followed immediately by R2 (written R1 + R2), and

Semantic rule. If the data base contains two different rings with names R1 and R2, which contain each other's name as entries (this is called an **intersection**) then

Action. Replace "R1 + R2" in the input string by R1.

Sentence (7b) contains 638 + BATTALION, so the syntactical requirement is satisfied. The data is then examined to determine if the semantic condition holds. It does, as Figure 14-3 shows, since "638" appears on the "BATTALION" ring and vice versa. The sentence becomes

WHO COMMANDER (R1) OF THE 638 (R2)?   (7c)

The next rule to be applied is "the + R → R," allowing us to drop a determiner. Note that in some cases this rule might not be applicable, because the determiner could be meaningful. The sentence is

WHO COMMANDER (R1) OF 638 (R2)?   (7d)

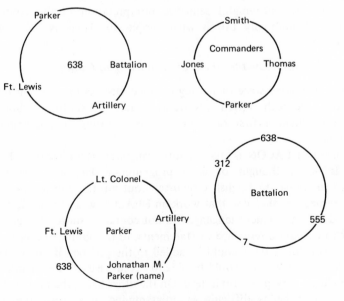

Fig. 14-3.   Data structure for DEACON example.

The next rule which DEACON applies is

Syntax. The input string contains the substring "R1 of R2"

Semantic. There is a set of connective rings R1, R2, R3 such that they all intersect each other.

Action. Replace "R1 of R2" by R3

There is an intersection between 638, COMMANDER, and PARKER in Figure 14-3, so the sentence is

$$\text{WHO PARKER (R3)?} \qquad\qquad (8)$$

This matches the rule

Syntax. Who + R

Semantic. None

Action. Output the external referent name of R.

PARKER is produced as the answer to the question.

Data are input to DEACON in much the same way as questions. The only difference is that upon receiving a sentence such as

$$\text{DATA:}\quad \text{THE 638TH IS A BATTALION} \qquad\qquad (9)$$

the program alters its data base instead of printing a response. In general, recognizing a verb activates a subroutine to alter a connection between rings.

DEACON can resolve syntactic ambiguities in natural language by noting that there is only one meaningful semantic interpretation in the context of the conversation. Undoubtedly this is what people do. There is only one possible interpretation of

John saw the Grand Canyon flying to California.

In the event that some stage of parsing in DEACON has to entertain two possible analyses, they are both carried forward as separate questions, and both answered unless one of them is first ruled out by its requiring an impossible semantic construction.

Reference to DEACON as "using natural language" is misleading. The command language is better thought of as a programming language with an external appearance so similar to English discourse about information retrieval that it can easily be learned. At the time that work on DEACON was suspended, the "English language" data management language did not contain a subroutine capability, the capability to execute a sequence of statements, or the ability to execute branching statements. No doubt these could be added to the program if one wished to take the trouble. Such a system would be able to execute easy-to-define inference rules, and so would be very powerful indeed. On the other hand, the proper statement of such rules might be as difficult as programming in a conventional computer language. To what extent is a compiler a model of comprehension?

14.1.3 DATA BASE STRUCTURES BASED ON MEANINGFUL RELATIONS; PROTOSYNTHEX III AND RELATED SYSTEMS

The basic terms of a data base can be related to each other in many ways. BASEBALL and DEACON are limited in their ability to reflect this, since the only way that either system has of stating a relationship is to specify the relative position of two items in the data base. An alternative method of data structuring is to link items together by labeled relationships. In this approach the data structure can be thought of as a graph in which the nodes are objects of the data base, and the labeled arcs between nodes specify relationships. Quillian (1968, 1969) has referred to such structures as *semantic nets*, and although this is not exactly what we mean by semantics, it is a shorthand term which we can use effectively. Figure 14-4 shows a semantic net specifying some elementary facts about man and his environment. We shall want to complicate this representation somewhat in a moment, but the basic idea will remain.

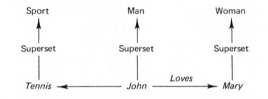

Fig. 14-4.   Data Structure represented by a labeled graph.

Semantic nets of some variety or another have appeared in several programs that attempt comprehension. One of the basic concepts of the semantic net is the type–token distinction (Quillian, 1968). Any universe of discourse will contain a number of objects. The objects themselves are defined by their relationship to other objects, thus forming a semantic net. Within this net there will have to be a node associated with the definition of every object. This is called the *type* node. In addition the net will have to contain other nodes referring to specific cases of an object as it is used in reference to other objects. These are called *token* nodes. To illustrate, imagine a data structure defining the entries in a dictionary. The token node of *man* would be defined as being in the *subset* relation to *male* and *Homo sapiens*. Now consider the definition of *lawyer*. A *lawyer* might be defined as a *man* providing that *man* is qualified by relations expressing the idea "who offers advice of legal type." The node for *man* in the definition of *lawyer* clearly would have to enter into relationships that were different from the node for *man* in the definition of *physician*.

The semantic net representation leads directly to the statement of inference rules. In effect, one can have an inference rule which says that if the data base explicitly states that relationship R_1 exists between nodes A and B, and R_2 between nodes B and C, then relationship R_3 may be inferred to exist between nodes A and C. To take a simple example, if the input data indicates that John is taller than Mary and Mary is taller than Sue, a comprehension program can infer the relationship John is taller than Sue. This is hardly a new idea. One of the classic ways to represent a deduction is by a graph. In programming comprehension, however, we are not restricted to the use of conventional rules of inference. For example, one could use a "psychologic" which states that if X is a subset of *man* and stands in the relationships *loves* Y who is a subset of *woman*, and Z is also a subset of *man* and in the relationship *loves* to Y, then the relationship X *dislikes* Z may also be inferred.

PROTOSYNTHEX III (Schwarcz, Burger, & Simmons, 1970) represents an ambitious effort to use the semantic net representation in information retrieval.[8] In addition to its semantic net, PROTOSYNTHEX contains quite complicated inference rules. The data structure will be described here and the inference rules in a subsequent section of this chapter.

The basic unit of the PROTOSYNTHEX data structure is the "event triple" XRY, in which X, R, and Y are either primitive objects of the lexicon (i.e., terms which have type nodes), tokens of type nodes, or event triples themselves. The interpretation of an event triple is that "X is in the relationship R to Y." Since R may be qualified and since XRY may itself be a term within an event triple, we do not represent the triple by an arc labeled by R connecting X and Y. Instead the triple itself is a node and is connected to its X, R and Y nodes by X, R and Y arcs.

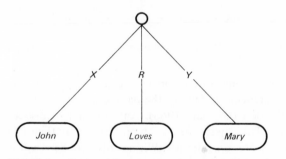

Fig. 14-5.   Event triple representation of *John loves Mary*.

This is shown in Figure 14-5. PROTOSYNTHEX III holds its data in a network of event triples. In addition, the program utilizes a network of semantic information about the sort of events and relationships which may occur. Semantic information can itself be divided into two classes. A network of hierarchies and equivalencies expresses relations between terms. This network indicates to the program the fact that *man* is a male *Homo sapiens, Socrates* is a *man, person* is equivalent to *Homo sapiens*, etc. In addition, PROTOSYNTHEX is given classes of *interpretable events* called semantic event forms (SEF), which are general classes of XRY events. Thus an SEF triple such as (ANIMALS EAT FOOD) can be instantiated by WOLVES DEVOUR MEAT. SEF's are particularly important in the inference stage, since rules of inference may be stated generally, as relationships between SEF's, and then applied to specific event triples.

PROTOSYNTHEX also contains a language preprocessor which maps English language sentences into event triples. Apparently this program is similar to the BASEBALL preprocessing program, in that it determines the internal form of a message without feedback from its partial analysis. This is unlike DEACON's technique of tying language analysis to data structure analysis. We shall not discuss the language analysis program beyond noting that failure to utilize semantic feedback is apt to be quite limiting.

The following example illustrates PROTOSYNTHEX's data structure and shows how a question can be answered without using any of the rules of inference. The input sentence is

> *The stones and iron that fall to earth from outer space*   (10)
> *are called meteorites.*

The basic references identified are *stones, earth, to, iron, space, outer, for, called,* and *meteorites.* In addition there are a number of "first-order" qualified terms. These are indicated by labeled arcs specifying the type of qualification. For example, "fall to earth" indicates a particular type of fall, falling to a specific location. This is diagrammed as FALL——$\xrightarrow{TO}$——EARTH. The following modified terms are labeled.

(T1.1) FALL TO EARTH

(T1.2) SPACE MOD OUTER (i.e., OUTER SPACE)

A modified term may modify a modified term as in

(T2.1) T1.1 FROM T1.2   (Fall to earth from outer space)

(T2.2) STONES T2.1 **   (stones fall to earth from outer space)

(T2.3) IRON T2.1 **   (iron fall to earth from outer space)

(T2.4) T2.2 MOD the   (the stones which, etc.)

(T2.5) T2.3 MOD the   (the iron which, etc.)

(The asterisks indicate a blank in the triple.)

The entire structure of (10) is shown in Figure 14-6a as an event triple consisting of two event triples, connected by the relationship AND, and specifying that the event triples involve qualified terms.

Semantic information about terms is also required. In this particular example we do not need inference rules, but we do need to know which terms are equivalent and which terms are subsets of other terms. Figure 14-6b shows this. TOP is a blanket term covering all other terms. Within this reference we see that *object* is made equivalent to *what, stone* and *iron,* and *meteorites* are subsets of objects, etc.

We are now in a position to answer

> *What is a meteorite?*   (11)

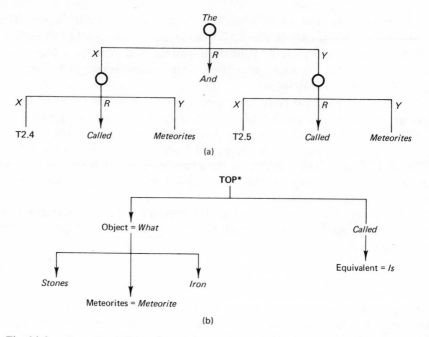

Fig. 14-6.   Data for PROTOSYNTHEX example. (a) Event triples. (b) Semantic event forms.

The answers that PROTOSYNTHEX derives are

$$\text{\textit{Meteorite be meteorite.}} \tag{12a}$$

$$\text{\textit{Meteorite be metorites.}} \tag{12b}$$

$$\text{\textit{Iron that fall to earth from outer space be meteorite.}} \tag{12c}$$

$$\text{\textit{Stone that fall to earth from outer space be meteorite.}} \tag{12d}$$

Answers (12a) and (12b) are determined by noting an equivalence relationship between two terms in the semantic information. Answers (12c) and (12d) are determined by detecting that (11) is equivalent to the triple

$$\text{\textit{object equivalent meteorite}} \tag{13}$$

and that the event triples

$$\text{T2.4 \textit{called meteorites}} \tag{14}$$

and

$$\text{T2.4 \textit{called meteorites}} \tag{15}$$

have the same form as (13).

Intuitively, semantic nets provide a natural way of expressing complex statements, but in practice they present formidable problems. The representation is costly both in terms of computer time and space. Schwarcz *et al.* (1970) report times of up to *20 minutes* to answer fairly simple questions using very small data bases. While these times were obtained using a now obsolescent computer (the AN/FSQ-32 military computer) and can now undoubtedly be improved, there is question as to whether they can be improved enough. For practical comprehension we have to increase both the speed and the storage capacity by at least two orders of magnitude. It is doubtful that hardware advances can achieve this in the near future. Similar problems have been noted in other systems which use semantic nets. Perhaps even more serious a problem is the number of relationships that would have to be specified in order to produce a system capable of serious reasoning. Ableson (1966) pointed out that simulation of human reasoning by computer often fails because we forget to include in our data base such prosaic facts as *People who stand in the rain get wet*. Since we cannot anticipate all the facts that might be needed by a comprehending program, we must include all relationships that might be relevant. Even if we had the machine capacity to deal with the necessary graph, how would we prepare data? On ·the other hand, what is the alternative? To achieve the ultimate in machine comprehension, it may be that we will have to read all the definitions of Webster's dictionary into a computer memory. This is impractical today, although it may soon be feasible to use semantic nets to represent nontrivial data bases for limited types of comprehensions in specific applications, such as toxicology or real estate law. Thus far, however, a practical example of the technique has yet to be produced.

14.1.4   A COMMENT ON DATA STRUCTURES AND COMPREHENSION

At present, we simply do not know if it is practical to construct large-scale question answering systems. Someone is going to have to try. One of the most ambitious attempts is the CONVERSE program under development at System Development Corporation (Kellog, 1968; Kellog, Burger, Diller, & Fogt, 1971). This is a very large system designed for execution on the third generation time-sharing computer (the IBM 360/67). As of 1971 the system was able to operate with a file of over 10,000 facts about 120 United States cities (Kellog *et al.*, 1971). Query times have not been reported. CONVERSE introduces no new ideas, although it does combine two important ones. Its data structures consist of sets of items (as the DEACON rings) with labeled arcs specifying the relationships between sets, rather than relationships between individual items. CONVERSE appears to be a very well programmed attempt to incorporate all the many solutions to little problems which have appeared in previous programs. In some ways it represents the best of our present understanding of data structures for computer comprehension. CONVERSE and systems like it will undoubtedly be attempted as computers become faster and memory hardware becomes cheaper. Quite possibly study of this system will indicate whether we need a new technology or new conceptual advances in information retrieval.

14.2   Deductive Inference in Information Retrieval

14.2.0   TECHNIQUES

A comprehending program ought to be able to reply to queries by determining what the data base implies as well as what the data base contains. In order to do this the program must be able to deduce facts from other facts. As the word "deduce" suggests, the procedures that are needed are closely related to theorem proving. There are, however, some important differences between mathematical theorem proving and inference in information retrieval.

An algorithm for fact derivation should always be valid. There seems to be no realistic situation in which one would be able to tolerate false answers. On the other hand, completeness—the ability to answer any answerable question—is not a *sine qua non*. As we saw in our discussion of theorem proving, completeness is often purchased only at great expense. In most realistic question-answering situations there will be many questions of one type and few questions of another. The goal of the system designer will be to maximize the utility of the system to the user,[9] so at times it may be advisable to trade away the capability of answering some questions at all in order to be able to answer other questions very quickly. As might be expected, such mundane economic reasoning has largely been ignored in the design of experimental deductive question-answering systems. Perhaps it should be.

We can distinguish several types of complexity in deductive procedures. At the lowest level a program might have only the capability of recombining stored facts in order to answer a query. This was illustrated in DEACON's answer to the question, *Who is the commander of the 638th battalion?* where a reply was constructed by finding the appropriate combination of entries in an existing data base. No new entries were produced as a byproduct of the question-answering process. A more powerful alternative is to provide specific operations for deducing new facts. Here questions of completeness, practicality, and problem-solving strategy are crucial. A program might contain a limited set of operators, such as implication and set inclusion, which are simple to execute but provide only a limited deductive capacity. At the other extreme a program could contain a complete inference system, such as resolution, and accept with this inference system the risk that some deductions would take an extremely long time.

A third approach is to allow the user to specify his own deductive procedures. In essence, the user asks a question and then tells the system how the answer is to be found. Slagle (1965), in DEDUCOM, and Dozstert and Thompson (1971) take this approach. It potentially places the entire power of the machine in the user's hands, but may also put on him the burden of being a programmer. Alternatively, an information retrieval system may contain preprogrammed deductive inference routines, but at the same time allow the user to specify a strategy if desired.

---

[9] Note that this criterion does not force us to treat all individual questions as equally important.

14.2.1   Systems Using Incomplete Inference

14.2.1.0   *The Reactive Library*

Our first example will be of a very limited incomplete inference system which was designed to experiment with the power of a few crude inference rules (Hunt & Quinlan, 1967). In the literature the term "computer comprehension" is virtually synonymous with question answering, but this program was not a classical question answerer. Instead it stored facts and made comments upon the relationship of old facts to new. For this reason we called the program the REACTIVE LIBRARY, by analogy to a librarian who publishes comments on books as they are received. The system was tested in a fairly realistic application, the analysis of literature on the physiology of memory. Our illustrations will be taken from this field.

The REACTIVE LIBRARY was a repository and collator of brief statements (facts) such as might be used to summarize the findings of an experiment. Whenever a new fact was received, its implications were considered as they related to previously stored facts. Two sorts of implications were produced by the program: two facts could either be in agreement and generalize to produce a new statement, called a *metafact*, or a new fact could contradict a previously derived fact, either directly or by generalizing to a contradictory generalization. Table 14-1 is a summary of the output for three consecutive additions to a data base taken from statements in Chapter 3 of Deutsch and Deutsch's (1966) *Physiological Psychology*.[10] To illustrate how the system makes inferences, we will consider the reactions to some further inputs once Table 14-1 was stored.

The fourth input statement was

THE POST-TRIAL INJECTION OF STRYCHNINE IMPROVES   (16)
DISCRIMINATION LEARNING IN TRYON-S3S.

The system replied

AGREEMENT WITH STORED FACT   (17)

THE PRE-TRIAL INJECTION OF PICROTOXIN FACILITATES
DISCRIMINATION IN WISTARS

METAFACT ON WHICH AGREE

INJECTION CONVULSANT IMPROVE DISCRIMINATION RAT

and

DISAGREEMENT WITH STORED FACT   (18)

IP INJECTION 1757-I HINDER AVOIDANCE LEARNING TRYON S-1

METAFACT ON WHICH DISAGREE

INJECTION CONVULSANT IMPROVE LEARNING RAT

---

[10] In following the example it helps to know that WISTARS, TRYON-S3's and TRYON-S1's are strains of rats used in psychological laboratories and that strychnine, picrotoxin, and 1757-IS are convulsant drugs.

TABLE 14-1
Sample Inputs and Output of the Reactive Library

INPUT: THE PRE-TRIAL INJECTION OF PICROTOXIN FACILITATES DISCRIM-
               INATION LEARNING IN WISTARS #D&D, CH 3

STORED AS: PRETRIAL INJECTION PICROTOXIN FACILITATE DISCRIMINATION
               LEARNING WISTAR

INPUT: INTRAPERITONEAL INJECTION OF 1757-IS HINDERS AVOIDANCE
               LEARNING IN TRYON-S1S #D&D, CH 3

STORED AS: IP INJECTION 1757-I HINDER AVOIDANCE LEARNING TRYON-S1
DISAGREEMENT WITH STORED FACT
               THE   PRE-TRIAL   INJECTION   OF   PICROTOXIN   FACILITATES
               DISCRIMINATION LEARNING IN WISTARS #D&D, CH 3

METAFACT ON WHICH DISAGREE:
               INJECTION CONVULSANT HINDER LEARNING RAT

INPUT: THE POST-TRIAL INJECTION OF STRYCHNINE IMPROVES DISCRIM-
               INATION LEARNING IN TRYON-S3S #D&D, CH 3

STORED AS: POST-TRIAL INJECTION STRYCHNINE IMPROVE DISCRIMINATION
               LEARNING TRYON-S3

AGREEMENT WITH STORED FACT
               THE PRE-TRIAL INJECTION OF PICROTOXIN FACILITATES DISCRIM-
               INATION LEARNING IN WISTARS #D&D, CH 3

METAFACT ON WHICH AGREE:
               ADMINISTRATION-TIME   INJECTION   CONVULSANT   IMPROVE
               DISCRIMINATION RAT

DISAGREEMENT WITH STORED FACT
               INTRAPERITONEAL INJECTION OF 1757-IS HINDERS AVOIDANCE
               LEARNING IN TRYON-S1S #D&D, CH 3

METAFACT ON WHICH DISAGREE:
               INJECTION CONVULSANT IMPROVE LEARNING RAT

Note that all the retrieved facts contain a verb which is either approximately a synonym or an antonym of a verb in the input fact. If the verb is a synonym, agreement is indicated; if the verb is an antonym, disagreement is indicated. Parenthetically, if the verb is "NOT z" it is interpreted as its own antonym. In addition, we see that non-verb forms also play a role in retrieval. Agreement or disagreement is determined by metafacts. All nounlike terms (*operands*) in the metafact represent either operands in the input or generalizations of an operand in the input. (Note the replacement of "strychnine" by "convulsant" in the example.) Each retrieved fact contains within its operand specializations of the generalization proposed in the metafact. This much is apparent to the user.

Now let us consider what happened at the level of program operations. The REACTIVE LIBRARY consisted of two parts, a program and a dictionary. The dictionary contained two classes of words, operands and verbs. Like DEACON, the

REACTIVE LIBRARY treated a sentence as an ordered set of the dictionary items it contained. The sentence

THE POST-TRIAL APPLICATION OF ECS OFTEN DISRUPTS MEMORY

(19)

would be stored as

POST-TRIAL EC DISRUPT MEMORY[11]   (20)

assuming that THE, APPLICATION, OF, and OFTEN were not stored in the dictionary. Each verb was assigned to a class of verbs. The class was further divided into positive and negative terms. For example, the *produce–destroy* class of verbs consisted of the positive terms

PRODUCE, FACILITATE, IMPROVE

and the negative terms

HINDER, DISRUPT, DESTROY.

We will refer to a verb as having a sign in addition to having a class. If the word NOT preceded a verb in an input sentence, the sign of the verb was changed. Although this does not correspond exactly with English usage, it proved to be close enough for most purposes.

Operands were related to each other by set inclusion. Thus strychnine was included in the set CONVULSANT. It was also possible to include an operand in two sets which were not included within each other. ELECTRO-CONVULSIVE SHOCK (ECS) was included in the sets TRAUMA and ELECTRIC-SHOCK in the physiological dictionary.

Each operand was represented internally by a code that permitted an immediate match between operands to determine their lowest common intersection. Let the coded operand name be a string of symbols, where the first symbol is the name of the most general class to which the operand belongs, the second symbol the name of the second most general class, etc. Thus if A were the code for animal, AM might be the code for mammal, AMR the code for rat, and AMR6 and AMR7 the codes for, say, TRYON S1 and TRYON S3 rats. By a simple masking operation the common denominator can be detected so that for code words, AMR6 and AMR7, the lowest common denominator would be AMR, the code for *rat*. Similarly, the names of all mammals could readily be retrieved by selecting all codes which had AM as their first two symbols. To handle a case in which a given term is a member of two sets which are not nested, as in the ECS example, an operand name could be assigned two or more codes. It would be inconvenient if very many operands had to have multiple codes, but this was not a problem in the applications (physiological psychology and forestry) studied using this program.

---

[11] Terminal "s" is always dropped. In fact, a fairly simple algorithm can be used to reduce an English word to its stem (Stone *et al.* 1967). The algorithm usually works.

Internally, sentences were coded by their verb class and sign, and by the set of left-hand and right-hand operands they contained. In example (19) the components are

$$\text{verb } = \text{DISRUPT (POSITIVE)} \tag{21}$$

$$\text{left } = \text{EC, POST-TRIAL}$$

$$\text{right } = \text{MEMORY}$$

As each new fact was entered a search was made of the file of facts already stored to find a stored fact whose verb was in the same class as that of the input fact. The new and retrieved facts were then compared by generalization. The steps in the generalization process were

1. removal of one or more operands from either the subject or the object, or
2. replacement of an operand by a more general operand.

The process of specialization was the replacement of an operand by one of its subjects. So, for instance, if

$$\text{CAT} \subseteq \text{FELINE} \subseteq \text{ANIMAL} \tag{22}$$

$$\text{RAT} \subseteq \text{RODENT} \subseteq \text{ANIMAL}$$

some of the constructed facts to which the fact

$$\text{CATS EAT RODENTS} \tag{23}$$

could be related by the above processes were

$$\text{CATS EAT RODENTS} \tag{24}$$

$$\text{FELINES EAT RATS}$$

$$\text{CATS EAT ANIMALS}$$

$$\text{ANIMALS EAT ANIMALS}$$

If a metafact could be found to which both the input fact and a stored fact could be transformed, then the system announced an agreement or disagreement, depending on whether the verbs of the matched facts agreed in sign.

At times users wished to suppress some or all of the retrievals the REACTIVE LIBRARY could produce. This facility was provided by a set of selective commands which allowed users to define new operands, or to restrict comparisons to certain operands. These conveniences are not part of the artificial intelligence program, and will not be discussed here.

After field testing, the REACTIVE LIBRARY was found to be interesting but, by itself, not adequate as an information retrieval system. Users reported that it would have been quite useful if it had been coupled with a conventional document retrieval system. This suggests a possible application in library automation. Within the artificial intelligence field the REACTIVE LIBRARY's chief interest is that it shows that comprehension is not limited to the answering of specific questions, and that a very limited program can construct interesting generalities. It is easy to produce an example for which the REACTIVE LIBRARY produces silly output, but that is not the point. People can recognize silly output easily. Where people need help is in being reminded that certain data, which they may have known once but have forgotten, may have application to the information which they have just received. The cost of telling them something noninformative is small.

14.2.1.2   *PROTOSYNTHEX Deductive Routines*

PROTOSYNTHEX III (Schwarcz *et al.*, 1970) contains some sophisticated techniques for dealing with the implications of the XRY triples that form its basic data base. PROTOSYNTHEX is a "true" question answerer, since it can respond to specific queries about the data base. As we saw in the BASEBALL and previous PROTOSYNTHEX examples, question answering may simply require a sophisticated search for the correct combination of previously input facts. PROTO-SYNTHEX can also respond to a question by inferring a new XRY triple from previously established triplets. The deductive inference techniques that were used closely resemble the theorem proving techniques used in rewriting systems such as FDS (Quinlan & Hunt, 1968) and GPS (Ernst & Newell, 1969). The rewriting rules of PROTOSYNTHEX are based upon five properties of relations which might occur in an XRY triple and five rules for combining relations into more complex relations. The details of these rules and their applications are somewhat cumbersome, so the reader is referred to the Schwarcz *et al.* article for a precise description. We will illustrate PROTOSYNTHEX deductive question answering by example, introducing the inference rules as they are needed.

PROTOSYNTHEX's basic strategy is to regard a question as the starting node in a problem solving (AND/OR) graph. If the question cannot be answered directly, subproblems are generated and either answered or expanded into subsubproblems, as appropriate. Thus the algorithms for expanding problem-solving graphs are directly applicable. In fact, PROTOSYNTHEX chooses which subproblem to expand next by an algorithm similar to Slagle and Bursky's (1968) *Multiple* algorithm. Questions and subquestions can be thought of as conditions that must be met by an event triple if that triple is to be regarded as the answer to the question. A question is answered if a suitable event triple exists in the data base, or can be inferred from existing triples by application of the inference rules.

Schwarcz *et al.* offer the following example. The data base is derived from the sentence

> NAPOLEON COMMANDED THE FRENCH ARMY WHICH LOST THE (25)
> BATTLE OF WATERLOO IN 1815.

In addition, the system was given a variety of semantic facts—NAPOLEON is a GENERAL, a GENERAL is a PERSON, WHO is equivalent to PERSON, etc. Figure

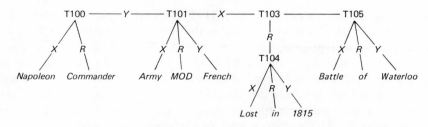

Fig. 14-7.   Event triples for *Napoleon commanded the French Army which lost the Battle of Waterloo in 1815.* (Modified version of the graph presented by Schwarcz *et al.*, 1970.)

14-7 shows a graph of the internal representation of the data base.[1,2] The question asked was

WHO LOST THE BATTLE OF WATERLOO?   (26)

PROTOSYNTHEX recognized the question as having the structure

WHO LOST (BATTLE OF WATERLOO)   (27)

which contains two question triples,

BATTLE OF WATERLOO   (28)

and

PERSON LOST (BATTLE OF WATERLOO)   (29)

Triplet (28) can be located directly in the data base, in a manner similar to that shown in the example of section 14.1.3. In order to answer (29) PROTOSYNTHEX used the inference rule "Complex Product" (C/P) which states

If the triple A R1 C and C R2 B are both true for some C, then the relation A(R1 C/P R2) B is true.

A specific relation term can be defined as the complex product of two other relations. Thus in the example the data base contained

LOST ⊆ (LED C/P LOST)   (30)

as part of its semantic information. What this says is that one of the ways of stating "X lost Y" is to say "X led Z and Z lost Y". Using rule (30) and the C/P inference rule, PROTOSYNTHEX detected that

NAPOLEON COMMANDED T101   (31)

is in the data base and is an example of the SEF class of triples PERSON LED

[1,2] We believe that Figure 14-7 is consistent with the definition of event triples given by Schwarcz *et al.*, but Figure 14-7 is not the same as their Figure 1, which clearly violates their own definitions.

GROUP. Further, by reference to 14-7 we find that

$$T101 \quad T103 \quad T105 \tag{32}$$

is a specification of GROUP LOST BATTLE. The program can then infer that

$$\text{NAPOLEON LOST T105} \tag{33}$$

Since (33) is a specific case of the question triple (29) both subgoals of the original question will have been answered, so an answer has been found.

PROTOSYNTHEX demonstrates two major advantages of the semantic net approach; intuitive reasonableness and the use of rewriting and graph searching within a question answering system. It also demonstrates some of the problems involved. The question of the practicality of semantic net data management has already been discussed. In PROTOSYNTHEX's inference system there is no way to express negation or quantification, thus it is an incomplete system. Schwarcz *et al.* point out that negation could easily be included, but that if they were to do so the system would be able to answer contradictory questions positively if the data base permitted it to. This is because PROTOSYNTHEX does not contain any check to prevent it from accepting contradictory event triples, such as

$$\text{SOCRATES IS A MAN} \tag{34}$$

$$\text{SOCRATES IS NOT A MAN}$$

Of course, one would not want a theorem prover to accept such statements, but is this a problem in a deductive question answering system? In other words, should a program reject an inconsistent data base? Perhaps not, since many interesting data bases are inconsistent. The experimental literature in practically any science is full of contradictions which deal with the most important topics of investigation. In law the most intricate legal problems arise when principles or specific laws are in conflict. A working PROTOSYNTHEX ought to follow the example of the REACTIVE LIBRARY: note inconsistencies but do not refuse to deal with them.

PROTOSYNTHEX's failure to deal with quantification is much more serious. In fact, quantification has not been dealt with adequately by any problem solver using rewriting techniques. In addition, PROTOSYNTHEX cannot deal with "how" questions, i.e., questions in which the response desired is a course of action which will result in a desired outcome. As we shall see in the following section, there is a natural way to deal with such questions using the resolution principle.

In summary, the semantic net approach is at once promising and frustrating. It is promising because it seems so reasonable. In practice semantic net systems seem to produce a set of clever examples which, on closer examination, depend on ad hoc solutions. Since there is no underlying formal theory, as there is for programs based on the resolution principle, it is hard to see what else we could expect. The artificial intelligence field badly needs a paper establishing some sort of theory for semantic nets. Such a theory would have to unite inference by rewriting, graph theory, and graph searching techniques, so we are asking for no small job.

14.2.2   DEDUCOM: Incorporation of Question Answering into
          the Data Base

An interesting alternative to reliance on preprogrammed rules of inference is
offered by Slagle's (1965) DEDUCOM program. DEDUCOM is an extension to the
LISP compiler (McCarthy *et al.*, 1963) and a brief description of certain LISP
constructs is needed before DEDUCOM can be explained.

LISP is an interpretive language whose expressions and data are both held
internally as list structures. Thus the distinction between what is a program and
what is a piece of data is arbitrary. In fact, programs can be defined and executed at
run time, since the LISP interpretive cycle reads and then evaluates a list structure.
The basic data types of LISP are *atomic symbols* (*atoms*) and *lists*, ordered sets
whose elements may be atoms or other lists. Three functions are defined on lists,
and contained in the interpreter. Let L be an arbitrary list. The function $car[L]$ has
as its value the first element of L, while $cdr[L]$ has as its value the remaining
elements of L. (Note that a list may be null.) The function $cons[L, M]$, where L
and M may be either lists or atomic symbols, has as its value the list (L, M). In
addition, the LISP interpreter contains a number of conventional arithmetical
functions and logical predicates. Thus $times(x, y)$ is a function whose arguments
must be arithmetic expressions, and whose value is the product of x and y. There is,
of course, a great deal more to LISP, but this brief introduction should be sufficient
to enable the reader to follow a description of how DEDUCOM works.

Slagle first added three new functions to the basic LISP interpreter;
$valueans[V; Q]$, $ans[V; Q]$, and the predicate $ansupset[Q_1; Q_2]$. The arguments to
the first two functions are the variable V and the question Q. A *question* is a
function of K arguments and so can always be expressed as
$G(X_1, X_2, X_3, \ldots, X_k)$. Consider the question

$$how\ many\ [finger;\ man] = (\text{how many fingers on a man}) \qquad (35)$$

Formally this is the function *how many* with arguments *finger* and *man*. Similarly

$$times[2, 4] \qquad (36)$$

is the product of 2×4. The difference between (35) and (36) is that the LISP
interpreter is capable of interpreting *times* directly, while the user must state how
to compute *how many* by use of *valueans, ans, ansupset* and the basic functions of
LISP. To define *valueans* and *ans*, suppose that, for $V = B$ the value of $Q(V)$ is A.
Then $valueans[V; Q]$ is the ordered pair $(V \cdot A)$, and $ans[V; Q]$ is A. From the
definitions of *car* and *cdr* it follows that for the ordered pair $(X \cdot Y)$

$$car[X; Y] = X; \qquad (37)$$

$$cdr[X \cdot Y] = Y \qquad (38)$$

so

$$ans[V; Q] = cdr[valueans[V; Q]] \qquad (39)$$

Let us pause for an example. Let *person* be a variable that can take the value John, James, Robert, Tom, and let *children* be a question. Further, let us assume that there is a known fact,

$$children(\text{Robert}) = \{\text{Tom, Dick, Beth}\}. \tag{40}$$

If we ask *ans*[Robert; *children*], the evaluation is, in order

$$ans[\text{Robert}; children] = cdr[valueans[\text{Robert}; children] \tag{41}$$

$$= cdr[\text{Robert}; \{\text{Tom, Dick, Beth}\}]$$

$$= \{\text{Tom, Dick, Beth}\}$$

The predicate *ansupset* $[Q_1 ; Q_2]$ is an assertion to LISP that any answer to question Q_2 is included in the set of answers to Q_1. Therefore, if Q_2 can be answered, Q_1 will be answered, although Q_1 may be answerable without answering Q_2. To continue with the example, "Tom," "Dick," and "Beth" would be legitimate answers to the question *child*(Robert). Only "Beth" would be an answer to the question *daughter*. Therefore *ansupset* [*child*; *daughter*].

For completeness, a DEDUCOM data base must include the fact that if variable V does not appear in question Q, and if there is any fact of the form $Q(X) = a$ then

$$valueans[v; q] = [anything \cdot a] \tag{42}$$

Also, by definition, the value of any question which is a constant is itself. Thus if Q is "5", the answer to Q is 5.

Suppose DEDUCOM is asked to evaluate

$$Q = g[q_1 ; q_2 \cdots q_n], \tag{43}$$

where g is a function and the q_i are questions. This, in effect, defines a way to answer question q in terms of a computation on the answers to other questions. The computing steps are

(*i*) Can the LISP interpreter evaluate Q directly? If so, do so. This will occur if Q is a constant or an atomic symbol.

(*ii*) Is g a function known to the LISP interpreter? If so, evaluate $q_1 \cdots q_n$ (perhaps using DEDUCOM) and then, given the arguments of g, evaluate g.

(*iii*) If neither (*i*) nor (*ii*) are true, set Q' to Q and ask if there exists a fact of the form *ansupset* $[Q_1', Q_2]$ where Q_1' is identical to Q' except for substitution of variables. If such a fact exists, go to step (*v*). Otherwise go to (*iv*).

(*iv*) If Q is of the form $Q' = valueans[V; Q'']$ (Q' is an answer to Q'' for some value of V) set Q' to Q'' and go to (*iii*) (try to answer Q''). Otherwise report failure.

(*v*) Use the DEDUCOM procedure recursively to evaluate Q_2. If Q_2 can be answered, its answer is an answer to Q. Otherwise go to (*iii*) and try to find a new question Q_2'. (Note that this step makes DEDUCOM a depth first search procedure, with all the disadvantages that entails.)

To illustrate this procedure, suppose DEDUCOM were given the facts already stated and the facts

    (*a*) If there are *M X*'s on a *V*, and if there are *N V*'s on a *Y*, then there are *M* x *N X*'s on a *Y*.

    (*b*) There are five fingers on a hand.

    (*c*) There is one hand on an arm.

    (*d*) There are two arms on a man.

For DEDUCOM to interpret these facts they must first be translated to LISP statements. This is not entirely a trivial process. Fact (*a*) is typical. It is written

$$ansupset\,[how\ many\,[x; y]\,]\,; ans\,[v; times\,[how\ many\ [x; v]\,; how\ many\,[v; y]\,]\,]$$

$$(44)$$

DEDUCOM users are required to make this translation. The disadvantage is obvious. The example question is also a LISP expression,

$$how\ many\,[\text{finger; man}]\qquad\qquad(45)$$

Tracing DEDUCOM steps;

    (*i*) *how many* functions cannot be evaluated directly but (44) permits substitution of

$$ans\,[v; times\,[how\ many\,[\text{finger}; v]\,; how\ many\,[v; \text{man}]\,]\,]\qquad(46)$$

    for (45).

    (*ii*) an *ans* function cannot be computed directly either, but by using (39)

$$cdr\,[valueans\,[v; \text{times}\,[how\ many\,[\text{finger}; v]\,; how\ many\,[v; \text{man}]\,]\,]\qquad(47)$$

    replaces (46)

    (*iii*) *cdr* is a LISP primitive that can be evaluated if its argument is known. To establish this, the next function to be evaluated is

$$valueans\,[v; times\,[how\ many\,[\text{finger}; v]\,; how\ many\,[v; \text{man}]\,]\,]\qquad(48)$$

    (*iv*) The procedure of answering is repeated, using a fact (not given here) about *valueans*. Eventually the question

$$how\ many\,[\text{finger}; v]\qquad\qquad(49)$$

    will be reached. This is answered by noting the fact

$$ansupset\,[how\ many\,[\text{finger; hand}]\,; 5]\qquad\qquad(50)$$

    which is the LISP version of fact (*b*). This leads directly to the question "5" which is its own answer.

    (*v*) The variable *v* is set equal to *hand*. The next question is

$$how\ many\,[\text{hand; man}]\qquad\qquad(51)$$

    which, by a fact similar to (50), is answered with the value 2.

(*vi*) By substitution of the values found for (49) and (51) the answer to (48) is determined to be (hand · 10). (47) has the answer 10, which is an answer to (46) and (45), the original question.

DEDUCOM can answer subtle questions, including the answer to a question which is the key to the plot of Gilbert and Sullivan's *Mikado* (Slagle, 1965). The program has the minor defect of being a depth first search for an and/or GRAPH, but this problem could be resolved fairly easily. A much more serious problem is that the DEDUCOM approach requires users both to state facts as LISP expressions and to anticipate how the search for an answer is to proceed. In other words, DEDUCOM is more of a programming language for question answering than an artificial intelligence program with its own built-in reasoning powers. However, the DEDUCOM approach ought to be seriously considered in future applications in which the user wishes to establish the inferences to be made.

14.2.3 DEDUCTIVE QUESTION ANSWERING USING RESOLUTION

Since question answering may require inference, it is not surprising to find that the resolution principle can be adapted to construct a question answering system. The first effective demonstration of how this might be done was by Green and his associates, with the QA2 (Green & Raphael, 1968) and QA3 (Green, 1969a,b,c) programs, which concentrated on the problem of answering questions after they had been translated to the predicate calculus format.

As one might expect, the biggest obstacle to applying the resolution principle to information retrieval is that the number of clauses needed to answer a question is likely to be very much greater than the number of clauses needed to state a mathematical theorem-proving problem. As a result the number of clauses generated in a deduction rapidly expands beyond any practical limit. Green's initial solution (Green, 1969b) was to divide the data base into two sets of clauses; a set of active clauses available to the deductive part of the program, and a much larger set of inactive clauses representing statements in the data base which were temporarily unavailable to the theorem prover. In QA3 a human user monitored the performance of the program and used his judgment in adding or subtracting clauses from the active set. Winograd (1972) has extended this idea by incorporating into the question answering system a statement of the conditions under which clauses can be chosen to be part of the active set. The conditions themselves are expressed in Hewitt's PLANNER language (Hewitt, 1972), which was discussed in Chapter XI.

In QA3 and the systems derived from it, both facts and questions are expressed in clausal form. This is easy to see[13] for simple forms. The clause

$$AT(GEORGE, HOME) \tag{52}$$

is an expression of the idea that *George is at home.*

---

[13] The reader who has not firmly grasped the idea of resolution principle theorem proving may wish to review Chapter 12 at this point.

Variables and quantifiers may be needed to express questions. The clause

$$(\exists x)(AT(GEORGE, x)) \tag{53}$$

expresses the idea *Where is George?* by asserting that there is some place, x, for which $(AT(GEORGE, x))$ is true. The way that (53) is shown to be true is by negating it and showing that the negation leads to a contradiction. The negation of (53) is

$$(\forall x)(7AT(GEORGE, x)) \tag{54}$$

which when instantiated, contradicts (52), proving that (53) must be true.

In most situations we want to know what the answer to our question is, not merely that an answer exists. To keep track of answers, Green introduced the idea of an ANSWER literal. Suppose S is a set of facts stated in clausal form, and $Q(x_1 \cdots x_k)$ is a query about these facts. The query is also stated in clausal form and contains k variables. An answer to Q is the set $A = \{a_1 \cdots a_k\}$ of values of variables such that $S \cup \{Q(a_1 \cdots a^k)\}$ is satisfiable. If A exists, the set of statements $S \cup \{7Q(a_1 \cdots a_k)\}$ will be unsatisfiable. A can be located by finding the instantiation needed to refute $S \cup \{7Q(x_1 \cdots x_k)\}$. We can summarize this rather formal statement by saying that a correct answer is a counterexample to the proposition that there is no correct answer. The problem of locating the counterexample remains. Green used a straightforward device called the ANSWER literal to keep track of the necessary instantiations. Somewhat more effective techniques for recording the crucial instantiations have since been developed (Luckham & Nilsson, 1971), but are difficult to include in an expository discussion.

The first step in the ANSWER literal method is to append a special literal, $ANSWER(x_1 \cdots x_k)$ to the literal $7Q(x_1 \cdots x_k)$, producing

$$(7Q(x_1 \cdots x_k), ANSWER(x_1 \cdots x_k)) = B^* \tag{55}$$

Resolution is applied to the set $S \cup \{B\}$ using the set of support strategy with $\{B\}$ as a set of support. Assuming that an answer exists, resolution of $S \cup \{7Q(x_1 \cdots x_1)\}$ will at some point, deduce $(Q(a_1 \cdots a_k))$, which then resolves with some other clause, either in S or deduced from the original set of clauses, to deduce (   ). If we follow the same deduction, but begin with $S \cup \{B^*\}$, then instead of producing (   ) we will produce $(ANSWER(a_1 \cdots a_k))$ which identifies the appropriate instantiation.

Consider the following example

$$S = \{(MAN(SMITH)), \qquad \text{"SMITH IS A MAN."} \tag{56}$$

$$(7MAN(x), ANIMAL(x))\} \qquad \text{"ALL MEN ARE ANIMALS"}$$

The question is *Is there an animal?*

$$(\exists x)(ANIMAL(x)) \qquad \text{"IS THERE AN ANIMAL?"} \tag{57}$$

Negating (57) and appending the ANSWER literal added produces

$$(7\text{ANIMAL}(x), \text{ANSWER}(x)), \qquad\qquad (58)$$

which has the intuitive meaning "Either there is no animal or there is an answer." The answer is constructed in the following steps

1. $(7\text{ANIMAL}(x), \text{ANSWER}(x))$	From (58)	(59)
2. $(7\text{MAN}(x), \text{ANIMAL}(x))$	From (56)	
3. $(7\text{MAN}(x), \text{ANSWER}(x))$	Resolve 1,2	
4. (MAN(SMITH))	From (56)	
5. (ANSWER(SMITH))	Resolve 3,4, after unification	

and question (57) is answered. Formally, the values of the variables in the ANSWER literal are values which the existentially quantifiable variables of the original set of clauses may take in order to produce a counterexample.

One of the key steps in question answering by resolution is the appropriate removal of existentially quantified variables. Recall, from the discussion of quantification in Chapter XII, that this is done by the use of Skolem functionals. Green (1969b) points out that this can cause a problem. Suppose that the axioms (imput facts) consisted of the single statement

$$(\forall z)(\exists w)(P(z, w)) \qquad\qquad (60)$$

and the question had the form

$$(\forall y)(\exists x)(P(y, x)) \qquad\qquad (61)$$

Negation of the question, conversion of the Skolem functionals, and the addition of the ANSWER literal, produces the clauses

$$C1: \quad (P(z, s_1(z))) \qquad\qquad (62)$$

$$B1: \quad (7P(s_2, x), \text{ANSWER}(x))$$

where $s_1(z)$ and s_2 are Skolem functionals. Note that s_2 is a function of no variables, i.e., a constant. By resolving the two clauses of (62) we have

$$(\text{ANSWER}(s_1(s_2))). \qquad\qquad (63)$$

produced. Literally (63) says that there is a constant s_2 such that a function of it, $s_1(s_2)$, is an answer. This will be meaningful to the user only if the origin of the Skolem functionals are known. QA3 provides this facility by allowing its user to request display of the clause used to create a particular Skolem function. Thus on seeing (63) a user could ask for the origin of s_1 or s_2, producing either $C1$ or $B1$ of (62). To see how this affects question answering, Green offered the following concrete example. Let us identify $P(u, v)$ as

Person u is at work and v is the person's desk.

The problem is

$$(\forall z)(\exists u)(P(z, u))$$ Every person at work has a desk   (64)

(1) $P(z, s_1(z))$ Same, with Skolem functionals
For every person y, $s_1(y)$ is
y's desk

(2) $(\forall y)(\exists x)(P(y, x))$ Is there a place at which
everyone works?

(3) $(7P(s_2, x))$ Negation of (2) with quantitifiers
removed. There is some person s_2
for whom there is no place of work.

(4) ANSWER$(s_1(s_2))$ The desk of s_2 is where s_2 works.

Given cleverness, one can phrase a great many questions in the resolution principle format. "How many" questions in quantification can be handled by devices similar to those used in DEDUCOM. For instance

If there are m y's on an x, and n y's on a z, then there are m x n y's on an x.

is expressible as

$$(7HP(x, y, m), 7HP(y, z, n), HP(x, z, \text{TIMES}(m, n)))$$ (65)

where HP(a, b, c) is interpreted as

a has c b's as parts

and TIMES(m, n) is a notation for the product of m x n. The question

How many hands has a man?

is written as,

$$(\exists n)(HP(\text{MAN, HANDS}, n))$$ (66)

"Does there exist n such that HP(MAN, HAND, n) is deducible?"

To illustrate that nontrivial question answering is possible, Green (1969a) used QA3 to answer examples taken from Cooper's (1963) more specialized system for answering questions about chemical compounds. Cooper's data base consisted of 38 facts either about chemistry (e.g., magnesium is a metal) or about equality and substitution (e.g., the symmetry of equality is written $(7EQ(x, y), EQ(y, x))$. An example of the proof to a simple question is the answer to

Is there a white oxide?

The response to this question is

1. $(7\text{OXIDE}(x), 7\text{WHITE}(x), \text{ANSWER}(x))$ Negation of question   (67)

    2.   (OXIDE(MAO))   Fact: Magnesium oxide
                                        (MAO) is an oxide

    3.   (7WHITE(MAO), ANSWER(MAO))   Resolve 1, 2

    4.   (WHITE(MAO))   Fact: MAO is white

    5.   (ANSWER(MAO))

QA3 answered all 23 of the questions which Cooper used to illustrate his specialized system, including several more difficult than the example.

Green (1969c) and Nilsson (1971) have considered the extension of the resolution technique from question answering to state–space problem solving. Note that this is different from the STRIPS application (Chapter XI), in which resolution is used to prove a fact about a particular state. The basic idea behind the application is to include axioms stating that one state can be reached from another by application of an operator. Consider the clause

$$(7P(s), Q(f(s))) \qquad (68)$$

where P and Q are properties of states. (68) can be read as

> *If state s has property P, then the state resulting from application of operator f to s will have property Q.*

An alternative formulation uses the axioms of the form

$$(7P(s), Q(f(a_1 , s))) \qquad (69)$$

which is interpreted as

> *If state s has the property p, then the result of applying operator a_1 to state s has property q.*

Green's QA3 solved a number of state–space problems including graph searching, the Tower of Hanoi puzzle, and even the generation of simple LISP programs by application of these devices. Nevertheless, it is the opinion of most workers in the field that problem solving based only on the predicate calculus is quite limited, because of the clumsiness of the problem statement and the tendency of resolution principle theorem provers to generate an unmanageable set of clauses when working with a large data base. The axiomatization of a problem is itself an art. Green cites the Tower of Hanoi problem as an example. There are many logically correct axiomatizations of this problem, but only a few of them lead to rapid solution of the puzzle. Green (1969a) reports that it took about 2 hours to axiomatize Cooper's facts about elementary chemistry although, as the examples of (68) show, most of these facts are easy to understand. This is another case in which artificial intelligence is stymied by our inability to find representations. Comprehension requires both that we choose a correct model of a situation and that we be able to manipulate the model. Resolution, like most problem solving methods, is only addressed to the second question.

14.2.4   Content Dependent Theorem Proving

We have repeatedly stressed that a major defect of the resolution method is that the number of clauses generated rapidly becomes unmanageable. In question answering this is a very serious consideration because of the number of clauses in the initial data base. Green's examples, in fact, were feasible only because the required deductions were quite short. One way to keep deductive programs from spending time producing clauses that are not needed in the proof is to confine resolution to clauses that are "relevant" or "likely to be relevant" to a proof. Consider the classical deduction

> *All humans are fallible. Socrates is a human. Therefore Socrates is fallible.*

In clause form the antecedent conditions are

$$(7HUMAN\ (x),\ FALLIBLE(x)) \tag{70}$$

$$(HUMAN(SOCRATES))$$

and the question

$$Is\ Socrates\ fallible? \tag{71}$$

is phrased

$$(7FALLIBLE(SOCRATES)) \tag{72}$$

The necessary deductions are

1.	(HUMAN(SOCRATES))	Axiom	(73)
2.	(7HUMAN(x), FALLIBLE(x))	Axiom	
3.	(FALLIBLE(SOCRATES))	Resolve 1,2	
4.	(7FALLIBLE(SOCRATES))	Negation of question	
5.	( )	Resolve 3,4	

Now suppose that we loaded memory with other, irrelevant facts—that Socrates is a Greek, that he is married to Xantipphe, that he is a Republican, that he dislikes hemlock, etc. How are we to keep a resolution principle theorem prover from wasting time considering these extraneous assertions?

Green's solution was to let a human controller determine which clauses were to be considered candidates for resolution. While this may be very practical, it is certainly not an advance in *artificial* intelligence. An alternative approach has been taken by Winograd (1972), which we will call *content dependent* theorem proving, amplifying on previous work by Hewitt (1969, 1970). We have already examined this technique as a planning device (Chapter XI); here we consider its implications for question answering.

To understand what we mean by content-dependent theorem proving and problem solving, it may be useful to look at a content *independent* strategy, the set of support strategy for resolution. The set of support strategy states that if **S** is an unsatisfiable set of clauses, and if there is a subset **C** of **S** such that **S** − **C** is satisfiable, then there exists a deduction of (   ) from **S** in which every step involves resolution in which one of the parent clauses is either a clause in **C** or a descendent of a resolution involving a clause in **C** (see Chapter XII for details). The proof that this strategy always works is independent of any "real world" interpretations of the clauses of **S**. Its validity depends on facts about logic, not facts about the interpretation of the data base.

In any realistic application of deductive question answering there will be a great many strategies which work for a particular data base. To take a somewhat whimsical example, suppose we were asked to write a deductive question answering procedure for use by tax lawyers. A question tax lawyers are frequently asked to answer is

Does the client enjoy a privileged tax status?

As a heuristic, we might try to prove the statement

Is the client a farmer?

and use the answer to the second question in order to answer the first. Similarly, to prove someone is a farmer we would ask questions about his economic activities and not his ancestry. Such strategies are content dependent. In actual applications we would expect them to play an important role in deduction. What we need is some way to let the user state content-dependent strategies to an inference making program. Winograd did so using Hewitt's (1972) PLANNER language, described briefly in Chapter XI in our discussion of planning in problem solving. The point is that planning is equally applicable to question answering. Thus in our tax example we could use PLANNER to issue instructions to search the data base to see if the client was a farmer, a veteran, a widow, etc. Another feature of PLANNER which is particularly useful in dealing with state–space problems is that the proof of a theorem can be treated as a command to be carried out, and a successful proof can be interpreted as an order to make certain assertions. For example if it is provable that Socrates is a man and that he is married to Xantipphe, then a "reasonable" man would immediately add to his data base the information *Xantipphe is a woman.* A PLANNER program can augment the data base in this way.

DEDUCOM also provided us with an example of a program which lets the user specify a search strategy. The principle differences between Winograd's project and Slagle's earlier one are that PLANNER, as a language, is much more suited for the task than is LISP. Perhaps the chief result of Winograd's work is that he has been able to show a method for translating from English to PLANNER programs. This will be discussed in Chapter XV. LISP, on the other hand, appears to be a poor target language. This is important because if we are going to rely on content dependent strategies the user must be able to state them in a language that is natural for him. There is little future in "Comprehension" programs if their users must first become proficient in PLANNER, LISP, MATCHLESS, IPL-V, or any of the many other languages for artificial intelligence programming.

14.3   Comprehension without logic

14.3.0   PSYCHOLOGICAL SIMULATION

If a comprehension program equipped with a complete, valid inference system is given an inconsistent set of facts, its conclusions are immediately suspect. Suppose that in dealing with a question and an inconsistent fact base, QA3 inferred (   ). There would be no way to determine whether the deduction relied on the inconsistency in the data base or an inconsistency between the data base and the negated form of the question. Casual observation shows that people do not seem bothered by apparent inconsistencies so long as they are not, in some sense, too blatant. During the Viet Nam war a presumably rational Army officer was quoted as saying *We destroyed the village in order to save it.* At a subtler level, political behavior offers numerous examples of what most observers admit is rational but agree is inconsistent. Lester Maddox, governor of Georgia in the 1950s and a man widely known for his "white supremacy" views, insisted that black citizens be represented on a number of public boards and commissions. Finally, Richardson (1956) noted that in the charter of the United Nations the phrase "peace loving nations" is used to refer to those national groups who have participated in the vast majority of the world's wars.

These examples are not illustrations of sheer hypocrisy. Governor Maddox's actions provide the clearest example of the rationality of inconsistency. From knowledge of this man's political actions it is reasonable to impute to him the following beliefs

1. White men are more capable than black men.
2. Those most capable should be appointed to public boards and commissions.
3. Both white and black residents of the state of Georgia are citizens of the state.
4. All groups of citizens of a state should be represented on its boards and commissions.

These beliefs imply contradictory policies on appointments, but we hesitate to say that a man is irrational (although he might be mistaken) to hold them.

A rewriting system can handle this sort of reasoning, since rewriting is not a rule of inference. We can imagine a program similar to PROTOSYNTHEX, GPS, or FDS, which could use facts 1–4 to derive either *Blacks should be appointed to public commissions* or *Blacks should not be appointed to public commissions*, depending on whether the program began with facts 1 and 2 or 3 and 4. A number of attempts to simulate "psycho-logical" reasoning of this sort have been made. Abelson and Reich's (1969) simulation of a political belief system will be used as an example. Similar programs have been written to simulate the reasoning of mental patients

(Colby & Pilf, 1970) or to summarize the belief system of a respondent in a psychiatric interview (Colby & Smith, 1969). Earlier work on psychological simulation of personality, including Monte Carlo simulations of group interaction, has been reviewed by Loehlin (1969).

Abelson and Reich's program attempted to simulate the political opinions of Senator Barry Goldwater,[14] an American politician known for his consistent and conservative point of view.[15]

The program's data structure is the "implication molecule," a set of statements that are in some sense chained together. Suppose we have the molecule *A does X to obtain Y*, consisting of the statements

A DOES X: X CAUSES Y: A WANTS Y.   (74)

The statements are themselves quite similar to the semantic event forms of PROTOSYNTHEX. (74) can be regarded as a molecule form, it is instantiated by specification of its variables in the normal way. A possible instantiation of (74) is

COMMUNISTS START RIOTS: RIOTS CAUSE DISRUPTION OF   (75)
SOCIETY: COMMUNISTS WANT DISRUPTION OF SOCIETY

The Abelson and Reich program began with a set of implication molecule forms and a set of initial beliefs. It was also given a dictionary indicating substitution rules (e.g., REDS EQUIVALENT TO COMMUNISTS, RUSSIANS SUBSET OF REDS) which, again, are similar to PROTOSYNTHEX's semantic information statements. The program received assertions and attempted to reconcile them with the assertions previously accepted as beliefs. An assertion was accepted when it could be used to construct an implication molecule by annexing it to other, previously accepted assertions. The program's action is illustrated by the following example of how the "NO WIN" molecule was used to accept a statement about British Foreign policy in the 1960s.

The NO WIN molecule states

LIBERALS FEAR STANDING UP TO COMMUNISTS: (76)

LIBERALS CONTROL WESTERN GOVERNMENTS;

STANDING UP TO COMMUNISTS PREVENTS SITUATIONS
 HELPFUL TO COMMUNISTS.

WESTERN GOVERNMENTS PROMOTE SITUATIONS HELPFUL
 TO COMMUNISTS:

[14] Abelson has never publicly identified Senator Goldwater by name, but his descriptive remarks (e.g., a "well known ex-ex Senator") make it clear who he means.

[15] The fact that Senator Goldwater's opinions are more internally consistent than those of most politicians has probably made the computer simulation easier to construct than it might be were one to try to mimic the behavior of a more Machiavellian leader. Friend and foe alike have commented that the Senator really believes what he says, and that once his viewpoint is understood his actions are quite predictable.

The assertion to be accepted was

BRITAIN DOES NOT INTERFERE WITH INVASION   (77)
OF CZECHOSLOVAKIA

By dictionary lookup, (77) is found to be an instantiation of the last line of (76), since "NOT INTERFERE" is, to the program, equivalent to "PROMOTE." The other substitutions are obvious. The program's task becomes one of finding other sentences to complete (78) with the same instantiation. In particular, SITUATIONS HELPFUL TO COMMUNISTS has been instantiated by INVASION OF CZECHOSLOVAKIA. The program needed the belief

STANDING UP TO COMMUNISTS PREVENTS INVASION   (78)
OF CZECHOSLOVAKIA.

and already had the fact

U.S. SHOW OF FORCE PREVENTS RED INVASIONS.   (79)

Apparently using an algorithm similar to unification,[16] the program determined that (79) is a compatible instantiation of (78). Note that this forced the instantiation of "STANDING UP TO COMMUNISTS" as "U.S. SHOW OF FORCE." The third line of (76) was easy, since the previous belief list contained

WILSON CONTROLS BRITAIN   (80)

and WILSON, then the leader of the Labour party of Britain, and BRITAIN, are obviously cases of LIBERAL and WESTERN GOVERNMENT. Finally, the statement

WILSON FEARS U.S. NUCLEAR ARMS   (81)

was on the belief list, and instantiated U.S. SHOW OF FORCE. The complete molecule was

WILSON FEARS U.S. NUCLEAR ARMS.   (82)

WILSON CONTROLS BRITAIN.

U.S. NUCLEAR ARMS STOP CZECHOSLOVAKIAN INVASION.

BRITAIN DOES NOT INTERFERE WITH CZECHOSLOVAKIAN
INVASION.

One can see that (82) would form the nucleus of a comprehension of world events which, although perhaps incorrect, is certainly coherent.

One of the most interesting features of the Abelson and Reich programs is what happens when the program cannot find a belief of the type it needs to fill out the molecule it is trying to complete. The program simply generates the required sentence and attempts to fit into some *other* molecule. If so, the generated sentence

---

[16] Abelson and Reich do not give details.

is treated as "presumptively true" and accepted. In the illustration, if (81) had not been in the belief list the sentence would have been generated. Now suppose that by appropriate substitutions, (81) could have replaced ** in the molecule

> LIBERALS FEAR STANDING UP TO COMMUNISTS = WILSON   (83)
>   OPPOSES BRITISH TROOP COMMITMENT
>
> LIBERALS OPPOSE ARMAMENTS = ***
>
> ARMAMENTS PROMOTE STANDING UP TO COMMUNISTS =
>   BRITISH TROOP COMMITMENTS AID U.S. SHOW OF FORCE.

This would have allowed the program to mark (82) as presumptively true. Loosely the sort of reasoning is

> *I cannot believe z unless I can believe x, but in light of y I'll believe x, so z must be true.*

Such reasoning may not appeal to a logician but it does not sound inhuman.

14.3.1   Conversing with a Computer under the Illusion of Understanding

In closing this chapter we wish to comment on a group of programs which, largely because they are fun, have generated a good deal of publicity about how computers understand people. The programs we have in mind are the ELIZA and DOCTOR programs designed by Weizenbaum (1966, 1967). These programs are all intended to be executed interactively. An example of an ELIZA conversation (offered by Weizenbaum, 1967) is

> PERSON: *You are not very aggressive but I think you do not want me*   (84)
>   *to notice that.*
>
> COMPUTER: WHAT MAKES YOU THINK I AM NOT VERY
>   AGGRESSIVE.
>
> PERSON: *You don't argue with me.*
>
> COMPUTER: WHY DO YOU THINK I DO NOT ARGUE WITH YOU.
>
> PERSON: *You are afraid of me.*
>
> COMPUTER: DOES IT PLEASE YOU TO BELIEVE I AM AFRAID
>   OF YOU.

This sort of conversaion can be continued for some time. What the program is doing is searching its input for a pattern of key words plus input text, and then executing an action associated with the pattern it finds. In most cases, the program simply rearranges the input words and prints them out. For example, the rule

> I THINK *X*   →   WHY DO YOU WANT TO BELIEVE *X*   (85)

is interpreted "*Search the input text for the words I THINK*" followed by any string
of letters. Let *X* be the string found. Output the words *WHY DO YOU WANT
TO BELIEVE* followed by *X*. A program that can do this is capable of exhibiting
the same sort of understanding as does a politician or administrator whose response
to petitions is to reply, "Yes, I hear you saying that. . . ." Such people may acquire
a reputation for sagacity.

Before we dismiss the ELIZA program as a clever trick, we ought to consider the
questions it raises. Pattern matching can be very sophisticated. Indeed, it is at the
heart of language analysis. Weizenbaum (1966) provides a number of examples
which show that even though ELIZA cannot begin to match all the patterns that
could occur in English, it can match a nontrivial subset of them. Also, there is no
reason that the action associated with a pattern match must be limited to printing a
variation of the input. Specifically, one could require the computer to perform a
computation. The following example (also taken from Weizenbaum, 1967)
illustrates the use of ELIZA with simple arithmetic and storage routines

INPUT: *The area of a circle is pi times the radius of the circle squared.*   (86)

*The area of a sphere is pi times the diameter of the sphere
squared.*

The area of a square is the side of the square squared.

The diameter of an object is twice the radius of the object.

The radius of the ball is 10.

What is the area of the ball?

PROGRAM: THE ASSUMPTION THAT BALL IS CIRCLE IS
CONSISTENT. SHALL I GO ON.

INPUT: *No.*

PROGRAM: THE ASSUMPTION THAT BALL IS SPHERE IS
CONSISTENT. SHALL I GO ON.

INPUT: *Yes.*

PROGRAM: IT'S 1256.6359.

Is this intelligent computation? Is the process of composing an intelligent reply
anything more than pattern matching followed by computation? Personally, we
hesitate to cite ELIZA as an example of comprehension, but we are uneasy because
we cannot say why we hesitate. Perhaps the real point is the one which
Weizenbaum makes in his own analysis of his work. When x says y comprehended
him, x is making an assumption about y's internal processes. This assumption is
often based on very weak evidence.

Chapter XV

COMPREHENSION OF NATURAL LANGUAGE

15.0   The Problem

15.0.1   INTRODUCTION

Most of our present computing equipment is used below capacity, because it is too hard to write adequate programs for tasks that are well within the machines' physical capabilities. If we write programs that are very closely tied to the order code of a specific machine, the machine's capacities are retained but the programs become so complex that they are difficult to understand. If we write programs in languages that lend themselves to the statement of certain types of problems—the "problem-oriented" approach of FORTRAN, COBOL, and BASIC, we generally lose the capacity to state all the computations a computer can perform. Much effort has been devoted to the design of languages for abstract machines that can be realized on actual computers, an approach which should allow the programmer to retain control over the details of the computation but not require him to be concerned with engineering. ALGOL and ALGOL 68 are the most conspicuous examples of this development. For reasons that are not entirely clear, these languages seem to be difficult to learn and, in fact, they give a programmer a capability that can be used only if he knows a good deal about computers. In this chapter a quite different approach will be discussed. Perhaps the biggest obstacle to the extension of computing beyond conventional applied mathematics and bookkeeping is not our inability to produce a language which displays the power of the computer to man, but our inability to move from man's natural language to the internal operations of the computer. In Chapter II we discussed the relation between machine construction and models of formal language, and showed how this relation helps us in understanding computers. In this chapter we will again look at formal languages, but this time we shall stress their limitations. Next we outline some new approaches which are conceptually more promising. Unfortunately these new conceptions of language contain their own limitations. What may soon be possible in principle may not soon be practical.

15.0.2   WHAT IS LANGUAGE?

In Chapters II and VII languages were defined to be sets of strings which satisfied some criterion for "well-formedness." Our primary concern was with the design of a machine that could decide whether a particular string of symbols met this criterion, although it was noted that at an abstract level, such recognition is equivalent to recognizing a sequence of machine executable orders. Let us shift our viewpoint, and consider the use of language in communication. Language is then regarded as a system of signs for describing events in the external world. There are philosophic objections to this definition. It is clear that we are using language in this way when we describe a baseball game or an apple pie, but it is not clear that the definition is satisfactory for more abstract concepts, such as love, jealousy, or freedom. This may be ignored. The concept of language as a model of the physical world is certainly sufficient to deal with any foreseeable conversations with computers.

The signs of a language refer either to objects in the external world, qualities of those objects, or relationships between two or more objects. The relationships themselves may be qualified. The phrases[1]

$$big,\ red\ box;\qquad John\ loves\ Mary \qquad\qquad (1)$$

describe objects and relations. In many situations, language utterances can be interpreted as assertions about the state of the world. Thus, the second example in (1) could be interpreted as the atomic statement

$$LOVES(JOHN, MARY). \qquad\qquad (2)$$

Intuitively, then, we ought to be able to make a connection between linguistic utterances and a set of computer manipulable expressions which constitute the machine's internal description of the external world. Similarly, we can regard questions as assertions that a certain clause is or is not compatible with the clauses describing the current world state. Imperatives can, in turn, be interpreted as orders to edit the internal world model. In Chapter XIV various ways were proposed for building internal computer models of real-world situations. If there is also a way to link natural language statements about situations to the representations of the same situations within a machine, then we can claim to have produced computer comprehension of language over some range of discourse. The question of comprehension has two aspects. Are there situations which we can discuss, and can model on a computer, but for which we cannot produce a linkage between the discourse and the model? Are there situations that we can discuss reasonably in natural language but for which we cannot produce an internal model?

The problem is that language can be used to express very complex relationships, including relationships between relationships. Language also allows us to treat a relationship as a thing to be either qualified or discussed in relation to other things.

---

[1] As in the preceding chapter, we shall number linguistic and mathematical expressions for ease of reference.

To achieve such complexity of expression, language provides rules for generating strings of symbols, in which the order of the symbols in the string indicate the relationship between the references for each symbol. In much simpler terms, you have to be able to unravel the structure of a language string—it is not sufficient to know only what symbols are in it. Only if you are aware of the structure can you detect that

$$John\ loves\ Mary. \tag{3}$$

$$Mary\ loves\ John.$$

are strings with decidedly different meaning.

Now let us consider comprehension from the computer's point of view. In the prefix notation every utterance has the form

$$fa_1, a_2, \ldots, a_n \tag{4}$$

in which the first term is an n-ary function, the value of a function is a term, and the n terms following an n-ary function are its n arguments. Thus if we see the term

$$-xy \tag{5}$$

we know that we are to subtract the term in the y position (which must be a number when it is evaluated) from the term in the x position (similarly a number when evaluated), eventually producing a number that may enter as a term into the argument list of some other function. It is natural to achieve "comprehension" of a statement like (5) in a three step process. In the *syntactic* phase we recognize that the first symbol of (5) is a binary function and we locate the terms which are its operands. In the *semantic* phase we note that the operation is negation, and determine any specific steps (e.g., evaluation of a subexpression) which are needed to find the values of x and y. In the *implementation* or *inferential* phase we execute the exact machine instructions (stores, fetches, additions, negations) needed to do the physical manipulations implied by the arithmetic. The third step is machine dependent, whereas the first two steps exist abstractly. The ideal computer programming language is one that is powerful enough to talk about those real-world situations for which a computational model is desired, and that permits an efficient three step translation to machine execution. Much of the research effort in computer science is directed toward design of more sophisticated control programs for each of these steps, so that machines can deal with ever more powerful programming languages.

Such an effort is certainly useful. It has and will continue to lead to better computing languages, especially if by "better" one means languages in which the user can exert greater control over machine execution. On the other hand, this may be a severely limited approach to the problem of expressing very complex computations on a computer.[2] No computational model can ever be prepared for computer execution unless a human can state it to himself, since this is the first

---

[2] For some additional arguments against the traditional approach to computer language, see Minsky (1970).

step in programming anything. Quite possibly, there are some problems that can be expressed only in natural language. However, the whole purpose of having the computer is so that people can state problems to it. If problems do exist that people can state only in natural language, then a way must be found to allow the computer to "comprehend" natural language. It is unlikely that this can be done in distinct syntax–semantics–comprehension stages, simply because natural language cannot be analyzed in this way.

Clearly this is a conjecture, not a fact. There is no satisfactory theory of human language, nor are we prepared to offer one. Our argument rests on a number of almost anecdotal observations. The most obvious is that a number of very talented people have tried to apply syntactic and semantic analyses to natural language and have not succeeded very well. This suggests that either the syntactic and semantic programs are complicated beyond belief, which seems unlikely since so many people learn to use language well, or that the approach is wrong. But why should the syntactic–semantic approach be such a poor way to analyze natural language, when it is demonstrably such a good way to handle the analysis of computational languages? Our answer to this is that computational languages were designed both with considerations of problem expression and machine execution in mind. Natural language evolved to be executed on a very different type of machine than any computer today. The form of that machine dictated the form the language had to have. We can accept only a certain (as yet imprecisely defined) class of languages (Lenneberg, 1967). Proofs about the capabilities of Turing machines to accept different abstract languages under different restrictions may not help us with the language comprehension problem. If we want to understand the structures of natural language, we should perhaps first consider the types of programs that are easily executable on a computing machine which has a system architecture similar to man's.[3]

This argument leads us to contrast two views of language, which we will call the "mathematical" and the "psychological" views. The mathematical view, due originally to Chomsky (1963), has been predominant in computer science, for the reasons detailed in Chapter II. To review the argument briefly, in the mathematical view a language is described by a system of rules capable of generating a well-formed set of strings, or *sentences*. The rule system can be regarded as a design for a machine which produces the sentences of the language and no other strings. Alternatively, the rules can be regarded as the specifications for a program capable of generating the language. There is a formal identity between a machine capable of generating a sentence in a language, and a machine capable of recognizing that a given string is or is not a sentence. In the case of the machine recognizing a sentence, we say that the machine *accepts* the string. In the mathematical analysis, accepting the string is equivalent to saying that the machine (or the interpreting program) has determined a way in which the string might have been generated. In the ideal language for computational analysis there will only be one way in which a

[3] For an elaboration of this point, see Hunt (1971, 1973).

given sentence can be generated, so accepting the string will be equivalent to determining "for certain" how it was generated. It seems reasonable (although the mathematical theory does not concern itself with this point directly) that if one knew the steps a speaker went through in generating a statement, one could easily determine the meaning of the statement. For example, having determined the structure of the string

$$A = (B + 2) * C \tag{6}$$

a FORTRAN compiler can determine what computations the programmer wished executed. For the vast majority of practical situations, this is all that is needed.[4]

In contrast to the mathematical view, the psychological view is chaotic. To the extent that it has a central point, the point is that we will understand languages only by understanding human capabilities and the broad laws that govern human behavior. Language is viewed as a specific activity of man to be derived from a broader understanding of psychology. In practice, this has meant that much of the psychological research on language has focused on variables that determine human language learning, such as Skinner's (1957) approach to language as a special case of operant conditioning. Another line of research seeks to determine the physiological basis of language (Lenneberg, 1967; Geschwend, 1970). Whereas such emphases are understandable in view of the psychologist's concern, they deal more with the question of *how* language arose in man than the question of precisely *what* has arisen or how a machine could be designed to use language. As a result the psychological viewpoint has had little impact on computer science. This is bound to be unfortunate, if it is true that we cannot design machines to comprehend natural languages until we understand more about how natural languages have to be comprehended. The argument rests on two assumptions; that the mathematical model does not lead to an adequate description of natural language, and that a psychological model can be used to construct computer executable algorithms for language analysis. The following sections present some evidence bearing on these assumptions.

15.1   Natural Language: The Mathematical Model

15.1.0   REMARKS ON CONTEXT FREE, CONSTITUENT STRUCTURE GRAMMARS

The idea of formal grammars has already been presented. In Chapter II the constituent structure, context free languages were introduced, and it was pointed

---

[4] There are a few troublesome situations in which either ambiguities do occur, or in which the removal of an ambiguity in the language also removes the capability of requesting a computation which the computer could do. A tremendous amount of research effort has been directed at extending the mathematical model to handle these relatively rare occasions. The study of ALGOL 68 is a case in point. One of the implied arguments of this section is that such an effort is of questionable economy, since there are major and not uncommon problems in the extension of computer languages which require us to abandon the mathematical model entirely.

out that every effort is normally made to construct computer programming languages so that they are constituent structure, and if possible, content free grammars. This is true even when it is proposed that the language be defined by example. All the grammatical inference algorithms discussed in Chapter VII assume a context free language. The following example illustrates why such languages are convenient for the computer scientist. Consider the language defined by the vocabulary

$$N = \{S, O, A, E\} \tag{7}$$

$T = \{$"any letter, $a \ldots z$," any integer from 0-1000", +, $-$ $\}$

and the grammar

$$S \rightarrow E; \tag{8}$$

$$E \rightarrow A;$$

$$E \rightarrow EOE;$$

$$A \rightarrow \text{"Any letter or integer"};$$

$$O \rightarrow \text{"+ or } -\text{."}$$

This language will generate strings of the form a, $a + b$, $a + 17$, $a - 17$, etc. It is a phrase structure language, as it is possible to construct a parsing tree for any string in the language by starting with the string, and then replacing any substring within the string which corresponds to the *right* side of one of the rules of G with the corresponding *left* side, until eventually the symbol S is reached. Figure 15-1 shows the tree for a simple string in the language defined by (7) and (8). The string is said to be parsed when the tree has been built. A successful parse is equivalent to recognizing that there is a way in which the language could have generated the string. Also, there is a direct way to translate a parsing tree into the semantics of computer operation. This can also be shown by Figure 15-1. The figure diagrams the parse as a tree structure; which can trivially be translated into the prefix (Polish) notation. Let us place parentheses around the string corresponding to each

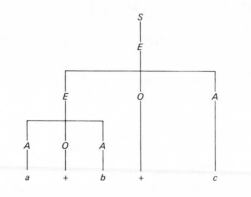

Fig. 15.1 Example of Parsing in a phrase structure grammar.

E in the string being parsed. This can readily be done. In the example the parenthetical structure is

$$(((a) + b) + c) \qquad (9)$$

Given this information, there are well-known mechanical procedures for changing to the prefix notation

$$+c + ba, \qquad (10)$$

which can then be calculated by a sequence of fetches and additions preceeding from right to left, i.e. by the sequence

Fetch a

Fetch b

Add the last two figures fetched, and store sum

Fetch c

Add to sum

The precise mechanics for executing these operations will, of course, depend upon the computer being used. Real programming languages, of course, are far more complex. Nevertheless, the basic principles are the same. The added complexity of the languages lies almost entirely in their having much larger grammars than we have used.

In summary, the program languages based on the context free, phrase structure model do generate a reasonable language for talking about arithmetic and algebraic operations. People can learn to speak these languages, and the languages are easily translatable into machine instructions. Therefore they are highly useful for some purposes. On the other hand, it is easy to show that these languages are not capable of handling some of the constructions of natural language. We will not try to characterize the problem in detail. Instead we illustrate, by noting that within the framework of phrase structure grammars there is no way to recognize that the two sentences

John picked up the book (11)

The book was picked up by John

are identical, since they would certainly generate different parses. One feels somehow that recognizing this sort of identity is an important part of comprehension.

15.1.1   TRANSFORMATIONAL GRAMMARS[5]

Many linguists feel that, in order to formalize languages of the complexity of natural languages, it will be necessary to consider an expanded class of grammars

---

[5] The basic reference on transformational grammars is Chomsky's (1965) book. Thomas (1965) provides a highly readable, nontechnical discussion of the use of transformational grammars in analyzing English.

called *transformational grammars*. These were briefly introduced in Chapter II, where it was pointed out that the full power of a Turing machine may be required to recognize strings from a transformational language. This suggests, on theoretical grounds alone, that formidably complex computations may be involved in language analysis. This is indeed the case. To see why, let us look at some of the information-processing requirements in human speech comprehension.

What happens when a sentence is generated? First, the speaker must decide what he wants to say. His idea is said to be represented syntactically by a string in a *deep structure* language, which is conceived of as a sort of internal language of thought. Mathematical linguists are little concerned with how the deep structure representation of the statement to be generated is connected to the idea it represents. We shall eventually question their lack of concern, since we maintain that it is precisely this question which must be dealt with in the computer use of natural language. For the present, however, the structure is assumed, and furthermore, it is assumed that the internal language in which the deep structure is expressed is a phrase structure language. The utterance is generated from the deep structure by application of a series of transformation rules which result in the spoken language sentence, whose structure is called the *surface structure*. The external language sentence must be analyzed by mapping back from the surface string to the deep structure, and then uncovering relations between the elements of the deep structure.

We will give two examples to illustrate the complexities this approach can involve. The first is the case of questions. Suppose one wishes to ask the question

Did Sherlock Holmes expose the evildoer?   (12)

Using a fairly obvious notation,[6] the deep structure of the question is shown in Figure 15-2. The diagram states that the sentence (S) consists of a question marker, a noun phrase, and a verb phrase. The noun phrase consists of the single (noun) referent "Sherlock Holmes," whereas the verb phrase consists of the verb plus auxiliary "did expose" and the noun phrase "the evildoer." English has a transformation rule that states that in sentences with Q markers the auxiliary verb may be moved in front of the subject noun phrase, which produces the final sentence. If we were to produce a phrase marker diagram from (12) directly we would no longer have a tree, since the adjacent elements of the terminal string in (12) are not always derived from adjacent nonterminal elements of the parsing tree. Although this poses no problem for sentence generation, it may pose a considerable problem in sentence comprehension, where one seeks the deep structure rather than starting with it.

A more complex example is offered by the sentence

Lady Agatha is believed to have been abducted.   (13)

---

[6] The following notation will be used throughout: Q = question, NP = noun phrase, N = noun, VP = verb phrase, V = verb, Det = determiner, Adj = adjective, Adv = adverb, Loc = location, Prep = preposition, T = time.

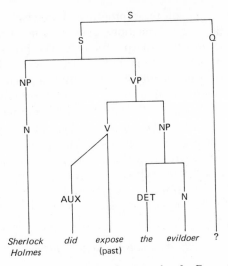

Fig. 15.2. Deep structure phrase marker for Example (15).

The correct interpretation of (13) is that some unspecified person(s) is of the persuasion that someone else, also unspecified, has abducted Lady Agatha. The deep structure is shown in Figure 15-3. The first noun phrase in the surface structure, Lady Agatha, is in fact the object of the verb in a subordinate clause. This clause, in turn, is the object of the main verb in the sentence. The subjects of the verbs in both the main and subordinate clauses are the indefinite "someone," but it is clear that they are different someones. Note that the sentence is

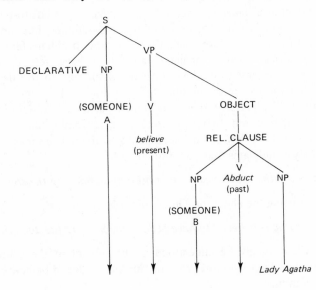

Fig. 15.3. Deep structure of *Lady Agatha is believed to have been abducted.*

immediately clear in spite of these problems. But why? There is no particular problem in constructing a transformational grammar containing rules with which to generate surface structures from deep structures. The problem is to go the other way, to recover deep structure from surface structure. In the case of the phrase structure grammar we can identify the nonterminals that might generate each terminal component in the surface string. This produces a string containing some nonterminals. Next we collapse adjacent symbols into other possible nonterminal symbols. At each step the collapsing of symbols in one part of the string is independent of the analysis of other parts. This allows us to parse the string progressively from left to right, without having to back up to rearrange trial parsings. The simple left–right scheme for reading a string will not work for language generated by a transformational grammar. To see this, consider the parsing necessary to locate "Lady Agatha" in relation to the proper verb in (13). Contrast this to the appropriate parse for

Lady Agatha is Sir Roger's fiancee.   (14)

In (14) the substring "Lady Agatha is" is properly parsed by assigning the NP "Lady Agatha" to be the subject of "is." In (13) the same NP is the object of the verb in a subordinate clause. In each example the proper role of the first noun phrase in the surface string cannot be determined until the characteristics of the words following "is" have been determined. Since the parsing of the initial noun phrase is dependent on the parsing of a surface string component not adjacent to it, the parsing algorithm must have either the ability to hold a parsing in abeyance until more information is received, or the ability to make trial parsings which can be corrected as more information becomes available.

The fact that natural languages cannot be analyzed by a left-to-right scanning algorithm is an inconvenience to the computer programmer, but more complex scanning algorithms could be developed. There are other problems that raise deeper conceptual difficulties. Natural languages appear to have very complex transformational rules. In many cases the choice of which rule to use depends upon information about the nature of the objects being discussed, rather than syntactic information about the parts of speech to which particular nonterminal symbols belong. The problem is not that some sentences are ambiguous in the natural language, but rather that they are not ambiguous to the native speaker, although a grammatical analysis indicates that they should be.In

Lady Agatha is believed to have been kidnapped by the spy.   (15)

the spy is seen as being the abductor. On the other hand, in

Lady Agatha is believed to have been kidnapped by the detective.   (16)

the detective will normally be understood as the subject of the main verb. Our choice between two deep structures rests on our knowledge of detectives and spies, not of English grammar.

To the mathematical linguist a grammar is a model of a language if it specifies a machine capable of generating all the strings in the language and no other strings. By this criterion phrase structure grammars cannot be used to explain natural language, while transformational grammars may be. To the computer scientist, however, language generation is not the point, language analysis is. What parsing algorithms can be developed that will recover the deep structure from the surface structure of a transformational grammar? We now turn to this question.

15.1.2   PARSING TRANSFORMATIONAL GRAMMARS

After an initial period in which a number of ways to handle the problem were proposed, a technique for analyzing transformational grammars appears to be developing. At least, a number of papers have reported the same basic method (Bobrow & Fraser, 1969; Kaplan, 1972; Thorne, Brately, & Dewar, 1969; Woods, 1970). It should be remembered, however, that parsing algorithms for transformational grammars have not, as yet been as intensively studied as have parsing algorithms for phrase structure languages, and it is not unreasonable to suspect that some quite new method for parsing transformational languages may shortly be developed.

Following Woods, the method to be described will be called *augmented transition network* method for analysis of natural language. It is based on an expansion of an unrealistically simple model of language analysis, *finite state transition network* analysis. To understand the complex method, a look at the simple model is in order.

A *finite state transition network* is defined by a set of nodes and directed arcs connecting them. Roughly, the nodes correspond to nonterminal symbols and the arcs to terminal symbols. A distinguished state S is designated as a starting node; state S^* is the finishing node. An example of a finite state transition network is shown in Figure 15-4. To use the graph to generate a string we begin at S and proceed as follows:

(*i*) Choose one of the directed arcs emanating from the current node and traverse it.

(*ii*) Each arc will be labeled either with a string termination symbol, #, or the name of a subset of the terminal symbols. When an arc is traversed, one of the terminal symbols in the subset associated with the arc should be emitted.

(*iii*) Continue the process until node S^* is reached. The string terminates at this point.

To illustrate, suppose we wanted to generate

$$\text{\textit{The big brown dog chased the little black cat \#}} \qquad (17)$$

from Figure 15-4. The nodes visited in order would be S, Det, Adj, Adj, N, V, Det, Adj, Adj, N, S*.

Now let us consider reception. Here we are given a string and asked if it could possibly be produced by the grammar defined by the network. To answer this

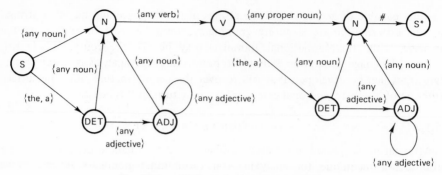

Fig. 15.4.   Finite state transition network.

question we begin at state S, and, taking each of the input words in order, find an arc that could be traversed in order to generate that symbol. If we are at S* after accepting #, the sentence has been accepted.

Finite state models are deficient in being unable to handle recursive generation rules. These are rules in which a symbol which is the sole symbol on the left is duplicated on the right. An example is

$$A \rightarrow s_1 A s_2 \tag{18}$$

Our natural language examples have had this form. The deep structures of (13), (15), and (16) are all

It is believed that(s). (19)

where the (s) may be replaced by any legitimate structure that can be generated from the head symbol—i.e., by any well-formed string in the language. In particular, (s) in (19) could be replaced by a second sentence containing an embedded (s), which could in turn contain an embedded (s), and so forth. Since there is no way to embody recursion as part of the circuit of a graph, finite state transition networks cannot recognize such a string.[7]

Recursion can be handled by augmenting the finite network model to allow one finite state network to call another finite state network, as a procedure to be executed at any node. A grammar is then represented by a set of finite state networks, each representing the parsing of some nonterminal component of the language. To analyze (generate) a string we proceed as follows:

---

[7] A natural question is whether or not arbitrarily deeply embedded strings do actually occur in natural language discourse. Obviously any given string has a finite level of embedding. A finite state network could be written to generate any language in which the level of embedding is limited. Linguists reject such models because of the potential capacity of the grammar to generate strings greater than this arbitrary limit. Psychologists, on the other hand, are more concerned with an analysis of strings that actually occur. We suggest that the computer scientist interested in designing a machine capable of conversing with man is, in fact, closer to the psychologist than the linguist in his concerns.

(*i*) Begin at S in the initial network. Completion of a path through this network to S* is equivalent to a successful parse.

(*ii*) At each step, traverse arcs and generate (or accept) nonterminal symbols as before. Except that

(*iii*) At certain nodes, instead of traversing an outgoing arc, control may be transferred to another finite state network in the grammar.

Call the network *from* which transfer is controlled the *calling* network and the second network the *called* network. The called network begins parsing at its own start symbol, using the next symbol in the string as its first input symbol. Upon reaching its exit node, the called network transfers control back to the appropriate node in the calling network. The "next symbol to be read" (generated) is now the first symbol after the symbols recognized by the (just completed) called network.

(*iv*) A called network may call other networks. Recursive calls (a network transferring to its own start state, either directly or through an intermediate network) are permitted.

In envisaging how a transition network analyzes a sentence it is useful to think of two separate components to the analysis algorithm: the network itself and a control program. The control program is responsible for keeping track of the word being read from the input string, the sequence of calls, and the network point which is currently active. In a finite state network without recursive capability the control program simply checks to see if the word just read is a possible label for one of the arcs emanating from the currently active node. When a calling capability is added the control program must be able to do two more operations, called PUSH and POP. Suppose the program is reading the jth word of the input string and is at node n in the network. This node will have associated with it the arcs emanating from it and, in addition, a list of networks which may be called from it. If the jth input word is not a permissible label for one of the arcs, the control program calls for a PUSH to one of the callable networks. The PUSH operation places a pointer to node n on a "pushdown list" and then begins parsing the called networks. The pushdown list is a list of node names which are read out in inverse order to the order in which the names are put on the list. (In operations research terminology, we would call this a "last in, first out" queue.) Thus if items are put on the pushdown list in the order n, r, s, they will be read out in the order s, r, n.[8] A POP operation is the inverse of a PUSH, it takes the first node name off the pushdown list and transfers control to it. The POP operation is used to transfer control back to the calling network when the end node of the called network is reached. POP is also used, with a failure indicated, if no path through the called network can be found.

Figure 15-5 shows a set of networks for a finite state transition network with the

---

[8] Theoretical aspects of pushdown lists were considered in Chapter II. Many variants of pushdown lists are used in systems programming and symbol manipulation by computer. See Knuth (1968) for details.

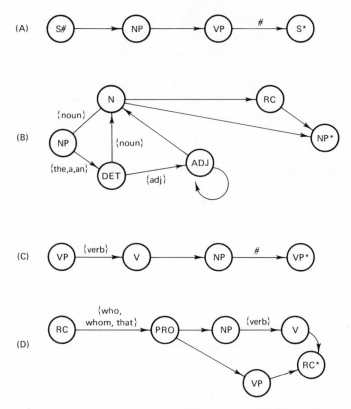

Fig. 15.5 Example of finite state network with procedure calls. The symbol $A(i)$ indicates node A in the subnetwork i. For example, NP(B) is the NP mode in (B).

ability to call other networks as procedures. Suppose this network is used to parse

$$\textit{The detective saw the man whom the woman heard.} \qquad (20)$$

Parsing begins at state S in network (A). Control is immediately transferred to NP(A), and the input word will still be "the." Network (B) will recognize "the detective" as a NP via the route NP-Det-N-NP*. We will place parentheses around this unit to mark it as a constituent of the sentence. Following a POP operation at NP*(B) control is returned to NP(A). Note that the return empties the pushdown list. The sentence now appears as

$$\textit{(The detective) saw the man whom the woman heard.} \qquad (21)$$

and the word being parsed is "saw." A second procedure call is made at VP(A), this time to network (C). Network (C) recognizes "saw" as a verb, and then, at NP(B), calls network (B). Following the necessary PUSH, control will be at NP(B). At this time the sentence analysis is

$$\textit{(The detective) (saw (the man whom the woman heard.} \qquad (22)$$

and the pushdown list is $(NP(C), VP(A))$. Network (B) can be used to recognize "the man" directly, but following "man" a call to network (D) is needed to recognize the relative phrase. When control is transferred to RC(D) the pushdown list will be $(RC(B), NP(C), VP(A)$ and the incomplete analysis of the sentence will be

$$(The \; detective) \; (saw((the \; man)(whom \; the \; woman \; heard. \qquad (23)$$

Network (D), in turn, calls (B) recursively to recognize "the woman." Note that this call requires a PUSH followed by a POP, which will successively place NP(D) on the pushdown list, then take it off. At that point control will be given to NP(D) with the incomplete analysis

$$(The \; detective)(saw(the \; man)(whom(the \; woman) \; heard. \qquad (24)$$

"Heard," the final word of the sentence, is read by V(D), and a series of POPs are executed, in order, at TC(D), NP(B), and VP(A). This empties the pushdown list and control ia passed to S*(A), which is the termination point of the highest level network. Parsing is now complete, with the sentence structure

$$(The \; detective)(saw(the \; man(whom(the \; woman) \; heard))). \qquad (25)$$

Although no formal proof has been offered, the example is hopefully adequate to convince the reader that a finite state transition network system with procedure calls can analyze sentences generated by a context free, constituent structure grammar. Thus this method is a possible, albeit somewhat clumsy, way of handling conventional computer programming languages.

We still have not dealt with transformations from deep to surface structure or vice versa, as no mechanism has been presented for rearranging the order of components in a string. To handle this problem Woods proposed adding to the finite state network a set of *registers* and a memory for the structure of a sentence. The registers control the parsing by holding information about the results of previous parsing actions. This information is used to change the order in which the control program examines different parts of the network, as it attempts to analyze the yet unparsed sections of the sentence. The information in the registers may also be used to rearrange the structure of the input sentence. Because the program is allowed to change the sentence structure or the information in the registers, the control program is able to make tentative assignments of parts of the input string to different sentence structures. These may be changed if subsequent analysis shows that the original assignment was incorrect. As a result, the control program is able to move from the surface structure of a sentence to its deep structure as more information about the sentence comes to light.

To illustrate how this happens, consider another sentence about the harried nobles. The network system we will use is shown in Figure 15-6. The figure also marks certain points which are not part of the network, but are points at which the control program will be working when significant actions take place in this example. The sentence to be parsed is

$$Lady \; Agatha \; was \; taken \; for \; a \; ride. \qquad (26)$$

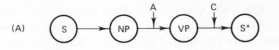

(A)

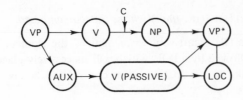

(B)

Registers

Subject _____

Verb _____

Object _____

Agent _____

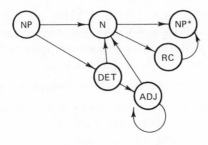

(C)

(D)

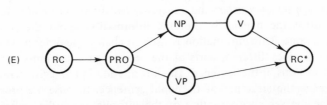

(E)

Fig. 15.6.   Finite state network with procedure calls and registers.

The steps in the parsing are as follows:

(*i*) Enter at S. Transfer to NP and push to network (B). Place NP(A) on pushdown list.

(*ii*) Recognize (Lady Agatha) as a noun phrase using network (C). POP returns control to NP(A). At point *A* place the phrase (Lady Agatha) in the SUBJECT register.

(*iii*) Enter VP(A) and PUSH to network (B). Recognize "was" as a verb. [Note that this is a preferred construction. The control program is trying to read from VP(B) to V(B). Only if this fails will it back up to try VP*-Aux.] At point *B* place (was) in the VERB register.

(*iv*) Control passes to NP(B), which is marked for a PUSH to network (C). Network (C), however, fails since the next word in the string, "taken," is neither a noun nor a determiner. The control program then backs up to the last decision point, the exit from VP(B) and takes the alternative branch to AUX.

(*v*) "Was" is recognized as an auxiliary and "taken" as a passive verb. (was taken) is placed in the verb register with the notation (take(past, passive))–i.e., the verb plus qualifiers.

(*vi*) Control passes to LOC(B), which PUSHes to network (D). The string "for a ride" is recognized as a prepositional phrase of location, and marked. A series of POPs move from LOC*(D) through VP*(B) to point *C*.

(*vii*) At this point the sentence has been parsed as (Lady Agatha) ((take(past, passive)(for a ride))). At point *C* the transformational capability is used. Having completed identification of the verb phrase, the control program discovers that the VERB register contains a marker for a passive form. The transformational rule contained in the problem is "For passive verbs, move contents of AGENT register to SUBJECT, and SUBJECT register to OBJECT." Since AGENT is empty, the indefinite "someone" replaces it. The rearrangement of the registers produces

$$(Someone)(take(past, passive)(Lady\ Agatha)(for(a\ ride))), \qquad (27)$$

which is the correct deep structure.

Augmented networks have the same power as a Turing machine. This means that any language that can ever be recognized by a computer program can be recognized by a program which uses the augmented transition network technique. Such considerable increase of power is obtained while retaining the conceptually simple device of a graphic representation of a grammar. There has been a price, however. The control program must be much more complex. In fact, the increase in control program complexity introduced by the use of registers and structural rearrangement is qualitatively different from the increase in complexity introduced by PUSH and POP operations. In order to go from analysis of one language to analysis of another using a finite state network without registers, all that must be changed is the networks. The control programs are invariant over languages. As soon as the control program assumes responsibility for checking and rearranging register information, the logic of the control program becomes part of the grammar. This has two important results. Analytically, the problem of stating what languages can be accepted by a particular augmented transition network analysis is changed from a problem of proving the existence of classes of paths through graphs to the much harder problem of proving theorems about the possible results of programs. Intellectually, we are forced to admit that a program offered as a description of a language might itself be too complex to comprehend.

15.1.3   A CRITIQUE OF THE MATHEMATICAL APPROACH

There are two levels at which one can critique an approach to language, or, for that matter, any other scientific model. One is that the approach is correct but the details may be wrong. This is essentially the argument for moving from a constituent structure to a transformational grammar analysis of natural language. In each case we retain the idea that a theory of language is a design for a machine for generating sentences in the language. The argument is over the details of the machine.

This is the position taken by the mathematical linguistics. Chomsky, in the very first pages of his major work on transformational grammars, is quite explicit in saying that formal linguistics is concerned with the study of *competence*, i.e., the assignment of structure to the sentences of a language, and not with *performance*, which he defines as the actual use of the language to transmit ideas. He points out (Chomsky, 1965, p. 11) that in actual use of the language we make a distinction between "acceptable" and "unacceptable" sentences which is distinct from the idea of "grammatical" and "ungrammatical". Thus

The man the boy the woman knew hit ran. (28)

is grammatical by the accepted rules of English, yet we find it unacceptable. On the other hand, there are any number of slang expressions that are acceptable but acknowledged to be ungrammatical. The best example we know of is the expression we have heard used (though not often) by Australian–English speakers

*Give us me tea. (29)

The speakers will, somewhat shamefacedly, admit that they used a poor construction. On the other hand, they will quite correctly point out that other speakers of the language knew what they meant. According to Chomsky, the notion of acceptability and the related notion of comprehension are part of the study of linguistic performance and, as such, are outside the realm of formal linguistics.[9] Chomsky further asserts, however, that he cannot see how one could develop a theory of linguistic performance without first having a theory of competence sufficient to assign structure to all sentences.

This is the point of disagreement. We believe that in comprehension there are no distinct, sequential phases of structural analysis, deep structure analysis, and mapping into meaning. Rather, it seems that the comprehender shifts back and forth from one mode to the other. Schank (1971) is more extreme, he likened the study of structure in the abstract to an attempt to understand thinking by cutting the head open! This may not be so, but it is still true that grammatical structure analysis cannot be understood in isolation from the listener's comprehension of the sentence. The psychological theory being espoused is that in natural language syntax is used as a guide to comprehension, but it is not a controlling element. In some cases it will be possible to comprehend a sentence without fully analyzing its

[9] In some of his writing Chomsky has retreated from this viewpoint. In a general introduction to the topic (Chomsky, 1967) he defined grammar as the process of mapping from a phonetic representation of a signal to the meaning of that signal. We would be willing to accept this definition, and then would have some reservation about the present stress on rewriting systems as a way of describing the mapping.

structure. In other cases it will be impossible to assign structure to a sentence without considering its possible meanings.

A most compelling argument for this view is that in natural language performance there is no single linguistic unit, such as a sentence, or in computer terms, such as a program or procedure, that can be comprehended in isolation. The analysis of a linguistic message depends upon the hearer's internal data bank, which has been built by comprehension of previous messages. Consider the paragraphs

> *Alice waded out of the stream. Looking up, she was startled to see the*   (30)
> *White Rabbit sitting on a rock, looking at her. She ran toward him,*
> *clutching her towel in front of her.*

and

> *Alice waded out of the stream. Looking up, she was startled to see Don*   (31)
> *Juan sitting on a rock, looking at her. She ran toward him, clutching*
> *her towel in front of her.*

The pictorial image evoked by Alice has probably changed considerably. Why? Because a new image was needed to obtain a reasonable data base describing the scene. Now one can object that this is a problem of assigning the correct reference to a noun, which is a separate question from grammatical analysis. This is the case in this example, but in other examples we can easily make the grammatical analysis dependent on comprehension. Consider

> *John and Mary have had the Beechcraft and Cessna repaired. They are*   (32)
> *flying planes now.*

and

> *John and Mary are bored with flying gliders. They are flying planes*   (33)
> *now.*

In these examples a grammatical ambiguity has been resolved by considering the meaning of the sentences surrounding the ambiguity. Unlike the "Alice" example there is no change in the referent of "planes" from (32) to (33). The key is that the ambiguous sentence can have only one interpretation if it is to become a meaningful part of the data base which represents the paragraph. Comprehension is the key to grammatical analysis, not the converse. Undoubtedly there are grammatical cues, which are used to determine the meaning of a sentence. At the same time, as the meaning of a sentence begins to unfold it exerts an influence over the grammar.

If our argument is correct, why is there now such stress on the analysis for formal languages? This is a perfectly proper pursuit for the mathematical linguist, since his goal is to provide a model for competence in detecting strings of a language, not competence in translation of these strings into a "correct" internal data base. At a more practical level, computer programming languages, which are useful but very restrictive, can profitably be analyzed in separate semantic and syntactic stages. The psychologist and the psycholinguist, who want to account for the performance, not competence, may have to look for other views of language. It is even questionable whether or not thinking about abstract automata will help the psychologist explain language behavior to himself.

The language comprehension problem in artificial intelligence is a compromise between these two views. The machines we are going to use are computers, and computers are the sorts of machines that can analyze languages by clear-cut divisions between competence and performance. In the foreseeable future computers will talk to humans only on specific topics, so there is no need to recreate the vast, and quite mysterious, human long-term memory capability. On the other hand, we are concerned with general comprehension, since the purpose of speaking to a computer is to get it to do something, and all a computer can do is change its internal data base. Perhaps we ought not to be so quick to disregard the style of operation of the only adequate comprehender we have available—*Homo sapiens.*

15.2   The Psychological Model

15.2.0   GENERAL

In what sense is it possible to write programs based on a psychological model? Certainly not in the sense that the programs will be based on a vague idea about the nature of language, since programs cannot be written based on a vague idea. It is not possible to write programs that are based on (or are) models of human linguistic behavior, since not enough is known about human comprehension. Rather, we shall say that a computer program for comprehension is psychologically oriented if (*a*) no attempt is made to keep distinct the syntactical and semantic phases and (*b*) the algorithms used are based upon intuitions about how a person might comprehend speech, rather than being justified by derivation from an abstract mathematical system. Such psychology admittedly owes more to William James and the German introspectionists than it does to modern experimental psychology. No apology is needed, because this is consistent with the goal of producing computer programs capable of reacting to natural language discourse. Ideas are where you find them. If a useful program can be produced by violating some set of mathematical conventions, or by translating into a program a psychological model that can be shown to be a false model of behavior, it is all right *for the purpose of the computer scientist.* The mathematical linguist or psychologist would not have such freedom.

Given such pragmatic approach, it is probably not surprising that the "psychological" theory of computer comprehension of language is not so neatly developed as the mathematical theory. Confusion and inconsistency are almost inherent in the approach. The ideas that appear to be sparking most current research in the field are the notion that knowledge can be represented by a semantic network (Quillian, 1968; McCalla & Sampson, 1972; Rumelhart, Lindsay, & Norman, 1971) and that parsing should be controlled by semantic as well as syntactic features (Schank, 1972; Winograd, 1972). It is too early to say what direction the field will take, and it would not be terribly surprising to us if some new idea were to be announced which would usurp all others. On the other hand, our discussion implies some of our guesses about how things are going to develop in this field. In particular, we have ignored a great deal of the earlier work, and some of the contemporary projects, simply because we feel that they are dead ends. We may be wrong. The reader interested in pursuing this topic further should see the more comprehensive review by Simmons (1970).

15.2.1   CONCEPTUAL PARSING

The basic idea behind the psychological approach to parsing is that structural analysis of a natural language sentence should be controlled primarily by the presumed meaning of that sentence. Syntactical cues can assist in establishing meaning but do not control the process. In part, this is a sort of "chicken and egg" sequence of events, since it is almost impossible to assign meaning until something is known about structure. The solution, therefore, is to write a computer program which assigns a tentative structural description to part of a string, then determines whether a meaningful interpretation can result, and, if it can, uses that result to guide the search for syntactical structure in the remainder of the sentence.

Since it is very important to understand the basic idea behind this process, and much less important to understand its details in a particular program, we shall try to illustrate with a nonprogramming example. Suppose you were trying to construct a model airplane under the following somewhat unusual conditions. You have available a small table that contains a position for the partially constructed model and some empty space onto which you may put parts that you are not yet ready to use. An assistant, or "transmitter" selects parts and hands them to you at a rate and in an order not under your control. To make the process more complicated, let us suppose that the blank area of the table is not large enough to hold all the parts in the box. Therefore your assembly of the model must be rapid enough so that whenever you receive a part you can either put it in position in the model or you can find space for it on the table. The analogy to speech is direct. In speech comprehension a speaker sends words to a listener at a rate under the speaker's control. The listener must keep up with the speaker in the assembly of a model of what the speaker is trying to say.

Like speech comprehension, this sort of model building is by no means impossible. Let us look at some of the ways in which it could be accomplished. One strategy for the model builder to follow would be to wait until the speaker handed him a "key piece" (e.g., the fuselage), which could be used as a frame around which other pieces would be placed. Probably most people would proceed in this way. Precisely how hard the task would be would depend upon a number of task characteristics which we have not yet specified. Contextual information would help a great deal—the mere fact that you knew that you were being handed airplane parts, rather than boat parts, would be a tremendous aid in recognizing where pieces should go. As the model begins to take form more contexual information will be available. The order in which the transmitter hands you the pieces will be very important. Ideally he will hand you pieces in an order such that, whenever you get a piece, you will know where it has to be placed in the final model. Under less than ideal conditions you might get pieces which, at the time you receive them, fit into one of several positions, forcing you to guess. If you guess wrong, then you will have to (partially) disassemble the model when further information uncovers the false start. Hopefully the amount of disassembly will be held to a minimum.

Now let us consider the effect of some constraints on the situation. Undoubtedly the major problem is one of guessing what the completed model is supposed to look like. Within a given context ("planes in general," "World War I planes," etc.) you will have to have a general plan of the permissible structures. For instance, you could be badly confused if you do not know about helicopters. As more and more pieces are identified your ideas about permissible structures will become narrower and narrower. In fact, you may be able to identify all major details of the model at some point before you have seen every piece. Returning to the speech analogy, we do not have to hear every word of most speeches in order to recognize the ideas behind them. It would also help if there were some constraints on the rate and order in which the speaker could hand the parts of the model to you. For instance, suppose that the transmitter was required to begin at the nose of the aircraft and work down the fuselage toward the tail, but that he was allowed to choose whether to go down the fuselage to the tail first, and then come back to the wings, or to go down one side, out onto the wing, and then back into the fuselage and down, and finally up the other side. The model builder could assemble parts fairly rapidly between choice points, but he would have to pause to determine which way the transmitter chose to go at each of the choice points. Finally, the more work space you have the easier it will be to recover from errors.

In speech comprehension the listener is much like the model builder. Comprehension is analogous to determining what the finished model should look like, and not analogous to reconstruction of the speaker's choices of what to transmit at a given time. To put this into linguistic terms, in comprehending speech we try to recognize the ideas that gave rise to the sentence. A structural analysis of the sentence is ancillary to this goal. Syntax is analogous to the rules which the speaker must follow in deciding which part to hand to the model builder. Knowledge of syntax helps to identify the relationship between pieces in some cases, in other cases it is not needed and sometimes it may not be a reliable clue.

Schank (1971, 1973) has developed these intuitive ideas into what he refers to as a *conceptual parsing system*. His work has been oriented toward computer implementation of a comprehension system (the SPINOZA program) based on conceptual parsing, although, as he points out, having the program is secondary to having the ideas on which it is based. In his programs phrases are identified as the basic agents and actions under discussion (the "concepts"). Dictionary definitions are used to determine the relation concepts may have to each other. Comprehension of

The big man took the book.   (34)

would proceed in the following steps:

(*i*) "The" is identified and held for further analysis. The dictionary definition indicates that a (possibly qualified) noun will be present.

(*ii*) "Big." The adjective is also placed in a temporary memory area, as no noun is available to be qualified. At this point we can visualize the partially completed structure of the sentence by the graph in Figure 15-7a, which shows two qualifiers waiting for an identifiable object.

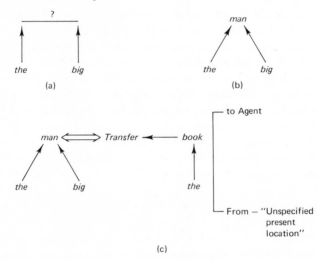

Fig. 15.7.   Steps in the comprehension of *The big man took the book.*

(*iii*) "Man" is recognized as a referent to an object. As Figure 15-7a indicates, a referent is expected, and can be connected. The incomplete structure begins to take place, by assembling one of its subcomponents. This is shown in Figure 15-7b,[10] when the possible actor has been identified. Schank regards comprehension as the construction of a picture of an actor completing an action—in some sense this is the basic unit of thought.

(*iv*) "Took." The dictionary definition of "took" identifies it as the action "take" modified by "past." The identification of the verb also provides a great deal of information about the permissible forms for the image we are trying to construct. In this case, the verb "take" has associated with it a particular graph, indicating that an agent Z transfers an object from position X to Y. This is shown in Figure 15-8. The image construction task now becomes one of trying to identify the components of Figure 15-8 in the construction of Figure 15-7.

[10] Note that one way of looking at this is to say that we are building up a visual image of what the sentence might mean. Psychologically it appears that the construction of visual images is, in fact, closely related to comprehension (Paivio, 1969, 1971).

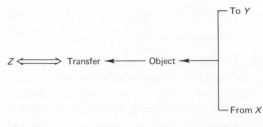

Fig. 15.8.   Skeleton image associated with "Take."

(*v*) The remaining words are used to fill in Figure 15-8. Note that in doing so the program (or the dictionary) must have access to a special rule which says that, for the verb "take," if the Y component is not specified in the sentence, then the Y component is the actor, and that if the X component is not identified, the phrase "present location of object" is to be substituted. The existence of special rules such as this will play havoc with an elegant mathematical description of a language. No matter, they still are needed for comprehension. Also, the sentence cannot be understood in isolation. As it stands, (34) contains a number of general terms. To construct a concrete image one must know *What big man are we talking about? What book?* and *Where is the book?* These questions can only be answered by reference to an immediate memory for referents to terms which have appeared in previous sentences.

Some complexities are presented by

$$I\ like\ books. \tag{35}$$

which is syntactically but not at all semantically similar to

$$I\ like\ Mary. \tag{36}$$

for in (35) "like" is to be interpreted as enjoyment of a specific activity (reading) involving a class of objects, while Mary is liked for a myriad of undefined activities associated with Mary. The correct structure for (35) is the one shown in Figure 15-9a, while the structure for (36) is shown in 15-9b. This example shows that like syntactic parsing, conceptual parsing is also context dependent. One can imagine situations in which (36) did or did not have a structure similar to (35), if we knew

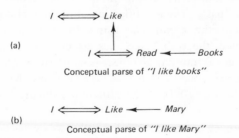

(a)

Conceptual parse of *"I like books"*

(b)

Conceptual parse of *"I like Mary"*

Fig. 15.9.   Two conceptual structures for sentences with syntactic similarity.

more about Mary. The question of which structure to use cannot be resolved unless the comprehending program can make a sophisticated analysis of the intended meaning of "like" in the context it is used.

Conceptual parsing rules refer to the relations that objects and actions can have to each other, rather than to the order of appearance of referents of objects in a string. The same rules for constructing a conceptual frame should apply to discourse about airplanes in English or Japanese, although the rules for establishing the referents for linguistic objects would vary. This is unlike the deep structure notion of a transformational grammar, which does not demand that all languages use the same grammar to construct the deep structure. If we had a complete conceptual parsing system, then, we would have the grammar for a universal "internal language of thought." Note that this grammar would determine what a well-formed expression was in thought, but would not specify the inference rules to be used in deriving new structures. The problem of writing a program to comprehend a specific language would be reduced to the problem of finding a procedure adequate to identify a structure in the internal language, given the evidence of the external string.[11] As in the airplane analogy, it might not always be necessary to have a complete analysis of the structure of the external language in order to do this.

15.2.2 SYSTEMIC GRAMMAR

Schank's group has done some programming, but most of their effort has been directed at theoretical analysis. A somewhat more concrete approach has been taken by Winograd (1972). In the previous chapter we referred to the program which he wrote to manipulate a robot arm in a simplified world of toy blocks. In fact, the main goal of Winograd's research was to test a particular approach to machine comprehension based upon the English linguist Halliday's (1967, 1970) notion of systemic grammar. In the terms we have been using, systemic grammar provides a set of heuristics for analyzing a linguistic string. Winograd uses these heuristics together with a consideration of the conceptual representation that is being built up in order to produce what Schank would call a conceptual parse of the meaning of a natural language input. This analysis is then incorporated into the data base of a deductive system. To illustrate how this is done we (as does Winograd) shall use examples that rely on the reader's knowledge of English in order to illustrate principles. The reader ought to remember this, and not draw the

---

[11] One implication of this position is that the structure of an external language will be determined in part by the ease with which one can map from the internal to the external language and vice versa. This is something of a reversal of the Whorfian hypothesis—we maintain that what people think about limits the form of the language they use, and not vice versa. The internal language itself cannot be of any logical structure, since it must use data structures which are in some sense easy for the human mind to handle. "Handle" here is meant in the mechanical sense of representation of data physically, which the brain must be able to do. Thus biology will limit the structure of our thoughts, and from this determine the structure of our language. For an elaboration of this philosophical viewpoint, see Lenneberg (1967, 1969).

conclusion that a program exists which can handle all the cases discussed. What Winograd's program does—manipulate imaginary blocks on a table-top world—is trivial. The principles it employs are not.

The key to the program's operation is that it contains within it a grammar that is capable of generating all possible graphs corresponding to the conceptual parses of the sentences it might receive. This relieves it of the problem of storing skeleton graphs in its dictionary, as in the "take" in the example of Figure 15-8. The way that this is done is to have the grammar represented *not* as a data structure (e.g., a transition network) but instead as a set of recursively callable procedures within a main program called PARSE. Grammatically, the use of a program to represent a grammar is similar to the use of recursively callable networks in Woods's augmented transition network analysis. An important additional feature, however, is that the procedures responsible for analyzing a given linguistic structure may resolve a syntactic question by calling programs which examine the data base to determine the most sensible semantic interpretation of a sentence. Thus the program would have the option of rejecting a syntactical structure because it leads to a semantic assertion that was inconsistent with or unrelated to previous assertions. We can imagine such a program's selecting the proper interpretation for "Alice" in the "Don Juan"–"White Rabbit" example of sentences (30) and (31). In general, one can follow that line of parsing which leads to a sensible interpretation, rather than having first to compute all possible parsings of the natural language string and then select the one which makes the best sense in context. This can be done because meaning is established in stages, by letting the particular flow of control within PARSE be established by results of both syntactic and semantic procedures called as subroutines within the PARSE program.

To demonstrate the general ideas behind the program, consider the sentence

$$\textit{The elk stand in the stream.} \qquad (37)$$

Clearly, we can establish some meaning for "elk" without knowing its role in the sentence. We cannot establish all its possible meanings, however, because we do not know if it is singular or plural until "stand" is parsed. Thus we would progressively learn that the sentence consisted of

   (*i*) Animate noun (tentative assignment subject).
   (*ii*) Animate noun plural (assignment subject),
         Intransitive verb (plural, present).

At step (*ii*) we know that the first noun phrase does indeed refer to the subject, that the subject is plural, and that the next part of the sentence is, predictably, some sort of adverbial construction. In other words, we are on our way to a conceptual parse. Instead of being satisfied with a graph expressing conceptual relations within the sentence, however, we must have some way of representing the information in the sentence in a form amenable to manipulation by an inference making system. Winograd makes the goal of the PARSE process the establishment of assertion in structures that can be manipulated by a PLANNER problem solving program (cf. Chapter 12). Thus (37) becomes

$$(\text{Location}(\text{Subset}(\text{elk-herd}), \text{stream})) \tag{38}$$

This clause has meaning in itself and, more importantly, in its interaction with other clauses which may be contained in a data base with it. (38) is a contradiction to the assertions formed from

$$\textit{Elk will not enter water.} \tag{39}$$

while it is an answer to the question

$$\textit{Why can't the dogs track the elk?} \tag{40}$$

In both cases a deduction is required to determine just what (38) means.

A basic concept in the process of finding meaning by moving back and forth from semantic to syntactic analysis is the idea of different levels of analysis. Based on Halliday's ideas, Winograd distinguishes three levels of syntactic structure; the clause, the unit, and the word. The clause, rather than the sentence, is the independent unit of thought. That is, it eventually translates into an expression in the data base, although it may be an expression contained within another expression. It is very important that the correct logical level in the data base be assigned to each clause. The logical structure of

$$\textit{I believe John loves Mary} \tag{41}$$

is

$$\text{Believe } (\text{I},(\text{Love}(\text{Mary, John})) \tag{42}$$

and does *not* contradict the assertion

$$7\text{Love}(\text{Mary, John}) \tag{43}$$

providing that (43) is on the same logical level as (42).

Within a clause, *units* are groups of words which either specify terms for logical discourse or specify a relation between terms. Four types of units are distinguished: noun groups specifying basic referents, and adjective, prepositional, and verb groups that state relationships between referents. Since a clause is itself a referent, the clause-unit structure may be used recursively, as is shown in (41). This syntactic structure fits nicely with the idea of a grammar as a procedure. The PARSE program attempts to assign structure by calling the procedure CLAUSE which, in turn, is largely a sequence of calls to procedures for recognizing different units. These procedures may, in turn, call CLAUSE as appropriate.

The lowest-level unit is the word. Words are recognized by a dictionary lookup, since several alternative meanings of a word may exist in a dictionary. The lookup program must be able to examine current structure of the sentence in order to determine which is the most acceptable meaning. Again we see the utility of representing a grammar as a program.

Parsing is basically from the top down, although no strict order of hierarchical analysis is followed. At each level the program "knows" that the structure it is working with must be one of several types, each with its distinctive features. Initially the task is to identify a major clause, which must be either an assertion, an imperative statement, or a question. Examination of a few words can determine which. This information will, in turn, define the possible choices for types of word groups. To mention just one case, if the clause is identified as an assertion, then the leftmost word group must be a noun group. Note how this forces a flow of control from one level to the next. Basically, of course, the dictionary meanings of words determine the interpretation of the input string, but the choice of alternate word meanings is determined by both the properties of the words which are found in the dictionary and the properties of the linguistic structure which have been found and the possible semantic interpretations of that structure. To illustrate, suppose the input sentence were

$$\textit{Who was that lady I saw you with last night?} \qquad (44)$$

At first PARSE would call CLAUSE (major) where the argument list (major) indicates a feature of the clause for which analysis is designed. Examination of "who" indicates (from dictionary lookup) that a "wh-" term has been encountered. Therefore CLAUSE can further restrict its search to clauses of the form (MAJOR, QUESTION). Once this restriction has been uncovered, CLAUSE can permit detection of a verb group as the next element. If a wh- term had not been detected, CLAUSE would have searched for a noun group. Other routines proceed similarly, including rearrangements of the features.

The similarity of this sort of analysis to the augmented transition network analysis is striking. In fact, Winograd points out that the two are formally equivalent, since both have the power of Turing machines with pushdown tapes. It appears to Winograd (and to us), however, that the view of a grammar as a procedure provides a more natural way to allow for procedures which control a parsing by reference to a previously established data base.

The following is an edited illustration of Winograd's approach. The input sentence is

$$\textit{Pick up the red brick,} \qquad (45)$$

which produces the following actions:

(*i*) PARSE calls CLAUSE(MAJOR). The CLAUSE procedure determines that the first word is a verb, which is a signal that the clause is an imperative clause. The program notes that the clause is (MAJOR,IMPERATIVE).

(*ii*) CLAUSE now calls for a parse of VERB-GROUP(IMPERATIVE) since this is necessarily the first part of an imperative clause. The VERB-GROUP procedure checks its argument list (IMPERATIVE) and transfers control to that part of the code which checks for imperative verbs. The only possible forms are infinitives or forms of the verb "do." Since "pick" is not a form of "do" the program VERB(INFINITIVE,MAIN VERB) is called.

(*iii*) VERB is a *word* program, i.e., it checks dictionary entries. In this case, VERB determines that "pick" is indeed an infinitive form of a possible main verb. It also notes that the verb in question is a transitive and can take a particulate. Therefore, when VERB returns to VERB-GROUP "pick" is incorporated into the sentence structure with the feature list (VERB MAIN VERB INFINITIVE TRANSITIVE VPRT). (The last term is an expression for "can take a particulate.")

(*iv*) On regaining control VERB-GROUP determines that only a main verb is needed if it is parsing an (IMPERATIVE) verb group, so it turns to CLAUSE. The CLAUSE procedure now knows that it is parsing a string of the form CLAUSE (MAJOR, IMPERATIVE . . .), and that it has just recognized a verb group. In such a case, a particulate is required if the main verb can take a particulate. By a check of the features in the developing structure CLAUSE finds that this is the case, so it calls the procedure PRT.

(*v*) PRT is again a word-oriented procedure. It determines from the dictionary that "up" is a particulate, and from the structure and then the dictionary, that "pick up" is a transitive particulate. Upon return from PRT these features are added to CLAUSE's feature list, so that CLAUSE is now analyzing CLAUSE (MAJOR IMPERATIVE PRT TRANSITIVE) and has just found the particulate.

(*vi*) At this point in CLAUSE the object structure must be found. CLAUSE has two ways to do this, by a call to NOUN-GROUP followed by successful recognition or by a call to CLAUSE(SECONDARY) to find a relative clause. The first of these two procedures will succeed. The string it incorporates may be assigned the role "object." Upon completion of this procedure all words in the string will have been incorporated, and the final string will have the structure

(CLAUSE MAJOR IMPERATIVE PRT TRANSITIVE)	(*Pick up a red block*)
(VERB GROUP IMPERATIVE)	(*pick*)
(VERB MAIN-VERB INFINITIVE TRANSITIVE PRT)	*pick*
(PRT)	*up*
(NOUN-GROUP OBJECT OBJ1 DET INDEF NOUN-SINGULAR)	(*a big red block*)
(DET INDEFINITE NOUN-SINGULAR)	*a*
(ADJECTIVE)	*big*
(ADJECTIVE)	*red*
(NOUN NOUN-SINGULAR)	*block*

In this example it is not necessary to refer to a developing data base to resolve parsing ambiguities. In other cases it might be. The point is that this is easy to do within the framework of grammatical procedures, since the grammatical procedure calls the semantic procedure using the same mechanism it would to call any closed subroutine. Winograd's other illustrations show that quite sophisticated use can be made of this feature to enable the program to figure out what the person instructing it must mean, even if the sentence itself is quite ambiguous.

15.2.3   COMMENTARY ON THE PSYCHOLOGICAL APPROACH

What sort of languages can be analyzed by the psychologically oriented method? This question turns out to be easy to answer since any program is allowable. A "psychological" analysis program can be written for any language that can be analyzed by a computer. This is too broad an answer for a mathematical linguist, since it denies him the possibility of developing a categorization of languages. On the other hand, it is comforting to someone who is simply concerned with producing a language-comprehending program for a specific problem. He knows that if it can be done, then this method can do it.

But what is the method? This is just what we do not know. Conceptual parsing and systemic grammars are not prescriptions for writing programs in the same sense that constituent structure, context free grammars do. They are ways in which one can think about the organization of large numbers of "special cases," such as the various tricks that must be used to analyze different forms of the English verb "to be." As soon as one sits down to write a language-comprehending program it becomes clear that there are many, many such special rules. Dictionary entries become amazingly complex, so that memory requirements push against the limits of our technology. Quillian (1968) exhausted the available memory of a 32,000 word machine with a program that detected the "in context" meaning of 60 words. Winograd's program, running on an 80,000 word computer, could store definitions for 200 words plus the information describing a moderately complex arrangement of blocks on a table. We seem to have quite a way to go before we reach the capacities of science fiction computers. Programs such as those of Winograd, Schank, and Quillian demonstrate that certain principles can be used to resolve fine points in the analysis of natural language. Producing useful programs for language comprehension seems to require a quantum jump in the design either of computer memories or of the addressing systems used with them.

If natural language comprehension is beyond our hardware capacities, then how is it that humans comprehend? Of course, we do not know. One speculation, though, is that human memory operates on a quite different principle than computer memory. Perhaps the brain contains records which activate themselves when the sensory apparatus delivers a "relevant" message to the sensory projection areas of the cortex. This would obviate the need for a "central processor," which would search a passive memory. The argument is detailed, and the evidence for it sketchy at best. See Hunt (1973) for a discussion of the functional model, and Arbib (1972) and John (1972) for discussions of possible physical mechanisms.

If the size of our machines is the problem, the problem will be solved. One of the lessons of the history of computer design is that machines will get bigger, faster, and cheaper, soon. Let us suppose for the moment that we could build the hardware needed to hold the dictionaries and data bases required for, say, a conversation about the criminal code of the United States. Would we then be ready to produce an automated District Attorney? We think not. Someone would still have to write the program which contained procedures for all those embarrassing special cases, and programming seems to have resisted automation in our computer world. How big a job would it be to produce a procedure-grammar, such as Winograd's, which contained the knowledge used professionally by a below average country lawyer? Remember that the person writing the program would have to be more than a competent programmer and a speaker of English, he would also have to be a sufficiently astute linguist to know the formal definition of the different variations of English irregular verbs. An offhand guess is that this project would, at the least, require the full-time services of 20 or more Ph.D.'s in linguistics or computer science for 20 or more years. Remember also that the programs they might produce would all have to fit together. The management problem will not be small!

We doubt that such an effort is in the offing. There is an alternative to it. Perhaps what we need is not a large, unmanageable project to create an English grammar directly, but rather a nucleus comprehension program which contains the capability of adding new rules to its syntactical and semantic routines as it is told about them. After all, isn't this the way that people learn language? Perhaps this is a more reasonable way to proceed. It reduces the problem from the intellectually messy one of trying to deal, simultaneously, with a host of small problems, to the problem of answering a single very difficult scientific question . . . how should the learning device be built? Admittedly, we do not know how to do this now. And also, admittedly, we prefer to advocate an attack on a single hard scientific question than to advocate a vast "state-of-the-art" technological project. Others, with other prejudices, might disagree.

In either case, programs that comprehend natural language in any general sense are not just around the corner. We do expect to see the *illusion* of such programs very shortly. This will be due to two developments. First, it should be possible to conduct discourse with computers within a strictly limited range of topics if one can extend the number of word definitions to be stored to, say, 500 words. This is not an unreasonable goal in the near future. We also expect to see, soon, some reasonable (though limited) solutions to the pattern recognition problems involved in speech recognition by computer. By 1980 you will probably be able to talk to one program to discuss stock market prices and to another program to ask for meat market prices. The two programs will not be interchangeable and, fairly frequently, they will have to ask you to reword your query. So long as the user simply wants information these programs will probably be quite adequate. If the user wants to demonstrate speech that is too subtle for a machine to follow, it will be easy to do so.

Chapter XVI

REVIEW AND PROSPECTUS

16.0 Things Done and Undone

I have tried to present a view of the fundamental mathematical and computing techniques underlying artificial intelligence research. I identified two well-defined classes of scientific questions—pattern recognition and problem solving—and have presented a variety of formulations and techniques for solution within each class. I feel on sure ground here. These problems have been carefully investigated and a number of ways of handling them have been developed. Much of the mystery of artificial intelligence research in these areas has been because the problems are such that their solution required a blending of mathematical techniques originally developed in a variety of fields. Pattern recognition is a good example. To explain pattern recognition, one uses analyses originally developed for statistical, psychological, and economic applications and finally, in discussing perceptrons, must add arguments based on number theory and formal logic. Problem solving by computer similarly requires us to think simultaneously in terms of graph theory and formal logic, with an occasional use of statistical reasoning. If it is hard to understand various efforts of artificial intelligence, it is not because specialized knowledge of any one field of study is needed, but because some knowledge of a great many fields is called for. I hope that by gathering together in one volume a number of basic analyses I will have made it easier for someone new to the field either to begin to specialize in it or to deal with a specific artificial intelligence application.

The discussion of machine comprehension was of necessity, on a much more intuitive basis. Comprehension itself is an intuitive term. While we can agree that a particular program did or did not solve a pattern recognition problem or prove a theorem, reasonable people may disagree about whether or not a program comprehended a statement, even though the facts about what the program did with the statement are quite clear. Another reason for the vagueness of discussions of machine comprehension is that comprehension is intimately tied to language analysis, and our understanding of language is itself primitive. We will never base a machine comprehension method on anything other than a formal theory of language, since, in the last analysis, the program controlling the computer implicitly contains such a theory. The approach to formal analysis of language used today is rooted in work that began in the 1950s. These are shallow roots indeed when one considers that pattern recognition can be traced directly to Bayes's writings in the seventeenth century, and that machine theorem proving is a fairly direct development of reasoning familiar to Aristotle.

In view of this state of affairs, it was still necessary to discuss machine comprehension. The techniques we discussed may or may not be fundamental techniques. Only time will tell. The problem is fundamental. Language is a unique signaling system for communication between members of our species. It bears little resemblance to the signaling systems used by birds or other mammals. We have not only specialized output devices in the pharynx and larynx, we also have special analytical areas in our brains, structures that are not found in rudimentary form in any other species, including the great apes (Geschwind, 1970). Given this degree of specialization it is doubtful that we can learn to communicate well in anything beside our natural mode. If our machines are to serve us, they must be able to receive the only transmission we can send well.[1]

It may be that our inability to communicate with our machines will be the ultimate limitation on the information-processing revolution. If we were near to this limit we would, perhaps, be best advised to avoid speculative discussions of machine comprehension. This is probably not the case. A recent study by the United States Department of Defense concluded that by 1984 there is a reasonable chance of constructing a computing system that could respond to natural language commands discussing nontrivial subject matter (Newell *et al.*, 1972). Whether a decade is the right time span, and what "nontrivial" is, are matters of debate. Our point is that a number of responsible, well-informed investigators are taking machine comprehension quite seriously. To be knowledgeable in artificial intelligence (and perhaps in computer science itself) one ought to have an idea of promise and performance in the machine comprehension field.

This book may have been a disappointment to many of the enthusiasts for artificial intelligence, since it concentrated on algorithms and abstract mathematical methods. This takes the fun out of the field. Where are the examples? Why did we not provide play from computerized chess, extensive dialogues from a computerized psychotherapist, or examples of difficult theorems proven by machine?

---

[1] One might object that, after all, people do learn to program. There are several counterarguments. Programming languages provide a very impoverished communication system. Only an infinitesimal percentage of humanity uses them now, and it is probably beyond the capacity of most people to learn to program in any but a rudimentary fashion. "Computers in education" enthusiasts who dispute this assertion are asked to consider a point made by the psycholinguist A. Liberman. Spoken language develops without formal instruction in over 99% of humanity. Reading requires extensive formal tuition. Societies such as our own, which spend literally years teaching reading and distribute rewards largely on the basis of reading skill are still plagued with a substantial number of functional illiterates. In view of this fact, why the enthusiasm for control of machines by universal programming?

   In fact, very few programs have been discussed. This was not done just to be boring, although that may have been the result. Discussion of specific examples in detail would have confused the central point—what are the fundamental algorithms? Take game playing as an example. The approach taken was to point out basic principles underlying game-tree searching. Suppose the "best existing" chess playing programs had been described. We would certainly have had more exciting illustrations! To explain them would have required going into great detail about how chess-specific problems were handled—secure in the knowledge that as soon as the book went to press a better chess playing program would be developed. Alternatively, examples of play could have been given, while leaving the reader mystified as to how the program developed the moves. Fundamentals have been presented instead of examples, in the belief that such a presentation, although duller, will be of more lasting value.

   There is another reason for avoiding too many striking examples. Almost by definition, artificial intelligence involves extension of computer applications to fields where one would not expect a computer application to exist. To a person not a specialist in the application field any success is apt to seem more spectacular than it is, since he did not expect progress and since he may not know what the problems are. Chess, speech recognition, and "robotology" provide excellent examples. Today's chess programs are reliable enough so that they can be used as advertising demonstrations at computer conferences. They beat most of the intelligent, casual chess players who go to such meetings. In a way this is spectacular, since in 1964 one of the most publicized programs was beaten by a (bright) 10-year-old boy (Dreyfus, 1971). But still today's programs are trivial opponents for master players. Tomorrow's may not be. Similarly, computer music has yet to produce an equivalent to Beethoven's sonatas, but humanity only did this once. What are the definitions of progress?

   "Robotology," which we have hardly discussed at all, is replete with interpretation problems. There are now in existence machines which move about under control of radio signals from a computer. They peer at their visual world through a cyclopean television camera eye, analyze the scene they see, and reason about the path they should take to move from one point to another (Nilsson, 1969, 1971). This is exciting! But .... The robot's visual perception is based on analysis of discrete cues from the visual scene (Falk, 1972; Guzman, 1969). There is no attempt to develop a representation of the metrics of three-dimensional space, although metric representations are extremely important if the machine's perceptions of and reasoning about space are to approach remotely human capability (Attneave, 1972). As of this writing, the robot's world is limited to a neater than average room full of large blocks. The machine's reasoning capabilities are those given it by programs with the potentials and problems we have seen in theorem provers. Many experts in artificial intelligence deride such remarks. They feel that the highly publicized robot projects provide a unifying theme for all aspects of artificial intelligence. At least, this has been the rationale for a small number of highly publicized (and heavily financed) robot construction projects. On the other hand, at least one reviewer of artificial intelligence in the 1970s, the British physicist Lighthill, in a report to the science research council of Britain, has suggested that fascination with robot building may have diverted attention from duller, but in the long run, more solid scientific problems (Hammond, 1973). I am inclined toward this view.

The point is not to belabor specific examples. I expect progressively better speech recognizers, chess players, and even robots. It is a mistake to focus on the characteristics of the technology at this moment. One should try to understand the capabilities and limitations of the analytic techniques on which that technology is founded.

16.1 Some Problems of Philosophy

Any discussions of artificial intelligence must either be conducted at a very technical level, or must come to grips with the question of how the study of thinking machines should or could influence our philosophical and psychological concepts. As promised in the introductory chapter, this discussion has been at the technical level. The broader questions remain and must be dealt with.

Philosophy poses two types of questions for artificial intelligence. One is "how should thought be represented by a mechanical device? This question leads to consideration of the appropriate internal symbolic representation of the external world and its problems. The specific questions that are raised seem to the non-philosopher to be technical ones. For instance, we might ask if Church's Lambda calculus is sufficient to express the key relationships between elementary objects in a given problem-solving situation. Similarly, we may want to know how we can represent inside a computer the fact that a particular action may have multiple effects besides those intended when the action was made. Such questions are aspects of the more general representational problem: How do we select a computer programmable model of a problem in which we are "really" interested? Various aspects of this question have come up throughout the book. In each case we have said "Little is known." The interested reader is referred to McCarthy and Hayes (1969) for further discussion. We have little to add.

The question *How should a machine think*? presupposes an answer to a prior question, *Can a machine think*? This is a much more exciting question to the layman. Unfortunately, it turns out to be too ill defined a question to answer directly. What is the answer to *How do you decide that anything is thinking*? This is not at all trivial. Some philosophers and many psychologists influenced by them claim that the concept of "thinking" is not a useful one. Instead they prefer to talk about specific behaviors which, if observed, might be characterized as "thinking" for purposes of a shorthand code, but without any commitment to belief in some common underlying process. In fact most of these writers would decidedly prefer not to use the word at all.[2] If this is to be an accepted criterion, then the question

---

[2] This philosophical view is epitomized by Skinner (1971), who feels that discussion of inherently unobservable mental operations cannot possibly be the basis of either a science or a technology.

of machine thought reduces to a series of empirical tests. Can theorem provers solve problems as well as professional mathematicians can? Certainly not. Can computer programs be written to solve the pattern-recognition problems found in intelligence tests? Yes. Can we, today, write programs that match human comprehension of natural language? No. Will we ever? Maybe. It seems then that an observational answer to the question, *Can a machine think?* is bound to be an arbitrary one. This might not be true if we had some justification for designating certain tasks as necessary or sufficient tasks for an intelligent machine. Without a theory of thought we cannot say what these tasks are.

A somewhat different question is *Does a machine think like a human being?* Here there is a temptation to assert that an observational test is appropriate: If a computer program mimics human behavior then that program is a model of the behavior. This is the argument that has motivated much of the modern research on computer simulation (Hunt, 1968; Newell & Simon, 1961; Simon, 1971). Somewhat surprisingly, we find ourselves at issue with this view. Human thought is based on a physiological system about which a little more than nothing is known. We do not feel that a psychological theory need to be completely reducible to a physiological one, but it does not seem wise to ignore physiology entirely. Specifically, I would reject a program as a model of psychological performance on a given task, even if it mimicked behavior perfectly, if the principles of information processing which the program applied were known to be incompatible with human performance in areas not simulated by the program.[3] Thus again the question about machine thought must be answered on a case-by-case basis. I would be willing to accept a program as a model in some situations, and would be very interested in noting similarities between reasonable simulation of behavior in different situations. The *general* question *Does the study of machine behavior tell us anything about psychology?* has no meaning.

16.2   A General Theory of Thought

Is there a general theory of thought? To the question, *Does one now exist?* the answer is certainly *No*. But is one on the horizon? I doubt it, but my answer requires some justification and even qualification.

It is generally agreed that intelligent behavior can only be produced by a system of information processing elements; feature detectors, theorem provers, and decision makers. A body of scientists and philosophers, known loosely as "general systems theorists," have asserted that there are nontrivial laws about how such systems must be organized (J. G. Miller, 1970). If the assertion is true, then systems theory ought to be applicable to the organization of intelligent machines as well as the organization of intelligent biological, social, and physical systems. Indeed,

---

[3] In the face of a perfect simulation I would be very careful about examining my prior psychological knowledge before making the rejection! All I am asserting is the right to do so.

Banerji (1969) has proposed the application of system and control theory to virtually all artificial intelligence. Banerji considers a *problem* to be a sextuple,

$$P = \langle S, C, D, M, S_L, S_W \rangle \tag{1}$$

where S is the set of possible situations, C the set of controls which apply to those situations, D is a set of disturbances, M a mapping from $S \times C \times D$ (situation plus disturbance plus control) into S (i.e., into a new situation), and $S_W \subseteq S, S_L \subseteq S$ are, respectively, desirable and undesirable situations. He then develops the formalism to apply it to a variety of games and problem solving situations. In doing so, he reveals some interesting similarities in superficially dissimilar problems. It is possible that further developments along these lines might lead to a useful taxonomy of problem solving situations. As Banerji himself admits, however, the formalisms have yet to lead to substantial theorems about the design of problem solving systems. At present Banerji's description is a perhaps useful way of describing what we have done after we have constructed an artificial intelligence program but it does not tell us how to proceed when the problem is first given to us.

A more intuitive but perhaps more useful application of general systems theory has been suggested by Simon (1969). He points out that all complex systems that work have certain features: the most conspicuous being hierarchical organization of components, decomposability of the total system into separate subsystems, and repeated use of similar components. Simon would simply have us keep these ideas in mind when attacking a given problem. This is certainly reasonable. In artificial intelligence research there are many outstanding examples. The study of machine comprehension is an example of a field in which almost no progress was made until Woods (1970) and Winograd (1972) rigidly adhered to Simon's dicta.

Still, this is guidance rather than a prescription for the design of intelligence. That is where our field of knowledge is. We have some general principles that should "usually" be followed .... We have techniques of varying utility and applicability. We are unable to say how thought ought to be organized. Neither were Descartes or Locke able to give us infallible rules. Since their time we have made slow progress. Our machines are faster, more complex, and more useful than most people dreamed of 50 years ago. I hope this book has helped to show how these machines display some intelligence today and can be made to show more tomorrow. Genius is yet undefined.

REFERENCES

Abdali, S. K. Feature extraction algorithms. *Pattern Recognition*, 1971, **3**, 3-21.

Abelson, R. P. Heuristic processes in the human application of verbal structure in new situations. *Proceedings of the XVIII International Congress of Psychology, Symposium 25*, Moscow, 1966, pp. 5-14.

Abelson, R. P., & Reich, C. Implication modules. A method for extracting meaning from input sentences. *Proceedings of the 1st International Joint Conference on Artificial Intelligence.* Bedford, Massachusetts: Mitre Corp., 1969. Pp. 641-648.

Allen, J., & Luckham, D. An interactive theorem proving program. In B. Meltzer and D. Michie (Eds.), *Machine intelligence*, Vol. 5. Edinburgh, Scotland; Univ. of Edinburgh Press, 1970.

Amarel, S., On machine representations of problems of reasoning about actions. The missionaries and cannibals problem. In D. Michie (Ed.), *Machine intelligence*, Vol. 3, Edinburgh, Scotland: Univ. of Edinburgh Press, 1968.

Anderson, R. & Bledsoe, W. A linear format for resolution with merging and a new technique for establishing completeness. *Journal of the Association for Computing Machinery*, 1970, **17**, 525-534.

Anderson, T. *Introduction to multivariate statistical analysis.* New York: Wiley, 1958.

Arbib, M. *Brains, machines, and mathematics.* New York: McGraw-Hill, 1964.

Arbib, M. *The metaphorical brain.* New York: Wiley, 1972.

Association for Computing Machinery, Curriculum Committee on Computer Science Curriculum. Recommendation for academic programs in computer science. *Communications of the Association for Computing Machinery*, 1968, **11**, 151-197.

Attneave, F. Some informational aspects of visual perception. *Psychological Review*, **61**, (3), 1954.

Attneave, F. Multistability in perception. *Scientific American* 1971, **225**, 62-71.

Banerji, R. *Theory of problem solving: An approach to artificial intelligence.* New York: American Elsevier, 1969.

Becker, J. The modeling of simple analogic and deductive processes in a semantic memory system. *Proceedings of the 1st International Joint Conference on Artificial Intelligence.* Bedford, Massachusetts: Mitre Corp. 1969. Pp. 655-668.

Berkeley, E., & Bobrow, D. *The programming language "Lisp".* Cambridge, Massachusetts: Information International, 1964.

Biermann, A. W., & Feldman, J. A. A survey of results in grammatical inference. In S. Watanabe (Ed.), *Frontiers of pattern recognition.* New York: Academic Press, 1972.

Bledsoe, W. Splitting and reduction heuristics in automatic theorem proving. *Artificial Intelligence* 1971, **2**, 55-78.

Bledsoe, W., Boyer, R., & Henneman, W. Computer proofs of limit theorems. *Proceedings of the 2nd International Joint Conference on Artificial Intelligence.* London: Univ. of London, 1971. Pp. 586-600.

Block, H., Nilsson, N., & Duda, H. Determination and detection of features in patterns. In J. Tou and R. Wilcox (Eds.), *Computers and information sciences*. Baltimore: Spartan Press, 1964.

Bobrow, D., & Fraser, J. An augmented state transition network program. *Proceedings of the 1st International Joint Conference on Artificial Intelligence*. Bedford, Massachusetts: Mitre Corp. 1969. Pp. 557-568.

Bongard, M. *Pattern recognition*, (T. Cheron, trans.). Baltimore: Spartan Press, 1970.

Botovinnik, M. *Computers, chess, and long range planning*, (A. Brown trans.). Berlin: Springer-Verlag, 1970.

Bourne, L. *Human conceptual behavior*. Boston: Allyn and Bacon, 1966.

Bruner, J., Goodnow, J., & Austin, G. *A study of thinking*. New York: Wiley, 1956.

Buchanan, B., & Headrick, T. Some speculations about artificial intelligence and legal reasoning. Stanford Univ. Computer Science Department. *Artificial Intelligence Memorandum* 123, 1970.

Busignies, H. Communication channels. *Scientific American*. 1972, **227**, 98-113.

Chang, C. The unit proof and the input proof in theorem proving. *Journal of the Association for Computing Machinery*, 1970, **17**, 698-707.

Chang, C., & Slagle, J. An admissable and optimal algorithm for searching and/or graphs. *Artificial Intelligence*. 1971, **2**, 117-128.

Chomsky, N. *Syntactic structures*. The Hague: Moulton, 1957.

Chomsky, N. *Aspects of the theory of syntax*. Cambridge, Massachusetts. MIT Press, 1965.

Chomsky, N. Formal properties of grammars. In R. Luce, R. Bush, & E. Galanter (Eds.), *Handbook of mathematical psychology*, Vol. II. New York: Wiley, 1963.

Chomsky, N., & Halle, M. *The sound pattern of English*. New York: Harper, 1968.

Chomsky, N., & Miller, G. Introduction to the formal analysis of natural language. In R. Luce, R. Bush, & E. Galanter (Eds.), *Handbook of mathematical psychology*, Vol. II. New York: Wiley, 1963.

Clowes, M. B. Pictorial relationships—a syntactic approach. In B. Meltzer & D. Michie (Eds.), *Machine Intelligence*, Vol. 4. Edinburgh, Scotland: Edinburgh Univ. Press, 1969.

Clowes, M. B. On seeing things. *Artificial Intelligence*. 1971, **2**, 79-114.

Cohen, J. *Statistical power analysis for the behavioral sciences*. New York: Wiley, 1969.

Colby, K. Computer simulation of change in personal belief systems. *Behavioral Science*, 1967, **12**, 248-253.

Colby, K., & Smith, D. Dialogues between humans and an artificial belief system. *Proceedings of the 1st International Joint Conference on Artificial Intelligence*. Bedford, Massachusetts: Mitre Corp., 1969.

Colby, K., Weber, S., & Hilf, E. Artificial paranoia. *Artificial Intelligence*, 1971, **2**, 1-26.

Coombs, D., Dawes, R., & Tversky, A. *Mathematical psychology*. Englewood Cliffs, New Jersey: Prentice Hall, 1970.

Cooper, P. W. Non-supervised learning in statistical pattern recognition. In S. Watanabe (Ed.), *Methodologies in pattern recognition*. New York: Academic Press, 1969.

Cooper, W. S. Fact retrieval and deductive question answering information retrieval systems. *Journal of the Association for Computing Machinery*, 1964, **11**, 117-137.

Corey, E. & Wipke, W. Computer assisted design of complex organic synthesis. *Science*, 1969, **166**, 178-192.

Cornsweet, T. *Visual perception*. New York: Academic Press, 1970.

Cover, T. Learning in pattern recognition. In S. Watanabe (Ed.), *Methodologies of pattern recognition*. New York: Academic Press, 1969.

Cover, T., & Hart, P. Nearest neighbor pattern classification. *IEEE Transactions on Information Theory*, 1967, **IT-13**, 21-27.

Craig, H., & Craig, V. Greek marbles: Determination of provenance by isotopic analysis. *Science*. 1972, **176**, 401-403.

Craig, J., Berezner, S., Carney, H. and Loveyear, C. DEACON Directo English Access and Control. *Proceedings of the Fall Joint Computer Conference, 1966.* American Federation of Information Processing Sciences, 29.1966.

Crespi-Reghizzi, S. An effective model for grammar inference. *Procedings of the International Federation of Information-Processing Societies.* Ljublijana, 1971.

Crespi-Reghizzi, S., Melkanoff, M., & Lichten, L. The use of grammatical inference of designing programming languages. *Communications of the Association for Computing Machinery.* 1973, **16**, 83-90.

Dale, P. *Language development: structure and learning.* Hinsdale, Illinois: Dryden Press, 1972.

Day, R. Visual spatial illusions: A general explanation. *Science,* 1972, **175**, 1335-1340.

DeGroot, A. Perception, memory, and thought: Some old ideas and some recent findings. In B. Kleinmuntz (Ed.), *Problem solving: Research, method and theory.* New York: Wiley, 1966.

Deutsch, J. A., & Deutsch, D. *Physiological psychology.* Homewood, Illinois: Dorsey, 1966.

Diehr, G. An investigation of computational algorithms for aggregation problems. Univ. California, Los Angeles. Western Management Science Institute working paper 155, 1969.

Diehr, G., & Hunt, E. A comparison of memory allocation algorithms in a logical pattern recognizer. University of Washington, Department of Psychology tech. rep., 1968.

Dostert, B., & Thompson, F. How features resolve syntactic ambiguity. *Proceedings of the Symposium on Information Storage and Retrieval.* Association for Computing Machinery, 1971, 19-32.

Dreyfus, H. *What computers can't do: A critique of artificial reason.* New York: Harper, 1972.

Duda, R., & Hart, P. *Pattern recognition and scene analysis.* New York: Wiley, 1973.

Elliot, R. Master's level computer science curriculum. *Communications of the Association for Computing Machinery,* 1968, **11**, 507-508.

Ernst, G., & Newell, A. *GPS: A case study in generality and problem solving.* New York: Academic Press, 1969.

Evans, T. G. Grammatical inference techniques in pattern analysis. In J. Tou (Ed.), *Software Engineering,* (Vol. II). New York: Academic Press, 1971.

Falk, G. Interpretation of imperfect line data as a three dimensional scene. *Artificial Intelligence,* 1972, **3**, 104-144.

Feigenbaum, E. Artificial intelligence: Themes in the second decade. *Proceedings of the International Federation of Information Processing Societies.* Baltimore: Spartan Press, 1968.

Feldman, J. A. First thoughts on grammatical inference. Stanford Univ. Computer Science Department, Artificial Intelligence Memorandum, **55**, 1957.

Feldman, J. A. Some decideability results on grammatical inference and complexity. *Information and Control.* 1972, **20**, 244-263.

Feldman, J. A., Horning, J., Reder, S., & Gips, G. Grammatical complexity and inference. Stanford Univ. Computer Science Department, CS 125, 1969.

Fikes, R., Hart, P., & Nilsson, N. Learning and executing generalized robot plans. *Artificial Intelligence* 1972, **3**, 251-288.

Fikes, R., & Nilsson, N. STRIPS: A new approach to the application of theorem proving in problem solving. *Artificial Intelligence* 1971, **2**, 189-208.

Frijida, N. Simulation of human long term memory. *Psychological Bulletin,* 1972, **77**, 1-31.

Fu, S. *Sequential methods in pattern recognition and machine learning.* New York: Academic Press, 1969.

Fu, S. On sequential pattern recognition systems. In S. Watanabe (Ed.), *Methodologies of pattern recognition.* New York: Academic Press, 1969.

Fu, S., & Swain, P. On syntactic pattern recognition. *3rd International Symposium on Computer and Information Sciences,* 1969. In Tou, J., *Software engineering.* Vol. II. New York: Academic Press, 1971.

Fukanaga, K. *Introduction to statistical pattern recognition.* New York: Academic Press, 1972.

Garnder, M. Mathematical Games. *Scientific American*, 1971, **225**(4), 114.

Garnatz, D., & Hunt, E. Eyeball parameter estimation with a computer. *IEEE Transactions on Systems, Man and Cybernetics*, **II**, 1973, **SMC-3**, No. 1.

Gelerntner, H. A note on syntactic symmetry and the manipulation of formal systems by machine. *Information and Control*. 1959, 9, 80-89.

Gelerntner, H. Realization of a geometry theorem proving machine. In E. Feigenbaum & J. Feldman (Eds.), *Computers and thought*. New York: McGraw-Hill, 1963.

Gelerntner, H., Hansen, J., & Loveland, D. Empirical explorations of a geometry theorem proving machine. In E. Feigenbaum and J. Feldman (Eds.) *Computers and Thought*. New York: McGraw-Hill, 1963.

Gelerntner, H., & Rochester, N. Intelligent behavior in problem solving machines. *IBM Journal of Research and Development*, 1958, **2**, 336-345.

Geschwind, N. The organization of language in the brain. *Science*, 1970, **170**, 940-944.

Gibson, J. *The perception of the visual world*. Boston: Houghton Mifflin, 1950.

Gillogly, J. The technology chess program. *Artificial Intelligence*, 1972, **3**, 145-164.

Gilmore, P. C. An examination of the geometry theorem machine. *Artificial Intelligence*, 1970, **1**, 171-188.

Glushkov, V. *Introduction to cybernetics*. New York: Academic Press, 1966.

Gold, M. Language identification in the limit. *Information and Control*, 1967, **10**, 447-474.

Green, B. *Digital computers in research*. New York: McGraw-Hill, 1963.

Green, B., Wolf, A., Chomsky, C., & Laughrey, K. BASEBALL: An automatic question answerer. *Proceedings of the Western Joint Computer Conference, 1961, American Federation of Information Processing Sciences*, **19**, 219-224.

Green, C. The application of theorem proving to question answering systems. Stanford Univ. Computer Science Department, CS 138, 1969. (Ph.D. thesis.)

Green, C. Theorem proving by resolution as a basis for question answering systems. In B. Meltzer and D. Michie (Eds.), *Machine Intelligence*, 4: Edinburgh, Scotland: Edinburgh Univ. Press, 1969.

Green, C. Application of theorem proving to problem solving. *Proceedings of the 1st International Joint Conference on Artificial Intelligence*. Bedford, Massachusetts: Mitre Corp., 1969. Pp. 219-239.

Green, C. & Raphael, B. The use of theorem proving techniques in question answering systems. *Proceedings of the 23rd Conference of the Association for Computing Machinery*. Baltimore: Spartan Press, 1968.

Greenblatt, R., Eastlake, D., & Crocker, S. The Greenblatt chess program. *Proceedings of the Fall Joint Computer Conference, American Federation of Information Processing Sciences*, **31**, 801-810.

Gries, D. *Compiler construction for digital computers*. New York: Wiley, 1971.

Guard, J., Oglesby, F., Bennett, J., & Settle, L. Semi-automated mathematics. *Journal of the Association for Computing Machinery*, 1969, **16**, 49-62.

Guilford, J. *The nature of human intelligence*. New York: McGraw-Hill, 1967.

Guzman, A. Decomposition of a visual scene into bodies. *Proceedings of the Fall Joint Computer Conference 1968*. American Federation of Information Processing Sciences, **33**, 291-304.

Halle, M. & Stevens, K. N. On phonetic features. *Proceedings of the 1972 Conference on speech communication and processing*. IEEE, 1972, 194-197.

Halliday, M. Notes on trasitivity and theme in English. *Journal of Linguistics* 1967, 3.

Halliday, M. Functional diversity in language as seen from a consideration of modality and mood in English. *Foundations of language* 1970, 6, 322-361.

Hammond, A. Artificial intelligence: A fascination with robots or a serious intellectual endeavor? *Science*, 1973, **180**, 1352-1353.

Harary, F., Norman, R., & Cartwright, D. *Structural models*. New York: Wiley, 1965.

Harman, H. *Modern factor analysis* (2nd ed.). Chicago: Univ. of Chicago Press, 1967.

Harmon, L. & Julesz, B. Masking in visual recognition: Effects of two dimensional filtered noise. *Science* 1973, **180**, 1194-1197.

Hayes, P. and Kowalski, R. Semantic trees in automatic theorem proving. In B. Meltzer and D. Michie (Eds.) *Machine Intelligence*, Vol. 4. Edinburgh, Scotland: Univ. of Edinburgh Press, 1969. Pp. 87-101.

Hebb, D. *The organization of behavior*. New York: Wiley, 1948.

Herscher, M. & Cox, R. An adaptive isolated-word speech recognition system. *Proceedings of the 1972 Conference on speech communication and processing*. IEEE, 1972.

Hewitt, C. PLANNER: A language for manipulating models and proving theorems in a robot. *Proceedings of the 1st International Joint Conference on Artificial Intelligence*. Bedford, Massachusetts: Mitre Corp., 1969.

Hewitt, C. Procedural embedding of knowledge in PLANNER. *Proceedings of the 2nd International Joint Conference on Artificial Intelligence*. London: Univ. of London 1971. Pp. 167-184.

Hewitt, C. Description and theoretical analysis (using schemata) of PLANNER: A language for proving theorems and manipulating models in a robot. M.I.T. Tech. Rep., AI-TR-258. 1972.

Hochberg, J. Perception. In J. Kling and L. Riggs (Eds.), *Experimental Psychology* (3rd ed.). New York: Holt, Dirchant, Winston, 1971. Pp. 395-550.

Hodes, L. The logical complexity of geometrical properties in the plane. *Journal of the Association for Computing Machinery*. 1970, **17**, 339-347.

Hoel, P. *Introduction to mathematical statistics* (4th ed.). New York: Wiley, 1970.

Huffman, D. Impossible objects in nonsense sentences. In E. Michie (Ed.), *Machine intelligence*, Vol. 6. Edinburgh, Scotland: Univ. Edinburgh Press, 1971. Pp. 295-323.

Hopcroft, J. & Ullman, J. *Formal languages and their relation to automata*. Reading, Massachusetts: Addison-Wesley, 1969.

Horning, J. A study of grammatical inference. Stanford Univ. Computer Science Department. CS 139 1969. (Ph.D. thesis).

Hovland, C. A "communication analysis" of concept learning. *Psychological Review* 1952, **59**, 461-472.

Hunt, E. *Concept learning: An information processing problem*. New York: Wiley, 1962.

Hunt, E. The evaluation of somewhat parallel models. In F. Massarik and P. Ratoosh (Eds.), *Mathematical Explorations in the Behavioral Sciences*. Homewood, Illinois: Dorsey Press, 1965.

Hunt, E. Utilization of memory in concept learning systems. In B. Kleinmuntz (Ed.), *Concepts and the structure of memory*. New York: Wiley, 1967.

Hunt, E. Computer simulation: Artificial intelligence studies and their relation to psychology. *Annual Review of Psychology* 1968, **19**, 135-168.

Hunt, E. What kind of computer is man? *Cognitive Psychology* 1971, **2**, 57-98.

Hunt, E. The memory we must have. In R. Shank and K. Colby (Eds.). *Computer models thought and language,* San Francisco: Freeman, 1973.

Hunt, E. & Kildall, G. A Heathkit method for building data management programs. *Proceedings of the symposium on information storage and retrieval*. Association for Computing Machinery, 1971, 117-132.

Hunt, E., & Makous, W. Some characteristics of human information processing. In J. Tou (Ed.), *Advances in Information Science* New York: Plenum Press, 1969.

Hunt, E., Marin, J., & Stone, P. *Experiments in induction*. New York: Academic Press, 1966.

Hunt, E., & Quinlan, J. The reactive library. Univ. Washington Psychology Dept. Tech. Rep. 67-1-03, 1967.

Irons, E. A syntax directed compiler for Algol 60. *Communications of the Association for Computing Machinery* 1961, 4, 51-55.

John, E. Switchboard vs. statistical theories of learning and memory. *Science* 1972, **177**, 850-863.

Johnson, S. Hierarchical clustering schemes. *Psychometrika* 1967, **32,** 241-254.

Julesz, B. *Foundations of cyclopean perception*. Chicago: Univ. of Chicago Press, 1971.

Kanal, L. and Chandresakaran, B. Recognition, machine "recognition", and statistical approaches. In S. Watanabe (Ed.), *Methodologies of pattern recognition*. New York: Academic Press, 1969.

Kaplan, R. Augmented transition networks as psychological models of sentence comprehension. *Artificial Intelligence* 1972, **3**, 77-100.

Kellog, C. A natural language compiler for on line data management *Proceedings of the Fall Joint Computer Conference*, 1968.

Kellog, C., Burger, J., Diller, T., & Fogt, K. The CONVERSE natural language data management system: Current status and plans. *Proceedings of the symposium on information storage and retrieval. Association for Computing Machinery*, 1971, 33-46.

Kelly, K. Early syntactic acquisition. Santa Monica, California: ARAND Corporation Report P-3719, 1967.

Kemeny, J. *Man and the computer*. New York: Screbner, 1972.

Kintsch, W. *Learning, memory, and conceptual processes*. New York: Wiley, 1970.

Kleinmuntz, B. The processing of clinical information by man and machine. In B. Kleinmuntz (Ed.) *Formal representation of human judgement*. New York: Wiley, 1968.

Kling, R. A paradigm for reasoning by analogy. *Artificial Intelligence*, 1971, **2**, 147-178.

Knuth, D. *Fundamental algorithms*. Reading, Massachusetts: Addison-Wesley, 1969.

Krantz, D., Luce, R., Suppes, P., & Tversky, A. *Foundations of measurement*. New York: Academic Press, 1971.

Lederberg, J. & Feigenbaum, E. Mechanization of inductive inference in organic chemistry. Stanford Univ. Department of Computer Science. Artificial Intelligence Memorandum 54, 1967.

Ledley, R. *Programming and utilization of digital computers*. New York: McGraw-Hill, 1962.

Ledley, R. High speed automatic analysis of biomedical pictures. *Science*, 1964, **146**, 216-223.

Lee W. *Decision theory and human behavior*. New York: Wiley, 1971.

Lefkovitz, D. *File structures for on-line systems*. New York: Spartan, 1969.

Lenneberg, E. *Biological foundations of language*. New York: Wiley, 1967.

Lenneberg, E. On explaining language. *Science*, 1969, **164**, 635-643.

Liberman, A. The grammars of speech and language. *Cognitive Psychology*, 1970, **1**, 301-323.

Liberman, A., Cooper, F., Shankweiler, D., & Studdert-Kennedy, M. Perception of the speech code. *Psychological Review*, 1967, **74**, 431-461.

Lindsay, P., & Norman, D. *Human information processing*. New York: Academic Press, 1972.

Loehlin, J. *Computer models of personality*. New York: Random House, 1968.

Loftus, G. Eye fixations and recognition memory for pictures. *Cognitive Psychology*, 1972, **3**, 525-551.

Loveland, D. A unifying view of some linear Herebrand procedures. *Journal of the Association for Computing Machinery*, 1972, **19**, 366-384.

Luce, R. D., Bush, R., & Galanter, E. (Eds.), *Readings in mathematical psychology*. New York: Wiley, 1965.

Luce, R. D., & Raiffa, H. *Games and decisions: A critical survey*. New York: Wiley, 1957.

Luckham, D., & Nilsson, J. Extracting information from resolution proof trees. *Artificial Intelligence*. 1971, **2**, 27-54.

MacQueen, J. Some methods for classification and analysis on multivariate observations. *Proceedings of the 5th Berkeley Symposium on Statistics and Probability*. Berkeley, California: Univ. of California Press, 1967.

McCalla, G. and Sampson, J. MUSE: A model to understand simple English. *Communications of the Association for Computing Machinery*, 1972, **15**, 29-40.

McCarthy, J. Programs with common sense. In D. Blake and A. Uttely (Eds.), *Proceedings of the Symposium on the Mechanization of through Processes*. London: H.M. Stationery Office, 1959.

McCarthy, J. A basis for a mathematical theory of computation. *Proceedings of the Western Joint Computer Conference, 1961*, 225-238.

McCarthy, J., Earnest, L., Reddy, D. R., & Vicens, P. A computer with hands, eyes, and ears. *Proceedings of the Fall Joint Computer Conference, 1968,* American Federation of Information Processing Sciences, **33,** 329-338.

McCarthy, J., & Hayes, P. Some philosophical problems from the standpoint of artificial intelligence. In B. Meltzer and D. Michie (Eds.), *Machine Intelligence,* Vol. 4, Edinburgh, Scotland: Univ. of Edinburgh Press, 1969.

McCarthy, J. *et al. LISP 1.5 Programmer's manual.* Cambridge, Massachusetts: M.I.T. Press, 1965.

McCulloch, W. & Pitts, W. A logical calculus of the ideas imminent in nervous activity. *Bulletin of Mathematical Biophysics,* 1943, **5,** 115-137.

Meisel, W. *Computer oriented approaches to pattern recognition.* New York: Academic Press, 1972.

Miller, G., & Chomsky, N. Finitary models of language users. In R. Luce, R. Bush and E. Galanter, (Eds.), *Handbook of mathematical psychology,* Vol. 2. New York: Wiley, 1963.

Miller, G., Galanter, E., & Pribram, K. *Plans and the structure of behavior.* New York: Holt, 1960.

Miller, J. Living systems: Basic concepts. *Behavioral Science,* 1965, **10,** 192-237. (a)

Miller, J. Living systems: Structure and process. *Behavioral Science,* 1965, **10,** 337-339. (b)

Miller, W. F., & Shaw, J. C. Linguistic methods in picture processing—a survey. *Proceedings of the Fall Joint Computer Conference,* 1968. *American Federation of Information Sciences,* **33,** 279-290.

Minsky, M. Steps toward artificial intelligence. *Proceedings of the Institute of Radio Engineers,* 1961, **49,** 8-30.

Minsky, M. Steps toward artificial intelligence. In E. Feigenbaum and J. Feldman (Eds.), *Computers and thought.* New York: McGraw-Hill, 1963.

Minsky, M. (Ed.), *Semantic information processing.* Cambridge, Massachusetts: M.I.T. Press, 1968.

Minsky, M. Form and computer science. *Journal of the Association for Computing Machinery,* 1970, **17,** 216-230.

Minsky, M., & Papert, S. *Perceptrons.* Cambridge, Massachusetts. M.I.T. Press, 1969.

Morgan, J., & Sohnquist, J. Problems in the analysis of survey data and a proposal. *Journal of the American Statistical Association.* 1963, **58,** 415-435.

Morris, J. E. Resolution: Extension of resolution to include the equality relation. *Proceedings of the 1st International Joint Conference on Artificial Intelligence.* Bedford, Massachusetts: Mitre Corp. 1969.

Muchnik, I. Simulation of process of forming the language of description and analysis of the forms of images. *Pattern Recognition,* 1972, **4,** 101-139.

Munson, J. Robot planning, execution and monitoring in an uncertain environment. *Proceedings of the 2nd International Joint Conference on Artificial Intelligence.,* London: Univ. of London, 1971. Pp. 338-349.

Nakano, Y., Ichikawa, A., & Nakata, K. Evaluation of various parameters in spoken digits. *Proceedings of the 1972 Conference on Speech Communication and Speech Processing.* IEEE 1972, 101-104.

Narashiman, R. Syntax directed interpretation of classes of pictures. *Communications of the Association for Computing Machinery,* 1966, **9,** 166-173.

Neisser, U. The imitation of man by machine. *Science,* 1963, **139,** 193-197.

Neisser, U. *Cognitive psychology.* New York: Appleton, 1967.

Neisser, U., & Weene, P. Hierarchies in concept attainment. *Journal of Experimental Psychology,* 1962, **64,** 640-645.

Newell, A. (Ed.) *Information processing language V manual* (2nd ed.). Englewood Cliffs, New Jersey: Prentice-Hall, 1965.

Newell, A. (Ed.) *Speech understanding systems.* New York: American Elsevier, 1972.

Newell, A., & Ernst, G. The search for generality. *Proceedings of the International Federation of Information Processing Societies*, 1965, 17-24.

Newell, A., and Shaw, J. C. Programming the logic theory machine. *Proceedings of the Western Joint Computer Conference*, 1957, 230-240.

Newell, A., Ernst, G., & Simon, H. Empirical explorations with the logic theory machine. *Proceedings of the Western Joint Computer Conference*, 1957, 218-230.

Newell, A., Ernst, G., & Shaw, J. C. Elements of a theory of human problem solving. *Psychological Review*, 1958, **65**, 151-166.

Newell, A., Ernst, G., & Shaw, J. C. Chess playing and the problem of complexity. In E. Feigenbaum and J. Feldman (Eds.), *Computers and thought*. New York: McGraw-Hill, 1963.

Newell, A., & Simon, H. Computer simulation of human thinking. *Science*, 1961, **134**, 2011-2017.

Newell, A., & Simon, H. An example of chess play in the light of chess playing programs. In N. Weiner and P. Schade (Eds.), *Progress in biocybernetics*. Amsterdam: Elsevier, 1965.

Newall, A., & Simon, H. *Human problem solving*. Englewood Cliffs, New Jersey: Prentice Hall, 1972.

Nilsson, N. *Learning machines*. New York: McGraw-Hill, 1965. (a)

Nilsson, N. Theoretical and experimental investigations in trainable pattern classifying systems. Technical report RADC-TR-5-257, Rome Air Development Center, Rome, N.Y., 1965. (b)

Nilsson, N. A mobile automaton. An application of artificial intelligence techniques. *Proceedings of the 1st International Joint Conference on Artificial Intelligence*. Bedford, Massachusetts: Mitre Corp. 1969. 509-520.

Nilsson, N. *Problem solving methods in artificial intelligence*. New York: McGraw-Hill, 1971.

Norman, D. *Memory and attention*. New York: Wiley, 1969.

Nyak, B. On acquisition of formal grammars. M.Sc. thesis, University of Washington Computer Science Group, 1972.

Paivio, A. Mental imagery in associative learning and memory. *Psychological Review*, 1969, **76**, 241-263.

Paivio, A. *Imagery and verbal processes*. New York: Holt, 1971.

Pietrzykowski, T. A complete mechanization of second order type theory. *Journal of the Association for Computing Machinery*, 1973, **20**, 333-364.

Polya, G. *Mathematics and plausible reasoning* (2 vols.) Princeton: Princeton Univ. Press, 1954.

Polya, G. *How to solve it*. New York: Random House, 1957.

Quillian, M. R. Semantic memory. In M. Minsky (Ed.), *Semantic information processing*. Cambridge, Massachusetts: M.I.T. Press, 1968.

Quillian, M. R. The teachable language comprehender: A simulation program and a theory of language. *Communications of the Association for Computing Machinery*, 1969, **12**, 459-476.

Quinlan, J. R. A task independent experience gathering scheme for a problem solver. *Proceedings of the 1st International Joint Conference on Artificial Intelligence*, Bedford, Massachusetts: Mitre Corp. 1969. Pp. 193-198.

Quinlan, J. R., & Hunt, E. A formal deductive system. *Journal of the Association for Computing Machinery*, 1968, **15**, 625-646.

Quinlan, J. R., & Hunt, E. The FORTRAN deductive system. *Behavioral Science*, 1969, **14**, 74-79.

Raphael, B. A computer program which "understands." *Proceedings of the Fall Joint Computer Conference*, 1964. *American Federation of Information Processing Sciences*, **26**, 577-590.

Rapoport, A. *Fights, games and debates*. Ann Arbor: Univ. of Michigan Press, 1960.

Rapoport, A. *Strategy and Conscience*. New York: Harper, 1964.

Reddy, D. R. Speech recognition: Prospects for the seventies. *Proceedings of the International Federation of Information Processing Sciences*, 1971, 15-113.

Reddy, D. R., Erman, L., & Neely, R. A mechanistic model of speech perception. *Proceedings of the 1972 Conference on Speech Communication and Speech Processing.* IEEE 1972, 334-337.

Reitman, W. *Cognition and thought.* New York: Wiley, 1965.

New York: Simon and Schuster, 1956.

Reiter, R. Two results on ordering for resolution with merging and linear format. *Journal of the Association for Computing Machinery.* 1971, **18**, 630-646.

Robinson, G. & Wos, L. Paramodulation and theorem proving in first order theories with equality. In B. Meltzer & D. Michie (Eds.), *Machine Intelligence*, Vol. 4. Edinburgh: Univ. of Edinburgh Press, 1969.

Robinson, J. A machine oriented logic based on the resolution principle. *Journal of the Association for Computing Machinery*, 1965, **12**, 23-41.

Robinson, J. A review of automatic theorem proving. *Proceedings of the Symposium in Applied Mathematics*, 1967, **19**, 1-18.

Robinson, J. Mechanizing higher order logic. In B. Meltzer and D. Michie (Eds.), *Machine Intelligence 4.* Edinburgh, Scotland: Univ. Edinburgh Press, 1969.

Robinson, J. A note on the mechanization of higher order logic. In B. Meltzer and D. Michie (Eds.), *Machine Intelligence*, Vol. 5, Edinburgh, Scotland: Univ. of Edinburgh Press, 1970.

Robinson, J. Computational logic: The unification algorithm. In B. Meltzer and D. Michie (Eds.), *Machine Intelligence*, Vol. 6, Edinburgh, Scotland: Univ. Edinburgh Press, 1971.

Rosenblatt, F. The perceptron: A probalistic model for information storage and organization in the brain. *Psychological Review*, 1958, **65**, 386-408.

Rosenblatt, F. *Principles of neurodynamics.* Baltimore: Spartan Press, 1962.

Rosenfeld, A. Picture processing by computer. *Computer Surveys*, 1969, **1**, 147-176.

Rosenfeld, A. *Picture processing by computer.* New York: Academic Press, 1969.

Rulifson, J. F., Waldinger, R. J., & Derksen, J. A. QA4 Working Paper. Stanford Research Institute Artificial Intelligence Group, Technical Note 42, 1970.

Rumelhart, D., Lindsay, P., & Norman, D. A process model of long term memory. In E. Tulving and W. Donaldson (Eds.), *Organization of memory* New York: Academic Press, 1972.

Samett, J. Programming languages: History and future. *Communications of the Association for Computing Machinery*, 1972, **15**, 601-610.

Samuel, A. Some studies in machine learning using the game of checkers. *IBM Journal of Research and Development*, 1959, **3**, 210-229.

Samuel, A. Some studies in machine learning using the game of checkers. In E. Feigenbaum and J. Feldman (Eds.), *Computers and thought.* New York: McGraw-Hill, 1963.

Samuel, A. Some studies in machine learning using the game of checkers. II. Recent progress. *IBM Journal of Research and Development*, 1967, **11**, 601-617.

Schank, R. Finding the conceptual content and intention of an utterance in natural language conversation. *Proceedings of the 2nd International Joint Conference on Artificial Intelligence,* London: Univ. of London, 1971, 444-454.

Schank, R. Conceptual dependency: A theory of natural language understanding. *Cognitive Psychology*, 1972, **3**, 552-631.

Schank, R. Identification of conceptualizations underlying natural language. In Schank, R., & Colby, C. (Eds.) *Computer models of thought and languages.* San Francisco: Freeman 1973.

Schwarz, R., Burger, J., & Simmons, R. A deductive question answerer for natural language inference. *Communications of the Association for Computing Machinery*, 1970, **13**, 167-183.

Sebesteyen, G. *Decision making procedures in pattern recognition.* New York: McGraw-Hill, 1962.

Sebesteyen, G., & Edie, J. An algorithm for non-parametric pattern recognition. *IEEE Transactions on Electronic Computers*, 1966, **EC-15**, 908-915.

Selfridge, O. Pandemonium. A paradigm for learning. In D. Blake and A. Utteley (Eds.), *Proceedings of the Symposium on the Mechanization of Thought Processes*. London: H.M. Stationery Office, 1959.

Shaw, A. C. A formal picture description scene as a basis for picture processing systems. *Information and Control*, 1969, **14**.

Shepard, R. and Metzler, J. Mental rotation of three dimensional objects. *Science* 1971, **171**, 701-703.

Sibert, E. A machine oriented logic incorporating the equality relation. In B. Meltzer and D. Michie (Eds.), *Machine Intelligence*, Vol. 4, Edinburgh, Scotland: Univ. of Edinburgh Press, 1969.

Sickel, S. & Hunt, E. Refinement compatibilities and extensions for use with the resolution principle, Technical Report 73-01-09, Computer Science Department, University of Washington, 1973.

Simmons, R. Natural language question answering systems, 1969. *Communications of the Association for Computing Machinery*, 1970, **13**, 15-30.

Simon, H. The theory of problem solving. *Information processing 1971* Amsterdam: North Holland, 1972. Pp. 267-277.

Simon, H. *Models of man*. New York: Wiley, 1957.

Simon, H. *The science of the artificial*. Cambridge, Massachusetts: M.I.T. Press, 1969.

Sinaiko, H. Translation by computer. *Science*, 1971, **174**, 1182-1184.

Skinner, B. F. *Verbal Behavior*. New York: Appleton, 1957.

Skinner, B. F. *Beyond Freedom and Dignity*. New York: Knopf, 1971.

Slagle, J. A heuristic program that solves symbolic integration problems in freshman calculus. *Journal of the Association for Computing Machinery*, 1963, **10**, 507-520.

Slagle, J. Experiments with a deductive question answering program. *Communications of the Association for Computing Machinery*, 1965, **9**, 792-798.

Slagle, J. Interpolation theorems for resolution in lower predicate calculus. *Journal of the Association for Computing Machinery*, 1970, **17**, 535-542.

Slagle, J. *Artificial intelligence: The heuristic programming approach*. New York: McGraw-Hill, 1971.

Slagle, J., & Bursky, P. Experiments with a multipurpose theorem proving heuristic program that learns. Univ. of California Lawrence Radiation Laboratory Tech. Report UCRL-70051, 1966.

Slagle, J., & Dixon, J. Experiments with the m and n tree searching program. *Journal of the Association for Computing Machinery*, 1970, **17**, 147-154.

Solomonoff, R. A formal theory of inductive inference I. *Information and Control*. 1964, 7, 1-22. (a)

Solomonoff, R. A formal theory of inductive inference II. *Information and Control* 1964, 7, 224-254 (b).

Stefferud, E. The logic theory machine. A model heuristic program. Santa Monica, Calif. RAND Corp. Tech. Rep. RM-3731-CC, 1963.

Stanfel, L. Tree structures for optimal searching. *Journal of the Association for Computing Machinery*, 1970, **17**, 508-517.

Stickel, M. & Hunt, E. An interactive theorem proving program for the first order predicate calculus. University of Washington Computer Science Group Tech. Rep., 1972.

Stone, P., Dunphy, D., Smith, M., & Oglivie, D. *The general inquirer* Cambridge, Massachusetts: M.I.T. Press, 1965.

Strasbourger, E. Recognizing a continuous spoken language using analytic cepstrum encoding. Ph.D. thesis. University of Washington Computer Science Group, 1972.

Strasbourger, E. The role of the cepstrum in speech recognition. *Proceedings of the 1972 Conference on Speech Communication and Processing*. IEEE 1972. Pp. 299-302.

Suppes, P., & Zinnes, J. Basic measurement theory. In R. D. Luce, R. Bush, and E. Galanter (Eds.), *Handbook of mathematical psychology* New York: Wiley, 1963.

Sussenguth, E. Use of tree structures for processing files. *Communications of the Association for Computing Machinery*, 1963, **6**, 272-279.

Swain, P. and Fu, K. Stochastic programmed grammars for syntactic pattern recognition. *Pattern Recognition*, 1972, **4**, 83-100.

Tatsuoka, M. *Multivariate analysis*. New York: Wiley, 1971.

Thomas, O. *Transformational grammars and the teacher of English*. New York: Holt, 1965.

Thompson, F. B. English for the computer. *Proceedings of the Fall Joint Computer Conference*, 1966. *American Federation of Information Processing Sciences*, **29**. Pp. 349-356.

Thorne, J., Bratley, P., and Dewar, H. The syntactic analysis of English by machine. In D. Michie (Ed.) *Machine Intelligence*, Vol. 3, Edinburgh, Scotland: Univ. of Edinburgh Press, 1968.

Thurlow, W. Audition. In J. Kling and L. Riggs (Eds.), *Experimental Psychology* (3rd ed.). New York: Holt, 1971.

Tulving, E. Episodic and semantic memory. In E. Tulving and W. Donaldson (Eds.), *Organization of memory*. New York: Academic Press, 1972.

Uhr, L. (Ed.) *Pattern recognition*. New York: Wiley, 1965.

Uhr, L., & Vosller, C. A pattern recognition program that generates, evaluates, and adjusts its own operators. In E. Feigenbaum and J. Feldman (Eds.), *Computers and thought*. New York: McGraw-Hill, 1963.

Uhr, L., Vosller, C., & Uleman, J. Pattern recognition over distortion by human subjects and by a computer simulation model for visual pattern recognition. *Journal of Experimental Psychology*, 1962, **63**, 227-234.

Vicens, P. Aspects of speech recognition by computer. Stanford U. Computer Science Department, AI-85, 1969. (Ph.D. thesis).

Von Neumann, J. The general and logical theory of automata. In J. R. Newman, (Ed.), *The world of mathematics*, Vol. 4. New York: Simon & Schuster, 1956.

Wang, H. Towards mechanical mathematics. *IBM Journal of Research and Development*, 1960, **4**, 2-22.

Watanabe, S. Information theoretic aspects of inductive and deductive reasoning. *IBM Journal of Research and Development*, 1960, **4**, 208-231.

Watanabe, S. Ungrammatical grammar in pattern recognition. *Pattern Recognition* 1971, **3**, 385-408.

Wegner, P. *Programming languages, information structures and machine organization*. New York: McGraw-Hill, 1968.

Weiner, N. *Cybernetics*. New York: Wiley, 1948.

Weiner, N. *The human use of human beings*. Boston: Houghton-Mifflin, 1950.

Weisstein, N. What the frog's eye tells the human brain. Single cell analysis in the visual system. *Psychological Bulletin* 1969, **72**, 157-176.

Weizenbaum, J. ELIZA. A computer program for the study of natural language communication between men and machines. *Communications of the Association for Computing Machinery*, 1966, **9**, 36-45.

Weizenbaum, J. Contextual understanding by computers. *Communications of the Association for Computing Machinery*, 1967, **10**, 474-480.

Williams, G. A model of memory in concept learning. *Cognitive Psychology* 1971, **2**, 158-184..

Winograd, T. A program for understanding natural language. *Cognitive Psychology*, 1972, **3**, 1-192.

Winston, P. THE M.I.T. Robot. In B. Meltzer and D. Michie (Eds.), *Machine Intelligence*, Vol. 6. Edinburgh, Scotland: Univ. of Edinburgh Press, 1972.

Woods, W. A. Transition networks for natural language analysis. *Communications of the Association for Computing Machinery*, 1970, **13**, 591-606.

Wos, L., Carson, D., & Robinson, G. The unit preference strategy in theorem proving. *Proceedings of the Fall Joint Computer Conference*, 1964, **26**. Pp. 615-621.

Wos, L., Carson, D., & Robinson, G. Efficiency and completeness of the set of support strategy in theorem proving. *Journal of the Association for Computing Machinery*. 1965, **12**, 536-541.

Zobrist, A. & Carlson, F. An advice taking chess computer. *Scientific American* 1973, **228**, No. 6, 92-105.

References Added in Proof

Edwards, W., Lindeman, T., and Savage, R. Bayesian statistical inference for psychological research. *Psychological Review,* 1963, **70**, 193–242.

Sokal, R., and Sneath, P. *Principles of numerical taxonomy*. San Francisco: Freeman, 1963.

AUTHOR INDEX

A

Abdali, S. K., 193-195
Abelson, R. P., 385, 405, 406
ACM Curriculum Committee, 3
Allen, J., 342
Amarel, S., 9
Anderson, R., 296, 305, 310, 311
Anderson, T., 11, 47
Arbib, M., 438
Attneave, F., 347, 442
Austin, G., 11, 256

B

Banergi, R., 9, 212, 444
Becker, J., 221
Bennett, J., 342
Berenzer, S., 376
Berkeley, E., 9
Biermann, A. W., 147, 162, 166
Bledsoe, W., 296, 305, 310, 311, 342
Block, H., 187, 191, 192, 195
Bobrow, D., 419
Bongard, M., 13, 201
Botovinnik, M., 252
Bourne, L., 11, 115, 141
Boyer, R., 342
Brately, P., 419
Bruner, J., 11, 256
Buchanan, B., 369
Burger, J., 382, 385
Bursky, P., 391
Bush, R., 255
Busignies, H., 358

C

Carroll, Lewis (H. L. Dodgson), 222
Carlson, F., 251
Carney, H., 376

Carson, D., 309
Cartwright, D., 210, 223
Chandresakaran, B., 129
Chang, C., 240, 317
Church, A., 281
Chomsky, N., 28, 29, 158, 358, 372, 412, 415, 426
Clowes, M., 171, 350, 351
Cohen, J., 88
Colby, K., 405
Cooper, W. S., 359, 400, 401
Corey, E., 4
Cornsweet, T., 349
Cox, R., 362
Cover, T., 87
Craig, H., 72, 83, 86, 376, 377
Craig, V., 72, 83, 86
Crespi-Reghizzi, S., 164

D

Dale, P., 154, 358
Dawes, R., 61
DeGroot, A., 252
Deutsch, J. A., 387
Dewar, H., 419
Diehr, G., 140-142
Diehr, P., 196
Diller, T., 385
Dirksen, J., 281
Dixon, J., 250
Dostert, B., 370, 377, 386
Dreyfus, H., 442
Duda, R., 59, 97, 187, 191, 192, 195, 202, 349

E

Earnest, L., 363
Edie, J. 100

SUBJECT INDEX

A
B   5
C   6
D   7
E   8
F   9
G   0
H   1
I   2
J   3